THE HISTORY OF
AIR CARGO
AND AIRMAIL
FROM THE 18TH CENTURY

THE HISTORY OF
AIR CARGO
AND AIRMAIL

FROM THE 18TH CENTURY

Camille Allaz

Christopher Foyle Publishing

in association with

The International Air Cargo Association

To Cécile

PAGE 2 **The old and the new – the massive Antonov An-124 Ruslan loading a Ju52 aircraft.**
Air Foyle

Photography Credits
Where possible photo credits are identified with the caption. Every attempt has been made to ensure that the correct credit is given for each photograph: we apologise for any errors which wll be corrected in future impressions..

First published in 1998 in French by ITA

This edition (first English language edition) published 2004

ISBN 1 902579 82 8

© Institut du Transport Aérien – Paris 1998
This design © Christopher Foyle Publishing, 2004

Published by CFP Christopher Foyle Publishing
in association with
The International Air Cargo Association TIACA

Camille Allaz has asserted his right to be identified as the author of this work.

John Skilbeck has asserted his right to be identified as the translator of this work.

British Library Cataloguing in Publication Data
A CIP catalogue record for this book is available from the British Library

Translation: John Skilbeck
Editor: George Grant
Design: Compendium Design
Maps: Mark Franklin drew the new material and reworked the French originals

CONTENTS

PREFACE

It is a pleasure for The International Air Cargo Association to join with Christopher Foyle Publishing to publish jointly the English language edition of the "The Great Adventure of Air Mail and Air Cargo From the 18th Century to the Present Day".

This first comprehensive history of over 200 years of air transport of mail and cargo was first published in French by the Institut du Transport Aérien in 1998, and received very favourable reviews. Through the publication of the English language edition, this remarkable work is now accessible to many more readers throughout the world. Accordingly, to bring the story of aircargo into the twenty-first century, this publication has been extensively updated and expanded to take into account the latest developments in the industry.

The author, Camille Allaz, served as Senior Vice President Cargo at Air France for more than 10 years, which gave him an insider's close-up view of his subject, a privilege not enjoyed by many historians.

There is no aspect of mail or cargo transport by air that has not been thoroughly researched and documented by Allaz, from the first brief transport of animals by balloon in France in 1783 to the vast global networks of the integrated express carriers in the 21st century. As a true scholar, he fits his narrative into the larger framework of political, military, economic and aviation history. This book should stand for years as the definitive work on the history of air mail and air cargo, and will be of immense value to the academic community, to the air cargo industry, the postal services, and to the general public.

We salute Camille Allaz for his contribution to our knowledge and understanding of the fascinating and complex story of those colourful persons and exciting events that transformed the slow, laborious and uncertain transportation of letters and goods into the reliable, speedy systems of air mail and air cargo that serve us today.

Dora Kay
President
The International Air Cargo Association

Publisher's note
There are considerable differences between this edition and Camille Allaz's original 1998 text. Apart from the obvious language change, so assiduously produced by John Skilbeck, there have been major additions and revisions covering recent history. Some of the additions – particularly those relating to Air Foyle and Antonov Airlines on pages 334–5; the listing of modern cargo airlines on pages 338–9; and the wealth of photographs – were inserted by the publisher, who would like to thank the following organisations and individuals for helping to produce this illustrated English language edition of the original French work:

- For invaluable general publishing advice: Alistair McQueen and Vivienne Wordley.
- For detailed help with the text and its revisions: Clare Weale and Linda McCash.

- For the two photographic reproductions of original paintings: Paul Jelleyman of Paul Martin Photography.
- For providing most of the photographs with great enthusiasm and cooperation: Air France, Boeing (Mary Kane), MAP (Brian Pickering), British Airways Museum (Paul Jarvis), Air Cargo News UK (Colin Ballantine and Nigel Tomkins), Lufthansa (Dagmar Bauer and Carola Kapitza), Royal Air Force Museum (Dr Michael Fopp, Director and Andy Rennick), Paul Duffy, Malcolm Nason, TNT (Veronique Simons), IATA (Joanna Grimble), Emirates (Ram Menen and Fawad Fazal), Cargolux (Jeanne Patrick), Channel Express (Philip Meeson and Stephanie Blevins), Airbus (Marie Bonzom), Air Atlantique (Annette Bowden), Air Rep (Simon King), Air Foyle, Air Foyle Heavylift, Heavylift.
- For creating the website David Creasy.

Christopher Foyle

ACKNOWLEDGEMENTS

In the first place I would like to express my thanks to the libraries that opened their doors to me. Among these are the Library of Congress in Washington, which deserves special mention for the richness of its collections, the helpfulness of its personnel and the openness of its admission criteria. I would also like to demonstrate my gratitude to the Public Library of New York, to the library of the Deutsches Museum in Munich, the Versailles Library, and the Service Historique de l'Armée de l'Air in the Château de Vincennes. The Library of the Musée de la Poste in Paris stands out for the great worth and ease of consultation of its documentation, as well as for the competence and considerateness of its librarians.

Among the organisations, which kindly agreed to put their archives at my disposal, I wish to mention the Musée de la Poste in Paris, the Air and Freight Museum in Washington (Mr. Paul McCutchon) and the Post Office in London (Mr. Andrew Perry). The researches of Mme. Gilotte, Head of the Archive Section at the Direction Générale de l'Aviation Civile, and of Mme. Sardain, in charge of the Archives of Air France, were a tremendous help. Various museums and postal services have afforded me very valuable assistance: the United States Postal Service (Mrs. Megaera Ausman and Mr. Michael Krop) and the National Post Museum in Washington (Mr. Timothy Carr), the Swedish Institute in Paris (Mme. de Ribaucourt), the Postal Museum in Stockholm (Mr. Erik Hanberg) and the Swedish Post Office (Mr. Sten Berglund) and finally the local museum of Quincy in California, which is so full of atmosphere and so lovingly cared for. I am also indebted to the Museum of Air France, represented by Mme Le Guernevé, whose researches for illustrations were of particular value, and to Captain Lasserre. I should also mention the Paris office of the great Japanese Daily Paper Asahi Shimbun (Mr. Shiina), who obtained for me and commented on first-hand information about the beginnings of commercial aviation in Japan, and the airlines KLM and Lufthansa with respect to their photographic contributions.

There are many who agreed to give me their time and enabled me to update my knowledge. In the hope that anyone who has been omitted will forgive me, I mention, in alphabetical order, Messrs. Berthelier (Singapore Airlines), Clément (Japan Airlines), Etien (Air Express International), Krainik (FIATA), Link (Lufthansa), Goudjil (China Airlines), Mariani (Aéropostale), Malès (KLM), Patureau (PDG Transvalair), Pelissier (Official representative of the DGAC), Pfab (President of the SNAGFA), Prochasson (Korean Air), Ress (Aéroport de Paris), Marie - Pierre Rogers (Federal Express), Rosselini (the French Post Office), Theil (Lufthansa) and Zwart (KLM).

I feel a particular appreciation, born of friendship and gratitude, towards all my former colleagues in the senior management of the Freight Division of Air France, and towards the team of François Bachelet. Amongst those whom I have most recently called upon, I would like to name (at the risk of appearing unjust to others) Messrs Avril, Boyer, Bizzi and Bour, Demeer, Desmaisons and Duroca, Jacques Feret, Foucault, Gilard, Hénon and Kutzuki, Le Quinio, Loze, Manus, Moreau and Mouza, Perlat, Pons, Scherret, Séréno, Anne Veyssié and Ann Wadman.

I would also like to express my sincerest thanks to the members of the Institut du Transport Aérien, and especially those who assisted me to input and format the text.

I thank M. Robert Espérou for having read through the entire text, and for giving me the benefit of his experience and his exceptional knowledge of historical matters. This work would never have seen the light of day if my father, whose long career in the field of airmail lasted from 1920 to 1962 with Lignes Aériennes Latécoère, Aéropostale and finally Air France, had not passed on to me the "airmail virus". May he see in this present work a token of my filial homage.

Acknowledgements to the English Edition

I would first like to express my particular gratitude to Christopher Foyle. Even before my book published in French, he demonstrated his interest in it, on the occasion of the Paris Air Cargo Forum in 1998. This English edition is the fruit of his personal commitment, and of his dual role in the worlds of air transport and publishing. To him, I offer my sincere thanks.

At the same time, I wish to show my appreciation to our translator, John Skilbeck. He has faithfully communicated by thoughts and respected the form in which they were written, reproducing the rhythm of phrase, and fine-tuning the choice of vocabulary.

Finally, I would also like to extend my gratefulness to Clare Weale for her kindness and her availability.

And finally, this enterprise could have been neither undertaken nor carried to fruition without the unceasing participation and support of my wife. Her ability to make contacts, linguistic skills, curiosity and constant desire to understand made her at once a powerful ambassador, an indefatigable researcher, a merciless critic, and an ever-precious associate. I thank her with all my heart.

Camille Allaz

GLOSSARY

Air Cargo Any property (freight, mail or express) carried or to be carried in an aircraft. Air cargo is comprised of the addition of Air Freight and Air Express and Air Mail.

Air Express Shipments for which the airline provides a guaranteed level of service — speed, door to door — at a premium charge.

Air Freight Goods other than Express Mail or Passenger Baggage delivered to an airline for carriage.

Air Mail Letters, postcards, documents and parcels carried under the terms of a postal convention or regulation.

Air Waybill (or **Consignment Note**) Document made out by or on behalf of the shipper, which evidences the contract between the shipper and the carrier for the carriage of goods over the route of the carrier.

Available Tonne-Kilometres (ATK) The total number of metric tonnes available for the transportation of passengers, freight and or mail multiplied by the number of kilometres over which this capacity is flown.

Class Rate A rate applicable to a specifically designated class of good (live animals, newspapers etc).

Consignee The person or firm whose name appears on the Air Waybill as the party to whom the goods are to be delivered by the carrier.

Consignment (or **Shipment**) One or more pieces of freight accepted by the carrier from one shipper at one time and moving under the contracted authority of one Air Waybill.

Consignor (or **Shipper**) The person or firm whose name appears on the Air Waybill as the party contacting with the carrier for carriage of the goods..

Consolidation (or **Groupage**) A number of separate shipments that have been assembled into one shipment for movement on one Air Waybill.

Consolidator An agent who provides consolidation services.

Container Rate Rate for the carriage of an entire container, igloo or pallet. Generally, the charge is uniform regardless of the weight up to a pivot weight beyond which an additional charge is levied.

Contract Rate A rate applicable in accordance with a contractual agreement specifying a minimum volume of cargo over a specified time.

Dangerous Goods (or **Hazardous Materials**) Items of goods that are inherently harmful and are only transported under certain conditions.

Deferred Rate A shipper using a differed rate agrees to accept a lower level of service in return for a lower rate.

Density Weight per unit volume.

Fare The amount charged by a carrier for the carriage of a passenger and his free baggage allowance).

General Commodity Rate (GCR) A rate which applies on all articles or commodities not specifically excluded.

Integrated Carrier (or **Integrator**) A carrier that provides door-to-door air cargo transportation using its own or contracted aircraft and trucks, and performs this service under the authority of a single Air Waybill.

Loose Cargo (or **Bulk**) Air Freight delivered to an airline as separate packages (as opposed to air freight delivered as ULDs).

Oversize Cargo (or **Outsize Cargo**) Term originally used by the USAF Military Airlift Command. Commonly used to designate unusually large or heavy cargo pieces that will not fit in the cargo areas of standard-body freighters or passenger aircraft.

Rate The amount charges by the carrier for the carriage of a unit of weight or volume of freight (or Excess Baggage).

Revenue Tonne-Kilometres (RTK) One tonne of revenue traffic transported over one kilometre. Revenue-tonne kilometres are computed by multiplying metric tonnes of revenue traffic (passenger, freight and/or mail) by the kilometres which this traffic is flown.

Shipment See **Consignment**

Shipper See **Consignor**

Specific Commodity Rate (SCR) A rate which applies only to a specific commodity or commodities that are specifically named.

Tariffs The published fares, rates, charges and/or related conditions of carriage of a carrier.

Tonne-Kilometres See **Available Tonne-Kilometres** and **Revenue Tonne-Kilometres**.

Unit Load Device (ULD) Aircraft pallet and pallet net and/or igloo, and/or aircraft container, enabling individual pieces of cargo to be assembled into a standard-size unit to facilitate rapid loading and unloading of aircraft having compatible handling and restraint systems.

Unitization Assembling multiple packages or items into a ULD.

Part One
The Age of Visionaries and Forerunners
1783–1914

"And they shall yet transport merchandise upon great flying vessels."

Marquis d'Argenson (1694-1757)

"In the field of aeronautics, they call an Aircraft any craft which can support itself in the atmosphere. Aircraft are divided into two groups: lighter than air or aerostats (balloons, dirigibles) and those which are heavier than air or aerodynamic (gliders, kites, aeroplanes, autogiros, helicopters, ornithopters)."

Edmond Pettit

1 AEROSTATIC VESSELS: BALLOONS AND DIRIGIBLES

It was cargo that initiated the age of flight on 19th September 1783.

On that day, a balloon created by the brothers Etienne and Joseph Montgolfier stood in the Cour des Ministres in the Château of Versailles. Made of Rouen cloth, it was painted blue and decorated with the royal monogram in gold letters. A few minutes after 1.00pm, in front of a considerable crowd and in the presence of the King, the Queen and members of the Académie des Sciences, the 32 ropes which held the balloon down were simultaneously released and, filled with hot air, it rose "almost vertically in a quick movement, carrying a wicker cage, which held a sheep, a cock and a duck".[1] This was the first airborne expedition in history.

The flight was short. The balloon, the "Montgolfière", propelled by the wind, landed 8 minutes later in Vaucresson Woods, where the animals were retrieved in good health, although the unhappy cock had endured a kick from the sheep. The latter, by order of the King, was lodged in the château menagerie "in order to preserve the first animal to open up the ways of the air." Since its state of health was considered satisfactory, the King then authorised manned air voyages: on 21st November 1783 the balloonist Pilâtre de Rozier took with him the Marquis d'Arlandes, and enabled him to overfly Paris without any difficulty, from the Jardin de la Muette to the Butte aux Cailles.

And so it was, thanks to a bellicose sheep, an injured cock and a discreet duck, that cargo took to the skies and acquired its letters patent.

1 VISIONARIES

As with many human activities, the transportation of post and goods by air had its prophets. Some studied the means of locomotion, imagining "flying vessels" founded on principles of physics and scientific intuition; others, in both civil and military fields, imagined the consequences of moving people and goods through the airways. These visionaries, whether physicists or utopians, flourished at the end of the 17th century and during the 18th century, an era when the natural sciences were making great progress. Among them were many churchmen with a taste for science, who had time for reflection.

In 1670 Father Francesco Lana de Terzi, an Italian Jesuit, published in Brescia a work which caused a considerable stir: "*Prodomo overo saggio di alcune inventioni nuove, premesso all arte maestra*" ("A defence or essay concerning certain new inventions, presaging a new art"). In it, Father Lana describes a design for an aerial ship, in the form of a boat suspended from four spheres and equipped with oars and a sail.

"*Let four spheres be made, each being sufficiently powerful to lift two or three men; make a vacuum therein and join them one to another by means of four beams of wood. Thereafter, construct a vessel in wood, similar to a boat, which shall be provided with a mast, a sail and oars. The four spheres shall be attached to the earth by means of four ropes of equal length, which shall, once the air has been exhausted, prevent them from flying off before the men shall have had time to board the machine. Immediately thereafter, the ropes shall be unfastened in order to release them all at the same time. The airship will then take flight, carrying with it a greater or lesser number of men, depending on the size of the spheres.*"[2]

Some decades later, another religious figure, Father Bartolomeo Lourenço de Gusmao, appears in Lisbon. He is said to have tested in 1709, in circumstances which remain rather unclear, a flying machine called "The Great Bird", which occasioned a letter to the King of Portugal, in which he demonstrated exceptional prophetic powers and a rare force of conviction.

"*With the aid of this machine it will be possible to cause the most important messages to arrive at army corps or remote provinces at the same or almost the same moment as they were despatched. Since the possessions of Your Majesty are separated by great distances, this fact will be more important for Your Majesty than for any other monarch, since it will be possible to avoid thereby such errors in the governance of conquered peoples, as are for the most part due to delays in the transmission of news. Moreover, Your Majesty shall be able to have brought with greater rapidity and security all such things as He shall require. The merchants will make short work of sending letters of exchange and sums of money, and it will be easy at any time to deliver supplies to the troops, and provisions and ammunitions to strongholds under siege."* [3]

In this wonderful quotation everything is conjured up: airmail – for the King and the merchants; airfreight – underlining its two fundamental qualities of speed and safety; and even military air lifts to send fresh supplies to besieged fortresses.

With Father Joseph Galien, a French Dominican and Professor of Theology at Avignon, we enter the realms of fantasy. A century earlier, in 1650, Cyrano de Bergerac had published his "*Histoire comique, ou voyage dans la lune*" ("A comic history, or a journey to the moon"). Father Galien published in 1755 his "*L'art de naviguer dans les airs, amusement physique et géométrique*" ("The art of navigating in the air, a physical and geometrical entertainment"), which was a best seller. He imagines an enormous contraption "wider and longer than the town of Avignon" which without doubt owes more to philosophical recreation than to scientific thinking. However, when Father Galien notes that his airborne vessel is capable of transporting "a numerous army with all its equipment of war and its victuals to the middle of Africa", how can one not be reminded of those hundreds of aircraft which within the space of a few weeks in 1990 and 1991 during the Gulf War, transported a whole army and hundreds of thousands of tons of provisions from the United States to the Middle East? A proof that reality often exceeds the wildest of fantasies.

Other than a shared propensity for Utopian speculations, and the fact that they both lived during the century of the Enlightenment, Father Galien and another visionary of air transport, the Marquis D'Argenson, have little in common. As the Minister of Foreign Affairs for Louis XV between 1744 and 1747, René Louis de Voyer, Marquis D'Argenson, came from a very ancient Touraine family, with a long tradition of serving the state. He was a powerful aristocrat, who was also a liberal who advocated political reforms – (we owe to him the statement: "Free elections have nowhere been the cause of disorder") – and who favoured free trade.

In his private writings he touched a wide variety of subjects. His "*Pensées sur la réforme de l'Etat*" ("Thoughts upon the reform of the State"), in which he touches on a wide variety of topics, devotes a chapter to "the invention of balloons".

"This is still an idea which men will call folly, but I am persuaded that one of the first discoveries to be made, and which is perhaps earmarked for our century, will be to find the art of flying in the air. In this manner men will travel fast and conveniently and they shall yet transport merchandise upon great flying vessels.

"There will be airborne armies. Our present fortifications will become useless. The custody of treasures, the honour of women and girls will be greatly endangered until they shall establish a constabulary of the air and shall clip the wings of impudent rascals and bandits. Wherefore artillerymen will learn to shoot in flight. And in the realm there shall be need of a new office of 'Secretary of state for the airborne forces'." [4]

And thus it was that the most enlightened spirits were prepared for the great event which took place at Versailles on 19th September 1783, bringing to a close the age of the visionaries.

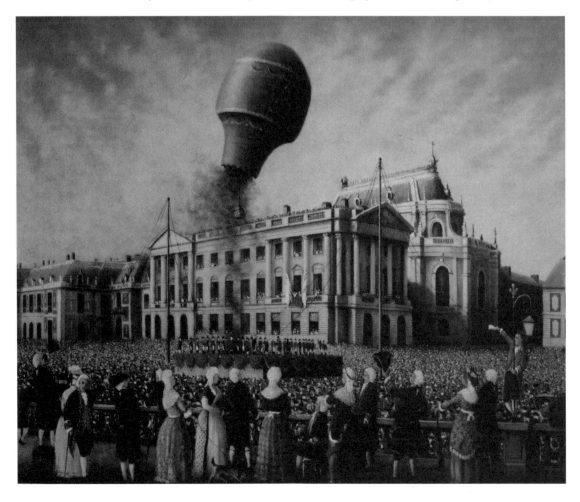

The sheep, cock and duck airborne in the "Montgolfière", Versailles, 19th September 1783. From a painting by Alan Tidy.
Paul Martin/Air Foyle

2 FIRST EXPERIMENTS 1784-1815

Civilian Achievements...

The first balloon ascent, which was soon followed by several others, began a wave of indescribable enthusiasm. "One could say that in France, people spoke of naught but balloons." [5] The ballooning craze soon reached Italy and then England.

The French aeronaut Jean-Pierre Blanchard organised several ascents in London in 1784. On one such occasion he took with him in the basket of his balloon Doctor John Jeffries, a native of Boston and a surgeon in the British Army. Jeffries had the idea of taking three cards with him and, after taking care to write on each of them "From the balloon above the clouds", he sent them to friends by throwing them overboard from the basket while they were flying over London.

This extremely primitive postal technique of throwing letters and postcards from the air, hoping that they would be recovered on the ground and taken to the post to be re-routed in the normal manner, became astoundingly popular. In the course of the 19th century it was frequently used in Europe and the USA during free balloon ascents, and reached its peak at the beginning of the 20th century during the triumphant tours of the Zeppelin dirigibles over Germany.

The team of Blanchard and Jeffries did not take long to rise to fame in a spectacular manner: on 7th January 1785 they crossed the Channel in a free balloon, taking with them a small sack of mail – the first international mail despatch and the first international air passengers, between the kingdoms of England and France, more than a century before Blériot! During their airborne crossing, Blanchard and Jeffries had to go to extreme lengths to save their sack of mail. They had left Dover at 13.05

The "Montgolfière", 19th September 1783.

hours and were not more than four or five miles from the French coast when the balloon started to descend rapidly. In order to avoid being swallowed in the waves, they were forced to throw overboard all the paraphernalia they could find in the basket. In vain! – the balloon continued its descent. They then had no compunction in undressing and throwing their clothes overboard – in mid January. Now lighter, the balloon resumed a safe altitude, and, driven by a favourable wind, landed at 15.00 hours between Cap Blanc Nez and Cap Gris Nez. Blanchard and Jeffries had saved the mailbag. It contained several letters, all addressed to the Mayor of Calais, to be re-despatched to their addressees, one of which was to the British Prime Minster, William Pitt. [6]

Military trials and successes

The wars of the French Revolution provided the opportunity for the first military application of aerostatic balloons. It was a field in which revolutionary France enjoyed a superiority. At the suggestion of the Convention, the Comité de Salut Public ("Committee for Public Welfare") decided to create a Company of Military Balloonists, provided with captive balloons anchored by ropes, which were used as vantage points from which observers followed enemy movements. The contribution of the captive balloon "L'Entreprenant" to the French victory at the battle of Fleurus on 26th June 1794 has become famous. [7] However, the attempts made by two fortresses in the north of France under siege from the Austrian army to communicate with the outside world using unmanned balloons were less successful.

In May 1793 General Chancel, commander of the fortress of Condé sur Escaut, used a balloon to try to send a message, Unfortunately, in spite of a favourable wind, the balloon fell into Austrian lines. The message was handed over to the Prince of Saxe Coburg, who was only too happy to receive this first-hand

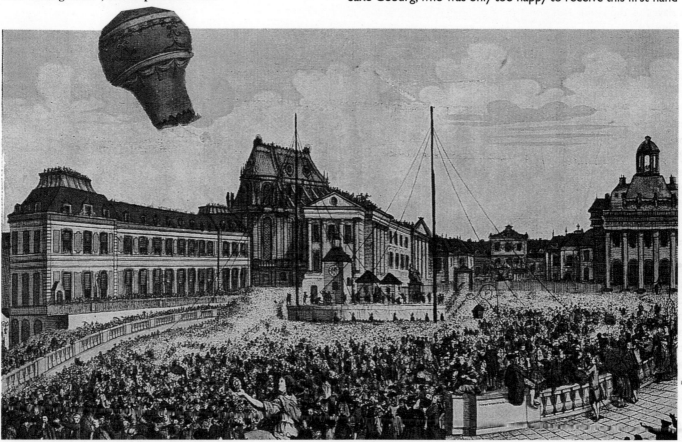

information concerning the precariousness of his enemy's position.

The second attempt occurred in Valenciennes on the 14th or 15th of June 1793. At the suggestion of Messrs Cochon and Briez, Commissioners of the Convention, a free balloon, transporting a pound of post (18 letters) and a carrier pigeon, was launched from the beleaguered fortress. This mail despatch had been very carefully prepared, and was preceded by the launch of a small pilot balloon carrying the following message:

"To all French Republicans,
The Representatives of the People in Valenciennes herewith notify the citizen finding this balloon, that a second balloon will pass, containing despatches for the National Convention. On the strength of his Patriotism he is entreated to use all possible means to cause it to reach its destination." [8]

This exhortation served no purpose as this attempt was no more fortunate than the first at the fortress of Condé sur Escaut: the balloon again fell into Austrian lines. The captured mail was sent to Vienna and lodged in the Military Archives. It consisted of the Report of the Commissioners to the Convention, a few notices, and several private letters, of which one is particularly interesting. It is addressed to Citoyenne L'Echelle, in the Canton of Mansle, in the District of Ruffec, in the Department of Charente, and carries the legend: "To Mansle by balloon". This is the oldest known letter to carry the equivalent of today's "Airmail" sticker.

There is no doubt that free balloons are a rather risky means of transport. Whether they are filled with hot air (the technique used by the Montgolfier brothers), hydrogen, the procedure used by Charles and Robert on 1st December 1783, or with town gas, as practiced by the Englishman Charles Green in 1821, they all share the same crippling weakness: they are slaves to the wind.

Nevertheless, the Dane Johann Peter Colding [9] managed on several occasions to harness the prevailing winds successfully. In 1808 Denmark was allied to Napoleonic France, and the British fleet was blockading the "Great Belt", the strait separating the island of Funen from that of Sealand. Colding proposed to the King [of Denmark] that he should re-establish postal communication between the two islands, using unmanned balloons filled with hydrogen. He recorded his first success on 2nd of June 1808: making clever use of the favourable winds, he succeeded in sending across a balloon containing royal messages, high over the British fleet. This feat was repeated on several occasions.

3 FREE BALLOONS IN EUROPE AND AMERICA 1815-1914

In Europe

After peace had returned to Europe in 1815, aerostatic balloon shows recommenced with demonstration ascents, using free or captive balloons, during which thousands of people had their "baptism of the air". Journeys by air made by scientists and established aeronauts also continued for the next hundred years. On many occasions, almost always for unofficial reasons, they carried mail, which was transported and thrown over the side of the basket.

On 7th November 1836, Charles Green, who made over 500 ascents, took off from Vauxhall, London, accompanied by two passengers. He established a new record, covering more than 375 miles in 18 hours' flight, and landed on 8th November in Germany (near Weilburg in the province of Nassau). During this flight, which was greeted with considerable acclaim, letters were released over Canterbury, Dover and various German towns, using for the first time the technique of the parachute.

In 1841, again in England, the aeronaut Gypson threw out a letter to a friend from his balloon high up in the air. This might all sound rather trivial, but for the fact that this letter is of exceptional interest in postal and philatelic history: franked with a "Penny Black", this is probably the first airmail letter to bear a postage stamp.

Continental Europe also enjoyed similar demonstrations, frequently organised by French aeronauts, until just before the First World War. Two of them are noteworthy.

On 19th and 20th of October 1887 Louis Godard carried out a flight lasting 24 hours 15 minutes. Starting from Leipzig, he landed at Tarnau in Silesia, after having covered a distance of 1,041 miles above Germany and Poland. He took with him a large number of postcards which show the postal despatch stamp "Leipzig 19.10.1897", and the arrival postmark, "Tarnau, 21.10.1897".

Another event which received an enormous amount of public attention was the odyssey of the "Mammoth". This English balloon, manned by the aeronaut Auguste Caudron, was launched from Crystal Palace in London on 12th October 1907. In addition to his two passengers, Caudron took several thousand postcards. He came to earth on 14th October near the little village of Tosse, in the west of Sweden, following an eventful landing during which the contents of the mailsacks were dispersed over a large area. The postcards were gathered up by the inhabitants and taken to the post office at Tosse, where they were postmarked and sent back to England with postage to be collected by the addressees!

In America

On 13th April 1844 the American newspaper "New York Sun" announced some "incredible news": "Atlantic crossed in three days!"

Once everyone's initial stupefaction had subsided, they asked: is it a hoax or an incredible feat? The story seemed all the more extraordinary since the crossing had been made from Europe to America, that is, against the prevailing winds, and without any particular difficulties if one was to believe the initial report.

"We are in sight of the low coast line of South Carolina. The great problem has been solved! We have crossed the Atlantic; we have crossed it in a balloon, easily and soundly."

All too easily, since this was a hoax signed Edgar Poe … [10]
John Wise, like Edgar Poe, was an American. He was a remarkable technician and a veteran of a considerable number of ascents, with a gift for popularising balloon travel. He was the first to found a commercial company for transporting post by balloon between America and Europe. After finding a rich backer, he decided to carry out his initial experiments by transporting post over land.

On 1st July 1859 at 18.45 hours John Wises's balloon, named "Atlantic", rose up over St. Louis, Missouri. It was heavily loaded: apart from the aeronaut and his assistant, his backer and a journalist, the balloon carried a mailbag entrusted to him by one of the most important American express freight companies. John Wise himself told how the "American Express Company" (which had been founded in 1850 by two East Coast business men, Henry Wells and William Fargo) wished to demonstrate its interest in the voyage, and asked them to take towards New York one of its transcontinental mail bags filled with mail from the Pacific coast and letters of greeting from the inhabitants of St Louis to their friends in the east, as if to show their approval for the new method of postal transport, which was inaugurated in this manner.[11]

The voyage started well. By midnight they were flying over Niagara Falls. Shortly afterwards the weather deteriorated and they were caught up in a terrible storm, which carried them out over Lake Ontario. In order to avoid being cast down into the waters of the lake, they decided, after having exhausted the ballast, to throw all their belongings overboard. When the situation got even worse, it was with heavy heart that John Wise resolved to do the unthinkable: to sacrifice the mailbag! Shortly afterwards, the balloon regained altitude, the violence of the elements abated, and the aeronauts succeeded in landing among the trees on the shores of the lake, not far from Henderson in the State of New York.

And the mail? As in any good American film, everything turned out for the best; two days later the mailbag was recovered on the shore, near Oswego, after having completed a record journey by air of over 750 miles. In spite of spending two days in the waters of the lake, the mail was found to be in good condition and was distributed to its recipients.

Although this had at first seemed a setback, some weeks later, impressed by the test flight and wishing to demonstrate their interest, the American postal services entrusted to John Wise "an official mailbag containing 120 letters and 23 pamphlets consigned to New York City".[12] The trial was a mixed success, however: after leaving Lafayette, Indiana, on 17th August 1859, the balloon soon encountered contrary winds and John Wise had to land four hours later at Crawfordsville, Indiana, after travelling a distance of 30 miles.

The overall success of John Wise's trials inspired emulators; it was now the turn of the American Thaddeus Lowe to throw his hat into the ring. In 1859, he constructed an enormous balloon of 20,000 cubic metres capacity, known as "The City of New York", in order to cross the Atlantic on a regular postal service. He suffered a number of reversals, until the start of the American Civil War put paid to his plans.

4 THE SIEGE OF PARIS AND THE ESTABLISHMENT OF AIRMAIL BY BALLOON 1870–71

The Franco-Prussian War in 1870 proved to be catalyst for the use of free flying, manned balloons to transport post in an official, organised manner, that was capable of being both regular and relatively secure.

War between France and Prussia was declared on 19th July 1870. Following the French Army's defeat at Sedan and its surrounding at Metz, its best units were destroyed or neutralised and the Prussian Army lost no time in laying siege to Paris. The Second Empire fell as a consequence of the defeat at Sedan and on 4th September 1870, a government of National Defence was formed in Paris. With increasing urgency for the French, the problem arose as to how the besieged positions could communicate with the outside world.

First Experiences in Metz

In Metz, where Marshal Bazaine had permitted himself to be entrapped with all his army, one Doctor Papillon, a surgeon in the ambulance service of the Imperial Guard, had the idea of using balloons to send ciphered or plain text messages. On 1st September 1870 he confided in Doctor Jeannel, the Pharmacist in Chief, who was later to write: "The idea of entering into communication with the rest of France by means of balloons launched above the Prussian lines caught my imagination, and I devoted some thought as to how it could be carried out."[13] Constrained by lack of means, he manufactured his balloons from tracing paper coated in varnish. The balloons were fragile and low in capacity, but since the weight of each letter was reduced to about 10 grams, Jeannel managed to send fourteen small balloons between 5th and 15th September. The balloons carried a total of approximately three thousand items of mail between the 5th and 15th September.[13] As in the earlier attempts at Condé sur Escaut and Valenciennes, these were unmanned free-flying balloons; but in Metz, the recorded results were much more encouraging because about half of the items sent arrived at their destinations. Doctor Jeannel well deserves the following commemorative plaque which was affixed to a wall of the former military hospital in Metz:

THE BIRTH OF AIRMAIL DURING
THE SIEGE OF METZ
The balloons which constituted the first
airmail service were produced
and launched from the military hospital
of Fort Moselle
on the 5th September 1870
at the instigation of

DOCTOR JULIEN F. JEANNEL

1814-1896

PHARMACIST IN CHIEF TO THE IMPERIAL GUARD

With the participation of the officers of the Medical
Corps[14]

The success of Doctor Jeannel's "balloon post" led to the concept being taken over on a grand scale by General Coffinières de Nordeck, the commander of the fortified city of Metz, who wished to place the balloon post "at the disposition of all those, whether soldiers or civilians, who were held prisoner in Metz". The task of manufacturing the balloons was entrusted to the School of Artillery and Engineering in Metz; the balloons measured from three to five metres in diameter, were inflated with town gas and could carry up to 30,000 messages. Between seven and 10 balloons were launched from 16th September to 3rd October, carrying more than 150,000 messages.[15] The balloon post had been made available to the public; a special post office was opened at the H.Q. of the Fifth Division, and the following notice was put up:

"In order to take advantage of despatch by balloon, correspondence should be set out on onion skin paper, bear the address on one side, and should not exceed 10 centimetres in length and 5 centimetres in width."

A contemporary lithograph showing the balloon launching field at place Saint-Pierre. The small departing balloon is "The Strasbourg".

Unfortunately, several of these unmanned balloons fell into enemy hands, providing them with a flood of information concerning the morale of the besieged troops. It was therefore decided to put an end to the "balloon post". Marshal Bazaine surrendered Metz on 27th October 1870.

Similar experiments in sending messages by free balloons took place at Belfort and Neuf Brisach, although these were of a much more modest and symbolic nature.

Siege of Paris: Organisation of airborne postal service
The siege of Paris by the Prussian armies began on the night of 18th–19th September 1870. During the morning of Monday, 19th September all communication with the outside world became impossible, other than by air. Faced with this situation, some individuals reacted very quickly. Three dates summarise the establishment of the first airborne postal service in the world, which was set up by the authorities and available to the public. This regular and secure service was provided by manned balloons.

• Thursday, 22nd September 1870 [16]
Germain Rampont, a committed, well regarded republican, was nominated as Director General of the Postal Service on 4th September by the Government of National Defence, and called a meeting of the Board of the Postal Service and the balloonists of Paris. Realising that the land route was closed (all

couriers on foot either having been made prisoner or having to return without being able to get through) and that the airways remained the only feasible solution, Rampont was to play a decisive role in organising an airborne postal service using manned balloons.

• Friday, 23rd September 1870
The pilot Jules Duruof (his real name was Dufour) was one of the best professional aeronauts of the period, and was the first to leave the besieged city of Paris on board his own balloon "Neptune". Duruof was a member of the Company of Military Balloonists founded by Nadar on 18th August 1870, before the fall of the empire, and which, in his own words, was "revolutionarily installed" at the beginning of September on the hill of Montmartre, which he considered to be particularly suitable for ballooning operations. He took off from Montmartre at daybreak, taking with him attached to the basket of his balloon three bags of mail with a total weight of 123 kilograms.

Two days later, on 25th of September, a second balloon, "La Citta di Firenze", piloted by Gabriel Mangin, left Paris. In addition to 120 kilograms of post and a particularly corpulent passenger, he took with him three carrier pigeons, "the first of the siege", which were intended to bring back to Paris news from the provinces. The two balloons landed without problems, the first near Evreux and the second near Médan. In both these cases, it was possible to hand over the mail to the French post, to be forwarded in the normal manner.

• Thursday, 29th September 1870
The Official Journal of the Government of National Defence

published two decrees carrying the date of 26th September, authorising the Post to use manned balloons to transport letters and postcards and establishing the maximum weights and the amount of stamp duty payable. These two decrees constitute the official "birth certificate" of an airmail service using manned balloons.

"The Government of National Defence issued under the date of the 26th September, two decrees having the following content:

First Decree

Art. 1 – The Administration of the Post is authorised to send by means of manned balloons ordinary letters destined for France, Algeria and foreign countries.

Art. 2 – The weight of letters to be sent on the balloons shall not exceed 4g. The duty to be charged for the transport of such letters is fixed at 20 centimes. The mail must be franked.

Art. 3 – The Minster of Finance is responsible for carrying out this decree.

Second Decree

Art. 1 – The Administration of the Post is authorised to transport by means of either free flying or manned balloons postcards bearing on one side the address of the addressee and the correspondence on the other side.

Art. 2 – The postcards shall be made of vellum card weighing a maximum of 3g, and shall be 11 centimetres long and 7 centimetres wide.

Art. 3 – Such postcards must be franked. The duty to be charged is 10 centimes for France and Algeria. The tariff for ordinary letters will be applied to postcards destined for foreign countries.

Art. 4 – The Government reserves the right to withhold any postcard, which may contain information of a nature capable of making it useful to the enemy.

Art. 5 – The Minster of Finance is responsible for carrying out this decree."

Airmail had thus become established, with official recognition. Its efficient operation is still subject to the twin conditions of the availability of high quality equipment and of experienced pilots.

The Director General of Postal Services placed its equipment orders with two suppliers known for their professional experience, skilled craftsmanship and ardent patriotism. They were the Goddard brothers, established in the station hall of the Gare d'Orléans, which was available because of the blockade, and two associates, Carmille Dartois and Gabriel Yon, who were established in the Gare du Nord.

This is the first example of series production in the history of aeronautics. The Postal Service had decided on certain specifications:

"The balloons shall have a capacity of 2,000 cubic metres, and made of first quality percalin varnished with linseed oil, and provided with a net of tarred hempen cord a basket capable of holding four persons and all the necessary apparatus: valves, anchors, sacks of ballast ...

"The balloons shall be capable of passing the following test: when filled with gas they must be capable of remaining aloft for 10 hours and after this test period shall still be capable of lifting a net weight of 500 kilograms."

The balloons from the siege of Paris were produced to precise standards: a sphere of 15.75 metres diameter, with a volume of 2,045 cubic metres, the envelope consisted of 40 strips, each made up of three pieces of cloth, with a basket of 1.40 metres x 1.10 metres x 1.10 metres high (not very much for a big man!). The total gross weight included ballast of 1,100 kilograms and had a payload of 500 kilograms. Manufacture took 12 days. The equipment, however good, would not have been any use without qualified pilots. In 1870 France had the most numerous and most experienced team of aeronauts in Europe. All the big names of the ballooning world played a role in the drama of the siege of Paris: Duruof – first to leave; Louis Godard, who was a member of "the largest dynasty of aeronauts of all time"; the brothers Gaston and Albert Tissandier; Wilfrid de Fonvielle and many others.

In spite of their skills, none of these men who left Paris with their balloons full of mail managed to return to Paris, since it was not possible to "steer" their craft. It was therefore necessary to call on volunteer pilots who were less and less well trained. Many were sailors who, although they may have possessed some notions of ballooning theory, had never actually flown. Two of them disappeared without trace with their balloons over the Atlantic: Alexandre Prince, on board the "Jacquard", who left Paris on 28th November 1870 with 250 kilograms of mail, and Emile Lacaze, on board the "Richard Wallace", who left Paris on 27th January 1871 with 220 kilograms of mail. We should pay tribute to these two first pilots who perished in the cause of airborne postal transport; the first of many.

The final assessment of the balloon postal service during the siege of Paris shows how much was achieved by the operation. From 23rd September 1870 to 28th January 1871 66 balloons left Paris. They carried:

• approximately 10,700 kilograms of mail and 2.5 million letters (the figures vary between 10,600 and 11,000 kilograms);

• around 400 carrier pigeons, of which only 57 returned to Paris;

• 102 passengers not including 66 aeronauts;

• somewhat over a ton of scientific equipment;

• an unstated, but certainly considerable weight of issues of the Official Journal, destined for the regional "Départements" and for the Government which had withdrawn to Tours, copies of various pamphlets and proclamations, to be scattered over enemy lines with the intention of undermining the morale of the Prussian troops, and, lastly, newspapers. The press in Paris showed remarkable creativity during the siege. It used new technical procedures (microfilm techniques and printing on ultra light paper) and launched a number of ephemeral titles with evocative names ("The Balloon Post", "The Balloon Despatch", or even "The Post Newspaper, Airmail Edition"). Overall, payload utilisation was excellent; above 90%. Modern airline companies can only dream of such figures!

If we look at quality of service, the airmail operation using manned balloons, organised by the General Postal Administration of the Government of National Defence, fulfilled the three criteria of public availability, regularity and security which characterise any high quality postal system:

• public availability: the service was open to the public at all post offices, at a specified weight and tariff. The system even incorporated a method for maximising utilisation which could be described as revolutionary in airmail terms: there was no surcharge for airmail (although the maximum weight of an ordinary letter for obvious reasons, was reduced from 20 grams to 4 grams, making it necessary to use special papers);

• regularity: this was remarkable when one considers the very severe climatic conditions in the winter of 1870-1871 (snow, frost, mist, freezing rain). Sixty-six balloons were launched, averaging out at about one every two days, with a low deviation from this mean. In order to maintain regular departures and escape Prussian gun fire, daytime flights were replaced by night flights: on 18th November 1870, by night and in a thick fog, the pilot Émile Lemoine took off in his balloon "Général Uhrich" carrying three passengers, four baskets of carrier pigeons and two mail bags; he had just inaugurated night airmail and blind flying. From then on, all departures except for one were made by night , even with the young and inexperienced pilots making their first flights;

• safety: almost 90% of the correspondence was distributed to its addressees. Only 900 kilograms of mail fell into enemy hands and 300

kilograms were lost at sea. This is an amazing result when one thinks of the conditions under which this service was set up.

Such was the world's first airmail service, the success of which was due to several factors: the courage and absolute devotion to duty of the balloonists; the active participation of the rural populations in France and Belgium in securing the balloons and their precious cargo; the mobilisation of the personnel of the postal system which continued to function in the occupied territories; the relatively low density of the Prussian occupying troops in the rural areas. This was why several balloons, which fell behind enemy lines, were spirited away by the peasants, while the pilots were concealed from the inquisitiveness of patrols and the mailbags were discreetly handed over to the post mistress in the next village.

The operation inspired Victor Hugo to write in fine poetic style:

"Paris surrounded, Paris blockaded, Paris cut off from the world's highways, and yet with the aid of a balloon, that bubble of soap, Paris corresponds with the rest of the world."

Night ascent of the balloon "Chemin du fer Nord" from a field in Paris.

It is true that Paris had managed to communicate with the outside world, but the rest of the world had had great difficulty in corresponding with Paris. Balloons are vehicles that go one way – the way of the wind. Although the best aeronauts gradually gathered in the provinces, no balloon, despite several attempts, managed to get back to Paris due to the relatively small area of the site under siege.

For communication from the provinces to Paris, another method was found, the carrier pigeon, using its special aptitude of being able to find its way back to its native pigeon loft, even from a distance of several hundred miles. The new director of telegraph lines, François Frédéric Steenackers, was instrumental in establishing this new pigeon post airmail between Tours and Paris. Since the weight lifting capacity of a carrier pigeon is obviously extremely limited, after several experiments stages a technique of "reduction by photomicroscope" was adopted. Based on chemical discoveries by Barreswill and perfected by Dagron and Fernique, the "pigeon-gram" was born:

"This procedure consisted of collecting at a central point all the telegrams for transmission, undertaking an initial size reduction by typesetting them, so that they were formed into columns as though in a large newspaper, and then photographing them down to a smaller scale and sending the films from the photomicroscope by pigeon. Although reduced to minimal dimensions, this telegraphic newspaper in photograph form arrived in Paris in very clear characters, which could be read using nothing more powerful than a strong magnifying glass. The films were inserted into goose quill tubes and fixed to one of the tail feathers of the pigeon, which caused it not the least inconvenience." [17]

Although initially reserved for official despatches, the pigeon post was then opened to inhabitants of the provinces with family members in Paris. However, it was not very reliable: out of 300 pigeons released towards Paris after previously being brought out by balloon, between 57 and 73 (according to reliable sources) returned to Paris.

In spite of its limitations, the experience of sending airmail via manned balloons during the siege of Paris made a great impression on the man considered to be the father of the modern international postal service: Heinrich Von Stephan, who was the Director General of the Prussian postal service and co-founder of the Universal Postal Union. In a remarkable speech given in Berlin on 24th January 1874, entitled "World postal services and ballooning", [18] he summarised the lesson to be learnt from the Paris experience: "The speed and direction of the balloon depend entirely on the wind, and there lies the nub of the problem". After enumerating the conditions to be fulfilled if ballooning was to become a secure and regular means of postal transport, he revealed his vision of the ideal universal postal union in which airmail could contribute to bringing the peoples of the world closer together:

"In the free realm of the air, space is available everywhere, the small intertwined territories of different states [here, Von Stephan is thinking of the political situation of Germany before 1870] whose rights of transit interrupt postal traffic, the frontiers with their customs posts and difficulties in crossing will no longer present a problem. Of all the discoveries made up to the present time, none will prove to be so favourable as ballooning in bringing about communication between the inhabitants of the Earth."

Forty years later, as a direct echo of Von Stephan, Count Ferdinand Von Zeppelin confessed: "It was this conference that kept alive in me the desire to create an airship of that nature."

5 DIRIGIBLE BALLOONS

The problem of how to direct balloons exercised many minds throughout the 18th and 19th centuries. All kinds of techniques were envisaged to provide balloons with an effective system of propulsion and guidance, from the physical principles of action and reaction, to muscle power, the steam engine, electricity and the petrol engine.

In October 1783 Joseph Montgolfier evoked "the power of the reactive force". Jean-Pierre Blanchard used successively a propeller powered by muscular arms, then one by a "fire engine" (steam engine). An important step was achieved by the engineer Henri Giffard, who had hitherto exercised his abilities on steam locomotives: on 24th September 1852 he took off on board a balloon with a very elongated shape, equipped with a steam engine driving a propeller. In spite of the low power developed, the balloon completed various aerial manoeuvres. Other researchers then turned towards a new energy source: electricity. On 9th August 1884 Captains Renard and Krebs achieved a round trip of over 4 miles in a "dirigible" balloon, the "France", fitted with an 8hp electric motor. The single, though major, difficulty was the weight of the batteries. The solution to the problems of powered flight was found in 1885 when Gottlieb Daimler invented the petrol engine.

In France, a young Brazilian, Albert Santos Dumont, carried off the Deutsch de la Meurthe Prize on 19th October 1901. On board his dirigible balloon "Santos Dumont No 6", fitted with a 20-horsepower engine, he took off from the Porte de Saint Cloud, doubled back round the Eiffel Tower and returned to land at his point of departure within 30 minutes. On 24th June 1903 the dirigible "Lebaudy", financed by a sugar magnate, covered the distance of 61 miles, thanks to a 40-horsepower Mercedes engine driving two propellers.

However, it was Germany which "went to the forefront of progress regarding dirigible balloons". [19]

Several ascents were made by Doctor Wolfert and the Austrian Schwartz, who was the first to design a rigid dirigible entirely in metal.

On 2nd July 1900 at 20.03 hours, Count Ferdinand Von Zeppelin took off from Manzell near Friedrichshafen on Lake Constance. He was with four other people aboard a large rigid dirigible, a "Zeppelin", measuring 128 metres long (within two metres, the same length as the Cathedral of Notre-Dame in Paris), and 11.7 metres in diameter. It was constructed using duralumin, with two nacelles, each fitted with a 14-horsepower Daimler engine driving two small air screws. The handling conditions were good and it covered a distance of 3,700 metres at an altitude of approximately 300 metres before returning to land without difficulty close to its floating hangar.

Count Von Zeppelin was born in Constance in 1838. During his brilliant military career he achieved renown by making an incredible horse ride of 25 miles inside the French lines at the beginning of the Franco/Prussian war. In 1890 he was promoted to Lieutenant General but soon afterwards resigned from the Army, apparently as a result of a difference of opinion on military doctrine – evidence of a strong character. At the age of 52 he began his second career, which would lead him to construct airships (German Luftschiffe) which circumnavigated the globe and established the first regular transatlantic passenger links. There are those who still dream of airships today, particularly for intercontinental freight transport.

In fact, Count von Zeppelin was interested in ballooning a long time before 1890. The entry in his personal notebooks for the 25th March 1874 reads:

> "The dimensions of an airship should correspond to those of a large marine vessel ... Take-off would be made using a motor and an altitude control rudder . . . At cruising altitude, the height control would be modified to keep horizontal in flight. In order to land, operate the height control and reduce speed." [20]

On 4th April 1875, more than 25 years before the launch of the first vessel to carry his name, he foresaw the functions of this "great aerial ship".

> "In the beginning balloons will on the one hand provide luxury transport and on the other hand serve to carry all things which require on a permanent basis a rapid, secure and easy link, which cannot be ensured by land or sea routes due to particular difficulties between two points." [21]

On 6th February 1896 in Stuttgart, he defined the possible uses of "dirigible air vessels" as being "post, navigation, the conduct of war, the exploration of the world". [21] The dual role of balloon transport – both civil and military – is clearly expressed. The great event of July 1900 was followed by many trials and tribulations and it was not until 25th September 1907 that the first post was transported on a Zeppelin balloon, when the LZ3 (Luftschiff Zeppelin No 3) released several letters over Romanshorn, a small Swiss town on the shores of Lake Constance, during a test flight. Following this inaugural flight, the history of the use of Zeppelins for postal operations before the First World War can be divided into two periods:

• First period: 1908–1909

Two kinds of cards were used: "Aerial release cards" (Abwurfkarten), embossed with the seal of the Zeppelin Construction Company and providing space for a limited amount of correspondence, and cards with reply forms (Findermeldekarten), which bore the following text:

> "Any person finding this card is most urgently requested to take one half of it to the Post. If he sends us this card, with an indication of the place where it was found, he will receive an expression of personal thanks from His Excellency Count Zeppelin." [22]

Only a very small number of these documents have survived, and have become objects of "very clever forgeries". [23]

• Second period: 1909–1914

In autumn 1909, the German Airship Navigation Company (Deutsche Luftschifffahrts Aktiengesellschaft better known under the name of DELAG) was founded and given the responsibility of the commercial exploitation of Zeppelin dirigibles. From 1909 to the summer of 1914, during 1,588 outings, the company transported without the slightest bodily injury 34,028 persons, of which 10,197 passengers actually travelled in a comfortable lounge. Many of these journeys were from one German town to the next, to give people "baptisms of the air" over their local town or rural district. DELAG also had a certain amount of postal traffic, but this was of limited value.

> "In order to transport postcards written on board by the passengers, they used small bags attached to large flags, which were easy to find after they were jettisoned from the balloon. The finder of the bag was requested to take it to the nearest post office, where he would receive his reward, amounting to 50 pfennigs." [24]

As can be imagined, this was not so much normal correspondence, as postcards for special occasions, philatelic souvenirs, or cards carrying advertisements. In 1912, the postal administration decided to install an employee aboard each balloon to receive and cancel the mail. But overall it amounted to a rather unsatisfactory postal operation using primitive techniques.

However, larger quantities of post were transported from town to town via dirigible balloons for special events, such as the Aeronautical Fortnight of the Grand Duchy of Hesse which took place at Frankfurt am Main on 10th to 23rd June 1912 and which became the first occasion in Germany when airmail was operated on a large scale.

2 AVIATION: AIRCRAFT AND SEAPLANES

1 FROM LEONARDO DA VINCI TO LOUIS BLÉRIOT

"Leonardo da Vinci was the first man of high scientific attainment to investigate the problem of flight." [1] He made detailed studies of bird flight and of its mechanical imitations, carried out research on the functions of propellers and made a sketch of a helicopter. However, due to the disappearance of his manuscripts shortly after his death in 1519 until their tardy rediscovery at the end of the 19th century, Leonardo da Vinci did not influence aeronautical history.

Instead, Sir George Cayley (1773-1857) was the great scientific visionary of aviation, "the true inventor of the aeroplane and one of the most powerful geniuses in the history of aviation". Wilbur Wright paid him a justly earned tribute:

"About 100 years ago, an Englishman, Sir George Cayley, carried the science of flying to a point which it never reached before and which it scarcely reached again during the last century."

Just as the Marquis d'Argenson embodies the French spirit of the 18th century, the baronet Sir George Cayley personifies the middle ranks of the English nobility in the first half of the 19th century. A practical agriculturist, preoccupied with the most modern techniques, a liberal man of politics, a mind with a penchant for philosophical and religious reflection, yet strongly attracted towards science, he combined with equal success research of a practical nature – he invented the caterpillar tractor – and the most advanced scientific speculations – he established the basis of modern aerodynamics.

A symbol of both his era and his social class, he was, in addition, a good husband and father. Although he exercised his aeronautical creativity only during two well-defined periods in his life, from 1799 to 1809 and then from 1843 to 1853, he never ceased to declare his faith in "aerial navigation": "I am well convinced that aerial navigation will form a most prominent feature in the progress of civilisation". Sir George Cayley, like all visionaries and pioneers of aviation, foresaw the transport of goods on the same basis as the transport of persons. He wrote in 1809:

"I fell perfectly confident, however, that this noble art will soon be brought home to man's general convenience, and

that we should be able to transport ourselves and our families, and their goods and chattels, more securely by air than by water and with a velocity of from 20 to 100 miles per hour. To produce this effect it is only necessary to have a first mover which will generate more power in a given time, in proportion to its weight, than the animal system of muscles."

Fifty years separate the work of Cayley from the first flights of the Wright brothers. During this half century many researchers, passionate about aeronautics and convinced that its future lay in heavier than air machines, contributed to the advance of knowledge. It is not within the remit of this book to list them all, but before we reach the exceptional achievements of the Wright brothers, three names stand out (at the risk of appearing to be unjust towards several others) – Alphonse Pénaud, Clément Ader and Otto Lilienthal.

Alphonse Pénaud (1830-1880) is little known to the public at large, but the English historian Charles Gibb-Smith paid him the finest of tributes: "The decade 1870/1880 was dominated by a great man, Alphonse Pénaud. He is one of the aeronautical giants ranking with Cayley and the Wrights". "Gentle and modest", a fine engineer and a remarkable theoretician, Alphonse Pénaud defined clearly the critical factors in aerial navigation (air resistance and lightness of motors).

Clément Ader (1841–1925) was completely different. He was an electrical engineer, the inventor of a number of patents, a great industrialist and a man of difficult character. From 1880 onwards, he devoted a substantial proportion of his resources to studies of mechanics and aeronautical theory. Over and above the findings which resulted from his work, one thing is certain: in an aeroplane named "Eole", entirely designed and manufactured by himself, equipped with a steam engine of remarkable ingenuity and lightness, Clément Ader was the first man "to leave the earth completely, skimming above the earth" [2] for a distance of about 50 metres and at an altitude of some tens of centimetres, solely as a product of motive power. The event occurred on 9th October 1890 at 16.00 hours in the park of the Château d'Armainvilliers, to the east of Paris. In addition, Ader bequeathed the French lan

The Wright Brothers' flight, 17th December 1903.
RAF Museum/Library of Congress

guage a word, which would have a great future: "Avion" – "Aircraft".

Otto Lilienthal (1848-1896), with the aid of a monoplane with a wing span of 7 metres and no form of motive power, succeeded in completely mastering the techniques of simply gliding through still air and of using winds and air currents, by dint of over 2,000 test glides. He was killed on the 9th August 1896 during one such flight.

Powered aviation was born on 17th December of 1903 in the United States at Kill Devil Hills, 4 miles south of Kitty Hawk in North Carolina, on the long, thin strips of sand which reach out into the sea to form Cape Hatteras.

On that day, between 10.30am and 12.00 midday, the brothers Orville and Wilbur Wright, who hailed from Dayton, Ohio, succeeded in flying and controlling an aeroplane of their own manufacture, fitted with a 12-horsepower engine, over a distance of more than 250 metres. "The flight lasted only 12 seconds, but it was nevertheless the first in the history of the world in which a machine carrying a man had raised itself by its own power into the air in full flight, had sailed forward without reduction of speed and had finally landed at a point as high as that at which it had started." [3] Orville and Wilbur Wright had made the first powered, sustained and controlled flight. Orville was to write:

"We stand at the beginning of a new era, the *age of flight*."

During the first few years following this event, the main question was that of the potential application of this new means of transport. At the end of 1904, Wilbur confided as follows to Octave Chanute, an engineer, pioneer and aviation propagandist: "It is a question of whether we are not ready to begin considering what we will do with our baby now that we have it." The realist, Orville provided the answer: "It is therefore our intention to furnish machines for military use first, before entering the commercial field."

Aviation's first calling was thus a military one and between 1908 and 1912, the new weapon – considered as a means of observation and reconnaissance – was introduced into the United States, France, Great Britain, Germany, Italy, Austria-Hungary and Russia.

On the initiative of Captain Ferber, France was one of the first to recognise the value of aviation: in September 1910 a group of 14 aircraft took part in large-scale manoeuvres in Picardy. Convinced of the advantages of this new weapon, the military would have a decisive influence on the development of aviation. They were the first to state their requirements and define specifications. A "competitive tender for military aircraft" was launched in autumn 1911.

In order to be accepted, designs would have to correspond to the following standards: [4] have a range of operation of 100 miles, be easily transportable by road or rail, be capable of landing on meadows and ploughed fields, have seating for two passengers in addition to the pilot, be capable of a speed of 40mph, carry a payload of 300 kilograms excluding fuel, and, finally, the aircraft and engine were to be of a French manufacture. Not all the competitors were able to fulfil the standards, but they reflected the technical possibilities of the time, and orders from the Armed Services were to determine the characteristics of civilian aircraft and engines to a large degree.

Aviation also owes its origins to sport. Its early years are marked by the setting of numerous records – speed, distance, altitude – and by organised airshows. On 13th January 1908, Henri Farman achieved a great performance in the presence of official sporting stewards at Issy-les-Moulineaux: he flew round the first closed circuit of one kilometre (0.6 miles) in a Voisin biplane fitted with a 50-horsepower Antoinette engine, manufactured by Levavasseur.

In order to establish itself commercially, aviation needed an act of extraordinary prowess, a sensational achievement which would act like a detonator – this was the first crossing of the Channel. On 25th July 1909, Louis Blériot left the locality of Les

Baraques near Calais at 04.41 hours in the morning. He landed near Dover, in a gap in the cliffs, at 05.13 hours. He had crossed the Channel in an aircraft, which he had designed himself, the "Blériot XI". This was a monoplane, 7 metres long, with wings 7.80 metres wide and having an effective aerofoil surface of 14 square metres. It was equipped with a 25-horsepower Anzani engine, and its total weight, including that of the pilot and fuel for 2 hours, was not more than 300 kilograms.

Louis Blériot was a great industrialist from the automobile industry, who had been converted to aviation. Two years later, in 1911, he underlined the commercial role of aviation when he declared: "We must prepare for the commercial aviation of tomorrow." From then on, there was a change of mind and pre-occupations changed: people no longer talked solely of records in speed, altitude and distance, but also of record payloads. The magazine "L'Aérophile", observed in 1911: "At present, the burning competitive spirit of the aviators seems to be concentrated on the record for the highest transportable payload."

The time was right for the beginnings of commercial aviation. While the first men and women passengers were transported from 1908 onwards, the first cargo flight took place in 1910, the first trials with airborne post in 1911 and the world's first regular air service began on 1st January 1914.

2 THE WORLD'S FIRST CARGO FLIGHT

The first cargo flight took place on 7th November 1910 in the USA, between Dayton and Columbus, Ohio.

In the evening of this memorable day, Milton Wright, Bishop in the United Brethren in Christ Church in Dayton, and father of Orville and Wilbur, wrote in his private diary: "Orville and Katherine went to Simms to see Mr Phil O. Parmalee start to Columbus with several bolts of silk in an aeroplane. He flew there in 61 minutes and delivered the goods." Thus it was that the father of the Wright brothers recounted in his most sober and factual manner one of the most significant events in commercial aviation: the first cargo flight.

LEFT Voisin with his Farman biplane. *RAF Museum*

RIGHT The first cross-Channel flight by Blériot, 25 July 1909. *RAF Museum*

BELOW Max Morehouse (left) and Roy Knabenshue photographed in the Wright factory in Dayton, one week before the world's first cargo flight on 7 November 1910. A Wright model B carried 200lbs (88 kilos) of silk from Dayton to Columbus for Max Morehouse. *Ohio History of Flight Museum*

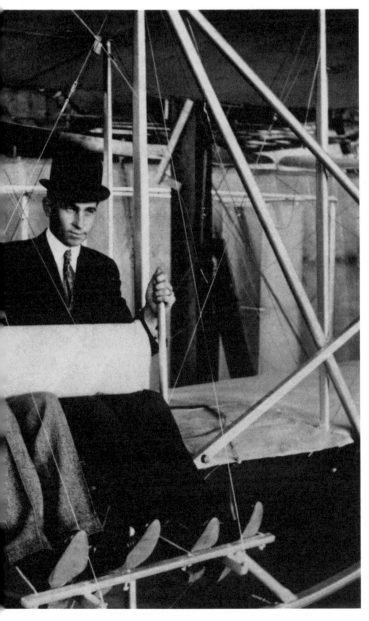

The key figure in this event was Max Morehouse.[5] He was an aviation enthusiast and a man of some influence in business circles in Columbus, where he ran the largest store, the Home Dry Goods Store. In a letter of 14th October 1910 addressed to the "Wright Exhibition Cy", Max Morehouse informs them of his idea of transporting a bolt of ribbon by plane from Dayton to Columbus to mark the annual autumn sale of the store. In order to ensure the greatest possible popular success and to benefit from maximum press coverage, Morehouse requests that "some aerial demonstrations" should be made above Columbus, in addition to the actual transport assignment. The Wright Exhibition Cy was fully qualified to provide this kind of service, since it had been founded in 1908 by the Wright Brothers and Glenn Curtiss for the purpose of organising flying shows and what amounted to aerobatic exhibitions, due to the lack of military opportunities and commercial activities.

After the usual bargaining, everything was ready for the great event. On Monday 7th November 1910 at 10.45 hours the young pilot Philip O. Parmalee took off from Dayton in a Wright Model B aeroplane. He was carrying a consignment of 200 pounds (about 88 kilograms) consisting of two parcels: one contained a bolt of pink silk and the other, nine pieces of silk of different colours. These nine pieces were intended to be sold in the store, whereas the bolt of pink silk would be cut up into small pieces on arrival. After being stuck onto souvenir post-cards, the pieces of material would be sold to the enthusiastic crowd, which had gathered on the Columbus airfield. And the profits were by no means small!

The flight proceeded under good conditions. The weather was clear and Parmalee was able to use a classic navigation technique: he followed the course of the Dayton-Columbus railway line. He landed shortly before midday in front of a crowd of over 3,000 people after travelling a distance of 70 miles and handed the goods over to their consignee.

After lunch, Parmalee went about the second part of the programme: the aerobatics: "He negotiated the most dangerous dives and the sharpest turns with superlative ease."

LEFT **First official air mail flight in Germany from Frankfurt to Darmstadt, 10th June 1912.**
Lufthansa

The first air cargo delivery was for more than a mere act of transportation: it was a brilliant marketing operation – "the main object for Morehouse was publicity". It was an entirely successful "advertising stunt" and the store's turnover increased so much that the cost of the operation, which at $5,000 was not inconsiderable, was covered "in a day or two". Morehouse had demonstrated that transport by airfreight increases the value of the goods transported and develops sales!

This flight of 7th November 1910 deserves a special mention in the annals of commercial aviation, because it was the occasion of several "firsts": the first airfreight shipment; the first "cargo only" flight, solely for the transport of goods; the first flight to be commissioned by a client – the first charter; and the first example of multimodal air transport, since the pieces of silk were transported by car from Columbus aerodrome to the store.

Recognising the future of combined transport, "Scientific American" observed "A striking demonstration of the conjunctive use of the aeroplane and the automobile in the delivery of mail and express". The consignment from Dayton was not followed up and examples of transportation of goods by air before the First World War are rare. In addition the few that did take place are not well known as, in contrast to the first postal flights which were the object of official authorisation delivered by the public administration, the first deliveries of freight by air were the product of private initiative.

As one author puts it, in a laconic phrase: "The origins of airfreight are obscure." [6]

None the less, it appears that the first shipments after those of Dayton were carried out in Great Britain:

• On 14th July 1911 a case of OSRAM lamps was sent by plane from Shoreham to Hove Lawns for the General Electric Company [7] (pilot H. Barber in a Valkyrie monoplane);

• Between 11th and 18th February 1913, the "Robert Sinclair Tobacco Company" organised an Aviation Week at Gosforth near Newcastle-on-Tyne. The pilot, B. C. Hucks, in his Blériot

aircraft transported several parcels of tobacco to destinations in nearby towns and villages (Blyth, Seaham Harbour, Ashington …). Each parcel bore a green label, showing a monoplane in flight.

Newspapers constitute an ideal transition between freight and post: they were formally included in post, but are now treated as freight shipments, and represented the market with the most obvious potential for airfreight, because of their extremely short shelf life. Moreover, the newspapers were quick to understand the value of the publicity that they could get by associating their image with that of aviation, and many newspapers sponsored air-shows. Some of the earliest examples of this are listed below:

• 13th August 1911, France: Jules Védrines transported newspapers from Issy-les-Moulineaux to Deauville. Jules Védrines might perhaps have had a claim to be the operator of the world's first cargo line if the engines of the day had been more reliable. In his autobiographical book "La vie d'un aviateur" ("The life of an aviator") he recounts how he "was persuaded to take on the role of an aerial postman between Paris and Trouville". The intention was for him to take every day letters, parcels and newspapers – although mostly newspapers – to Mantes, Evreux, Lisieux, Trouville and Deauville.

The first flight took place on 13th August 1911, departing Issy-les-Moulineaux at 05.10 hours and arriving at Deauville at 06.50 hours, carrying the Paris morning papers. "I tried to set out again as often as I could," writes Védrines, "every day if I could manage it, and I got in to the habit of doing this journey in an hour and a half."

It all ended on 16th August 1911 with a violent and involuntary dip in the sea off the beach at Deauville after the engine had suddenly cut out.

• 19th August 1911, Germany: the "Berliner Morgenpost" chartered an aeroplane. The pilot Siegfried Hoffmann transported papers from Berlin-Johannisthal to Frankfurt on the Oder. In his

RIGHT Promoters, pilots, mechanics and postal officials of the first aerial mail.
RAF Museum

PROMOTERS, PILOTS, MECHANICS, & POSTAL OFFICIALS OF THE FIRST AERIAL MAIL

RIGHT Promoters, pilots, mechanics and postal officials of the first aerial mail.
RAF Museum

Harlan monoplane, he beat the train from Berlin by an hour.

• 2nd October 1911, Norway: the Swedish Baron Karl Cederström undertook a tour by air financed by the daily newspaper "Tidens Tegn" from Kristiana (Oslo). When he arrived above Trondheim, he threw out copies of the newspaper bound with a tape bearing the message: "Tidens Tegn – first airmail in Norway. Dropped by Baron Cederström from the 'Nordstjernen', 500 metres above Trondheim. The finder is kindly requested to deposit this package in the nearest letter-box."

• June and August 1912, England: the "Daily Mail", of which the proprietor, Lord Northcliffe, was a great aviation fan, financed several flights from Bath to Falmouth, and then between South Coast holiday resorts.

• 8th October 1913, Canada: W. C. Robinson loads newspapers on board the first flight from Montreal to Ottawa.

3 THE FIRST REGULAR PASSENGER OPERATION

The world's first regular air service was operated in Florida in the United States from 1st January to 31st March 1914, between the towns of Tampa and St Petersburg, two coastal resorts separated by a marshy bay. Instead of once-off flights,

BELOW Arrival of the mail aircraft "Yellow Dog" at the Darmstadt air mail office, 10 June 1912.
Lufthansa

this was a daily airline service open for the regular transport of goods and passengers. The flight time was short – only 20 minutes – and the service was provided by a seaplane, "Benoist type XIV", weighing 1,400 pounds, of wood and cloth construction, fitted with a 75-horsepower engine and flying at a speed of about 60mph.

The Tampa/St Petersburg airline operated for three months with a regularity that was exemplary for the time – eight flights cancelled out of 90 planned. It was the forebear of the modern passenger airlines, or "mixed lines", which take all types of traffic – passengers, post and freight – and which even today carry as much goods traffic as cargo aircraft specially designed for the purpose. Since it did not have a contract with the American Post, the "St Petersburg-Tampa Airboat Line" only transported passengers and goods. The airfreight rate was specified on a "warehouse to warehouse" basis: we still use the same definition today.

At the end of the three-month operating period, the commercial income (supplemented by a subsidy from the town of St Petersburg) consisted of 92% passenger receipts, and 8% in receipts from freight and excess baggage. Today the proportion of revenue derived from airfreight transportation by the major American passenger airlines is lower.

4 THE DEBUT OF AIRMAIL

A distinction needs to be made between unofficial and official flights. The former have more to do with airmail philately than with the history of transportation. The latter, given official authorisation, are concerned with the testing of the actual capabilities of a new mode of transport on behalf of an administration, which is always intent on employing the fastest means of conveying the mail.

Unofficial Flights

From 1909 onwards, a large number of Aviation Weeks and flying meetings were held and various philatelic documents – commemorative postcards or token stamps – were issued during the events. In all cases, the documents sent may only unofficially be classified as "Post", and it is often very difficult to determine whether they were in fact transported in an aircraft. At best, they were placed on board an aircraft, which carried out a brief flight over the airfield before landing at its point of departure: one cannot therefore really describe these as "postal transport".

The official postal authorities first became involved when they opened temporary post offices at airfields during air shows. The first official airmail postmark was applied in August 1909 on mail handed in to the temporary post office during the "Grand Aviation Week" of Bétheny sur Marne near Reims. It bore the inscription "Bétheny Aviation-Marne".

Special airmail postmarks were used in Germany during the Chemnitz Aviation Week (black postmark "Chemnitz Flugplatz"), and in Great Britain during the first Blackpool Flying Meeting in August 1910, during which the pilot Graham-White carried several pieces of private post on board his aircraft. [8]
A detailed study of the documents issued, and possibly transported during these events, is outside the scope of this work. However, some examples of "private post", have become part of the history of airmail:

• 13th/20th September 1911, Morocco. The "Petit Journal" decided to make "a practical demonstration of airborne post",
in the French protectorate, with the semi-official support of the French civil and military authorities. The pilot Bregi, accompanied by Lebaut, transported several letters from Casablanca to Rabat on 13th September 1911, and then from Rabat to Mèknes on the 18th and from Mèknes to Fez on the 20th.

• 7th October 1911, United States: During a convention in St Louis, Missouri a seaplane manufactured by Curtiss, took off from the surface of the Mississippi and then landed back on the river with mail on board. This is believed to be the first instance of such a flight.

• 18th February 1912, Germany: On this date a private postal flight was carried out between Bork and Brück, to municipalities in Brandenburg, near Potsdam and Berlin. Earlier, during the spring of 1910 in Bork, the engineer Hans Grade had set up an aircraft manufacturing workshop and a famous flying school, which was to operate into the year 1945. The initiative of operating a postal flight between Bork and a neighbouring town came from the dentist in Bork, who was also president of the local transport association (Verkehrsverein). With his encouragement, the postal link was organised: on 18th February 1912 the pilot Hermann Pentz, an ex-pupil of the Grade flying school, conveyed a mail sack containing 400 to 500 items from Bork to Brück. The letter bearing the number one was addressed to the Kaiser Wilhelm II. Although privately organised, since the Reichspost had not authorised it, this flight caused a considerable stir within Germany. As a historical footnote, this famous flight was not only unofficial, it was illegal, since Pentz only received his pilot's license two days afterwards! [9]

Official flights

From an official point of view, airmail was born in Allahabad – in Northern India – on 18th February 1911. At that time India was administered by Britain as part of its empire and a great many British civil servants lived there with their families.
In 1911 "The Annual United Provinces (of India) Industrial and Agricultural Exhibition", an event with both cultural and commercial aims, was held at Allahabad, a city situated at the confluence of the Ganges and the Yamuna.

To liven up the show, the organisers called upon the Englishman Walter Windham, who was a skilled motorcar driver and an aviation enthusiast, to carry out or organise a series of demonstration flights. At that point, a clergyman of the Church of the Sacred Trinity of Allahabad, (whose flock consisted principally of British civil servants), had the idea of linking a demonstration flight with the transportation of mail for charitable purposes. His strategy was exactly the same as that of Morehouse in Columbus, although the aims differed: charitable rather than commercial. With the authorisation and under the control of the Postmaster General, any persons wishing to send mail in support of the good works of their clergyman (to wit, the building of the hostel for Indian students) were invited to pay a surcharge of 6d over and above the normal postage to enable their mail to be transported by air, over a short symbolic route.

On 18th February 1911 the French pilot Henri Péquet, to whom Windham had entrusted this aerial mission, transported 6,500 letters and postcards over the few miles, which separate Allahabad from Naini junction.

Over 60 years later, Hénri Péquet still remembered the flight, in a recorded interview: [10]

Henri Péquet completes the first airmail flight on 18 February 1911 from Allahabad to Naini Junction.

"What were the conditions under which the first airmail post operated? First of all, what kind of aircraft was it?"

"It was a Sommer, with a 50-horsepower Gnome radial engine. A two-seater biplane.'

"What instrumentation on the instrument panel?"

"Don't go thinking that we had instrument panels at that time! All we had in front of us was empty space. I had a watch on my right wrist and an altimeter on my left knee.'

"No rev counter?"

"No. When you started off you set the engine speed at about 1,200 rpm by means of the 'bell' (the oil distributor cover) which you could hear sounding, and which you checked with your watch!'

"Now what about the airfield?"

"It was a polo ground.'

"And the mission?"

"To link up with Naini, about 10 kilometres [6 miles] from Allahabad and to transport a sack containing 15 kilos of mail: 6,000 letters and cards, with some for the King of England, the King of Italy, the King of Belgium, the Queen of Holland, and a lot of very superior personalities."

"Was there a special postmark?"

"Of course. Because the organisers attached a lot of importance to the affair. The postmark consisted of the words: 'First aerial post'."

"Have you still got one?"

"Naturally. I wrote to myself that day!"

"What was the date exactly?"

"18th February 1911."

"Was it fine weather?"

"Of course. Otherwise you couldn't have flown!"

"Speed?"

60 kilometres an hour [38mph] in flight, and 50 for landing [31mph] ..."

"Flight time?"

"27 minutes."

"Terrain?"

"Flat. I followed the road through the middle of forest."

"What about the flight itself? Any recollections? Was there a crowd when you took off?"

"No, mostly the buffalo! On take off you had to pass above the Ganges. I didn't feel too comfortable ..."

"Is it wide?"

"Yes, 300 or 400 metres... it wasn't so much that I was frightened of getting wet. It was the crocodiles!"

"And on touchdown, was there a crowd?"

"No. There was one official from the Post to whom I handed over the bag."

"Altitude during the trip?"

"40-50 metres. Not more."

"And did the press talk about it?"

"Yes. Here is a cutting from a newspaper at the time: I read: 'In London, at the end of the week, letters were received from India, bearing a postmark which is novel in postal history, the first postmark recognised by the authorities for franking letters transported by air ... These are the first letters to be officially distributed by aeroplane. A supplement for this mode of transport amounted to 6 annas per letter.'"

The first official airmail flight was only of a symbolic nature, since the mail was re-despatched via the traditional land and sea routes after it had completed its demonstration flight between Allahabad and Naini, but it was nevertheless of major significance since for the first time the postal authorities had demonstrated their interest in aviation, which was still in its infancy.

From then on, there was a series of official postal trials continuing right up to the declaration of the First World War in August 1914:

• 9th/26th September 1911, Great Britain: On the occasion of the coronation of King George V, an airborne postal service was organised between London/Hendon (the cradle of British aviation) and Windsor Great Park. It operated from 9th to 26th September 1911 and enjoyed the approval of the Postmaster General.

The correspondence transported consists exclusively of envelopes and postcards specially printed for the occasion by an Air Mail Committee. It carried the inscription: "A.D. Coronation 1911 – First U.K. Aerial Post by Sanction of H.M. Postmaster General."

Always prudent, and anxious not to be held responsible for any problems, the postal administration asked for the following text to be printed on the lower left hand corner of the envelopes: "To be forwarded by aeroplane from London to Windsor. The Postmaster General is not responsible in case of loss, damage or delay."

Each card was adorned with an official commemorative postmark: "First United Kingdom Aerial Post."

In contrast to the experience at Allahabad, this was not an isolated flight but a series of flights: although temporary, this was the first attempt to set up a regular service by air.

The operation of the service was entrusted to The Graham-White Aviation Co Ltd, which laid on a service using four French aircraft: two Blériot and two Farman.

The outcome of the service was mixed. On the one hand, 21 flights were made, with the largest number being carried out by the French pilot Gustave Hamel, and 130,000 cards transported. But on the other hand, there were flights postponed due to fog, interrupted flights, mechanical setbacks, damaged aircraft and one pilot seriously injured. "The official verdict of the experiment was that the airmail would have no scientific value, but it might under favourable conditions permit of more rapid communication than by any other means of transport, but that it was too dependant upon weather to be of use as a regular and ordinary mode of conveyance." (Brigadier General Williamson).

Since the income from the sale of the postcards exceeded the total of the costs incurred, a cheque for £1,000 was sent to the King Edward VII Hospital in Windsor: "that was the principal result of the experiment."

Aviation did not yet possess the qualities of regularity and safety, which are required by any postal administration.

• 23rd September/1st October 1911, the United States: On 14th June 1910, the Texan Democrat representative Morris Sheppard introduced a bill in the House instructing the Postmaster General of the USA to study the possibility of operating an experimental postal airline between Washington and some other town to be designated.

The bill never got past the Committee stage in Congress but the Postmaster General, Frank H. Hitchcock, did not need convincing: he was an aviation supporter. So when the organisers of an international aviation meeting at Garden City Estates, Long Island, near New York, informed him of their intention to operate a special airmail service, he agreed immediately.

The first postal flight was carried out between Garden City Estates and Mineola, New York, on 23rd September 1911 by the pilot Earle Ovington on a Blériot monoplane christened "Dragonfly". The cockpit of the aircraft was so cramped that the pilot had great difficulty in jamming the mailbag, containing 640 letters and 128 postcards, between his legs! [11] Since the Postmaster General was detained in Washington, he was unable to attend the departure of the flight, to his great regret, but he went to the airfield on 25th and 26th September and had himself photographed in the act of handing over a sack full of mail to Earle Ovington. This was the first time in history that the Chief Executive of a postal service publicly demonstrated such a high degree of interest in airmail.

In total, eight pilots took part in this airmail service and transported 32,415 postcards, 9,953 letters and 1,062 other documents [12] during the nine days of operation. Greatly impressed by the experience, Frank Hitchcock wrote in the US Post Office's Annual Report for 1911. "The progress being made in the science of aviation encourages the hope that ulti-

mately the regular conveyance of mail by this means may be practical." Now that he had got into his stride, he asked Congress in January 1912 for an appropriation of $50,000 to test an airmail service in some mountainous area where access was difficult, such as Arizona or New Mexico. The request was rejected – it was too early. In November 1912 Woodrow Wilson was elected President of the United States and shortly afterwards Albert S. Burleson was appointed as Postmaster General. Like his predecessor, he asked Congress every year to grant a special appropriation of $50,000. In March 1915 Congress demonstrated its interest in aviation: it authorised the creation of the National Advisory Committee for Aeronautics (NACA). Made up of representatives of the Army, high profile institutions and the scientific community it was given the mandate "to supervise and direct scientific study of the problems of flight, with a view to their practical solution."

In 1916, the activities of the NACA and the perseverance of the Postmaster General, ably supported by his assistant Otto Praeger, overcame the reservations of Congress, who released an appropriation of $50,000. Burleson and Praeger, after sidelining an unrealistic idea for establishing a start-up link between Chicago and New York, allied themselves to a project for an experimental airmail service between Washington and New York, proposed by the NACA.

• September/October 1911, Italy: There is no doubt that Italy is the country in which it is most difficult to distinguish between official and unofficial flights.

Towards the end of September 1911 an air speed competition over a number of stages was organised by a newspaper from Bologna on a route between Bologna, Venice, Rimini and Bologna under the title of "First Flying Circuit of Bologna". Officially it was not intended to transport post, but thanks to a set of coincidences, mail was indeed conveyed from Bologna to Venice on 19th September 1911. Taking advantage of the late departure of the youngest competitor, Lieutenant Achille Dal Mistro, due to technical problems, the Provincial Director of Postal Services in Bologna used his own initiative and opened a temporary post office on the Bologna airfield. The few cards which were handed in were collected together to make up a despatch of post from Bologna to Venice, and given to the young aviator. The landing in Venice on the Lido beach was rather eventful, but the pilot and the small mailbag came out unscathed. The delivery of post was solemnly received by the Venice Post Office for immediate distribution.

The first truly official postal trial in Italy took place at the suggestion of the Turin Aviation Committee on 29th-31st October 1911 during the International Aeronautical Congress, on a route between Milan and Turin. [13]

Eight pilots took part in a kind of postal competition on a course from Milan to Turin and back. The results which were recorded give a good idea of the low degree of reliability of aircraft and engines in those early days of aviation: although eight aircraft managed to take off, one crashed shortly after take off, another had to land immediately afterwards, and three others had to turn back. Out of the eight competitors who entered the competition, only two, pilots Verona and Manissero, managed to complete the round trip in a proper manner.

As was always the case in this kind of event, the mail was primarily composed of illustrated postcards issued specially and printed with the declaration: "Servizio Postale Aereo Milano-

Torino Torino-Milano".

About 20 kilograms of mail were carried from Milan to Turin and about 10 kilograms in the opposite direction.

• December 1911/January 1912, South Africa: E. F. Driver, one of the pilots from the temporary London/Windsor service, came from South Africa. He founded The African Aviation Syndicate Ltd and organised an event – the Cape Peninsular Flying Fortnight – in December 1911. He obtained official authorisation from the Postmaster General to transport post.

As usual, special postcards were printed and sold in the Cape. They are marked: "First South African Aerial Post". [14] Over 2,500 cards were sent on 30th December 1911 from Kenilworth (on the Cape) to Muizenburg and on the return journey on 3rd January 1912.

• June 1912, Germany: The German airborne postal service officially came into being during the Aeronautical Fortnight of the Grand Duchy of Hessen in Frankfurt on Main on 10th-23rd June 1912.

Here, as at Allahabad, airmail was closely linked with a charitable activity. It was indeed envisaged that special postcards, sold for the benefit of a charitable organisation presided over by the Grand Duchess would be sent by air, with the authorisation of the Imperial Post.

In view of the considerable quantity of mail to be transported by air (460,700 Flugpostkarten) on one section of the circuit Frankfurt/Darmstadt/Worms/Mainz/Frankfurt circular route, [15] the organisers decided to use both airship and aircraft. They combined the transport capacity of Zeppelin LZ10 "Schwaben" with that of the Euler aircraft named "Gelber Hund" (Yellow dog), piloted by Lieutenant Ferdinand von Hiddesen of the 24th Dragoons Regiment, who carried 297 kilograms of mail with him. All the postcards were over-stamped with a large black postmark: "Flugpost am Rhein u. am Main". This was the birth of airmail by aeroplane, in tandem with airmail by balloon which had existed in Germany since 1907.

• 1st June 1912, Japan: The first Japanese postal flight took place on 1st June 1912 from Tokyo (Shibaura Beach) to Yokohama. It was undertaken by the American W. B. Atwater in a Curtiss sea-plane, and lasted 23 minutes. It carried around 1,000 letters and commemorative cards stamped with a triangular commemorative postmark bearing the bilingual inscription, in Japanese and English: "Japanese Aerial Post". [16]

• 31st July 1912 and 15th October 1913, France: France, distracted by sporting events and absorbed by military applications, took its time in trying out commercial applications for aviation, although paradoxically it was often French aircraft and pilots which helped to support postal trials abroad!

The first French experiment took place on 31st July 1912 during an aviation meeting at Nancy, on the Jarville Racecourse, which had been transformed into an airfield. The event was organised by the Association of the Friends of Aviation (Association des Amis de l'Aviation) in a patriotic cause: the collection of funds to build hangars for military flying activities.

"In order to confer an official character on the first airmail flight on French territory, M. Chaumet, Under Secretary for the PTT, authorised the creation of a special token adhesive stamp." [17] The post office employees of Nancy were "authorised to cancel in the usual manner this commemorative sticker, which was affixed in addition to the normal postage, as a postage stamp from the Postal Administration. Its selling price to the public was set at 0.25F and the sums so collected should be used for the purpose of building hangars." A special postmark "Nancy Aviation" was created.

Although the flight was planned for 29th July, it was postponed until the 31st because of bad weather. Lieutenant Nicaud took off at 07.16 hrs in his Farman biplane with three sacks of mail weighing about 50 kilograms. He landed 17 minutes later in the Champ de Mars in Lunéville, 17 miles away.

Aware of the limitations and uncertainties of flying, the Postal Administration had previously drawn up a regulation in the following terms:

"Envelopes posted on the days of 27th and 28th July 1912, bearing the special stamp, will be transported to the central office in Nancy and postmarked with the date. They will be then conveyed on board an aircraft and transported to a destination within the area and transferred to another post office, which will distribute them further, after having

The aviator Lieutenant Ronin shows the box which carries the mail on his monoplane to M. Massé, Minister of Post and Telegraphs.
Musée de la Poste, Paris

stamped them with a second dated postmark, which, together with the first, will provide evidence of the journey by aeroplane."

However, the flight made by one Lieutenant Ronin made much greater impact. On 15th October 1913, in a Morane-Saulnier aircraft, fitted with a 60-horsepower Gnome engine, he ferried a mailbag containing 10.6 kilograms of mail from Villacoublay (near Paris) to Pauillac (near Bordeaux). On arrival at Pauillac the mailbag was loaded on board the postal steamship "Pérou", bound for the West Indies.

In order to appreciate the significance of this trial, one needs to know that at the time one postal vessel sailed every 14 days for the West Indies out of Bordeaux-Pauillac. By passing on the post which had been collected in Paris the previous evening (after the post train normally linking with the steamer had already left) the aeroplane had shortened the delivery time for this correspondence by two weeks!

The flight of 15th October 1913 is of major importance in the history of airmail, because it broke a number of records and achieved in one fell swoop two "firsts": distance covered – around 310 miles; time saving achieved – two weeks for the type of mail transported; the first carriage of proper correspondence instead of the usual commemorative postcards; and lastly, the first instance of the combination of airmail/sea mail.

• January 1914, Egypt: An Aviation Week was held in Heliopolis, near Cairo from 4th to 12th January 1914. Several postal activities were organised for the occasion: a temporary post office was opened on the airfield, a special token stamp was issued, and, above all, the first airmail link in Egypt was inaugurated. The honour for this goes to the French pilot Marc Pourpe who, after leaving Cairo on 4th January, reached Khartoum on the 12th, after a flight of over 1,250 miles via Luxor, Wadi Halfa and Abu Hamed. After landing in Khartoum, Marc Pourpe handed over to the British authorities an official sack of mail which had come straight from Cairo.

• 12th May 1914, Denmark: In spite of its modest size, Denmark occupies an eminent place in European aviation history: it was in fact a Dane, Lillehammer, who was the first to fly an aeroplane under power in Europe: on 12th September 1906 on the small island of Lindholmen.

From the postal point of view, the example of Denmark and indeed of Scandinavia as a whole shows the difficulty of making a clear distinction between private initiatives and official measures. According to official records, the first airmail flight in Denmark goes back to 12th May 1914. On that day Lieutenant Ussing, in a Farman aircraft, carried several thousand special postcards from Copenhagen to Roskilde, travelling a distance of about 25 miles.

However, there are instances of special airmail operations had already been carried out in Denmark and the rest of Scandinavia without official approval having been granted:[18]

• In Denmark, on 1st September 1911: At the instigation of a daily newspaper, pilot Robert Svendsen transported postcards and copies of the newspaper "Mittelfart Avis" across the Little Belt from Mittelfart on the island of Funen to Fredericia in Jutland.

• In Sweden in early February 1914, the National Guard in Kalmar, perhaps sensing the approach of war, organised a patriotic event: it wanted to collect funds to purchase machine guns. It was supported by two local newspapers, who published special editions devoted to aviation. The centrepiece of the whole activity was a flight over the strait of Kalmar to the island of Ölan, made by Enoch Thulin, the future Swedish aircraft manufacturer, who piloted the "old" Blériot plane which he had just bought from Cederström. During the flight on 8th February 1914 Enoch Thulin carried a small amount of post – the inevitable commemorative postcards – and some copies of the two local newspapers, for the benefit of the Kalmar National Guard. Since the ground at Öland was drenched with rain, he could not land and had to "drop" the mail and newspapers.

• Again in Sweden, on 1st June 1912, Danish pilot Peter Nielsen transferred a hundred or so postcards between two municipalities in Skania – Eslöf and Marieholm. Since special permission had been requested from the local Director of Post, an airmail postmark, "Svensk Flygpost", was used for the first time.

• 16th/17th July 1914, Australia: The French pilot Guilleaux, in a Blériot aircraft, took off from Melbourne on 16th July 1914 with 18 kilograms of post consisting of 1,785 postcards, each purchased for the price of a shilling. After a difficult flight over four stages, during which he endured violent rainstorms without any protection, Guilleaux landed in Sydney on 17th July. When he appeared out of the cloud, for it was a poor day, the crowds gave him a roaring tribute. Clutching a letter from the Governor of Victoria to the Governor of New South Wales, the Frenchman was carried on the shoulders of his admirers to deliver the letter in person."[19]

The above list of the airmail flights completed between 1911 and 1914 may not be exhaustive, but an attempt has been made to recognise the rôles played by each nation in the birth of air postal services, as well as the contribution of each pilot and each aircraft manufacturer.

These flights have many points in common: their experimental nature, the relatively short distances covered, the frequent interrelationship between airmail and charitable or patriotic activities, the preponderant rôle played by French pilots and aircraft and the conveyance of commemorative postcards rather than regular mail items.

From many points of view, one flight stands out above all the others: that of Lieutenant Ronin on 15th October 1913 from Villacoublay to Pauillac. The novelty of this flight did not escape newspapers at the time: "Both in France and abroad, people had already tried to transport urgent communications and correspondence by aeroplane: however, although interesting in themselves, these attempts were always in the nature of exceptional events. The trial flight happily completed by Lieutenant Ronin, at the behest of the Minister of Trade and Public Works, was aimed at providing a targeted improvement in postal services: it therefore represents the first official trial of postal aviation, and its first success."

However, on the eve of the First World War, in spite of all these experiments, there still existed only one example of a regular airborne postal service: that provided by manned balloons during the Siege of Paris.

Part Two

The First World War 1914–1918

"A bird may be a dove or a hawk. It made itself a hawk.
"The war was a tremendous lever for aviation."

Le Corbusier

1 THE CONSEQUENCES OF THE WAR

It was during the First World War that the world definitively entered the age of flight. For a period of more than four years the warring nations engaged in a gigantic race in terms of investment and performance to win the mastery of the air. In spite of the progress evidenced from 1903 to 1914, the war gave aviation an enormous kick-start.

> "*The war was a tremendous lever for aviation. In a feverishly accelerated rhythm, at the command of the State every door was open to discovery. Success was achieved, the aim reached, astounding progress made ... War was the hellish laboratory in which aviation became adult and was shaped to flawless perfection.*" [1]

Although it represented a jump forward for powered aviation, the war was also a major factor in the development of lighter-than-air craft. At the outbreak of hostilities, various observers predicted a division of roles between aircraft and dirigible balloons: "heavier than air" would service short and medium distances, while "lighter than air" would provide the inter-continental link.

1 THE BREAKTHROUGH OF AVIATION

A change of scale ...
The war multiplied the production of airframes and engines by a factor of 100 and brought the aircraft industry into a totally new realm.

A very rapid transition was made from what had more or less been a craft industry into full-blown industrial mass production, based on research departments and series production. From 1914 to 1918 almost 200,000 aircraft and over 250,000 engines left the factories of the warring countries. The annual production figures for the French aircraft industry in 1914 and 1918 grew as follows:

	Aircraft	Engines
Year 1914	600	480
Year 1918	35,000	52,000

The number of French aeroplanes available for battle grew from about 400 in 1914 to over 13,000 at the time of the armistice. This production level was accompanied by a considerable increase in the numbers of particular models: the production volume of the French fighter plane Spad XI, in which Captain Guynemer rose to fame, was 8,472 units.

Major technological developments...
At the same time the average performance figures for a single-seater combat aircraft developed thus:

	In 1914	In 1918
Engine Power (hp)	80/90	200/300
Speed (mph)	55/75	120/140
Rate of climb (m/s)	3,000m in 45sec	3,000m in 45sec
Operating ceiling (m)	3,000	8,000

This improvement in performance was a result of progress in two main areas: engines and production techniques for airframes and wings.

• Engines
Engines were manufactured in very large series quantities (the production of the Hispano-Suiza V8 engine reached a total of 35,000 in France) and achieved substantial increases in power in horsepower:

	In 1914	In 1918
Gnome	80	200
Renault	70	230
Daimler	100	240

Rolls-Royce reached 360hp and American Liberty engines, 400hp.

• Airframes and wings
One design engineer, Hugo Junkers, dominated all his competitors with the modernity of his ideas. The undisputed British expert on the subject, Charles H. Gibbs-Smith,[2] has written:

> "*It was in Germany that one of the most fundamental and far reaching aeronautical innovations took place during the war years ... Hugo Junkers had in 1910 patented his thick-*

section Cantilever wing, without external bracing with struts or wires. It was not until 1915 that this epoch making invention was successfully implemented …

"The influence of Junkers was to affect the whole course of aircraft evolution. He may be fully and fairly credited with the design and construction of:

a) First practical Cantilever wing aeroplanes.

b) The first all-metal aeroplanes

c) The first practical low wing aeroplanes, all of which he continued to develop successfully over the years."

ABOVE **Junkers Ju10.** *MAP*

BELOW **Handley Page O400 G-EALX, crashed 1920**. *RAF Museum*

BOTTOM **DH4.** *MAP*

…Well-defined missions

For each mission in military aviation – whether reconnaissance, combat or bombing – there were corresponding types of aircraft which became increasingly specialised. Combat aircraft were too small, too fragile and had too large a fuel consumption to be interesting to a civilian operator. However, some bombers were used for many years in civil aviation after modification as they bombers offered the greatest flying range and "useful" load, which could be up to 800 or 1,000 kilograms. Low speed was their greatest disadvantage. Examples include:

HANDLEY PAGE O/400 "HEAVY BOMBER"
Biplane equipped with two 360hp Rolls-Royce engines.
Considerable flying range: 8 hours – speed: 60-75mph.
Payload for transporting bombs: 800 kilograms.

DE HAVILLAND DH4
"The most outstanding high performance daylight bomber of the First World War." (Jane's)

Single-engine biplane equipped with a 12-cylinder Rolls-Royce engine, of which several thousand units were produced from 1916 onwards. When fitted out with a 400hp Liberty 12 engine, it was to become, among others, the workhorse of the US airmail service in 1920.

FARMAN F60
Night bomber, biplane, originally fitted with 2 x 230hp Salmson engines, rectangular fuselage.
Cruising speed: 70mph – high payload of up to 1,000kg.

In its civil version, "Goliath", it was "one of the most successful aircraft of all time." (Dollfus)

Vickers Vimy. *British Airways Museum*

BRÉGUET 14 B2
Lightweight daylight bomber biplane combining the new material of duralumin with fabric; fitted with a 300hp Renault V12 engine. In the A2 version (Army Corps two-seater) it was adapted for civil transport ("addition below each lower wing, of a small tapered coffer to contain mail and parcels"), [3] and it became the legendary aircraft of Lignes Aériennes Latécoère.
Cruising speed: 80mph – Operating range: 280/310 miles.
Payload between 250 and 400kg

CAPRONI 32
Italian biplane bomber, fitted with three 150hp engines.
Payload approximately 500kg.

JUNKERS JU10
Assault aircraft produced in 1918. Low-winged monoplane converted into a passenger version (one passenger or a small quantity of freight).

"This aircraft can be regarded as the true ancestor of the metal transport aircraft of the 1920s and 1930s and certainly of the extremely successful Junkers Ju52 which was produced on a massive scale." ("Jane's")

Aviation wins its halo ...
On both sides, aviators enjoyed an extraordinary prestige during the whole of the war. Compared with the large infantry units, who were massacred anonymously, the aviators embodied a new kind of chivalry, the values of which were fearlessness and contempt for death, self-mastery and cool aggression, camaraderie and a respect for the enemy. From among their number, some names stand out: Frenchmen such as Guynemer, Fonck and Nungesser, Germans such as Manfred Von

Richthofen and Immelmann, American captains like Rickenbacker and Lufbery, the Briton Albert Ball, the Belgian Lieutenant Coppens de Houthulst, the Canadian Don MacLaren and the Italian Francesco Baracca. These were the "Aces". Through their gallantry and their sacrifice they built the aviation legend which inextricably combined heroism and technology, and which was to carry over into the early years of civil aviation, particularly in the USA and France. They endowed aviation with an image "sans pareil".

... Unanticipated Limitations
Aviation made considerable progress during the war, but only for military purposes as the emphasis was on absolute speed, rate of climb and the manoeuvrability of aircraft.

The attrition rate for military aircraft was extremely high: to end up in possession of 3,618 airworthy aeroplanes on Armistice Day, France had built over 40,000 aeroplanes and 64,000 engines in 1918 alone!

The engines were not reliable and moreover were designed to fulfil specialised operational needs, rather than for use in regular air services. After every three flying hours they had to be inspected by specialist mechanics, and their life expectancy was a mere 100 hours.

Bombing missions particularly showed up their limitations, on both sides, and with a few exceptions their effect was more psychological than actual. For example, the most famous of the French bomber squadrons only dropped 16,500 kilograms of bombs in 41 sorties, ie an average of 400 kilograms per raid. If the weather was bad the payload often had to be reduced by significant amounts.

There were many who underestimated these limitations

Farman Goliath. *RAF Museum*

However, some individuals were aware of them, like this anonymous English writer who wrote: "The great advances made in aviation during the war have been largely artificial and unnatural." [4] The truth doubtless lies somewhere between the enthusiasm of some and the scepticism of others.

2 PROGRESS IN BALLOON DEVELOPMENT

The siege of Przemysl: aeroplanes and free-flying balloons
As in Condé-sur-Escaut in 1793, free-flying balloons were used in 1914 and 1915 to carry post from besieged positions during the war.

Przemysl, a Polish town on the borders of the Ukraine and Slovakia, was at that time part of Austrian Galicia. It occupied a strategic position and its fortress was held by a large Austro-Hungarian garrison. It was the scene of fierce fighting from summer 1914 onwards, and was besieged on two occasions by the Russian army: the first time from 18th September to 10th October 1914 and the second time from 7th November 1914 to 21st March 1915. The eternal problem arose as to how to re-establish communications between the besieged fortress and the GHQ in Krakow, 150 miles away, which the Austrians attempted to solve using both aircraft and free balloons.

The Austrians were concerned about the morale of their troops, and quickly organised a military airborne postal service, publishing the following communiqué: "The post will be conveyed by aeroplane, weather permitting."

The military post was composed mainly of letter cards (Feldpost Korrespondenz Karten) bearing the airmail legend "Fliegerpost Przemysl".

Free flying balloons were also used during the siege on several occasions, with little success. The last mail was despatched on 19th March 1915, two days before the garrison capitulated: one aircraft and three balloons managed to leave the besieged fortress. The aircraft landed inside Austrian lines, while the balloons, irresistibly driven by winds blowing towards the north, fell into the hands of the Russian Army, who sent the letters to the Red Cross after censoring them. Once again it had been demonstrated that free balloons were a risky and unpredictable means of transport. Sadly, these beautiful spherical balloons will not feature in this story of air transport until much nearer our time, when American crews achieved sensational crossings of the Atlantic and the Pacific.

Progress and use of dirigibles
The Italian army is believed to be the first to use dirigible balloons in a military offensive, during the bombardment of Turkish positions on 10th March 1912 in Tripolitania.

During the First World War the Allies used dirigible balloons to fight against submarines, and to protect convoys at sea. However, the Germans used them in far more varied missions.

Zeppelin dirigibles from DELAG were assigned to Army use immediately after the declaration of war, and their production was intensified. Zeppelin Luftschiffbau in Friedrichshafen produced more than one balloon per fortnight, and its number of employees rose to 13,600. The operating performance of the Zeppelins improved continuously from 1914 to 1918 (see table on next page).

German dirigibles carried out many reconnaissance and surveillance missions over the North Sea; during 284 bombing missions, they carried and dropped 480,780 kilograms of bombs chiefly over England, but also Belgium and France. [5] In practice, however, the low speed of the large dirigibles represented a major restriction in their use for military purposes.

	LZ16 (1913 Version)	LZ113 (1918 Version)
Volume in m³	19,500	68,500
Payload in kg	6,000	51,500
Power in hp	540	1,560
(Maybach engines)	(3)	(6)
Speed in mph	45	70/75
Operating range at full power in hours	20	100

They also carried out a number of transport operations, the exploits of LX104 "L59" being the most famous.

In autumn 1917 the troops in German East Africa were surrounded by British troops and needed aid. On a mission to take them fresh supplies, Zeppelin LZ104 "L59", a large rigid balloon 226 metres long with a volume of 68,500 cubic metres, left Jamboli in Bulgaria on 21st November 1917. It was carrying a cargo of arms, ammunition, food and medical supplies with an incredible total weight of 13,870 kilograms. After the captain received a radio message informing him that the last centres of resistance had fallen, he decided to turn round over the Sudan and fly back to his point of departure in Bulgaria. He landed after a record flight of 95 hours, covering 4,220 miles. No one had ever before transported such an enormous load over such a distance by air. During the voyage of nearly four days, the LZ104 had proven in a spectacular manner the capabilities of dirigible balloons for the transportation of goods. The magazine "L'Aéronautique" described perfectly the comparative advantages of the aeroplane and the dirigible in an article headed "The question of lighter-than-air craft and their future" which appeared in 1919: "Although the speed of the dirigible is less than 50% of that of an aeroplane, it can carry a commercial load 15 to 20 times heavier." Dirigibles thus still had some advantages when compared with aeroplanes.

3 THE BIRTH OF MILITARY AIRMAIL

The chief driving force of armies is morale, even above disci-pline, and the regular and speedy forwarding of mail is one of the surest means of maintaining the determination of the troops. It was therefore hardly surprising that the military leaders very soon had the idea of using air transport to speed up postal services to their armies.

The first instances of military airmail took place before the First World War. In 1911, during the confrontations between Italy and the Ottoman Empire in Tripolitania, civilian pilot volunteers carried military post from Tripoli to Derna on 25th November 1911 and to Tobruk on 28th November. [6]

The official beginnings of military airmail can be traced to early 1916. The theatre of operations was not in Europe, but Mexico, which was just ending a long period of revolution in which General Pancho Villa had been one of the most famous leaders. This redoubtable warlord, at the time in charge of his Divisione del Norte, who came from a very modest country background, had a violent and passionate temperament and found it difficult to submit to authority, even revolutionary authority. During 1915 he returned to his province of Chihuahua and resumed his guerrilla activities. On 10th January 1916 his men stopped a train and executed 18 Americans who were working in a nearby mining company. On 8th March 1916 he personally led an attack on the small American town of Columbus in the state of New Mexico in which eight Americans were killed. The President of the United States was infuriated and by way of retaliation sent out a punitive expedition, which he placed under the command of General Pershing, who was later to take charge of the American troops in Europe. The ensuing battle is now recognised as a classic encounter between a conventional army and an adversary expert in the art of guerrilla warfare, who knew the area like the back of his hand, waged across difficult terrain totally lacking in means of communication. The First Aero Squadron, consisting of Curtiss JN4 "Jenny" spotter aeroplanes under the command of Captain Benjamin D. Foulois (of whom more later), was put at General Pershing's disposition. Captain Foulois allocated his aircraft to observation missions – all the more valuable because it was impossible to capture the enemy

German airmail 1914–1918.
Lufthansa/German Post Museum

– and to the transport of official despatches and military post.

"Between 27th and 31st March we managed to make about 20 flights carrying mail and despatches ... By the end of our first 10 days of operations it was obvious that our six planes were incapable of fully performing the task assigned." [7] The engines could not stand the combined effects of heat and altitude. Despite the failure of this operation, which some even considered an aviation scandal, it was to lead to the development of military airmail.

In Europe, the first initiatives in military airmail can be traced to Germany and Austria. The length of the Eastern Front line posed serious transport problems for German military postal officials. In order to speed up the distribution of the mail they established an air route over 600 miles long between Dünaburg (Daugavpils in Lithuania) and the Crimean Peninsula during 1917. On the Western Front, in order to relieve some of the overcrowding on the communication routes by land, a postal airline was opened at the end of 1917 between Berlin, Hanover and Cologne – an exact precursor of later civil operations.

From the beginning of 1918 onwards, Austria established its own military airmail. On 11th March 1918, under the command of a former fighter pilot, A. R. Von Marwil, an air route was started through Vienna, Krakow, Lemberg (Lvov in Ukraine) to Kiev, with a temporary extension as far as Odessa. The service was provided by military aircraft, but it was open to civilian correspondence, cancelled with a postmark "Flugpost". In response to this first success, another line from Vienna to Budapest was inaugurated in July 1918. Then followed two purely military services restricted to letter cards: the first by aeroplane between Lemberg (Lvov) and Brest-Litovsk, and the second by seaplane along the Dalmatian coast of the Adriatic, from Pola in the north (Pula in Croatia) to Durazzo in the south (Durrès in Albania).

As far as France was concerned, although it had the most powerful aircraft industry, the need for military airmail was different. On its main war front, the relative stability of the lines of combat, the short distances involved and the quality of the communication routes on the ground meant that it did not

have to adopt any exceptional measures. It was the massive arrival of American troops after the United States entered the war in 1917 which was to justify the employment of new measures: in order to speed up the conveyance of American mail, a service for airpost was opened between Paris and Saint Nazaire – the principle port of disembarkation – via Le Mans. The route was operated by the Postal Administration, with crews and equipment made available by the Army "in return for remuneration". On 17th August 1918 Warrant Officer Houssais, in a Letord aircraft, transported the first sack of mail from Paris-Le Bourget to Saint-Nazaire-Escoublac in a time of 5 hours 4 minutes. The airline was to operate up to 10th January 1919.

A "Par avion" label had to be stuck onto the envelopes and the Post over-stamped them with the following wording: "Ligne Postale Aérienne de Paris à Saint Nazaire Escoublac" ("Air Post Line from Paris to Saint-Nazaire-Escoublac").

As a group of islands, Great Britain was placed in an unusual situation regarding airmail. It first experimented with the transport of civilian mail by military aircraft in 1917 and 1918. In order to counteract the danger from the presence of numerous German submarines in the Irish Sea, a regular airborne postal service using military hydroplanes was set up between Windermere in the Lake District and the Isle of Man. This was not in the proper sense of the word an airmail line as the hydroplanes, which were carrying out numerous submarine missions over this route, were authorised to carry post without surcharge or any special postmark.

The most pressing need, however, was to speed up the transmission of military mail and official despatches between Great Britain and the Continent. Several experiments were carried out and from May to October 1915 air links departing from Folkestone were operated to destinations in Northern France and to the very small part of Belgium which was still in the hands of Allied troops. (Hence the name "King Albert Line" which was sometimes given to these services.) The services were taken up again in 1917, this time entrusted to the Belgian Army.

2 PERSPECTIVES OF PEACE

1 THE PRECURSORS OF PEACE

Even before hostilities had ended, people in many countries were thinking about the requirements for establishing aviation on a commercial basis. The French MP M. D'Aubigny forcefully made the point in a report entitled "L'Aviation et La Paix" ("Aviation in peacetime") which he presented to the Inter-Allied Parliament in London on 24th October 1918:

> "One factor has emerged from the world cataclysm which will bring about a profound change in the relations between human kind: it is the progress of aerial navigation." [1]

In the United Kingdom the Civil Aerial Transport Committee was set up on 22nd May 1917. In its conclusions of 7th February 1918, it advocated "State action for the development of aerial transport services" and stressed "the need for Empire services and the necessary Empire route surveys". This summarises clearly the two major principles which would dominate the creation and expansion of commercial aviation from 1919 to 1939.

In the spring of 1917 Italy instigated a commission responsible for studying "the possibilities for establishing air post links within the country", presided over by Professor Righi, a celebrated physicist and senator. In view of the positive conclusions of the committee, Italy proceeded with various trials:

• On 22nd and 26th May 1917, between Turin and Rome, 68 kilograms of post and 200 copies of newspapers were carried on the outward flight. Since there was no airmail stamp, a stamp from 1903 intended for express letters, "Expresso", was used to frank the letters and was cancelled with a special postmark "Esperimento Posta Aerea Maggio 1917 Torino-Roma Roma-Torino" ("Air Post Trial May 1917 Turin-Rome Rome-Turin").

• From 27th June to 31st September 1917, between Civitavecchia (on the Tyrrhenian coast north of Rome) and Terranova Pausania in Sardinia, a military fleet of eight seaplanes (type FBA) carried 2,344 kilograms of mail, without surcharge, special stamp or any particular postmark. The maximum weight per hydroplane was 75 kilograms.

• On 28th and 29th June 1917, between Naples and Palermo (Sicily), a postal seaplane was piloted by Ruggero Franzoni, the Italian aeronautical pioneer. Starting out from Naples, the aeroplane transported a generous quantity of mail, a message from the Mayor of Naples to the Mayor of Palermo and 200 copies of a special edition of the newspaper Il Mattino. All the correspondence was cancelled with a special postmark: "Idrovolante Napoli Palermo" ("Seaplane, Naples Palermo").

This operation roused enormous postal and philatelic interest, and gave rise to a rather harmless subterfuge, which was confessed to 25 years later in the very serious journal "The Postal Union", published in Berne by the Universal Postal Union:

"The success of this initiative was extraordinary. In Naples, items of airmail post accumulated by the thousand awaiting flights, which were constantly being delayed due to all kinds of difficulties. With the payload capabilities of the time, dozens of aeroplanes would have been required to fulfil their transportation. They resorted to a heroic remedy (after 25 years we can reveal the secret, since we were its protagonists): in an undercover operation, involving the sorting staff on the Naples-Messina and Messina-Naples post trains, several sacks of mail were transported from Naples to Palermo, where they reappeared in the light of day just on the arrival of the seaplane." [2]

To think of those poor, bamboozled philatelists!
With the experience of these trials with airborne post, and possessing a strong aeronautical industry which had moved towards producing bombers (Caproni) and seaplanes, Italy prepared itself for civilian air transport by looking forward to its future uses. "London and Paris, Paris and Rome, Berlin and Vienna, New York and San Francisco will all have their air links", predicted the President of the Aeronautical Section of the National Scientific and Technical Committee. His thoughts on the subject of goods and mail were prescient:

> "We won't waste time talking about an airborne postal service, the organisation of which we await with impatience; sending post by air will mean the immediate exchange of correspondence.

"The idea of using the airways for transporting urgent goods should not occasion the least mirth. If we think back to the comfortable lifestyle during peacetime, the moneyed classes have needs, which they will not stint in satisfying: fresh flowers, the latest cinematographic films, trade samples. We have had occasion to read in an enumeration on this subject, the case of a lady of note who would have willingly paid a large sum of money to get hold of a particular evening gown by a certain time, and of a modern Amphytrion, a gourmet host, who wanted a certain type of fresh fish for his dinner table as a matter of greatest urgency."

In France, the Inter-Ministerial Commission for Aeronautical Matters proposed to the Government in December 1917 that it should start up two international air services (Paris-London and Paris-Rome) and make the necessary studies for a plan of internal services. Later, in October 1918, it suggested "further investigations with the aim of setting trans-Saharan and transatlantic routes and preparing rapid communications between France and the Empire of the Rising Sun."

For its part, Germany, with engineers such as Junkers or Dornier possessed an advanced aeronautical industry, and had all the advantages necessary for building the foundations of a future civil aviation industry. Shortly before the Armistice, the International Company for Aerial Communications in Berlin established the outline of a very logical air network. It was concentrated around Central Europe and composed of short stages of 125 or 200 miles, suited to the actual performance of the aeroplanes in service. It covered the traditional areas of German influence, being structured around three major axes:

• Hamburg/Constantinople via Berlin, Dresden, Prague, Budapest, Belgrade and Sophia;

• Metz/Warsaw via Frankfurt, Leipzig, Dresden;

• Strasbourg/Constantinople via Stuttgart, Munich, Vienna, Budapest and Bucharest.

Such forward-looking measures, which would form the base for the postwar civil aviation industry, were not the sole prerogative of the great powers involved in the war. The Scandinavian countries, The Netherlands, Switzerland and Greece also developed similar projects. The whole of Europe was preparing for the coming of commercial aviation. All, however, underestimated the difficulties in passing from military activities to exploitation in a civilian context.

2 THE FIRST FLIGHTS IN PEACETIME

Immediately after the signing of the Armistice on 11th November 1918, it became obvious that there was an urgent demand for a rapid means of communication within Europe. Whether in supplying aid to the populations in devastated areas, providing official links between the Allies or in establishing a new civil order in Germany, only aviation was in a position to fulfil the requirements.

Aid to devastated areas

Belgium and northern and eastern France had suffered enormously during the war: towns and villages were destroyed, factories were demolished and communication links were impassable or fractured.

The first humanitarian operation involving air transport started on 1st February 1919. At the request of the Belgian Government, an airlift was established between Folkestone and Ghent to supply the war-torn provinces with essential goods needed by the population (bedding, medicines and food). Flights were organised by the English air company Aircraft Transport and Travel, which had been founded by George Holt-Thomas on 5th October 1916. It used De Havilland DH4 light bombers, piloted by the Royal Air Force: an example of the collaboration between civilian organisations and military resources in terms of men and equipment.

Like Belgium, France was confronted with the problems arising from the massive destruction of the rail network in occupied regions in the north and the east of the country. the solution was to open several temporary airmail routes out of Paris, beginning in February 1919: Paris/Lille, Paris/Maubeuge/Valenciennes, Paris/Longwy, Paris/Mulhouse, Paris/Strasbourg and Paris/Brussels. A route from Paris to Bordeaux via Chateauroux was also set up. Once again, civilian and military operations co-operated, characteristic of the immediate postwar period. These air links were operated by the Aeronautical Directorate, using military aircraft on behalf of the General Directorate of Post.

Since these were only temporary peace time links to overcome the consequences of the war they were closed down as soon rail transport was re-established. The air links from Paris to Valenciennes and Strasbourg lasted only three months, and Paris to Longwy and Paris to Mulhouse just one month. The Paris to Lille link registered the largest amount of traffic: 378 mailbags were sent between 7th February and 10th April 1919, at which date the operation was taken over by a private company – La Compagnie des Messageries Aériennes.

By 1919, the French Post Office had acquired considerable experience with airmail. Added to the previous operations

DH4 of AT & T, Belgian service.
RAF Museum

DH4a.
RAF Museum

were the route between Paris and Saint Nazaire, temporary routes with liberated regions, the experimental link between Nimes and Nice, and experimental seaplane flights between Nice and Corsica. The Post Office was then in a position to carry out its first appraisal of the operations, which was positive although qualified with some serious reservations. The gains had been considerable: it had been demonstrated that under certain circumstances an airborne postal operation was technically possible. However, these first practical experiences clearly underlined the limitations of postal aviation due to the technology of the time.

"To free aviation of the legends which paralyse it, and reduce to reasonable proportions the hopes with which it has been burdened , is to perform a valuable service. It can only be good for the progress of aviation if we say frankly that it is far from coming up to the mark, that its productivity has been mediocre and that for the time being it is neither safe nor regular nor, to call a spade a spade, practical,"

as one reads in the Annals of the PTT for 1919: [3]

• *"The aeroplane does not provide regular service, it does not fly every day (fog), it does not fly by night (this was a major handicap for the postal executives, since post trains ran by night and acted as a facility for sorting the mail) and two times out of 10 it obstinately refuses to take off.*

• *"The aeroplane is expensive because its service life is extremely short and its depreciation costs are very high.*

• *"The aeroplane is not safe: on 7th April 1919, the post plane Paris/Bordeaux caught fire on landing and the pilot was seriously burned; on 20th April 1919 the aeroplane from Paris to Strasbourg overturned near Saint Dizer, resulting in two people dead and one seriously injured."*

The author (who, interestingly, was both a postal executive and a lieutenant in the Air Force) then posed a difficult question, the eternal struggle between caution and risk taking: One has the right to question whether it is appropriate to risk on a daily basis human lives in order to carry out, via the airways, the transport of correspondence which the present ground communication routes already assure in a satisfactory manner." Perhaps wary of sounding too pessimistic, the author concludes: "I know that sooner or later aviation will fulfil its promise."

Fast links between Great Britain and the Continent

As soon as France and Great Britain had entered the war, they had realised the paramount need for a communication system which was permanent, fast and safe. All means were used: coded messages, official despatches and liaison officers. Because of its speed the aeroplane was the ideal means of transport for urgent correspondence and official passengers. One of the first people to use it in an organised manner was Captain Louis Pierron. He was attached to the French Aviation Mission in England, and, until his disappearance in 1918, flew a practically regular service between the aerodrome of the Lorraine-Dietrich factory at Argenteuil near Paris and Hounslow aerodrome near London, making over a hundred flights. [4]

The opening of the Paris Peace Conference on 18th January 1919 brought an even greater need for fast communication between the two Allies. In order to meet this requirement, the Royal Air Force had, from 10th January, opened an official link for passengers and post between London (Hendon) and Paris (Buc, near Versailles, where some of the delegations had gathered). Two transport squadrons, one based at Hendon and subsequently at Kenley, and the other based at Buc, were placed under the command of Major J. R. McCrindle (who for 40 years was to be one of the leading figures in British air transport) to operate the service up to the end of September 1919. In total, 749 flights were made, carrying 946 passengers, 1,008 sacks of mail and 46 despatches. In the main, two types of aircraft were used: a light bomber, the De Havilland DH4, and a heavy bomber, the Handley Page O/400. [5] Shortly after the Armistice, the British Army Post Office and the Royal Air Force decided jointly to organise a Forces Airmail Service serving France, Belgium and the British occupied zone of Germany.

For an initial period from 17th December 1918 to the end of February 1919, the marine section of the route between England and France continued to be covered by boat. All the flights left from Marquise, near Boulogne-sur-Mer, destined for Valenciennes, Namur and Spa. They were operated by De Havilland DH9A light day bombers, fitted with a more powerful engine. The first flight left Marquise on 17th December 1918 at 12.50 hours and dropped the post by parachute over Valenciennes before continuing its route towards Namur. The Christmas mail was distributed in good time to all the troops, thanks to the airborne postal service. The flights were extended to Cologne on 18th January 1919, and an additional service between Marquise and Cologne was added on 5th January 1919.

During the second period, commencing on 1st March 1919, the point of departure for postal services was transferred from Marquise to Hawkinge near Folkestone. From then on, transport was effected completely by air and was done in two stages: from Hawkinge to Maisoncelles, near Boulogne-sur-Mer by Bomber Squadron No 120, and then from Maisoncelles to Cologne by Bomber Squadron No 110.

This airmail service for the forces ended on 31st August 1919. But maintaining the regularity of the service had presented numerous difficulties. The RAF had to put up with very unfavourable weather conditions during the winter of 1918–1919 – in particular the presence of thick banks of fog above the Belgian Ardennes. It was only after considerable resources had been commissioned (five Bomber Squadrons, emergency airfields along the route, radio telegraphy equipment and weather stations) that the reliability of the service reached a high level.

Period	Flights planned	Flights completed	Reliability
17.12.18/01.03.19	1,017	917	90%
01.03.19/31.08.19	1,842	1,770	96%

The injection of resources had been vital, as had – to an even greater extent – the courage of the pilots: "Pilots who had survived the intense air fighting of 1918 perished in the Channel or the mountains of the Ardennes and Eiffel as flying postmen." [6]

The Weimar Republic
Military defeat brought about the fall of the German Empire. The Kaiser abdicated at the end of 1918 and took refuge in Holland. The Social Democrats proclaimed a republic and a Constituent National Assembly convened in Weimar, a town in Thuringia steeped in history as the former home of Cranach, Goethe and Schiller. Fast and safe communication links between Berlin, the capital where the ministries and administration departments were located, and Weimar, which had been promoted to the temporary political capital 150 miles away, had become a matter of absolute necessity. At that time Germany was shaken by waves of political agitation and social upheaval,

L.V.G. C.VI CKD 1919.
Lufthansa

the railways were disorganised by strikes and there were shortages of coal. Consequently an express letter took between four and five days to get from Berlin to Weimar. To remedy this parlous situation, an air service between Berlin and Weimar was opened on 5th February 1919 by a company called Deutsche Luft Reederei, or DLR, which had been founded on 17th December 1917 with a number of prestigious company names among its shareholders (including AEG, Hapag and Zeppelin). Although the first flight on 5th February was more or less taken up with the transportation of newspapers (4,000 copies of the "Berliner Zeitung Am Mittag"), the flight on the morning of 6th February left Berlin-Johannisthal aerodrome carrying airmail, albeit in a mailbag containing only 14 letters. Despite these small beginnings the service operated until September 1919, carrying official passengers and newspapers as well as the post for which it had been set up. A small notice was put up in post offices defining the conditions for the conveyance of mail:

• Transport by aeroplane and onward delivery by express (Eilboten);

• Weight scale for airmail surcharge: 1 Mark up to 20 grams and 1.5 Marks from 20 to 250 grams;

• "If an aeroplane breaks down, the airmail surcharge will be reimbursed to the sender on presentation of the envelope." All eventualities were provided for!

For transporting the post, DLR generally used old AEG JII former reconnaissance planes fitted with a 200-horsepower Benz engine and carrying a maximum payload of approximately 200 kilograms.

It is difficult to summarise the exact nature of the limited number of flights made in the first months after the Armistice in France in Belgium and in Germany. They were operated by both civilian and military authorities, using either civilian or military aircraft, although they were always former warplanes. In the peacetime flights which emerged straight out of the war, war and peace overlapped with unclear boundaries – on either side of the Armistice line between the Allies and Germany.

RIGHT **During the rail strike in February 1922, express mail is flown between Berlin and middle Germany.**
Lufthansa

BELOW **L.V.G. C.VII biplane, March 1919.**

Part Three
The Age of Pioneers
and Organisers
1919–1939

*"I have re-done my calculations: our idea is unworkable.
There is only one thing left to do: make it work."*

Pierre-Georges Latécoère

*"I have always asked myself how it is possible
to live without enthusiasm or passion."*

Jean Mermoz

ABOVE **Passengers boarding Handley Page O/10 G-EATN.**
RAF Museum

BELOW S. Instone & Co Ltd Aerial Transport Vickers Vimy.
MAP

1 JUBILATION AND DISILLUSIONMENT IN THE POST WAR PERIOD

Once the Armistice was signed all the factors necessary for the rapid development of commercial aviation were assembled: aircraft, capital and individual enthusiasm.

In the former warring nations, thousands of military pilots returned to civilian life. Many of them only had one idea in their heads: to fly, at any price. Mermoz was one of them:

"To live is to fly. I have never questioned it. It is a fact. I could not conceive of existence except in the air." [1]

And there were even more aeroplanes available than pilots. Some were second hand, but most of them had just come off the production lines a few weeks before the end of the war. The aircraft manufacturers, whose companies had shown spectacular growth, were interested in investing capital to create air transport companies in order to obtain new outlets for their production. The high profile of shareholders in the German company, DLR, has already been mentioned but the most striking example is that of the Compagnie des Messageries Aériennes. The list of people at its board meetings contains the biggest names in French industry: Blériot, Bréguet, Caudron, Henri Farman, Morane, Renault and Saulnier. In this favourable economic climate, the next few months saw a blossoming of initiatives: there was a starburst of ideas, with swarms of projects ensuing. Hordes of air companies were founded, sometimes generously capitalised but mostly impoverished. The intensity of this period of jubilation and creativity was matched only by its brevity.

Four important lessons emerged from these very first years of commercial aviation.

1. Military aircraft were not suitable for civilian use. Their purchase price may have been low or zero, but maintenance costs – in particular for the engines – were prohibitive.

2. The regular operation of civilian air services presupposed a minimum amount of infrastructure (airfields, marshalling areas, weather information offices etc). In most cases, none of this existed.

3. The transport of mail constituted the main, and sometimes the only, source of income. It is no exaggeration to say that

the Post acted as godmother when aviation was christened. During the whole of the period from 1919 to 1939 the Post Offices around the world provided air companies with over half of their commercial income.

4. Commercial aviation, with the then current state of technology, was not a profitable activity. It had to be supported by governments providing direct subsidies, or through generously calculated postal fees:

"For some years into the future, civil aviation will not be self-sufficient . . . It is therefore important to keep it alive, even artificially, during this difficult period. It is a matter of major national interest, not only because of the vital importance of peaceful applications, but also because civil aviation provides indispensable reserves for military aviation." [2]

*   *   *

It is not the purpose of this chapter to retrace the complexities of the birth of air transport. However, some examples demonstrate how mail, and to a lesser extent freight, were able to contribute to the launch of commercial aviation in Europe and on the other continents during the period 1919–1922 .

I IN EUROPE

In Switzerland Major Isler started an air service between Zurich (Dübendorf aerodrome) and Berne (Kirchlindach aerodrome) in January 1919. In a process which would often be repeated, the service was initially restricted to transporting post and goods; then, on completion of a running-in period, it was opened to passengers. In addition providing an essential source of finance, the Post played a ground-breaking rôle in opening up the airlines.

"The Postal Union", the official mouthpiece of the Universal Postal Union, informed all the postal services of the world in its June 1919 issue about the establishment of an airborne postal service:

"As of 30th April 1919, following an agreement between the Swiss postal authorities and a company based at Dübendorf, all consignments of letter post and newspapers may be conveyed by aeroplane, subject to a unit weight limit of 250 grams, and the payment of a surcharge, between Zurich, Berne and Lausanne."

Two points need to be emphasised. The first, of general relevance, is that there is no form of airmail without a surcharge. The second, which is specific to central European countries, is that newspapers represent an important element of post sent by air.

As in the case of the German service between Berlin and Weimar, the railway could make up for any defects in the developing aviation service. "If the aeroplane is obliged to land en route, the consignments of airmail will be sent by the next post train."

In France, a number of air companies were founded immediately after the Armistice. Some of them were responsible for establishing commercial aviation in France, notably Lignes Aériennes Farman on the Brussels run; La Compagnie Générale Transaérienne, La Compagnie des Messageries Aériennes and La Compagnie des Grands Express Aériens on the Paris-London section; La Compagnie Franco-Roumanie de Navigation Aérienne bound for the Balkans; and the Lignes Aériennes Latécoère between Toulouse and Casablanca. Others such as Aèro Transports Ernoul had only a fleeting existence.

All these companies, as was usual among the European air transport companies, operated a complete service from the beginning, carrying passengers, goods and post. However, for many, the latter two types of traffic were of particular importance.

On 18th April 1919 La Compagnie des Messageries Aériennes (CMA) took over from the Postal Administration the operation of the Paris/Lille service, which was exclusively devoted to post and goods. On this basis, CMA was probably the first company in the world to operate a regular cargo-only service. In July 1919 it released the following information to the press: [3]

"La Compagnie des Messageries Aériennes has been operating since 18th April last a two-way service between Paris and Lille; the service flies daily, with complete regularity. On this service, it has carried up to time of writing:

- *80,000 daily newspapers*
- *20,000 periodical journals*
- *600 assorted parcels*
- *1,200 bags of letters*
- *50,000 telegrams."*

During the summer of 1922, between Paris and London the same company opened a post and parcel service, using a timetable which prepared the way for night flights, starting from Paris Le Bourget and London-Croydon at 06.00 hours each morning.

In competition, the Compagnie des Grands Express Aériens devoted a half-page advertisement to the transport of goods, with the following message: [4] "Send your parcels by aeroplane. you will save time and money."

In Britain, as in France, companies were created which would form the basis of British commercial aviation prior to the formation of Imperial Airways in 1924, notably Aircraft Transport and Travel Ltd, founded in 1916 by George Holt Thomas; Handley Page Transport; Instone Air Line and Daimler Airways.

Aircraft Transport and Travel Ltd inaugurated on 10th November 1919 the first regular airmail service between Paris and London, [5] leading the way in European air transport. In April 1920 [6] Handley Page Transport made a three-fold innovation on its London-Paris route: at the same time as it took into service "a new aircraft specially designed for the transport of goods", it reduced the freight rates and introduced a modern tariff structure by weight classification, which was to have an exceptional length of life [a method which is still in use today].

Rate Structure	Rate	Index
Minimum charge	5s	
Weight breaks		
< 10lb (4.5kg)	2s 6d per lb	100
10-20lb (4.5-9.0kg)	2s 3d per lb	88
20-50lb (9.0-22.6kg)	2s per lb	77
50-100lb (22.6-45.3kg)	1s 9d per lb	73
> 100lb (45.3kg)	1s 6d per lb.	61

Note: In pre-decimal UK currency, 12 pence (d) = 1 shilling (s); 20 shillings = £1

In addition to these large companies, a number of smaller ones, which often disappeared without trace, launched themselves into the operation of "cargo only" services. It was in the field of transporting exclusively goods that these young air companies experienced the highest degree of jubilation and the greatest disillusionment; they faded away as fast as they appeared. In this game, it has been the British who, from the beginnings up to the present day, have demonstrated an indefatigable spirit of enterprise and unfailing confidence in airfreight. Two examples of these first enterprises are listed below.

North Sea Aerial and General Transport Ltd opened in June 1919 a daily express parcel service between Leeds and Scarborough. On 6th March 1920 it inaugurated a cargo only line, which did not last long, between Leeds and Amsterdam, using a converted Blackburn Kangaroo bomber.

On 13th September 1920, using a Westland Limousine, *Air Post of Banks Ltd* started up a London/Paris service, essentially for the purpose of transporting bank documents. On 2nd November 1920, the operation was halted. It had only lasted six weeks but pre-dated by 60 years the activities of today's courier and express freight companies.

In Germany, the development of commercial aviation was very disorganised, reflecting the social and political situation of the country. In spite of the obstacles imposed by the Treaty of Versailles, companies were set up but operations were frequently disturbed by fuel shortages. In spite of the frequently chaotic operations, the main outlines of German air transport between the wars became clear at a very early stage: the two main aspects were the high density network which focused on "Mitteleuropa", and the dedicated postal activities of a Hanseatic Service connecting the ancient cities of the Hanseatic League from Tallinn to Hamburg, which extended towards Scandinavia on the one side and towards Amsterdam and London on the other.

DH16 at Amsterdam Schiphol, after completing the first flight
from London in 1920.
KLM

German Airmail Traffic (in kg)

	Letter Post	Parcels	News	Total	% News
1919	2,385	-	7,537	9,922	76%
1920	2,237	72	3,421	5,730	60%
1921	3,914	1,323	18,928	24,165	78%

The "air newspaper" service available on a domestic basis and
to the free town of Danzig benefited from attractive rates: the
surcharge for a 20-gram newspaper was only 5 pfennigs, as
against 20 pfennigs for a letter of the same weight.

However, the dirigible balloon was the greatest novelty in
German aviation in 1919. Before the Zeppelin company was
forced to hand its dirigibles over to the Allied nations, DELAG
had time to give them a brilliant demonstration, operating a regular service between Friedrichshafen and Berlin-Staaken for passengers, post and goods from 24th August to 5th December
1919, and carrying out a special flight from Berlin to Stockholm
on 8th October 1919. For these flights it used the "Bodensee", [7]
a medium-sized dirigible built in 1919, which was 120.8 metres
long and had a volume of 20,000 m³. During these three
months the "Bodensee" transported 2,250 passengers, 3,000
kilograms of goods and over 4,000 kilograms of post. Record
loadings were achieved during the German rail strike in mid
November 1919, with 744 kilograms on the 11th, 754 kilograms on the 13th and 800 kilograms on the 14th of
November.

The special flight from Berlin to Stockholm on 8th October
1919 was a real postal star performance. In addition to the
usual postcards written on board the airship, the "Bodensee"
unloaded "a considerable quantity of regular post" [8] and a small
green cachet "Bodensee-8, Oct 1919" was stamped on all correspondence.

In Scandinavia the hesitant beginnings of commercial aviation were closely linked to experiments with airmail. There are
numerous examples.

During the winter of 1919–1920, Estonia, at the extreme
edge of Scandinavia, was isolated from the rest of the world: the
sea-lanes were closed off by ice and land routes were blocked
by hostilities between the new Baltic republics and Russian
troops, and some German Free Corps. In these exceptional circumstances an airmail service was opened on 7th February to
15th March 1920 between the Estonian capital Tallinn and the
Finnish port of Helsingfors about 110 miles away. In spite of the
high rate of the airmail surcharge and the short distance, the
success was such that special measures had to be taken to limit
the traffic. The first flight on 7th February 1920 carried 164
kilograms of mail. The aeroplane had broken the isolation of
Tallinn and few objected to the airmail surcharge!

Some hard lessons had to be learned from these early
experiments in airmail. In the summer of 1920, from 18th
August to 15th October, the Norwegian company Det Norske
Luftfartsrederi operated an airborne postal service between
Bergen and Stavanger using sea-planes. Although it was a technical success, with a reliability rate of 94%, this was outweighed
by commercial failure: only 2,600 letters were carried. Unless
there were exceptional circumstances, the public was reluctant
to pay an airmail surcharge of 40 öre for a distance of around
125 miles.

However interesting these efforts, they did not lay the basis for future commercial aviation in Scandinavia. That lay in the establishment of a regular airmail link between continental Europe and England, via Germany. The first attempt dates from summer 1920 and united three companies: the German company Deutsche Luft Reederei opened a postal service between Warnemünde, Malmö and Copenhagen on 1st October 1920, soon to be followed on 7th August by the Danish Det Danske Luftfartselskab, and on 31st August by the Swedish Svensk Lufttrafik A.B. on the same route. Warnemünde was the entry point to the German air network in the direction of Berlin. After hard-fought postal negotiations with Germany, the Danish company, as sole carrier, set up a service from Copenhagen to Hamburg on 15th September 1920, offering direct connections to Amsterdam and London, using flights from a Dutch company created on 7th October 1919: the Koninklijke Luchtvaart Maatschapij Voor Nederland En Kolonien, or more simply KLM. The flights were interrupted on 30th October 1920, at the end of the summer season (many services in Europe only worked during the good weather for some years), and these links were only reopened in 1923.

At the other end of Europe, in Spain, two postal services (open to passengers) operated in 1922 between Seville and Larache (a part of Morocco which at that time was under Spanish control) and between Barcelona and Palma de Majorca. In both cases, aircraft were used over the marine sections of the routes.

2 IN AFRICA

Belgium was the pioneer of air transport in Equatorial Africa within its colony, the Belgian Congo – known today as the Congo.

It was an immense colony, 80 times the size of Belgium, covered with thick equatorial forest for a large part of its surface and traversed by a mighty river – the Congo – which was interrupted by rapids at several points. Sparsely populated, difficult to penetrate and rich in mineral resources, the Belgian Congo seemed to be made for air transport.

At the suggestion of King Albert I, a "Committee for the Study of Aerial Navigation in the Congo" was set up in 1919. This committee conferred the task of establishing an air link along the River Congo to an organisation named Ligne Aérienne du Roi Albert, or LARA, using Lévy-Le Pen seaplanes, which carried a maximum load of 590 kilograms. During a period of almost three months, and by dint of considerable efforts, the pilots from LARA travelled upstream from water table to water table and set up the required waterside bases necessary to operate a permanent air link. Leaving from Leopoldville (Kinshasa) on 22nd February 1919, they opened the first stretch from Leopoldville to Gombé on 1st May 1919 and then the second stretch from Gombé to Coquilhatville (Mbandaka) on 1st May 1921. The last stage from Coquilhatville to Stanleyville (Kisangani) was completed on 1st June 1921.

With a length of 1,150 miles, the route between Leopoldville and Stanleyville consisted of nine stages and took three days. Linking up with the Malle d'Anvers, the postal steamer bringing the mail from Belgium, it reduced by two weeks the average time for conveying correspondence to the Belgian civil servants and colonists in the area of Stanleyville and beyond. Whereas it used to take 17 days to travel up river by boat and porters, only three were needed by aeroplane.

Having made its point, LARA ceased activities a year later in June 1922, having transported 95 passengers and 1,800 kilograms of post in 80 flights.

3 IN SOUTH AMERICA

In South America, Guiana and Colombia were the pioneering nations.

French Guiana was sparsely populated, marshy, covered in jungle and difficult to get to. It was felt that certain economic activities, although of limited extent, "may offer items of airfreight having high value for low volume", [9] for example, the production of gum from Balata (a reddish coloured wood which produces latex) or resupplying the work camps which panned gold-bearing sediments. Conditions seemed favourable for air transport and some high profile shareholders, among whom were Louis Bréguet, founded the Société des Transports Aériens Guyanais on 7th June 1919. Initially equipped with George Lévy seaplanes, and later with Bréguet 14 A2s, this company encountered enormous difficulties and was dissolved on 30th October 1922.

However, the operation was of interest on two counts. Firstly, the ambitions concerning cargo were innovative: in an advertisement, which appeared in 1922, the company proposed to carry out "the transport of supplies for placers and production operations for Balata gum". This was an attractive idea, but the production units concerned were much too primitive to provide enough business for an airline. Secondly, the postal aims of the operation were noteworthy, as is evidenced in a decision taken on 8th July 1921 by the Governor of Guiana:

"In view of the interest which the Colony would have in the organisation of the transportation of despatches between Cayenne, Saint Laurent du Maroni, Inini and vice versa,
It is decided:
• Article 1: An airborne service for the transport of the mail will be organised between Cayenne, Saint Laurent du Maroni, Inini and vice versa.
• Article 2: In addition to the postage charge, a surcharge will be collected by the Postal Service to the benefit of the Société de Transports Aériens Guyanais. This surcharge will be represented by a token stamp issued by the Aviation Service."

Thus, the airmail surcharge took an unusual form: that of a sticker issued, not by the Post Office but by the "Aviation Service". In fact, it was issued by the airline itself.

Because of its terrain, Colombia is one of the most suitable countries in the world for air transport: the port of Barranquilla on the Caribbean Sea is separated from the capital Bogota, situated at an altitude of 2,600m, by sheer walls of rock and sudden changes in ground level. The overland link, which combined the river route (travelling up the Rio Magdalena) with the railway, lasted a dozen or so days.

The year 1919 witnessed a number of air transport initiatives in Colombia. On 18th June 1919 the American pilot Knok Martin made the first postal flight in Colombia, indeed in all of South America, by transporting a mailbag containing 160 letters from Barranquilla to Puerto Colombia on board a Curtiss aircraft.

On 22nd September 1919 a group of Franco-Colombian businessmen founded the first Colombian air company: the

De Havilland DH4 operated by the US Air Mail Service in 1920.

Compañia Colombiana de Navigación Aérea. The "CC de NA" with a fleet of two Farman aircraft, won a tender from the General Postal Directorate in Bogota to establish three airmail services from Bogota, to Barranquilla, Pasto and Cucuta. But the problems started from the very first flights at the end of February 1920: the aircraft which were put into service had not been designed for the rough terrain, high altitude and difficult climate of Colombia. The operation was stopped after two fatal accidents, and the company was liquidated in 1922.

On 5th December 1919, a group of German-Colombian businessmen and pilots founded the "Sociédad Colombo-Alemaña de Transportes Aereos", better known by its initials SCADTA. But that is another story.

4 IN NORTH AMERICA

As we shall see in Chapter 3 of this part, the United States occupies an eminent position in the history of airborne post, but the epic story of its domestic postal system should not eclipse the contribution of a number of smaller US companies in the field of international post.

Between 1920 and 1923, the American Postal Administration issued the first Foreign Airmail Contract (abbreviated to FAM). This was the start of a system of assigning international postal routes by tendering, to transport American post to foreign countries. The system is very similar to the policy applied today by an increasing number of Post Offices.

The first contract – FAM1 – was issued on 15th October 1920 to Florida West Indies Airways to transport mail between Florida (Key West) and Cuba (Havana). This company was soon

bought up by Aero Marine Airways, which in turn disappeared in 1923.

The second contract – FAM2 – went to the Seattle Victoria Air Mail Line, which is often known as Hubbard Air Transport, after the name of its owner/pilot/and chief of everything, Eddie Hubbard, who was a flying instructor at the San Diego airbase during the war, and later a test pilot with Boeing.

As is clearly declared in its official name, this company specialised in the transport of post between the town of Seattle (in Washington State, USA) and the port of Victoria (in British Columbia, Canada) which was the first or last port of call in North America for transpacific postal steamers. Although the first trial flight to test the route was made on 3rd March 1919, carrying 60 letters and William E. Boeing on board, regular operations, using a Boeing B1 aircraft did not start until 15th October 1920 after the negotiation and signature of the contract – FAM2 – with the American Post. This contract covered a maximum of 12 return flights per month, with 600lb of post per flight.

Why open an air service between two towns, which were less than 100 miles apart? The answer was to speed up the transport of post by sea by bringing in air transport to cover the first or last link between the port of Victoria, and Seattle, the point of entry into the United States. Thus Eddie Hubbard, on his first flight, made a connection with the Japanese ship "Africa Maru", out of Yokohama. Thanks to a 50-minute flight, the mail destined for the United States gained several precious hours on the traditional transhipment system involving sea and rail links between Victoria and Seattle.

This airline, which operated uninterruptedly until 30th June 1937, recorded annual traffic of between 10 and 20 tons throughout this period.

The third contract – FAM3 – was similar to the second, but dealt with a different part of the world. On 9th April 1923, after the contract was signed, a little company, The Gulf Coast Airline, opened a short service of 85 miles between New Orleans and Pilottown at the mouth of the Mississippi, a port of call for ships coming from South America and the Caribbean. As was the case with Victoria and Seattle, it was a matter of saving a few hours on the last section of the route by using an aircraft to replace transhipment overland.

Although a neighbour of the United States, Canada came to air transport late. Its first airmail trial, which was in fact unplanned, took place in June 1918. Canada had been at war for four years and needed to recruit still more pilots. In order to encourage people to join up, the Montreal office of the Aerial League of the British Empire decided to organise a demonstration flight from Montreal to Toronto. The flight was planned for Saturday, 21st June, without any post on board. Everything was planned, except for the bad weather: the flight was postponed until Monday, 23rd June but the visibility remained practically zero. Finally, taking advantage of a gap in the clouds, the aircraft – a Curtiss JN4 "Jenny" manufactured in Toronto – piloted by Captain Brian Peck took off at 10.12 hours carrying a sack of mail, and landed at 16.55 hours at Camp Leaside near Toronto, after making two technical stopovers. In fact, advantage had been taken of the successive delays to make this arrangement to carry the sack of mail as originally this flight was not supposed to carry any post. There is even an apocryphal story that this flight even carried cargo: a case of Old whisky! [10] After the end of the war, Canadian politicians were too busy keeping the railway system, which was really the backbone of the country, from going bankrupt, and did not invest much energy in air transport. One Minister even made the following peremptory declaration: "I do not believe that Canada will ever have any need for air transport." [11]

Finally, in Mexico, on 3rd October 1921 a bi-weekly service started between Mexico City and the port of Tampico. The service was open to passengers and first class post.

5 IN ASIA

The first postal flight in China took place on 7th May 1920 when English veterans made a test flight from Peking to Tientsin and return, intended to demonstrate the commercial advantages of Handley Page bombers. Letters were loaded on board, although the quantity is not recorded, and carried a bilingual postmark in Chinese and English from the Chinese postal service. In spite of the long period of disturbance which the country had entered into, the Chinese Government was interested in aviation. In 1919 the Bureau for Aviation proposed a draft statute on aviation, outlining the creation of a Chinese air network and, as a matter of priority, the opening of a service between Peking and Shanghai. Rather than trying to connect Peking and Shanghai, which were over 600 miles apart, entirely by air, the solution adopted consisted in combining an aeroplane from Peking to Tsinan, the capital of Shantung situated just to the south of the Yellow River (about 185 miles), with the railway from Tsinan to Shanghai. The first flight by Peking Government Air Company was on 1st July 1921; conditions were good and the post arrived in Shanghai on the following day. Unfortunately, as a consequence of increasingly unstable internal conditions, the flights were suspended from 10th July. From these first flying operations, China soon established an extremely sound system of regulations for airborne post. "A

contract for the transport of aerial post" was signed on 26th April 1921 between the Aeronautical Department and the Directorate General for Post. It established a direct link between the air surcharge, which was set by the Aeronautical Department but collected by the Post, and the remuneration to the transport company, fixed at 80% of the income from the sale of air postage stamps. [12]

In Siam (now Thailand) the Administration itself operated a weekly airmail line serving several localities on the Korat Plateau in the east of the country (Ubon, Roi-Et, etc). "The Postal Union" published the news in 1922. One unusual feature of these operations was that no airmail surcharge was collected.

In Japan, various historical and political factors favoured the rapid start-up of air transport. The popularity of kites in all forms and colours; the interest shown by the Emperor Meiji in military balloons from 1877 onwards; the participation of the first unit of Japanese balloonists in the capture of Port Arthur in 1904 during the Russo-Japanese War; the appearance of an aircraft building activity carried out by artisans and very much inspired by French models; the presence of Japan beside the Allies during the First World War; and the rôle of British and French military missions in 1919–1921 were all vital factors. To these should be added the very considerable influence of the Imperial Aeronautical Association, founded in 1913 under the presidency of General Nagaoka, which was at the forefront in the birth and development of Japanese aviation. Between 1919 and 1922 it was responsible for organising airmail flying contests, [13] during which the participants had to complete a course in the best time. These unusual competitions were endowed with prizes, and had more in common with exhibition flights and sporting trials than with air transport, but their aims were clear: to establish airmail links inside Japan. The principal competitions were:

• 22nd October 1919. The first airmail flying contest took place from Tokyo to Osaka and return, in which Japanese manufactured Itoh and Nakajima aeroplanes took part. Pilot Yozo Sato in a Nakajima 4 won the trial in 6 hours 58 minutes, along with the first prize of 10,000 yen.

• 20th November 1920. The second airmail flying contest from Osaka to Zentsuji, Oita and Kurume (on the island of Kyushu) was won by pilot Ishibashi in a French-made Spad 13.

• 21st August 1921. The third airmail flying contest took place over a course from Tokyo to Morioka (340 miles to the north) and return. No participants finished the course due to fog.

• 3rd November 1921. The fourth airmail flying contest was held from Kanazawa, on the Japan Sea, to Hiroshima in the south of the island of Honshu.

• November 1922. The fifth airmail flying contest was organised on a larger scale over the original Tokyo/Osaka/Tokyo course. It brought together 14 civilian pilots, and continued for a whole week, giving a measure of the progress accomplished within three years. The record time was reduced from 6 hours 58 minutes to 4 hours 49 minutes, thanks to a Nakajima B6 aircraft fitted with a Rolls-Royce Eagle engine of 360hp. The number of letters transported during the competition rose to 8,897.

The first regular service in Japan started on 12th November 1922. It was principally devoted to transporting newspapers and parcels between the towns of Sakai (Osaka Prefecture) and Tokushima, and was operated by the Japanese Air Transport Research Institute (JATRI) which had just been set up by Choichi Inouye, one of the fathers of Japanese commercial aviation.

The aircraft used was a seaplane type Itoh EMI31 inspired by the Curtiss Seagull, fitted with a 200hp Hispano-Suiza engine.

The fifth airmail flying contest proved that the idea of a regular service between Osaka and Tokyo was no longer just a dream. The interest in aviation development shown by one of the world's largest newspapers, "Asahi Shimbun", helped to bring the service into being. The Japanese daily's powerful support was instrumental in founding the East/West Air Transport Company, Tozai ("East/West" in Japanese), in 1923, and the company immediately began to operate an airmail service between Tokyo and Osaka. The aeroplanes, for the most part Nakajima 5s, left Tokyo and Osaka at the same time, and crossed at Hamamatsu, according to the following timetable:

Tokyo	08.00hrs	12.00hrs
Hammamatsu	09.30hrs	10.30hrs
	10.30hrs	09.30hrs
Osaka	12.00hrs	08.00hrs

The Osaka/Tokyo service commenced in the middle of winter and on 22nd February 1923 pilot Takeo Shimada on board his Shirato 25 Kuma Go was on the stretch from Hammamatsu to Tokyo when he was caught up in a snow storm above Hakone near Mount Fuji. Off course and in zero visibility, he crashed on the Myojingatake Mountains, adding his name to the world's roll of pilots who have sacrificed their lives for airborne post.

The service was initially reserved for post and goods. On board the first flight there were messages addressed to the mayors of Tokyo and Osaka and to the Prime Minister, merchandise including a consignment of socks and "anything which the clients felt they could send in the conditions of that time". The history of the Tozai between 1923 and 1929 can be divided into seven periods, as described by its President, Mr Muroyama. [14]

During the second period, from August 1923 to March 1924, the following statistics were recorded: 74 flights, 128,000 letters, 780 parcels, 793 photos, 50 telegrams, a quantity of newspapers and no passengers. The service was opened to passengers only in 1925; once more the Post had fulfilled its function of opening up a service. (However, it does not appear that anyone followed up an initial plan to parachute parcels out over Nagoya and two other towns.)

In 1924, the Aviation Department of the "Asahi Shimbun" took direct control of the operation of Tozai.

6 IN AUSTRALIA

As in Japan and the United States, the post was at the roots of commercial aviation in Australia.

Australia is an island – an immense continent. The main part of the population is distributed around its circumference in areas of settlement which are often very remote from one another. "In Australia, conditions are ideal for aviation." During the initial period, for technical and financial reasons, there was no question of trying to put a girdle around the Australian continent in one continuous airline. The Australians restricted themselves to setting up individual sections of the service in order to link settlements which were not so well served by

In Australia, a Queensland and N.T. Aerial Service Avro aircraft.

post carried overland or by sea. The first three services were opened between 1921 and 1924 and were operated on the same pattern: private companies subsidised within the framework of postal contracts agreed with the Government of the Commonwealth of Australia.

• The first service was inaugurated on 4th December 1921 between Geraldton and Derby, along the western coast of Australia, by Western Australian Airways. It operated very regularly once a week over a distance of 1,250 miles, joining a number of small, very isolated centres of population: Geraldton, Carnavon, Onslow, Roehourne, Port Hedland and Derby. It was first extended southwards from Geraldton to Perth on 17th January 1924 and then northwards from Derby to Wyndham on 13th July 1934. Despite an accident during the first flight, in which the pilot and his mechanic lost their lives, this air service was a great success:

> "… the service was carrying about 10,000 letters a month and made a real dent in the armour of isolation which had closed upon the North West for so many years. Life was really transformed for the men and women of the North West who had previously been confined to a single monthly boat." [15]

• The second service was opened on 2nd November 1922 between Charleville and Cloncurry (600 miles) via Tambo, Blackall, Longreach, Winton and MacKinley, in the state of Queensland in northeast Australia. In contrast to the first service, it united settlements in the outback, where the population was very widely dispersed. It was provided by a company, which was registered on 16th November 1920 as the Queensland and Northern Territory Aerial Services Limited and which has since become better known under the name of Qantas.

• The third service started up on 2 November 1924 between the two large East Coast cities Adelaide and Sydney, via Mildura, Hay, Narrandera, and Cootamundra, over a distance of 860 miles. It was operated by Australian Aerial Services Ltd. Following the classical formula, the service was first restricted to mail, and after a running-in period, was opened to passenger traffic on 1 January 1925.

* * *

This world survey shows the great debt which commercial aviation, springing to life on every continent, owed to the various postal authorities. It also underlines the interdependence and complementary roles of the different modes of transport.

LEFT **Sir Sefton Brancker.**
RAF Museum

ABOVE **The three first Australian airmail routes: the first from Perth to Derby; the second from Cloncurry to Charleville; the third from Sydney to Adelaide.**

2 THE INTERNATIONAL LEGAL FRAMEWORK IS PUT IN PLACE

Although the aeroplane was considered as a domestic means of transport in such vast countries as the United States, Australia or China, this was not the case in Europe in the early years. In this small continent, fragmented into numerous states, aviation was necessarily international and its harmonious development required the definition and application of a body of common rules.

In less than two years, from 1919 to the end of 1920, the infant commercial aviation industry was given a very complete international legal framework, covering the aeronautical relations between states, the relations between carriers and the status of aerial post. The delicate problem of the nature and liability limits of airline companies in respect of passengers and the shippers of goods was resolved somewhat later in 1929. Without wishing to analyse things too deeply, it is appropriate to trace the essential characteristics of this system which promoted the development of commercial aviation, and which even today remains to a certain extent the foundation of international air regulation.

I IATA: AN UNUSUAL TYPE OF RELATIONSHIP BETWEEN COMPETING COMPANIES

On 25th August 1919, 12 men, representing six air companies, some of which had not yet begun to fly, met in The Hague at the initiative of George Holt Thomas, the Chairman of the British company Aircraft Transport and Travel Ltd, which had on that very day inaugurated its regular London/Paris service. [1] The six companies were:

- Aircraft Transport and Travel Ltd (UK)
- Det Danske Luftfartselskab A.S. (Denmark)
- Det Norske Luftfartrederi (Norway)
- Deutsche Luft Reederei (Germany)
- Svenska Lufttrafik A.B. (Sweden)
- and lastly a Dutch company which was still in the process of formation, and would soon become Koninklijke Luchtvaart Maatschappij voor Nederland En Kolonien, or KLM.

Although it has been rarely commented on, it is remarkable that the initial core of IATA, with the exception of the four

companies from four neutral countries – The Netherlands, Sweden, Norway and Denmark – consisted of an English company and a German company, at a time when the Peace Treaty had not yet been signed. This is a fine example of the breadth of vision possessed by the founder and chief promoter of IATA, and his right-hand man, the British General Sir Sefton Brancker, who chaired the meeting, less than 10 months after the Armistice.

On 28th August the six companies signed a short document, only one page long, written in longhand by Sir Sefton, to set up an association entitled the International Air Traffic Association (IATA), "with a view to co-operate to mutual advantage in preparing and organising international aerial traffic". At the dawn of commercial aviation, half a dozen young companies, which were very vulnerable (in spite of some of them having illustrious shareholders), had decided to assist one another in order to develop this new method of transport. From these beginnings, IATA grew into an association which was always open, and which sought to assemble the largest possible number of carriers and to go beyond its European framework. In 1939, in spite of various mergers which had occurred, it included 29 companies from four continents (Africa, America, Asia and Europe). However, it was still dominated by European companies, and Europe as a geographical area represented its main area of activity, since the long-haul imperial and postal services fell outside its competence.

The actions of IATA between the two wars enabled enormous progress to be achieved in simplifying formalities and procedures, ensuring uniformity of transport documents and standardising technical norms. Its major achievement was the coordination of timetables and the organisation of a European system of connecting flights. The Conference on Timetables and Accounting, established in 1929, regularly met in Berlin.

At that time fares and rates were not considered to be within the competence of IATA. This at least was the theory, because in practice "meetings of specialists on traffic matters during IATA conferences provided an opportunity for getting into unofficial discussions around a restaurant table." [2] In addition, the spread within Europe of the system of pools [3] contributed greatly to the unification of tariffs, particularly for passenger transport.

948

KLM founder Albert Plesman and Anthony Fokker in 1930.
KLM

In its early days, IATA devoted a considerable amount of time and energy to questions of parcel services and postal problems. It played a decisive role in the negotiations with the Universal Postal Union, pushed for a study concerning a European night post network, held discussions with the distribution services of the press, made great efforts to bring some order into the field of rates, etc.

Dr Albert Plesman, the founder Chairman of KLM – one of the major figures in commercial aviation – assessed the achievements of the first IATA in the years 1919–1939 thus:

"IATA has played an important role in the development of aerial transport, by making all possible efforts to lead the companies to cooperate on a friendly basis and to try to find common solutions to all the problems which are capable of being treated jointly." [4]

2 INTERNATIONAL PUBLIC LAW ON AIR TRANSPORT: THE PARIS CONVENTION OF 13th OCTOBER 1919

The debate concerning air space and its legal status goes back to before the First World War, the doctrine preceding the law. Even before any actual international air links existed, a marked split was apparent between the advocates of freedom of the air and the supporters of the sovereignty of the states below.

At the beginning of the century the question had arisen in connection with balloons drifting from one country to another. The crossing of the Channel by Blériot made the problem more acute and precipitated the calling of several international conferences. In 1913 the Madrid Conference sought to resolve the differences between the French and German delegates on the one hand, who favoured the principle of freedom of the air, and the British delegates on the other hand, who defended the principle of states having sovereignty over the airspace above their territories. The idea emerged that freedom of the air could not be realised without applying a certain number of policing regulations, which should naturally fall under the control of the states being over-flown.

"The end of the First World War marks the true birth of practical air law", [5] whether it was a matter of internal legislation within states or of international law. The latter was developed within the framework of the Peace Conference. An Aeronautical Commission of the Peace Conference met in Paris at the beginning of 1919 and quickly agreed on the text of an International Convention for the Regulation of Aerial Navigation. It was approved on 27th September 1919 by the Supreme Council of the Allied Powers and their associates, and the convention was opened for signature by the states on 13th October 1919. Signatory states were obliged to ratify the convention and non-signatory states were free to observe its terms.

The 1919 Paris International Air Convention took effect on 11th July 1922. Its first article answered the fundamental question of freedom of the air versus national sovereignty. There was no doubt: "the Contracting Parties recognise that each

Power has complete and exclusive sovereignty over the airspace above its territory." [6] Discussions only concerned the nature and the limits of exceptions to be applied to the principle of sovereignty in order to facilitate the development of aerial navigation. The principle of freedom of passage for non-scheduled flights was admitted in peacetime. On the other hand, "the establishment of international routes for aerial navigation is subject to the approval of the States who would be overflown." [6]

The convention consisted of nine Chapters and Technical Appendices, which had the same legal status. The Chapters deal with general principles, the nationality of aircraft, certificates of airworthiness, patents, the permission for flights over a foreign state, regulations applying to departure, during the flight and on landing, and concerning prohibited transport and state aircraft. Moreover, the Paris Convention provided for the creation of a permanent organisation in order to develop international regulations in line with technical progress and the rapid expansion of civil aviation – the International Commission of Air Navigation – or ICAN. With its headquarters in Paris, the ICAN had the status of a permanent international commission placed "under the authority of the League of Nations". It consisted of representatives of the states and was provided with a permanent secretariat. It was organised in Sub-Committees (operational, legal, wireless telegraphy, meteorology, medicine, cartography, equipment) and in Committees (Customs and standardisation). The ICAN exercised considerable regulatory power: the amendments which it applied to the technical appendices of the Convention were rendered applicable by simple notification to member states, providing that they had been adopted by a three-quarter majority. "Until the Second World War it was a remarkable instrument for legislative and regulatory unification, since the States had to model their legislation and regulations on the provisions of the Convention and its appendices. [7]

Unfortunately, several countries, and not the least important, remained outside the Convention either because they did not join – Germany, Soviet Union and China – or because they did not ratify it – the United States. However, these countries felt the need to have available an agreement comparable to that of the Paris Convention, in order to facilitate the development of their commercial aviation: this was the "Pan-American Convention on Commercial Aviation" signed in Havana in 1928 and ratified by 22 countries. The United States supplemented the Havana Convention by means of several bilateral agreements.

3 THE LEGAL FRAMEWORK FOR RELATIONS BETWEEN THE POST AND THE AIR COMPANIES

Although domestic traffic is a matter for each postal administration concerned, international postal dealings fall under the competency of the Universal Postal Union or UPU. It was created on 9th October 1874 on the initiative of Heinrich von Stephan, the Director General of Post, first for Prussia and then for Germany.

It addressed the concern of ensuring freedom of transit for international correspondence from one state to another. To this end, the states are considered to form a single territory, as is robustly expressed in Article 1 of the Universal Postal Convention:

"The countries between which this present Treaty is concluded shall form under the title of 'General Postal Union' a single postal territory."

"The Earth constitutes a single territory", such is the revolutionary affirmation which the postal executives the world over have made their slogan since 1874. In this world-encompassing postal territory, the mail can pass freely: "Freedom of transit is guaranteed within the entire territory of the Union" (Article 4).

As it was in charge of international postal relations, the UPU was concerned with the most efficient means of conveying mail. Indirectly, the UPU itself fixed the remuneration of sea and rail transport companies, through fixing the transit fees between postal administrations with respect to "ordinary services". In contrast to these, the rare "extraordinary services" were the object of special regulations.

"The transit rates specified in the present article do not apply to conveyance within the Union by means of extraordinary services specially established or maintained by one Administration at the request of one or several other Administrations. The conditions for this class of conveyance are regulated by mutual consent between the Administrations concerned." (Article 4, paragraph 5 of the text of the Convention finalised by the Congress of the Universal Postal Union in Rome in 1906.

The regulations concerning the application of the Rome Convention specify: "The extraordinary services of the Union which give rise to special charges, the fixing of which is reserved, according to Article 4 of the Convention to arrangements between the administrations concerned are exclusively:

1. Those which are maintained for the accelerated overland transport of the Indian Mail Service,
2. That which is established for the transport of mail by rail between Colon and Panama".

This was the situation in 1920 when the Congress of the Universal Postal Union met in Madrid. In less than 20 years, between 1920 and 1938, the relations in the international field between postal services and the air companies would pass through three phases: the recognition phase (1920–1927), the integration phase (1927–1938), and finally the phase in which it became common place (1938).

Recognition phase: 1920–1927
In a postal world, which was exclusively dominated by sea and rail transport, the first objective of the still infant air transport sector was to have its existence recognised. This it was quickly able to do, thanks to the far-sightedness of a number of postal administrations.

Great Britain, to whose postal administration falls the great merit of bringing about the official recognition of air transport by the Universal Postal Union, proposed to add to the main Convention a supplementary article as follows: [8]

Article 4b – Aerial Services
"Aerial services established for the conveyance of correspondence between two or more countries are considered as analogous to the extraordinary services to which Article 4 §

6 refers. The conditions of conveyance are settled by mutual consent between the Administrations concerned. The transit charges applicable to each aerial service are, however, uniform for all Administrations which use the service...".

We would do well to recall the reasons behind the British proposition:

"In view of the expansion of aerial postal services which give rise to extraordinary expenses, and to which the provisions of the present Convention manifestly do not apply, it appears desirable to provide for an exceptional treatment for these services, notably with regard to the fee rates for postage and transit."

After the intervention of delegates from Sweden, Switzerland and France, the new text of Article 4b was adopted, except for one minor modification. On 22nd November 1920, during the second plenary session of the Congress, aerial transport was recognised by the UPU as an "extraordinary service" on the same basis as the legendary Indian Mail Service and the Panama Railway. At this initial stage, it was a great victory for a mode of transport which could hardly yet fulfil the three inseparable requirements of the Post, namely speed, regularity and safety – not to talk of price.

The following UPU Congress was held in Stockholm in 1924. In spite of a rewriting of the text, it did not bring any appreciable change to the international postal status of aerial transport. It remained grouped with the "extraordinary services" and was not subject to any uniform regulation common to different companies or different air routes. On the contrary, "The postal administrations of countries directly served by air services shall determine, by agreement with the companies concerned, the transport fees to apply to mail taken on board in airports in their respective territories for journeys effected by means of such companies." [9]

Sweden, whose ideas on airmail were among the most progressive, attempted to use its role as the host country in order to help air transport to cross a decisive new hurdle, that of integration and standardisation: "The Swedish Postal Administration has the honour of proposing to the Stockholm Universal Postal Congress that the question of the establishment of international provisions for aerial transport should be put up for discussion... This question is of great importance." [10] Hence Sweden proposed to replace "arrangements" from case to case with "international provisions". However the majority of the Congress was not yet ready to pass to the next phase, although an increasing number of delegations began to underline the inadequacies and limitations of simple recognition.

"No rules at all applied in the establishment of international postal communications via the airways. The prices for transport varied from one country to the next, and sometimes even from one service to the next. Some offices demanded that the surcharges paid at despatch should be wholly reimbursed to them, whereas others demanded remuneration based on the weight of mail, though the unit of weight itself varied." [11]

In order to put an end to a situation which was becoming more and more anarchic with the increasing number of air services,

and under pressure from business interests for whom the International Chamber of Commerce acted as spokesperson, the Universal Postal Union decided to call a special conference at The Hague on 1st September 1927, without waiting for the London Congress of 1929.

The phase of integration and standardisation: 1927–1938
The "Airmail Conference of The Hague" was opened by the Dutch Minister of the Waterstaat, who defined its mission as follows:

"You have been summoned to work out a plan for regulating international airmail traffic. Regulations should be put into force, as an experiment, at the commencement of 1928, and should in this case serve as a basis for the revision of the Universal Postal Convention at the Congress of London in 1929... The new regulation must fix cheap, uniform rates; a just compensation for the air navigation companies; regulate transhipment of the mail; a marked simplicity of international accountancy." [11]

In practice, the Conference of The Hague did provide the international transport of airmail with a system of universal regulation. It was no longer considered as an "extraordinary means". It was integrated into the array of modes of transport codified by the UPU, while at the same time remaining a means of transport distinct from the others and therefore justifiably qualified to the payment of a surcharge. Air transport had been integrated and its regulations had been standardised, but it was not yet commonplace.

The International Chamber of Commerce played a considerable role in the preparations for and the course taken by the Conference at The Hague. It presented a group of "proposals concerning aerial post" which had the distinction of simultaneously expressing the point of view of users and that of the airlines. It declared itself in favour of "maintaining the surcharge, but on condition that its application be made uniform, systematic and general". With regard to the remuneration of the air companies it proposed "a remuneration to be as uniformly applied as possible for each kilogram transported by day within Europe". The air companies requested a charge of 6 to 7.5 gold francs per ton/kilometres, on European daytime flights, and a considerably higher charge for European night flights and intercontinental links.

During the entire period of the debates, the Universal Postal Union was concerned not only to listen, but also to involve in its debates the representatives of the users (the International Chamber of Commerce) and of the air transport companies (IATA). Its attitude is all the more worthy of note since at the time no one spoke about consumer protection or about supplier-client contracts. Progressing in an atmosphere of mutual agreement, the Conference of The Hague quickly drew up and then adopted, with the full agreement of the representatives of the users and the transport companies, a number of "Provisions concerning the Conveyance of the letter post by Air" which were thenceforward to constitute the charter for international airmail. What were its chief points?

1. *"All the articles mentioned in Article 33 of the Universal Postal Convention are admitted for aerial conveyance over the whole or part of the distance, namely: letters, single postcards or postcards*

with reply paid, commercial papers, patterns and samples of merchandise, printed matter of all kinds including that for the use of the blind, and money orders."

2. *"The right of free transit provided for in Article 25 §1 of the Universal Postal Convention is guaranteed for air-carried correspondence throughout the whole territory of the Postal Union."*

3. *"Articles to be conveyed by air are charged, in addition to the ordinary rates, a special surcharge, the amount of which shall be fixed by the administration of the country of origin. This surcharge shall not exceed 25 centimes per 20 grams and per 1,000 kilometres [625 miles] of the distance travelled."*

4. *"The basic rate to be applied in the settlement of the accounts for air transportation between the administrations has been fixed at 6.5 centimes of gold franc for every indivisible fraction of 100 grams net weight and 100 kilometres [62.5 miles]… The above prices do not apply to transport over long distances and carried out by service, the creation and upkeep of which give rise to extraordinary expense."*

As a rule this basic rate was limited to some European routes. Consequently there was an explosive increase in extraordinary services by means of extremely lucrative charges which subsidised the airlines' growth.

5. *"Registered correspondence is subject to the postage rates and general conditions decided by the Universal Postal Convention."*

6. *"All correspondence to be carried by aeroplane must bear a blue label with the words 'Par Avion' and their corresponding words in the language of the country of origin."*

7. The transport of postal parcels by air was the subject of special provisions. In fact this was the sole topic where there was any serious disagreement between the postal administrations, who were eager to extend the benefits of air transport to postal parcels, and the air transport companies, who were concerned that they should not be inundated with traffic which was mediocre in quality due to its volume, and less well paid than "letter post", but nevertheless benefiting from postal priority in loading. Following a memorandum of dissent, it was decided that postal parcels would only be transported by aeroplane "in communications between countries of which the postal administrations had declared themselves to be in agreement on this matter."

This was the only sour note in a conference which produced a complete system of universal regulation, and which "unquestionably marked the beginning of a new era for the airmail." [12]

The phase of generality and assimilation: 1938
The following passage is taken from the report of the Conference at The Hague: "At the request of one delegation" – from the radical nature of the idea expressed, it might have been The Netherlands or Sweden – "the Chairman states that it is understood that the prescription of a surcharge is optional." That is how the problem of the collection of a surcharge was raised. Over the years, the Post has always used the most rapid means of transport: to make the use of the aeroplane subject to the payment of a surcharge, amounts to introducing

discrimination between the means of transport. "In international postal services, it is admitted as a general rule," writes Major Martin Wronsky, Managing Director of Deutsche Lufthansa "that all closed mail should go by the fastest and most direct route." It is clear that the sender would be entitled to make a protest if the postal authorities intended to convey his letters by horse-drawn van or steamboat. No one could seriously oppose the suppression of surcharges. Those sending mail, the air transport companies and the postal authorities were all agreed that surcharges represented an anomaly. The main obstacle to their immediate withdrawal in Europe, and to their progressive withdrawal within the intercontinental system, was of a financial nature. Knowing that the user would hardly be willing to pay a higher postage rate for intra-European communications, how should the decrease in earnings due to the withdrawal of the surcharge be apportioned among the postal administrations and the air transport companies?

In order to obtain the first elements of an answer to this question, the International Bureau of the UPU called an International Airmail Conference in Brussels from 13th to 15th October 1929, which was restricted to the European postal administrations. The official reason for the conference was to "examine the situation created by certain European postal administrations who convey by aeroplane, principally on night flights, mail for which no surcharge has been collected." (This concerned the Reichspost, which had in 1929 initiated night post services run by Deutsche Lufthansa.)

Since it was unable to solve the problem, the Conference proposed two principles:

1. The time would come when all European first class mail would be sent by air – at least in cases where an aeroplane would permit a saving in time. However such developments would imply an appreciable reduction in operating costs and a regularity of operations, particularly by night, comparable to that of post trains.

2. In the meantime postal administrations were free to transport by aeroplane, either by night or by day, non-surcharged mail without having to request the authorisation of the country of destination.

This was an enormous breach driven through the surcharge system.

In the wake of the Brussels Conference, a further European Conference met in Prague in 1931 to discuss the creation of a European airmail network. This was the time when Europe was sinking into economic depression, and major projects were put on hold. Nevertheless the idea of withdrawing the surcharge continued to develop in people's minds, and the Cairo Postal Congress of 1934 confirmed the direction in which the Brussels Conference was moving. "The administrations have the possibility of not collecting any air transport surcharge, providing that they inform the country of destination." (Article 5 of the Convention.)

As is often the case, events would force the law to evolve: after the partial failure of the Brussels Conference, several European postal administrations decided, officially and unilaterally, to withdraw the surcharge for all or some of the European destinations. Sweden and Norway set an example in 1930, followed by Germany and The Netherlands in 1935, and Great Britain in 1936, whilst the Finance Act of 1937 authorised the French postal authority to carry mail without surcharge within Europe.

Once the economic crisis had passed, this tide of initiatives left countries no other choice than to follow the conference route in search of an overall solution: the "European Airmail Conference" met in Brussels from 16th to 25th June 1938.

"The delegates of the postal administrations ... considering that the moment has come for generalising the transport of non-surcharged airmail in Europe, whenever delivery can benefit by such transport ..." crossed the last hurdle: that of the complete assimilation of the aeroplane into the overall range of means for postal transportation. From now on, to use the words of the French Post, "the aeroplane is regarded as a normal means of transport". It had become common place.

Naturally, in order to achieve this result, which was translated into a substantial growth in traffic, the airlines who were from that time onwards operating more economical aircraft with greater load capacity, had to make concessions: they accepted that their transport rates for European routes would be reduced from 6 to 2.5 gold francs per tonne and per kilometre during a trial period of three years, and then to 2 gold francs.

This compromise appeared equitable to all concerned. The Conference expressed the wish that the surcharge could be generally suppressed "before 1st August 1939". How were they to know that the Second World War would break out on 1st September 1939!

4 INTERNATIONAL PRIVATE LAW: THE WARSAW CONVENTION

The harmonious development of international air commerce brings with it the need for the settlement of disputes between air companies and their customers, whether passengers or shippers of goods, on the basis of legal principles common to all countries.

If there were no international regulations, what law would be applied in the case of damage suffered by merchandise of Spanish origin, sent by plane "charge collect" from Paris to Riga, handed over at Le Bourget to Lignes Aériennes Farman and conveyed from Paris to Amsterdam by Farman, from Amsterdam to Hamburg by KLM and from Hamburg to Riga by Deutsche Lufthansa with a transfer in Berlin? The solution of such brain-teasers requires the adoption of transport documentation standardised both in form and content, and the specification of regulations regarding liabilities which are identical for all international air transport companies.

France played a key role in this process. On 17th August 1923 Raymond Poincaré, the President of the Council of Ministers and Minister for Foreign Affairs, proposed that all states should meet in Paris for a conference with the object of "drawing up a convention concerning the liability of the air carrier, and to decide whether it would be desirable to pursue the international unification of private law regarding aeronautical matters."

It may be that the topic did not really inspire the governments, or that Poincaré may have had rather strained relations with a number of countries, but nothing happened until 1925. Aristide Briand, the Minister for Foreign Affairs, renewed the

French proposal on 30th June 1925. He took the precaution of enclosing a draft convention: "The First International Conference on Private Air Law" met in Paris on 26 October 1925, with the participation of 43 countries.

In view of the quantity and the importance or the issues, the First Conference did not succeed in exhausting the subject. The problem of carrying through supplementary studies was conferred to a group of government experts known as: the International Technical Committee for Experts in Air Law" or CITEJA. This committee carried out the preparatory work for the "Second Conference" held in Warsaw in October 1929, which ended on 12th October 1929 with the signature of the "Convention for the Unification of Certain Rules relating to International Carriage by Air", more usually known as the Warsaw Convention. This was a document of fundamental importance, not the least of its achievements being to reconcile the two great streams of legal thought, the "Civil Code" approach resulting from the Code Napoléon, and the "Customary [Common] Law" approach derived from the English tradition.

Just as IATA, ICAN or UPU each refers to its own domain, the Warsaw Convention applies only to international transport, although its influence extended to cover numerous examples of national legislation which included its main provisions. It is concerned with passengers, luggage and goods. Airmail was governed solely by the provisions of the Universal Postal Convention.

The Warsaw Convention deals with two topics: transport documentation and the civil liability of air carriers.

The air consignment note

The "air consignment note" is for goods what the "passenger ticket" is for the air traveller. The Warsaw Convention replaced the International Despatch Note, an anachronistic denomination redolent of horse drawn transport, with the "Air Consignment Note" or ACN. This is the "essential document" for airfreight, the "instrument reflecting the contract between the consignor and the transport company." [13]

In Article 8, the Convention enumerates a long list of the particulars to be contained by the ACN. Let us mention specifically the place and date of execution of the document, the place of departure and destination, the agreed stopping places, the names and addresses of the consignor, the consignee and of the first carrier, the nature of the goods, the characteristics of the packaging, the weight, the quantity, the volume or the dimensions of the goods, the freight payable, etc. .... In total, no less than 17 headings: people lost no time in criticising the complexity of the Air Consignment Note. Nevertheless, it was on the basis of these provisions that the member companies of IATA in Antwerp in 1931 succeeded in defining a standard model of the Air Way Bill.

Of all carriers, the air companies were the only ones to possess a standardised transportation document which was universally accepted within the Association: as a new means of transport, airfreight is also a simple one.

The liabilities in civil law of the air carriers

Those responsible for drafting the Warsaw Convention had a dual concern: to guarantee that the passenger or consignor should receive just compensation in case of damage, and to promote the development of a means of transport which was still very vulnerable. The outcome was that: "the burden of the carrier was lessened, by taking into consideration that the passenger (or the consignor of goods) accepted some degree of risk." [14] In the compromise which they eventually retained and which came down in favour of the carriers, the authors of the Convention affirmed the principle of presumption of liability by the carrier, but they provided it with exemptions and limitations.

Article 18 of the Convention sets out the principle of presumption of liability:

"*The carrier is liable for damage sustained in the event of the destruction or loss of, or of damage to, any registered luggage or any goods if the occurrence which caused the damage so sustained took place during the carriage by air.*"

Article 19 states the principle of the liability of the carrier in case of delay.

"*The carrier is liable for damage occasioned by delay in the carriage by air of passengers, luggage or goods.*"

In practice, carriers endeavoured to limit the application of this Article by introducing into the general terms of carriage conditions restricting such application, the validity of which has been called into question by some legal experts. Delay per se does not constitute a "damage".

The presumption of liability by the carrier was thus affirmed, and the authors of the Convention then went on to palliate its effects by adding several exceptions:

1. "*The carrier is not liable if he proves that he and his agents have taken all necessary measures to avoid the damage or that it was impossible for him or them to take such measures.*" (Article 20 – paragraph 1)

    "*In the common law of transportation, a proof of the absence of fault is not sufficient: the carrier cannot exonerate himself simply by establishing the existence of an outside cause for which he is not responsible.*" [15]

    The air carrier is in a more acceptable situation, since it is sufficient for him to prove that he has not committed any fault in order to avoid liability. The more so, since as a general rule, jurisprudence has interpreted the concept of "necessary measures" in a sense favourable to the carriers.

2. "*In the carriage of goods and luggage the carrier is not liable if he proves that the damage was occasioned by negligent pilotage or negligence in the handling of the aircraft or in navigation and that, in all other respects, he and his agents have taken all necessary measures to avoid the damage.*" (Article 20 – paragraph 2)

    This is an exoneration from liability due to aeronautical faults, which has its source in maritime law (negligence of the captain in the management of the vessel).

3. Finally, the liability of the carrier is modified in case of negligence on the part of the victim.

    "*If the carrier proves that the damage was caused by or contributed to by the negligence of the injured person the court may, in accordance with the provisions of its own law, exonerate the carrier wholly or partly from his liability.*" (Article 21)

    It is up to the carrier to prove the link of cause and effect between the damage to the goods and the negligence of the consignor, the most usual cause being defective packaging. In case of a claim, the liability of the air carrier is tempered by Article 22 which puts a ceiling on the total damages: "In the carriage of registered luggage and of goods the liability of the carrier is limited to a sum of 250 francs per kilogram" or its equivalent in local currency. The franc concerned in this case is Poincaré's gold franc, which is defined as a weight of 65.5 mg of gold of millesimal fineness 900.

    However, the limit to liability may be annulled in three cases: if the consignor declares a higher value and consequently pays a special charge, if no ACN exists, and finally in the case of an intentional fault on the part of the carrier – "by his wilful misconduct or by such default on his part as … is considered to be equivalent to wilful misconduct." (Article 25)

    The Warsaw Convention remained the basis for settling litigation between carriers and the consignors of goods by air until November 2003.

3 THE US POST OFFICE CREATES THE WORLD'S LARGEST AIR NETWORK

No Mr President (Wilson), you were not wasting your time on 15th May 1918 when you attended the launch of the Washington-Philadelphia-New York airmail service. When the take-off got behind schedule, it is said that President W. Wilson leaned over to his wife and whispered – rather too loudly not to be heard: "We are wasting valuable time here." [1] In fact, 15th May 1918 was one of the red letter days in the history of world aviation: the start-up, in the middle of wartime, of the first regular air postal operation.

The history of airmail in the United States between 1920 and 1940 shows an exceptional richness. It reflects a number of traits of American civilisation: the belief in technical progress and the power of the resources devoted to it, the interventionism of the administration in favour of powerful capital interests, the high value placed on human life and the extraordinary public attention paid to the conquest of the West. To give it the epic dimension which it deserved, it only lacked the talent of a pilot and author such as Saint Exupéry praising the courage of those who, in peril of their lives, fought against the fogs of the Allegheny Mountains, the snowstorms of the Sierra, or the blizzards of Wyoming.

I FIRST PHASE: 15th MAY 1918–30th AUGUST 1927. THE POST OPERATES ITS OWN AIRMAIL SERVICES

In contrast to Europe, aviation in the United States was for almost ten years practically synonymous with the transportation of mail. A number of factors contributed to this peculiar situation: the scarcity of aerodromes, the speed and comfort of the railways, the lack of interest from business circles, and a certain mistrust on the part of the American public. In contrast to this, the faith which a few people in authority in the Federal Postal Administration placed in air transport, together with the enthusiasm and boundless devotion of the pilots, achieved the establishment of the world's first airmail network.

It may be recalled that Congress had in 1916 made available a credit of $50,000, and that a sub-committee of the National Advisory Committee for Aeronautics recommended in 1917 "that the Post Office operate an experimental route between Washington and Philadelphia or New York". On the strength of this recommendation from the most prestigious aeronautical

institution in the United States, the Postmaster General Albert Burleson, instructed his assistant Otto Praeger to pull out the stops and do everything possible to open the service. Like his boss, A. Burleson, Otto Praeger was a Texan and a journalist and had since his nomination at the end of 1915 given ample proof of his administrative abilities. "He was the key man in the creation and development of the air postal services" [2] up to his departure in April 1921. He left such a mark on the U.S. Airmail Service that several American historians have conferred upon him the title of "Father of the Airmail".

It was the Army which, on its own initiative, opened the Washington-New York service – daily, excepting Sundays. It operated it at the Post Office's expense for a brief period until 11th August 1918, using modified Curtiss JN4 -D Jenny aircraft (after fitting a more powerful engine and conversion of the front pilot's position into a post compartment). The operating system was based on a relay principle because of the limited range of the Jenny. Two planes left simultaneously from New York–Belmont Park and Washington–Polo Field bound for Philadelphia-Bustleton Park, where the relay was taken over by another pilot in another aircraft flying towards Washington or New York.

The inaugural flight from Washington gave rise to some rather comical scenes. First of all, the plane obstinately refused to start, to the annoyance of President Wilson! When they checked everything, they found the cause of the breakdown: they had forgotten to fill up with fuel ...[3] Finally, to everyone's great relief, the plane took off with a young inexperienced pilot at the controls. He proceeded to follow the wrong railway line – at the time, railway lines were the most sophisticated instrument of aerial navigation – got completely lost and landed in the countryside about 25 miles. south of Washington, damaging his aircraft. Thank goodness that the post leaving New York was entrusted to more proficient pilots: Lieutenants Webb and Edgerton completed the journey impeccably.

Soon after the service had been started, relations between the Post Office and the Army began to deteriorate. In the middle of the war, the military had better things to do than running an experimental airmail route 230 miles long. Moreover, the operating principles of Otto Praeger and the Army proved to be irreconcilable. The former demanded that the planes left on time whatever the weather; the latter insisted on making allowances for the meteorological conditions. Both sides exhibited a certain diplomacy: the Army was not too annoyed to make a discreet withdrawal, and the Post Office was not unhappy in taking the postal flights under its control. It became the sole master on board.

A review of the first few months of operation gives mixed results. On the operating side, the outcome was satisfactory, with a regularity rating of above 92% after a difficult start. It was disappointing from a commercial point of view: over too short a distance, daytime flights were not able to demonstrate any advantage over the night-time post trains which, with never-failing timetables, had for many years been adapted to the needs of commerce. On top of that came the imposition of a high airmail surcharge: the postage for an ordinary letter was 3 cents, and 10 cents for a letter delivered by messenger, but 24 cents for an airmail letter delivered in the same manner. The air postage was reduced from 24 to 16 cents on 15th July 1918 and then taken right down to 6 cents excluding special delivery, on 15th December 1918. In spite of these rate incentives, surcharged mail continued to make poor sales, and the majority of airmail traffic consisted of first class mail [4] without surcharge. Learning its lessons from this commercial failure, the Post Office abolished the airmail surcharge on the Washington-New York service on 18th July 1919: it had known for more than a year that the future of airmail in the United States lay elsewhere.

Otto Praeger, of whom it was said that "he could hardly tell a monoplane from a biplane" might have been lacking in aeronautical knowledge, but he did have a vision of the future. During the summer of 1918 he had thought up a grandiose development plan, of which he lost no time in convincing Burleson. He imagined two great transcontinental routes: one east-west from New York to San Francisco via Cleveland, Chicago and Salt Lake City, and the other north-south from Boston to Key West (at the outermost edge of Florida) via New York, Philadelphia, Washington and Atlanta. These two trunk routes would be joined by feeder lines coming from St. Louis, Dallas or Minneapolis, while two international airmail routes would extend the lines from Key West, one towards Cuba and the other towards South America. On 27th August 1918, the Postmaster General, Burleson, rather over-optimistically, wrote to the Secretary of State for War: "I am anxious to inaugurate beginning October 1st, regular aeroplane mail service between New York and Chicago."

They still did not possess an aeroplane capable of carrying out this great plan. Since the ideal aircraft – a multi-engined plane capable of transporting 150 kilograms of mail for 200 miles at a speed of 100mph – was not available, the choice of the Post Office lighted on the De Havilland DH4, "the most outstanding high performance daylight bomber of the First World War" (Janes). It bought 100 units which, since they could not be used as purchased, were subjected to numerous modifications: the pilot's position moved rearwards, reinforcement of the fuselage, and relocation of the landing gear. Like all aeroplanes of the time, the DH4s were very sensitive machines, which required intensive and costly maintenance. The 400hp Liberty engines needed practically one hour of maintenance for every flying hour, and the economic operating life of the aircraft was no more than 2,000 flying hours. Altitude had a considerable influence on the payload, so that this was reduced by 25%

on the highest stretch of the transcontinental route between Cheyenne and Salt Lake City. Granted that the payload was modest – around 180 kilograms – but the volume available to contain the mail was so restricted that it was not always possible to make full use of this limited weight allowance [5]: the volume limit was often reached before the weight limit. In order to reduce this disadvantage, a container was included under the belly of the fuselage in 1922.

Now the US Post Office was able to get on with carrying out its master-plan: to operate in all weathers, day or night, a daily transcontinental airmail route of 2,750 miles in length, linking New York with San Francisco. It managed it in record time – on 1st July 1924, thanks to the will power of the managers, the self sacrifice of the pilots, the extreme energy of all concerned, and the allocation of considerable material resources. As Central Pacific and Union Pacific had done 60 years before when building transcontinental railways, the Post Office started almost simultaneously to operate the route from both ends:

• to the West, the San Francisco/Sacramento section in California, on 31st July 1919;

• to the East, the New York/Chicago route was opened in two stages: first section Chicago/Cleveland on 15th May 1919, followed by the second section New York/Cleveland on 1st July 1919. A total of 760 miles.

The operation of the New York/Cleveland sector was particularly complicated and treacherous due to the crossing of the Allegheny Mountains. It was an inhospitable region, with very uneven terrain, covered in forest and frequently hidden under thick layers of cloud or submerged in fog – the enemy Number One as far as the pilots were concerned. One of them recalled: "When the clouds were low you had to fly near the ground, close enough to see it. The lower the clouds, the lower you flew." With all the risks that that entailed. The deterioration of flying conditions pushed the already strained relations between the pilots and Otto Praeger to breaking point. However, at the price of some apparent concessions, he managed to hold his position. The pilots had to fly in bad weather, and it was not up to the pilots, but to the field managers to judge the weather conditions. For Otto Praeger on the Cleveland/New York route, as for Didier Daurat on the Toulouse/Casablanca route, the mail had to "get through", and the "chain" had to be forged, even at a heavy cost in terms of human life: one death in 1918, five in 1919, fifteen in 1920 (the blackest year), and six in the first half of 1921. On 16th September 1920, the New York Times observed: "While it is gratifying to know that the Post Office is doing remarkable things in establishing long-distance airmail routes… success at an unnecessary cost of life would be deplorable." [6]

The year 1920 brought a resounding success. After the Chicago/Omaha section had been inaugurated on 15th May 1920 and the feeder lines had been opened from St. Louis and Minneapolis, the Omaha/Sacramento link was opened on 8th September 1920 via North Platte, Cheyenne, Rawlins, Rocksprings, Salt Lake City, Elko and Reno. The New York/San Francisco transcontinental airmail service, with a length of 2,750 miles was well and truly open. It traversed the barrier of the Rocky Mountains, swept in winter by snow storms, the vast deserts of Nevada and the precipitous slopes of the Sierra. With the precision of a tracing rule, it followed the routes of the railways which had been laid by teams of Irish and Chinese navvies or, less certain and under the unremitting onslaughts of nature, the trails which had been followed for more than half a century by hundreds of thousands of immigrants in their legendary covered wagons. For the first aeroplanes, as for the ox carts or the first locomotives, the same names signal the way to the West.

It was a magnificent achievement, with incomplete results. Since aircraft were not able to make night flights, the post could not be conveyed from end to end by plane. The transcontinental airmail route was in fact a mixed air/rail service. Until the month of July 1924, the "air" transport of mail between New York and San Francisco was an intermittent operation, combining day flights with night trains, combining the diurnal speed of the former with the nocturnal safety of the latter. A prophetic sign: the air surcharge was not re-established, and the aeroplanes continued to be used for carrying first class mail. As an economy measure, the Washington/New York service was closed on 31st May 1921.

At this point, it seemed absolutely clear that the only way to compete against the rail service would be to operate the air route from end to end, uninterruptedly, night and day. Night flights had become a decisive issue.

The Democrat Otto Praeger relinquished his role in April 1921 after the victory of the Republican Warren G. Harding in the White House. Between 15th May 1918 and 15th March 1921 the postal planes had covered 1,755,921 miles and carried over 700 tonnes of mail.

Paul Henderson was appointed Second Assistant Postmaster General – the former post of Otto Praeger – in 1922. As the second great figure in American airmail history, his policy was dominated by three major concerns:

• to prepare the routes of the USA Airmail Service for transfer to private enterprises, in keeping with the philosophy of the Republican Party;

• to continue and strengthen the "safety first" campaign which had been initiated with spectacular success by his courageous predecessor Edward Shaughnessy, in spite of his short period of office: a single death in 1922, compared with 15 in 1920. Henderson issued an instruction, which there was no gainsaying : "Stop killing the men";

• to investigate and commence night operations. A study commissioned by Henderson when he took up office concluded that night flights were feasible, subject to the carrying out of substantial investments to improve the airports, adapt the planes and to mark the air route itself by means of beacons. Assisted by his influential political connections, Henderson obtained the necessary support in order to fit out the central Chicago/Cheyenne link over a length of 890 miles, and to adapt 60 DH4 aircraft for night flight. The lighting for the Chicago/Cheyenne flight path was a spectacular feat in itself, requiring:

• the installation on the aerodromes of Chicago, Iowa City, Omaha, North Platt and Cheyenne of giant lighthouses – "the most powerful artificial light ever produced by man",

• the laying out of 34 emergency airfields, at intervals of about 25 miles from one another, lit by powerful incandescent beacons,

• the installation across the prairies of 250 acetylene beacons on 6-foot pylons, every three miles.

On 1st July 1924, the US Airmail Service opened the world's first night flight route – The Lighted Airway, which operated in winter and summer alike.

In the initial stages, it was not absolutely necessary to fit out the transcontinental route over its entire length in order to ensure an uninterrupted air service. It was sufficient to take off from New York and San Francisco in the morning in order to arrive at Chicago or Cheyenne in the evening: aircraft entered the lighted route and left it on the following morning. The first airmail flights were carried out in 34 hours 45 minutes in one direction and in 32 hours 21 minutes in the other – compared with 91 hours for the fastest trains. Now confident in its competitive advantage against the railway, the Post Office proceeded to take a logical and expected decision: it reintroduced the airmail surcharges which had been withdrawn on 18th July 1919. Against all expectations, the traffic figures for the first months from July to December 1924 were disappointing. The number of surcharged letters transported varied between 770,000 and 855,000 depending on the month, without any very clear upward trend. The American Post Office had pulled off a remarkable technical feat, but the forecasts were not achieved. Perhaps they had been too optimistic: the Post Office had got into the habit of filling its aircraft with non-surcharged mail and transporting considerable quantities of letters depending on the capacity available and its own policies. As is shown in the table at the top of the next page, the situation changed, immediately after the user had to pay a surcharge.

Business users, who provided three-quarters of the traffic, were still not completely satisfied: they thought that the timetables were unsuitable. These had been designed to meet a single imperative: to use the beaconed Chicago/Cheyenne section overnight. This is why the planes left New York in the morning at 11.00 hours and San Francisco at 08.45 hours. They arrived the following afternoon at 16.30 hours in San Francisco and at 18.00 hours in New York.

18.00 hours in New York meant the post was only distributed on the following day. The commercial companies called for departures in the late evening and arrivals during the course of the morning. An extension of the night beacon system to cover the whole length of the route was the only means to remove the operational constraints and satisfy the requirements of the largest clients. The equipment installation was finished during 1927.

On 1st July 1925 the night airmail line between Chicago and New York was opened. It had been decided on as a result of the important intervention of Paul Henderson with the Illinois Association of Bankers. It had required considerable infrastructure work between New York and Cleveland via the small airport of Bellefonte in the heart of the Allegheny Mountains. In addition to the setting up of three main airports, there were no less than 29 emergency airstrips and 46 guidance beacons along a route of 400 miles: "The night route between New York and Cleveland was a marvel in the initiation of commercial aviation."[7] In spite of the large amount of ground equipment and the introduction of instrument flying, a night flight over the

Development of traffic of the US Airmail Service: 1918–1927 [8]

Fiscal year (30 June)	Miles Travelled	Forced landings		Number of letters carried
		Mechanical Reasons	Meteorological Reasons	
1918	21,389	6	6	713,240
1919	194,986	37	56	9,210,040
1920	648,400	155	185	21,063,120
1921	1,770,658	810	954	44,834,080
1922	1,727,265	281	479	48,988,920
1923	1,809,028	176	279	67,875,840
1924	1,853,251	154	353	60,001,360
1925	2,501,555	174	586	9,300,520
1926	2,547,992	155	707	14,145,640
1927	2,583,006	140	881	22,386,000

Notes: Years 1918–1924: Post not surcharged.
Years 1925–1927: Only surcharged post.

Alleghenies during thick fog or a snowstorm still remained quite a performance. The instrument flying pioneer, Charles Ames, was killed on 1st October 1925 when he crashed at full speed into a mountain near Bellefonte.

The timetable of the daily run between Chicago and New York corresponded precisely to the expectations of its customers.

21.30 hours	New York	05.00 hours
0530 hours	Chicago	19.30 hours

Mail posted in the special boxes up to 18.00 hours in Chicago or New York would be distributed on the following morning at their destination: the transit time for cheques and other banking documents had been reduced by 24 hours. It was an immediate success: the daily traffic very soon exceeded 100 kilograms, and peaks in excess of 250 kilograms justified the introduction of supplementary aeroplanes.

The definitive proof of airmail's future had been provided. The time was ripe, both from the political and economic points of view, for the routes of the US Airmail Service to be transferred to private airlines.

2 SECOND PHASE: 15th FEBRUARY 1926–9th FEBRUARY 1934. PRIVATE COMPANIES CARRY THE MAIL, BUT THE US POST OFFICE SHAPES THE AIR NETWORK OF THE UNITED STATES

The first two phases of American airmail history overlap: the first ends on 30th August 1927, the day on which the Post transported its last mailbag, and the second begins on 15th February 1926, the date when a private company conveyed its first bag of mail. Between these two dates there is a transition period during which the airborne activities of the Post progressively diminished.

During the eight years from 1926 to 1934, the face of American air transport was completely transformed. From an exclusively postal operation carried out on behalf of the Postal Administration, it was replaced by the world's largest network for the transport of passengers and post, served by a small number of airlines controlled by three major finance groups, who were openly supported by the Government and who did not shrink from any means of ensuring that they controlled the market. Legal, technical, financial and human factors all contributed to this absolute change.

As R. E. G. Davis underlines in his remarkable work Airlines of the United States since 1914, the development of civil aviation took place in a "legislative vacuum". The void was filled by two fundamental legal documents adopted in 1925 and 1926.

The Contract Airmail Act of 2nd February 1925, more usually known from the name of its author as the Kelly Act, had the object of "encouraging the development of commercial aviation and authorising the Director General of Post to conclude contracts for the transportation of air post" following a procedure of invitation to tender. The remuneration of the contracting companies was fixed at 80% of the amount of the surcharges. In addition, under certain conditions, the Post could use the available capacity to convey first class mail. The Air Commerce Act of 20th May 1926, which has been called "the cornerstone in the development of civil aviation", provided the United States with a complete set of aeronautical regulations, whether it was a question of the qualifications and licences for pilots, aids to aerial navigation or the way airports functioned. In order to provide the basis for their new air transport activities, the private companies henceforth had access to two basic legal texts, drafted by the Postal Administration and Congress, who were very receptive to their concerns.

From a technical point of view the years 1925–1930 witnessed a considerable number of improvements in the fields of instrument flying, aerodynamics and the performance of engines. Among the American aircraft of the period, the Ford Tri-Motor and the Boeing 40A have particular significance. The Ford Tri-Motor, which made its maiden flight on 1st June 1926, had a considerable resemblance to the Junkers aircraft: like them, it was made entirely in metal, and fitted with three air-cooled engines. It had a cruising speed of 106mph and could transport a payload of around 1,500 kilograms. When it was fitted out for transporting mail and passengers – with up to 14 seats – it was one of the main workhorses of commercial aviation. A single-engined cargo version, produced in 1931, met with little success. The smaller Boeing 40A, which made its initial flight at Seattle on 20th May 1927, was designed for transporting mail along with two passengers.

From 1925 onwards, major American capital interests began to look at commercial aviation, which seemed to be developing into a profitable activity. Considerable investments were made in the aviation industry and air transport.

Two men, different as chalk and cheese , played a decisive role in the metamorphosis of civil aviation in the United States. One of them became a worldwide celebrity and legendary hero, and the other, a lawyer and politician, became the omnipotent Postmaster General. The former was Charles A. Lindbergh, and the latter Walter F. Brown. They had one thing in common: their faith in aviation.

Today, it is difficult to imagine the demonstrations of enthusiasm which swept through American and European public opinion when Lindbergh crossed the North Atlantic from Long Island to Le Bourget on the 20th to 21st May 1927 at the controls of his little single-engined Ryan, christened "Spirit of St. Louis". In the United States, his exploit dramatically fired the growth of air passenger transport.

Walter Brown, who was appointed Postmaster General in March 1929, enjoyed the support of President Herbert Hoover. A lawyer from Toledo, and a member of the Republican Party, he was an authoritarian force for centralisation, who pursued a single objective for the whole duration of his mandate: to use the absolute weapon of the postal contracts to provide America with a dependable, coherent and profitable air network.

In fulfilment of the Kelly Law, the Post proceeded to put out the first calls for tender. With some wisdom, it decided to hand over the operation of the airmail network in stages. The feeder lines were be allocated in an initial period, followed by the allocation of the transcontinental line itself in the second stage.

The first five postal contracts were issued on 7th October 1925. In American terminology, they were referred to as Contract Airmail or CAM, followed by an order number. Let us look at the main characteristics of these contracts: route – start date – contracting company.

- CAM1 – New York/Boston – 18th June 1926 – awarded to Colonial Air Transport – CAT. This company was a product of high finance in the north east (William A Rockefeller, Governor John H. Trumbull etc) Its first Managing Director was Juan Trippe, who left to found Pan American Airways. In contrast to many other companies, CAT operated a complete range of air services from the start: passengers, post and parcel service.

- CAM2 – Chicago/Saint Louis – 15th April 1926 – awarded to Robertson Aircraft Corporation. In striking contrast to Colonial Air Transport, everything here depended on one man, Major William Robertson, who in 1921 with the help of some friends and family, had founded a company, which specialised in buying up and modifying military aircraft.

The Robertson Aircraft Corporation has a double claim to fame: it included Charles Lindbergh among its

pilots – which explains the name of the plane in which he crossed the Atlantic – and was among the distant ancestors of American Airlines, along with Colonial Air Transport.

- CAM3 – Chicago/Dallas – 12th May 1926 – awarded to National Air Transport (NAT), which emerged from New York and Chicago financial circles, and with an old friend as its Managing Director: Paul Henderson!

NAT, the ancestor of United Airlines, got its hands on a much sought after route, that linked the oilfields of Texas, which were expanding apace, with the capital of the Midwest.

- CAM4 – Los Angeles/Salt Lake City – 17th April 1926 – signed with Western Air Express, a Los Angeles company, run by a very colourful character, the former racing car driver, Harris M. "Pop" Hanshue, and supported by big money from South California. To some extent, it signified a reaction against San Francisco which had been chosen as the terminus for the Transcontinental line.

- CAM5 – Pasco/Boise/Elko – 6th April 1926 – north-south line joining two states of the North West, Washington and Idaho, with the Elko-Nevada station of the Transcontinental route. The service was awarded to Varney Airlines, which was less a company than a man: Walter T. Varney was an aviation enthusiast and a veteran of the Great War who, as he had foreseen, was the only one to make a bid for this route.

After these first five contracts, the Post Office made further calls for tender before relinquishing the Transcontinental service.

- CAM6 – Detroit/Chicago

- CAM7 – Detroit/Cleveland

Without waiting for the Kelly Law to come into force, Henry Ford had on 3rd April 1925 set himself up to operate a "daily private express service" restricted to transporting his own freight between Detroit and Chicago. He extended this link out to Cleveland in July the same year. Hence he was well placed to win both the contracts concerned and to become the first to start up operating airmail services on 15th February 1926.

- CAM8 – Seattle/San Francisco/Los Angeles – 15th September 1926 – fell to Pacific Air Transport founded by Vern C. Gorst who owned a bus company in Oregon. This was a difficult, very mountainous route in the north, feared for its storms and fogs.

- CAM9 – Minneapolis/Chicago – 7th June 1926 – awarded to Charles Dickinson, this contract was taken up three months later on 1st October 1926 by North West Airways, whose shareholders were Detroit and Minneapolis businessmen. It gave birth to North West Airlines in April 1934.

It still remained to hand over the Transcontinental Airmail Route. This was divided into two sections on either side of Chicago. It had been tacitly understood that they would be awarded to companies which were already operating feeder

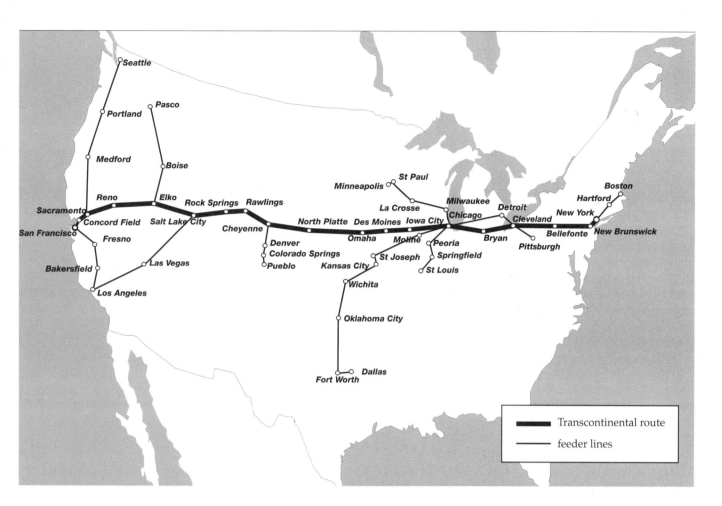

ABOVE **Map of United States airmail network in 1926.**
Union Postale, 1926

RIGHT **Operated by Boeing Air Transport a Boeing 40A carries the mail between Chicago and San Francisco in 1927.**

lines and would have acquired sufficient experience to take on this route.

• The Chicago/San Francisco section (CAM18) seemed almost certain to go to "Pop" Hanshue who was already operating the Los Angeles/Salt Lake City route with Douglas M2 postal aeroplanes, adapted to transport two passengers. To general surprise, it was actually awarded to Boeing Air Transport (BAT) which had been established a short time before with capital from William Boeing, although at the instigation of his friend Eddie Hubbard, who continued to operate FAM2 (Foreign Airmail Contract) between Seattle and Victoria. Confident in the performance and the profitability of the Boeing 40A, BAT had submitted an offer considerably below that of its competitor. It started operations on 1st July 1927. The Chicago/New York section (CAM17) ended up with National Air Transport – to no one's surprise. In order to ensure service from 1st September 1927 NAT purchased from the Post Office a group of 18 Douglas M4 aircraft, machines which had been basically designed for transporting mail, and the first of which, "Douglas Airmail 1" or DAM1 had flown in July 1925. The M4 version, fitted for instrument flying, could take a load of over 500kg.

Thus the Post Office completed the handover of its network to private enterprise. During the following years it continued to make calls for tender, and to award new postal routes as traffic developed. This showed spectacular progress from August 1928, when the air surcharge was reduced for the first ounce. Apart from the mail contracts, there was a great deal of freedom in the choice of routes and the establishment of passenger fares. Passenger traffic, which had hitherto been non-existent, grew rapidly from 1927 onwards, leading to the creation of a number of companies. Would this lead to an anarchic explosion in air transport in the United States? That would have been without reckoning on the decisive involvement of one man, Walter Brown, who, in three years, succeeded in providing American commercial aviation with its definitive structure.

By the time he relinquished his responsibilities in 1932, Walter Brown had fully achieved his aim: to turn a patchwork quilt of lines without logic or financial stability into a viable national network robustly anchored on three large intercontinental companies and a few smaller regional airlines.

In order to impose his vision, Brown moved in three stages.

• First stage: non-renewal of contracts.
For a transitory period of six months, he decided not to renew the postal contracts which were expiring.

• Second stage: modification of the Kelly Act.
At his instigation, the Kelly Act was amended by the Watres Act (29th April 1930) which introduced three essential conditions:

1. the validity period of the contracts was increased from four to 10 years for companies which had more than two years' experience;

2. the principle of paying the companies according to the weight of post transported was replaced by the principle of payment for the space made available, whether or not this was used by the Post Office. In parallel, the minimum rate per mile was reduced ($1.25 maximum per mile). Since it encouraged the companies to introduce larger capacity aircraft, this condition had a considerable impact;

3. the Postmaster General was authorised to "extend" and "consolidate" the airmail routes "when in his judgement the public interest will be promoted thereby".

• Third stage: between 15th May and 9th July 1930, Walter Brown organised in his office a number of meetings to award postal contracts.

At these meetings, which enjoy enduring renown under the evocative name of "Spoils Conferences", he took care to invite only companies supported by powerful financial groups, who in his eyes were alone capable of providing the framework for a homogeneous airline system. After concluding the "Spoils Conferences", and without the least shadow of doubt falling upon the personal honesty of Walter Brown, 20 contracts out of 22 were awarded to the three large capitalist conglomerates, which controlled the aviation industry, engine manufacture and transportation. These were:

• General Motors North Aviation Group, with Transwestern Air Express and Eastern Continental and Transport;

• United Aircraft and Transport Corporation with the companies which formed United Airlines;

• Aviation Corporation of Delaware with American Airways.

Between 1929 and 1933 the companies belonging to these financial groups always received more than 90% of the annual payments from the Post Office to the totality of the air lines in America. In 1933 the postal "manna" was shared out as follows: [9]

GM-North Aviation:	29.6% ˇ	
United Aircraft:	34.3%	} 91.1%
Aviation Corporation:	27.2% °	

In spite of the penetration of passenger activities, the companies remained totally dependent on the payments from the US Post.

Revenue of domestic airmail contracting companies (breakdown in percent)

Years	Mail	Passengers	Freight	Total
1931	85.0%	14.8%	0.2%	100%
1932	80.0%	19.7%	0.3%	100%
1933	74.6%	24.6%	0.8%	100%

Reading this table, one can easily understand that an authoritarian Postmaster General who was prepared to expand the limits of his powers, might have been able to reconstitute the American air transport system within a very short period of time, based on the three main Transcontinental routes and a branch from Boston to Miami.

During the five years from 1929 to 1933, the contracting air companies received $84.1 million from the Post. The receipts from the air surcharges collected by the Post did not exceed $27.9 million. Therefore the Post Office had paid out to these national companies the enormous sum of $56.2 million over and above its own receipts. How is one to describe this "discrepancy"? Subsidy or reimbursement of costs? "Subsidy is something in addition to cost. We are not asking anything in addition to our costs", declared a representative of the companies in 1925. Whether it was a subsidy or a reimbursement, one thing is certain: it was the Post Office which financed the birth and development of American commercial aviation.

3 THIRD PHASE: 9th FEBRUARY 1934–1940. THE POST OFFICE, PLACED UNDER SUPERVISION, REMAINS THE PRINCIPAL CLIENT OF THE AMERICAN AIR COMPANIES

On 9th of February 1934, at 16.00 hours, a thunderbolt exploded into the world of air transport. President Franklin Roosevelt, having taken the advice of the Attorney General, announced the cancellation of all airmail contracts. He decided to transfer the operation of the postal routes to the Army for a transitory period starting on 20th January. This was after consulting General Benjamin Foulois, whom we already met when he commanded the 1st Aero Squadron of General Pershing's Mexican expeditionary force.

What had happened? In short, in January, he had received Senator Hugo Lafayette Black, President of the "Special Committee of Investigation on the Airmail and Ocean Mail Contracts" to breakfast in the White House. Senator Black had come to the conclusion that the manner in which the Postmaster General Brown had awarded the postal contracts during the Spoils Conferences was totally illegal, due to the secretive nature of these meetings. He communicated his feelings to President Roosevelt, who took a rather hasty decision of engaging the assistance of a somewhat over-confident general.

While American historians are divided in their evaluation of the activities and the results achieved by Walter Brown, they are unanimous in their judgement about the Army taking back the airmail services: "it was an instant fiasco" [10] accompanied by several fatal accidents, which turned it into a media sensation. Three elements contributed to the fiasco: absolutely horrendous weather conditions, the inexperience of the military crews, and the unsuitability of their aircraft for civil missions. President Roosevelt was quick to learn from this disastrous experiment. On 30th March 1934 the Post Office published a new call for tender with the following features:

1. The air companies which had taken part in the suspect conferences were eliminated. Contrary to what one might think, this measure had minimal consequences. The companies merely made slight changes to their trading names: thus American Airways became American Airlines; United Airlines, whose contract had been signed in the name of its subsidiaries, needed to make no efforts to adapt. The final names under which we now know the major American air lines are a direct consequence of the postal crisis of 1934.
2. The contract was signed on a provisional basis.
3. Quotations were not to exceed 45 cents per mile. Only mail actually transported qualified for payment.
4. Long-distance mail services were reserved for companies equipped with multi-engined aircraft.

The 1934 crisis had profound repercussions, which carried far beyond the domain of airborne mail. It permanently transformed the American air transport scene and brought to light the weaknesses of the Army Air Corps.

From the legal point of view, the Airmail Act of 12th June 1934 constituted the new legal basis in America. It divested the Post Office of part of its prerogatives: although it left with the Post Office the power of signing renewable annual contracts with the airlines, it transferred to the ICC (Interstate Commerce Commission) the authority to fix postal rates, expressed in cents per mile (cent/mile). It provided for a dual system of remunerating the companies: based on the actual weight transported for the principal traffic routes, according to a minimum set weight on secondary routes.

In addition to the postal regulations, the Airmail Act included two conditions with far-reaching implications:

1. The first establishes the principle of financial independence of the contracting companies with respect to the aviation industry. This meant the end of holding companies uniting both manufacturers and transport companies. The companies had until 30th December 1934 to conform to the law. They would comply all the more rapidly since mail still represented 56% of their income;

2. The second authorised the President of the United States to nominate a commission with the responsibility of producing a plan for the organisation of civil aviation. At the end of a lengthy procedure, its work culminated in the signature of the Civil Aeronautics Act on 23rd June 1938. This monument of American air law, with the aim of "promoting the development of a commercial air transport system and fulfilling the needs of the internal and international trade of the United States, the postal service and national defence" was to regulate the operation of American aviation in all respects for more than 40 years. This law conferred upon the CAB (Civil Aeronautics Board) the task of setting the payment levels for mail transport. The Federal Postal Administration was placed under supervision and appeared to be excluded from the field of play. In fact "the Post Office Department assumed an active role as an intervener in every airmail proceeding" and, like the CAB it "was subjected to many pressures by Congressmen, government bodies, the airline industry and other pressure groups" which had any influence on the setting of rate levels. [11] The process of development for postal rates was much more complex than could be assumed from the documents.

The Airmail Act of 1934 was amended on 14th August 1935: according to these new conditions, the duration of the contract was extended to three years and the Postmaster General retained an important part in the judgement of the replies to the calls for tender: "Postmaster General is authorised to adjudicate contracts for the air transport of mail between towns of his choice and for initial periods of a duration not exceeding three years, to bidders offering the lowest price and sufficient guarantees for a loyal execution of the service." [12]

From a military viewpoint, the crisis of 1934 had revealed the deficiencies of military aviation. There followed some soul searching on a national scale, which resulted in Congress voting for important modernisation programmes. "The transport of the mail turned out to be a blessing for the army and the country", as General Foulois wrote later in his memoirs. "Otherwise, I am convinced that we would never have recovered so quickly after the disaster of Pearl Harbor."

For the public, the taxpayer or the airmail user, the fallout from the crisis of 1934 was very positive. Whereas the total of the surcharge was reduced, the length of the "airmail routes" increased from 25,248 miles in 1933 to 28,548 in 1935 (+13%). Four new states and 19 additional towns were added to the network. At the same time, for an improved service, the total of the payments from the Post Office to the contracting companies reduced by 55% (see table below at top of page 68).

For the airlines, the crisis of 1934 weakened the position of the major players and accelerated the developments which had already started. Although the share of the Big Four [13] was reduced from 91.1% in 1933 to 72.7% in 1938, they retained the majority of the postal payments. The large companies already in place usually made the best offers and got their contracts again – although at a less profitable level! A new transcontinental company, North West Airlines, appeared between Chicago and Seattle, while Braniff and Delta became the principal companies to gain from the new policy. The reduction of the share of postal revenues in the total revenues of the airlines, which had already begun, continued at a faster rate (see bottom table on page 68).

Revenue of US Post Office Department from domestic airmail and payments to contractors ($ 000)

Fiscal Year	Payments to domestic airlines	Post Office revenues from domestic airlines	Excess of payments over revenue
1930	14,618	5,273	9,345
1931	16,944	6,210	10,734
1932	19,938	6,016	13,922
1933	19,400	6,116	13,284
1934	12,130	5,738	6,392
1935	8,814	6,590	2,224
1936	12,104	9,702	2,402
1937	13,088	12,440	649
1938	14,666	15,301	-635
1939	16,625	16,326	299

Notes: 1. Postal expenses (payments to domestic airlines) do not include costs of the ground handling of airmail
2. Only domestic transport

Source: Lisbeth Freudenthal, "The Aviation Business", New York, 1940, p.312 (an inspired and inspiring work).

The airlines overcame this reduction of their postal income – or the fall-off in subsidies – pretty well. There were two reasons: technical and economic. The entry into service of a new generation of aircraft turned the history and economics of air transport on its head, by introducing a factor which had been hitherto missing: profitability. After the Boeing 247 and the Lockheed Electra, the Douglas DC-2 was rolled out in 1934 and American Airlines introduced the legendary DC-3 on 25th June 1936 between Chicago and New York. At the same time, following the Great Depression, between 1929 and 1934, the revival of the American economy took hold, under the influence of the New Deal of President Roosevelt and his advisors. While the airlines brought onto the market new capacities, provided at declining unit costs, passenger traffic experienced formidable growth, and postal traffic doubled in four years, from 4,900 tonnes in 1935 to 9,700 tonnes in 1938. In the meantime, postal revenue had expanded strongly and the Post remained the prime client of the airlines, bringing in 36% of their sales in 1939.

On the eve of the Second World War, American air transport had already gained a dominant position in the world. It encompassed over half the passenger traffic and more than a third of the mail.

From whatever point of view – historical, economic or political – "Airmail has been the foundation of air traffic development in the United States." [14] It had brought into being the largest network in the world.

Development by type of revenue of contracting airlines
(in percentages)

Business year	Domestic contracting airlines				For comparison: postal revenues as % of PAA total revenues*
	Mail	Passengers	Freight	Total	
1931	85.0%	14.8%	0.2%	100%	86%
1933	74.6%	24.6%	0.8%	100%	76%
1935	40.8%	56.9%	2.3%	100%	67%
1937	36.6%	60.1%	3.3%	100%	56%
1939	35.9%	61.0%	3.1%	100%	52%

*PAA: Pan American Airways

4 THE SOUTH AMERICAN EPIC

The conquest of the South Atlantic to provide airmail services remains one of the great exploits in the history of commercial aviation. The Germans and the French, at first competing and then working together, each brought to bear their own particular talents: the French, with a concept of "the Line" of epic, almost mystic import, justifying all the sacrifices of the new knights of the air, embodied by Mermoz and immortalised by Saint Exupéry; the Germans through an approach less rich in panache, but more economical in the means it used, and symbolised by the mastery of Dr Eckner at the controls of his dirigible balloon, or by the power of the catapult ships launching seaplanes over the face of the ocean.

And yet our European egocentricity should not lead us to underestimate the role played by a third group of actors: the Americans. With the encouragement and guidance of a lordly leader, Juan Trippe, Pan American Airways, supported by the US Administration, acted for 20 years as the sole representative of the economic and financial power, the confident and prudent operations, the clever and crafty imperialism of the American flag in the Caribbean Sea and in South America.

As for the South Americans themselves, they succeeded admirably in turning the situation to their benefit. Profiting from the competition between German, American and French interests, the nations of South America, including the poorest among them, succeeded in acquiring at a very early stage a good air transport infrastructure and in establishing well organised national airlines which in at least some cases, still figure today among the oldest in the world.

I THE BEGINNINGS OF THE FRENCH EPIC: TOULOUSE TO DAKAR

An audacious project
Two dates, two steps stand out towards the fulfilment of this grand design:

• 25th December 1918: Pierre-Georges Latécoère leaves the aerodrome of Montaudran in Toulouse, on board a "demobbed" Salmson 2A2, piloted by Cournemont. Two hours later he lands on the racecourse at Barcelona "after an uneventful flight".[1] First step.

• 8th-9th March 1919: Latécoère leaves Toulouse on Saturday 8th March at noon in a Salmson piloted by Lemaitre. After stopping over at Barcelona, Alicante, Malaga and Rabat, he disembarks at Casablanca on Sunday 9th March at 16.15 hours. He has covered 1,156 miles in five stages, taking 25 hours and 15 minutes in total, with 11 hours 45 minutes flying time. The link between France and Morocco has been forged. This was an enormous personal success for Latécoère who with a mixture of subtlety and sentiment handed over to Lyautey a copy of the newspaper "Le Temps" dated 7th March and offered to Madame la Générale, a bouquet of Toulouse violets. In order to appreciate these tokens of esteem at their true value, it should be realised that the time taken by sea mail between France and Morocco (then a French Protectorate) varied between five and ten days depending on the season.

From that moment on Latécoère could count on the full support of Lyautey, the General Representative in Morocco from 1912 to 1925, later promoted to Marshal of France in 1921. Great administrator that he was, he immediately understood the advantages of fast air links between the Protectorate and France. Lyautey instructed the Director General of the Moroccan postal service to draw up a draft agreement providing for an annual subsidy of 1 million francs. Latécoère, quite overwhelmed, left Casablanca on 12th March with an official sack of mail and an "official paid" letter addressed to the Minister for War by General Lyautey. A destiny had been sealed: the connection between Toulouse and Casablanca was to become the model for all airmail routes. The second step towards the fulfilment of the grand design had been taken.

The grand design was to connect France with South America, Toulouse with Buenos Aires, through an airmail service. It was to use both air and sea transport in its initial phase, but then operate entirely by air as soon as there appeared a machine capable of regularly crossing the South Atlantic.

Latécoère conceived of his project during 1918. At that time he was manufacturing in his Montaudron factory a series of 1,000 Salmson 2A2 two-seaters which had been ordered by the Ministry for Armaments. As an engineer and "enterprising industrialist" who before the war had specialised in the manufacture of railway equipment, Latécoère was well known in political and military circles. On 8th September 1918 he sub-

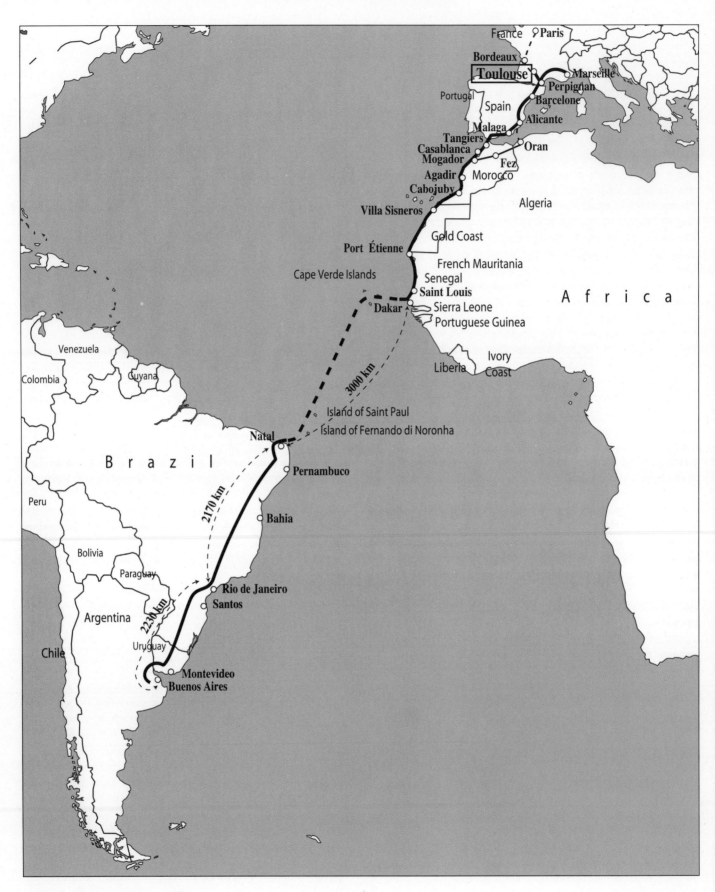

ABOVE **Latécoère Airlines – 1927**
Toulouse-Dakar service and projected Dakar-Buenos Aires Line.
Latécoère Airlines

mitted to the Under Secretary of State for Aeronautics a memorandum presenting the broad outlines of his plan, at the Aeronautics Ministry. On 2nd December 1918 he completed the dossier by submitting a draft concessionary contract for a Toulouse-Rabat service. We know the rest.

First section: Toulouse-Casablanca

In order to move from the experimental flight of 8th March 1919 to a regular operation, it would first be necessary to solve two problems: those of relations with Spain and relations with the Government. The latter became the object of two agreements: the first dated 7th July 1919 for a period of five years, and the second dated 9th July 1924 for a period of ten years. They were based on identical principles: the Government provided subsidies in exchange for services undertaken by the operator (with respect to route, frequency and regularity of service). In contrast to the United States, where the Post Office indirectly subsidised the air companies by paying them a remuneration in excess of the amount received in surcharges, in France, the Government paid an amount of subsidy directly to the concessionary, with the calculation method varying from one agreement to another.

In the agreement of 1919, the Government paid an annual subsidy corresponding to the service provided; in exchange "the concessionary shall provide free of charge the transportation of mail to be picked up from or delivered to the post offices of Toulouse or Rabat"; he was free to carry goods and passengers up to the limit of the remaining load capacity. The agreement of 1924 introduced a more elaborate system of subsidies and payments; it provided for a system of multiple contributions, known as "route subsidy", "operating cost subsidy" or "management subsidy", and even a "supplementary route subsidy" in case the operating accounts showed a negative balance after the various other subsidies had been applied. The transportation of mail was paid for on the basis of the actual weight carried, but "the remuneration allocated by the Postal Administration may not exceed the total of the surcharges received".

As far as the question of relations with Spain was concerned, this was settled by a Franco-Spanish Convention of 28th August 1919. The last obstacle had fallen.

The regular Toulouse-Rabat service, via Barcelona, Alicante and Malaga (the night stopover point) was opened on an experimental basis on 1st September 1919, and officially on 1st October by the "Lignes Aériennes Latécoère" or LAL. This "completely unofficial company name adopted by the founder" [2] was legalised on 11th April 1921 when Latécoère founded "La Compagnie Générale d'Entreprises Aéronautiques" – CGEA.

In spite of Latécoère's sentimental attachment to Salmson aircraft manufactured in his factories, the "Service de la Navigation Aérienne", which was the authority responsible for commercial aviation, specified the Bréguet 14. The Bréguet 14A2 was a single-engined two-seater biplane used by the Army Corps for reconnaissance and observation purposes. It owed its remarkable longevity to "the use of a new material – duralumin, and to an over-powered engine – the 300hp Renault 12-cylinder V-engine." [3] Its cruising speed reached 78mph with an operating range of about 300 miles. Like other aircraft of the period, it was fitted with no navigation instruments worthy of the name: navigation was done by eye. Where the pilots of the US Airmail Service had found guidance in following railway lines, those from LAL followed the coastlines first of Spain and then of Morocco. Due to lack of space in the minute cabin, they had fitted containers on the underside of the wings to carry the mail. But not only mail, "it has been known for the mechanics to travel inside these containers … an opening in the side provided them with air and an unrestricted view of the scenery below." [4] In total, over 100 of these "cumbersome machines, heavy and unresponsive" [5] were put into service by Lignes Aériennes Latécoère.

Although passengers were carried exposed to the elements, without the least protection, and goods under the name of "aéropaquets" were permitted on the Toulouse-Rabat service, it was essentially designed for the transportation of mail. By putting all their money on airmail services, the directors of Lignes Aériennes Latécoère would in a few years succeed in turning the France-Morocco service – extended from Rabat to Casablanca in June 1920 – into the archetype for all airmail services. This air link possessed a number of in-built advantages: the presence in Morocco of 80,000 Europeans; the personal interest of Lyautey ; the gain in transportation time compared with the sea mail service (two days by plane, compared with five to ten by boat). But these favourable factors would not have been enough to endow airmail with the important position it occupied on this route, if it had not been for the close collaboration of the Directorate General of Post and Lignes Latécoère. They worked together on five parameters: three of a technical nature – frequency, timetables and regularity of service – and two of a commercial nature – the amount of surcharge applied and publicity. First, the technical aspects:

• Weekly frequency grew in stages from twice per week on 1st September 1919 to seven times per week on 1st September 1922.

• The departure time from Toulouse, which was initially set at 08.00 hours was put back to 10.30 hours in order to ensure a link-up with the night train from Paris which arrived at 10 o'clock at Toulouse station; in summer, a letter posted before 18.00 hours in Paris arrived in Casablanca the following evening!

• The regularity of the service became an obsession with Lignes Aériennes Latécoère and later with Aéropostale: "in the conveyance of airmail there is no room for delays or irregular service." [6]

It is difficult to imagine the amount of effort, courage and heroism needed to fulfil this demand of regular service, when aircraft had no navigation instruments and when engines were subject to "never ending breakdowns." [7] To get his way, Latécoère even had to appeal to Didier Daurat, the head of the Malaga aerodrome, at a time when "certain pilots had got into the habit of not going to the aerodrome as soon as the wind rattled the shutters in the Hôtel du Grand Balcon (in Toulouse), where they had established their headquarters." [8] It will be recalled that in the United States Otto Praeger was confronted with the same situation at about the same time. Although they were from different backgrounds, the two men were similar in many respects. They brought the same response to the same question: in (almost) any weather conditions, the mail had to "get through". Even though the price was too high . In total, from 1919 to 1939, "there were one hundred and twenty one pilots, navigators, radio operators, mechanics, engineers and sailors, who fell in the service of their country to ensure that the mail got through." [9]

By way of memorial, representing the "comrades who, on some day or night in obscure fog, went to their eternal rest", [10] let us mention the two first crews who disappeared over Spain within 72 hours of one another: Rodier and Marty on 2nd October 1920 and Genthon and Benas on 5th October 1920.

Thank goodness that postal discipline did not always demand such human sacrifice. But it did insist on absolute devotion from its servants. Listen to Raymond Vanier, one of the pioneers of airmail:

> *"One Sunday afternoon I came back from Rabat 24 hours late. At Montaudron airfield (in Toulouse) there was nobody but the guards; I had announced the breakdown and there was no one waiting for me. So I shouldered the two bags of mail, and suitcase in hand went to the tram stop and delivered my precious cargo to the main post office. Happy days!"* [11]

Once the technical requirements for developing the service had been fulfilled, the Post and Lignes Latécoère were free to join forces on the commercial front.

Within two years, considerable reductions were made in the amounts for postal surcharges:

Surcharges	1919	1920
Up to 20 grams	1.25F	0.50F
20-100 grams	2.50F	1.00F
100 to 200 grams	3.75F	1.50F

At the same time the maximum permissible weight went up from 200g to 1.5kg for letters and to 3kg for printed matter.

Between the two wars, the airlines for their part did not restrict their activities to merely conveying the mail. They made an active contribution to the popularisation of airmail thanks to a major "propaganda initiative directed at the Post Offices and at the Users." [12] All the classical commercial activities were utilised, from selling door to door right through to publicity. The installation of "special airmail letter boxes" at judiciously selected sites in the major cities proved to be the most original and effective initiative. This allowed airmail to be separated from the classic, centralised postal system based on the railways, and to replace it by means of a "lateral transport system" which was much faster.

Brégeut 14-A2.

Development of activities of Lignes Aériennes Latécoère

Year	Number of passengers	Freight in kg	Mail in kg	Number of letters
(1919)				(9,124)
1920	225	9,948	3,418	182,061
1921	455	25,555	6,707	327,805
1922	920	46,494	35,398	1,407,352
1923	1,416	70,373	68,159	2,958,863
1924	1,976	15,436	105,234	4,026,593
1925	1,666	18,600	194,360*	7,502,191
1926	1,464	15,154	145,710*	6,149,489
1927	1,547	17,451	116,077	6,454,977

*Traffic in years 1925–1926 is artificially inflated by considerable amounts of military post connected with the Rif War in Morocco.

Second section: Casablanca-Dakar

Important as it was, the Toulouse-Casablanca line was not the ultimate objective. It was merely the first stage on the route to South America. Once the first sector was firmly in place, they went on to the second: the 1,780-mile-long stretch from Casablanca to Dakar

Although the route continued to follow the Atlantic coastline, it traversed a desert region over which Spain and France exercised an authority which was often of a rather theoretical nature, challenged by "indomitable" nomadic tribes in perpetual revolt. Thus, the permanent risk of a forced landing in the middle of the Sahara resulting from a mechanical failure was compounded by the formidable danger of finding oneself in the hands of these "rebellious" tribespeople, whose sole wealth lay in their proud poverty. Several pilots became victims, or suffered a long captivity. Here are remembered the names of Mermoz, Guillaumet and Delaunay.

The weekly service from Casablanca to Dakar via Agadir, Cape Juby, Villa Cisneros (where crew and aircraft passed the night), Port Etienne and Saint Louis du Sénégal, opened on 1st June 1925, using Bréguet 14A2 aircraft. Initially it was restricted to mail and goods transport, but was opened to passenger traffic after a running-in period. It put Dakar four days away from Bordeaux instead of ten days away by sea.

With a length of 2,938 miles, the Toulouse-Dakar route was 188 miles longer than the American Transcontinental line, which it was far from equalling in terms of quality of infrastructure.

Provisional assessment

Whichever criterion we take, Lignes Aériennes Latécoère occupied an unusual position in the French air transport industry around 1925: it remained a carrier of airmail.

• Development of traffic
From 1920 to 1927 passenger traffic increased about sevenfold, cargo traffic doubled, but mail increased by 34 times! In 1927, the average daily load consisted of four passengers, 48kg of freight, but 318kg of mail, ie 17,684 letters (see table above).

• Number of letters
We can make an astounding comparison: in 1927, six million surcharged letters were transported between France, Morocco and Senegal, compared with only 22 million within the United States. Between France and Morocco, 25% of mail on the outward journey and 45% on the return leg was sent by air in 1930. [13]

• Percentage of postal revenue in the income of LAL
In 1926 the subsidies provided 78% of revenue (which was a normal situation at the time), and the mail provided 78% of commercial income.

• Ranking among French airlines
In the same year, out of the total for all French airlines, Lignes Latécoère flew 47% of the miles operated, 24% of the air passengers, 6% of the parcels carried, but 97% of postal traffic.

At that time airmail was synonymous with Latécoère. Soon it would become Aéropostale.

These last few lines of Saint Exupéry's "Courier Sud" written in the form of a telegram, [14] express far more than matters of postal policy – they embody the whole mystique of the airmail:

"From Saint Louis du Sènègal to Toulouse: (Aircraft) France-America located East Timéris. Enemy force nearby. Pilot killed plane wrecked mail intact. Continuing to Dakar."

The next stage would reach Buenos Aires.

2 LINKS BETWEEN EUROPE AND SOUTH AMERICA: A FRANCO-GERMAN ACHIEVEMENT

"From the beginning, one of the declared aims of Deutsche Lufthansa was to bridge the South Atlantic in order to open an airmail route of over 8,750 miles in length connecting Germany with pro-German countries, and with regions in South America to which Germans had traditionally emigrated." [15] Like the French, the Germans did not possess an aircraft capable of crossing the ocean. They were also obliged to proceed in stages, though they were handicapped by not having colonies on the route, but possessed the advantages of maintaining good relations with Spain and of having active minorities working for them in many of the destination countries.

South America under the influence
Two Latécoère study missions visited South America in 1924 and 1925 to prepare commencement of operations on the section Natal/Rio/Montevideo/Buenos Aires. They found that the French were not alone and that the German aviation industry was already very much in evidence. Here are a few key dates:

• 5th December 1919: foundation in Barranquilla, Colombia, of Sociedad Colombo-Alemaña de Transportes Aereos or SCADTA, precursor of Avianca, by a group of German and Colombian businessmen.

• 5th May 1924: creation in Berlin of Condor Syndikat, by SCADTA and Deutsche Aero Lloyd (one of the forerunners of Deutsche Lufthansa). Condor Syndikat was a research and testing company and was to play a major role in the development of commercial aviation in South America.

• 4th December 1924 two Junkers aircraft fly over the Andes during the second expedition of Ugo Junkers.

Pierre Georges Latécoère finally decided to go to South America himself. He arrived in Rio on 3rd December 1926 where he was received by Paul Vachet, who did a remarkable job in opening up the future connection between Natal and Buenos Aires. It is entirely by chance, but nevertheless a significant coincidence, that Latécoère's journey took place at just about the same time as the famous "Luther flight" during which the ex-German Chancellor Hans Luther flew from Buenos to Rio on board a Dornier Wal seaplane belonging to Condor Syndikat.

What would be the attitude of the South American countries towards the clearly declared ambitions of the two parties? In most respects, Brazil was attracted to Germany and Argentina was inclined towards France. The year 1927 was to be decisive for both camps.

On 26th January 1927 Brazil granted to Condor Syndikat a concession for the transport of mail and passengers between Rio de Janeiro and Porto Alegre. This was then extended to cover the whole of the northern route from Rio to Natal, and to the ocean section between Fernando do Noronha and the coast in September 1927. Elsewhere, another airline was being born: on 7th May 1927 Varig (Impresa de Viaçao Aerea Rio Grandense SA) whose main shareholder was … Condor Syndikat. The latter soon handed over to a direct subsidiary of Lufthansa on 1st December 1927: Syndicato Condor Lta.

These two companies of Brazilian nationality but with German capital demonstrate an interesting peculiarity in terms of airmail philately: like SCADTA in Colombia, they were both authorised to issue and use their own stamps for the payment of airmail surcharges. On the other hand, the Compagnie Générale Aéropostale and Pan American Airways never used anything other than official Brazilian stamps.

After the failure of negotiations concerning an airmail contract with Brazil in 1926, fortune smiled on the French in Argentina in 1927.

On 8th February 1927 a postal contract was signed between CGEA and Argentina, thanks to the intervention of Vincent Almondos de Almonacid, an Argentinean who was a great friend of France, and to the savoir faire of Marcel Bouilloux-Laffont, a French businessman who was well established in Brazil. This contract, which would have a decisive influence on the opening of airmail links between South America and Europe, contained six essential conditions:

1. The company undertook to set up a weekly airmail service between Argentina and Europe;
2. The duration of the journey should not exceed seven and one half days at the commencement of the service (a period which was later increased to nine days for the first six months). This was then to be progressively reduced to four days after three years of operation;
3. The company received from the Argentinean postal service a remuneration of 18 centavos per gram of mail transported, equivalent to 210 dollars per kilometre. This was the equivalent to the level of surcharge paid by the user;
4. The company was protected against the entry of any new competitor as long as the number of letters transported should not exceed 25% of the total of the mail between Argentina and Europe;
5. The General Directorate of the Argentinean postal services was permitted to cancel the contract in the case of repeated delays or cancellations or if another company, over a period of 12 consecutive months, succeeded in providing faster transport with identical regularity;
6. The contract was signed for a period of ten years and had to be put into effect at the latest seven months after its ratification by the Argentine Government. The contract was ratified on 10th June 1927.

Similar airmail contracts were signed with Uruguay on 16th June 1927 and with Chile on 9th January 1928, while on 6th December 1927 Brazil granted rights to overfly and make stopovers on its territory from the island of Fernando do Noronha in the north to the Uruguay frontier in the south. All the legal and commercial conditions for the commencement of an airmail link between Europe and South America had now been fulfilled.

But on 10th April 1927 the unexpected happened: Latécoère threw in his hand and sold his airline to Marcel Bouilloux-Laffont (though he retained his aircraft manufacturing operations). Bouilloux-Laffont was to put his financial resources at the disposal of the airline, in addition to the subsidies from the French state. Hardly had Bouilloux-Laffont completed the purchase of Lignes Aériennes Latécoère which had now become Compagnie Générale Aéropostale – or Aéropostale for short – than he started work on fitting out the 13 aerodromes (or stopover airfields) which marked out the route from Natal to Buenos Aires.

The Natal/Buenos Aires route, with a length of 2,906 miles was opened on 22nd November 1927. It was divided into two sectors with two chief pilots: Paul Vachet in Rio and Jean Mermoz in Buenos Aires.

Now, they only needed to conquer the major obstacle: the South Atlantic.

"The Atlantic Reef" [16]
Two dates, two questions:

• Buenos Aires, 1st March 1928 – 03.15 hours – Mermoz's Latécoère 26 takes off with 36 bags of mail. The airmail link between South America and Europe, the world's first transoceanic airline, has opened. Airmail or air/seamail?

• Friedrichshafen – 18th May 1930 – The dirigible "Graf Zeppelin" LZ127, a superb "ship of the air" 236.60 metres long, rises up, loaded with mailbags, bound for Brazil. It reaches Recife on 22nd May and Rio on 25th May 1930. One-off flight or regular service?

The truth is that in 1928–1930 no one had the ability to cross the Atlantic at a single stretch at any time of year, whether in a dirigible, a seaplane or a conventional aircraft. Up to that point, the South Atlantic had only been the object of sporadic "air raids". Only six crews had succeeded in crossing the ocean: two Portuguese, one Spanish (Commander Franco in a Dornier Wal seaplane), one Italian (General De Pinedo in a Savoia S55) and one French (Costes and Le Brix on board a Bréguet 19). The

first Portuguese crew, consisting of Sacadura Cabral and Gago Coutinho, deserves a special mention: in spite of an incredible amount of bad luck it succeeded in blazing the trail, thanks to the uncommon obduracy the crew members. They left Lisbon on 30th March 1922 in a Fairey Seaplane called "Lucitania" and only reached Rio de Janeiro on 17th June! The second Portuguese crew, led by Sarmient de Beires, crossed the South Atlantic in 1927. The Germans and the French applied different tactics to the problem of crossing the Atlantic, which were at first opposite and eventually complementary.

The "Atlantic Reef": the French solution
When it opened the first regular weekly airmail service between South America and Europe on 1st March 1928, Aéropostale captured a lead of several years over its competitors. To achieve it it adopted a mixed solution, teaming air transport with sea transport according to the following initial schedule.

• Toulouse to Saint Louis du Sénégal in a Latécoère 26 aircraft.
• Saint Louis du Sénégal to Porto Praïa (Cape Verde Islands) in a CAMS51 seaplane.
• Porto Praïa to Recife by advice boat.
• Recife/Buenos Aires by Latécoère 26.

The Laté 25 and 26 aircraft had left the production line during 1927. Fitted with a 450hp Renault engine, they were designed to carry a payload of 800kg over a distance of 500 miles at a cruising speed of 110mph. They were almost identical, except for the fuselage: the Laté 25 was a passenger plane with an enclosed cabin; the Laté 26 was a postal aircraft with a large hold of 5.8 cubic metres, without an enclosed cabin. The Laté 26 were soon provided with an invaluable communication tool: radio. "It was the Laté 26s with radios which carried out the majority of the regular night flights" recalls Marcel Moré, a mechanic and stopover station manager at Pelotas, in southern Brazil. [17] Between Toulouse and Buenos Aires the line thenceforth extended over a distance of 7,750 miles. The outward flights were called FRAME (France/Amérique du Sud), and the homeward flights were AMFRA (Amérique du Sud/France).

After a disastrous start-up and the loss of one seaplane, it was quickly decided to simplify the itinerary by carrying out the whole of the ocean stretch from Dakar to Natal by boat – some 1,910 miles.

The sea service was initially provided by a fleet of six advice boats ("Péronne", "Lunéville", "Épernay", "Belfort", "Reims" and "Révigny") and auxiliary vessels. These advice boats were former submarine hunters built in 1917 and leased from the French Navy at a nominal price, but their cruising speed was not above 16 knots and they suffered from numerous mechanical faults. This is the perfect example of a bad "good deal". They were replaced in 1930 by four 61-metre ocean-going patrol boats. They were christened "Aéropostale I" to "Aéropostale IV" and remained in service until Air France introduced aircraft capable of flying the South Atlantic on a regular basis in January 1936. In spite of the legendary storms in the "Doldrums" they exhibited a remarkable regularity of service. It is no doubt

Jean Mermoz.

The LZ127 "Graf Zeppelin" dirigible.
Lufthansa

during one of these tempests that patrol boat "Aéropostale II" was lost with all hands on 12th August 1932, with 24 men on board – Frenchmen, Brazilians, Portuguese, Senegalese and Chinese. They also sacrificed their lives for the Line.

The average speed of the patrol boats was not more than 16 knots, whereas Latécoère had wished to have ships operating at 20 knots. The impossibility of speeding up the sea crossing, which on average lasted four and a half days, boded ill for the future: they were unable to fulfil their obligations to the Argentine postal authorities. From 1928 to 1933, in spite of improvements achieved by putting more rapid aircraft into service and generally introducing night flights, only 20% of the weekly services were accomplished in less than eight days in the north/south direction and in less than nine days from south to north.

Nevertheless, in comparison with seamail, which took at least three weeks, but which often took one month, Aéropostale's weekly flights leaving Toulouse on Sundays and Buenos Aires on Saturdays, brought a very considerable improvement in the speed of the mail. This benefit was subject to the payment of a very high surcharge: 8.50F per unit weight of 5 grams. Naturally, the South American service was classified by the UPU amongst the "extraordinary services".

Aéropostale was alone in operating the South American service for almost six years, from March 1928 to February 1934, at which date Deutsche Lufthansa opened its own service. During this period, it had transported, by week and per single direction, an average of 100kg of mail between the two continents, principally consisting of business correspondence.

In spite of the constant development of the traffic, only a small fraction of the mail was sent by plane (figures for the year 1931):

- Leaving Europe:

France	10.7%
Germany	2.7%
Great Britain	1.1%

- Leaving South America:

Argentina	3.2%
Brazil	1.1%
Chile	8.6%.

The last stretch from Buenos Aires to Santiago de Chile had been inaugurated on 15th July 1929 by Mermoz and Guillaumet in a Potez 25 A2 aircraft, extending the total length of the service from 7,750 miles to 8,500 miles. It was on this last section, which consisted of crossing the Andean Cordillera, that some of the finest pages in the history of French aviation were written. It was there that Guillaumet, exhausted after an uninterrupted march of five days and five nights through the snows confided in his friend Saint Exupéry: "I swear to you, what I have done, no animal would have ever done."

Development of airmail in the South Atlantic Aéropostale, 1928–1933

	France/ S America	S America/ France	Total	Weekly Average*
(1928)	(310kg)	(948kg)	(1,258kg)	
1929	1,630kg	3,481kg	5,111kg	49kg
1930	3,464kg	5,913kg	9,377kg	90kg
1931	3,951kg	6,201kg	10,152kg	98kg
1932	4,165kg	6,752kg	10,917kg	105kg
1933	6,510kg	7,710kg	13,220kg	127kg

*Based on 52 theoretical round trips, ie 104 one-way journeys.

"The Atlantic Reef": the German response

As soon as it was able, Deutsche Lufthansa took its turn in attacking the commercial crossing of the South Atlantic. Where the French solution had now proved to be simple and stable, the German response was complex, took a long time to put into practice, but was finally more effective. It went through a number of stages.

• First stage: 1929–1931 – "À la française"

Between 1929 and 1931 Deutsche Lufthansa tested a formula aircraft/steamer/aircraft which did not get past the experimental stage. It did not call upon dedicated ocean facilities, but used the services of German steamship lines.

In 1929, it started several "express postal flights" to extend its Stuttgart/Barcelona service via Seville and later as far as the Canary Isles. It was then in a position to organise a series of experimental airmail services combining the following participants:

1. Deutsche Lufthansa from Stuttgart to Las Palmas: "small quantities of mail for South America were put on board a plane leaving from Stuttgart, thrown to earth over Cadiz, and from there transported by seaplane to Las Palmas to be put on board high speed German steamers;" [18]

2. The "Hamburg-America Line", from Las Palmas to the vicinity of the island of Fernando do Noronha, off Brazil, on the postal steamers "Cap Polonio" and "Cap Arcona";

3. Syndicato Condor from Fernando do Noronha to Natal by seaplane, and then from Natal to Rio by conventional aircraft.

In total a dozen mixed airmail crossings were made between 22nd March 1930 and 6th September 1931. They enabled experience to be gained, at the same time as showing the limitations of the service. The excessive time intervals between the German steamer services on the South Atlantic did not permit the establishment of a weekly link, which was the minimum frequency for any airmail service – even very long haul.

So something else had to be found.

• Second stage: 1930–1933 – "Germany's great originality": the solo exploitation of the dirigible "Graf Zeppelin"

The "Graf Zeppelin" dirigible LZ127 was one of the most beautiful flying machines of all time: with a length of 236.60 metres and a diameter of 30.50 metres, it had a volume of 105,000m³. Propelled by five Maybach engines, each with a power of 530hp, it had an available payload of 30 tonnes. Launched on 18th September 1928, it made four experimental crossings of the South Atlantic, one in 1930 and three in 1931, in association with Lufthansa on the one hand and with Syndicato Condor on the other. During these crossings it transported mail (990kg in 1931) consisting more of philatelic covers than regular mail.

This operation put into effect an old plan developed in the 1920s with certain Spanish organisations. In September 1922 it had resulted in the establishment of the company Transaera Colon, under the aegis of the Zeppelin Company, with the object of establishing a regular Friedrichshafen/Seville/South America dirigible service.

The situation changed radically in September 1931 when DELAG decided to finalise a plan for regular though seasonal services between Friedrichshafen and Rio de Janeiro: in this context it carried out nine two-way crossings in 1932 and the same number in 1933. These flights carried passengers, mail and goods; it was now only five days from Berlin.

Whereas until 1940 seaplanes and conventional aircraft had only transported mail, the "Graf Zeppelin" dirigible operated the first regular transoceanic service which was entirely airborne and open to passengers, freight and mail. This achievement did not prevent the German postal services from making a down to earth judgement, at once laudatory and critical: "These results are no doubt remarkable, but the connection thus established comes nowhere near to fulfilling the requirement for a regular and rapid communication service." It is impossible to provide a weekly service with a single dirigible! Back to the drawing board.

• Third stage: 1934 – Commencement of a weekly service

Since 1929 Deutsche Lufthansa had been gaining experience in the North Atlantic with combined airmail transport using seaplanes and steamships with a catapult-launching facility. After carrying out a number of tests, it decided to introduce this formula systematically in the South Atlantic by locating a catapult ship in the middle of the ocean to provide a relay base.

It opened a regular airmail service between Stuttgart and Buenos Aires on 3rd February 1934. Initially running twice a month, it changed to a weekly schedule on 21st July 1934. When operations began, Deutsche Lufthansa had only one vessel available, the steamship "Westfalen" which had been converted to a "floating airbase". It was a solidly built cargo ship 125 metres long, specially modified to provide launching and retrieval facilities for seaplanes. It was fitted with a catapult for launching and with a "trawled sail system" for retrieval.

• The great K6 catapult manufactured by Heinkel was installed in the bows of the ship. It was 40 metres long and capable of launching in two seconds a 14-ton seaplane, with all its engines roaring, at an initial velocity of 95mph, by means of a compressed air pump at a pressure of 160 atmospheres. Inside the seaplane, "the four-man crew were firmly attached to their seats; the headrests were provided with generously proportioned fillings to protect them from injury during the short period of high acceleration during launching." [19]

ABOVE **South Atlantic, 6th June 1933, a Dornier WAL flying boat is hauled by crane on to the "Westfalen" where she was serviced and then relaunched by catapult.**
Lufthansa

BELOW **Heinkel He 70.**
RAF Museum

• The "trawled sail" trailed in the water behind the stern of the ship, slightly submerged, creating a kind of "calm zone" where the seaplane could land. The plane was then hoisted on board by means of a crane mounted at the rear of the ship. Thanks to its radio and direction-finding installations, the "Westfalen" was in permanent contact with the seaplanes, so as to give them precise guidance during the delicate phase of landing on the sea.

At the beginning of the operation, the connection was organised as follows:

• Stuttgart-Marseilles-Barcelona-Seville via the postal aircraft Heinkel He 70 Blitz which had a cruising speed of over 190mph (departure airport transferred to Frankfurt in April 1936) — first day;

• Seville airport/Cadiz seaplane base, by car;

• Cadiz/Las Palmas/Bathurst (British Gambia) by seaplane – second day;

• Transatlantic crossing Bathurst/Natal in a Dornier Do J WAL seaplane – third and fourth days.

The Do J WAL was a two-engined aircraft weighing 8 tonnes, with a cruising speed not above 110mph, and which had been used since 1926 for the sea crossings between Germany and Scandinavia. It left Bathurst to land in the "calm zone" behind the steamship "Westfalen" in the middle of the ocean. The ship then continued for some hours of night-time sailing and then launched the seaplane from its catapult towards Natal;

- Natal/Rio/Buenos Aires via the Syndicato Condor – fifth day.

The operation was modified in autumn 1934 with the arrival of a second catapult ship, the "Schwabenland" and the entry into service of a more powerful seaplane, the 10-ton Do J WAL.

ABOVE **Lufthansa Dornier WAL "Taifun" on deck.**
Lufthansa

BELOW **Dornier WAL on "Westfalen".** *Lufthansa*

Each of these floating airbases was stationed about 100 miles off the African or Brazilian coast: the seaplanes came to these bases from Natal or Bathurst respectively, to be catapulted for an Atlantic crossing in a single stretch. A third catapult ship, the "Ostmark" was introduced in 1936.

This new air service, together with the 12 Zeppelin flights recorded between May and December 1934 permitted the German flag to offer a regular weekly airmail service between Europe and South America from May 1934.

This was quality conveyance: five days to Rio.

• Fourth stage: 1935–1937 The integrated air service "aircraft, seaplane, dirigible"
The year 1935 was marked by progress in two important respects. The introduction of systematic night flying allowed the duration of the Stuttgart/Rio flight to be reduced to almost three days, and the Syndicato Condor opened the Buenos Aires/Santiago de Chile service – which Aéropostale had inaugurated in 1929 – after obtaining the necessary postal concessions from the countries concerned.

It was also in 1935, on 1st April, that the Deutsche Zeppelinreederei, or DZR, was founded as a company for commercial operations, which had as its principal shareholders the Zeppelin Construction Company and Lufthansa: "a token of the close collaboration between aeroplanes and dirigibles on the South Atlantic route".

The integrated employment of all existing means of aerial transport – land-based planes, seaplanes and dirigible balloons, is the most original feature of the German airmail operation between Europe and South America, and remains a unique case in the history of commercial aviation.

During the years 1935 and 1936, the airmail was transported both by plane – the greater part – and by dirigible between Las Palmas and Natal, where the mailbags, mostly filled with philatelic mail, were thrown down to the ground. This practice allowed the saving of approximately six hours compared with a normal landing at Recife. The dirigible even completely replaced the seaplanes from 15th November to 2nd December 1935 while the two catapult ships were taken out of service to be overhauled; at that time the "Graf Zeppelin" carried out three consecutive return flights between Bathurst and Recife, known as *Pendelfahrten* – "pendulum flights".

ABOVE **LZ129 "Hindenburg".** *RAF Museum*

BELOW **Dornier Do 26 seaplane with the Nazi swastika clearly visible on the tailplane.** *MAP*

BOTTOM **Dornier Do 18 on the water.** *MAP*

The "Graf Zeppelin" carried out 16 return crossings in 1935 and 20 in 1936. Although the dirigible had not yet made a winter crossing, it was moving towards a regular bi-monthly operation in addition to Lufthansa's weekly postal service. The commercial activity of DZR was targeted towards the transport of passengers and freight, and in advertising material produced at the end of 1936 encouraged users "to use the new regular schedule to send printed matter, business mail, samples and parcels". But they did not only transport small scale items on board the "Graf Zeppelin". The lists of goods taken on board features one car and two light aircraft!

From 1936 the "Graf Zeppelin" was no longer alone. It was joined by a second dirigible, the "Hindenburg" LZ129. It was also filled with inflammable gas and was even larger. The "Graf Zeppelin" took off for Rio de Janeiro on 26th April 1937: it was to be its last flight, since a few days later at Lakehurst, near New York, the "Hindenburg" caught fire during landing, causing 35 fatalities and putting an end to the commercial operation of dirigible transport balloons – but for how long?

• Fifth stage: 1937–1939
From 1936 onwards, Deutsche Lufthansa was alone in operating a weekly service from Europe to South America devoted exclusively to airmail.

For the transoceanic leg it introduced faster seaplanes: the Dornier Do 18 in 1935 and then the Dornier Do 26 at the end of 1938. The Do 26 was a seaplane fitted with four Junkers-Jumo engines rated at 600 or 700hp, depending on the type, and capable of carrying a payload of freight or post of 900kg at a cruising speed of 165mph over long distances. Whether for the Do 18 or the Do 26, Lufthansa continued to use the catapult system.

On 1st April 1939 one last legal adjustment occurred which brought the law into harmony with reality: Lufthansa took over direct responsibility for the operation of the Natal/Santiago line to connect with their transatlantic route.

Towards "entente" between Deutsche Lufthansa and Air France
On 1st March 1928, when Aéropostale opened the South America/Europe service by plane and advice boat, it seemed that the results achieved would never allow it to honour its undertakings to the Postal Administrations involved. The introduction, and then the early widespread general use of night flying – from 1929 onwards – along with the introduction of faster aircraft – Laté 28, Wibault 283T – all played their part in reducing the average time for conveying the mail to round about six days. But that was still a long way from the target of four days.

The solution to the problem seemed to lie either by following the German example or in the construction of an aircraft, whether land or sea based, capable of crossing the South Atlantic in a single stretch. A competition for tender was opened in 1928 by the French aeronautical authorities.

Since answers were slow in coming, Aéropostale decided at the end of 1929 to give Mermoz the task of carrying out a series of trial flights from Dakar to Natal. As there was no suitable aircraft available, the choice fell on a single-engined 'land' aeroplane fitted out for passenger transport, the Laté 28. "An excellent aircraft in the international class," [20] the Laté 28 fulfilled the following specifications: it carried a load of 850kg over a distance of 625miles at a cruising speed of 135mph. Although at the outset it was not a long-distance airmail aircraft, a few machines would be subjected to special modifications to adapt them for this new function.

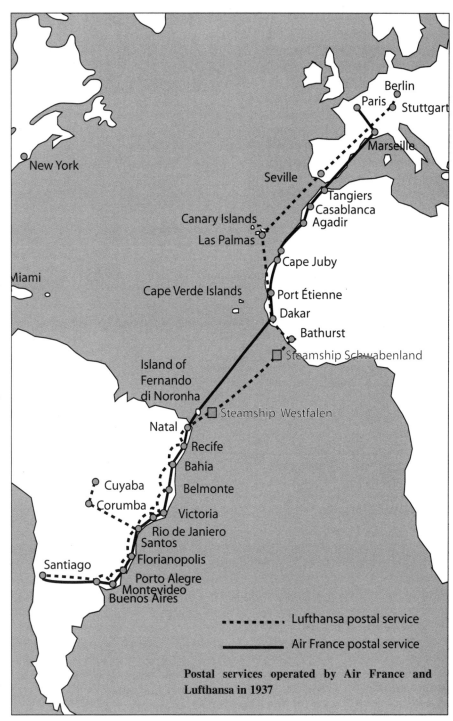

Postal services operated by Air France and Lufthansa in 1937

- - - - - - - Lufthansa postal service
————— Air France postal service

• Four machines were adapted for service as long-haul airmail planes: thanks to an auxiliary fuel tank in the cabin, their operating range was increased to 125 miles, but the payload was reduced to 540kg (Laté 28-1 LC).

• Four further machines were transformed into three-seater airmail seaplanes with floats, fitted with a 600hp Hispano-Suiza engine, with an augmented aerofoil surface and auxiliary fuel tanks (Laté 28-3).

It was in an aircraft of this type, called "Comte de la Vaux", that a crew consisting of Mermoz, Dabry and Gimié left Toulouse on 11th May 1930 carrying the mail on scheduled flight FRAME No 19.

So this was not merely a one-off effort, but a proper airmail flight, carrying "three large mail bags (130kg), more than 20,000 letters, from the whole of Europe, destined for Brazil, Uruguay, Argentina, Paraguay, Chile and Bolivia." [21] The "Comte de la Vaux", still with the same crew, took off from Saint Louis du Sénégal on 12th May at 11.00 hours. Mermoz made a sea-landing in Natal on the following morning, after having flown through a terrible cyclone which flooded the cabin: he had crossed the 1,983 miles in 21 hours 24 minutes! The mail to Buenos Aires had taken less than four days.

The first end-to-end airmail flight from Europe to South America gave rise to considerable enthusiasm. However, with his usual sense of realism, the director [22] of the journal "L'Aéronautique" cooled the general excitement: "What is the significance of this exploit? It confirms the manifest valour of the crew. It does not mean that the problems raised by the commercial crossing of the South Atlantic have been solved overnight."

Subsequent events would provide cruel confirmation of this opinion and show that that flight of 12th May 1930 was a one-off, which everyone had hoped so much it would not be. In fact, "inexplicable delays in the delivery of the aircraft they had ordered, linked with financial difficulties within L'Aéropostale which appeared towards the end of 1930, would prevent the company from having the aircraft available, with which it was planning to make regular Atlantic crossings before the agreed date in March 1932 on which its exclusive postal contracts could be rescinded if it did not succeed." [23] The next crossing was not accomplished until three years later.

This was because the next two and a half years were filled with a succession of tests, trial crossings and more or less short-lived periods of operation involving four different types of aircraft, built by four different manufacturers. This was blinding proof of the dissipation of effort within the French aeronautical industry and at the same time of the lack of political cohesion on the part of the authorities in charge. From January 1933 to March 1935, trial crossings followed one another:

• 12th January 1933: three-engined Couzinet 70 aircraft "Arc-en-ciel";
• 3rd January 1934: four-engined seaplane Laté 300 "Croix du Sud";
• 27th November 1934: three-engined seaplane Louis Blériot 5190 "Santos Dumont";
• 3rd June 1935: four-engined Farman 2200 aircraft "Centaure".

From its foundation in 1933, Air France was confronted by the problem of the South Atlantic. The company had been born of the fusion of four companies – Air Orient, Air Union, CIDNA and SGTA Lignes Farman – and had in fact taken over Aéropostale which had gone into liquidation on 28th March 1931. The situation took a turn for the worse when Deutsche Lufthansa opened its airmail service in February 1934. The board of Air France had to act fast in finding answers to a double question: which operating policy and what attitude to take regarding the new competitors?

• Which operating policy?
The reply was simple: to resume the objective of operating as soon as possible a wholly airborne service, as defined by Aéropostale. The number of planes available did not allow them to put this policy into immediate application , so they proceeded in stages:

1934:   7 crossings by aircraft; 45 by advice boat;
1935:   21 crossings by aircraft; 23 by advice boat.

The weekly route between France and South America was launched on 5th January 1936. Mail now took only three days to Buenos Aires (the terminus for the service was moved from Toulouse to Paris in April 1936).

During 1937, the operation gained a degree of stability and regularity which had hitherto been unknown, thanks to the exclusive utilisation of five Farman 2200 aircraft, called after the cities of "Mendosa", "Dakar", "Montevideo", "Saint Louis" and "Natal". The Farman 2200 was a monoplane with wings cable-stayed from above, fitted with four Hispano-Suiza engines each of 600hp. It had a cruising speed of 125mph and its operating range was over 2,500 mile. From 1936 to 1940, the Farman 2200 made 366 South Atlantic crossings, carrying only mail.

• What attitude to Deutsche Lufthansa?
The question of how to treat the new arrival, or more exactly the German flag in general, led to people taking passionate stands, causing violent clashes, both within Air France and across public opinion in France. It set the realists, who considered that an agreement with Lufthansa was inevitable and desirable, against the nationalists/idealists who, like Mermoz, considered that the work so far achieved and the lead established could not under any circumstances be shared with the German company.

After an attempt at compromise by Lufthansa [24] had been rejected in 1931, in spite of its according to France in recognition of its lead a larger share of the business than was awarded to Germany, a period of out and out competition commenced on 3rd February 1934. It could not do other than cause severe damage to Air France since it had previously obtained 25% of its business from the German Post, and from 1934 to 1935 recorded considerably longer transit times than its competitor. We should add that this competition did not bring the slightest advantage to the public, since the two operators left Europe on the same day.

At the end of a year of competition, national pride was put aside, and gave place to a policy of mutual understanding embodied in two conventions signed between Air France and Deutsche Lufthansa. The Convention of 16th May 1935 which entered into force on 1st July 1935 contained the following principal provisions: fixing of different departure days so as to offer the customers a bi-weekly service; equalisation of rates;

Air France Farman 2200 "Ville de Montevideo" operated the route to South America from 1935 until 1940. *Air France*

coordinated publicity and mutual technical assistance. The Convention of 7th July 1937 extended technical collaboration and initiated a system of financial pooling.

Within this narrowly specified framework of relationships, traffic expanded as is shown in the table below. If one considers the period between 1928 and 1938, the last complete year before the Second World War, approximately 265 tonnes of post were transported between Europe and South America by all the operating companies; 160 tonnes under the French flag and 105 tonnes under the German flag. At the end of this period, the average weekly traffic in each direction exceeded 500kg., an altogether remarkable figure if one considers the high value of the air surcharges, and it reflects the intense "propaganda" efforts in favour of airmail expended by Air France in the wake of Aéropostale and Latécoère and by Lufthansa (see table below).

Right up to the end, crews were laying down their lives to pay for the transportation of airmail across the South Atlantic: on 10th February 1936 Ponce and his crew disappeared seven

hours after leaving Natal on board the Laté 301 seaplane "Ville de Buenos Aires"; during the night from 14th to 15th February 1936 the Dornier Do J Wal seaplane "Tornado" with "Flugkapitäne" Bielenstein and Scheffler at the controls, lost radio contact nine hours after their catapult launch; on 7th December 1936, the Laté 300 seaplane "Croix du Sud" at the hands of Mermoz and his crew sent its last message – "cutting right rear engine". All of them, before they disappeared, could have subscribed to the fine words of Saint Exupéry: "Alone in the vast courtroom of the tempestuous skies, the pilot defends his mail before three elementary divinities: the mountain, the ocean and the storm."

Here, as with many other services, the war halted the operation: Lufthansa made its last crossing on 25th August 1939; Air France on 2nd July 1940.

Postal traffic Europe-South America and vice versa in gross weight of mail (in kg)

Years	Air France Europe-S America	S America-Europe	Lufthansa Europe-S America	S America-Europe	Comments
Actual 1934	6,566	8,746	3,731	3,215	DLH opens in March
Actual 1935	6,827	9,590	7,929	7,929	Agreement from June onwards
Actual 1936	9,961	11,217	10,077	10,832	
Actual 1937	13,288	13,508	14,010	11,073	
Estimate 1938	15,300	15,000	18,000	11,000	

Source: For years 1934–37, Hirschauer Report of 21st July 1938.

5 THE IMPERIAL LINES

Colonialism, which reached its zenith between the two World Wars, is a system of geopolitical organisation in which one dominant mother country exercises its authority over an empire consisting of territories which are very often at large distances from one another. In such a spatial structure communications play a determining role: an imperial network is a medium for economic interchange between different territories living under the same flag, and an organ of command for the dominant country. [1]

The concern for speeding up links with distant parts of their empires caused Belgium, France, Great Britain and The Netherlands to open up air routes towards Asia and Africa. Admittedly, none of these great imperial lines was exclusively for airmail, since they fulfilled more complex needs: the rapid movement of high-ranking civil and military officials, the conveyance of urgent parcels, the transportation of private mail and official despatches. In spite of this, post in all these cases played a fundamental role in the process of starting up the lines and in their economics.

1 IMPERIAL LINES TO ASIA

The British and the route to India

The Indian Empire was the jewel in Great Britain's crown, and the establishment of an air link between London and Calcutta stood out as having an absolute priority. From July 1922, the Civil Aviation Advisory Board declared itself in favour of speedily putting into operation an "Imperial airmail service" to India and Australia.

Without waiting for the official recommendations, pioneers had already shown the way. From 12th November to 10th December 1919, the Englishmen Ross Smith, Keith Smith, J. M. Bennett and W. H. Shiers had established the link between London and Darwin in Australia via Karachi, Delhi, Calcutta and Singapore, with a number of other stopovers, in a Vickers Vimy bomber. They thus pocketed the prize of £10,000 offered by the

Australian Government to the first demobilised veterans who succeeded in flying from Europe to Australia in less than 30 days. This is a detail which is interesting for us: "they had privately taken with them 'mail' of some 200 letters which were officially accepted by the Australian Post Office as the first airmail from England to Australia." [2]

At the same time, or almost, the way was marked out for the future "air route to India". Since there was no question at the outset in trying to establish a regular air service from end to end, the method adopted was that of "small steps", combining a number of airborne sections with a basically marine routing – involving three points of note:

• Bombay/Karachi section: An airmail section was launched on 24th January 1920 with the aid of the Royal Air Force. The aircraft took off immediately after the arrival of the mailboat from England to carry surcharged letters, marked "via Bombay-Karachi Air Service". The experiment, which had little impact and made large losses, ended on 9th March 1920;

• Paris/London section: Thanks to a good connection with the night mail train, the aircraft allowed a much quicker link-up with the Indian mail boat at Marseilles. "From the beginning of 1920 to September 1921 it was possible in London to post late letters for India up to 11am on the morning following the general dispatch and also to extend by several hours the time of posting in provincial towns." [3]

• Cairo/Baghdad section: "The Desert Airmail Route". Egypt, which Britain had taken officially as a protectorate in 1914, was of major strategic importance due to its position on the sea route to India (the

British stamp celebrating the first air mail service from England to Australia between 12 November and 10 December 1919.

The DH-10 seen here in 1919, carried airmail between Hendon and Renfrew and went on to open the Desert Air Mail in 1921. *MAP*

Suez Canal). On the other hand, Iraq, which had formerly been under Ottoman influence, was placed under British mandate in 1920. One can therefore understand more easily the political interest in a fast airmail link between Cairo and Baghdad, the key link in the future air route.

After undertaking two test flights on 24th February and 11th March 1919, the Royal Air Force undertook to set up The Desert Airmail Route in 1921. It established rudimentary landing fields, installed petrol filling stations, and at certain points laid out a road across the ground by means of which the planes could find their way in a desert terrain without landmarks. The RAF opened the route on 28th June 1921 using De Havilland DH9 and DH10 aircraft, subsequently going over to Vickers bombers.

Initially reserved for official mail, the service was opened to the public on 8th October 1921. "The Postal Union" in Berne published the following communiqué on December 1921. "In consequence of an agreement between the British Ministry of Aviation and the British Post Office, the public will be able to send mail, both ordinary and registered, from Egypt to Iraq by means of an airborne service which operates once a fortnight, using [British] Government aircraft."

Depending on the weather conditions, the journey was made in one or two days. The reduction in postal transit time, normally at least 20 days, was spectacular. In Port Said the plane linked up with the mail boat of the Peninsula & Oriental Company in order to speed up to a maximum the conveyance of mail between Great Britain and Iraq. The Desert Airmail Route was an immediate success: the average number of letters transported by plane went from 980 in 1922 to 3,700 in 1923. After two years of operation, 22% of the first class mail to Iraq was sent by air.

It was now necessary to make the last step: that of preparing and opening up the future route. The first test flight from London to Rangoon (Burma) was made between 10th

November 1924 and 17th March 1925 by a pilot of exceptional qualities, Alan Cobham, of whom it is said that he frequently carried with him as private post, a number of letters and postcards. "The impression gained from the flight was that an aeroplane service from England to India and Burma was feasible from a technical standpoint." [4] On 15th November 1925 the Air Ministry and the Imperial Airways Company (formed on 31st March 1924 as a result of the re-grouping of four private companies) signed an agreement providing for the opening, at the latest on 1st January 1927, of a twice-monthly service between Egypt and India in return for a subsidy, the value of which was fixed for five years.

It turned out that Imperial Airways, confronted with serious problems of aeropolitics (prohibition of overflight and landing), was only able to take over from the Royal Air Force on 7th January 1927 by opening to passengers the desert airmail route between Egypt and Iraq. The weekly service from London to Karachi, which was purely airmail, and only later extended to passenger service, did not begin until 30th March 1929 according to a very complicated operating plan, which resulted from the length of the route, the obstacles encountered and a particular policy regarding the machines used. This combined in succession the plane from London to Basel (Armstrong Whitworth Argosy) with the train from Basel to Genoa, followed by a seaplane from Genoa to Alexandria (Short S8 Calcutta) and finally a plane from Alexandria to Karachi (De Havilland – 66 Hercules). A total of 20 stops over a voyage of seven days. As an example of an imperial route, the connection between London and Karachi gained the majority of its income from the mail, even though as a result of the high level of the surcharge, the actual postal traffic remained limited. Whereas the postage for a letter via sea mail cost 1.5 pence per ounce, the airmail surcharge amounted to 6 pence per half ounce. Under these conditions it was urgent mail, principally consisting of business letters and official communications, which was sent by air. Although the gain in time was appreciable (eight days in 1929 to twelve days in 1935) only a low proportion of the traffic was sent by air: 11% in 1935.

But Karachi was by no means the final goal. It was merely one stage in the journey towards Australia and Hong Kong. Delhi was reached by a regular service on 30th December 1929, Calcutta on 1st July 1933, Rangoon and Singapore on 23rd September and 9th December in that same year. The last thing left to do was to connect Britain with Australia and Hong Kong.

Postal traffic on the British India Line

	London/Karachi	Karachi/London	Total
1932/33	23,838	20,882	44,720
1933/34	29,648	27,987	57,635

The Post was to play a major role in the preparation and opening up of the longest route in the world: London to Brisbane. The British General Post Office, breaking with its traditional policy of prudence which caused it never to send post on board trial flights, decided to make its own contribution. It put appreciable quantities of mail aboard three experimental return postal flights carried out in 1931. The first two, made between 4th April and 14th May and between 25th April and 27th May, linked Imperial Airways with the Australian companies Australian National Airways and Qantas; the third, made between 22nd November 1931 and 22nd January 1932, was

ABOVE Vickers Victoria. *RAF Museum*

RIGHT DH9A. *MAP*

LEFT DH66 "City of Cairo". *British Airways Museum*

BELOW LEFT DH66. *British Airways Museum*

BELOW Short "Calcutta". *RAF Museum*

RIGHT Vickers Vernon.
MAP

BELOW RIGHT Vickers Victoria V.
MAP

reserved for Christmas mail coming from Australia and for New Year's mail coming from Great Britain. It was flown entirely by Australian pilots.

There are several Australian pilots who grace the annals of airborne post. Kingsford Smith and G. V. Allan gave their support to each of these three flights. C. P. T. Ulm, for his part, at the controls of his modified Avro 10 Faith in Australia, inaugurated the official airmail connection from New Zealand to Australia on 17th February 1934 and from Australia to New Zealand on 11th and 12th April in that year.

This series of experimental flights, marred by numerous technical failures, was not judged to be a complete success, and the London/Brisbane service was not inaugurated until 8th December 1934: the Christmas mail arrived at its destination on 21st December after an interminable journey which contained no fewer than 49 stops of which 19 were in Australia. The Singapore/Brisbane section, operated by Qantas Empire Airways, was reserved to postal traffic until 13th April 1935. Shortly afterwards, on 6th May 1935, the pressure of business permitted a doubling of the frequency.

The Hong Kong service was opened on 14th March 1936. Here again, passenger traffic appeared to play very much a secondary role when compared with post. Let us hear the story of the arrival of the first Imperial Airways flight arriving in Hong Kong at Kaï Tak airport on 24th March:

"The honour of being the first passenger to land at Kaï Tak (Hong Kong airport) went to a Kuala Lumpur man, Mr Ong Eee Lim, who sat all the way from take-off to touch-down on 16 mailbags the aircraft was carrying. This event inaugurated the weekly air service between Penang and Hong Kong which connected with the Imperial Airways route to Australia and the United Kingdom." [5]

One could have imagined oneself on the Latècoére service 10 years before!

The Dutch and the East Indies

Since the East Indies were even more valuable to The Netherlands than the Indian Empire was to Great Britain, thought was given at a very early stage to the establishment of an airmail link between Amsterdam and Batavia (Djakarta), which was the seat of the General Administration for the East Indies.

The first airmail trial flights, the complicated details of which we need not consider further, were made in the East Indies (Indonesia) between 1920 and 1923 by seaplanes of the Dutch Navy. By way of example, we will mention the 28th April 1920, when a postal link was established between Tandjong-Priok (the Port of Batavia) on the island of Java and Telok-Betong on the island of Sumatra, with a small load of 91 items of post. [6]Other isolated experimental flights followed, without any overall plan.

We have to wait until 1923 to see the operation of a regular, though temporary, service from 28th July to 12th August, between Batavia and Bandung, in order to speed up the conveyance of local post and European mail during the Bandung Fair. "This service was success from every point of view. There were 16 flights from Bandung to Batavia and 19 in the opposite direction. They transported 621kg of mail from Bandung to Batavia and 845 from the capital to the interior." [6]

At the same time a committee had been formed in The Netherlands in order to form an airlink between Amsterdam and Batavia: the "Commit Vliegtocht Nederland/Indie". It was on their initiative that the first flight was made towards the end of 1924. Carrying 281 official items of mail "overprinted with a special circular stamp" the aviator Thomassen a Thuessink Van der Hoop took off from Schiphol on 1st October in his Fokker VII. After serious mechanical problems had detained him in Europe for a month, he landed at the aerodrome of Tjilitan in Java on 24th November. This spectacular flight was never followed up.

The committee then turned to more restricted objectives: to reduce the transport period (33 days) by linking sea transport with airborne sections at either end. On 26th May 1926, KLM and Lloyd of Rotterdam collaborated in a postal flight from Rotterdam to Marseilles to make immediate connection with the steamboat "Indrapoera" leaving for Batavia – gaining four days. The same operation was carried out in the reverse direction on 6th June 1926 (with steamboat "Patria").

The experiment was taken up again in 1927 and extended to both ends of the marine service: between Rotterdam and Marseilles on 18th March and 22nd April 1927 and between Sabang (at the north west end of Sumatra) and Surabaya (at the eastern extremity of Java) via Batavia on 2nd and 4th of April. All these attempts of limited importance were soon to be completely eclipsed by the masterly "Postal air raid" by Lieutenant Koppen. G. A.. Koppen, a lieutenant in The Netherlands Air Force, had been for some years preparing a flight from Amsterdam to Batavia. After lengthy negotiations, he made an agreement with the Government on the following basis: in return for his undertaking to transport all the mail presented to him within the payload limits available on his aircraft, he would receive half of the airmail surcharges, while The Netherlands and the East Indies would each pay to him a contribution towards costs of 12,500 florins.

He left Schiphol on 1st October 1927 in a three-engined Fokker FVIIA which had been christened "De Postduif", or "The Postal Dove", for the occasion and landed 10 days later in Java with a load of 2,092 items of mail (in spite of the very high level of airmail surcharge: 10 florins for one letter !). Lieutenant Koppen spent a week in Java and started out on his return on 17th October with a record load of post consisting of 4,642 letters and cards. He landed at Schiphol on 28th October 1927: for a journey time by sea of 30 days he had substituted an air transit period of 10 days, a gain of almost three weeks.

In the face of this unmistakable lesson, all the interested parties – commercial companies, shipping companies and airlines, and public authorities – pooled their efforts from that moment on, in one of those movements of national unanimity of which the Dutch possess the secret, in order to bring about the speedy opening of a regular service from Amsterdam to Batavia. They worked on the two ends of the future link.

In Batavia, the KNILM or Royal Dutch Indies Air Navigation Company, was founded in 1928 with the dual aim of establishing an interior network, and establishing links with neighbouring countries. The company took charge of four Fokker VII planes, which as they flew out from Schiphol to Batavia in September and October 1928 were used to transport quite respectable amounts of post: 225kg per aircraft.

On 31st October 1928 KNILM opened the first regular internal service between Batavia and Bandung and had soon developed a veritable network serving the principal towns on the isles of Java and Sumatra which was extended to Singapore. An airmail service with surcharges was opened at the same time and experienced rapid growth, so that over nine tonnes of post (9,097kg) were carried in 1930.

At more or less the same time as KNILM was created, KLM (through an agreement signed with the Dutch Government providing for the payment of a subsidy) undertook to make 12 return airmail flights between Amsterdam and Batavia from 1928 to the end of 1930. It established the first links at the end of 1928 and then made a series of eight return flights at fortnightly intervals from 12th September 1929 to 15th January 1930. For the first time the post for Christmas and the New

Junkers F.VII. *RAF Museum*

LEFT **KLM DC-2, PH-AKH.**
RAF Museum

BELOW **Dewoitine D.332 at
Amsterdam Municipal
Airport.**

Year were transported by plane on the payment of a surcharge of 70 cents for a letter of 20 grams: 1,772kg on the outward and 1,487kg on the return journey. The flight of 18th December 1929 from Batavia reached a record load of 384kg and 942 grams (at that time mail was considered to be so precious that it was weighed in grams).

After being interrupted at the request of the British authorities who, in order to modernise the Indian airports, considered it necessary to forbid access only to foreign companies, the KLM airmail flights were resumed on 25th September 1930, still at a frequency of once a fortnight, not to cease again. In line with the practice in other countries, The Netherlands and the Dutch East Indies introduced an airmail surcharge of 30 cents for letters not over 5 grams. During the first year of operation, from September 1930 to September 1931, over 10 tonnes of post (10,832kg) were sent by air between Amsterdam and Batavia, that is an average of 401kg for each outward or return flight.

However, a frequency of two flights per month would not satisfy businesses. They obtained an undertaking from the Government that it would negotiate a new contract with KLM, which opened a weekly service between Amsterdam, Batavia and Bandung on 1st October 1931. This service took 12 days at the beginning, which was soon reduced to 10 days in winter and eight to nine days in summer, including 15 stopovers. It exhibited three remarkable characteristics:

• Length: 9,063 miles;
• Means of transport used: only aircraft, even over the maritime sections, in contradiction to the teachings of the usual doctrine;
• Type of operation: the same aircraft, piloted by the same crew carried out the whole of the journey.

But the most original feature lay in the conditions of the contract between KLM and the Dutch Postal Ministry. In the contract, which could be described as "American" [7] KLM undertook to carry up to 500kg of mail in each direction and the Post undertook to reimburse KLM at the rate of 42.50 florins per kilogram on the basis of 500kg irrespective of the weight of post actually transferred to the company. With hindsight, this contract appears to have been particularly effective: it ensured that the operator had a guaranteed postal income, and encouraged the Post to make the maximum of publicity for the promotion of surcharged airmail (36 cents for an airmail letter against 6 cents for the same letter by boat). The publicity campaign paid off, since in 1933, almost 25% of the letters between The Netherlands and the Dutch East Indies were carried by plane.

As with the other imperial services, the Amsterdam/Batavia line also transported goods and passengers, for which the company actually won the business, but the association between KLM and the Dutch Post was so close that the French commercial attaché in the Hague wrote, incorrectly, in his note of the 6th December 1935: [8] "There is one service which is operated by the Postal Administration, which is the Amsterdam/Bandung service which connects The Netherlands to their overseas colonies in the Far East." Once they were solidly installed on the East India route, the Dutch concentrated their efforts on three factors: increasing frequency (two per week from 12th June 1935 and three per week on 2nd October 1937); speeding up flights by eliminating intermediate stopovers and putting into service faster aircraft (the Douglas DC-2 reduced the journey by six days); and finally, extending the network beyond Batavia, thanks to a close collaboration between KLM and KNILM (Singapore from 1933, Australia in 1936 and Indo-China in 1938). The volume of post transported reached 46,766kg in 1934 and 62,237kg in 1935.

The French and the route to Indo-China
Just as the British founded their Indian route on specific anchor points, which they possessed in Egypt and Iraq, the French used the Lebanon and Syria for which they had received a Mandate of Administration from the League of Nations, in order to provide support for the service to Indo-China.

Before any service was opened with France, the military were the instigators of the first airmail demonstrations in the countries of the Levant and in Indo-China:

• In Syria, a small and rather original airmail service started on the 14th August 1925 [9] as a collaboration between the military authorities and the Postal Administration. The letters were posted in post-boxes and transferred by the Postmaster to the

head of the military Post Office, transported on military aircraft and then at their destination returned to a civilian postal official by the warrant officer in charge of post. This small network was composed of three lines:

1. Aleppo/Antioch, which could take 75kg of civilian mail, but which did not work on fixed days due to the violence of storms in the mountainous region over which they flew;

2. Aleppo/Deir-Ez-Zor, where the weight of civilian post could not exceed 50kg;

3. Damascus/Palmyra/Deir-Ez-Zor, for which there was no limitation.

• In Indo-China [10] numerous military reconnaissance or survey flights provided the first postal transport, generally consisting of official mail and military post, between 1921 and 1927. We mention by way of example a Saigon/Luang-Prabang reconnaissance flight in April 1921 using an adapted Bréguet 14 with 1kg of mail on the return flight, or a flight Saigon/Hanoi on the 11th April 1923 with over 100 letters on board, or again in 1926 a number of experimental postal flights for the purpose of opening up routes in Laos.

As was the case for Great Britain or The Netherlands, the object was not to operate colonial regional services, however useful they were, but to connect the colonies with France. In 1925, "the French air ministry put forward the idea of a France/Lebanon service, which at the time was of paramount strategic importance." [11]

The first reconnaissance flights, without post, were carried out in 1926 by Maurice Noguès in a Schreck amphibious seaplane, fitted with a Gnome et Rhône engine. Noguès was distinguished with war honours, and had been a pioneer in night flying in the Balkans. He had just left the Compagnie Internationale de Navigation Aérienne or CIDNA and was about to earn his reputation as "airline trailblazer" on the Indo-China route.

The beginnings proved laborious: the first attempt did not get past Cap Corse, and the second was broken off in Athens: but the work of opening up the route had started.

The company Air Union-Lignes d'Orient, founded in 1927 with Maurice Noguès as its Director, obtained a Government contract for making five survey flights between Marseilles and Beirut. After the completion of a considerable amount of work in providing equipment and infrastructure, seven trial airmail flights were completed at the end of 1928 between Marseilles and Beirut. There were quite a few similarities with the KLM flights at the end of 1929 between Amsterdam and Batavia. The result was the inauguration of a regular weekly service between Marseilles and Beirut, on 6th June 1929, via Naples, Corfu, Athens and Castellorizo, on board a Cams 53 seaplane. This was a seaplane built by Chantiers Aéromaritimes de La Seine, a biplane in wood and fabric, fitted with two 500hp Hispano-Suiza engines. Cruising speed reached 106mph, with a range of 700 miles and a payload of up to 250kg.

Once the first segment was established, the new company Air Orient, which had been founded at the beginning of 1930 from the amalgamation of two companies, Air Union Lignes d'Orient and Air Asie, progressed in stages and according to the

LEFT **Cams 53 Flying Boat.** *Air France*

BELOW LEFT **Dewoitine D.338.** *MAP*

speed, endurance and operating reliability, seemed to be combined for the first time so that a true, end-to-end, long haul airmail operation could be considered." [12] After testing by Mermoz on the Paris/Dakar route, the "Émeraude" was assigned to the Oriental services. It took off on the 21st December 1933 to make the inaugural Paris/Saigon/Paris flight. On the return flight it was caught up in a snowstorm and crashed in Morvan, 125 miles southeast of Paris on the 15th January 1934. Among the victims was Maurice Noguès, the "trailblazer of the Indo-China route".

classic formula. It started by marking out the two ends of the route: the stretches from Damascus to Baghdad and Saigon to Bangkok were opened in January and October 1930 respectively.

The connection between Baghdad and Bangkok was accomplished in April 1931. The twice-monthly service between Marseilles and Saigon, which was reserved for mail and cargo, began weekly operation in May 1932. It was run according to an English model: by seaplane over the sea route from Marseilles to Beirut and by conventional aircraft over the land route from Damascus to Saigon (with a section from Beirut to Damascus by bus).

At that point, Air France, which had only just been formed, took delivery of a new three-engined aircraft, the Dewoitine 332, christened "Émeraude", which had been developed from a single-engined long-range aircraft. In Paris, Noguès, who had created Air Orient and had become the Assistant General Manager of Air France, had immediately recognised the advantages that could be obtained from an aircraft for which "the

It was not until 1938, when the Dewoitine 338 was put into service on this sector, that the Indo-China route, extended as far as Hong Kong, was operated from end to end using the same type of machine. This was a sleek and well-proportioned aircraft of metal construction throughout, manufactured by Emile Dewoitine. It became one of the great success stories of the French aeronautical industry, due to its technical performance, its comfort and its economy of operation. It was produced in three versions – short-, medium- and long-haul. Air France owned 29 units in 1939: it combined a payload of 1,700kg, a cruising speed of 160mph and an operating range of approximately 1,250 miles.

Until it ceased to operate in June 1940, the French Indo-China service remained "a highly characteristic example of an imperial service", and even of "a double imperial service: France/Levant on the one hand and France/Indo China on the other." [13] Like all imperial services, it transported passengers, parcels and post, which provided the large proportion of its income.

Development of traffic on the Indo-China service

	Passengers (number)	Cargo	Post
1934	831	11,395kg	17,369kg
1935	1,042	20,225kg	16,312kg
1936	651	19,078kg	17,508kg
1937	634	21,484kg	20,909kg
1938	1,139	18,557kg	27,615kg

The above figures apply to all traffic streams taken together, France/Levant and France/Indo-China. In 1937, the post from France to Indo-China and on the return journey was not more than 16,119 kilograms. However it is true that the carrier was remunerated at a rate of 102 gold francs per kilo!

2 THE IMPERIAL ROUTES TO AFRICA

The Africa of 1920 was an immense colonial continent divided up between European countries. It fell to three nations, Belgium, France and Great Britain, to survey, equip and operate two African imperial routes, each over 6,250 miles in length. One British line linked England with South Africa through the Nile valley and the great Rift Valley lakes, and one Franco/Belgian line crossed the continent diagonally, linking Belgium and France to the Belgian Congo and Madagascar via the Sahara and French Equatorial Africa. The first service was inaugurated on 20th January 1932, and the second, which was set up after some delay, was opened in stages between February 1935 and April 1936.

Rather than describe the setting up of these lines, as was done with Asia earlier in the book, this chapter highlights the significant developments of each route, the continuity of the British route, the impatience of the Belgians when confronted with the equivocations of France, and finally the particular role of Madagascar in French aero-postal history.

British continuity

Apart from a few local peculiarities, the establishment of the Cape route was a repetition of the creation of the Indian service.

• The first aerial assault on the route between Great Britain and South Africa was made in 1920 by a Vickers Vimy bomber, followed by a survey flight carried out between 16th November 1925 and 13th March 1926 by the indefatigable Alan Cobham, who was known as "the flying Ambassador of the British Empire". [14]

• Instead of proceeding in one fell swoop, as the Dutch had done with the Amsterdam/Batavia line, the British continued to favour the strategy of small steps. Imperial Airways opened a regular weekly service between Great Britain and East Africa (Croydon/Mwanza on the shores of Lake Victoria) on 28th February 1931. This service was extended as far as the Cape from 20th January 1932.

• Each new stage was at first reserved for the transportation of post. Passengers were admitted later, once the service had been run in. Thus the section between Kisumu (also beside Lake

ABOVE RIGHT **Imperial Airways AW Argosy in 1928.**
RAF Museum

RIGHT **Imperial Airways Handley Page HP42 Hercules at Croydon Airport.**
RAF Museum

Armstrong Whitworth Atalanta "Astraea".
RAF Museum

Victoria) and the Cape, which was inaugurated in January 1932, was not authorised to carry passengers until 27th April 1932.

• The operations for the Cape route were as varied and complex as those on the route to India. After a Handley Page "Heracles" aircraft left London for Paris, there followed a train journey from Paris to Brindisi, a Short S17 Scipio seaplane flew from Brindisi to Alexandria, there was a further train journey from Alexandria to Cairo, an Armstrong Whitworth Argosy aeroplane then flew from Cairo to Khartoum, a Short S8 "Calcutta" seaplane travelled from Khartoum to Kisumu, and finally a De Havilland 66 Hercules went from Kisumu to the Cape. In all the journey took 11 days, with 30 stop-overs.

• As with the routes to India and Australia, very special attention was paid to the transportation of Christmas mail: even before the Cape service existed, the East Africa flight of 9th December 1931 was extended into South Africa to carry the Christmas post.

• Once the Imperial route had been established, further development only required speeding up, simplification of flights and increase of frequency.

• With identical postal rates (the amount of surcharge for destinations to Calcutta or the Cape was fixed at 6 pence per half

ounce), the traffic was also similar: the weight of post sent by air from the Union of South Africa reached 17,050 kilograms during the fiscal year 1934–35.

Belgian impatience

Although a Franco/Belgian convention had been signed on 23rd May 1930, providing for the creation of a Belgium/France/Congo/Madagascar service, the Belgians had not seen much by way of results. The establishment of a direct air link between Belgium and the Belgian Congo continued to be dependent on the good will of the French.

Having become tired of waiting, the Belgians seized their opportunity and organised a brilliant postal "air raid" towards the end of December 1934, just before Christmas. This was at the initiative of a former fighter pilot in the Belgian army, Maurice Franchomme. [15]

A short time previously, an air race from England to Australia had been held (the Mac Robertson England-Australia Air Race) which had been won by an aircraft specially built for the competition, the De Havilland DH88 Comet which had just beaten the Douglas DC-2 Series machine of KLM. Franchomme's idea – to use the DH88 Comet to convey the Christmas post to Leopoldville – captured the imagination of the Australian owner of the aeroplane. Not content with putting a pilot at his disposition, he took charge of a good part of the expenses. The affair took on such a magnitude that King Leopold, tipped off by the British Embassy, demonstrated his interest, and Queen Astrid consented to the aeroplane bearing her name.

After a certain amount of work to adapt the aeroplane for this special mission (it was necessary to reduce the volume of the fuel tanks in order to be able to load around 120 kilograms of post), the De Havilland DH88 "Reine Astrid" left Brussels-Evere airport on 20th December 1934 at 10.40hrs, with the Australian pilot Ken Waller and Maurice Franchomme at the controls. After spending the night at Niamey, and battling with a terrible storm, which completely blacked out the sky before they made an impromptu stop at Point Noire, they landed at Leopoldville aerodrome on 22nd December at 14.46hrs. All the airmail speed records had been beaten: the Christmas post and a few newspapers had reached Leopoldville in two days, on board a long-range aircraft flying at 230 mph! It had been a veritable postal air raid!

The Belgians were about to complete their airmail route. Since October 1934, regular airmail flights by the Régie Air Afrique under Captain Jean Dagnaux had been linking Algeria with Brazzaville using a Bloch 120 three-engined aircraft. Using the infrastructure of the Régie Air Afrique spanning the French territories, the Belgian company Sabena was at last able to start its own service from Brussels to the Congo on 23rd February 1935: each of the two companies operated the route once a fortnight so as to offer overall a weekly service.

For six months from October 1934 to April 1935 Régie Air Afrique loaded nothing but post and parcels on the service (Paris) Algiers/Brazzaville. But the Director of the Institut Pasteur in Brazzaville considered the humanitarian role of the new service also to be invaluable, as he recorded in the Bulletin of the PTT of October 1935:

"I the undersigned, (René) Boisseau, Director of the Institut Pasteur in Brazzaville, certify that I consigned to the care of the pilots of Air Afrique Alger-Congo during their voyages of December 1934 and January 1935 a quantity of BCG anti-tuberculosis vaccine, which permitted the vaccination of 688 natives. Since this vaccine had to be used within 10 days of its preparation, it could not have arrived within the required period by any other means of transport than the aeroplane.

"The regular service of Air Afrique Alger-Congo also permitted the completion of an analysis of the water of the Kasai River which the Ministry had been requesting for some years, and which had not given satisfactory results due to the excessive duration of the voyage from Bangui to Brazzaville by boat.."

The particular role of Madagascar in French airmail policy

Madagascar, a French colony located 7,500 miles from France, out in the ocean at the southeast end of Africa, made its appearance in airmail history on 29th July 1934, when "the great pilot René Lefèvre, "who had already on two occasions forged a link between France and the 'Great Island' in single engined sports or touring planes" [16] inaugurated the first Tananarive/Maintirano/Mozambique/Quelimane/Tete/Broken Hill airmail flight. He opened up Madagascar by connecting it with the British Imperial route from London to the Cape, on which Broken Hill, a Rhodesian mining town, was an important stopping point. From then on, the mail from France took 10 days instead of 30 by the traditional sea route.

Run as part of the public service, this line was devoted exclusively to mail (there were 30 kilograms of post on the first flight) and was run under state control using two SPCA 218 aircraft leased by the French state to the Governor General of Madagascar at the peppercorn rent of 1 franc. These machines

were piloted by two men – Lefèvre and Assolant – who need to be considered together as the creators and pioneers air transport in Madagascar and who took turns in operating the service on the Broken Hill route.

In summer 1935 the two SPCA 218 aircraft were taken off the route and replaced by three-engined Bloch 120 machines which had already been used by Régie Air Afrique on its service from Algiers to Brazzaville. The Tananarive/Broken Hill service opened to passenger traffic in the month of August, and was then extended to Elizabethville (in the south of the Congo – today known as Lubumbashi) in November 1935: it connected alternately with Régie Air Afrique and Sabena. Madagascar was now linked directly to France.

Régie Air Afrique took over responsibility for the Algiers/Tananarive service from end to end on 1st September 1937, when the duration of the journey was reduced to six days. Airmail between France and the Great Island then experienced a remarkable period of growth. The major factors were:

• The gain in time achieved: six days by aeroplane against 30 by boat.

• The care taken in distributing the airmail:

"At Tananarive, the sorting of the airmails only takes half an hour. A siren installed on the roof of the PTT offices announces to the users that the letters can be handed out at the counter to people requesting them. The postmen set off on their delivery rounds immediately, and the whole of the mail for the capital is delivered a maximum of 3 hours after the arrival of the plane." [17]

(It cannot be overemphasised that, in 1938, airmail and air-freight were truly considered as express products.)

• The practice of innovative postal policies: there was an appreciable reduction of the airmail surcharge on 1st September 1937, and customers were attracted by the possibility of sending by air "postcards and visiting cards carrying wishes expressed in a maximum of five words, on the occasion of Christmas and the New Year" without airmail surcharge.

The result was that more than 60% of correspondence to Madagascar was sent by aeroplane.

Thus Madagascar was opened up from the outside. It now remained to access the interior.

On this great island, larger than France and sparsely populated, the communication routes were few in number and of bad quality, particularly during the rainy season. With the support of the local authorities and Lefèvre and Assolant, the idea of complementing the long-haul mail links by connecting with internal postal routes serving the majority of towns made rapid progress. On 27th October 1936, the Governor General of Madagascar created the Malagasy postal network. It was organised under government control and was initially operated using two SPCA 218 aircraft taken from the Tananarive/Broken Hill service, and then in 1937 by fast single-engined Caudron Simoun postal aeroplanes (cruising speed 175mph).

Although the French Post was normally a conservative body, the object of this government controlled service was remarkably progressive: to provide without surcharge the

ABOVE **Caudron Goeland.** *RAF Museum*

BELOW **Madagascan airmail routes 1938.** *From Aviette postale, No 135, Dec 1937, p. 147*

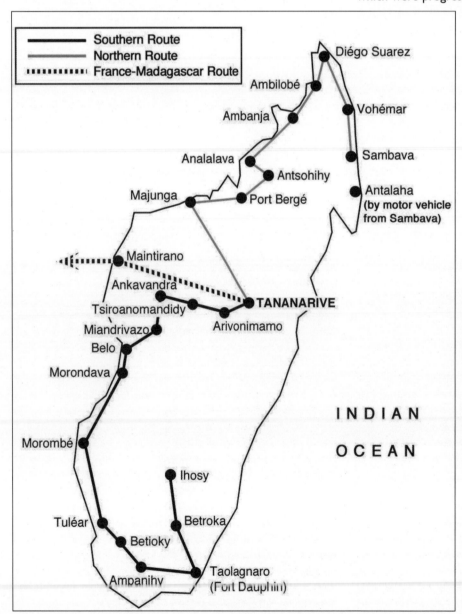

Southern Route
Northern Route
France-Madagascar Route

Diégo Suarez
Ambilobé
Vohémar
Ambanja
Analalava
Antsohihy
Sambava
Majunga
Port Bergé
Antalaha
(by motor vehicle from Sambava)
Maintirano
Ankavandra
TANANARIVE
Tsiroanomandidy
Arivonimamo
Miandrivazo
Belo
Morondava
INDIAN
Morombé
OCEAN
Ihosy
Tuléar
Betroka
Betioky
Taolagnaro
Ampanihy
(Fort Dauphin)

weekly transport of post by air between Tananarive and as many localities as possible.

In 1939 the Malagasy postal network consisted of two lines, which were progressively developed and expanded:

• The Northern Line was inaugurated on 13th December 1936 after the preparatory work had been carried out for several months by military aviation. It connected Tananarive with Diego Suarez, providing a service to six locations: Majunga, Port Bergé, Antsohihy, Analalava, Ambanja and Ambilobé. Moreover, due to the absence of ground facilities (the mail was thrown overboard to deliver it to the six landing fields),[18] the modernisation of the operation allowed the line to be extended to Vohemar and Sambava, and to link Sambava to Antalana, an important centre for vanilla production, by means of a post van. On the other hand, the low-set wings of the Caudron Simoun made parachute launches [ie when throwing mail overboard] dangerous, and obliged the service to retract this method of delivery at the sites without proper facilities, and to replace it with vehicle services. An extra delivery point at Madirovalo was introduced between Tananarive and Majunga.

• The Southern Line was opened on 31st October 1937. It connected Tananarive with Ihosy, serving 14 locations: Arivonimamo, Tsiroanomandidy, Ankavandra, Miandrivazo, Belo, Morondava, Manja, Morombé, Tuléar, Betioky, Ampanihy, Tsihombe, Behara (Fort Dauphin) and Betroka.

An attractive sticker, in either red or violet, was affixed to all mail loaded onto the first flight:

Mail Carried by Air

Destination	Time gained by aeroplane (days)			Percentage of mail by plane		
	Year opened	1935	1936	Year opened	1935	1936
India	5/8	8/12	8/12	3%	11%	16%
East Africa	8/23	10/23	10/23	5%	15%	20%
South Africa	6/8	8/10	8/10	1%	5%	9%
Australia	-	12/20	12/20	-	5%	9%

"AIRMAIL

First weekly service between TANANARIVE AND THE SOUTH OF THE ISLAND with a connection to the France-Congo-Madagascar route.

31st October-2nd November 1937."

In each direction, the two services linked up with the Europe/Congo/Madagascar service. They made considerable reductions in the postal delivery times to the interior of the island: two days against 16 from Tananarive to Sambava, and a few hours to Manja instead of nine days.

As a result of increased traffic, the administration was forced to slow down the development of the two-way postal service due to the limited capacity of the Caudron Simoun, and to forbid the transport by aeroplane of air parcels, newspapers and printed matter. On each route, the traffic exceeded 250 kilograms per week – 25 tonnes over a full year. It had to consider putting to work an aircraft with a larger carrying capacity, and the two-engined Caudron Goeland was introduced in April 1939.

But the public was not entirely satisfied. "The public, far from not recognising the advantages of the speed of aircraft, wanted all overseas letter mail carried by air, without any surcharge, on the same basis as the British colonies which used the services of Imperial Airways." [19]

So what was happening in the British colonies?

3 A POSTAL REVOLUTION: "THE EMPIRE AIRMAIL SCHEME"

A key date in airmail history is 29th June 1937: the inauguration of the Empire Airmail Scheme.

On that date a Short S23 seaplane named "Centurion" belonging to Imperial Airways left its sea base at Hythe near Southampton bound for South Africa, after having loaded an unusual weight of post – 3,000lb or 1,360 kilograms – exclusively consisting of un-surcharged first class mail. [20] Britain had just accomplished a postal revolution of the first order.

The gestation of a decision

Since the beginning of the 1920s, the British authorities had been considering the establishment of an Empire airmail system, which would develop communications, speed up correspondence and reinforce cohesion at the heart of the empire. The motivation was not so much postal as political. The creation of Imperial Airways constituted to some extent the first phase of the enactment of this plan. The GPO – General Post

Office – for its part did not remain inactive and undertook various activities to prepare the way, both technically and commercially. To simplify the system, it introduced two measures:

• For the calculation of air surcharges, the use of standard unit weight intervals of half an ounce (14 grams) on the long-haul Empire lines classed as "extraordinary services" and one ounce (28 grams) on the European lines classed as "ordinary services" as defined by the Universal Postal Union.

• The fixing on the Empire sectors of two uniform postage rates: one of 3 pence per half ounce for the Near East, and the other of 6 pence per half ounce for India and South Africa.

However, in spite of these incentives and an advertising campaign on the benefit of airmail, its proportion in the total postal despatches remained minimal: the business mail went by air, and personal and family correspondence by boat.

Despite the growth shown by the figures in the table above, the expectations of the political authorities were still not fulfilled. The speeding up of communications across the empire was a prime objective of national interest.

After its conception in 1933, and extensive trials in 1933 and 1934, the Empire Airmail Programme was adopted on 20th December 1934 by the British Government. From 1937 the whole of first class mail would be transported by aeroplane from the United Kingdom to the territories of the British Empire as well as from these countries and territories participating in the programme into the United Kingdom. The execution of the plan was conferred upon Imperial Airways.

The conditions for success

Considering that these were long-haul routes, the revolutionary decision was matched by ambitious objectives.

The quantities of mail involved were considerable for that time. The weekly traffic leaving Great Britain was expected to be at least 20 tonnes: two tonnes to Egypt, five to East and South Africa, seven to India, Singapore and Hong Kong and six to Australia. In reality, since the majority of the territories had decided to participate in the programme, Imperial Airways would handle a volume of Empire Post of about 2,000 tonnes per year. [21]

Confronted with this formidable challenge, Imperial Airways and its controlling authorities had only a limited time to build up the necessary capacity, negotiate new contractual arrangements, fix an appropriate set of postal regulations and establish a timetable for their progressive introduction.

Imperial Airways Short S23 Empire Flying Boat. *MAP*

• Necessary capacity

Since the aircraft then in service could not offer sufficient capacity, Imperial Airways took a bold decision: it placed an order on the basis of drawings with the manufacturers Short Brothers, and bought 28 Short S23 or C class flying boats, which it was to operate under the name of Empire Flying Boats.

The Short S23 C class was a monoplane flying boat with a high cantilevered wing fitted with four Bristol "Pegasus XC" 790hp in-line engines. Designed to this specification by engineer Arthur Gouge, with the potential to cover distances of 1,00 miles at a speed of approximately of 150mph, it could, depending on how it was fitted out, transport from 16 to 24 passengers and 1,500 kilograms of post or goods. The fuselage consisted of two decks. The mail was loaded into a vast hold situated on the upper deck behind the crew and into compartments built in the lower deck, one forward and one aft.

The maiden flight of the Short Empire Flying Boat took place on 3rd July 1936. It was put into commercial service on 30th October 1936 on the sector from Alexandria to Brindisi.

• Contractual arrangements

After the publication of a White Paper on the subject, the British Government entered into a 15-year contract with Imperial Airways, commencing on 1st January 1938. Under the terms of this new convention:

1. Imperial Airways undertook to carry out nine return flights per week leaving from Southampton, four towards Africa and five towards Asia, all passing via Alexandria in Egypt.

   In return for these undertakings in terms of frequency and capacity, Imperial Airways received, in the context of the Empire Airmail Scheme and in addition to its receipts from passengers and goods traffic:

2. A remuneration from the British Post Office (corresponding to traffic of 1,200 tonnes per year for the first seven years and 1,500 tonnes per year for the remaining eight years) and from the postal services of the participating territories.

3. A decreasing subsidy granted by the British Government and the 31 participating territorial bodies.

In total, in each of the first three years Imperial Airways was to receive an annual sum of £2,150,000 of which £935,000 was in the form of subsidies.

This contract gave rise to criticism from liberal circles, concerned both about the Imperial Airways monopoly, and about the amount of the subsidy, and also from certain Territories and Dominions, who thought the bill was too costly and continued to charge airmail surcharges.

• New postal rates

The scale of weights was modified and the airmail surcharge was discontinued. From then on the customer did not have to choose between the aeroplane – fast but expensive – and the boat – economical but slow. As is usual, the Post used the fastest transport method to get to the destination.

1. Previous situation:
   Seamail: 1½ pence for the first ounce
   1 penny per additional ounce
   Airmail: Normal postage + surcharge of 6 pence per ½ ounce

2. New situation:
   1½ pence per ½ ounce for letters
   1 penny for postcards

• Introduction in stages

There was no question of introducing such an ambitious project in a single operation. Apart from a few exceptions, the plan was built up in three stages:

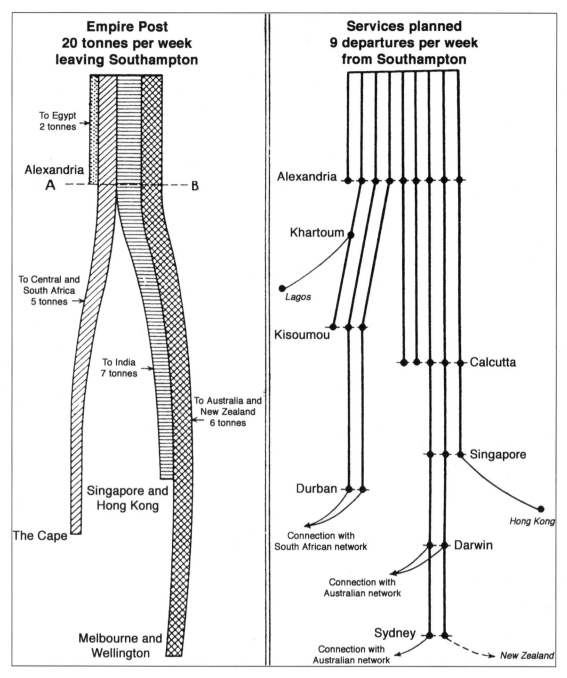

**Empire Post
20 tonnes per week
leaving Southampton**

To Egypt
2 tonnes

Alexandria
A ——————— B

To Central and
South Africa
5 tonnes →

To India
7 tonnes →

To Australia and
New Zealand
6 tonnes →

Singapore and
Hong Kong

The Cape

Melbourne and
Wellington

**Services planned
9 departures per week
from Southampton**

Alexandria

Khartoum

Lagos

Kisoumou

Calcutta

Singapore

Durban

Hong Kong

Connection with
South African network

Darwin

Connection with
Australian network

Sydney

Connection with
Australian network

New Zealand

LEFT Diagram for
weekly distribution of
first class Empire Post
(excluding America)
leaving Great Britain
and the air services
planned for its trans-
portation.
*"L'aéronautique",
February 1939*

1. 29th June 1937: Sudan, East Africa and South Africa (Nigeria was not involved in this plan).
2. 23rd February 1938: Egypt, India, Burma, Malay States.
3. 28th July 1938: Australia, New Zealand, Papua-New Guinea. Hong Kong was only integrated on 2nd September 1938 and Iraq on 15th May 1939.

A startling success
Tinged with a dash of jealousy, an American aviation expert wrote in 1939:

"Now a 'Crofter' on the shores of Scapa Flow in the Orkney Islands off the northeast coast of Scotland can send a letter by air in about 10 days to his cousin over 13,000 miles away in Sydney, Australia, for a penny – ha'penny or three cents. Formerly it cost him a shilling, three pence or about thirty cents."

To clarify his thoughts a little further he added the following

note at the bottom of the page: "A New Yorker can send a half-ounce airmail letter to his army cousin in Manila, Philippines, 11,000 miles away in 6 days for 50 cents." [22]

The Empire Airmail scheme, sometimes called the "all up mail scheme" because it was designed to convey all the first class mail by air, brought considerable tonnages to Imperial Airways. The traffic leaving Great Britain reached 1,100 tonnes in 1938, which would be in the order of 1,500 tonnes in a full year (around 500 tonnes to India and Hong Kong, 500 tonnes to Australia and 500 tonnes to Africa), and more than 2,000 tonnes in both directions added together.

The success even exceeded the initial forecasts and swamped the available capacity. This was the case for the Christmas post bound for Australia in 1938. In order to cope with an influx of 240 tonnes during the seven weeks just before Christmas, Imperial Airways had to reduce its passenger traffic, press into service every available aircraft, call upon the Royal Air Force and even – the ultimate disgrace for an empire line – use a foreign airline. [23]

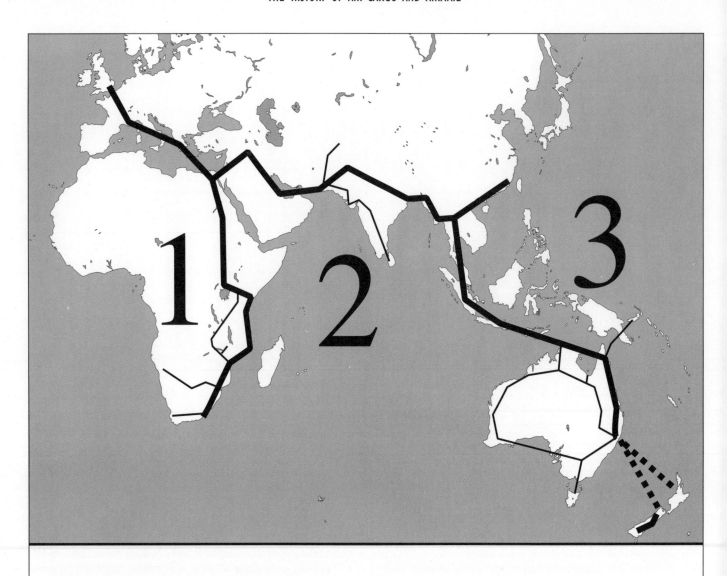

Timetable for start up of operations for Empire Airmail Scheme
Stage 1 29th June 1937: Basutoland, Bechuanaland, Kenya, Mauritius, Northern Rhodesia, Nyasaland, South and West Africa, Southern Rhodesia, Sudan, Swaziland, Tanganyika, Uganda, South Africa, Zanzibar

Stage 2 23rd February 1938: Aden, Bahrain, Brunei, Burma, Ceylon, Dubai, Egypt, India, Labuan, Malay States, Mascate, North Borneo, Palestine, Sarawak, Seychelles, Gulf States, Tibet, Transjordan

Stage 3 28th July 1938: Australia, Banks Islands, Cook Islands, Fanning Island, Fiji Islands, Gilbert & Ellis Islands, Hong Kong, Nauru, New Guinea, New Hebrides, New Zealand, Norfolk Island, Papua New Guinea, Samoa, Salomon Islands, Tonga

Source: "La poste aérienne dans L'Empire Britannique" ("Airmail within the British Empire") in "Bulletin d'information", Ministry of PTT, Paris, 1939

The infectiousness of good examples
Following the British initiative, The Netherlands eliminated their airmail surcharge for mail to the Dutch Indies on 5th June 1937 and decided to send all first class mail by air, while changing the postal rates in the following manner (in Dutch cents):

	Before 5 June 1937			After 5 June
	Sea mail	+ Surcharge	= Total	1937
< 5 grams	6	+ 30	= 36	12.5
to 10 grams	6	+ 50	= 56	25
10 to 20 grams	6	+ 75	= 81	

The Convention between the Dutch Government and KLM was modified as a result: "The Postal Administration guarantees for each week, on the outward and homebound services, a minimum freight load [24] of 1,100 kilograms which will be paid for at the rate of 42.50 florins per kg for 600kg and 12.50 florins per kg for 500kg." [25] Thus, each of the interested parties made its own contribution: the old sea mail postage rate was doubled, KLM's average unit remuneration was reduced by over 50%, and the administration of the PTT transferred all first class mail to airmail.

In 1938 KLM transported over 168 tonnes of post on the Amsterdam/Bandung service, compared with 62 in 1935.

Unfortunately, not all the colonial nations followed the same example.

6 AIRMAIL IN EUROPE

In contrast to what happened in the United States, the history of the beginnings of commercial aviation in Europe is not intimately linked to that of airmail.

On the contrary, the three categories of traffic – passenger, goods and post – each contributed to the start up of airlines. No doubt the European public found aviation appealing, distinguished as it was by the exploits of the war, and there was an eagerness to transport goods by air across a Continent bristling with Customs barriers.

I THE OBSTACLES TO THE DEVELOPMENT OF AIRMAIL IN EUROPE

Let us recall the judgement recorded in the Annals of the French PTT in 1919:

"In theory aircraft are fast; in practice they are irregular, prone to frequent accidents and expensive. They have another major disadvantage: no night flights. Compared with such inadequacies, the railways only show advantages: no doubt they are slower on paper, but they are regular, safe and inexpensive. And above all they travel through the night, this enchanted period beloved of postmen, which allows them to convey and sort the mail while their customers sleep."

The attitude of the Post Offices was more or less the same everywhere: the aeroplane would become a competitive means of transport from the moment when it flew regularly, throughout the year and on every night of the week. It was against this background, in principle rather unfavourable, that the infant airlines fought so doggedly to obtain a few scraps of particularly profitable business: surcharged airmail.

The London-Paris service offers a good example of the limitations of airmail in Europe, in spite of the obstacle of the Channel.

Without waiting for the end of hostilities, Holt Thomas, the founder of the Air Transport and Travel Company, had already proposed in 1917 the creation of an Express Airmail Service between London and Paris. Gifted with a fertile imagination, he even suggested that postal aircraft should land on the roof of the Central Post Office Building in London! In that same year,

the French PTT had approached the Post Office proposing a similar service. Contacts were renewed after the Armistice and led to the signature of an Airmail Agreement concerning aerial post between France and Great Britain. Following this Airmail Agreement, the Air Transport and Travel Company and its French associate, La Compagnie Générale Transaérienne, opened a daily Paris/London service on 10th November 1919. In normal circumstances, aeroplanes left Paris-Le Bourget and London-Hounslow at 12.30hrs and landed at their destinations at 14.45hrs.

On the face of things, this service seemed excellent. Airmail letters could be posted in France at all post offices, but only in certain large towns in Great Britain. Special collections, as late as possible, were made at eight post offices in Paris and seven in London. These letters, which were handed in by 10.30hrs at the Hotel des Postes in the Rue du Louvre in Paris or at the Post Office in Lombard Street in London, were distributed on the same day between 17.00hrs and 18.00hrs in London or Paris respectively. All items of correspondence were accepted, both ordinary and registered, subject to the payment of a surcharge in addition to the normal postage and to the statement on the envelope "Londres par avion" for post leaving Paris and "Airmail Express" for that leaving London. In reality, it was quickly recognised that the surcharge was too expensive, the time saved was minimal or illusory, and the reliability erratic.

The surcharge had been fixed at the outset at a very high level. Too high: 3 francs per price band of 20 grams on departure from Paris and 2 shillings and 6 pence per ounce (28 grams) for post leaving London. Initially, this almost deterrent surcharge included the cost of special delivery by a post boy on arrival; it was reduced on two occasions in 1920, so that from July onwards it only amounted to 0.25 Fr from Paris and 2 pence from London.

The time saving was more theoretical than actual, since the timetables were not based on the habits of commercial companies, who were accustomed to signing mail at the end of the afternoon. Letters posted in the morning in the special letter boxes in Paris and London were actually the letters from the previous evening. In practice, the transit time was not 7 or 8 hours but 24 hours. The night mail train on which the letters posted on the previous evening were sorted, still maintained its advantage.

ABOVE **Farman Goliath.**
RAF Museum

LEFT **Loading mail onto an Air France aircraft.**
RAF Museum

grams per day as a result of the reduction of the surcharge, it then fell back from 1921 onwards (2,130kg for the whole year).

The failure shown by the Paris/London service is instructive. It demonstrated that the development of airmail over short and medium distances, barring exceptional circumstances, was subject to three conditions: absolute regularity, low or zero surcharges and finally an indisputable saving in time which can only be achieved through night flights.

Saint Exupéry wrote: "Each night we lose the advantage which we have gained over railways and mail boats during the day." A view confirmed by Major Wronsky, the Managing Director of Deutsche Lufthansa: "The development of night flights is a factor which is essential for the progress of aerial post in Europe."

The Royal Air Force made the first experiment in regular night-time airmail connections on 14th May 1919 between Hawkinge and Cologne, for the transport of military post. On the Paris-London route, chief pilot René Labouchère carried out an experimental link in a Farman Goliath aircraft during the night of 7th-8th June 1922. Maurice Noguès was instrumental in the transition from the experimental to the operational phase. In September 1923 the Compagnie Franco-Roumaine, of which Noguès was chief pilot, opened the first regular night service over the 375 miles between Belgrade and Bucharest, the last section of the Paris/Bucharest service.

Germany was also concerned to develop at an early stage regular night services. The first flights intended for mail transport, were carried out in 1924 over the Baltic on the Warnemünde (near Rostock)/Karlshamn/Stockholm route. Joseph Kaspar was at that time a pilot with Junkers Luftverkehr:

"The route had been designed in such a way that one took as reference points the lighthouses for sea navigation, and reached one's destination by proceeding from lighthouse to lighthouse. The only difficulty in bad weather was how to

As the last straw, the operational regularity during the first few months was deplorable: only 48% of the planned flights actually took place between November 1919 and March 1920. As in Switzerland and Germany during the same period, it was necessary to fall back on a procedure for redirecting mails by train in case the flight schedule was interrupted.

It should be no surprise therefore that the service never established itself. At the beginning of 1920 it did not carry above 40-50 letters a day, and although it reached 10-15 kilo-

ABOVE **Loading a Dornier Merkur mail plane at Cologne, 1929.**
Lufthansa

BELOW **Inland European night mail service with Lufthansa, 1929.**
Lufthansa

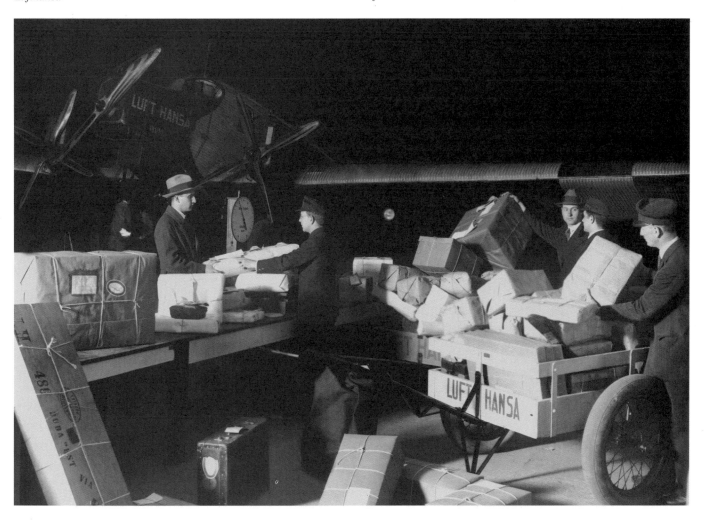

Luftfracht-Verladung auf das Nachtflugzeug
der Lufthansa Berlin-London.

ABOVE LEFT **Loading cargo onto a Lufthansa Junkers G34 operating the Berlin-London nightflight.**
Lufthansa

BELOW LEFT **Lufthansa Junkers F13.**
Lufthansa

ABOVE **Loading cargo into a Lufthansa Junkers G24.**
Lufthansa

BELOW **Loading cargo into a Lufthansa Fokker FIII.**
Lufthansa

locate these lighthouses, often at a distance at over 110 kilometres [c60 miles]." [1]

These were still only experimental flights. The first regular night service which was open to passengers and post was started on 1st May 1926 between Berlin and Königsberg (now Kaliningrad) after the installation of the "Illuminated route" between the two towns (with revolving search lights, neon lamps or gas burners installed on masts).

The Swedish company ABA in the person of Captain Karl Florman carried out a particularly promising series of airmail flights in 1928 between Stockholm and London, via Malmö, Hamburg and Amsterdam on board a Junkers F13. During the first flight, made between 18th and 20th June 1928, over 12,000 items of mail were conveyed in each direction. Sweden, which was off the beaten track, had recognised the advantages of aerial post in 1920. Whereas a letter posted in Stockholm on a Monday evening, and conveyed by the normal route, was only delivered in Paris or London on Thursday morning, the same letter sent by a daytime flight was distributed on Wednesday morning; by using a night flight one could save a further 24 hours. This was proved by a flight on 18th June: mail posted in Stockholm at 15.30hrs was distributed in London on the next day, 19th June, between 14.30 and 17.00hrs. The Swedish Postal Authority, one of airmail's pioneers, had fulfilled a postal dream: the mail had got through in under 24 hours.

It was not until 1929 that night mail flights began to proliferate throughout Europe. The first services were regular but not permanent: in most cases the services only operated in summer. Air Union was the first to open a Paris/London service on 9th April, then Sabena began a Brussels/London service on 14th April, while Deutsche Lufthansa launched a series of four routes on behalf of the Reichspost, and the different Scandinavian airlines united their strength to cover the long route Helsingfors/Stockholm/Malmö/Copenhagen/Hannover.

2 THE EUROPEAN NIGHT-TIME POSTAL NETWORK: THE DREAM

Comparisons between the United States and Europe were unavoidable. On the one side was a coherent postal network, designed on a continental scale, the product of a global vision imposed by an omnipotent administration with the agreement of Congress. On the other side, there were routes without an overall plan, launched at the whims of postal administrations from different countries and by different airlines. The idea of integrating these disjointed operations into a European night post network germinated from 1930 onwards, and gave rise to three projects in the space of six years. All were failures, for lack of a common purpose.

The first project came from Captain Karl Florman. It was presented at the Annual General Meeting of IATA in Antwerp during September 1930. This "Project for the itineraries of night time postal air services in Central Europe" covered a geographical area which extended from Riga and Helsingfors to Paris and London, and from Oslo to Budapest. Centred on Germany, it was constructed around half a dozen mail platforms: Berlin, Königsberg, Hannover, Cologne, Copenhagen and Brussels. (Note that Cologne, Hannover and Brussels became the principal platforms of Europe's express freight operators – TNT, DHL and UPS.)

Captain Florman's project, which included several night-time links, was no doubt premature. It was received without enthusiasm. The airlines hid behind the undeniable difficulties of carrying it through and did not follow it up.

The second project had postal origins. The international bureau of the Universal Postal Union convened a European Airmail Commission in Prague from 8th to 18th June 1931, bringing together the European Post Offices and the airlines. Placed under the active chairmanship of Brigadier General F. H. Williamson, the delegate of the British Post Office, the commission voted in favour of a "Project for a European Postal Network – night-time services with extensions by means of daytime services". This project was much more ambitious than the Florman proposal: it covered the whole of Europe from Moscow to Lisbon and from Oslo to Athens.

Unfortunately, the efforts of the Commission could not have come at a worse time: the world economic crisis was beginning to make deep inroads into the European economies, and the various states had other priorities than subsidising an airmail network. The European Airmail Commission, fully aware of the problems, showed great realism in its conclusions:

"In presenting its plan for the creation of a general air network for Europe, the Commission was under no illusion that the realisation of this plan might encounter many and diverse difficulties ... But it expresses the hope that in setting out the first markers for the rational organisation of air connections for European post, it will have succeeded in making some contribution to the development of postal aviation." [2]

It was a vain hope: to this day, the Continental postal authorities have not managed to construct a European postal network. The task was finally taken over in the 1980s by their most redoubtable competitors, the large private express transport companies!

The third project was the work of Professor Karl Pirath, a German academic and aeronautics expert. Professor Pirath's plan, published in 1936 [3] when Chancellor Adolph Hitler was beginning to worry the European capitals, stood no chance of being carried out. Like the plan put forward by the Prague Postal Commission, it covered the whole of Europe through a dozen interlinked platforms. Today, one would describe it as a multi-hub night-time network. In contrast to the first two projects, it was not reserved exclusively for postal traffic. It would be a mixed network, with freight and post, operated by cargo aircraft – Junkers 52, as the author imagined. Both in the nature of its services and the location of its platforms, it anticipated by almost 50 years the system operated by modern providers of express freight and mail services.

The failure of these projects on a European scale did not prevent the opening of new night postal services between different states (Paris/Brussels/Cologne/Berlin in 1933, London/Cologne/Berlin in 1936 etc). But the European dream had been shattered.

3 BACK TO REALITY: THE DOMESTIC POSTAL NETWORKS

In the absence of a Europe-wide network, the postal administrations continued to develop their national networks, using the capacities from scheduled services or adopting special

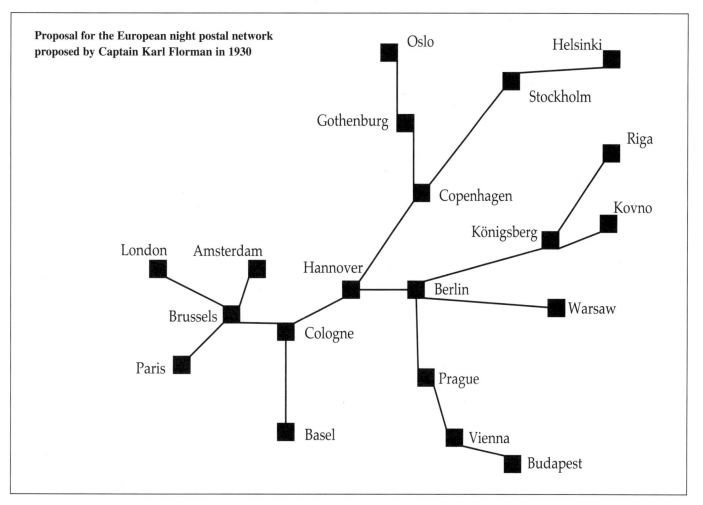

Proposal for the European night postal network proposed by Captain Karl Florman in 1930

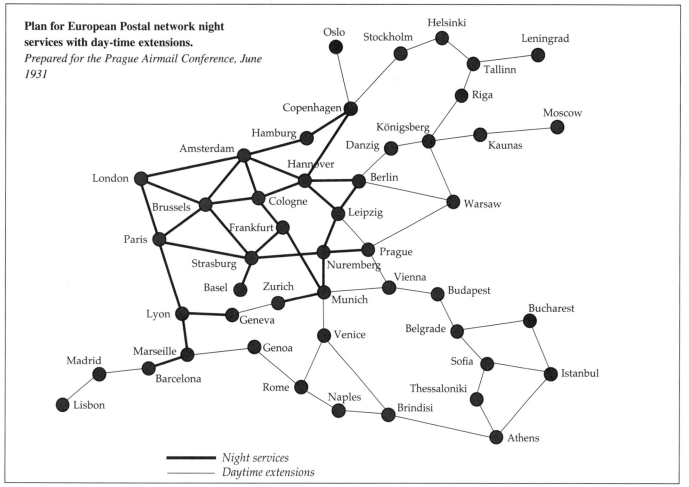

Plan for European Postal network night services with day-time extensions.

Prepared for the Prague Airmail Conference, June 1931

Night services
Daytime extensions

ABOVE A Lufthansa Junkers Ju 52.
Lufthansa

BELOW **Lufthansa Junkers Ju 52 loading freight, 1933.**
Lufthansa

ABOVE **Loading cargo into a Lufthansa Junkers W33.**
Lufthansa

BELOW **Loading a Lufthansa Heinkel He 111 in 1936.**
Lufthansa

measures. The domestic airmail networks started to take shape at the beginning of the 1930s, alongside the international links which had appeared from 1919.

The evolution of the internal postal services in three countries – Germany, Great Britain and France – are instructive.

Germany

Germany was the first to set up an autonomous postal network, beginning in 1929. At the time it possessed the densest air network in Europe. Deprived of its colonies by the Treaty of Versailles, it had been able to concentrate all its efforts on the construction of a remarkable air system, which linked the major German towns and covered the whole of central Europe. However, these numerous connections had been established as a result of the demand from passengers, and rarely fulfilled the requirements of the Post, particularly with respect to the timetables. This led to the forward-thinking idea of the Reichspost to create its own air services.

The first night services were launched in 1929. They were reserved exclusively for postal traffic, and were generally operated on a sub-contract basis by Deutsche Lufthansa on behalf of the Post. Initially, they only operated during the fine season but in spite of being isolated and seasonal, these services already formed part of larger concept, which was methodically developed over the years by extending the operating periods and opening new services.

In 1935 [4] the night-time airmail network consisted of five routes operated by Junkers Ju52s:

Berlin/Hannover/Cologne/London
Berlin/Halle/Leipzig
Hannover/Frankfurt/Stuttgart
Cologne/Brussels/Paris
Cologne/Frankfurt/Munich/Nuremberg

The majority of the airborne post was therefore conveyed over the Reichspost's own network: 64% in 1936, 61% in 1937.

The airmail network expanded considerably from 1937 onwards within the context of an aeronautical policy, which was more the reflection of military preoccupations than of postal requirements. In 1939, the postal network consisted of 14 lines and covered a length of 4,250 miles. The total of German airmail traffic, by far the largest in Europe, rose to 6,132 tonnes (including 9% of the surcharged letters, 4% of airmail parcels, 10% of newspapers and 77% of non surcharged post).

Great Britain

Great Britain was a latecomer to adopting domestic airmail services. It should be said that a priori the attitude of the Post Office was not favourable to air transport: "On the whole, the public is satisfied with the speed and regularity of the present mail transport" in Europe, wrote the Director General in 1923. Between 1923 and 1928, there were only a few unsuccessful attempts. One series of experimental airmail flights started on 15th September 1923 on a Belfast/Manchester/ Birmingham/ Plymouth route, but the weather was uniformly bad for almost a month, and put paid to all Alan Cobham's efforts.

A second attempt made from April to June 1924 by Northern Airlines fared no better. Like the previous attempt, this Belfast/Liverpool service was aimed at speeding up the distribution of sea mail arriving from the USA and at transporting

newspapers, but it survived for less than three months in disastrous weather conditions.

Things only got moving seriously in 1934. The Highland Airways Company received the first Royal Mail Pennant on 29th May 1934, authorising it to carry six times per week, without surcharge, first class mail (letters and postcards) between Inverness in the north of Scotland and Kirkwall in the Orkney Isles. This section by air was later integrated into a very comprehensive system of postal transport joining the Shetland Isles (north of the Orkney Isles) and Glasgow, and successively combining the steamer between the Shetlands and the Orkneys, an aircraft between Kirkwall and Inverness, the train between Inverness and Glasgow and then either an express train or an aeroplane from Glasgow to London. Although an extreme example, it shows clearly that the aeroplane is not an autonomous method of mail transport but an essential component of often very complex postal routing systems.

The Inverness/Kirkwall service had been initiated in order to resolve a very local postal problem, without reference to any national airmail plan. The same thing happened with the Isle of Man service by the Blackpool and West Coast Services Company from 3rd February 1935, and the Channel Islands service (Southampton/Jersey on 1st June 1937 and Southampton/Guernsey on 8th May 1939).

Postal traffic on UK domestic airlines reached 541 tonnes in 1938.

France

If the German national postal network is an illustration of the methodical Germanic mind, and if the British postal services are a demonstration of English pragmatism, the belated creation of the domestic French network in July 1935 is a shining example of the Gallic preference for centralising and systemising. There were three phases in this short and eventful history.

• Phase 1 – Air Bleu, first approach: surcharged post and daytime flights – 1935–1936
The foundation of Air France had left several first class players of the great age of Aéro Postale (B. de Massimi, Didier Daurat etc) on the touchline. The latter, with the support of the Ministry for Post, proposed the creation of an airline to be entrusted with operating a postal network inside France. The contract between the Postal Administration and the new company, known as Air Bleu, was approved in February 1935. With the benefit of hindsight, it is difficult to understand how these airmail specialists could have started out on a path which, even at that time, contained all the ingredients for failure: daytime post, with a surcharge, over short and medium distances!

The surcharges applying to airmail within metropolitan France were published in the JO (Official Journal) of 30th June 1935: 2.50 F for a letter of 10 grams (and per fraction of 10 grams) in addition to the normal postage of 0.50 F. Therefore, a letter for Bordeaux would be charged at a total of 3.00 F (instead of 0.50 F) to be sent by air ... in the daytime.

In close liaison with the French Post Office, Air Bleu had organised a very comprehensive and coherent postal network, consisting of seven routes, obviously centred on Paris, serving the majority of the country (see map). As France did not possess the ground support services necessary for night flights, only day-time flights could be considered.

The first flight took place on 10th July 1935 from Le

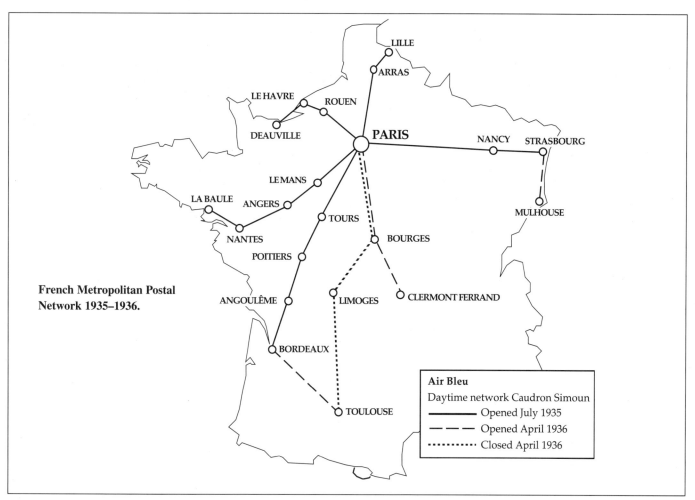

**French Metropolitan Postal
Network 1935–1936.**

Air Bleu
Daytime network Caudron Simoun
——— Opened July 1935
– – – Opened April 1936
········ Closed April 1936

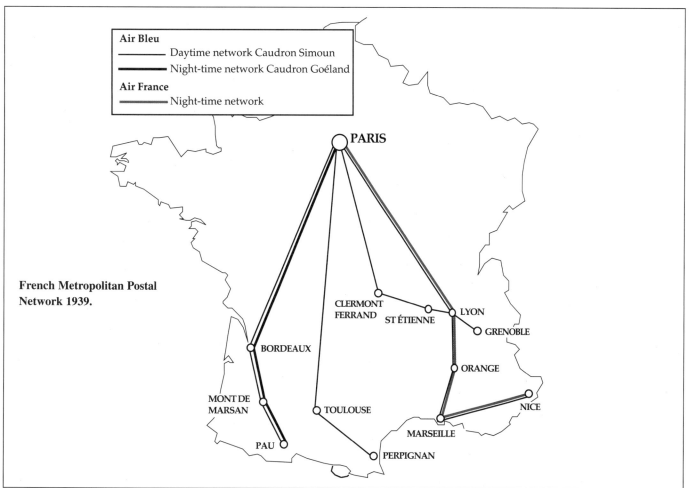

Air Bleu
——— Daytime network Caudron Simoun
——— Night-time network Caudron Goéland
Air France
——— Night-time network

**French Metropolitan Postal
Network 1939.**

Air France Bloch 220 at Paris Le Bourget.
Air France

Bourget, to Tours/Poitiers/Angoulême/Bordeaux. Raymond Vanier, the airmail pioneer, was at the controls: "On 10th July 1935 at 11.00, Monsieur G. Mandel, the Minister for Post handed over to me the first bag of mail."

The Air Bleu network was operated with a fleet of 11 Caudron Simoun low-winged single-engined monoplanes, of metal and fabric construction, fitted with Renault engines, with a cruising speed of approximately 175mph. They were equipped with the latest navigational instruments to permit all-weather flying (to ensure the regularity of the mail) and could carry a payload of 150-200 kilograms, which soon proved to be over-generous, in proportion to the traffic.

The proposed service (with a weight surcharge for a negligible or zero saving in time, although delivery was assured in the same way as for telegrams) was nothing like what the public expected, and the results in terms of mail carried were way below even the most pessimistic of forecasts. Air Bleu made great efforts to redress the situation via a number of corrective measures: the introduction of a sliding scale of charges, advertising regarding "samples and parcels", and adaptation of the network. The most important change, effective from the month of October 1935, was to modify the timetables so that Paris was no longer treated as the centre for receiving and despatching mail, but as "the hub at the centre of postal transfers between the provincial cities".

Nothing came of it all. The handicaps were insurmountable. The traffic continued to be insignificant (298 letters a day on average in May 1936) and the operation was terminated in August 1936. As often happens in France, it gloried in the technical success, and drew a veil over the commercial failure.

• Phase 2 – Air Bleu, second approach: mail with no surcharge and day flights
This predictable failure did not deter the French Postal Service from its objectives, which it set itself as follows:

"A letter posted during the evening at any point in the Territory must reach its addressee in any Department in Metropolitan France on the following morning."

In order to achieve the, the Post decided to adopt a new and modernistic strategy with three goals: [5]

"1. To provide France with an airmail system not requiring the direct collaboration of the client.

2. To integrate air transport into the general organisation for conveying mail.

3. To eliminate all airmail surcharges within the internal regime of Metropolitan France."

This was a volte face: from now on the choice of the fastest method of transport would be made by the Postal Authorities themselves, as a function of their general objectives. Air transport

Line-up of the Air Bleu aircraft in July 1935.
Air France Museum

had become an everyday matter. The Post now had an obligation to produce the end results, but was free to choose the means.

The Société Nouvelle d'Aviation Postale, or new Société Air Bleu, was founded on 1st July 1937. The game plan was clear: the state possessed the majority of the shares (52%) while Air France and the former Société Air Bleu each held 24%.

The new Metropolitan Postal Network started up in July 1937. It consisted of three routes operated by Air Bleu (Paris/Pau, Paris/Perpignan and Paris/Grenoble) and of one route Paris/Lyon/Marseilles/Nice operated by Air France flying a Bloch 220 from 16th February 1938.

After a reorganisation which completely integrated the air-mail sections into the overall transport links, the Post managed to reduce transit times by 8-24 hours, depending on individual circumstances. However, in the absence of night flights it still could not achieve its objective. Not without a note of regret, it wrote: "On the question of night flights, it is still the technical considerations which determine the rate of progress." From this observation, one can judge how backward France was in the field of airport equipment and the optical marking of air routes, compared with the United States – or even Germany.

• Phase 3 – Air Bleu, third approach: Mail without surcharge and night flights

The long-awaited day finally dawned on 10th May 1939: "Air Bleu inaugurated the service towards which all the efforts of its promoters had been directed: the night mail service" on the Paris/Bordeaux/Mont de Marsan/Pau route flying a two-engined Caudron Goéland aircraft. The mail collected at the end of the afternoon from local letterboxes in the Paris area was delivered in Pau the next morning.

With this Air Bleu service, the French Postal Authority was at last able to implement its policies. The homogeneous fleet of 14 Caudron-Renault, 11 Simoun and three Goéland aircraft were to be used for night flights and the following flying programme was established:

1. July 1939: Paris/Marseilles
2. end of 1939: Paris/Clermont Ferrand
3. beginning of 1940: Paris/Toulouse

Air France opened the Paris/Marseilles night mail service on 25th July 1939 in a three-engined Dewoitine D338 aircraft carrying 1,230 kilograms of post.

From 1st January to 2nd September 1939, the Air Bleu services transported 204 tonnes of post (or 22,565,500 letters) and those of Air France carried 315 tonnes between Paris and Marseilles: a total of 518 tonnes. However, the declaration of war halted the night-flight development programme.

7 THE NORTH ATLANTIC, OR THE CONQUEST OF THE "ROYAL ROUTE"

"My dear Elsie
Just a hurried line before we start. This letter will travel with
me in the official mailbag, the first mail to be carried over
the Atlantic. Love to all.
Your loving brother,
Jack" [1]

This short missive, scribbled on 14th June 1919 by Captain John Alcock just before his take-off from Newfoundland, is surely the most stirring letter ever to have crossed the Atlantic.

1 GREAT DEEDS WITH NO FUTURE

The North Atlantic, which had been the key sector for the shipping industry since the beginning of the 19th century, became the "Royal Route" [Ed: as it is known in French; the closest English language equivalent is "Blue Riband"] for air transport in the middle of the 20th century. Between 1919 and 1939, this long-haul mail run was the ultimate air transport goal, inspiring the largest number of individual forays, record breaking attempts and test flights until Pan American Airways started operating the commercial New York/Azores/Lisbon/Marseilles service on 20th May 1939.

The year 1919 witnessed an extraordinary triple success: within less than two months the North Atlantic was successively conquered by a seaplane, a conventional aircraft and an airship.

On 16th May 1919, an American Navy seaplane, a long-range ocean patrol type Curtiss NC4, under Lieutenant Commander Read left All Souls Bay in Newfoundland, and landed at Horta in The Azores on 17th May at 13.28hrs. This was the first crossing, but it carried no mail.

Around this time a number of British crews were hurrying to Newfoundland, hoping to make their mark. Lord Northcliffe, the proprietor of the Daily Mail, a very wealthy man and a great aviation enthusiast, had just renewed his offer of a £10,000 reward – originally published on 1st April 1913 – for the crew of the first aeroplane to fly non-stop from North America to Great Britain. All the great names in British aircraft manufacturing were there: Sopwith, Vickers, Martinsyde . . .

It was then that the Director of Postal Services in Newfoundland, aware of the exceptional advantages which a transatlantic airmail service would bring, wrote to the Director of the Sopwith team. He asked what would have to be done to send a small bag containing some official mail and a number of ordinary letters on the first flight. Thus, the Sopwith crew, consisting of Hawker and Mackenzie-Grieve, carried an official mailbag when they left Newfoundland for Ireland on 18th May 1919. Their attempt failed due to mechanical problems, but they managed to come down safely in the sea not far from the Danish cargo steamer Mary, which picked them up. This was a real piece of luck for the crew, who were feared lost for several days since the cargo steamer did not have a radio, and also for the mailbag, which was delivered to the nearest Post Office when they disembarked at a British port. A finer example of the impromptu combination of air and sea transport can hardly be imagined. The letters, stamped with a "Caribou" Canadian stamp, carried a special postmark stating: "First transatlantic Air Post. April 1919."

The second attempt was successful. Captain John Alcock and Lieutenant Arthur Whitten Brown, at the controls of their Vickers "Vimy" bomber, left St John in Newfoundland at 16.15hrs on 14th June. They made a rough landing in Ireland on the following day, 15th June 1919, at 8.40hrs. They had completed the first crossing of the North Atlantic by aeroplane, and carried a mailbag containing one letter-packet and 196 letters, including that addressed to "My Dear Elsie". [2]

The airship might have been the last to overcome the obstacle, but it made good its delay with a flourish, and entered the show with a two-way crossing. This exploit, which had been planned and organised during the war, was carried out by a British team of 31 men under the orders of Major Scott. The airship, R34, made in Britain but following a German design, was a colossal vessel, 204 metres long, propelled by five Sunbeam engines and containing 55,000m³ of gas. It left Scotland on 2nd July 1919, not carrying mail, and landed on 5th July in New York-Mineola; it left again on 10th July, carrying an official mailbag, and landed in Pulham, England, on 13th July 1919.

There were few attempted postal or commercial crossings during the 20 years between these first exploits and the opening of the scheduled North Atlantic air service on 20th May 1939. The best known is that of Commodore Richard E. Byrd. He took off from Roosevelt Field, Long Island, New York, for Le

Alcock and Brown crossing the Atlantic in their Vickers Vimy, 14 June 1919, by Coulson.
Paul Martin/Air Foyle

Bourget on 29th June 1927, a month after the triumphal flight of Lindbergh who, wishing to make the maximum possible weight reduction in his single-engined machine, had not even carried a single letter. Byrd's aeroplane was a powerful three-engined Fokker 7, named "America". It had been fitted out with the latest technical refinements including wireless telegraphy and equipment for instrument flying. In addition to the crew of four (Bert Acosta, Bernt Balchen, George Noville and Richard Byrd), the American carried an official mailbag containing 250 letters. It had been handed over to Richard Byrd by the Postmaster of New York, John Kieley, who had made him swear a formal oath to carry it duly to Paris, and had delivered to him a "Certificate of the Oath of Mail Messengers".

During the flight, which encountered rain and thick fog, a failure of the navigation instruments brought the aircraft off course. Once they had got back onto the right heading, they flew over Brest and St Brieuc, and sent out a distress call. Byrd decided to land his plane, which was running out of fuel. Rather than risking a crash landing on the ground, he managed to bring her down abruptly into the waves near the beach at Ver-sur-Mer, Calvados, France at 02.30 hours on the morning of 1st July 1927, after 40 hours in the air.

When they left the "America" the crew took refuge with the keeper of the Ver-sur-Mer lighthouse. The mail bag was handed by Byrd to Mme Decaux the postmistress at the local

post office: it was the first mail delivered by air from the United States to France. It gave rise to an exchange of greetings between the two postal administrations as is evidenced by the following transcription of the official document from the United States Post Office and the reply from the French Post:

"Post Office of the United States

BULLETIN OF VERIFICATION -
Despatch No 171 from the Exchange Office in New York for the Exchange Office in Paris

Despatch of June 21, 1927, 2.00 PM
By Airplane "America"

"THE POSTMASTER AND EMPLOYEES OF THE NEW YORK POST OFFICE SEND GREETINGS TO THE POSTMASTER AND EMPLOYEES OF THE PARIS POST OFFICE ON THIS OCCASION OF THE FIRST DIRECT AIRMAIL SERVICE BETWEEN NEW YORK, USA AND PARIS, FRANCE."

Madame Decaux answered on the same document. Her translated reply was:

"The Postmistress and staff of the Post Office of Ver-sur-Mer where the aircraft 'America' made its sea touch-down on 1st July 1927 acknowledge the good wishes of the Postmaster and his employees of the Post in New York and in turn extend their sincere good wishes and congratulations on the occa-

sion of the inauguration of the first mail 'PAR AVION' received directly in France from the United States."]

Another first was the two-way crossing of the North Atlantic made 10 years later, between 9th and 14th May 1937, by Dick Merril and Jack Lambie, pilots of Eastern Airlines, in a Lockheed Electra fitted with additional fuel tanks.

The initial purpose of the flight had been to fetch the film of the coronation of King George VI from London. However, events transformed this first two-way commercial flight between the United States and Europe, which originally should have only carried freight on the return leg. As it happened, on 9th May 1937 at 21.15 hours the crew left the Floyd Bennett Airport in New York, carrying with them the first photographs of the disaster involving the giant German airship "Hindenburg" which had occurred on 6th May. And so this became the first transatlantic flight to carry express freight in both directions.

In both the above cases, these flights were considered to be isolated exploits, great deeds that did not lead to anything. Immediately after the First World War, the state of technology in aviation did not allow anyone to contemplate a regular transatlantic service. However, these exploits did succeed in demonstrating the strategic value of certain logistic bases: Newfoundland, Ireland and The Azores.

2 THE ALLIANCE OF SEA AND AIR

"How can sea mail times be reduced?" was a question that numerous postal, shipping and airline organisations had tried to answer by making different combinations between the main sea passage and substitution of part of the route with complementary air links. This relay between sea and air transport took two different forms, depending on whether the baton – in this case the mailbags – was handed over at sea or on land.

Handover at sea

It seems that the Americans were the first to try and adopt for civilian use a technique that was reserved for the military: aircraft carriers. In August 1927 [3] tests were carried out in the sea off Boston to prove the feasibility of a link up between ships and aircraft at sea. The test was made in two directions: from ship to shore, and from shore to ship.

The ship-to-shore attempt was made on 1st August 1927 in good conditions: a Fokker 5 aircraft piloted by Clarence Chamberlain was launched from the deck of the American steamship "Leviathan" about 80 miles off the coast, and crossed the distance to terra firma without incident.

The shore-to-ship attempt was due to take place on 20th August 1927 with the official blessing of the New York Postmaster, who authorised the experiment, subject to the limitations of a maximum weight of mail of 100lb or 45 kilograms. In fact, it was a fairly hairy undertaking, since it was necessary to lower two sacks of mail by means of a rope onto the deck of the "Leviathan" whilst the aircraft flew over the ship with reduced speed and at low altitude – airmail acrobatics!

The "Leviathan" steamed out of Boston on 20th August 1927, and Lieutenant Schildhauer took off several hours later in pursuit with the mailbags. After flying 100 or so miles, he encountered heavy fog and had to turn back. The mail, brought back to land, was sent on the next boat, but the postal authorities had had time to overprint each item with an accusatory black postmark: "Airmail failed to SS Leviathan".

The experiment had hardly been convincing. The shore-to-ship formula, which was much too risky and difficult to master, was discontinued. All efforts went into the ship-to-shore technique, which was perfected by the French in 1927/1928. "In 1927, 10 years before there was any question of creating a regular airmail service to cross the North Atlantic, the President of the Compagnie Générale Transatlantique, John Dal Piaz, had the idea of combining the steamer and the aeroplane in order to save one day's time for the mail on the New York route." [4] It was done by catapulting amphibious aircraft, which had been loaded on departure, from the deck of the steamer, some hundreds of miles out from the American or European coast depending on the direction. The time saved corresponded to the difference in speed between the ship (about 28mph) and the aircraft (between 100 and 125mph).

In order to carry this project through to fruition, the Société Transatlantique Aérienne, "the first airline on the North Atlantic", was founded in 1927. The Penhoët yard was given an order for the design and manufacture of a catapult, which was installed on the rear deck of the "Ile-de-France", the newest vessel on the transatlantic route. The catapult was 35 metres long, weighed 57 tonnes and could project a mass of 4 tonnes at 110mph.

Two test flights carrying mail were completed in 1928 using a Lioré et Olivier 198 seaplane piloted by Navy Lieutenant L. Demougeot. On the voyage to New York, the first catapult launch took place on 13th August 1928, 450 miles from the American coast, with three mail bags on board.

The second launch was on the 3rd December, 700 miles from the coast, and resulted in a saving of over 27 hours: the objective had been achieved. On the return journey to Le Havre,

"the seaplane was launched on 23rd August at 7.00am while 'Ile de France' was approximately 300 kilometres [190 miles] from Bishop Rock, at the entrance to the Channel. It landed at 14.52hrs at Le Bourget airfield …The 'Ile de France' did not arrive at Le Havre until the following day, whereas the mail had already been distributed the previous evening." [5]

To mark the occasion a special sticker was affixed to each letter:

"August-September 1928
FIRST TRANSATLANTIC AIRMAIL LINK
By seaplane launched by catapult from the Ile de France
Pilot: Navy Lieutenant L. Demougeot"

Although the operation was continued on a minor scale during the summers of 1929 (eight flights) and 1930 (six flights) using an amphibious Cams 37 aircraft, the experiment was abandoned for several reasons: the low amount of traffic – less than 25 kilograms per flight, due to the high rate of the surcharge (11.50 F) and the irregularity of the service; the complexity of the launching manoeuvres as a result of the fixed position of the catapult; and finally the development of fast steamers reducing the crossing to a little over four days.

Perhaps because of their geographical situation in Europe, being further from America, the Germans proved to be the most persevering operators of this system of speeding up the mail through catapult launches and made 198 flights using this method between 1929 and 1935.

At the instigation of the Ministry of Commerce, which was eager to promote commercial relations between Germany and the United States, Deutsche Lufthansa and the shipping company Norddeutsche Lloyd decided in 1928 to join forces to create a seasonal accelerated postal service. The maiden voyage of the new steamer "Bremen" provided the opportunity for its commencement. On 22nd July 1929 the floatplane Heinkel He12 piloted by Captain Jobst Von Studnitz was launched towards the American coast by a Heinkel K2 catapult. Two and a half hours later he made a sea landing in the port of New York, with several mailbags. On the return voyage the He12 was catapult-launched 5 miles to the west of Cherbourg. It then travelled the 500 miles to Bremerhaven where a special aeroplane took over the relay for Berlin, thus gaining 24 hours for 18,000 letters. Once the experimental period had been judged satisfactory, regular operation, programmed at the beginning of the season at a more or less weekly frequency to link up with the arrivals and departures of the steamers, started up in May 1930. Until 1935, around 32 flights were made each summer, between May and September. In order to provide this service the shipping company equipped the two steamers "Bremen" and "Europa" with a movable catapult in order to facilitate the launching operations. Three types of aircraft were used: Heinkel He12 and He58 seaplanes, and then, from 1932, Junkers Ju46s – a reinforced version of the W34 which was particularly suitable for this type of activity due to its cruising speed of 125mph and its long flying range of 750 miles.

This seasonal accelerated service was put at the disposal of all post offices, as witnessed by this notice which appeared in the Information Bulletin of the French PTT Ministry in June 1932:

"Utilisation of the air services from the German steamers Bremen and Europa on the New York Line.
Since 31st May 1932 airmail of French origin with destinations in the United States and beyond, can be conveyed by means of the air link 'German steamships Bremen and Europa – New York'.
Time saving: approximately 24 hours.
Air surcharge: 4 francs per 10 grams or a fraction of 10 grams, for all categories of mail."

Handover on land

The technique consisted of reducing to an absolute minimum the length of the sea crossing, and to supplement this by the fastest possible air transit. Depending on the direction, the link between aeroplane and ship was made at the last or first port of call, preceding or following the transatlantic crossing.

The British tried out this procedure at a very early stage. For short periods in September 1923 and April 1924 they used Plymouth/Belfast and Liverpool/Belfast flights to connect with transatlantic steamers calling at Belfast. No doubt the trials were judged inconclusive since they were not followed up.

It was the Canadians who used this solution in a more consistent manner to speed up the European mails during the season when the navigation of the St Lawrence River was not blocked by ice. The handover point from ship to aircraft was at Rimouski, a riverside township about 300 miles downstream from Montreal.

Pilot H. S. Quigley [6] made the first liaison flights, each with 200 kilograms of mail, in an HS-2C seaplane, an aircraft "which played a leading role in the history of Canadian aviation." [7] The flights took place on 4th September 1927 along the Montreal/Trois Rivières/Rimouski route to connect with the "Doric", and on 16th September in the return direction, connecting with the "Express of Australia". These flights were far from being easy outings. It is said [8] that a seaplane of the Royal Canadian Air Corps, piloted by Squadron Leader J. H. Tudhope, crashed in the choppy waters of the Saint Lawrence. "They managed to save the crew and recover the mailbags. By an irony of fate, the ship finally arrived at Montreal well in advance of the mailbags. However, not to be beaten, the Authorities decided to set up an aerodrome at Rimouski. They sent mail to the coast on small boats. From there it was taken to the aerodrome."

Once it was working properly, the operation of the Montreal/Rimouski airmail service resulted in a considerable

BELOW **Particularly in Germany, "catapult messenger" flights enjoyed some degree of success, in spite of their limitations, and carried an average per flight of over 10,000 letters, all marked with a special postmark like this.**

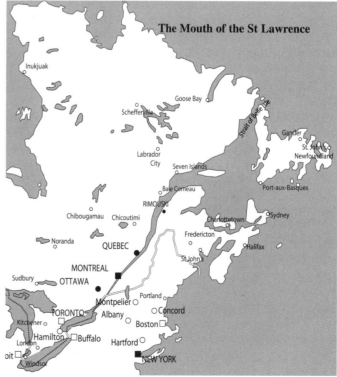

The Mouth of the St Lawrence

RIGHT **Heinkel HE-58.**
Lufthansa

BELOW **Junkers JU-46.**
MAP

RIGHT **Dornier DO-18.**
MAP

BELOW **Westland Wessex.**
MAP

BOTTOM **Focke-Wulf FW 200
Condor.**
Lufthansa

shortening of the times for transatlantic mail (48 hours inbound from Europe, 72 hours outbound), and reduced by half the interminable journey on the Saint Lawrence from its mouth to Montreal. The service went on operating until the beginning of the Second World War.

In 1932, the gathering at Ottawa of the Economic Conference of Commonwealth Countries, which adopted the famous doctrine of "Imperial Preference", was the occasion for a particularly interesting experiment in combined airmail. At the initiative of the Canadian authorities, special flights linking directly with the mail steamer "Empress of Britain" were carried out at each end of the crossing in July and August 1932, thus reducing to approximately five days the time taken to convey mail from London to Ottawa. On three occasions, the mail was brought to Cherbourg by a Westland Wessex aircraft of Imperial Airways, and loaded onboard the "Empress of Britain" and shipped to position just off Red Bay at the entry of the Straits of Belle Ile which separate Labrador from Newfoundland. It was unloaded from the ship and sent on by air to Ottawa (over 900 miles) in three stages using three different aircraft.

Due to its situation at the mouth of the Channel, the port of Cherbourg was best suited for this type of operation. The Swiss and the Germans used it regularly between 1930 and 1939. On 5th July 1930, the Swiss Post began a seasonal Basel/Cherbourg/Le Havre air service, linking up with the departures and arrivals of the transatlantic steamers which, depending on the circumstances, reduced the transit time by between one and four days. The service, operated by Air Union and CIDNA, functioned for 23 months before being cancelled in 1933 because of its cost, but over seven million items of mail had benefited from the accelerated, non-surcharged service.[9]

Deutsche Lufthansa maintained the operation of a seasonal Cologne/Cherbourg line on behalf of the Reichspost which ran for over 10 years from 1929 to 1939. Coupled with "catapult messenger flights", it contributed to a significant, though seasonal, reduction in the mail transit times between Berlin and New York, as an official from the German Patent Office testified:

"I was thus able in due course to send a patent registration to America, for which the documents signed in Frankfurt on Main were sent by air to Cherbourg, and from there on the steamer Bremen as far as the American coast, when they were then conveyed by aeroplane to Washington via New York. My American correspondent wrote to me that with this exploit a record for patent registrations from Germany had been established." [10]

With the catapult flights and the flights from Cologne to Cherbourg, Deutsche Lufthansa forwarded 8-10 tonnes of accelerated mail per year.

To a lesser extent, Italy also showed interest in combined airmail flights when a postal seaplane took mail, which had been posted at the last minute in Genoa some hours after the ship sailed, to Gibraltar to catch the Italian steamer on the Genoa/New York service.

3 THE COMMERCIAL CONQUEST OF THE NORTH ATLANTIC

The history of the start-up of commercial operations over the

North Atlantic is a brilliant demonstration of the aeropolitics of the airways, and provides at the same time a lesson in the harsh realities of aviation. It demonstrates that despite the desires of political prestige, in the long term no-one can operate an airline without the required traffic rights and the appropriate means of transport, capable of covering the target distance with an economic payload.

It was the fulfilment of these two requirements that enabled Pan American Airways to commence the commercial exploitation of the North Atlantic on 20th May 1939. This was the inevitable conclusion of a complicated scenario which had brought on the scene four competing nations – Germany, The United States, France and The United Kingdom – with three possible means of transport – the dirigible, the seaplane and the conventional aircraft – on two potential routes – one to the north via Ireland and Newfoundland, and the other to the south via the Azores and Lisbon. (Due to the strategic location of the Azores Portugal also played a leading, though passive role.)

Because Germany and France had neglected these basic but constraining commercial realities, they found themselves eventually pushed back into the wings. However, in 1936, Germany had seemed to possess the best technical assets to open an airmail service between Europe and the United States. Germany had been spoiled for choice: both the airship and the seaplane were available to her. The airship LZ129 "Hindenburg", the bigger sister-ship to "Graf Zeppelin", was 245 metres long with a volume 190,000m³, and had on 14th May 1936 begun to make a series of 10 commercial return flights to New York-Lakehurst. The journey took two and a half days and carried passengers, parcels and mail, although this was of an essentially philatelic nature, due to the absence of a postal contract with the Americans, and due to the lengthy period between the flights (two to three weeks). Hopes were high for the airships: in February 1937 the operating company Deutsche Zeppelin Reederei GmbH, founded on 22nd March 1935 with one H. Goering as President, published a programme of 18 return crossings extending from May to October 1937 at a rate of about three flights per month. This was the start of a regular service, which came to a brutal halt with the terrible conflagration at Lakehurst on 6th May 1937, destroying the airship filled with hydrogen, and claiming 36 lives. The impact of the catastrophe on the mail can be measured exactly: out of the 17,609 items of mail on board, the fire-fighters only recovered a small number, and the American Post redirected a mere 147 letters to their addressees.[11]

However, the Germans had already started trialling a second means of transport on 5th September 1936 with the first of a series of six experimental airmail flights using a well-tried technique: that of catapulting an aircraft from a steamer equipped as a floating base. The first test took place on 9th September 1936 off Horta in the Azores, catapulting a two-engined Dornier Do18 Zephir seaplane from the steamer "Schwabenland" bound for New York. The seaplane, under the command of two experienced pilots, Joachim Blankenburg and Baron Von Gablenz, the chief pilot of Deutsche Lufthansa, touched down in Fort Washington, the seaplane base for New York, after 22 hours and 12 minutes flying time.

Deutsche Lufthansa continued its technical trials on a larger scale during the following two years. It carried out 14 flights in 1937 and 28 in 1938, from two floating bases, the one

RIGHT The Short-Mayo Composite-Mercury and Maia separating.

CENTRE Pan American Airways Boeing 314. *RAF Museum*

BELOW Pan American Boeing 314 "Yankee Clipper" boarding passengers from an Imperial Airways launch. *RAF Museum*

The Short-Mayo Composite-Mercury and Maia separating

moored at Horta and the other at Port Washington, using three HE139 aircraft manufactured in Hamburg by a subsidiary of Blohm & Voss at the naval dockyard. These seaplanes, named "Nordwind", "Nordmeer" and "Nordstern" had been specially designed in collaboration with Deutsche Lufthansa for the North Atlantic airmail service. They were fitted with four Junkers Jumo 205 C engines and could carry a payload of 500 kilograms for a distance of 3,000 miles at a cruising speed of 150mph. At the end of the trials in 1938, which had been carried out with rigorous precision, the official publication of the German Post observed:

> "*Since 1938, if the American Postal Authorities had given the authorisation, German aviation would have been capable of establishing an airmail service between Europe and the United States.*" [12]

Deutsche Lufthansa took up the same refrain in its Annual Report published in 1938:

> "*Lufthansa is now ready to open a scheduled airmail service across the North Atlantic, as soon as the international arrangements give us the freedom to do so.*"

Whether knowingly or not, the Germans were deluding themselves. Neither Britain, which had the legal power to bar the northern route, nor the United States, where President Roosevelt had got the true measure of the Nazi regime, would allow them to negotiate the necessary "international arrangements" indispensable to their plans. The feat accomplished on 10th August 1938 by a four-engined Focke

Wulf 200 Condor 'landplane', which flew directly from Berlin to New York in 24 hours and 36 minutes, changed nothing. It simply showed that the days of the supremacy of seaplanes for long-distance maritime crossings were probably numbered.

In France, some people took an early interest in the North Atlantic service. In 1929 two great captains of industry, Marcel Bouilloux-Laffont and Paul Louis Weiler, founded the Société pour L'Exploitation des Lignes Aériennes du Portugal in order to acquire a monopoly for the stopover rights in the Azores. Unfortunately the conditions imposed were so onerous that they could not be fulfilled and the agreement was cancelled by Portugal in 1932. 1934 saw the formation of a Group for the study of the crossing of The North Atlantic and in 1936 the Committee of the North Atlantic was constituted, uniting Air France, the Compagnie Générale Transatlantique, and representatives from the Government. In June 1937, this led to the creation of the company Air France Transatlantique.

France might have got on the right road, but its famous "prototype policy" [13] had been taken to ridiculous extremes, dispersing efforts and prolonging the production process and so ruining any chance of coming up with an aircraft which could do the job when required. In 1939, when time was running out, it at last obtained all the necessary stopover rights. France made six experimental return flights on the southern route with a Laté 521 flying boat named "Lieutenant de Vaisseau Paris" and a Laté 522, "Ville de Saint Pierre". The Laté 521, fitted with six Hispano-Suiza engines, was for a time the world's largest aircraft, with a wing span of 49.31 metres and a length of 31.62 metres.

There is no doubt that the flight of 14th July 1939 by Guillaumet and his crew, on board the "Lieutenant de Vaisseau Paris", was a great achievement. They flew non-stop from Port Washington to the sea base of Biscarosse, south of Bordeaux, following the Great Circle route (3,672 miles non-stop in 28 hours 27 minutes).

However, in spite of all the added technical refinements, the Laté 521 was an aircraft with a design going back to the start of the 1930s. It was not capable of coping with the difficult North Atlantic weather conditions in all seasons. In fact, "this flying boat would not permit us to envisage regular services following a pre-determined timetable." [14]

Other aircraft specially designed to ensure non-stop commercial services across the North Atlantic, particularly the promising Potez Cams 161, were not yet ready to fly in 1939.

Once Germany and France were out of the game, Great Britain and the United States were left as the sole combatants. Great Britain possessed a decisive legal advantage over its competitor: it had close control of the stopover rights on the northern route. It was able to impose on the Americans – in fact, on the company Pan American Airways – a convention based on the principles of reciprocity and equality of opportunity.

Following a series of discussions in Ottawa and Washington in November 1935 and 1936, the two parties reached an agreement on the conditions for operating a New York/Southampton service via intermediate points in Canada, Newfoundland and Ireland. Then, in 1936, to the great chagrin of Germany and France, Portugal granted regular stopover rights in the Azores and in Lisbon to Pan American Airways and Imperial Airways. The United States and Great Britain had now acquired all the necessary administrative authorisations needed to launch commercial operations in the North Atlantic, whether on the northern or the southern routes, or even on both. They were then able to devote all their energies to solving the technical questions.

In this respect, the British seemed to hold a trump card: among the 28 Short S23C Class aircraft ordered in 1934 by Imperial Airways for its Imperial Airmail Programme, there were two machines, named "Caledonia" and "Cambria", which were specially adapted for crossing the 2,000 miles between Foynes in Ireland and Botwood in Newfoundland. The first commercial trial flights with these two machines took place in the months of July and August 1937. There was no doubting their capabilities, but since they offered no useful payload, they were not in a position to provide a commercial link on the North Atlantic. Another solution would have to be found pending delivery of the more powerful Short S-26 seaplanes at the end of 1939. Imperial Airways turned to temporary solutions strictly reserved for postal traffic.

The "Mayo Composite", tested in 1938, was a most ingenious system, employing two seaplanes, and was the fruit of research by the chief engineer of Imperial Airways. The formula was simple in theory, but rather tricky in practice: it consisted of a specially designed four-engined seaplane with additional floats, named "Mercury", taking off on the back of a powerful Short S-23 called "Maia". Once the cruising altitude was reached, the two aeroplanes separated and "Mercury" crossed the Atlantic carrying several hundred kilograms of payload while "Maia" returned to land at its point of departure. Using this unusual tandem arrangement, the British achieved the first commercial flight across the North Atlantic, officially carrying 270 kilograms of mail between Great Britain and Canada on 20th and 21st July 1938. But this successful trial was not repeated.

Another solution was considered: air-to-air refuelling, intended to increase the operating range of the refuelled plane. Imperial Airways carried out a series of eight regular postal flights between Southampton, Montreal and New York in August and September 1939, using two modified Short seaplanes baptised "Caribou" and "Cabot". But it was too late.

By 20th May 1939, the Americans had won the race. They had been victorious across the board: in the north and in the south, for passengers and for post/express freight. As a wily captain, Juan Trippe, had been the first to hold the two winning cards: the stopover rights and the Boeing 314 seaplane – the incomparable Boeing Flying-Boat (R. E. G. Davies) – which Mrs Eleanor Roosevelt named the "Yankee Clipper".

4 THE NORTH ATLANTIC, OR THE CONSECRATION OF PAN AMERICAN AIRWAYS

Pan American Airways, for so long one of the world's leading international airlines, and for over half a century the incarnation of American might, was the achievement of one man, Juan Trippe, and of one organisation, the US Post Office.

There were no doubt many good fairies who came to bless the cradle of Juan Trippe. He was the scion of a good New England family, an intelligent and a shrewd diplomat who could be tough when necessary – and good looking into the bargain. At Yale University he founded the Yale Flying Club, afterwards served in the Navy, and counted among his friends and acquaintances all the financial bigwigs in the northeast of the United States. In 1926, as Managing Director of Colonial Air Transport, he had managed to land the first domestic postal contract – "CAM-1", between Boston and New York. Several years later

Pan American Airways System Boeing 314 "Yankee Clipper".

he said with pride: "I won the first post contract." In fact, the Post was to become his destiny, when he became Managing Director of Pan American in 1928. On the same basis as the domestic airlines, Pan American Airways owed its rapid expansion and its prosperity to the generosity of the American Post, as shown by the accumulated results for the 10 years 1929–1938:

• During this period, mail revenue represented 70% of the total income of Pan American ($65.91 million compared with a total $95.4 million).

• At the same time the sum total of airmail surcharges received by the American Postal Services from the public did not exceed 30% of the sums paid out to Pan American. The company operated on 30% revenues and 70% subsidy, to put it bluntly.

All American historians are agreed on the generosity of the postal remuneration, which still accounted for 54% of income in 1938: "in the United States, generous postal rates served as indirect subsidies."

Or again . . .

"Thanks to the very liberal mail subsidies it received, the overseas airline flourished exceedingly well during the intense business slump of 1929–1933." [15]

Once it was solidly propped up, the expansion of Pan American Airways evolved in three stages, corresponding to the three principal geographical zones of operation: Central and South America, the cradle of the company; the Pacific; and finally the North Atlantic.

It all began between Key West (at the southern most end of Florida) to Havana (Cuba) in October 1927. As the successful bidder for the Key West/Havana postal contract, which was

extremely important because of the busy trade between Cuba and the United States, the young company was confronted with a dramatic problem: under the terms of the contract, it was obliged to commence operations on 19th October latest, but did not yet actually own an aircraft! Everything turned out well, due to the unexpected arrival of a Fairchild, FC-2 seaplane. It was chartered on the spot and on 19th October transported seven bags of mail weighing 114 kilograms from Key West to Havana on behalf of Pan American Airways. (This preceded the flight which many consider, wrongly, to be the first scheduled airmail flight. That did not occur until 28th October 1927 in a Fokker F-VII piloted by Hugh Wells and assisted by Ed Musik, the future chief pilot of the company, bearing 350 kilograms of mail on board.)

By a happy coincidence, some weeks later, on 7th December 1927, President Coolidge sent a message to Congress recommending the creation of a network of airmail services in South America. Following this presidential recommendation, Congress passed the Kelly Foreign Airmail Act on 8th March 1928. This law was an exact equivalent for international post of the Kelly Act of 2nd February 1925 concerning domestic post. It authorised the Director General of Postal Services to make contracts with a duration of 10 years for the air transport of mail to Latin American countries, subject to a call to tender. He was not obliged to choose the company submitting the lowest quotation, providing that he did not exceed a remuneration of $2 per mile travelled, for a fixed weight of 800lb maximum (360 kilograms). On top of that, the company received a supplementary remuneration, and further, was guaranteed a minimum total payment.

In pursuance of the Kelly Law of 8th March 1928, the Postmaster General put out for tender seven contracts for Mexico, the Caribbean Sea, Central America and South America between 29th May 1928 and 24th September 1930. They were all awarded to Pan American Airways at the maximum authorised rate of 2 dollars per mile for both the return and the outward journey, except for a single contract (FAM9) [16] for the zone from the Panama Canal to Santiago de Chile and on to Buenos Aires. With his habitual combination of shrewdness, audacity and toughness, Juan Trippe had succeeded brilliantly in establishing his total supremacy in just two years, either by eliminating his weaker competitors or by making allies of the most powerful (the Grace Shipping Company on the east coast of South America). However, it must be said that "rightly or wrongly, depending on the interpretation of the loosely written Kelly Foreign Airmail Act of 1928, the Post Office Department and Congress by its appropriations, tolerated and indeed encouraged monopoly in the foreign airmail service from the beginning." [17]

By the end of 1929 the Pan American Airways System operated 71 airports, 26 radio command stations and 44 multi-engined aircraft. At the end of 1930, its grid of services covered the whole of the Caribbean area, along with Central America, and clasped South America in two long routes, one to the east and the other to the west, joining up at Buenos Aires. From 15th September 1928, Miami became the company's operations centre.

Instead of a long explanation, a simple list of the postal contracts (see table below) is the best way of following the extremely rapid establishment of the Pan American network. [18]

Although mail, consisting for the most part of letters and business papers, provided 86% of its total revenues in 1931 and 81% in 1932, Pan American Airways was never in the true sense of the word "a postal airline". Juan Trippe always imagined air transport as a global activity, directed at passengers and freight as well as mail.

The Sikorsky S-40, a four-engined flying boat, fulfilled Trippe's requirements. In its day it was the largest aircraft in the world and could carry 40 passengers. This was the first type of flying boat called a "Clipper" – a denomination which Pan American faithfully retained for many years – and was baptised "American Clipper" by Mrs Hoover on 12th October 1931. On 19th November 1931 it made the inaugural flight from Miami to Cristobal with Colonel Charles Lindbergh, the technical advisor of the company, at the controls.

The Pacific was the next area of development, although less by choice than by necessity. The North Atlantic had been objective number one since 1930, but the British held the keys and, with a realism which Juan Trippe well understood, were only prepared to grant access as it suited them, and in their own time. Thus, Trippe turned towards the Pacific and ordered studies to be made for a San Francisco/Manila route, almost 6,250 miles long.

After the 1898 war with Spain, the United States had inherited some of the remnants of the historic Spanish presence in Asia. Thus, and not without some embarrassment, they became a colonial power, and in addition to the Philippines possessed a whole series of Pacific Islands which could represent many potential stopover sights: Hawaii, Midway, Wake and Guam. Along this route the only difficulty consisted in the length of the ocean sections (2,440 miles between San Francisco and Honolulu) and Juan Trippe was confident that his problems would be mainly technical. Once these had been solved, the first scheduled trans-Pacific flight left the sea base at Alameda, in San Francisco Bay, on 22nd November 1935, bound for Manila-Philippines via Hawaii, Midway, Wake and Guam. The aircraft was a Glenn Martin M130 flying boat fitted with four 900-horsepower Pratt and Whitney type 1830 "Wasp" engines, capable of carrying a payload of 1,900 kilograms with the maximum fuel load and luxuriously furnished to receive 48 passengers. Like the Sikorsky S42, which was only called into regular service somewhat later, this aircraft was the result of a Pan American call for tender in 1931 in search of a long-haul flying boat. Once again, the Post had fulfilled a dual mission: the financing and the launching of a service.

As might be expected, the inaugural flight of 22nd November, under Captain Ed Musik, exclusively transported mail. It carried exceptional quantities of correspondence: 58 sacks weighing 920 kilograms, with 110,865 letters when it left San Francisco – and approximately 730 kilograms, 98,000 letters, on the return journey from Manila. One might think that all the philatelists in the world had made a date of it! Subsequently, the weights became more reasonable. This service was reserved for mail for about a year: passengers were only admitted on 21st October 1936.

In fact, the first months of operation had been more difficult than foreseen, due to disastrous weather conditions. One flight took more than a month to travel from San Francisco to Manila

Postal Contracts of Pan American Airways

Contract	Route	Contract Date	Date of first flight	Weekly frequency
FAM 4	Key West/Havana (Miami/Havana)	29.05.1928	29.05.1928 (15.09.1928)	7
FAM 5	Miami/Cristobal (Panama Canal Zone) via Cuba and Central America (extended to Paramaribo)	13.06.1928	4.02.1929	1
FAM 6	Miami/Puerto Rico (extended to Port of Spain)	13.07.1928	9.01.1929	3
FAM 7	Miami/Nassau (Bahamas)	24.10.1928	2.01.1929	3
FAM 8	Brownsville (Texas)/Mexico	16.02.1929	10.03.1929	7
FAM 9	Cristobal/Santiago de Chile (extended to Buenos Aires and Montevideo)	2.03.1929	17.05.1929	2
FAM10	Paramaribo/Santos (extended to Buenos Aires)	24.09.1930	27.11.1930	1

– an illustration of Juan Trippe's systematic refusal to have his crews take excessive risks. The postal contract (FAM14) between Pan American and the Post included one unusual condition: for the first six months it only obliged the company to make an average of two return journeys per month, abandoning the principle of weekly flights. The conditions of the rest of the contract conformed to the general model: duration of 10 years and remuneration of $2 per mile up to the limit of a maximum weight of 800lb or 360 kilograms. It turned out that this remuneration, when added to revenues from passenger and express freight traffic, did not allow a profitable return on the enormous investments that had been made to fit out and operate the service. After lengthy investigations, the new Civil Aviation Authority, born of the Civil Aeronautics Act of 1938, accepted as justified Pan American's requests for a revision of the contract, and decided to increase the postal remuneration from $2 to $3.35, commencing on 1st April 1939.

The true objective of the Northern Trans-Pacific line was not to provide a service to the Philippines, but to China. This was achieved in April 1937 when Pan American aircraft from Manila linked up in Hong Kong with those of the China National Aviation Corporation, or CNAC, a 45% subsidiary of Pan American, arriving from Shanghai.

There only remained one last jewel to the crown: the North Atlantic. Pan Am, which now held all the landing rights, obtained the necessary technological solution in March 1939. In April 1936 it had put out a call to tender for a long-haul aircraft to the following specifications: to transport a payload of at least 4,550 kilograms over stages of 2,375 miles at an altitude of 3,000 metres and at a cruising speed of 160mph. Boeing received the contract for its Boeing 314. This was a monoplane flying boat, entirely in metal, fitted with four Wright Cyclone engines, each developing 1,500 horsepower. It had twin decks, the cabin for the crew and the holds for the mailbags and luggage were on the upper deck,

and the passenger cabins on the lower deck (72 passengers in the daytime or 40 couchettes for the night). Supplementary holds were situated under the lower deck. In spite of a delay in production due to manufacturing difficulties, "the performance of the Boeing 314 proved to be better than had been expected." [19] Everything was ready for the launch of a commercial air service across the North Atlantic. Everything, except for one small detail: the amount of the postal remuneration/subsidy. Following fierce discussions, the American authorities had accepted to make an annual guaranteed payment of $2,454,000 against the company's claim for $3,189,000 dollars, based on a frequency of two flights per week. Now everything was indeed ready: on 20th May 1939, the Boeing 314 "Yankee Clipper" made the first scheduled New York/Azores/Lisbon/Marseilles link with a total load of 820 kilograms of mail, some 112,574 letters. Some weeks later the northern route – New York/Southampton – was inaugurated and both lines were opened to passenger traffic. Pan Am had truly become an American institution and "the instrument of National Policy".

ABOVE RIGHT **Pan American Sikorsky S-40.** MAP

RIGHT **Pan American Martin M-30.** *RAF Museum*

8 AIRBORNE FREIGHT TRAFFIC UP TO THE EVE OF 1939

The Post occupied such a dominant position in the history of air transport between the two world wars that it almost obscured freight traffic, to such a point that some people have thought that airfreight only started after the Second World War. That was not the case, since the world's airlines – excluding the Soviet Union – transported around 57,000 tonnes of goods in 1938, divided between three groups of countries:

• Europe, the cradle of airfreight, where the aeroplane became one complementary means of transport between large economic centres.

• Up-and-coming countries, where the aeroplane became an irreplaceable instrument in the exploitation of natural resources, in areas without ground-based communications. These countries represented almost two-thirds of the total traffic.

• The United States, where Air Express was only a new embodiment of an old American tradition going back to the mid–19th century.

On the other hand, goods traffic on the long-haul international and imperial routes remained at a fairly modest level up to 1940. There were two reasons: the low payloads available, and the strict application of the principle that airmail got priority. Thus, in 1938, Sabena only carried 20,030 kilograms of parcels on its major colonial route to the Congo, and Air France only took 21,379 kilograms on the Marseilles/Saigon/Hanoi service. The exception was KLM, the undeniable pioneer of airfreight, with a goods traffic of 93,381 kilograms on its flagship line from Amsterdam to Batavia (Djakarta) during the same year.

Deutsche Lufthansa which in 1938 was the world's leading scheduled airline for freight, deserves special mention, for introducing the first long-haul transoceanic freight charter for humanitarian purposes. From 15th to 18th February 1939 it transported 567 kilograms of medical supplies in a Dornier Do26 seaplane from Warnemünde (on the Baltic Sea) to Santiago de Chile for the benefit of victims of an earthquake.

Distribution of goods traffic sent by air in 1938

Area	Traffic (tonnes)	Distribution in %
Europe	15,000	26
Up-and-coming countries	36,000	63
United States	5,000	9
Imperial/transcontinental lines	1,000	2
Total	57,000	100

I EUROPE

Immediately after the end of the First World War, Europe saw the simultaneous start up of passenger, post and goods activities. Certain airlines such as Air Union [1] or KLM even devoted particular attention to this last activity right from the start, and quickly demonstrated spectacular increases.

	Air Union	KLM
1920	50	22
1924	514	147

(figures in tonnes)

Even Lignes Aériennes Latécoère, the archetypal postal airline, devoted important coverage in its commercial publications for the transport of "Aéropaquets" (air parcels). The brochure "Les Instructions Générales Relatives au Transport des Aéropaquets" in 1924 states that parcels should not exceed 0.50m x 0.30m x 0.30m, nor weigh more than 30 kilograms, that despatches could be made charges collect, and that "light parcels will be charged on the basis of 1 kilogram per 4 cubic decimetres".

The sales arguments
The development of European airfreight was influenced by factors typical of the period. "Les Instructions pour le transport des Marchandises par avion", [2] published in 1929 in Zurich by "L'Union Suisse pour le transport Aérien" emphasises some of these:

• The speed of the aeroplane: "with an average speed of approximately 150 kilometres per hour [95mph], the aeroplane is the world's fastest means of transport."

• The safety of air transport: "packaging can be reduced to its simplest form" due to the "careful treatment of the merchandise."

• The speed of Customs formalities: no doubt the most important competitive advantage of air transport in Europe. It highlighted the picture of a small continent carved into a multiplicity of territories, bristling with barriers, both duties and regulatory. In seaports and railway stations, the Customs formalities took a long time. In the airports, at the hands of specialist Customs officers, they were "quick and easy".

• The simplicity of using airfreight: from 18th April 1927 all member companies of IATA used a uniform document, the International Despatch Note, which became the Air Way Bill.

• Flexibility of rates: in parallel with the public rate structure, the airlines illustrated a remarkable ability to adapt to the market. The airfreight rates had not yet been ossified by regulations which were pernickety and excessively restrictive. Quite officially, there was room for "special arrangements": "batches of over 500 kilograms" – we would call them large consignments – and "regular shipments" – that is, regular loads – could be the subject of "contractual arrangements". On reading such a forward-thinking document, one cannot help thinking that a little teaching from history might bring progress to the present!

• A first class quality of service.

On the subject of the Paris/London traffic, the journal "L'Aérophile" wrote in its issue of 1st May 1920: "one only has to deliver the goods in Paris before 11.00 o'clock in the morning, either at the offices of the Company Agencies or at Travel Agencies, for them to be delivered, with Customs clearance, to their destination in London on that same evening."

During that period, airfreight was truly an express service: one cannot repeat enough that the speed of airfreight transport in the years 1920–1940 was comparable to the speed of express freight in the 1990s. The attitude of Lufthansa is typical, when it called their freight service Luftexpressdienst – "Air express service".

Speed and safety, simplicity and quality: this list of selling points was, on the whole, very similar to that developed and systematised after 1945.

Product categories
Since the rates were high and the capacities low, the only goods sent by air were very perishable, very urgent and/or of high value.

• Newspapers: Due to an extremely short shelf life, the daily press was the airlines' first freight client from 1919/1920. After a number of trials with rather variable timings, official negotiations started in 1927 between IATA and the press despatch offices in order to establish transport conditions for considerable tonnages of newspapers. IATA made rate concessions and entered into operational commitments: daily services for 12 months a year from 1930 onwards (many routes were still only functioning during the fine season), with a regularity of 95% during at least six months of the year. These proposals did not seem to be adequate and no global agreement was reached. However a number of individual agreements were concluded between airlines and press enterprises. Air France, KLM, Deutsche Lufthansa and several British companies operated regular night freight flights restricted to transporting newspapers.

For example, from 1929 KLM made a seasonal daily flight from London to some of the Dutch and Belgian beaches on the North Sea so that British tourists could read their usual paper at breakfast; Air Union, Air France and a number of small British freight companies – Wright Ways and Air Despatch – carried up to 500 tonnes of newspapers per year between Paris and London; and some forwarding agents for traffic between London and Paris, like Dawson, actually specialised in handling press consignments.

In Germany, the transport of newspapers by plane, assumed an unusual form: newspapers took advantage of favourable

KLM has always specialised in the transport of live animals. Here "Nico" the bull boards a special flight between Rotterdam and Paris in 1924.

postal rates, and represented a very important part of the airmail (78% in 1925). The "Air newspapers" had to be packaged by the publisher before sending them to the Post Offices, to be conveyed to three different user groups: individual subscribers, group consignments to the same destination, and large batches.

• Bank notes and precious metals: For reasons of safety and insurance rates, airfreight became the normal means of transport for gold bars inside Europe. After the onset of the economic crisis of 1929 and the revaluation of the gold price by President Roosevelt, the transport of gold between the central banks reached such a volume that KLM made six special flights per day.

• Perfumes, haute couture, garments: According to a survey of 1935, [3] these made up 18% of the European freight market. This was the main activity for Air France: gloves sent to Scandinavian destinations, perfumes for Great Britain, and haute couture for Germany and Central Europe.

• Spare parts of all kinds for machinery and vehicles: These made up 25% of the market, according to the same survey. This was the top category of merchandise transported by air, particularly for Imperial Airways and Deutsche Lufthansa.

• Live animals: This cargo varied from small domestic animals to day-old chicks (a British and Dutch speciality), and included racing pigeons, which were among the most regular and profitable clients of Sabena, departing from Brussels (needless to say, they returned under their own wing power!).

Even larger animals, such as cows or horses, were carried. It is said that KLM managed to get a cow into a Fokker biplane in 1920: not without difficulty, one imagines. Some years later Air Union had some trouble in getting two circus horses on board a Lioré 213 converted as a cargo plane: "a sloping gangway led up to a padded cabin which was provided with tethering straps to prevent the animals from being thrown from side to side during the journey. On several occasions they tried to get the horses to go up the gangway – without success. At his wits' end, the trainer had the idea of leading them up to the sound of the music, which accompanied their entrance into the circus ring. There were no bagpipes available in the immediate vicinity but they managed to find an accordion, thanks to which the embarkation was eventually effected." [4]

• Cut flowers and perishable goods: KLM sent fresh flowers cut that very morning, to destinations all over Europe, which represented 40% of the traffic through Amsterdam airport.

Distribution network
The European airlines, whose parcel activities were of more or less marginal importance within the volume of intra-European commerce, were immediately confronted with the major problem of distribution. They showed much pragmatism in making their freight product as widely available as possible. Once again the instructions of the "Union Suisse pour le trafic aérien" from 1929 are instructive. Originally published in French, English, German and Italian, the excerpt below is from the 1929 English version (note the wording of the time!):

"The consignment of merchandise to be transported by air may take place as follows:

'Parcels for conveyance by airplane can be handed in at the aerodrome, at one or other of the offices specially opened for the purpose in the town, at the offices of the large transport agencies, or, if it is a question of a combination conveyance (airplane-railway), at all the railway stations of the Federal Railways organised for express parcel delivery service.'"

Of particular interest are the following points:

1. "Either at the aerodrome or in one of the specially opened . . . offices in town" – ie offices of the airlines and certain travel agencies.
2. "At the offices of large transport agencies" – ie via forwarding agents.

In Europe, some forwarding agents became interested in transporting goods by aeroplane at a very early stage and contributed to the creation of modern airfreight. Although it only appeared in the United States in 1942, airfreight had existed in Europe since 1919, examples of these pioneers being: Air Express Company and LEP (who opened a special office on the London-Hounslow aerodrome in 1919) in Britain, Transports Michaux and Leygonie in France, and Crowe and Danzas in Switzerland.

3. "Or if it is a case of combination conveyance (airplane-railway), at all the railway stations of the Federal Railways organised for express parcel service."

From 1926 onwards, the air transport companies made agreements with the railway companies relating to distribution or marketing, so as to benefit from their large number of operating sites:

• 1926 – Sweden: An agreement was made between Swedish railways and ABA, limited to three principal railway stations.
• 1927 – Germany: A global agreement was signed between Deutsche Lufthansa and German Railways for the joint organisation of a combined air/rail traffic system. Clients could hand in their air parcels in any stations open for the express parcel service and benefit from a very simple single rate integrating the two modes of transport. These combined consignments, known as Flei-Sendungen, an acronym for *Flugeisenbahn*, [5] represented between 13% and 16% of the export business of Deutsche Lufthansa between 1930 and 1938. [6] (For example, in 1937 150,019 kilograms was carried in 12,402 consignments.)
• 1928 – Switzerland: "By means of this combined transportation, all localities in Switzerland are in practice connected with the international air network" of Swiss Air and Balair.
• 1930 – Great Britain: Imperial Airways introduced a combined rail-air service in conjunction with the British railway network.
• 1933: IATA and the International Railway Union adopted a single, combined transport document.

By 1935, agreements between airlines and railway companies had been signed in the majority of European countries. The air-rail co-operation had then achieved a level which it was never again to regain.

The freight offer and aircraft
The freight availability of the general companies who carried passengers, mail and goods was, as today, a mixed capacity

Junkers G31.
RAF Museum

consisting of two elements: the uncertain residual load on mixed transport aeroplanes which remained after taking on post and passengers, and a guaranteed capacity (except for the uncertainties of the weather) on all-freight or cargo planes.

In the beginning, the freight capacity of passenger aeroplanes was very limited, with few exceptions such as the Farman Goliath or the Handley-Page O/400. The goods were stowed in small compartments situated fore or aft of the cabin, if they existed at all.

Very frequently parcels had to be stowed with some difficulty either under the passenger seats or even between the passengers' legs! Packages were even to be seen strapped beneath the wings! The first holds in the belly of aeroplanes did not appear until the 1930s.

The cargo-only aircraft were often merely passenger planes, which had been summarily converted: it was just a matter of taking out the seats and installing some rudimentary cargo restraint system. Cargo versions of the Fokker VII or Junkers F13, De Havilland DH86 or Farman 306 were all operated in this way.

However, a number of aircraft manufacturers became interested in producing aeroplanes which were specially designed for carrying cargo. One of the first projects to attract attention was that of the British aircraft builder Blackburn, in 1920. This was a gigantic monoplane, with an immense wing span of 48 metres, designed to carry a payload of 4 tonnes. It was called the "Pelican", a name which will evoke many memories within Air France. This "air truck" had one special feature, far ahead of it's time, which was later taken up on various civilian and military freighters: in order to simplify the loading and unloading of large-sized packages, the front of the cabin could be opened like a door, pivoting around vertical hinges.

The manufacturer which placed airfreight highest on its priority list was undeniably the German company Junkers. Its passenger aeroplanes, with their metallic structure and the almost

square cross-section of the cabin, could be easily adapted for freight transport. Many F13s were converted to cargo aeroplanes and we will see later what an extraordinary cargo aeroplane the Junkers G31 was to become in New Guinea. Junkers also manufactured aeroplanes originally designed for freight transport, which were later adapted for passengers, for example, the W33-W34 and the legendary Ju52.

• The Junkers W33, developed from the F13, was defined as follows: "a freight aeroplane with a possibility for transporting passengers". It had a volume of 4.8 cubic metres, and in its original version had no portholes. It was operated by Lufthansa for its postal network and by many South American companies controlled by German capital. The W34 version, which did have portholes, was "a combined aeroplane for passengers and freight".

• The legendary Junkers Ju52 was originally a cargo plane. The engineer Ernst Zindl, who was a great believer in the future of airfreight, decided to manufacture an "all cargo" aeroplane capable of transporting a load of 2,000 kilograms over a distance of 500 miles at a speed of 150mph. This was the birth of the Ju52/1m, a single-engined "removal van" which made its maiden flight on 13th October 1930.

The cabin was in the form of an elongated rectangular box, designed to facilitate the handling of goods. The main cabin hold (6.4m x 1.6m x 1.9m) had a volume 16.7 cubic metres, to which was added a secondary hold positioned to the rear of this cabin and four small compartments placed under the main deck. The facilities for loading were exceptional, combining vertical

handling – thanks to a trap door of 1.81m x 0.90m built into the roof of the cabin – and horizontal handling – with a large cargo door of 1.8m x 1.25m on the left-hand side, and three small doors on the right-hand side.[7] This was the first modern cargo plane, but it could not have arrived at a worse moment: right in the middle of the world economic crisis. Only five units were built.

It gave rise to a three-engined passenger version, the Ju52/3m, which flew over every continent for more than 40 years. As usual, Junkers manufactured a number of different versions of what became nicknamed "good old Auntie Ju". The version with the widest distribution among the airlines was the Ju52/3 m g 4c version, which was described as follows:

> *"an aircraft for the transportation of passengers and freight with a reinforced floor, large loading doors on the left-hand side and on the cabin roof, and a tie-down facility made of steel tubes to ensure that parcels are stowed securely."* [7]

Although there were many airlines which operated cargo-only aircraft, there were very few European cargo-only airlines between the two wars. Most of these airlines were British – their profitability was always very questionable, and their lifespan was often short. Some of them specialised in transporting

LEFT Loading cargo into a Lufthansa Junkers Ju 90 with the help of a conveyor belt.
Lufthansa

BELOW Curtiss Condor.
MAP

newspapers, as on the Paris-London route. Others started off carrying general freight, such as International Airfreight, which opened a London/Amsterdam route on 29th September 1937, and then a London/Brussels service on 3rd May 1938, using modified Curtiss Condors.

In 1938, the intra-European traffic reached 15,000 tonnes. This was a disappointing total after the promising start in the years 1920–1925, and it was even somewhat derisory in view of the intensity of trade. The limited capacity, the high level of rates, the density of surface transport and the short transit distances were all factors which played their part in giving a secondary role to the air transportation of goods within Europe.

In spite of this, new airports which opened towards the end of this period, such as Le Bourget in Paris or Tempelhof in Berlin, devoted large areas and modern equipment to goods traffic. In June 1939, the review of the German Airport Association described the Tempelhof installations as follows:

"Commercial freight arrives by either on road vehicles or by rail on a special connecting line, into the large goods hall. This latter contains sections for Customs, which can be locked, cold rooms for perishable goods and safes for consignments of valuables. The freight is transported to the aeroplanes on electric wagons."

Le Bourget airport, which achieved a traffic in parcels and large luggage of 2,146 tonnes in 1938, had similar facilities.

In both cases, in order to simplify the loading of mixed aeroplanes, the freight area was located within the passenger terminal.

For the whole of the period under consideration, the Paris/London axis was the main artery of European freight: it carried 100 tonnes in 1920, 400 in 1922 and 1,400 in 1937, roughly 10% of the total European traffic. It was when opening a new night cargo service between Paris and London on 31st March 1935, in a three-engined Farman 306, that Robert Bajac, the chief pilot of Air France, lost his life. One of his colleagues wrote of him: "Of Bajac, I have kept the memory of a gentleman to whom I would not have wished Good Day without raising my hat." [8]

2 THE NEW NATIONS

Rather than looking at each developing nation, we will concentrate on the four countries, or groups of countries, for which the domestic traffic exceeded 5,000 tonnes per year: Canada, the countries of Central America, Colombia and, the most remarkable example, New Guinea.

Canada

In 1920, Canada was the perfect example of a new nation with a great future. The immense distances, the rigours of the climate, the low population density and the location of natural resources in regions bereft of communications were precisely the factors which favoured the development of air transport. From its beginnings, Canadian civil aviation appears to be a substitute transport method, closely linked with mining activities and life in the far north.

The first teetering steps, albeit with little significant results, were made in 1920. In October, two pilots took a fur trader, Frank Stanley, on his annual round of visits to the trappers, 500 miles north of Winnipeg. In November, the Imperial Oil Company leased two Junkers F13 aircraft to send prospecting

crews and equipment to the valley of the River McKenzie, which was iced up at the time. This brief experiment illustrated a general feature of "bush aviation", in which men, mail and merchandise were carried indiscriminately, even if, in some circumstances, the last of the three assumed a particular importance.

In 1921 and 1923 the centre of attention moved across to the island of Newfoundland, where some airmail trials were made which are of considerable philatelic interest: the flights between St John and St Anthony on 26th February 1921 and between Newfoundland and Labrador from February to May 1923.

Since aviation did not enjoy any official encouragement, the first scheduled service, operated by Laurentide Air Services, was not opened until spring 1924, between the gold mines of Rouyn in Quebec Province and the railway terminus at Angliers. It carried 35 tonnes of mail and goods, and 1,000 passengers during its first six months of activity. This pioneering service was joined by a number of others in the same sector, leaving from Haileybury and Trois Rivières in 1925 and 1926. The operators used aircraft fitted with skis in winter and floats in summer, because of the region's many lakes.

From 1926 onwards, a number of small companies were created to keep up with the development of new mining centres in Ontario, Manitoba (Red Lake District) and the Northern Territories.

"The main impetus for commercial flying in this period was the lure of the vast trackless North, rich in minerals and forest resources and almost totally devoid of regular transportation links – here the new breed of 'Coureurs des bois' had to master hazardous challenges – intense, cold Arctic blizzards, rough landings in unknown countries." [9]

As the carrying capacity of the aircraft increased, all sorts of mining equipment, right up to tractors, were taken to the most remote sites. Goods traffic grew from 30 tonnes in 1925 to 1,131 in 1929.

Two events brought a new dimension to Canadian commercial aviation: the change in postal policy in 1927 and the revaluation of the gold price by President Roosevelt in 1933.

Up to 1927, the Canadian Postal Administration had not organised any form of airmail service. Nevertheless, the private airlines, which carried letters to places without any form of communications links, were authorised to issue airmail stamps on their own behalf, albeit under very strict control from the Post Office. These companies were remunerated through a surcharge, which they received directly, in addition to the normal postage collected by the Post. This is how Laurentide Air Service and Northern Air Service flying to the mines of Rouyn, Elliott-Fairchild Air Service and Patricia Airways and Exploration Co in the Red Lake district, Yukon Airways, Klondike Airways, Commercial Airways, Cherry Red Airline and Canadian Airways in the valleys of the Yukon and the McKenzie came to issue their own postage stamps, which are today much sought after by collectors.

In 1927, the Canadian Post changed its attitude and started to organise airmail links, the operation of which it entrusted to private airlines. The first experiments were carried out in regions where the post was often interrupted in winter: the mining districts of Red Lake in Ontario, Pelée Island, lost in the midst of Lake

Erie when it was iced up, and villages on the northern bank of the Saint Lawrence River, buried beneath the snows. Thus it fell to Romeo Vachon, a Quebec personality well known in Canadian aviation, and nicknamed "The flying mailman of the ice", [10] to make the Christmas post delivery to a whole string of villages dotted along the Saint Lawrence River between Malbaie and Sept Iles, to the east of Quebec. Since there were no landing fields, and due to the isolated situations of the hamlets, he had to fall back on an unusual form of aerial distribution:

"The aeroplane flies over the communities situated along the coast, and the sacks of mail are thrown out as near as possible to the small post offices. One can understand how disagreeable it would be for the local Postmaster to have to clamber through thick snow in search of heavy airmail deliveries, which had not fallen anywhere near his office. One day, when one of the Postmasters had complained about the lack of accuracy, the matter was communicated to the flight operator and rigorous preparations were made by the pilot.. On the following journey, he distributed the mails with bulls-eye accuracy, straddling the roof of the Post Office itself." [11]

Once things were set in motion, the Post continued to develop the airmail network, with constantly growing traffic: 7 tonnes in 1927, 215 tonnes in 1930, 512 tonnes in 1935 and 1,231 tonnes in 1940. By then, Canada benefited from an interrelated system consisting of three main elements:

1. A transcontinental route, which was eventually opened on 1st March 1939 by Trans Canada Airlines (which became Air Canada on the 1st January 1965), between Vancouver and Montreal, and extended to Halifax on 1st April 1941.

2. A number of seasonal services.

3. A group of air links to provide a postal service in the prairies, leaving from Winnipeg and Calgary; and towards the Yukon and the North West Territories, leaving from Edmonton on one branch towards Whitehorse and Dawson on the frontier with Alaska, and another branch towards Fort Revolution, with tributaries out to Yellowknife (Great Slave Lake), Coppermine (Arctic Ocean) and towards Fort Norman and Aklavik at the mouth of the McKenzie River. For these destinations, all mail traffic was conveyed by air without airmail surcharge, in contrast to the surcharges for the Transcontinental Route destinations.

President Roosevelt's decision to raise the value of an ounce of gold [12] to $35 fired the starting pistol for a world-wide race for gold. In Canada, new gold-bearing deposits, as well as mines for radium and soon afterwards uranium, began to be exploited around the Great Slave Lake in the Northern Territories. Still closely linked to mining activity, airborne goods traffic registered a dizzying growth rate, accompanied by wild swings.

Development of Canadian Airfreight Traffic

Year	Tons
1929	1,131
1934	6,500
1935	11,980
1939	9,800

Excluding the Soviet Union, Canada occupied the top position in the world for goods traffic carried by air between 1935 and 1939. [13] This business consisted for the most part of items of equipment, the majority of which was non-scheduled charter traffic, with an important proportion being private carriage. At that time, freight brought in approximately 75% of the revenue of the airlines operating in the far north.

TACA: The world's leading freight company in 1940 (12,600 tonnes)

TACA (Transportes Aereos Centro-Americanos) was founded in 1931 to transport passengers, mail and goods around Central America, and within a few years had succeeded in establishing an international network covering the republics of Guatemala, Honduras, Costa Rica, Nicaragua and El Salvador. In countries where the terrain was often extremely rugged, and covered in thick tropical vegetation, freight transport soon became the main activity, providing roughly 60% of the company's income. Its goods traffic soon reached levels that would make the American and European airlines envious. [14]

By 1940 TACA was operating a fleet of 50 aircraft – including 25 Ford Tri-motors, and was serving 236 airfields, of which 85 were on the basis of scheduled services and 151 as "on demand" or charter services.

Development of TACA freight traffic

Year	Tons
1937	5,150
1938	7,000
1939	9,100
1940	12,640

The secret of TACA'S success has been summarised as: "The conveyance of bulk freight at low rates in a country where surface transport is difficult." [14] Alongside the goods, it transported mail at the same rates as the normal post carried by donkey! It introduced differed freight rates, 50% below those for express freight, and thus enjoyed a permanent reservoir of traffic, which ensured maximum loading factors.

In a region devoid of efficient land communication routes, all sorts of products were transported by aeroplane. The choice of products was completely different from those current in Europe. TACA carried perishable goods alongside steel sheets, bags of cement or bags of rice. The two principal goldmines in Nicaragua, Neptune and La Luz, were completely dependant on the air-link, even for petrol, which was brought in aeroplanes specially fitted out as flying tankers.

The most colourful activity of TACA, beginning in 1935, was the "Chewing Gum Express". Chiclé, the juice of the sapodilla, which provides the base for chewing gum manufacture, was produced in the district of Peten in Guatemala, 155 miles from Puerto Barrios on the Caribbean Sea, from which it was exported to the United States. This short distance required a lengthy journey: two weeks on mule-back. The immediate replacement of pack animals by the aeroplane revolutionised the transport system: it provided a guaranteed capacity for transporting the entire production, and it enabled the local authorities to collect their export taxes. In 1937, TACA carried 610 tonnes of chiclé, and almost 1,000 tonnes in 1939.

Colombia, pioneer in the routine air transport of goods
It will be recalled that a number of German and Colombian pilots and businessmen had founded South America's oldest airline on 5th December 1919: Sociedad Colombo-Alemana de Transportes Aereos, or SCADTA, which became an ancestor of Avianca.

The idea behind the creation of this company was to make a saving of approximately 10 days in the endless journey between the capital Bogota, situated on a plateau at an altitude of 2,500 metres, and the port of Barranquilla on the Caribbean Sea. At the end of an extremely detailed study and after over a year of trial flights, SCADTA opened its service in September 1921 flying Junkers F13s, which travelled up the valley of the Rio Magdalena from Barranquilla to Girardo, the railhead for the Bogota railway. At the time, this route took about 80% of Colombia's internal trade. After a difficult start, especially with regard to passengers, SCADTA made regular progress, and from the 1930s onwards endowed Colombia with the densest and best-organised network in South America. The Bogota/Barranquilla line remained the main axis, but many other services were created, connecting Barranquilla with the great centres of Cali and Medellin and to the port of Buenaventura on the Pacific coast. These main routes were met by a large number of feeder services. In view of the increase of traffic, SCADTA put into service Junkers W34 passenger and freight aircraft. Besides the passenger service, which remained of minor importance in its trading results, it developed its own mail activity and considerable goods traffic.

SCADTA is of major interest in the history of air philately: it was authorised to issue and use its own stamps for a period of approximately 10 years, in return for a royalty of 2% of the face value of the stamps to the Colombian Government. This went on until 1931, when the Airmail Administration of the Republic of Colombia was created. These private, although official, postage stamps were widely distributed in Colombia and sold in a certain number of Colombian consulates in Europe.

SCADTA did not only issue its own stamps, but also had its own Post Offices in Colombia (70 in 1932) and itself undertook the delivery of airmail to its addressee's door, sometimes combining a section by air with delivery by mule or even by Indian bearer! [15]

It was in the field of goods traffic that SCADTA showed the greatest success. Between the two world wars, Colombia was the pioneer country for the regular air transportation of merchandise. This resembled the situation in Canada and New Guinea regarding charter transport or private carriage. Colombia's freight traffic showed a constant growth, and from 1935 onwards achieved proportions far superior to those of the European airlines:

1930	468 tonnes
1935	2,500 tonnes
1938:	5,432 tonnes

SCADTA based its development on a policy of service quality and always charged relatively high rates, which was made easier by the inadequacy of traditional means of transport. It distributed regular dividends to its shareholders until 1940, when it was replaced by Aerovias Nacionales de Colombia – Avianca.

New Guinea: The first air lift in the history of aviation
The eastern part of New Guinea, which the League of Nations placed under Australian administration in 1919, provided the setting for the first air lift in history: from 1930 until the Japanese invasion in 1942, the open-cast goldmines in the valley of the Bulolo were exclusively supplied by air.

In 1922, Cecil J. Levien, Deputy District Officer of Morobe, was informed about the discovery of gold-bearing formations. He left his job and returned to Australia. On his return in 1923 he located the richest gold-bearing deposits in the valley of the Bulolo. The country was as inhospitable as could be: the terrain was extremely rugged, mountains covered with thick tropical jungle, and the climate very hot and humid. The coast was only 30 miles away, but it took 10 days to reach it over a very difficult track, which only allowed goods to be carried on the shoulders of bearers. Even this solution was risky, due to the opposition of the local population against Australian prospectors invading their territory. Hence, from the moment of its creation, the Guinea Gold No Liability Company, founded in Adelaide in May 1926 for the purpose of exploiting the gold-bearing site, was confronted with a crucial problem: that of transport.

All the possibilities were examined. Overland delivery had its supporters, but Levien, who in the meantime had become the Director of the new company, preferred the air solution.

"Pard" Mustar, a veteran of the Royal Australian Air Force, began to operate air links between the coastal town of Lae and the mining centre of Wau, commencing on 6th April 1927 in a De Havilland DH37. The aeroplane was an immediate success. "This changes the way of life there," said the prospectors and other gold diggers. The first airlines were created. The Guinea Airways Ltd, of which Mustar was the Director, was registered in November 1927. In order to find an answer to the main difficulty – the lack of capacity – Mustar left for Europe and placed an order for the aircraft which seemed to him most suitable, both for its sturdiness and its carrying capacity: the Junkers W34. In its first two years of operation, Guinea Airways

133

1928 to 1936 by Deutsche Lufthansa to carry passengers on its European services (fitted with 15 seats). The cargo version was only manufactured in three examples to meet the specifications of Guinea Airways. It was equipped with three 535hp Hornet-BMW engines, and presented a remarkable feature in the form of a vast loading door of 3.50 metres x 1.80 metres built into the cabin roof, making vertical handling by crane and slings extremely easy. The passenger cabin had been transformed into a vast cargo hold measuring 7.31 metres x 1.96 metres x 2.08 metres, offering a volume of 40m³ and allowing the transport of particularly bulky components and packages, right up to cars and light trucks. The G31 cargo version could carry a useful load of 3,200 kilograms over short distances.

The first Junkers G31 cargo landed in the aerodrome of Bulolo on 31st March 1931, marking the start of the first airlift in the history of aviation. Almost a year later, 21st March 1932 was a day of great festivities on the operating site: Dredge Number 1 was taken into service, followed in October by Dredge Number 2. During the start-up ceremony, a director of BDG declared: "The transport of mining machinery by aeroplane is being watched with considerable interest by engineers the world over." [16] At the end of 1939, eight dredges were operating in Bulolo Gold Fields, all delivered by air

In somewhat under 10 years of operation, between March 1931 and January 1942, the three Junkers G31 cargo aircraft, named "Peter", "Paul" and "Pat" carried 35,750 tonnes of goods.

3 THE UNITED STATES

Air Express

The United States was a special case in the transportation of goods by air, which was largely undertaken by Air Express until well into 1940. Since the mid–19th century, the express carriage of packages by private companies, either complementary to or in competition with the Post Office, had been a major factor in the American communications system. The railway companies controlled the transport network, and had been the object of fundamental reforms on 1st January 1918. On this date the American government, anxious to ensure a coherent express transport network for all the firms participating in the war effort, compelled all the express service companies to regroup into a single one operating nationwide: The American Railway Express Company. After being entirely privatised just

returned remarkable results, thanks to the performance of the Junkers 34s, of which the airline took delivery of a third model in 1930. The company transported 2,792 passengers and 1,170 tonnes of freight between December 1927 and January 1930. Without receiving a penny by way of subsidies, the profits they recorded were nothing short of remarkable: the company paid large dividends and in 1930 distributed one free share for every share held. Incidentally, this move had a disastrous effect on the small companies and individual operators who were the competitors of the powerful Guinea Gold. Highly critical of the "usurious rates" charged by Guinea Airways which some people called "God Almighty", these small air transporters managed to make life difficult for Guinea Airways in spite of their limited means, and forced it to reduce its prices on several occasions.

A new company, intended to exploit the rich pickings of the Bulolo valley on a large scale, was founded in February 1930 in the midst of the world crisis. It was the task of the Bulolo Gold Dredging Ltd – BGD – to install and operate enormous dredges, capable of processing gigantic quantities of gold-containing gravels. Once again, the operators were confronted with a transport problem, but of such size and difficulty that it appeared to be insoluble: how were they to transport dismantled dredges, of which the single heaviest component (the vital tumbler shaft) weighed over three tonnes, onto the site by aeroplane, within an acceptable time scale? There was only one manufacturer who could meet the challenge: Junkers, with a specially adapted cargo version of the G31. The G31 was an all-metal monoplane in the Junkers tradition, and was used from after the war, this new company was endorsed by the Transportation Act of 1920, and approved by the Inter-State Commerce Commission in spite of its monopolistic character.

The "World Almanac", a work intended for the general public, provided the best explanation of an express service:

"*Express service is a nationwide system for the expedited transportation of packages and larger shipments direct from senders to receivers in some 23,000 cities and towns located on railroad lines.*" [17]

We should take good note of this definition. Fifty years ahead of its time, it encapsulates admirably the policy and ambitions of the two present American giants in the field: Federal Express (Fedex) and United Parcel Service (UPS).

In spite of its name and

American Railway Express Company

AIR EXPRESS TARIFF No. 1

Applying on Traffic Carried by

AIRPLANE

From and To

BOSTON, MASS., NEW YORK, N. Y., CHICAGO, ILL., DALLAS, TEX., SALT LAKE CITY, UTAH, LOS ANGELES, CALIF., SAN FRANCISCO, CALIF.

And the Intermediate Landing Points named herein

ISSUED August 24, 1927.   EFFECTIVE September 1, 1927.

ROB'T E. M. COWIE, President, New York, N. Y.   F. S. HOLBROOK, Vice-President, New York, N. Y.   Issued by GEO. S. LEE, Traffic Manager, 46 Trinity Place, New York, N. Y.

tions, and which would be paid wholly to the operator, that was not the same for the share allocated to air transport activities. This amount was to cover the transport activity carried out by the airlines, as well as the sales and marketing activities provided by the American Railway Express Cy. Since the latter had the upper hand for the time being, it imposed its point of view and received 25% of the share of income attributed to the air transport activity.

The transcontinental Air Express service was launched on 1st September 1927 with the support of the four main airlines: Colonial Air Transport between Boston and New York, National Air Transport between New York and Chicago and also between Chicago and Dallas, Boeing Air Transport between Chicago and San Francisco, and Western Air Express

its railway connections, American Railway Express realised very soon the role that air transport could play in a national express freight system. It organised a trial in November 1919, with a four-engined Vickers Vimy Bomber between New York and Chicago. Buffeted by violent winds and suffering from mechanical problems, the aircraft was forced to land 20 minutes after take-off. The express freight was unloaded and taken to the nearest railway station. The experiment was premature and produced no immediate consequences, but the plan for a regular night service between New York and Chicago had aroused considerable interest among the shippers.

Contacts between American Railway Express and the new airlines were established in 1926. Following a conference held in Chicago in summer 1927, an agreement was finally signed as they were well aware that their interests were converging. On one side, the President of the American Railway Express made a realistic estimate of the potential risk presented by private airlines which operated mail contracts on favourable terms; for the other side, the airlines in 1927 were attempting to gain access to a pick up and delivery service on a national scale (a goal that still eludes them today). There was therefore a niche for a service integrating the air transport capacity of one group with the terrestrial distribution network of the other: it became Air Express, marketed by the Air Express Division of the American Railway Express Cy. As one can imagine, the financial aspects of the agreement were the subject of dogged negotiations. Although there was no difference of opinion regarding the proportion of the rate which would be allocated to ground opera-

between Salt Lake City and Los Angeles.

Some days previously, on 24th August, a four-page document had been published containing the terms and conditions for transportation, and the rating regulations for this new service, under the title of Air Express Tariff No 1. The rates between the 26 towns served by air were all-inclusive rates from the sender to the consignee. The unit rate on which the tariff was based was a quarter of a pound or 4 ounces (113 grams) and there was no diminishing scale for weight. The maximum weight per package was limited to 200lb (90 kilograms) and each package was regarded as a separate consignment. These few tariff conditions allow us to see exactly the kind of market that Air Express was aiming for: urgent small- and medium-sized consignments despatched from door to door.

The other airlines subsequently joined in with this agreement, which offered many advantages: the ease of combining express air and rail services, the creation of an enhanced network effect due to the unification of sections of routes operated by individual companies, and, to an even greater extent, the marketing of available capacity. For its part, American Railway Express changed its identity on 1st March 1929, following a change in its shareholders, and became the Railway Express Agency, better known under its initials REA.

Relations between the airlines and REA became very strained when, in 1932, seven airlines, led by TWA, decided to break free of the control of the railways and founded a rival company, the General Air Express Company.

This incident would not be particularly important if it did not contain a lesson, which is still valid today: "He who has no powerful distribution network should not dabble in express delivery companies". The splinter group was immediately confronted by the problem of door-to-door collection and delivery. In search of a solution, it decided to join forces with the Postal Telegraph Cable Company, which possessed its own vehicle transport network. The new group was not short on ambition, since it envisaged that "items would initially be transported by both passenger and mail planes, but that special types of aircraft would be created for the exclusive transport of goods once the need had become established." [18] In fact, General Air Express was unable to assert itself against the formidable nationwide infrastructure of REA. The revolt came to an end in September 1937, when TWA returned to the fold. However, the rebellion of a few airlines was not without one happy result: it forced REA to reduce its remuneration rate from 25% to 12.5% of the air transport revenues in summer 1932.

In 1938, the Civil Aeronautics Board fixed the rate for the air transport element of the Air Express Service to $0.80 per ton-mile.

The Air Express traffic was hit head on by the Great Depression of 1929–1933 and only properly got under way from 1933/1934 with the economic upturn and the use of aircraft with increased capacity.

In 1940, 18 airlines belonged to the Air Express Agreement with REA, whose 23,000 offices ensured complete coverage of American territory. In spite of its brilliant development, Air Express played a modest role in the grand scheme of things: it only represented 0.7% of the global activity of REA (1 million consignments out of a total of almost 149 million) and only brought in 3% of the airlines' revenue. Typically, it was an activity for small, urgent consignments, of low unit weight, and consisted for the most part of replacement parts, printed matter and articles of a very high unit value from the major department stores.

Air Express was not restricted to serving domestic requirements, since Pan American Airways opened an express freight service in 1930, followed by its subsidiary Panagra in 1931. The latter presents a particularly interesting case: it developed simultaneously an express freight service for goods from the United States, and a service for ordinary freight, consisting of investment goods carried between the South American locations on its network. In August 1934 Pan American and REA made a similar agreement to that which linked REA to the domestic airlines. REA agreed to issue Pan American's own particular despatch documents, whereas all domestic consignments were covered by an Air Service Uniform Express Receipt which was common to all the airlines.

Development of Air Express Traffic 1928–1940

Year	No of consignments	Weight in kg	Av weight/ consignment
1928	17,006		
1931	9,074		
1935	200,222	700,272	3.5kg
1938	715,410	2,148,182	3.0kg
1940	1,078,189	3,500,000	3.2kg

Source: "Air Express & Freight", REA Inc., Jan 1942.

Development of Pan American Airways express traffic

	Latin American Division	Pacific Division	Total
1930	5,525kg		5,525kg
1934	436,800kg		436,800kg
1938	396,800kg	8,500kg	405,300kg
1940	489,000kg	31,400kg	520,400kg

Express freight provided 3.7% of Pan American Airways income in 1938 and 4.5% in 1940.

What became of ordinary airfreight?
Although it was never completely absent, ordinary airfreight was never more than the object of temporary exploitation, and almost always remained of limited scope.

With the optimism of novices, a few small airlines rushed into untimely experiments. The best known of these was Aéro Marine, which had the courage, or the rashness in view of its limited means, to run a publicity campaign self-confidently announcing "the dawn of an era of freight by air"! Its efforts received their just reward, and the company can be proud of a world "first" which Harry Bruno (cf bibliography) announced with some humour. [19]

"Our ship, the 'Buckeye' (F5L seaplane) piloted by Ed Musik was the first aeroplane to carry a Ford car from Detroit to Cleveland. The old model T was a light car, but 1,500lb was a spectacularly heavy load for even as big an aeroplane as the 'Buckeye' to carry. The word that we were going to attempt it brought droves of reporters and photographers to our landing float. The roadster was driven down to the dock under its own power and photographed as it came to a rattling stop. Then it was rolled to the freight shed to be taken down, in order to pack it into the cabin of the plane. Reporters watched the various sections of the car being pushed aboard and at four men's efforts to bring in a box labelled 'Motor'. They cheered with the rest of the crowd as the 'Buckeye' took off without mistake.

After 20 years I regret my role in this 'First'. The motor, which embraced about half of the weight of the roadster, was not in the box put aboard that day. The irony of it is that it might just as well have been on board the plane. The 'Buckeye' could well have borne this load, as we learned much later."

(This is why one should be very chary about the different "firsts" which were reported!)

In the United States, as elsewhere, the transport of daily newspapers to coastal resorts during the tourist season provided some airlines with an ephemeral living, such as the Balsam Air Service between Garden City near New York and Dixville Notch in New Hampshire during summer 1922, and the Curtiss Metropolitan Airplane Company during winter 1923 across the short stretch between Miami and West Palm Beach.

In its triple role as car builder, aircraft constructor and airline, Ford made the only attempt to use airfreight on a large scale. For four years from 1928 to 1932, the Aeronautical Division operated daily cargo links on behalf of the Automobile Division between the factories and warehouses of Dearborn (Detroit) and Chicago, Cleveland and Buffalo. In total, more than 14 million pounds (approximately 6,500 tonnes) of components were conveyed by air to feed the assembly lines. This was the first example of the integration of airfreight into a logistic process, but the experiment was not convincing. The distances between the towns served were too short and the surface transport facilities too efficient for an aircraft to bring a significant quality advantage. No public traffic was accepted on board these aeroplanes.

In terms of aircraft production, Ford's efforts produced no reward. In this period of great economic depression, not a single purchaser came forward to buy a cargo plane. In spite of all these negative aspects, the Ford trial remains paradoxically positive: during the four-year cargo operation, numerous industrialists came to Detroit to find out about it. Although they didn't order aeroplanes, they did learn from their visits that air transport applied to general cargo, as much as to mail or passengers.

Despite the Ford Motor Company's pioneering airfreight operations, all other attempts at transporting air cargo for the public at the time in the US were very limited:

• For a few months in 1931, Western Pacific Airfreighters operated a Ford Tri-motor to transport poultry and perishable products between San Francisco, Seattle, Boise and Reno.

• Also in 1931, Air Ferries Cy of San Francisco flew merchandise across the bay between San Francisco and Oakland, until the construction of the bridge dealt it the death blow!

Two other trials deserve special mention since, though short lived, each shows an interesting approach:

• In winter 1932–1933, Air Express Inc, which had been founded by a Denver business man and supported by New York capital sources, launched a transcontinental night cargo service between New York and Los Angeles using a Lockheed Orion, one of the fastest aeroplanes at that time. It carried flowers one way and lobsters on the return journey, before ceasing after a few months.

• At the end of 1936, TWA undertook a large survey of potential clients to assess the sensitivity of traffic to rate reductions: an innovative marketing approach for a short-lived service.

However, there was one state, which then was still a Territory, in which airfreight was already enjoying great success. In Alaska, traffic reached 1,900 tonnes during 1938–1939. [20] As in the Canadian far north, the small mining communities, isolated in the snow and ice, were completely dependant on the bush pilots. Robert Reeve was one of them. On a fine spring day in 1932, he disembarked at Valdez, a small port on the southern coast of Alaska, with $2 in his pocket, attracted by the lure of gold, the camaraderie of the pilots and the prospect of being his own master. [21] He decided he would become a bush pilot, first with a Fairchild 51 and later with a Fairchild 71, which was convertible for cargo flights.

"That first winter, Reeve also learned the vital importance of the bush pilot to the inhabitants of the isolated communities around the territory. He was supposed to serve as mailman, a message carrier and purchasing agent. Each trip, people clustered around the aeroplane to see what the pilot had brought. He once forgot to pick up some snuff for an old Swedish miner; his oversight was talked about for a long time. The bush pilot was a lifeline to the rest of the world; to be forgotten was in Reeve's words 'a crushing, and often humiliating blow'.

"Many times, he went out of his way to get crates of fresh fruit for the isolated villagers – the greatest treat of all."

As in Canada and in New Guinea, the revaluation of the gold price by President Roosevelt started off a veritable gold rush, causing the reopening of mines situated in inaccessible locations – except to the bush pilots. When they reopened the Big Four Mine, only 30 miles from Valdez, but at 2,000 metres above sea level, Reeve made 60 flights in a single month, landing 30 tonnes of equipment on the Brevier Glacier, which served him as an airstrip.

In the final analysis, due to its size and diversity, the United States offers a broad insight into the air transport of goods between the two wars, illustrating the development of express, the attempts at airfreight services, and the bush pilots of Alaska.

9 THE SOVIET EXPERIENCE

The early history of the air transport of goods and mail would not be complete without a special chapter on the newly formed USSR.

I DETERMINING FACTORS

Commercial aviation in Russia was born with the Soviet regime. But its development resulted from the relationship between two factors: one external – geography – and the other adopted from within – Marxist-Leninist doctrine. Where there was conflict between these two elements, the second, often carried more weight than the first.

Geography

For the great Russian novelists, as in military campaigns, the mighty features of Russian geography play a dominant role: the immensity of the USSR (with an area of 22 million square kilometres [13.75 million square miles], it is twice as vast as Canada, China or the United States); the rigours of winter; the chaos of the thaw ("the most impressive climatic phenomenon of the year, accompanied by the liquefaction of the soil)";[1] the sheer extent of the forests and marshes; the hydrography, running north/south, a barrier to east/west human communication. The widely dispersed population and the inadequacy of communication routes, together with the presence of minable deposits in inaccessible regions, served to accentuate the conditions which were naturally favourable to the creation of a massive air transport activity.

Political philosophy

Confronted with these realities, what was the response of Marxist-Leninist doctrine, and what was the place of aviation in the general transport theory of this first state to be governed under the principles of socialist economics? Such an economy is founded on two basic rules:

1. The collectivisation of means of production: "the economic basis of the USSR is constituted by the system of socialist economy and by the socialist ownership of the instruments and means of production." (Article 4 of the Constitution)

2. The planning of the economy: "the economic life of the USSR is determined and directed by the State Plan." (Article

11) It operated to the rhythm of the Five-Year Plans. The Plan was prepared at the summit of government by a gigantic planning organisation – The "Central Commission for the Plan of the Union" – and was the product of collective work issuing from various commissariats for production and transport, which themselves relayed the requirements of other regional and local bodies. In reality, the much-vaunted flexibility of these mechanisms, and the principle of decentralisation, were never converted into fact; the Soviet economy always suffered from excessive centralisation.

Between the two world wars, the object of the Five-Year Plans was essentially to provide the country with a basic industrial infrastructure and with a communication network. "As the transport problem presents itself more urgently in the USSR than in any other country of the world",[2] the role of planning lay in optimising the utilisation of means and in rationalising choices:

• Optimising the utilisation of means: since it was engaged in an unprecedented effort at industrial development, the Soviet Union did not possess the capital necessary to carry through all its projects. Faced with a scarcity of means, it favoured production. The ideal balance between production and transport was that which minimised the volumes transported with respect to a given level of production.

• Rationalising choices: Soviet theory considered that each means of transport should only be exploited as a function of its own particular qualities and advantages, and that the competition between different means of transport was a source of waste, unless it was strictly controlled. It was the railways and waterways which corresponded to the industrial emphasis of the first plans and satisfied the taste of the regime for grandiose achievements and therefore enjoyed the greatest share of investment. The functions of air transportation, for which the Second Plan reserved an important role, were clearly defined in keeping with the general doctrine; on the one hand its principal mission was to contribute to the development of remote areas lacking in ground communications, in central Asia, Siberia and the Arctic; on the other hand it had a secondary mission to complement the existing means of surface transport whenever urgent delivery was economically or politically justified (newspapers and political literature).

2 THE GREAT LEAP FORWARD OF THE SECOND FIVE-YEAR PLAN

During the course of the 1920s, the creation of a civil aviation system was not among the primary preoccupations of the new communist power, which had inherited a disorganised country ravaged by war. The first signs of air transport were few and far between. The authorities were not concerned solely with airmail, but, as in western and central Europe, handled official passengers, post and certain urgent goods. Instead of following the meanderings of this complex story, we will limit ourselves to recalling individual events or achievements in the period 1920–28.

The first experiment in air transport occurred between May and October 1921 on the Moscow/Kharkov (Ukraine) route. Three converted Ilya Murometz bombers under the command of Captain Tumansky made 43 flights at a rate of about two per week conveying 6,000 kilograms [3] of mail in addition to about 60 passengers. This was a short-term service, and ceased on the re-establishment of normal rail links, but it is interesting from two points of view: its primarily postal role, and the operation of an aircraft which has been unjustly forgotten, the Sikorsky Ilya Murometz.

The Ilya Murometz, designed in 1912/1913 by the young engineer Igor Sikorsky and tested in 1914 just before the declaration of war, was the first giant aircraft of its time. It was fitted with three in-line engines, and intended to carry six passengers installed in an enclosed cabin. Some even called it the "Aerobus".

The next episode, organised by the company Deruluft, was not a trial but a permanent service. Before the birth of the Soviet Union, the Bolshevik authorities had signed a separate peace treaty with Germany at Brest Litovsk on 3rd March 1918 which permitted them to concentrate their forces against the internal opposition which was supported by the Allied powers. Thus, Germany was the only power which had established legal links with the Soviet regime. In 1921, negotiations were commenced between the German company Aero-Union and the Commercial Representation of Soviet Russia. On 11th November 1921 they founded an airline, of which the capital was held 50/50 by the two parties: the company was Deruluft-Deutsch-Russische Luftverkehrsgesellschaft mbH. The signing of the Treaty of Rapallo on 16th April 1922, under the terms of which Germany recognised the legal existence of the Soviet Union, removed the last obstacle to the establishment of a permanent airlink between the two countries. On 1st May 1922, a symbolic date, Deruluft opened its service between Königsberg (a city that was then situated in East Prussia, now Kaliningrad) and Moscow via Kaunas and Smolensk. As a general air transport company, Deruluft handled all types of traffic, but post and goods (which also included the excess baggage of the passengers, a usual practice at the time) represented a notable part of its activity, as if shown in the following figures:

Traffic, freight and mail from the company Deruluft [4]

	Mail	Freight	Total
1922	1,047kg	19,919kg	20,962kg
1925	5,410kg	38,543kg	43,953kg
1930	27,244	49,933	77,177
1935	72,200	329,000	401,200

From May 1922, until it ceased operations in March 1937, Deruluft flew Fokker FIII, Dornier Komet and Merkur, Junkers 52, and then the Russian Tupolev ANT9 aircraft.

Before the enactment of the first Five-Year Plan, the known cases of goods transported by air in the Soviet Union are few and fragmentary, including the modest traffic in 1922 between Moscow and Niznhy Novgorod on the occasion of the annual fair. More important was the establishment in 1925 of a link-up between a station on the Trans-Siberian railway and the gold fields of Bodaibo on the River Aldan, a tributary of the Lena, in eastern Siberia. A trek of 35 days through the forest on mule back was replaced by an air journey of a few hours.

The First Plan (1929–1932) was devoted to the development of heavy industry, and did not include air transport among its primary objectives. However, it did include production forecasts, as for all sectors of the Soviet economy. These forecasts were too ambitious, and were far from being fulfilled.

Objectives and results from the First Five-Year Plan

	1928	1932 Objectives	Results
Mail	93 tonnes	1,700 tonnes	450 tonnes
Merchandise	155 tonnes	1,600 tonnes	550 tonnes
Total	248 tonnes	3,300 tonnes	1,000 tonnes

The results fell far short of the targets. However, scheduled airfreight operations began to appear, whilst the mail, as elsewhere, fully played out its role in supporting the build-up of new services.

On 15th May 1929, the company Dobrolet – one of the forebears of Aeroflot – opened a regular Moscow/Sverdlovsk/Novosibirsk/Irkutsk (later extended to Vladivostok) service. This route, laid along the Trans-Siberian railway, became the backbone of the Soviet air network, and for two years, from May 1929 to May 1931, was reserved exclusively for mail transport, before being opened up to passengers. The same happened with the service to central Asia. Consistently in Soviet civil aviation, the Post opened up the way. These would be observed much later in the introduction of the supersonic aircraft Tupolev 144.

However, freight was the decisive factor in the launch in 1928 of a scheduled service between Irkutsk and Yakutsk in Central Siberia, of which one branch served the Bodaibo gold deposits. It was operated using Junkers W33s, aircraft designed primarily for goods transport. This was a line typical of a developing country. The route enabled the opening up of a hostile landscape, isolated and sparsely populated.

The distribution by air of the complete type blocks for "Pravda" (the official daily newspaper for the Communist Party) within European Russia illustrates the second Soviet use of air transport: to complement surface transport in exceptional circumstances. In this case the more rapid circulation of official views justified the recourse to the aeroplane. A trial service was begun on 3rd June 1930 between Moscow and Kharkov. On 16th June, a special air transport section was created to convey in the shortest possible time the type blocks for "Pravda" from Moscow to Kharkov, Leningrad, Sebastopol, Pyatagorsk, Grozny, Odessa, Kazan, Rostov, Tblisi and Sverdlovsk.

The Second Five-Year Plan, however, saw the start up of civil aviation in earnest. In socialist economics, political imperatives

Junkers W33.
MAP

replaced private initiative and the 17th Congress of the Communist Party passed a resolution in February 1932, stating: "Air transport shall be developed in all directions." Henceforward, transport aviation was one of the priority sectors of the Second Plan, 1932–1937. The planners, who were no doubt more smitten with Marxist theory than with the economics of transportation, assigned altogether unrealistic objectives: 60,000 tonnes of post, "corresponding to 40% of the total internal mail traffic", [5] and 230,000 tonnes of cargo (some sources even mention 2.3 million tonnes, which must be wrong since this figure is so unfeasible).

Whatever the forecast, air transportation did make a spectacular leap forward during the Second Five-Year Plan, due to the use of aircraft of Soviet manufacture, the introduction of a new organisation for civil aviation and the zeal of certain individuals.

From the beginning of the 1930s, Soviet aircraft production slowly took over from foreign aircraft, mostly German, thanks to the talents of three designers:

• Constantin Kalinin, whose single-engine cable-stayed K5 monoplane, characterised by its elliptical wing, was equipped to transport eight passengers at approximately 100mph over a distance of 300 miles. This was the most popular aircraft in the USSR in the 1930s.

• Andrei Tupolev, whose ANT9 was designed to carry nine passengers (or an equivalent weight of goods) at 105mph over about 600 miles, and which in its three-engine or two-engine versions was operated right up to the end of the Second World War. The four-engined ANT6, which could carry 12 passengers, was manufactured in a very large production series (over 600 units) but was essentially operated in its military version, except in Arctic aviation.

• Nikolai Polikarpov, whose two small-sized single-engine aircraft were operated on a large scale. First was the U2, later called the Po2, which was for over 30 years the best known

aircraft in the USSR, a legendary biplane, entrusted with all imaginable missions in times of war and in times of peace. The second was the P5, a civilian version of the R5 military aircraft, owned in large numbers by Aeroflot and used for transporting mail. None the less, the Soviet authorities felt that they had fallen behind compared with American aircraft construction and this led them to obtain a manufacturing licence for the Douglas DC-3. After being introduced in 1940, and renamed "Lisunov Li2" in 1942, it became the workhorse among Soviet transport aircraft, whether civilian or military, for passengers or cargo.

The job of fulfilling the ambitious objectives of the Five-Year Plan fell to the main board of the Civil Air Fleet, or Aeroflot. Founded on 26th March 1932, Aeroflot was far more than an straightforward airline in the classic sense of the term. In its eight sections it encompassed all aspects of civil aviation, from air transport using gliders, to airfields, airships and agricultural aviation. From a territorial point of view, it was organised in 13 regions, each provided with a regional management board.

Equipped and organised as such, Aeroflot attacked the grandiose objectives of the Plan. Admittedly, it did not achieve them – far from it – but the progress was such that for mail and goods transport it took the Soviets to the top of the world rankings in 1940.

It is difficult to interpret the results recorded in the USSR, since the various kinds of performance and their numerical representation were both systemically accepted and praised by some, and contested and vilified by others. Against this background of caustic criticism and sycophancy, it is exceedingly difficult make a clear assessment.

Objectives and results from the Second Five-Year Plan [6]
(in tonnes)

	1932	1937 Objectives	Results	1940 Results
Mail	450	60,000	9,040	14,600
Freight	550	230,000	36,950	47,540
Total	1,000	290,000	45,990	62,140

The figures summarised above are at least plausible. Bearing in mind that two airlines in two small countries, Guatemala and New Guinea, carried 15,000 tonnes of goods in 1938, it is probable that Aeroflot in 1940 carried over 47,000 tonnes of freight, considering the fleet of aircraft available, the size of the country and its immense needs. Being perfectly adapted to the physical and human characteristics of the USSR, the aeroplane became an irreplaceable tool in the exploitation of distant regions in Siberia, Central Asia or in the Arctic far north. Likewise, the Soviet regime was quick to understand the advantages of possessing such an incomparable instrument for spreading official views via the press.

Until 1936–1937, there were many long-haul lines which, beyond a certain point, only carried mail: Moscow/Vladivostok (5,120 miles) was opened to passengers and mail as far as Novosibirsk, but thereafter only carried the mail; Moscow/Tashkent took passengers as far as Samara, and only post beyond: the Moscow/Leningrad service was reserved exclusively for the transport of mail. [7]

In spite of the apparent remarkable volume of traffic, Aeroflot was confronted with immense difficulties. In spite of the initial investment, civil aviation was soon to be sacrificed to military aviation, due to the growing danger of a coalition between Germany and Japan. At the same time, hundreds of civil servants and engineers were dismissed, arrested or deported under accusations of sabotage or espionage during the great Stalinist purges. Finally, the irresistible love of the regime for achievement reports showing quantitative figures, in preference to qualitative evaluations, handicapped Aeroflot:

"The result of this situation (in 1936) is that the Soviet airlines, which are ill equipped, poorly provided with tools, and badly served by incompetent personnel, disciplined on the surface but who in fact were only out to avoid even a minimum of responsibility, have fallen far behind the foreign airlines. Traffic is irregular, accidents frequent. Most services only operate episodically, either when the weather is good, or when there is no shortage of personnel, equipment or fuel, which is relatively rare ... For lack of money and trained mechanics, the infrastructure of the airlines is still very rudimentary, and even non-existent on most of the secondary routes." [8]

In spite of this gloomy picture, which has a strange resemblance to certain descriptions made over 50 years later, there were still some encouraging signs:

"The improvement in the general situation allows the government to devote larger credits than in the past to developing and equipping the airlines. The appointment to the top positions in Civil Aviation of leaders known for their energy, should improve discipline and above all the application of the personnel." [8]

Aeroflot, responsible for all branches of aviation, thought of using airships and gliders to link up with distant areas lacking in the ground-based infrastructure. The experiments were not very convincing, and plans to operated scheduled goods services by airship, and connections by means of "glider trains" composed of three to five gliders towed in a "V" arrangement behind a single aircraft were shelved.

3 SOVIET POLAR AVIATION

Towards the end of the 1920s, the Soviet Union discovered a new frontier, in the American sense of the word: the far north beyond the Arctic Circle, the endless shoreline, most of the time blocked by ice, extending from Archangel to the Behring Strait. "The conquest of the Arctic was included among the gigantic labours of the First Five Year Plan." [9]

A Commission for the Arctic was constituted in 1929, and the mission of exploring and setting up basic facilities in the region was conferred upon the Central Administration for the Northern Sea Route. On 1st September 1930, the latter created a Polar Aviation Department, otherwise known as Aviaarktika, which established itself in Krasnoyarsk in central Siberia. Aviaarktika's fleet of aircraft originally consisted of Junkers F13s fitted with skis or floats depending on the season, and Dornier Wal seaplanes, and was later reinforced with four-engined Ant-6s.

Whilst Aeroflot established a network which frequently followed the layout of the railways, Aviaarktika opened new routes through virgin terrain, lacking any lines of communication. Its aircraft frequently worked in horrendous conditions: snowstorms, frequent fog, intense cold. It fulfilled multiple missions, carrying cargo, as well as mail and passengers, and living as much from charter transportation as from regular traffic. The mining deposits and the scientific and weather stations extending along the northern sea route, which is theoretically the shortest route between Europe and Japan, were entirely dependant on supply by air – as was the case in the far north of Canada. In order to supply the mining centre at Norilsk, in the extreme north of Siberia, Aviaarktika opened a branch off the Krasnoyarsk/Dikson route, joining central Siberia with the icebound Arctic Ocean. But the great achievement of Aviaarktika, which is too frequently forgotten these days, remains the opening up of the Moscow/Petropavlovsk (in Kamchatka) service, first stretch by stretch, and then the full scheduled operation on 1st February 1940. It involved a journey of 5,000 miles in nine days, along the northern route following the coast of the Arctic Ocean, past the mouths of the great Siberian rivers, then crossing the Anadyr Massif.

Between 1931 and 1937 the Arctic was the scene of events which were abundantly exploited by Soviet propaganda, a number of which involved airfreight or airmail.

At 21.30 hours on 27th July 1931 a remarkable first took place on the diminutive Hooker Island, which is part of Franz Joseph Land – the first "aeronautical link-up in the Arctic" [10] between the German airship "Graf Zeppelin" and the Soviet icebreaker "Malygin". The icebreaker's boat approached the nacelle of the airship and handed over 400 kilograms of mail. Of course, this was not correspondence from individuals overwintering in the scientific and weather stations in the area, but philatelic mail, and was an opportunity for the two nations to celebrate their technical prowess and friendship.

Once the handover had been made, the icebreaker continued on its way, and the airship went on cruising eastwards towards the Severnaya Zemlya, which it reached on 28th July. Then things started to go wrong: a thick fog enveloped the whole region and it proved impossible to find the weather station and deliver the mail to its snowbound inhabitants.

The next event was the Papanin expedition of 1937, an extraordinary operation in combined air/sea transportation. Ivan B. Papanin was the director of a scientific station on Cape Chelyuskin on the Arctic Ocean, when he submitted the plan for a new Polar expedition. Its mission was: "To set up camp on a moving ice flow and to live on it as it is drawn along by the current." [11] The originality of the project lay less in the idea of a "drifting expedition", which had already been suggested in 1881, than in the choice of the North Pole as the expedition's point of departure. The project proved attractive and Papanin found himself nominated to prepare and lead the expedition. Following detailed studies, he decided to transport all the equipment for the future North Pole station by aeroplane from Rodolph Island, the northernmost of the islands in Franz Josef Land which offered natural landing strips. Due to the extreme thoroughness in dealing with the transport problems, the Papanin expedition is a remarkable example of adapting the packaging of equipment and goods to suit the peculiarities of air transport. However, in spite of all the efforts at reducing the weight to be transported, it reached about 10 tonnes, of which 3 tonnes consisted of food packaged in 70-kilogram drums.

Between 21st May and 5th June 1937, four ANT-6 aircraft transported the four members of the expedition and all their equipment from Rodolph Island to the North Pole. The cargo was piled up in the cabin and loaded into compartments situated in the wings.

The first arrival was "Pilot Vodopianov, who made a masterly landing on the ice" on 21st May 1937 at 11.00am, 13 miles from the Pole. He had just accomplished the most astounding example of combined transport: the link up between an aircraft and a floating sheet of ice, which would take the Papanin expedition to a position just off Greenland, where it was picked up on 19th February 1938 by two Soviet icebreakers.

27 July 1931, a courier goes out over the ice to the "Graf Zeppelin".

Part Four
The Disruption of the Second World War 1939–1945

"Uncommon valor was a common virtue."

Fleet Admiral Chester Nimitz (1885–1966)

1 CIVILIAN AND MILITARY AIRMAIL

The world's airlines as a whole had just begun to form a coherent network when the invasion of Poland by German troops on 1st September 1939 triggered the Second World War. Regular operations across the North Atlantic had been initiated only three months before and the South Atlantic route was still reserved to postal traffic. In the absence of ground equipment and adequate means of navigation, no long-haul line was yet carrying passengers by night.

Although it would create enormous specific demands for transport, the war began by immediately interrupting air communication routes. States used their sovereign powers to close their air space to foreign airlines, and civilian aircraft fleets were requisitioned to fulfil the needs of national defence.

1 CIVILIAN AIRMAIL: INTERRUPTIONS AND ADAPTATIONS

The first measures to restrict air transport were taken in Europe a few days before the outbreak of hostilities, when international tension was reaching its peak.

Switzerland forbade any aircraft to over fly its territory on 29th August 1939. On the same date France finalised its war plans, and suspended all air services on 2nd September, the date of the general mobilisation, although it was to resume the operation of long-haul lines and a few European services (Paris/London) later. A few days before the declaration of war, Great Britain collected on its territory all the aircraft, which had been scattered throughout Europe, and the air fleet was put at the disposition of the Government. Germany was forced to suspend its airmail links with South America.

The situation became more dramatic in June 1940 after the German invasion of the Netherlands and Belgium, the collapse of France and the entry of Italy into the war. KLM transferred the terminus of its Batavia service to Lydda in Palestine, which was under British mandate. Connections between Great Britain and Europe were reduced to the Stockholm and Lisbon services, whilst the strategically important imperial services were broken off.

Civilian airmail was obviously affected. Wisely, the different postal administrations adopted measures to restrict the volumes down to the level of the reduced and often unreliable capacities available.

On 2nd September Great Britain cancelled the Imperial Airmail plan and re-established the surcharges: the cost of an air-letter for Hong Kong – via the United States – leapt from 1½ pence to 5 shillings! The expected consequence did not take long: the average weekly traffic of British airmail fell from over 20 tonnes to about 3 tonnes.

For its part, the Canadian Post Office informed the public and its own employees regarding the restrictions, which would affect the conveyance of airmail:

"Post masters are kindly requested to remember that the only places in Europe for which correspondence by air can be accepted are Gibraltar, Portugal, Spain, Switzerland, the State of the Vatican City, and the non-occupied territories of France ..." [1]

Whilst the volume of mail being exchanged was diminishing, the transport times were increasing under the dual effect of lack of capacity and the introduction of censorship. The Post Offices had to show considerable imagination in finding new routing circuits. When leaving Europe, they mostly used the services of Pan American – officially the United States was neutral – which departed from Lisbon for Asia and the Americas.

Surprisingly, the Axis powers (Germany and Italy) did not have to fall back on complicated and expensive strategies to maintain their airmail links with South America. On 21st December 1939, with the war raging, the Italian Company LATI – Linee Aeree Transcontinentali Italiane – inaugurated a regular airmail link between Italy and Brazil. It was operated by four Savoia Marchetti S83 seaplanes and this weekly service followed the Rome/Seville/Villa Cisneros/Cape Verde Islands/Recife/Bahia/Rio route. It continued to function after Italy entered into the war against Great Britain and was extended to Buenos Aires in July 1941. On this occasion the Brazilian postal authorities affixed a violet sticker to the mail items: "Voo Inaugural Brazil – Argentina, Julho 1941 XIX". [2]

The service came to an end in December 1941 when the United States entered the war. At that point the American Government firmly requested the Brazilian and Argentinean authorities to discontinue any supply of fuel to the Italian seaplanes. For two years they had provided an excellent postal service, and had permitted the German press to be distributed by aeroplane to Brazil. Thus the issue of the "Frankfurter Zeitung" for 1st May 1940 was put on sale in Rio with a sticker: "*Gefördert durch Transatlantikflug*" – "Transported on transatlantic flight".

The role of Lisbon: Thomas Cook and PO Box 506
In spite of the state of war, the belligerent nations soon felt the need to have a point of contact which wold allow their citizens to continue corresponding with relatives living in enemy territory. Lisbon occupied this role as meeting point during the whole period of the war.

With its harbour, its seaplane base on the Tagus, and its airport, Lisbon became the "doorway to Europe." [3] Crews and aircraft met up peaceably – Italians from Ala Littoria (Rome/ Lisbon), Germans from Deutsche Lufthansa (Berlin/Stuttgart/Lyons/ Barcelona/Madrid/Lisbon), Spanish from Iberia (Barcelona/Madrid/ Lisbon) and British from British Overseas Airways Corporation (or the Dutch, since KLM had retreated to London, putting its resources at the disposal of the British, and operated the London/Lisbon route on its behalf). And we should not forget the Portuguese of Aero Portuguesa, nor, above all, the Americans of Pan American Airways, who offered connections with the long-haul routes which started from Lisbon and the United States.

From May 1940 onwards, Lisbon functioned as the airmail exchange centre for the Germans and the British.

At the beginning of 1940, the British Post Office had organised a routing circuit for mail destined for Germany and occupied territories, for the benefit of families separated by the war. In order that the Post Office, as an official body, would not be directly involved in the process and accused of consorting with the enemy, the British Government designated an official intermediary to carry out the operation: this was the famous London Travel Agency Thomas Cook & Son Ltd. Amsterdam served as the handover point until Holland, a neutral country, was invaded by German troops on 10th May 1940. Another city had to be found, and Lisbon was elected.

In its role as official forwarding agent, Thomas Cook & Son maintained for the duration of the hostilities the operation of the famous PO Box 506, Lisbon, through which millions of letters between Great Britain and Germany or the occupied territories made their transit in both directions. The inhabitants of the Channel Islands, which were occupied by the Germans, were among the largest users of the system. The regulations governing the service were drawn up in 1940 by the General Post Office, but only reached their final formulation in 1943:

"*Conditions under which letters may be sent to relatives or friends in Enemy Countries or Enemy-occupied Territory.*

"*The territories included in these arrangements are: Belgium, Bulgaria, Czechoslovakia, Danzig, Denmark, Estonia, Finland, France (zone left unoccupied by the enemy in 1940), Germany, Greece (mainland), Greek Islands and Crete, Holland, Hungary, Italy and Italian possessions not occupied by the United Nations, Latvia, Lithuania, Luxembourg, Norway, Poland, Romania and Yugoslavia.*

1. *Communications must be clearly written . . . (without erasures) . . . and should not exceed two sides of a normal size sheet of notepaper. Only one letter may be placed in each envelope . . .*

2. *Letters and envelopes must omit the sender's address. They must only refer to matters of personal interest . . . (a) no reference may be made to any town (other than Lisbon), village, locality, ship or journey . . . No indication may be given that the writer is not in Portugal . . . (b) (mention of a letter . . . received from or written to enemy or enemy occupied territory is not permitted . . .*

3. *Each letter must be placed in an open unstamped envelope . . . fully inscribed to the addressee, who should be asked to address any reply to your full name, care of Post Box 506 LISBON, Portugal. Poste Restante addresses are not accepted . . .*

4. *The open envelope containing the letter should be placed in an outer stamped envelope and sent to THOS COOK & SON, LTD, Berkeley Street, Piccadilly, London W1, together with a memorandum plainly written IN BLOCK LETTERS containing in the name . . . and full address of the sender . . .*

5. *The communication to THOS COOK & SON LTD must enclose a postal order value 2s . . . which fee will cover the postage of one envelope containing one communication to the neutral country . . . also of a reply (if any) from the neutral company to Messrs Cook's Head Office in London . . .*

For an extra fee of 6d pence each, letters can be sent Airmail between London and Lisbon.

6. *Business letters . . . must not be sent . . .*

7. *Communications for Prisoners of War . . . and Civilian internees, cannot be sent under the foregoing arrangements . . .* " [4]

Although this formula was not meant for prisoners of war or civilian internees, the transit via Lisbon was frequently used on both sides to send mail to these two categories of people, as is witnessed by the arrangements introduced in 1941 between the British and the German authorities:

"*The German authorities undertook to carry by air free of charge between Lisbon and Germany correspondence to and from British prisoners in return for the free conveyance by air between Lisbon and the United Kingdom of correspondence to and from German prisoners. The combination of British and German air services reduced the actual transit time between the United Kingdom and Germany (excluding censorship at both ends) to two or three weeks, a great improvement on the previous transit time, which frequently ran into months. A similar arrangement was made with the Italian authorities in the spring of 1942.*

"*The services offered for correspondence in the outward direction were: postage-free letters and postcards which were carried by sea to Lisbon and then by air to Germany or Italy, as the case might be, and an airmail service at 5d for the first ounce and 3d for each subsequent ounce for letters, postcards at 2½d each and an air letter service on special forms sold by the Post Office at an inclusive charge of 3d each. The latter proved very popular and constituted about 80% of all letters sent to Germany and Italy. Airmail correspondence was carried by air to Lisbon and so received air conveyance all the way to Germany or Italy. The total traffic in the last years of the service was about 200,000 items per week."* [5]

Naturally, the liberation of France brought the arrangements with Germany to an end and at last simplified communications with Switzerland. From then on, the correspondence for prisoners of war was transported between the United Kingdom and Switzerland via Lyons.

At this point, Geneva should be mentioned, and the invaluable role of the International Committee of the Red Cross (the ICRC), whose volunteers dealt with 100,000-200,000 letters per day in 1944. However, the history of the ICRC is not part of the history of airmail, due to the fact the Switzerland was land-locked in the midst of belligerent countries.

2 MILITARY AIRMAIL: FROM CONCERN TO INNOVATION

In wartime, military mail is a priority, since an effective means of getting letters to the troops and back to their relatives and friends is a necessary requirement for keeping up the troops' morale, as illustrated in this quotation from 11th December 1943, taken from the newspaper of the First Canadian Division, fighting in Italy: "The Canadians were always quick to understand the importance of morale in winning the war. We can boast of having the best postal service of any army." [6]

Twenty-five years later, a German review of postal history reiterated this point: "Today, it is difficult to imagine what it meant to the soldiers on the front and to their families, in their distress and affliction, that every day these millions of letters reached the people to whom they were addressed." [7]

In many cases, the aeroplane was the only means of providing the service required. Both the Germans and the Allies used it widely, but in different ways: the British, and to a lesser extent the Americans, strove to reduce the volume and weight of mail transported over long distances, whilst the Germans organised a veritable military airmail network on the Eastern Front.

The Airgraph Service [8]
At the end of 1940 the quality of most postal communication lines to the soldiers of the British Army in Egypt was deplorable. Direct air communication with Great Britain had been interrupted since Italy had entered the war on the side of Germany. Military mail used the fast ship services of the Union Castle company as far as South Africa, and then the aircraft on the famous Horseshoe Route between Durban and Cairo. The transit times in practice could take several months, against one month in theory. No commander could accept such conditions, which did considerable damage to the morale of the troops.

The British Post Office returned to a proposal which the Kodak Company had made to it in 1932: to use a special machine called "Recordak" to photograph documents of standardised format onto a cinema film at great speed. Once the

documents were reduced in this manner, it was only a question of transporting a few relatively compact films by air in place of the voluminous traditional mail bags. The machine had been originally designed to reproduce bank cheques, and could record any kind of correspondence providing that only standardised formats were used.

Ignoring the objections, which had been raised in peacetime (the need to equip stations with a reproduction system, lack of confidentiality in correspondence), it was decided at the end of 1940 to introduce the system between London and Cairo. This technique, which curiously recalls the "Pigeon-grams" of the siege of Paris, was called Airgraph, from the name of the Airgraphs Company founded before the war under American law for the purpose of exploiting various patents including the "Recordak" patent, and in which Eastman Kodak, Imperial Airways and Pan American Airways owned equal shares.

The "Airgraph Service" was first restricted to mail for the British forces in the Middle East, and was introduced to mail departing from Cairo from April 1941 and for mail to Cairo during the month of August. It produced an immediate and very significant reduction in the average time for conveying the mail, which fell from two months or more, to a fortnight.

The geographical extension of the Airgraph Service on a large scale, and its progressive opening to civilian mail necessitated the establishment of a whole organisation.

Airgraph forms were made available to the public free of charge in Post Offices, and the postage fixed at 3 pence. The senders had the choice of handing the completed forms in at their usual Post Office, which would then send them to the "Foreign Section" of the London Postal Region or, in the interest of confidentiality, could themselves send the forms directly to the "Foreign Section". The forms were then sorted by desti-

Airmail letter for Christmas 1944.

Chronology of development of the Airgraph System

Year	Departing from GB	Destination GB
1941		
April		Middle East
August	Middle East	
December		Canada
1942		
February		India
March	East Africa	
April	Fiji	
May	Bahrain-Burma-Egypt	South Africa-Rhodesia
	(Civilians)-India-Seychelles	Egypt (Civilians)-Sudan
June		Transjordan-Seychelles
		Cyprus-Palestine-Aden
		Somalia-British
July		USA American Forces
August	Canada-Newfoundland	Zanzibar-Mauritius
September	Madagascar-Mauritius	Iraq
	Rhodesia-South Africa	
	Nyasaland	
1943		
March	Ireland-North Africa	USA British Forces
April	New Zealand-Tonga-	
	New Hebrides-Persia (Civilians)	
May	Madagascar (Civilians)	
June	Australia-USA	Persia (Civilians)
	(British forces)	
July	Saint Pierre and Miquelon	
October	Eritrea (Civilians)	Eritrea (Civilians)
1944		
March	Réunion-Gambia-Nigeria	
	Gold Coast-Sierra Leone	
		(Civilians)
June	Central Mediterranean	
July	Turkey	Turkey
September	Cyrenaica-Tripolitania	
	(Civilians)	
October	Belgian Congo	

nation and arranged in bundles of 1,700 corresponding to the number which could be photographed on a 100ft (30.48 metres) length of 16mm film.

The bundles of forms were then sent to Kodak-UK to be photographed, the films were developed and packed in a cardboard container. The Post collected the containers with a unit weight of only 5½ ounces or 142 grams, and put them into mail bags which never weighed more than a few pounds, so that they always qualified for "first priority" status on the aircraft.

On arrival, the negative films were treated so that the text from the forms regained its original appearance. The forms then only had to be put in envelopes and distributed. Naturally, this meant that certain points of call, near zones of the front, or adjacent to large concentrations of troops, had to be equipped

with the necessary photographic equipment and provided with certain specialists. Airgraph stations for both reception and distribution were initially installed in 1941 and 1942 in Cairo, Toronto, Nairobi, Johannesburg, Bombay, Melbourne and Wellington. As the military situation evolved, other stations were opened in Algiers, Naples, Calcutta and Colombo.

The treatment process for mail leaving London reached such a degree of efficiency that forms arriving before 16.00hrs on day one were processed and ready to be put on board aeroplanes at 12.00hrs on day two, although they commonly exceeded a total of 250,000 per day. The Airgraph traffic experienced two spectacular peaks on the occasions of the Christmas and New Year holidays in 1943/44 and 1944/45. The Post Office issued forms for special Christmas greetings Airgraphs, selling around 12,000,000 copies in each of the two years.

All of the Post Offices in the Commonwealth encouraged their customers to use Airgraph messages, although they did not guarantee any confidentiality in their correspondence,[9] in preference to normal airmail which had become unreliable, as in the following notice in the Weekly Bulletin No 1136 of the Canadian Post Office for December 1942:

"In consequence of the increasing requirements for space in aeroplanes for the transport of essential war equipment, it is only possible to send a limited quantity of airmail by air. This situation deteriorated to such an extent during the last week that almost all mail stamped at the airmail rate had to be sent from Canada to Great Britain by ship. In view of these circumstances the Canadian public is advised to use the Airgraph Service to correspond with civilians and troops in Great Britain."[10]

The British Military Authorities even had the generosity to allow access to the system to Italian prisoners of war held in Ethiopia and Eritrea so that they could correspond with their families after a station was opened in Naples.

The Airgraph Service ceased to operate on 31st July 1945. It had enabled 350 million messages to be sent on standardised forms, for a weight of less than 50 tonnes, giving an extremely valuable weight saving of some 4,000 tonnes.

"Airgraphs had been the means of maintaining a speedy postal communication at a time when the human value of such a service was too great to be estimated."[11]

"The V-Mail" for Victory

The Americans also employed the Airgraph system, but they were evidently dissatisfied with such an ugly name. With their love of catchy slogans, they gave the Airgraph a far more positive and seductive ring: "V-Mail" (V for Victory = Victory Post).

In spite of its inspiring title, it does not appear that the V-Mail met with as much success as the British Airgraph. No doubt this was because, at least between the United States and Europe, the normal airmail continued to function satisfactorily. However, the instructions from the Postal Authority were clear: "The use of V-Mail rather than the regular mail between foreign theatres and the continental US should be encouraged",[12] and the priority in loading the Victory Post was clearly stated. In practice, the American soldiers and their families were able to use the two systems together, and could compare V- Mail versus airmail.

This is reflected on several occasions in the letters of Keith Winston.[13] He was an insurance underwriter in Pennsylvania, who was married and the father of two children. He was the epitome of an American pacifist and was mobilised in 1944 at the age of 32 and drafted to 2nd Battalion, 398th Infantry, 100th Division as a combat medic. In many respects, he was an anti-hero, obsessed with the idea of getting back home, but he was nevertheless proud of belonging to a fighting infantry unit, to such an extent that on 14th December 1944, when his battalion was fighting somewhere in Alsace, he wrote to his wife Sarah: "God bless the infantry".

Forty years later, in 1985, Sarah published Keith's letters. In a moving preface she recalls "the interminable waiting, waiting for some word, waiting for the mailman". The mail occupied such an important place in the lives of Keith and Sarah that they examined the advantages and disadvantages of V-mail and airmail with the greatest of care. In October 1944, onboard a troop carrier taking him to Marseilles, Keith wrote:

"There seems to be some arguments as to whether airmail or V-mail is better. Of course you can't enclose anything with V-mail and must use the prescribed envelope. Also it takes extra time to photograph V-mail, so the consensus is that airmail is faster. For the time being, mail airmail – getting the 6¢ airmail envelope. Also, rather than wait for the mail man to pick it up, put it in the mail box immediately, as a delay of one pick up could mean a delay of a week, more or less."

On 21st October he returned to the topic:

"As usual, today I'm thinking of you and longing for you terribly. Perhaps even more so, as some of the boys received a mail from home. I know you're writing and as all mail received was airmail and I suggested you to write V-mail when I left, I'm sure that is the reason. Now we'll try airmail unless that proves unsatisfactory."

On 25th October he buried the V-mail for good: "Today received your first letter – the first V-mail! It's been a long time en route, so, in the future use only airmail."

German military post

The Germans, just like the Allies, assigned particular importance to the organisation of the military postal system. The Feldpost, or "Field Postal Service", consisted mostly of professional postal employees, and amounted to almost 12,000 men. Even before the Nazi attack against the Soviet Union, it had to fulfil the requirements of army units dispersed from the far north of Europe to the fringes of the Egyptian desert. To achieve these aims it made considerable use of air transport facilities in both directions.

To the north, in order to maintain contact with troops deployed north of the Arctic Circle in Norway and Finland, the Feldpost used two services operated by Deutsche Lufthansa which were essentially restricted to the transport of military post, consisting of correspondence and large volumes of newspapers.[14] The first line, opened towards the end of 1940, served the Norwegian coast from Trondheim to Kirkenes (on the Finnish frontier, and today on the frontier with Russia).

A second line from Oslo to Rovaniemi (in the north of Finland) provided a service to Finnish Lapland.

To the south, air links covered the requirements of troops deployed in the Balkans and those of the Afrika Korps in Libya and then in Tunisia.

The mail for the Balkans and Greece were carried either by regular flights of Deutsche Lufthansa, sometimes with supplementary assistance, or by the military postal services based in Zagreb, flying to Dalmatia, the Ionian Islands and the island of Crete.

Postal links with the Afrika Korps in the Egyptian/Libyan desert were provided by a series of services, which were developed as the front line moved back and forth, flying between southern Italy and Tripolitania, such as the Naples/Tripoli, Bari/Benghazi and Brindisi/Crete/Tobruk services, as well as Taranto/Derna.

Airmail network on Eastern Front

Lines time	Itineraries	Distances	Flying
A (North)	Biala-Podlaska-Vitebsk Dno-Gatschina/Return	1,291 *miles*	10.75 *hours*
B (Centre)	Biala-Podlaska-Vitebsk-Smolensk-Roslawl-Orel-Orscha-Smolensk-Vitebsk-Biala Podlaska	1,265 *miles*	10.15 *hours*
C (South)	Biala-Podlaska-Kiev-Kharkov-Stalino-Mariupol-Simferepol-Nikolajev/Return	2,430 *miles*	19.30 *hours*
Total Network		4,986 *miles*	40 *hours*

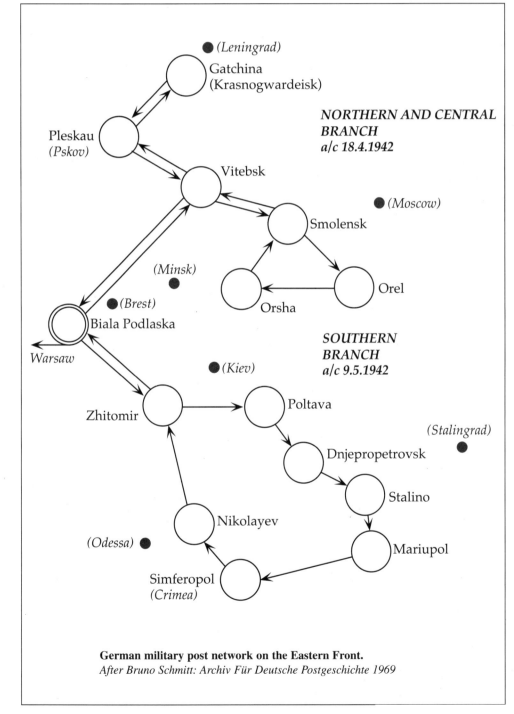

NORTHERN AND CENTRAL BRANCH a/c 18.4.1942

SOUTHERN BRANCH a/c 9.5.1942

German military post network on the Eastern Front.
After Bruno Schmitt: Archiv Für Deutsche Postgeschichte 1969

But from winter 1941–1942, the Feldpost was confronted with problems of an altogether different magnitude on the Russian front, following the first Soviet counter-offensive. In order to resolve them, it created in April 1942 a full-scale postal air network, the Luftfeldpostdienst Osten or "Military Airmail Service for the Eastern Front".

The following communiqué was published on 15th April 1942:

"*In order to provide the possibility for soldiers on the Eastern Front and their relatives in the Fatherland to exchange two new letters per month by the most rapid means possible, it is proposed to create a military airmail service in addition to the normal conveyance of mail by the military post.*" [15]

It seemed clear, even before winter 1941-42 had ended, that only a large-scale deployment of air transport would be capable of surmounting the numerous obstacles which had been encountered in conveying and distributing mail along the Russian Front – the destruction of the railways by retreating Soviet forces; roads which became rivers of mud after the melting of the snows, bogging down the postal vans; and the constant harassment by partisans.

What were the main characteristics of the military airmail network on the Eastern Front?

• Aircraft and fleet sizes. The aircraft used was, of course, the Junkers Ju52, which had just the right performance characteristics; a fleet of six aircraft, later increased to 12 in October 1942, was drafted to the network.

• Hub airport. The choice of the airport to be used as the main base had to fulfil several conditions: it should occupy a central position in relation to the various branches of the front, which extended from Leningrad in the north to the Crimea and the River Kuban in the south; it should not be used by fighting air units; and it should be easily accessible by rail. The choice fell on the airport of Biela Podlaska, on the Russian-Polish frontier near Brest Litovsk, which had a good rail connection with Berlin.

• The network. The initial network was built up on the basis of the number of available aircraft, the layout of the front line, and the number of divisions employed on the northern, central and southern sectors. It was made up of one northern and central branch, and one southern branch and consisted of three services which were run every day.

In this network based on Biala-Podlaska, the airport of Vitebsk occupied a strategic position at the junction of the northern and central lines, and was known as Feldpost Luftkreuz des Ostens, "Eastern air hub for military post".

• Operation of the network. The northern branch started operating on 18th April 1942, whereas the instability of the front lines in the south, which were subjected to a vigorous Soviet offensive, meant that the opening of the southern branch had to be delayed until 9th May. The ground personnel were provided by the Luftwaffe, and the flight personnel came from Deutsche Lufthansa, who had sent their most seasoned pilots. In the best airmail tradition, they had to get the mail through in all weathers, fog, snow or storm, and to land on any terrain, dodging the attacks of enemy fighters, which were not too obtrusive at the outset, but made themselves increasingly felt.

• The postal system. Each soldier on the Russian Front received four airmail stamps per month: two to write to his family and two to send to them so that they could in turn send him two air letters back (what a difference from the daily letters sent by Keith Winston . . .).

Following the success of this system, a notice from the postal authorities to the Armed Forces on 26th May 1943

meant that the number of airmail stamps would be doubled from 1st June 1943; which would enable the despatch and receipt of one air letter per week, independently of the surface mail, which was known to have been subject to numerous uncertainties.

• Evolution and final results: The network reached its maximum extent (9,375 miles) during autumn 1942 at the time of the German offensives on Stalingrad and the Caucasian oilfields. The withdrawal of the German armies, which started on 19th November 1942 when the Russians unleashed their great winter offensive, brought about a shortening of the front lines, and the progressive reduction of the postal network. It underwent a considerable reduction at the end of the summer 1943 after the loss of Smolensk and Orel.

The front came ever nearer to Biala Podlaska, which the Russian troops reached on 28th July 1944, after which there was no more Russian Front, nor any postal planes. The network had been closed down on 24th July 1944.

In its 27 months of operation, from 18th April 1942 to 24th July 1944, the Ju52 aircraft of the military airmail network on the Eastern Front had covered 2,686,458 miles and transported 7,477 tonnes of mail, including 4,574 tonnes of airmail and 2,903 tonnes of regular post.

*　　*　　*

The efforts made by the warring nations and the ICRC (International Committee of the Red Cross) to ensure that the fighting units and the prisoners of war received a regular and rapid mail service could lead one to believe that everyone during the Second World War enjoyed the benefits of airmail. Unfortunately, this was not the case. Innumerable prisoners, internees and deported persons never received a single letter.

2 MILITARY TRANSPORT AVIATION: AIRLIFTS

"The Second World War witnessed an enormous development in aviation." [1] It applied a formidable accelerating force, which historians, according to their philosophies, have assessed differently as to its effects. The more cautious among them have considered that the war brought an advance of a dozen or so years; at the other end of the spectrum, "it was commonly said that World War II advanced the airplane by 50 years." [2] Whatever one thinks, the war completely changed the scale of aviation.

The aeroplane had become a means of mass transport, capable of fulfilling all the needs of a fighting force, in terms of men, armaments and munitions, supplies and even fuel. The transport aircraft of the two sides would in total transport several millions of tonnes of supplies of all types between 1941 and 1945.

Supply by air had become a major component in logistics and the art of war. Military doctrine endeavoured to codify its usage. The Americans placed the emphasis on the concept of distance, distinguishing between strategical airlift, supplying armies engaged in distant theatres of operation, and tactical airlift, referring to the placement of goods and equipment as near as possible to fighting units. For their part, the Germans favoured the concept of control in the regions over which their aircraft flew, distinguishing between *Luftversorgung[en]* or "Air supply operations" – a situation in which the aeroplane is the sole means of supplying an army or region encircled by the enemy – and *Lufttransport*, or "Air transport operations", which covered all activities for transporting men and equipment within a space controlled by the German army. These finer points of military theory reflect situational differences in situations, rather than a basic contradiction of doctrine.

The airlift is the most complete and spectacular form of supply by air. The notion of the "air bridge", whether the airlift is civilian or military, does not require terrestrial or maritime communications to have been broken, but implies the simultaneous fulfilment of several criteria: 1) the definition of a precise mission, specific in space and time; 2) the employment of significant airborne resources in order to counteract the inadequacy or temporary interruption of traditional communication links; 3) the concentration of the service between two specific points or areas; 4) the continuity of flights during several weeks or months.

It would appear that the first military operation of this kind was carried out in Tripolitania by the Italian army, long before the Second World War. For a period of three months, from February to April 1922, Caproni CA3 aircraft supplied a battalion under siege in Azizia, carrying 44 tonnes of food and equipment, as well as 331 soldiers. [3] The first airlift of a significant magnitude was carried out in 1936, when General Franco ferried several elite units back to Spain from Morocco, using Ju52 aircraft put at his disposal by Germany.

Yet it was only during the course of the Second World War that airlifts developed their full potential. Moreover, with few exceptions, they were not achieved using aircraft newly designed for the needs of war, but through the massive utilisation, in a manner which until then had been inconceivable, of civilian aircraft which were already in service or on order, and their military versions (Douglas DC-3 and DC-4, Junkers 52).

I ACHIEVEMENTS AND LIMITATIONS OF GERMAN MILITARY TRANSPORTATION

The Luftwaffe used air transportation on a large scale, both for men and materiel. During the whole of the war, it carried 826,078 tonnes of food, materiel and ammunition and 75,000 tonnes of fuel: [4] it took 1,199,291 soldiers to the front and evacuated 664,053 wounded back behind the lines. [5] The figures are both impressive in their magnitude, and surprising in their precision ...

Yet whatever the figures, the Luftwaffe transport missions were hampered for the entire duration of the war by lack of aircraft.

"The Ju52-3m, although already outdated in 1940/41, remained the basic machine for transport units." [6] It supported all the major supply operations and airlifts. In spite of its exceptional robustness, it suffered from a low useful load, the fact that it had to be loaded from the side, and its need for a hard-surfaced runway of around 500 metres in length.

The German Air Ministry (*Reichsluftministerium*, or RLM) which had been aware of the limitations of the Ju52 since the beginning of the war, turned to manufacturers Henschel and Arado for the construction of a military transport aircraft to the following specification: a two-engined aeroplane with a

Luftwaffe Junkers Ju52-3m.
MAP

Arado Ar232.
MAP

payload twice that of the Ju52, with a horizontal deck and length-wise loading from the rear, equipped for sending out loads by parachute. That is to say, all the characteristics of future military transport aircraft built by both the Americans and Russians after 1944.

The Arado 232 made its maiden flight during summer 1942 and was converted to a four-engine aeroplane. In spite of its good flight characteristics, it never managed to fulfil the specifications required, and its payload never exceeded 3.3 tonnes. Nevertheless, "it was the first aircraft to be designed and manufactured as a true multipurpose military transport aircraft. Industrial limitations prevented its production on a large scale and only 22 machines were delivered." [7]

In order to have available a heavy transport aircraft, the RLM in October 1942 ordered the development of the Messerschmitt 323 Gigant. It was derived from the Me321 assault glider at the beginning of 1942 and became the first "wide-bodied" aircraft. This enormous mammoth of a machine was fitted with six Gnome-Rhone 14N engines, and was considered as one of the "milestones of the air", [8] combining most of the qualities required of a modern military cargo plane: a large volume of 103m³ (cabin dimensions: 10.97m x 3.12m x 3.35m), a large payload for its day at 12.3 tonnes, axial loading from the front by means of a door 3.35m high, which opened in two halves, a horizontal deck very near to the ground in order to assist loading and special landing gear, defined to "absorb" small obstacles. On the other hand, its low cruising speed (130mph), together with its considerable size, made it the choice target for enemy interceptors. It could cope with heavy equipment (tanks, artillery, various kinds of vehicle) or could transport 120 fully armed men, and was used intensively between Italy and Tunisia from November 1942 to May 1943. A total of 201 units were produced.

We would like to mention another transport aircraft which was developed from an assault glider, the Gotha Go244. This transport machine was a failure due to its lack of engine power, but it was the first aircraft to have a twin boom tailplane.

Although they were often handicapped by inadequate means, the Luftwaffe transport units played an active role in many operations, notably during

ABOVE **Gotha Go244.**
MAP

BELOW **Messerschmitt Me323 Gigant.**
MAP

BOTTOM **Heavy artillery being loaded into a Messerschmitt Me323 Gigant.**
DNP and FAMA

the invasion of Norway, the campaigns in Tripolitania and Tunisia, and on the Eastern Front. On this last sector, the breakdown of the air supply action to the 6th Army encircled at Stalingrad is well known, the brilliant yet two-edged success of the Demjansk airlift has been under-sung.

The Demjansk airlift – a hollow victory

The scene was set roughly half way between Moscow and Leningrad towards the end of autumn of 1941. Winter had closed in early, with particular vehemence. With the intense cold and snow, "General Winter", the ancient ally of all Russian armies, had arrived. The Soviet Army, informed of the disarray of the Germans, returned to the counterattack and was regaining territory. The large German units, weighed down with equipment unsuitable for the rigours of winter, were not falling back quickly enough. After a fast encircling manoeuvre, the Soviet troops arriving from the northeast and the southwest, took the German 2nd Army in a pincer movement, which closed on it at the River Lovat, at the beginning of 1942. Six German Divisions (95,000 men) were completely cut off from their lines and surrounded at Demjansk. There was only one way out: by air.

The First Air Fleet received the order to ensure the supply of the entire 2nd Army, which, in order to maintain its fighting capacity, was estimated to require 300 tonnes per day. The first airlift of any significant size in the Second World War commenced on 19th February 1942. It connected the bottled-up army at Demjansk, which had two airstrips without ground installations, with a chain of six airports between 150 and 300 miles away to the west, stretching from Pskov in the north to Daugavapils (Lithuania) in the south, passing by Riga (Latvia) in the centre. For a period of almost a year, from February 1942 to January 1943, the First Air Fleet made 32,427 transport missions and carried to the besieged zone 64,844 tonnes of material of all kinds. In addition, it flew 30,500 soldiers into Demjansk and evacuated 35,400 sick and injured.

This airlift allowed the German Second Army to resist the siege for almost a year, until it could be relieved. Five factors in the success of this first airlift can be identified:

1. The establishment of a proper logistics organisation placed under a single hierarchical and operational authority, short-circuiting the normal chain of command.

2. The availability of a homogeneous fleet of Ju52/3Ms, 500 strong, which enabled around 150 machines per day to be put into service.

3. The setting-up of an extremely powerful ground-based organisation capable of ensuring the maintenance of a fleet of 500 aircraft in temperatures of -40°C.

4. The definition of extremely rigorous and detailed procedures which enabled very tight turnaround times (operations being, of course, limited to daylight hours). The greatest difficulties in this respect were encountered during the period of the thaw, when the mud invaded all the parking area.

5. Domination of the skies: this was an absolute precondition for the success of any airlift. On the whole, the Soviet fighters inflicted limited damage.

It was a brilliant success, but deceptive. The positive outcome of the Demjansk airlift was largely instrumental in maintaining the illusion of the German High Command that the 6th Army, when it was encircled at Stalingrad at the end of 1942, could also be supplied from the air.

The Stalingrad airlift: an inevitable disaster

"ARMEE EINGESCHLOSSEN, MUNITIONSLAGE GESPANNT, VERPFLEGUNG RECHT FUER SECHS TAGE." [9] – ("ARMY SURROUNDED, AMMUNITION TIGHT, SUPPLIES ENOUGH FOR 6 DAYS").

This famous radio telegraph message, sent on 22nd November 1942 by General Paulus, Commander of the German 6th Army at Stalingrad, marked the turning point of the Second World War.

In order to understand the military situation, it is necessary to look back to the end of summer 1942. Though the German troops had succeeded in making spectacular breakthroughs, particularly towards the Caucasus, they had not reached any strategic objective – the Baku Oilfields were still out of reach, Leningrad was still resisting capture and the German 6th Army at Stalingrad was still unable to overcome the fierce resistance of the Russian 62nd Army under General Tchuikov, "with their backs to the river and no place to retreat", [10] and reinforced by workers' militias.

At the beginning of September 1942, Generals Zhukov, Vassiliensky and Voronov began to prepare a major Soviet offensive against the flanks of the German advanced formation, which had Stalingrad at its apex. They concentrated their efforts on the weak points of the enemy – the areas of contact between the large German units and the troops of their allies (Italy, Hungary, and Romania). After a violent artillery barrage, the Russian offensive was launched in the morning at 05.00hrs on 19th November 1942. In one fell swoop, the troops of Rokossovsky in the northeast and Vatontin in the southwest pierced the German line and met up behind their enemy on 22nd November near Kalatch, surrounding the German 6th Army and the IV Corps of the 4th Armoured Brigade, some 300,000 men.

What were the Germans to do? They had two options:

• Either they could abandon Stalingrad and order the 6th Army to fight through the still thin wall of Russian forces in order to rejoin their own forces. This was the preference of General Von Weichs, Commander of Army Group B, who in a message on the evening of 22nd November considered "that it is not possible to supply an army of 20 Divisions by air".

• Or they could pull back into Stalingrad and to hold out, whatever the cost. This was of course the solution preferred by Hitler, bolstered in his blindness by the boastfulness of Goering, who on the 25th November declared: "The Luftwaffe will deliver a daily average of 500 tonnes of provisions by air. The delivery of supplies to the German troops who were besieged last winter for three months in Demyansk confirms that this operation is feasible." This was a total, and fatal, delusion: the 4th Air Transport fleet, which had been put in charge of the operation, was incapable of carrying the 300-500 tonnes per day which were necessary to maintain the 6th Army at a state of readiness. It would have required 1,000 Junkers 52s, but the Luftwaffe could only line up a total of 750. And even then, part

Luftwaffe Junkers Ju52-3m.
MAP

of this fleet had been mobilised to deal with the consequences of the recent American invasion in North Africa.

To make matters worse, the Luftwaffe, unlike at Demyansk, no longer had command of the skies. Russian bombers and fighter aeroplanes destroyed a considerable number of transport aircraft on the ground: "a strike made against Salsk on January 9, where some 150 transport aircraft were based, was especially successful. Seven Il-2s, commanded by I. P. Batkin, with fighter escorts, were sent to destroy them. The attack on the airfield was made without warning, out of the clouds. The ground-attack aeroplanes made six runs on the target. They put out of commission more than 70 Ju52s." [11]

The history of the Stalingrad airlift can be divided into two periods: before and after 16th January 1943, when the Russian army captured the Pitomnik airfield, in the western part of the surrounded area.

• From 29th November 1942, when the airlift started, until 16th January 1943, the Luftwaffe never fulfilled the objectives it had been set: the average lift of supplies had never exceeded 110 tonnes per day, whereas the absolute minimum required had been estimated at 300 tonnes. The causes for this failure were many: the attacks by Russian fighter aeroplanes and the constant bombardment of Pitomnik by the artillery; the weather conditions, which were particularly hostile (cold, snow and fog); the employment, for lack of anything better, of unsuitable aircraft (Heinkel He 111); the progressive lengthening of the distances for the airlift due to the progress of the Russian army towards the west; and finally, the psychological difficulties of increasingly young and inexperienced crews, traumatised by the sight of an entire army slowly starving.

• After the fall of Pitomnik, the Gumrak airfield, which was further east, soon proved to be unusable, due to the thickness of snow, and the intensity of the artillery bombardment. There remained only one makeshift solution: to parachute or throw overboard, into the snow, sacks of bread and cases of ammunition. The supply rate fell to 60 tonnes per day. And even then, half of the rations were lost, either because the containers fell behind Russian lines or because the soldiers in their weakened state were incapable of pulling them out of the snow.

The lessons were clear:

"The German attempt to organise an aerial supply service for the large number of surrounded troops was a complete failure. Favourable conditions were created for the destruction of entire troop concentration." [12]

The Germans capitulated on 1st February 1943. In total, since 29th November 1942, they had airlifted 6,691 tonnes of aid.

Tactical logistical support
The Eastern Front was characterised by its immense plains, the massive use of armoured vehicles, the speed of movement of large infantry units and the decided preference of the German generals, mirrored by the Russians, for large encircling manoeuvres. It was an ideal terrain for applying the "*Kampfeinsatz*" of German theorists, or the "tactical airlift" of the American strategists. Many examples could be cited. The most striking occurred in the Ukraine, on the right bank of the Dnieper, in January and February 1944.

On 5th January 1944, General Koniev had unleashed a major winter offensive based on Cherkassy. He pushed his armoured divisions rapidly forward, and by 28th January had succeeded in encircling the German 8th Army in the region of

Korsun-Chechenkovsky to the southeast of Kiev. In a classical enveloping manoeuvre, the Russian generals had thus formed an internal ring with the 4th Guards Division, while the 5th Armoured Guards Division and the 6th Armoured Division faced outwards in order to ward off any German attempts at help. During the manoeuvre, some of the Soviet armoured units had advanced so far that they themselves were in a critical situation. At this stage, the adversaries were so interlocked, and the transport situation on the roads had reached such a parlous state due to the thaw, that, on both sides all possible air transport units were mobilised to provide the fighting units with supplies, ammunitions and fuel. It was surprising how similar the priorities and solutions of the two sides became.

On the Russian side – as the besiegers – they reported as follows: "When the thaw set in, the air supply of fuel and supplies to the advanced armoured units became most important, since the roads had become impassable to all categories of vehicles. A number of airborne regiments using PO-2 aircraft were transferred to airfields situated near a railway line, in order to speed up the transfer of the supplies. Between 8th and 16th February 1944, 820 rescue missions were flown, by day and by night, in extremely bad weather conditions, and carried 49 tonnes of fuel, 49 tonnes of supplies and over 500 shells to the ground forces." [13]

The Germans, under siege and whose sole objective was to avoid another Stalingrad, almost echoed these sentiments:

"Because of the thaw, the roads had become almost impassable, so that it became impossible to send supplies to the III Armoured Corps (which had the task of breaking the encirclement). Air transport was the only solution, and supplies of petrol, ammunition and food were dropped in containers along the tank columns." [14]

The soil had become so liquid that the aircraft could not land, except at night when the frost took hold again.

For both armies, logistical support by air, or tactical airlift, had remained the only practical form of delivering supplies.

Eventually, III Armoured Corps joined up with the German 8th Army on 16th February 1944, ending the siege. In 17 days the latter had received 2,000 tonnes of aid, delivered by air.

2 SPECIAL FEATURES OF SOVIET MILITARY TRANSPORTATION

With regard to Soviet air transport, we do not have such a complete and well-recorded overview as for German military transport. In the absence of complete records, we will restrict ourselves to considering a few significant points.

When the German troops entered the USSR on 22nd June 1941, they benefited from an incredible surprise effect, in spite of the information and warnings sent to Stalin by the British. Despite its heroic resistance, the Red Army had to abandon enormous tracts of territory. From autumn 1941, the two principal cities of Moscow and Leningrad were under threat. The destruction and disorganisation of the terrestrial transport routes reached such a point that air transport seemed to be the last resort. But the Soviet Air Force had also suffered terrible losses: almost half its machines had been destroyed on the ground during the first two days of the war. It was in this context, which demanded the highest degree of courage in the face

of this complete disorganisation, that we must consider the role of Soviet transport aviation during the first months of the Great Patriotic War.

The siege of Leningrad

A German army of some 20 divisions began to surround the city of Leningrad in September of 1941. When the terrible winter of 1941–1942 closed in, during which hundreds of thousands of the inhabitants would die of hunger, the city possessed only meagre reserves: flour for 15 days and sugar for 30 days. Leningrad only remained connected to the Soviet Union by means of a fragile lifeline – the Lake Ladoga road – which was subjected to intense German bombardment. Theoretically, the airways were still open, but they were threatened by German air supremacy, and endangered by the lack of resources of the Soviet Air Force, whose main task was to defend Moscow.

The President of the Soviet Union, Mikhail I. Kalinin, a former worker from the Putilov factories in St Petersburg, then appealed to Stalin on behalf of the population which was beginning to starve:

"The situation in Leningrad has become palpably worse. It seems essential to find and establish reliable routes of supply during the winter season – by sleigh, by car and by plane." [15]

Kalinin's entreaty was listened to, as much as was possible at a time when there were desperate demands from all quarters. The decision to supply Leningrad by means of an airlift was made on 16th November 1941. The Air Force [16] was given the instruction to provide 34 aircraft to transport 200 tonnes of energy-giving foodstuffs per day. Even these objectives, which were insufficient in themselves as the total needs of the population were evaluated at 1,000 tonnes per day, were not achieved. In total, approximately 6,420 tonnes of aid were sent by air from October 1941 to the beginning of 1942 – 130 tonnes of post, 310 tonnes of blood, 1,660 tonnes of military equipment and 4,320 tonnes of food. On the return journey, the aircraft loaded shells and military equipment which Leningrad factories were continuing to produce until supplies ran out.

Limited in scope, this airlift did not save Leningrad on its own, but although the aeroplane in this case was only one factor among others, it certainly made a large contribution.

One lesson emerges from the battles of Demyansk, Leningrad and Stalingrad: in times of war, airlifts are irreplaceable logistical tools, but only given certain conditions: the possession of a powerful and renewable transport fleet, and supremacy in the air.

Supplies to the Partisans

The most original, and perhaps the most important, aspect of the air transport activities of the Soviets during the Great Patriotic War was the supplying of the Partisans. Originally, the Partisans were groups of a few dozen up to hundreds of fighters who had been cut off from their units during the rapid advance of the German armies in the summer of 1941. They were underestimated by the German Command, who were too confident of a rapid victory, but they played a leading role in Soviet strategy. Later, they were reinforced by the Young Communists and became solidly installed in regions of

Polikarpov U2.
MAP

Byelorussia covered in immense forests and swamps. They harried at the heels of the German army, with actions which went from classic guerrilla warfare to medium-scale engagements with mortars and ordnance, attacking isolated troops, destroying communication routes and maintaining a permanent atmosphere of insecurity.

To a large degree, the logistical support of the Partisan groups consisted in continuous supply by air, particularly of radio equipment (essential for coordinating their activities with headquarters), heavy armaments for infantry, ammunition, explosives, signal equipment and medical equipment. In the same way, all personnel link-ups were made by air.

The system for supplying the Partisans by air grew appreciably from the summer of 1942, when the task was given to an airborne force specially trained for night supply operations, using parachutes or landing on makeshift landing strips marked out at the last minute. On any day, the number of night-time missions carried out behind German lines varied between 250 and 1,000 for the single group [by this force] working with the Central Armies. [17] The aircraft usually employed for this type of mission were the U2, the Li2 and C-47, as well as A7 cargo gliders.

The Polikarpov U2 was an exceptionally robust aircraft. With a single engine, and carrying a payload of 100-150 kilograms, it was truly the kingpin in the support operations for the Partisans (supply drops, evacuation of the wounded etc) as it needed only extremely short airstrips for landing and take-off. Larger supply operations (pieces of artillery, relief of troops etc) as well as parachute missions were carried with Li2 aircraft – the Russian version of the Douglas DC-3 manufactured under licence in Tashkent, and originally called the PS-84 – and

by Douglas C-47s, the military version of the DC-3 which from 1942 onwards had been supplied to the USSR by the United States in large quantities under the Lend-Lease Act (700 units).

> "The Partisan units would not have been able constantly to increase and improve their armaments, nor to carry out combat missions of increasing complexity, without the aerial supply operations. They ensured an important flow of arms, ammunitions, explosives, rockets and if necessary food rations and clothing, as well as specialists and training personnel. They also provided a system for transmitting orders and instructions, a military post service, a propaganda service for the Partisans and the civilian population, and any other means of maintaining the combat strength and morale of the troops." [18]

According to figures from the Soviet Ministry of Defence, 17,000 tonnes of goods were conveyed by these means to the groups of Partisans, and 88,000 sick and wounded men were evacuated in the course of more than 109,000 air sorties.

3 THE POWER AND PARTICULARITIES OF AMERICAN MILITARY TRANSPORT

From the declaration of war in 1941, the United States built up in stages the world's largest air network in order to carry supplies of men and materiel for the American forces and their allies dispersed across all the continents.

Progressive involvement
Between 1935 and 1937 Congress successively passed four laws on neutrality. This reflected a strong isolationist feeling in the United States, particularly represented in the Senate. It is greatly to the credit of President Franklin D. Roosevelt that, aided by his Secretary for State, Cordell Hull, he managed to

USAAF C-47 aircraft in Normandy during World War II.
RAF Museum

move the United States by stages from a concept of rigorous neutrality to an active commitment towards Great Britain, which in July 1940 stood alone in facing the Axis powers. An important stage was reached when the Republican candidate in the presidential election declared on 2nd November 1940: "We are in favour of affording our aid to the heroic people of Britain. We should put our industrial production at its disposal." Although not yet at war, the United States was not altogether neutral.

When Winston Churchill personally met Roosevelt on 8th December 1940, he obtained an immediate agreement for assistance. On 20th December, President Roosevelt declared in a broadcast message: "We should become the great arsenal of Democracy."

The massive American aid accorded to Britain, and later to the China of Chang Kai Chek, and to Stalin's Russia, was to be based on a document which has remained famous: the Lend Lease Act, signed on 11th March 1941. This document conferred very extensive powers on the President of the United States. It authorised him to deliver to any country, the defence of which he considered to be vital for the United States, any civilian or military equipment which it may need, while leaving it the greatest possible latitude with regard to the methods of payment.

Although they were committed from that moment on, the Americans were not yet at war. They first had to take certain precautions regarding the supply of the military equipment which had been ordered. Rather than having recourse to official means, the American Government, for this delicate mission, decided to rely on the only airline which already possessed a powerful international presence: Pan American Airways. In November 1940 it was instructed to set up a series of airports situated in British territories in the Caribbean region.

Although it was initially limited to setting up the infrastructure, the military engagement of Pan Am was extended to the operational level in June 1941 when it used an Anglo-American subsidiary to ferry American bombers to the Royal Air Force in Egypt.

Finally, on the instructions of the President, Pan Am set up a regular and permanent service between the United States and Africa for the delivery of large quantities of military equipment to the British forces in Egypt. The first link from Miami to Khartoum was made on 21st October 1941, and the service from Miami to Leopoldville, via San Juan, Port of Spain, Belem, Natal, Bathurst and Lagos, was opened on 6th December 1941. Throughout the war, the parallel involvement of civilian airlines working under contract, and specific military resources, would become one of the characteristics of American military transport.

ATC: the world's most formidable airline
The balance finally tipped on 7th December 1941 when the Japanese attacked the United States at Pearl Harbor.

After a short experimental period, General Arnold, who was in charge of Aviation, ordered the creation of the Air Transport Command, or ATC, on 20th June 1942. Placed under the command of Lieutenant-General Harold George, the ATC combined in a single organisation all the air transport activities within the Army: convoying new aircraft, transporting equipment and men and setting up air bases. The ATC quickly became the largest and most powerful air network in the world, developing services to suit the fluctuations in the various front lines. It fulfilled its mission partly by giving contracts to civilian airlines, which as we shall see made a considerable contribution, but in the main ATC used its own dedicated transport fleet.

USAAF C-47 over Burma.
RAF Museum

The geographical organisation of the Air Transport Command adapted itself to follow the movements in the theatres of operation.

The following sectors were opened in succession:

June 1942	North Atlantic-Caribbean
	Pacific-South Atlantic
	Africa/Middle East
5th October 1942	Alaska
1st December 1942	Indo-China
15 December 1942	Sector Africa/Middle East
	split into 2 sections –North Africa
	and Central Africa
January 1943	Europe

The activities of the ATC encompassed the entire globe. As examples of its achievements, the following quotations from two of its serving officers are instructive:

• Major-General Smith, Assistant Commander of the ATC, declared during a congress held in Oklahoma City in 1944:

"Today, the organisation of Air Transport Command is composed of more than 200,000 men and women located throughout the world. Today our flight operation is measured in millions of miles. Our first job was the ferrying of aircraft . . . Our other principal job, one which outstripped the ferrying of aircraft, was the operation of a system of world transportation . . . In total, the operation of Air Transport Command emerges as the greatest transport operation in history and contributed essentially to the solution of our problems of logistics, accelerating the tempo of war and contributing to the shortening of the conflict. The war is moving too fast and must move too fast to be bound down by the limited speed of surface transportation." [19]

• Colonel James Aston, described the magnitude of the operation before a conference of air transport users which met in Washington in July 1945:

"One of the accomplishments of Air Transport Command has been to transport about 6,000 tonnes of cargo per day." [20] (By way of comparison, all the American airlines had transported 4,700 tonnes of freight [21] during the entire year of 1938.)

In 1945 the American military traffic in goods and equipment of all kinds, transported by companies working under contract, the American Air Force [USAAF] and the Navy reached almost 1.8 billion (ie thousand million) ton kilometres. This level of traffic would not be exceeded by the whole of the world's airlines together (excluding the USSR) until 1960.

These results, which were staggering for the period, were achieved with the transport aircraft already in existence, or which were already being built, at the beginning of the war, deployed in massive air fleets. Three main types of aircraft were used:

• Douglas DC-3, or C-47 in its military version (known to the British as the Dakota), which became "the backbone of allied transport aircraft throughout the war". [22] More than 10,000 units were produced of this aircraft.

• The Douglas DC-4, or C-54 Skymaster in its military version (with reinforced deck and side cargo door). The DC-4 was a four-engine aircraft, with a payload of about 8 tonnes. It made its maiden flight on 14th February 1942, and was then progressively introduced onto the long-haul sectors (North Atlantic,

Pacific, and South America). Produced in 1,163 units, the C-54 was by general acclaim, "a splendid aircraft" which "worked wonders".

• The Curtis C-46 A Commando, which was a two-engined transport aeroplane originally designed for civilian use, but which in its military version, ordered in 1940, offered twice the payload of the Douglas DC-3 (6.8 tonnes).

Alongside these three classic aircraft should be mentioned the Boeing 307 Stratoliner, which was also a civilian aircraft, introduced by TWA on 8th July 1940 on the transcontinental route; the C-69, a military version of the Lockheed Constellation; and the transport version of the B-24 Liberator Bomber, known as the C-87.

Loading a C-46 on "The Hump".

This short history of the ATC should also mention its naval equivalent, the NATS, or Naval Air Transport Service, created on 12th December 1941.

The contribution of the civil airlines

The Transport Association of the American airlines [23] had proposed to the Department for War in 1936 that a mobilisation plan should be set up in case of national emergency. The plan was established, and then regularly updated. On 7th December 1941, the companies were ready. For the whole of the war they fulfilled a dual role as civilian carriers, although directly linked to the war effort, within the United States, and military carriers, in the form of transportation contracts with the ATC or the Navy, in all four corners of the world. This enabled them to acquire unequalled know-how.

Due to the continual increases in the resources of the Air Transport Command, the contribution of civilian transport companies to the military traffic decreased regularly in percentage terms from 1942–1945. Nevertheless, they made an extremely valuable contribution.

Development of air traffic in military material [24]

	1942	1943	1944	1945
By military aircraft	18	170	851	1,510
By airlines	71	267	330	280
Total	89	437	1,181	1,790
Share of airlines	80%	61%	26%	16%

Unit: Revenue tonne kilometres

The strategic sector of Alaska gives an example of the range of military transport activities of the American airlines during the war. General Billy Mitchel, the enfant terrible of American aviation, declared to Congress a few months before the Japanese attack: "Alaska is the most central point in the world as far as aviation is concerned. Whoever holds Alaska holds the world." On 3rd June 1942 the Japanese bombarded Dutch Harbour and some days later captured two of the Aleutian Islands: Attu and Kiska.

The Americans decided to do everything necessary to keep control of Alaska and prevent the Japanese from setting foot on the North American continent. They started an enormous plan for constructing strategic routes, military bases and airports. All the airlines would participate. Although the records are incomplete, they give some idea of the performance of the American airlines. In June 1942 American Airlines made 182 flights between Edmonton (Canada) and Nome (Alaska). Western Airlines, which was more accustomed to the sun of California, did such a noteworthy job during winter of 1941–1942 that its aircraft were called the "Alaska Phantoms". United Airlines made 1,800 flights to Alaska from the beginning of 1942 to November 1944 and carried over 10,000 tonnes of military freight. Pan Am maintained two flights per day out of Seattle on behalf of the Navy. But Northwest Airlines was incontestably the main transport airline to Alaska, operating a number of regular services from Minneapolis, its principal base. When the Americans recaptured the Island of Attu in May 1943, Northwest immediately opened up a Minneapolis/Attu service with three return flights per day!

"The Hump": the greatest airlift of the Second World War

On 13th May 1942, the Japanese 15th Army achieved its strategic objective: to cut the last ground communication route which still linked Chang Kai Chek's China with the outside world. It was a fragile link, consisting of a railway from Rangoon to Lashio, followed by a narrow and tortuous mountain road, scaling dizzy slopes, from Lashio to Pao-Shan and Kun Ming in the Chinese province of Yunnan. Its monthly capacity was limited to 10,000 tonnes but those 10,000 tonnes were vital.

The Allies, particularly President Roosevelt, considered that keeping Nationalist China in the war was a key strategic objective, to retain the largest possible number of Japanese divisions inside China, and to use the south of China as a base for long-range bombers capable of hitting Japan. There was only one means to achieve this end: the supply of arms, ammunition and fuel by air. Air links were set up between airports in Assam, in the northeastern limb of India, and Kunming. They were operated using DC-3s belonging to CNAC – a Chinese subsidiary of Pan Am – and of the 10th Air Force. But the resources committed bore no relationship to the needs. Although the ATC had taken direct responsibility for the operations in December 1942, the operation became difficult to sustain in April 1943 due to lack of aircraft and a sufficient number of crew members.

It was then that an exceptional character appeared on the scene, Lieutenant-General Claire L. Chennault, "One of the USAF's Greats", a controversial iconoclast [25] who was in command of the 14th Air Force, based in South China. In view of the turn of events, and regardless of any thunderbolts which might descend from headquarters, he made a direct approach to President Roosevelt, who appreciated the problems. The greatest airlift of the Second World War was given the green light. It linked half a dozen airports in the north of Assam with Kunming. Although the distances covered were relatively short (500-600 miles), the operational difficulties were considerable: no navigation aids, frequent fog, monsoon rains of exceptional violence, and, above all, mountain chains forming a great "hump" reaching heights of 3,500 to 5,000 metres – hence the name under which this airlift has remained famous: "The Hump".

In order to fulfil its objectives, the ATC set up additional facilities. It built new airports, opened a warehouse in Agra, organised an assembly line at Bangalore, introduced night flying, and replaced the DC-3s which were too limited in their maximum cruising height and load, with Curtiss C-64 Commandos, which became the real battle horse for "The Hump". From then on, traffic grew quickly, increasing from 3,450 tonnes in July 1943 to 10,000 tonnes per month at the end of the year, reaching 23,675 tonnes in August 1944, 44,000 tonnes in January 1945 and finally the record figure of 71,042 tonnes in July 1945. In total, 650,000 tonnes were transported over "The Hump".

4 LINES OF FORCE AND THE SPREAD OF JAPANESE MILITARY TRANSPORT

There are many reasons why the Japanese army should have given priority to the use of air transport to deliver supplies.

• The fascination of aviation for the Japanese public: This was evidenced in the many aviation associations, all controlled, at the behest of the military, by the Aeronautical Association for a Greater Japan.

• The reorganisation of Japanese commercial aviation. In August 1939: the company Dai Nippon Koku KK, or "Airlines for a Greater Japan", was created, in which the state had a 37.3 % shareholding. This company operated a network consisting of a number of very busy domestic services (Osaka/Tokyo, Sapporo/Tokyo) and connections serving the territories which

were either under Japanese control (Korea, Formosa, Dairen), placed by the League of Nations under Japanese mandate (Marianas Islands, Marshall Islands, Caroline Islands and Palau Islands), or which they had recently conquered (Manchuria). Its greater objective was to implement its Fifteen-Year Plan. This had been worked out in 1935 by the Imperial Aviation Society to serve, in particular, a "second zone of expansion for Japanese commercial aviation" which included Siam, Indo-China, the Dutch East Indies, Malaysia and New Guinea. These territories were considered to belong to a future "region of joint prosperity" which the Japanese envisaged. The inauguration in June 1940 of a weekly Tokyo/Bangkok airmail service was the first stage in this plan.

• The extent of the front lines at the commencement of hostilities: After the rapid fall of Singapore, Malaysia and the Dutch East Indies, and with the arrival of Japanese forces in Burma and New Guinea, the Japanese front line on the ground formed an immense arc, more than 6,000 miles long, with no other means of communication than by sea or air.

• The domination of the air: The Japanese enjoyed almost total supremacy in the air until 5th June 1942, when the main Japanese aircraft-carrier fleet was annihilated by Admiral Nimitz off Midway Island in the Central Pacific.

In spite of all these favourable factors, it does not appear, in the absence of comprehensive statistical information, that supply by air played a decisive role in Japanese operations, apart from some exceptional cases (for example the capture of the Palembang oilfields on the island of Sumatra).

Two principal reasons explain this situation, which initially is rather surprising. Firstly, "The low amount of interest shown by the Army and the Navy in transport aviation". [26] The term "transport aircraft" does not appear [in military records] until 1937. All attention had been devoted to fighters and bombers, particularly, as a peculiarly Japanese feature, 70% of the total aircraft fleet was in the Navy.

Secondly, the excessive degree of dispersal of transport aircraft among too many units. The Army did not collect all its transport aircraft into sufficiently large units to achieve a critical mass and to operate proper airlifts. It spread them among too large a number of Armies, Divisions and Airborne Brigades. The Navy, which owned a total of 750 transport aircraft, of which 250 were for mail and despatches, created Naval Transport Units to counteract the effect of having their capabilities too thinly spread. There were four such units, each flying 100 machines, which could be used at any point in the theatre of operations, as needed.

The Army and the Navy each operated a regular air transport network. [27] These two networks were very similar, but not interchangeable. If the lines of engagement were identical (Japan/Singapore and Japan/Philippines), the naval network was turned more towards the Pacific Ocean, while the army network was orientated more towards the continent of Asia (Manchuria, China and Burma). These regular routes served in particular to supply spare parts to the numerous airbases and aircraft repair centres spread out near the front lines. In order to operate them, the Army and the Navy used their own air fleets, and called upon the civil airlines to provide supplementary services.

Kawanishi H8K.
RAF Museum

In addition to these regular services, both the Army and Navy made many special flights to suit the needs of operational units. Because of the lack of transport aircraft, such missions were often carried out by heavy bombers or reconnaissance aircraft summarily adapted for the purpose.

The Japanese military air transport fleets were made up of three main types of aircraft:

• The Douglas DC-3
Manufactured under licence from 1940 onwards, the DC-3 was modified (cargo door, reinforced deck, freight anchoring rings) to make it more like the military C-47 model of the Americans. It was manufactured in over 450 units.

• The Mitsubishi KI-57 [28]
This aircraft was developed in 1939 on the basis of the KI-21 heavy two-engined bomber to meet the requirements of the Army (transport of troops and equipment) and the specifications of Dai Nippon Koku (payload of 1,300 kilograms and a range of 1,250 miles). This was the workhorse of the Imperial Army, used as a troop transport and a logistical support aircraft, shuttling across every theatre of operation. An improved version was manufactured from 1942, and a total of over 500 units came off the production lines.

• The Kawanishi H6-K2-L and H8-K2-L [29]
These were transport versions of the four-engined flying boats used as long-range marine reconnaissance aircraft and as bombers, in versions H6K and H8K. In spite of its speed, the Kawanishi H6-K2-L proved to be an extremely fragile aircraft, due to the lack of reinforcement of the airframe and the absence of protection for the fuel tanks.

It was replaced by an aircraft which was much better protected – the Kawanishi H8K, "the most remarkable combat seaplane in the Second World War". Only 36 units of the transport version were constructed in 1943–1945, exclusively for the Navy. With a cruising speed of 190mph and a maximum speed of 275mph, a range of 2,875 miles and a payload of around 4 tonnes, it out-performed the British Short Sunderland and the American Consolidated Catalina.

5 THE RICHNESS AND DIVERSITY OF BRITISH AIR TRANSPORT

The distinguishing characteristic of British air transport during the Second World War was the variety of missions: re-establishment of communications with the Empire; organisation of new "strategic air routes"; "overseas ferrying"; transport of men, materiel and mail to and from theatres of operations in Egypt, North Africa, Burma and later Europe; tactical missions in support of ground-based forces; support and equipment of resistance movements in France and Yugoslavia; and even humanitarian missions. These many and various tasks were carried out by a single airline – BOAC – and one military organisation – the Air Transport Command of the Royal Air Force.

BOAC and the re-establishment of air communications with the Empire
BOAC, the British Overseas Airways Corporation, was established on 24th November 1939, officially taking over the activities of Imperial Airways and British Airways on 1st April 1940.

After the collapse of France and the entry of Italy into the war, Great Britain was obliged to undertake a complete reassessment of its air links to Egypt and South Africa on the one hand, and to Egypt, India and Australia on the other, since it was no longer possible to fly over France, Italy and the Mediterranean. BOAC's first mission was to re-establish these broken communications with the empire. It was necessary to find an alternative to the sections of the service between Great Britain and Cairo: this became the Poole/Lagos (Nigeria) route via Lisbon, Bathurst and Freetown. After a survey flight of 6th August 1940 by Captain A. C. Loraine, the chief pilot, the route

BOAC Mosquito.
MAP

was operated on a scheduled basis, and extended to Khartoum. There it made connections with the famous "Horseshoe Route". This was an immense curve or horseshoe over 7,500 miles long, consisting of the Durban/Cairo section of the old South Africa route, and the Cairo/Calcutta section of the old route to India. After the uprising in Iraq endangered the Cairo/Karachi section of the Horseshoe Route, an alternative had to be found. This was the Hadramaut, or South Arabian, route via Aden, Riyan, Salalah and Masira Island. In record time, it was surveyed and equipped with the necessary infrastructure (radar/weather stations and airports), in spite of the particularly hostile, difficult conditions. "The Southern Arabian route, intended as an emergency standby, has become an important strategic link much used by the US Air Transport Command en route to the supply line for China as well as by the Royal Air Force and the [BOAC] Corporation". ("Jane's", 1942–1943)

In addition to its role, so vital to Great Britain, of re-establishing, maintaining and opening up transcontinental links across the North Atlantic, BOAC was also called upon in certain circumstances to participate directly in military operations. Examples of this activity occurred in April/May 1941 during the evacuation of the island of Crete, and in November/December 1942 between Cairo and the front in the Western Desert. "Military operations required Cairo-Western Desert services, and BOAC had to suspend Cairo-Lagos and Cairo-Takoradi flights because of shortage of aircraft. More than 200 flights were made in each direction between Cairo and the Western Desert by the end of December." [30] However, of all the operations carried out by BOAC the most dangerous was undoubtedly its ball-bearing run to Sweden.

Sweden played an unusual role in the course of the Second World War. As a neutral country, it could be a point of contact between diplomats, and as the world's leading producer of ball bearings, it supplied the arms factories of the warring powers. While Germany, after the bombing of its principal manufacturing centre in Schweinfurt on 17th April 1943, could easily obtain supplies from Sweden by sea, this was not the case with Great Britain. The regular supply of indispensable ball-bearings could only be guaranteed to the British arms factories by means of a night-time link. This was extremely risky as it over-flew Norway and Denmark, which were occupied by the enemy.

BOAC was entrusted with the mission. In February 1941, in the middle of winter, it started up a service between Leuchars (an airbase near St Andrews in Scotland) and Stockholm, flying a Lockheed 14, registration number G-AGBG. This service, which is still regarded as one of the great exploits of British air transport, was given many titles and nicknames: from the sober " ball-bearing line" to the picturesque "bashful Gertie, the terror of the Skagerrak", as well as being known by its military code name, "Scrutator". Various types of aircraft operated the route, some being piloted by the Royal Norwegian Air Transport.

The highest-performance aircraft used on this route was the De Havilland Mosquito introduced into the service on 6th August 1942 by the Royal Air Force, and operated by the civilian pilots of BOAC from February 1943 onwards. It was unusual for a commercial (though rather special) transport service operating with an aircraft such as the Mosquito. One of the most revered machines in the RAF, the Mosquito was a remarkable aircraft, with a structure made entirely of wood. It was originally designed as an unarmed bomber, its sole defence being its outstanding performance – it was fitted with two 12-cylinder Rolls-Royce Merlin engines, and was exceptionally fast. When it was delivered to the RAF in July 1941 it proved to be remarkably adaptable for a variety of uses.

Characteristics of the Mosquito

Bomb load	Up to 4,000lb
Weight: empty	14,622lb
Loaded	22,587lb
Speed: max	425mph
Speed: cruising	315mph

In spite of the aircraft's speed, five Mosquitoes were shot down by German fighters. The last flight took place on 17th March 1945. In total, 530 return flights were completed with this aircraft, carrying some passengers, a certain amount of official mail, and a large quantity of vital freight (ball bearings).

The Air Transport Command of the Royal Air Force
The Air Transport Command of the Royal Air Force was not established until 11th March 1943. This organisation fulfilled the dual function of carrying out a large number of missions, and coordinating all the British air transport means. It was composed of four sections:

• Regular military services carrying passengers, mail and freight
• Ferrying
• Close support operations
• Supplying of forward ground forces (and evacuation of the wounded)

Charged with organising and opening a network of strategic air routes, the Air Transport Command constructed a veritable "World System". [31] The main routes in this world-wide network crossed the North and South Atlantic, connected to the United Kingdom and Egypt and Ceylon, as well as with West Africa, and joining Canada to Australia by passing across North America and the Pacific. In a single month (December 1944) the traffic figures amounted to 47,000 passengers, 350 tonnes of post (Airgraph mail) and 2,300 tonnes of freight.

RAF Transport Command used many different types of aircraft: Douglas C-47 Dakota, Bristol Bombay, Lockheed Hudson and Lodestar, Vickers Warwick and Wellington", Armstrong-Whitworth Albemarle, Avro York and Consolidated Liberator.

RAF Transport Command tactical support and supply missions
There were too many such missions to be able to refer to all of them, but two illustrate the diversity of the tasks.

• Burma: The Siege of Imphal, March/June 1944
On 4th February 1944 the Japanese launched a major offensive in Burma. The object was to open the way to India. They managed to pierce the British front and to encircle the West African Division and the 5th and 7th Indian Divisions. However, following a massive intervention with C-47s of the RAF and C46s from the US Transport Command, which dropped over 2,000 tonnes of supplies within a few days, these units managed to break out of the containment and to rejoin the main force.
In spite of the relative failure of this first phase of their offensive, the Japanese went on to a second phase and launched an assault against the towns of Kohima and Imphal, which barred the way to India:

"Imphal was the nodal point on which hinged the defence of Assam and vital to any force invading Burma from India and vice versa." (Lord Mountbatten).

On 29th May 1944, the Japanese managed to surround Imphal completely, trapping 150,000 men of the 14th Army. Unlike General Paulus at Stalingrad, Lord Mountbatten, countermanding the instructions personally received from President Roosevelt, decided on his own authority to put the relief of Imphal before the continuation of the "Hump" airlift, and transferred a large number of C-46s and C-47s from this latter operation.

The requirements of the besieged army were estimated at 400 tonnes per day. In fact, in spite all the efforts of the Troop Carrier Command, the air supply operation never achieved more than 270 tonnes per day. The food rations were reduced to 65% of normal. But thanks to the domination of the air by Spitfires and Hurricanes, the 14th Army was maintained on a fighting footing. The Japanese were attacked from the rear by American forces based in China, and began to release their stranglehold on Imphal. In June 1944, the garrison was freed via overland routes.

The Royal Air Force, in its official history, is very clear about the conclusions to be drawn about this operation: "The meaning of domination in the air had once more been proved." [32] For his part, Lieutenant-General William Slim, who was in command of the ground forces in Burma, expressed a much more qualified opinion about airlifts:

"Among the most strategically dangerous ideas that half-baked thinking on air supply provoked, was that even if surrounded, positions could be held for months provided that they might be maintained from the air. In fact, troops thus cut off, even if fed and maintained, eventually lost heart and air supply is so easily interrupted . . . Air supply is only half the answer. The other half is an adequate relieving force." [33]

• The Rhine – March/May 1945
During the last weeks of the war, British mechanised and armoured divisions were pushing eastwards. They were in danger of being slowed down in their advance by an acute logistical problem – the renewal of fuel supplies. The task was taken over by an enormous fleet of 2,000 aircraft which transported, as near to the front as possible, thousands of tonnes of fuel – almost 3,000 tonnes (669,000 gallons) on 4th April 1945, and over 2,000 tonnes per day (500,000 gallons) during the following week, using Dakotas, Halifaxes and Stirlings.

Help for the resistance movements in France and Yugoslavia
The support activity for resistance movements was carried out by units specially trained for missions involving cargo drops and parachuting operations, namely the 138th and 161st Squadrons of the RAF, reinforced towards the end of 1943 by a transport group, and in February 1944 by two squadrons of the US Air Force flying Liberators. These so-called "special duty operations" were carried out from 14 aerodromes situated in Great Britain which witnessed a rapid growth in operations from 1943 onwards.

In 1943, 1,349 special duty sorties were made into France alone, of which 615 were successful, and 578 tonnes of materials were dropped in containers which could hold 320 pounds of stores, small arms and ammunition, explosives, wireless equipment, medicines and food. From August to October 1943 a special drive was made to equip the Maquis fighters of Haute Savoie, shortly after the battle of Glières Plateau, with 10,000 sten guns, 20,000 grenades and 18 tonnes of explosives. "Warning that the supply drop was to be made was given out by the BBC on the French news. Cryptic phrases such as 'Adolphe a deux soeurs' sent brave men and women out in the night with torches and with their lives in their hands." [33] However, the largest supply of aid to resistance fighters was

ABOVE Lockheed Hudson.
MAP

BELOW Vickers Wellington.
MAP

TOP **Douglas Dakota, June 1944.** *RAF Museum*

ABOVE **Armstrong Whitworth Albemarle, June 1944.** *RAF Museum*

ABOVE RIGHT **Liberator C.VIII.**
RAF Museum

OPPOSITE PAGE
ABOVE **Vickers Warwick.** *MAP*

CENTRE **RAF Avro York C1.** *MAP*

BELOW **Lockheed Lodestar.** *British Airways Museum*

made to the Yugoslavian Partisan Army, using British, American and Russian air transport units.

Humanitarian missions
On several occasions RAF Transport Command was involved in humanitarian missions, often unsung.

The civilian populations of France, Belgium and The Netherlands, suffering in the conflict, benefited from such campaigns and received aid by air in the form of foodstuffs, medicines and clothing. The largest such operation was code named "Manna" and was carried out from 29th April to 8th May 1945 over Holland. More than 3,000 bombers dropped 6,685 tonnes of foodstuffs to the starving populations of Rotterdam and The Hague. The least known humanitarian airlift involved the British colony of Aden in April and May 1944. After three years without rain, the inhabitants of the Hadramaut Valley, who were even deprived of the money normally sent to them by their relatives installed in Malaysia and Indonesia, were suffering under conditions of famine. The British Government sent aid to the Port of Al Mukalla and the first famine relief flight took place on 29th April 1944. A fleet of six Wellington aircraft made three round trips per day for the whole of the month of May between the airport of Riyan, and the landing strip at Quatn in the Hadramut Valley. Over 400 tonnes of corn were distributed to the famished population, and reserves sufficient for four months' consumption were re-established.

Thus, in addition to their war activities, Air Transport Command and Bomber Command of the RAF "were to bring comfort to the afflicted and thus to show that the power of the air may be gentle and healing, and not only terrible and strong". (History of the Royal Air Force)

ABOVE **Bristol Bombay.**
RAF Museum

LEFT **C-46 of USAAF, Burma.**
RAF Museum

BELOW **RAF Avro York.**
RAF Museum

Part Five
The Time of "Safe and Orderly Growth" 1945–1970

"Het luchtruim verbindt alle volkeren."
("Airspace unites all peoples.")

Albert Plesman (1889–1953) Founding President of KLM

The part title is taken from "*Convention concerning International Civil Aviation*", Second part, Chapter VII, Article 44

1 THE NEW ORDER FOR THE INTERNATIONAL AIRWAYS: A REGULATED WORLD

The war was still raging when the Allied powers, with the personal endorsement of President Franklin D. Roosevelt, decided to create a new international organisation with the responsibility of setting up a collective system of security, more effective than that of the League of Nations. The United Nations Declaration was adopted on 1st January 1942 and the United Nations Charter was signed in San Francisco on 26th June 1945, coming into force on 24th October 1945. The United Nations Charter was ambitious in its intentions and generous in its principles, extending its competence over all aspects of international life. The Security Council was given "the primary responsibility for the maintenance of international peace and security".[1] The Economic and Social Council, which, through the influence of its numerous dependant Specialised Agencies, covered all the economic, technical and cultural aspects of international life, was given the task of promoting "higher standards of living, full employment and conditions of economic and social progress and development "for all peoples".[2] Thus, the United Nations Organisation, founded by those who for 15 years had known nothing but the devastation of an economic crisis without precedent and the horrors of a war without equal, embarked on two inextricably linked objectives: the preservation of peace and economic progress.

In order to leave the apocalyptic years behind, the statesmen imagined a world which was ordered and pacified. They defined the operating rules for a new international order, based on co-operation and the development of trade. In the same spirit they approached all aspects of international relations, whether monetary, with the Bretton Woods Agreements and the creation of the International Monetary Fund, commercial, with the International Trade Organisation and later the General Agreement on Rates and Trade (GATT), agricultural, with the Food and Agriculture Organisation (FAO), or aeronautical, with the International Civil Aviation Organisation, etc. The object of these many regulations, which were sometimes restrictive, was not to eliminate competition but to re-establish and expand all forms of trade and exchange in a fragmented world.

1 PUBLIC LAW OF THE AIR

Whilst the war was still running its course, the United States and Great Britain felt it necessary to call a conference for the purpose of establishing and expanding the international regulations which would be most appropriate for the development of international civil aviation.

The conference was called by President Roosevelt, and opened in Chicago on 1st November 1944, with the Soviet Union absent. It assembled 54 nations, of whom 25 were already signatories of the Paris Convention of 1919. The Chicago Conference examined two main areas. The technical area was the easier to resolve, since it had already been considered by ICAN. The other area concerned economic issues, and these soon proved to be the stumbling block of the conference, particularly concerning the mutual grant of traffic rights, the definition of air routes, and the determination of capacities and mechanisms for fixing rates.

In short, two different economic philosophies, which went to the heart of the balance of power and of national interests, confronted one another during the course of the conference. The United States, strengthened by its crushing superiority in the air, argued in favour of the widest possible multilateral exchange of freedoms of the skies, and for an automatic regulation of capacity by allowing the free play of market forces. The US declared itself in favour of an international organisation which would deal principally with technical matters. On the other side, Great Britain, bruised by five years of conflict, advised a more limited exchange of access to air space and proposed the creation of an international organisation – the International Air Authority – which would be given extremely wide powers regarding economic and commercial matters (granting of air routes, definition of flight frequencies, control of capacities). A kind of international CAB!

These two points of view were so difficult to reconcile that the Chicago Conference halted on the question of the reciprocal exchange of freedoms of the air. From a legal point of view, there are five recognised freedoms of the air. The first two are generally considered to be technical rights:

• The first freedom refers to the right of an airline of country A to over fly country B.
• The second freedom refers to the right of an airline of country A to make a stopover in country B for technical reasons, without any commercial activity.

The three following freedoms are known as " traffic rights":
• The third freedom is the right of an airline of country A to disembark traffic (passengers, freight and mail) in country B.
• The fourth freedom is the right of the same company to take on board traffic in country B destined for country A.

The third and fourth freedoms are closely linked.

The fifth freedom is entirely different in nature, since it introduces a third agent, ie a third country:

• The fifth freedom is the right of an airline of country A to disembark or take on traffic in a country B which has come from or is travelling to a country C.

In order to appreciate the importance of this fifth freedom, which brought the conference to a halt, we should remember that the long-haul lines after the war still included many stopovers, out of the weakness of the markets lack of demand and the limited range of the aircraft. A prohibition of loading or unloading commercial traffic on intermediate stopovers would have seriously compromised the profitability of long-haul services. The Americans intended to make liberal use of this freedom. The British, supported by a number of delegations, wished to grant it only sparingly.

Since it could make no further progress, the conference ended on 7th December 1944 with the signature of various documents which would later become the "Convention concerning International Civil Aviation", more commonly called the "Chicago Convention". It entered into force on 4th April 1947.

The Chicago Convention
Without going into details about the Convention and its appendices, it is instructive to identify its essential features to understand the framework of public law in which international civil aviation was to develop.

Article 43 of the Convention established that "an organisation to be named Civil Aviation Organisation is formed by the Convention. It is made up of an assembly, a council and such other bodies as may be necessary", otherwise known as the ICAO. Article 44 defined its mission: "The aims and objectives of the organisation are to develop the principles and techniques of international air navigation and to foster the planning and development of international air transport."

There than followed an enumeration of some of the general objectives which were particularly representative of the thinking at that time (Article 44). These included:

a) "Ensure the safe and orderly growth of international civil aviation throughout the world …
b) Meet the needs of the people of the world for safe, regular, efficient and economical air transport.
c) Prevent economic waste caused by unreasonable competition."

Those who had drafted the Chicago Convention were convinced that an "organised and limited competition" was the best way of guaranteeing the sure, effective development of international civil aviation in postwar conditions. Moreover, they had before them a model of organised air transport where competition was controlled: that of the American domestic transport system, placed under the strict governance of the Civil Aeronautics Board.

With just as much vigour as the Paris Conference of 1919, Article 1 of the Chicago Convention confirmed the absolute sovereignty of states over their airspace:

"The contracting States recognise that every State has complete and exclusive sovereignty over the airspace above its territory."

Having reaffirmed this inviolable principle, the Chicago negotiators examined the most suitable manner for enabling the mutual grant of traffic rights, or "freedoms of the air", between the contracting states. To this end they prepared two documents:

• The Transit Agreement, which provided for a multilateral exchange of the first two freedoms of the air or "technical rights" for scheduled international services. This text was signed and ratified by the majority of the states, and entered into force on 30th January 1945.

• The Transport Agreement which proposed "the exchange on a multilateral basis of all five freedoms of the air". The controversial content of this document, which introduced a kind of "general freedom of the air" through the introduction of complete multilateralism, had no chance of being accepted by the majority. Over-ambitious, it was never put into practice.

In terms of the "freedoms of the air", the Chicago conference ended up simply with a mutual grant of the technical rights. It referred back the difficult question of the grant of traffic rights, to be dealt with in bilateral negotiations between states, the sovereignty of which had been reconfirmed in the first article of the Convention.

The Bermuda Agreement and the "Triumph of Bilateralism" [3]
The United States and Great Britain met in Bermuda at the beginning of 1946 to try to find solutions to the problems which had been left unresolved by the Chicago Conference: capacity determination , traffic movements under the fifth freedom, and a mechanism for fixing rates. They reached an agreement which was signed on 11th February 1946.

The Bermuda Agreement was a subtle compromise between the American open skies policy, and the very control-orientated British policy, covering each of the three main issues dealt with.

• Capacity Determination
Capacities were defined in a bundle of conditions, often considered very vague, known as the "Bermuda Clauses" and which could be summarised as follows:

1. Capacities deployed must correspond "to the needs of the public" (ie to market expectations). Based on this principle, "the American airlines observe that nothing in the wording of the Bermuda Agreement would permit the predetermination of frequencies and capacities (by the aviation authorities) and the establishment of such matters falls solely within the competency of the operating companies." [4]

2. The capacities of an air route should be determined in order of priority, taking firstly the traffic under the third and fourth freedoms and secondly according to the traffic under the fifth freedom.

3. The agreement introduced an a posteriori or ex post facto control mechanism for clauses on capacity and other measures. In order to quantify the damage suffered by a party, it was first necessary to establish that it had been caused. Moreover, the clause concerning the settlement of differences was not binding, since these were simply submitted to the opinion of the ICAO in a consultative capacity.

• Mechanism for fixing tariffs

Since the British side had made concessions regarding the fifth freedom, which was subject to limitations, but acknowledged and taken into account when calculating capacities, the American side demonstrated its flexibility in the field of tariffs. The tariff system which was agreed had three conditions:

1. The fixing of the structure and the level of tariffs was delegated to the IATA Traffic Conferences.

2. "The rates shall be fixed at reasonable levels, due regard being paid to all relevant factors such as cost of operation, reasonable profit and the rates charged by any other air carriers." (Paragraph H of Annex II of the Bermuda Agreement)

3. The tariffs adopted by the IATA Traffic Conferences would not be allowed to be put into effect by the designated airlines, until they have been approved by the Government authorities of the two contracting parties.

For the Americans, the CAB – "an independent regulatory agency charged with the economic regulation of civil aviation" – immediately approved the IATA rate making machinery.[5] This explicit approval was absolutely necessary from a legal point of view, so that the IATA tariffs, which had been decided as a result of an understanding between competing companies, could benefit from an exemption from the effects of anti-trust legislation.

The Civil Aeronautics Board, whose powers were originally limited to domestic routes, was thus accorded by the Bermuda Agreement formidable powers which it would use to the full: it was now able to reject international rates or regulatory conditions submitted to it for approval.

• Definition of "Air routes"

This definition followed certain principles, which once again, referred to a number of bilateral agreements:

1. Multiple designation of departure points in the country of origin.

2. Uniqueness of arrival point in the country of destination.

3. A "flexible and precise" course for the route through the enumeration of a number of intermediate points between which a choice can be made.

This was the main outline of the Bermuda Agreement.

"The United States had advocated a policy of bilateralism prior to the Chicago conference. For a brief period, the policy had changed to one of multilateralism at the Chicago conference, and then at Bermuda in 1946 it had reversed to bilateralism." [6]

From then on, bilateral air agreements, diplomatic documents negotiated between sovereign states, would without exception dominate the organisation of international air transport. They can be divided into two families, depending on their content:

1. Bilateral agreements of the Bermuda type, in which capacities are not predetermined by the aeronautical authorities, but fixed as a function of the "demand for traffic between the country of origin of the company, and the country served by the last stop",[7] and which were much appreciated by the airlines concerned.

2. Bilateral agreements of a non-Bermudan type, which were the largest in number. They did not contain that type of clause: the capacities were fixed within the bilateral agreement itself, which was therefore more restrictive. There is a predetermination, often on a 50/50 basis, of the capacities employed by both contracting parties.

By 1960, over 400 bilateral agreements had been registered with the ICAO. In spite of their rigidity they made a considerable contribution to the "safe and orderly growth" which was desired by the writers of the Chicago Convention.

"Indiscrimination"

This word means that the sources of public air law in their original state – the Chicago Convention, the Bermuda Agreement and the bilateral agreements until the 1970s – do not admit a distinction in the application of their terms and conditions, between the three traditional types of traffic: passenger, mail and freight. The agreements therefore cover all types of traffic without distinction ie discrimination.

Nevertheless, international cargo lines were operating from 1946 onwards. The question of possibly inserting particular clauses relating to cargo-only flights into the bilateral agreements was therefore raised. "The European multilateral agreement concerning the commercial rights for non-scheduled air transport in Europe", signed in Paris on 30th April 1956, is one of the first documents to have recognised the existence of "exclusive freight services", both scheduled and non-scheduled. In spite of a multitude of reservations and limitations, it associates for the first time the notions of "exclusive freight services" with "liberalisation" of the regulations. In fact, cargo services frequently served as a proving ground for deregulation policies.

With the increasing number of cargo lines, there was a gradual tendency towards the individualisation of rights regarding freight traffic in the bilateral agreements. However this movement was too slow to fulfil the requirements of the market. The law was in danger of lagging behind practice. The executives of the airlines concerned therefore found an escape route out of the legalistic restrictions, with the tacit acquiescence of their Government authorities, who were loath to reopen diplomatic negotiations with a doubtful outcome for the sake of a mere cargo service. By common accord, while remaining within the classic bilateral context, they proposed a form of official approval for such services through the simultaneous creation and/or joint operation of cargo services, which were not covered by the air traffic agreement. It would suffice to include such services within the official framework on the occasion of the next revision or negotiation.

This ingenious formula met with considerable success, and is still widely practised today.

As can be imagined, the United States always upheld that the Bermuda clauses were sufficiently flexible to authorise the creation of any cargo service, according to market demand.

2 "THE NEW IATA"

The IATA of 1945 appeared to be a resurrection of the IATA that existed immediately after the First World War. The logo remained unchanged, as a symbol of permanence. The name was only slightly changed: the International Air Traffic Association became the International Air Transport Association. But whereas the early Association was the product of individual initiatives on the part of the leaders of private companies, the new IATA was born in the shadow of the Chicago Conference.

• The renaissance of IATA
On 6th December 1944, on the eve of the signature of the Chicago Convention, 34 representatives of airlines, who were attending the conference as advisors or experts in their national delegations, "happened to meet" and "it was agreed to set up the committee charged with drawing up the statutes of a new organisation." [8] The partial similarity in the identities of the individuals drawing up the convention and the initiators of the new IATA leaves one to expect that the views of the ICAO, an organisation of sovereign states, and IATA, an association of airlines, would be largely identical. The ICAO and IATA form the two pillars on which rested the safe and orderly growth of postwar air transport, within the framework of reasonable competition.

The statutes and organisation of IATA
The aims and objectives of the association, as expressed in Article III of its statutes, express the complete agreement between the two organisations.

Article III
"*The aims and objectives of IATA shall be:*

(1) to promote safe, regular and economical air transport for the benefit of the peoples of the world, to foster commerce and to study the problems connected herewith.

(2) to provide means for collaboration among the air transport enterprises engaged directly or indirectly in international air transport services.

(3) to co-operate with the International Civil Aviation Organisation and other international organisations."

In October 1945, the first annual general meeting, which met at Montreal, the seat of the association, nominated Sir William Percival Hildred as Director General. He was a former Director General of Civil Aviation in Great Britain and by virtue of his past experience, his convictions and his personality, he helped to perpetuate the hybrid character of IATA, a quasi-public body consisting of private members.

Sir William was an eminent figure in postwar commercial aviation, constantly voted back into office for a period of over 25 years, and he left a profound imprint on the International Air Transport Association. He was a cultivated and humanist, warm but able to keep his distance, adept in his use of language, who managed to win the approbation of all in world dominated by the Anglo-Saxon powers. He was very much preoccupied with the financial management of airlines, while remaining concerned for the general economic good, and despite his often strained relations with Government authorities, he was able to combine outspokenness with diplomacy. He possessed a clear vision of the future, based on solid technical knowledge, and a global appreciation of the trends of the time. He was a realist, without ever appearing insensitive, and was convinced – perhaps overly so – of the future of airfreight, being always acutely aware of the inestimable contribution which IATA made to the development of air transport after the war. During the Annual General Meeting of 1954 he gave his own definition of IATA, which is at the same time the expression of his philosophy:

"*IATA is the solution by means of which the airlines have attempted to work out for themselves in a very diverse world the unity of aims and methods which represents the condition sine qua non for any international public service.*" [9]

Sensing that future changes were inevitable, Sir William wrote in 1961: "Whilst we shall always be an essential public service, we are more and more a consumer industry."

The Association, whose Director General was both its motor and its kingpin, was composed of the following main entities:

• The Annual General Meeting
The AGM was "The ultimate authority of the Association", consisting of representatives of its active members. It met once a year.

"*Any air transport enterprise is eligible to become an active member if it exploits on its own behalf a regular air service for passengers, post or freight open to the public against remuneration between the territories of two or more States, under the flag of a State eligible to be a member of ICAO.*"

Here, as in the bilateral agreements, no distinction is made between companies operating mixed services (passengers, mail and freight) and companies operating services exclusively for freight. Note that IATA is an "open association" to which any eligible company is free to belong, unlike a cartel, which is a closed association.

• The Executive Committee
This is elected by the AGM and exercises "the function of managing the Association". It deals with the big issues. It is theoretically the strongest body within the Association but, in reality, its influence on the Standing Committees and Traffic Conferences – where the real work is done – is limited. As a prestigious committee, consisting of a few very senior executives, it has a tendency to withdraw into the lofty regions of aeropolitics.

• The "Standing Committees" and "Traffic Conferences"
These are supposed to assist the Executive Committee. Numbering five at the outset, the Standing Committees were

reduced to four: the Financial, Legal, Technical (which absorbed the Medical Committee) and Traffic Committees (the latter covering all commercial regulatory and tariff questions).
Around these Standing Committees revolve various sub-committees, working groups etc.

Activities and operating principles of IATA

IATA embraces all aspects of freight transport activity. Its competence covers not only the technical and legal aspects, but also financial and commercial issues (rates and regulations). In all domains, the work of the Standing Committees is dominated by two key goals, equally significant: harmonisation and standardisation.

This standardisation of technical procedures and the harmonisation of commercial regulations and transport documents, both create savings and are a prerequisite for the free circulation of persons and goods and have made a powerful contribution to the development of civil aviation. In many respects, the ICAO and IATA seem to be two faces of the same entity. It is only due to the tremendous expansion of the world economy and of air transport that the administrative aspects of the one and the commercial aspects of the other have received increasing emphasis.

Below is a summary of the basic principles under which IATA operates:

1. At the heart of IATA and the bilateral agreements, is the original standpoint − the complete lack of discrimination with regard to freight activities.
The agreement, which establishes the powers of the Traffic Committee decrees: "the Traffic Committee shall take charge of all the questions concerning passengers, freight and the handling of post."
Within IATA it was only recognised very slowly, under the dual effect of an increase in traffic and the particular nature of the problems encountered, that freight activities were sufficiently different to justify the creation of permanent specialist bodies. One major hurdle was overcome in 1964 with the organisation of Traffic Conferences specifically for regulating and setting rates for freight. But specialisation did not yet mean autonomy.

2. Within IATA decisions are taken unanimously. This rule of unanimity, which has been widely criticised, since it systematically generates compromised solutions, has one rare merit: that of respecting the point of view of the smallest company in a sector dominated by a few large operators. However, in the field of rates the rule of unanimity presents a major disadvantage: it means that tariff agreements can only be achieved if based on the costs of the least efficient companies.

3. All member companies have the binding obligation, on the threat of internal fines, to apply the regulatory tariff decisions, which have been unanimously adopted and approved by the Governments concerned. There is not only a "mutual understanding on rates" approved by the Governments, but any company which causes a client to benefit from a rate more advantageous than that adopted unanimously, lays itself open to sanctions.

Within this restrictive framework of tariffs and regulations, which nevertheless corresponded to the needs and views of the postwar world freight transport presents itself like a boisterous and undisciplined pupil. It is within the freight field that the binding rates structures were most frequently violated. Thus, in the IATA Bulletin of December 1956 we read: "The tariff agreements for cargo are being violated on a considerable scale." In modern parlance, one would say that freight transport offered a "window of opportunity"!

3 THE UPU, A SPECIALIST INSTITUTION OF THE UNITED NATIONS

Immediately after the war, many postal executives thought that the Universal Postal Union would be able to preserve its "splendid isolation". This was an illusion, as was recognised in a speech by Joseph-Jean Le Mouel, Director General of the French Postal Service, on 15th September 1949 when he addressed the fifth Annual General Meeting of IATA at The Hague:

"Relations of the UPU with the United Nations:
Since the last Paris Congress,[10] the UPU has been attached to the United Nations as a specialist institution, on the same basis as ICAO, UNESCO, the ILO and many other organisations of which you are aware. People have sometimes disapproved of this partial abandonment of an independence which has lasted 75 years, and regretted that the UPU, which hitherto had not answered to any other higher authority, had entered into a path of collaboration with an organisation whose essential activity is concerned above all with politics. For my part, I have no regrets at being one of the supporters of the UPU becoming attached to the United Nations. In spite of this attachment, everything, which is concerned with the technical and professional spheres relating to international post, remains the exclusive responsibility of the UPU, whose declared aim is to keep itself apart from any disturbances of a political nature. Undoubtedly, it may occur that we in the UPU deal with politics, but it is only incidentally, and in some ways in the manner of a photographer. For the UPU, a country exists or does not exist; it is created, dissolves or disappears. We observe the fact without seeking to analyse it, without wanting to comment on it, and only draw such conclusions as are useful for organising our Union. Nothing more."

2 THE AGE OF AIRFREIGHT

The war completely changed the statistical distribution and the volume of traffic.

• Statistical distribution

Where airmail had formerly been dominant, freight increasingly gained the upper hand. The age of airmail gave way to the age of airfreight.

Comparative development of mail and freight traffic (in million RTK [1])

	Mail	Freight	Total	Relative percentages	
				Mail	Freight
1938	36	17	53	68%	32%
1946	100	120	220	45%	55%
1950	200	770	970	21%	79%
1951	230	870	1,100	20%	80%

Source: ICAO

• Volume

The quantities carried postwar were of a completely different magnitude. This applied to all aspects of commercial aviation: by 1950, compared with 1938, passenger traffic had multiplied 17-fold, mail six-fold and freight traffic, which stands out as the most dynamic element, 45-fold, due to the increase in tonnages and the growth of average distances travelled.

In 1951, the world's scheduled freight traffic [2] divided into three more or less equal components:

	Freight traffic	Proportion of total
Traffic within the United States	315	36%
Traffic within other countries	275	32%
International traffic	280	32%
Total (unit: million RTK)	870	100%

If one considers that a large proportion of international traffic was generated by the USA, one can see to what extent the might of America dominated commercial aviation following the Second World War. The American flag carriers made up 61.6% of the world traffic in passengers, 48.5% in freight and 58.1% in mail. In addition, all airlines, or at least those with the freedom

or the means to do so, dreamed of buying aircraft of American manufacture.

1 A NEW AMERICAN INDUSTRY: AIRFREIGHT

The United States became successively interested in airmail in the 1920s, passengers in the 1930s and freight in the 1940s. It did not pioneer airfreight, but gave it such an energetic push forward that some people thought that the United States was indeed its birthplace, whereas that honour might more fairly be given to European nations or even Colombia.

From Air Express to Airfreight

Until the beginning of the 1940s, the freight traffic of the American airlines more or less amounted to Air Express: a product organised and marketed by the Railway Express Agency, and limited to small parcels. The entry into service of a new generation of passenger aircraft, which offered a higher payload and larger cargo holds, fired the imagination of managers within the American airlines. In answer to the concerns of the time, the Air Transportation Association created a research company called Air Express Inc, in June 1940. Less than a year later, in March 1941, the "Big Four" – American Airlines, Eastern Airlines, TWA and United Airlines – founded another research company named Air Cargo Inc. This change in nomenclature is extremely important as it reflects the changing view of cargo.

Air Cargo Inc, which had 50 employees, carried out research on behalf of its members into the technical and commercial requirements for establishing a "new" mode of air transport, Airfreight, which would be open to carry any quantity or type of goods. From then on, two forms of goods transport by air would coexist in the United States: Air Express and Airfreight. The latter gained increasingly at the expense of the former, until the revolution of the 1970s.

To return to 1940, practical experience soon fleshed out the theory. American Airlines and United Airlines each took a decisive step, though in different fields. United, showing operational courage, was the first to begin operating cargo aircraft, whilst American took the initiative on innovative tariffs in a commercial gamble.

On an experimental basis, United Airlines launched a daily cargo service from New York to Chicago on 23rd December 1940, exclusively reserved for express freight and mail. It was operated with DC-3 passenger aircraft, and remained traditional in its commercial approach. It closed down on 31st May 1941.

Although the entry of the United States into the war slowed the growth of civilian airfreight, it brought about a rapid development of military freight. From then on, civilian and military activities were tightly knit. In March 1942, the airlines began to operate the first domestic military freight services under contract. Pennsylvania Central Airlines ran the Washington/Chicago sector, while Continental opened the first transcontinental freight service from San Francisco (California) to Harrisburg (North Carolina). The privilege of providing the first scheduled cargo link goes to a regional airline of modest size: Hawaiian Airlines. This was a civilian service, but directly linked to the new war footing of the United States. After the Japanese attack on Pearl Harbor on 7th December 1941, the sea connections between the different islands in the archipelago were temporarily broken. The Hawaiian Airlines Company was given the job of re-establishing a certain minimum of communications for passengers, mail and urgent freight. After receiving United States Air Cargo Certificate No 1 from the CAB, it began to operate a little "inter-island cargo network" on 20th March 1942, with the aid of two converted Sikorsky amphibian aeroplanes. [3]

After interrupting its "one-way line" from New York to Chicago at the end of May 1941, United operated a new New York/Chicago/Salt Lake City cargo service for seven months, between November 1942 and June 1943. It achieved its goal on 16th October 1943 when it established its first scheduled civilian transcontinental cargo service from New York to San Francisco using Douglas DC-3 Cargoliners. Although it was a civilian service, it was of course primarily devoted to the requirements of the war effort.

American Airlines could not remain in the background for long. In reply to the operational initiative from United, it countered with a commercial innovation. On 14th September 1944, it threw off the yoke of the Railway Express Agency, and published the first airfreight tariff in the modern sense of the word: "American Airlines Airfreight tariff No 1". [4] United Airlines, which up to that point had shown a certain amount of institutional caution, speeded its pace and published its own first "tariff" in February 1946. In the meantime, in July 1945, American Airlines and TWA had started up their own transcontinental freight service.

A new American product: airfreight

Airfreight became the up-and-coming new sector for the American companies. They threw themselves into it with enthusiasm. Airfreight has its own characteristics and philosophy. Nowhere else is it possible to gain better insight into its true nature than in a remarkable brochure, much ahead of its time, published in 1944 by American Airlines. In particular, one section reads:

"Airfreight is designed to move merchandise at air speed in a regular flow on a volume basis ... A new fleet of airfreighters is coming   with large capacity for Air Age distribution needs. But it is not too early to investigate possibilities

now, so you'll be ready when war restrictions end. We invite you to take advantage of the services of our sales engineering staff now, because it sometimes takes months to engineer for airfreight, to determine its potential benefits for any particular commodity." [5]

In addition to this visionary text, many more superficial documents were predicting a glorious future for airfreight. Some even announced that "the time is not far off when airfreight will attain passenger volume in revenue and then go beyond". [6] Others imagined transporting raw materials by air:

"Most of the nations of the world will become America's next-door neighbours in the post-war air age, when vast fleets of sky giants make regular ports of call, bearing processed goods, raw materials and passengers ...

"Utilisation of the 'Air Ocean' for transportation makes every community in the world a port. There is no shoreline in this air ocean, the harbor is any space large enough to land a plane. For example, rubber from South America need not be carried to New York, then sent by surface transportation to a tyre factory in Ohio. In the future it can be carried by air from South America and unloaded alongside the tyre plant."

This text did not come from just anybody: it was signed "Jack Frye", the prestigious President of TWA. [7] For many, there was a confusion between the hard necessities of a war economy and the rules of an economy at peace. The greater the illusion, the deeper the fall and the disappointment.

Airfreight differed from Air Express in several respects. First of all the marketing was different. Air Express was marketed by a single agency on behalf of all the participating companies whose capacities were pooled and made available to all. Airfreight was a product specific to each airline, and was marketed by the company itself or by intermediaries – freight forwarders.

Secondly, it differed in its rate structure. The rates for airfreight were at once much lower than those for Air Express, and had a different structure:

Rate levels in US cents per ton-mile

	Rates	Dates effective
Air Express	80	1938
	70	15.07.1943
	61	01.01.1946
Airfreight		
United Airlines Tariff	26	01.02.1946

Finally, it differed in respect of the ground equipment required. The physical processing of airfreight required installations and handling equipment, which were not available in most airports in 1947. The expansion of airfreight demanded costly investments, both for the airlines and for the airports. Without them, any time gained in the air would have been lost on the ground.

The "veterans" move centre stage

In June 1948 a young Senate representative from Massachusetts, one John F. Kennedy, sent a vitriolic letter to the Air Transportation Association of America, the symbol of the Establishment as far as the American airlines were concerned:

"It was in World War II that air cargo was really developed on a large scale, and the young men who are now veterans suffered a great deal to build it up. Unfortunately, a lot of the top officials in the established airlines did not have to go through such an experience, or, if they did, it did not affect them very much , and many of them appear to be managing their companies as they did before the war, when air transportation was largely a matter of passengers and mail and a few packages in the luggage compartments . ...The fact that these veterans' companies, even without operating certificates, already carry more freight than do the established lines, which are members of your association, is to me a pretty good indication a) that they want to go into this new activity on a big scale and have been working hard to pioneer this new business, and b) that your members, who possess far more capital and other resources, have been making only half-hearted efforts in that direction.

ABOVE RIGHT **American Airlines DC-3.**
RAF Museum

RIGHT **The "Flying Tigers" – the US Volunteer Group – flew Curtiss P-40s with distinctive tiger shark markings.**
Air Cargo News UK

BELOW **Flying Tigers C-46.**
MAP

Flying Tigers C-54.
MAP

"*As Americans, we have always believed that the access door to business should not be slammed in the face of the next generation, and we are not going to forget that principle now.*" [8]

In order to appreciate the tone of this letter we should go back three years, to the moment when hostilities ceased. Peace returned a large number of pilots to civilian life, and thousands of aeroplanes, DC-3s and C-46s, were put onto the market for a fistful of dollars. The former military pilots, these young "veterans", rushed into air transport. A surprising number of cargo companies sprang up, with only a single aircraft, lacking capital, with no experience and no certificates for regular operation, but driven by the enthusiasm of an owner. It is difficult to say how many there were. Perhaps 100; 70 for certain, of whom the majority would soon be swept away, due to their own inexperience and the fierce competition from the existing airlines, who were so scathingly denounced by Kennedy.

The reaction of these established companies towards these little charter operations took two forms: price wars or administrative obstruction through the CAB.

The price war raged for two years, from 1946 to July 1948. On 1st February 1946, United Airlines registered a rate of 26.5 cents per ton-mile with the CAB. In 1947, the cargo charter companies counter-attacked by reducing their rates to between 22 and 15 cents per ton-mile but no one doubted that the large companies with scheduled services had finally won. They offered the capacity in the holds of their passenger flights to numerous destinations, operated transcontinental cargo services, and had the slack to support the losses from their "freight only" activities, which were very much the lesser part of their businesses, thanks to their passenger traffic, which was

rapidly growing, and their mail income, to which the charter companies had no access. They were able to reduce the rates. American Airlines reduced its price for full loads on its Douglas C-47s (2,700 kilograms) to 13 cents, and then to 11 cents. Finally, after many of the charter airlines, known as "non-scheduled", had disappeared, the CAB decided to intervene to re-establish healthier conditions of competition. On 1st July 1948 it issued a Minimum Rate Order fixing the minimum rate of 16 cents per ton-mile for the first 1,000 miles and 13 cents thereafter. This minimum tariff was to remain in force until September 1953.

Since the CAB did not move fast, the tactic adopted by the large scheduled airlines was to string out as long as possible the examination of the requests for schedule operating certificates submitted by the charter companies.

After the price war and the procedural go-slow had taken their toll, only six charter freight-only companies were still in contention by the end of 1948. After over three years of procedural delay, the CAB brought the Airfreight Case to its conclusion, and on 24th April 1949 issued four companies with certificates for operating regular freight lines, for an experimental period of five years, known as Experimental Five-Year Scheduled All-Freight Certificates. The two biggest and best run companies, Slick Airways and The Flying Tiger Line, were granted scheduled operations on transcontinental services between California and the East Coast: the southern route fell to Slick Airways and the northern route, the famous "Route 100" via the Mid-West, was accorded to Flying Tiger.

A real American story: Bob Prescott and the Flying Tiger Line
Robert William Prescott was born in 1913 in Fort Worth into a family of seven children. When he was 20 he left for California. While studying law at Loyola University in Los Angeles, he worked at various trades in order to finance himself through college. One day, his friends dragged him along to the navy flying school at Long Beach and Bob was captivated.

Flying Tigers BUDD-RB1 Conestoga.
Air Cargo News UK

He threw in his studies: he'd found his calling — he would become a military pilot.

By nature an adventurer, in 1941 he was among the group of voluntary pilots who in peace time left the Army or the Navy with the consent of President Roosevelt to fight the Japanese invasion of Southern China under the orders of Claire Chennault, the outstanding senior officer already encountered in this book. He joined the American Volunteers' Group, or AVG. Dressed in civilian clothes, and receiving payments by results (they got a bonus for every Japanese aeroplane they brought down), these volunteers piloted P-40 Tomahawk fighters, marked with the emblem of a roaring Bengal tiger, framed in the "V" for Victory – they were known as the "Flying Tigers".

Everything changed after Pearl Harbor. Claire Chennault was taken back into the Army, promoted to the rank of general, and put in charge of the 14th Air Force. His volunteer Tigers were then given their liberty. "Some of the A.V.G. stayed on, but many went home." [9] Bob Prescott was one of the second group. After his return to Fort Worth, the legend of the Flying Tigers already having gone before him, he was interviewed by Helen Ruth, a charming journalist from the Fort Worth Press. In 1943 he returned to China. Naturally he participated in the "Hump" airlift over Burma but his confirmed love of freedom, and his past as a Flying Tiger, led him to join the China National Airways Corporation – the subsidiary of Pan American working for Air Transport Command – in preference to the US Air Force.

At the controls of his C-46, he made over 300 flights and returned to the United States at the end of 1944, where, in the purest tradition of American romance, he married Miss Helen Ruth. End of Act I.

Act II began in April 1945 in one of the select places of American political life, the Hotel Mayflower in Washington, where Bob Prescott met a Californian businessman Sam Mosher, whose activities ranged from oil to flower farming. Bob explained to him an idea for transporting his flowers by aeroplane from California to the consumer markets on the East Coast, which Sam Mosher found attractive. With Mosher's financial backing, Bob contacted former Flying Tigers who were enthusiastic at the prospect of getting back into a charter airfreight company. On 25th June 1945 he founded the National Skyway Freight Corporation, or NSFC. Sam Mosher was the President and Bob Prescott, Managing Director of the new company, which carried the slogan "The Line of the Flying Tigers" below the company's rather forbidding official title.

In order to start up the operation, Bob bought a fleet of 14 Budd-RB1 "Conestoga" aircraft. These machines did not possess great flying characteristics, but had a double advantage for cargo operations, with a horizontal deck and a vast doorway located at the rear of the fuselage

Business got off to a modest start in July 1945 with a planeload of grapes from Bakersfield, California to Atlanta, Georgia. The producer was pleased to find that the consumers accepted paying a higher price for grapes transported by air because of their improved freshness. This was proof that airfreight could increases the value of the goods transported. More flights followed: flowers to Detroit, furniture, ballpoint pens, Dutch tulip bulbs, racehorses and all kinds of animals. It was fortunate that Sam Mosher was there to give confidence to the company's backers, enabling them to get through the winter of 1945–1946, and introduce some more rigorous management procedures. On this last subject, it is reported [10] that during the hiring of the company's first accountant, the following dialogue took place:

Accountant: *"Where are the books ?"*
Bob (surprised): *"Which books?"*

However, neither the zeal of the Flying Tigers nor the exceptional atmosphere of the young company, reminiscent of a

One of Slick Airways's C-46s.
MAP

The start-up of the domestic American market
The growth in the American market, though spectacular, was deceptive. Only a minute proportion of freight within the United States was sent by air – 0.03%.

Domestic scheduled traffic (in ton-miles)

	Air Express	Airfreight	Total
1938	2	-	2
1951	40	175	215

college, a squadron and a large family, all at the same time, were able to sweep away the hard facts: there was no market for a air cargo charter company. Therefore Bob on 6th August 1946 registered a request with the CAB for a certificate to operate scheduled services, at a time when the financial situation was looking desperate. Would this be the end of the Flying Tigers? End of Act II.

Act III brings the rescue. It is also an illustration of the intricate interlocking of civilian and military activities in the world of the Cold War, which was just beginning.

The Flying Tigers were saved, thanks to a remunerative contract signed up with the Air Transport Command of 28 flights per week over the North Pacific. The Army provided the aeroplanes, but the NSFC found the pilots and carried out the maintenance. Originally for six months, the contract was extended to November 1947.

For the new company, 1947 was an annus mirabilis. The contract with ATC allowed it to hold fast during the rate war, the Budd aircraft were replaced by C-47s and C-54s and they diversified their activities into domestic and international passenger transport. To the great satisfaction of the Flying Tiger veterans, the company changed its name to become the Flying Tiger Line Inc.

The Flying Tiger Line changed its business in summer 1949 to become a scheduled carrier, and started operating on Route 100 from Los Angeles to New York. Whether by luck or a premonition, at the beginning of 1950 Bob Prescott bought a fleet of 25 Curtiss C-46 Commando aircraft – the same aeroplanes that he and his companions had piloted over the "Hump". Then on 25th June 1950 communist North Korea invaded South Korea. The United States reacted: some days later, the C-46s of Flying Tiger Lines disembarked the first reinforcements in Korea. The Korean airlift had begun. True to their image, which combined a spirit of enterprise with love of a good scrap, the Flying Tigers could regard the future with equanimity.

For many years they would be safe. End of Act III.

Air Express, which represented about 20% of the total traffic, was carried exclusively by 16 scheduled companies, in accordance with their agreements with the Railway Express Agency. Airfreight, which had taken the lion's share of 80% of the traffic, was divided between passenger airlines and cargo airlines. All the passenger companies carried freight in the holds of their passenger planes, and the main airlines had started operating regional and transcontinental cargo services. This was the case for American, United, Transworld, Northwest, Eastern and Continental. With regard to the cargo companies, the majority of the traffic was carried by Flying Tiger and Slick Airways, founded by Earl F. Slick in 1946, which experienced a remarkable expansion, thanks to its fleet of 10 C-46s.

The list of products, which were usually sent by air, bears a strange though not surprising resemblance to the list of goods transported in Europe in the years 1930–1939. Richard Malkin, the most remarkable airfreight chronicler of the last 50 years, has drawn up the list: [11]

"... flowers, machine parts, fashion articles, pharmaceutical products, machines and accessories, electric equipment, jewellery, fruit and early vegetables, fish, day-old chicks, handbags, shoes ..." The most fragile flowers (lilies, roses, and camellias) were put on aeroplanes from California and Florida to bring them to Chicago, Boston or New York. The most easily damaged varieties of fruits and vegetables (cherries, strawberries, raspberries, French beans, asparagus) provided regular customers for airfreight – the difference in time to market for asparagus, depending on whether it went by express rail or airfreight, was between 4 and 11 days.

Even more perishable than perishable goods was the daily press. The Atlanta Journal called upon the services of Delta

Straits Airfreight Express Bristol 170 Freighter.
MAP

Airlines in 1945 to distribute its newspapers to Savannah and Augusta, while The New York Times launched an International Air Edition in 1946, aimed at 39 countries in Latin America, Europe and the Near Easter, entirely distributed by air.

In 1949, American Airlines pulled off a spectacular coup. In record time, it distributed throughout the whole of its American territory, a new type of razor blade – 112 tonnes, 25 million blades, distributed by 12 cargo aeroplanes and the whole of its passenger fleet.

In a different but equally promising area, Flying Tiger and TWA got into the business of regular deliveries, entering the market for distributing textile products and fashion items to the large department stores.

2 DOMESTIC TRAFFIC IN OTHER COUNTRIES

Apart from the United States, four other countries had the largest proportion of internal air traffic in 1950 – Australia, Brazil, Canada and Colombia.

The Australian Example: The Beefsteak Airlift [12]
In Australia, goods traffic sent by air leapt from 800 tonnes in 1939–1940 to 34,000 tonnes in 1948–1949.

In this immense and under-populated country, where the ground communication network was both limited and loosely structured, the main artery for air traffic was paradoxically only a few hundred miles long. It joined Sydney to Hobart in Tasmania, the island situated off the southeastern flank of Australia, separated by frequently very rough seas. This marine barrier makes air transport 10 times more competitive. At one time, a farmer chartered an aeroplane to transport a herd of 43 milk cows out to Tasmania. Another day, a whole printing works took to the air.

As happened almost everywhere, scheduled transport provided the largest proportion of traffic, but it was the once-off charter services which added the touch of colour and got people talking. This was the case with Air Beef Limited, a company founded in 1948.

Kimberley in North-Western Australia was an immense stock-raising area, divided up into vast ranches which sometimes reached areas of several thousand square miles. Every year, during the dry season, over 30,000 head of cattle were herded to the port of Windham to be slaughtered. The problem was how to run the cattle in the best possible condition, over a distance which, in the case of the most distant ranches, could be over 300 miles. There were a few different methods possible:

• The traditional method was to drive the herds over the trails, through what was often very rough country. Although this was a very low-cost method, it had two disadvantages: the loss of weight by the beasts and the reduction in the quality of their meat.

• The solution of the future was transportation in fleets of trucks, but this could not get under way until the road network had been improved, involving the construction of bridges. The Federal Government had released credits as a result of signing a 15-year contract with Great Britain, but it would take some time to carry out the work. Under these circumstances, air transport was given a trial for a limited period. This trial meant that the supply line had to be completely reorganised. It was impossible to consider transporting cattle on the hoof in aeroplanes for both economic reasons – the cost per kilo – and for practical reasons – the young bullocks were more or less wild. Under these conditions, it was necessary to set up a small abattoir and cold storage facilities in Kimberley area, nearer the cattle ranches.

The mover and shaker, who got the enterprise going, was Gordon Blythe, from Mount House Ranch. It was his determination that got the support of the Government of Western Australia, enabled the construction of an abattoir and a cold storage warehouse at Glenroy Station, and oversaw the creation of the company Air Beef Ltd (from two pioneers of Australian air transport – Mac Robertson-Miller Aviation and Australian National Airways). The final and absolute requirement was the support of three major ranches (the cattle from Fossil Downs Ranch only had to travel 100 miles across the trails to the abattoir, instead of 280 miles to the Windham refrigerated warehouse!). In May 1949, everything was ready to operate the air

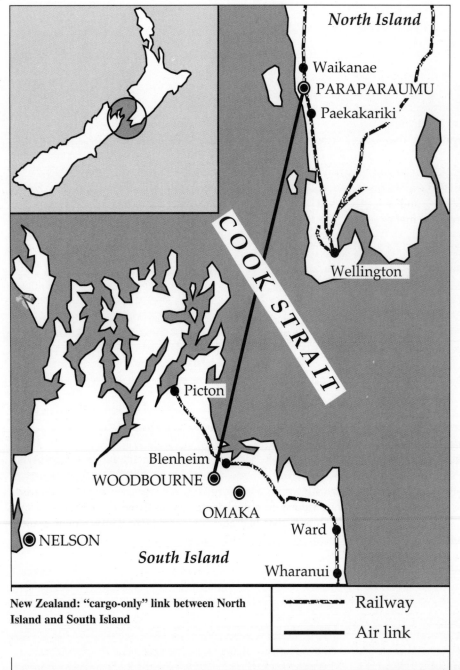

New Zealand: "cargo-only" link between North Island and South Island

Legend:
- Railway
- Air link

mile-long cargo route between Paraparaumu on the North Island and Woodbourne on the South Island.

The goods were brought by road and rail to the two airports and then were loaded onto air shuttles, which operated five days a week.

The service, which was at first run by the Royal Air Force and then by New Zealand National Airways Corporation, operating DC-3 Dakotas, met with considerable success. In September 1950, traffic reached 300 tonnes per week (equivalent to 15,000 tonnes per year). Following a call for tenders, the operation of the line was transferred to Straits Airfreight Express Ltd, which employed Bristol Freighter 170 cargo aircraft fitted with a loading door situated at the front of the fuselage.

Ten years later, in 1959, Straits Airfreight Express ran a fleet of three Bristol 170 cargo aircraft and transported over 30,000 tonnes per year. This is a rather unusual example of air/rail integration for goods traffic.

3 INTERNATIONAL TRAFFIC

International traffic represented the third part of world freight traffic. In the main, two geographical areas were involved: Europe and the Americas.

Europe

The European scene still bore the scars of war. Lufthansa, which had been the top freight airline in 1938, did not rise from its ashes until 1955. Alitalia, a new Italian company founded on 16th September 1946 with a 40% participation by Britain, began operations on 7th May 1947. LOT and CSA, the pre-war Polish and Czech airlines, were soon absorbed into the Soviet sphere of influence, though they continued to belong to IATA. In Western and Northwestern Europe, the large scheduled national airlines took up the torch once more: Air France, Sabena, KLM, Swissair, the Scandinavian airlines which would soon regroup under the banner of SAS, and the British companies BOAC and BEA, which resulted from the break up in 1946 of the British Overseas Airways Corporation, which itself was the outcome of a merger between Imperial Airways and British Airways on 24th November 1939.

Beside these large scheduled airlines, which made up the great proportion of the traffic, numerous charter airlines appeared. The reasons were the same as in the United States — immobilised pilots and cheap ex-military aircraft.

It is in France that we find the best "veteran story". Captain Louis-Jacques Ottensooser (known as Captain Charles) and Captain Eugene Weismann both combined business experience with an exemplary military history. One had been called up, the other had joined as a volunteer in 1914, and they both started

transport solution. The process entailed slaughtering and refrigeration to -20°C at Glenroy Station; loading of the best quality front and hind quarters into a DC-3 in 13 minutes, and later onto Bristol 170s; flight to Windham; rapid unloading and transfer to the refrigerated warehouse. The final assessment of the air solution was satisfactory with regard to quantity: 1,360 tonnes were transported in four years, approximately 1,800 animals per year (6% of the cattle slaughtered) but rather more undecided with regard to quality as the improvements in weight were not as high as expected, due to the time it took to assemble the top-quality animals at Glenroy Station.

In neighbouring New Zealand, a country consisting of two islands, North and South, separated by Cook Strait, internal transport links were always confronted with the problem of non-continuous carriage.

In 1947 New Zealand Railways decided to speed up communications by joining the northern and southern rail networks by means of an air ferry. On 10th February 1947 they launched a 70-

fighting in the infantry. After they were both badly wounded and rendered unsuitable for infantry service (Eugene Weismann had both feet amputated in Verdun on 1st June 1916) they took up flying and ended the war with the rank of Lieutenant.

After returning to civilian life, they acquired business experience, Ottensooser as the President of the Paris Employers' Federation for Leather and Exotic Hides, Weismann as Director of the Établissements Weismann, the distributor for Ford, Mercury and Lincoln cars in the Paris region but they both went back into uniform in September 1939.

Neither accepted the humiliation of defeat: Jean-Jacques Ottensooser reached London on 17th June 1940 – a few hours before the appeal of General De Gaulle – and Eugene Weismann immediately joined the Resistance. They met again in the Air Force in 1944.

On 16th July 1945 they made a joint proposal to the French Air Ministry with a project for creating an airline, specialising in taxi services, photography and "air-trucking", a picturesque expression to describe airfreight over short distances. As they explained in their introductory letter:

"The undersigned, who submit this present project in the name of a group of their aviation comrades, are officers in the Air Force Reserve. In addition, they have industrial or commercial experience and they believe in the future of French Civil Aviation and would be glad to contribute to its development, which would allow them to continue to serve their country when they return to civilian life.

"Moreover they have a desire to obtain for those of their comrades, who are unable to or do not wish to remain in military aviation, an employment conforming to their wishes and aptitudes." [13]

They eventually founded the Compagnie Air Transport, which, through many trials and tribulation, would operate for 30 years. Its name will always be linked to a "Camembert Airlift" (as the Americans would say), during which they transported several hundreds of tonnes of cheese between Caen and London during the summer of 1947, together with another French charter company, Transports Aériens Intercontinentaux, or TAI.

In France, the creation of the Compagnie Nationale Air France did not prevent the Government from adopting a pragmatic policy with regard to these small private charter companies. They were granted operating licenses, which were "provisional and revocable" subject to two conditions: that they would not compete against the national airline and that they would use French equipment. It was against this rather uncertain legal background that some 40 companies hastened to try their luck. There are too many to enumerate, but they all present certain common points:

• An attraction toward the territories of the French Union, where services caused less problems with traffic rights, since the French authorities were in sole charge. There was single exception: cargo charter flights between the Continent and England (fruit, vegetables, cheeses);

• The frequent presence of shipping interests among the shareholders: this was a precautionary investment in case air transport became a serious competitor to sea transport;
• An extremely precarious financial situation: in spite of the hos-

tile legal framework, they made great efforts to develop their freight chartering activities more in the direction of mixed schedule operations.

Two companies merit particular consideration: TAI (Transports Aériens Intercontinentaux) and SATI (Société Aérienne de Transports Intercontinentaux).

"For the public, the TAI logo was synonymous with freight transport" [14] – perishable goods and live animals. In 1946 it provided a Paris/London airlift to convey fruit and vegetables, and in 1948 it acquired a Bristol 170 all-cargo aircraft, which it used especially for transporting racehorses between France and Britain. But no sooner had the Douglas DC-4s appeared on the scene then TAI changed its policy and turned towards passenger transport and Africa.

The creation of SATI is a wonderful freight story, which is told by one of its founders:

"With the benefit of what we'd seen in the United States, and the spectacular results already obtained by airlines such as Flying Tiger or Seaboard, who were operating at the margins of the scheduled services, we were trying to work out the opportunities and likelihood of success for such an enterprise... One day – or rather one night – in June 1948, we made up our minds to give it a try. A quick study caused us to opt for long-haul freight transport, as there seemed to be sufficient demand to justify starting up." [15]

This is how Roger Loubry, Flight Captain, and Jean Combard, a Constellation mechanic, left Air France to throw themselves into the great adventure. They founded the Société Aérienne de Transports Intercontinentaux with three Liberators – former bombers that had been converted. The Government granted them an operating licence, which was "temporary and revocable" to operate out of ... Cormeilles-en-Vexin.

They must have had a lot of a trust in airfreight, and not a little recklessness, to swap Constellations for Liberators and to operate from a village like Cormeilles-en-Vexin!

The first flight took place on 15th April 1949 to Fort Archambault: "the rough landing strips of post-war Africa were to become the destinations most favoured by the Liberators". Strange to say, it was not in Africa that SATI flew its finest missions, but over the ice-sheets of Greenland. The French Polar Expeditions, led by Paul Emile Victor, were undertaken for the purpose of studying the Greenland icecap. At the centre of the island, at an altitude of 3,000 metres, they were to set up a scientific station, in which teams of scientists and technicians would spend the winters of 1950 and 1951. The setting up of the station required some 100 tonnes of equipment to be installed on site, and Paul Emile Victor decided to have part of this work done by plane, due to the difficulties of moving across ice, covered in deep corrugations.

The Liberators got involved the first time from 12th to 14th July 1949, when they parachuted aid to Paul Emile Victor's team blocked 600 metres above sea level. Once the convoy had been freed, and had arrived at base camp, further parachute missions were made between 26th July and 7th August 1949 to supply material for equipping the station: more than 60 tonnes were parachuted down, in conditions which were sometimes extremely dangerous, due to the great sensitivity of the Liberator to trim.

However spectacular these "stunt flights" may have been, they didn't bring in enough money to keep the show on the road. The Chargeurs Réunis Group bought SATI and created a new company on 13th October 1939, the Union Aéromaritime de Transport – UAT – which was authorised to operate in French sub-Saharan Africa services which would be complementary to those of Air France.

In fact, it was Air France, which carried the majority of goods traffic under the French flag in 1950, with figures of 38.2 million tonne-kilometres and 28 670 gross tonnes. The national airline Air France, which was constituted in its new form on 1st September 1948, pursued a policy which was at once prudent and innovative in this field. Due to the lack of suitable equipment, it was obliged for economic reasons to limit its all-cargo services to North Africa (the Paris/Lyons/Marseilles/Algiers service, operating six times per week with Ju52s in 1948), in spite of the "obvious inadequacy" of capacity on long-haul services to the French Union. In order to remedy this situation the company optimised the utilisation of capacity in the holds of its passenger aircraft, and forced itself in "in spite of seasonable variations in passenger traffic, to assign a certain minimum capacity to freight transport throughout the year." [16] Although it was conservative in some respects, Air France's freight policy was resolutely innovative in the commercial and pricing field on the North African services which were not subject to IATA regulations. They introduced contract rates for regular clients, variable rates, depending on the prices of perishable goods, and rates with a margin for negotiation for large consignments. These were three areas in which IATA companies had never managed to reach agreement.

A snapshot of trade carried by air for France in 1950 gives an accurate picture of the politico-commercial situation of the country (see table below). The table gives cause for reflection on three points:

• France was still a colonial power: 70% of trade by air was with the French Union.

• The aeroplane was a means of transport for medium distances: 85% of the traffic was with North Africa and Europe.

• Streams of traffic corresponding to transhipment of maritime goods (France/North Africa and France/Great Britain) represented 80% of the total traffic. It was an undeniable point of weakness of which few people were aware.

Nevertheless, there was room for clarification: "The traffic between Metropolitan France and North Africa has become unquestionably the most heavy air route in the European area, [17] but to what extent it rests upon a temporary condition of inadequate surface transportation is difficult to say." [18]

The same questions can be asked regarding traffic between the Continent and Great Britain, since in both cases sea transport had been seriously disturbed by the war and its aftermath.

Like France, Great Britain experienced the co-existence of private charter airlines and national airlines. Even more than in France, the climate was right for the growth of charter companies concentrating on freight transport. In Britain, as elsewhere, there were two obstacles to overcome: the unsuitability of the old military aircraft (Haltons; Lancastrians) and the restrictions of the legal regulations on "independent British airlines". The Berlin airlift (see Chapter 4) in 1948/49 would reveal the extraordinary vitality of British independent transport companies, which were often financially vulnerable and threatened with closure, but always springing up again in a variety of forms and full of enthusiasm.

The two British national airlines, BOAC for long-haul flights, and BEA, moved towards operating cargo services shortly after the end of hostilities, complementing the capacity available in the holds of their passenger flights.

With regard to long-haul flights, the North Atlantic Return Ferry Service was demilitarised on 30th September 1946. BOAC decided to continue to operate the London/Montreal service as a civilian venture using old Liberator bombers, for which the air-worthiness certificates did not permit the transport of passengers. In the event, BOAC operated a service reserved for mail and freight. During the following two years it extended its freight services towards the Dominions, which had played a major economic and military role during the war, and which possessed enormous sterling balances on their accounts with Great Britain. On 2nd December 1947 it opened cargo services to Australia, flying Lancastrians, and to South Africa in summer 1948, in collaboration with South African Airways. Neither the Liberators nor the Lancastrians had been designed for civilian operations, and their profitability was disastrous. BOAC cancelled the cargo services to Montreal and Johannesburg. For the Far East and Australia it replaced the Lancastrians with a cargo version of the York, although this also was hardly an ideal freight aircraft.

With regard to the medium-haul services, BEA stood out with its early creation of a "Cargo Division", which was given a certain degree of autonomy. It opened the first daily

Analysis of French external trade carried by air in 1950

Destinations/Origins	Exports		Imports		Total	
	Tons	%	Tons	%	Tons	%
Franc Zone Territories	9,213	69.5	7,323	70.0	16,536	69.7
Of which, North Africa	8,104	61.2	7,259	69.4	15,363	64.8
Foreign Countries	4,042	30.5	3,135	30.0	7,177	30.3
Of which, Europe	3,536	26.6	1,409	13.5	4,945	20.9
Of which, USA	170	1.5	1,500	14.4	1,670	8.8
Total	13,255	100	10,548	100	23,713	100

BEA DC-3.
British Airways Museum

London/Brussels/Prague service on 10th August 1947 using DC-3 cargo planes, followed by a London/Nice/Rome/Malta service in April 1949 and a London/Paris service in March 1950.

The North Atlantic
For over 50 years, the North Atlantic never ceased to be the primary route for air transport, including all traffic categories across the board.

North Atlantic traffic of scheduled airlines

	1948	1949	1950
North America-Europe	2,385	2,792	3,179
Europe-North America	1,432	2,097	3,036
Total	3,817	4,889	6,235
		+28%	+28%

Units = tonnes; Source : IATA

This table does not give a complete picture of the trade in goods carried by air across the North Atlantic. It does not include traffic from the charter lines, and in particular that of the American freight carrier Seaboard and Western. A conservative estimate of the total traffic would give a figure of over 7,000 tonnes in 1950. That was already, and by a long chalk, the principal long-haul connection in the world, adding freight, mail and passengers together.

Looking back from a standpoint beyond the year 2000, an annual traffic of 7,000 tonnes – about 70 tonnes per week in each direction – looks derisory. But in 1950, compared with the activities of the long-haul services before the war, it was impressive.

Apart from its absolute value, it reflects the enormous growth rate which airfreight seemed destined to make (+28% per year) and the speed of recovery of the European economies, partly under the effect of the Marshall Plan. After 1950, trade carried by air between Europe on the one hand and the United States–Canada on the other was approximately in balance, and the North Atlantic was confirmed as the sector with the most promising development. Hence, although the majority of the goods traffic continued to be transported in the holds of passenger planes, "some airlines created scheduled services for cargo planes, so as to guarantee their clients that all the freight they wished to send would be conveyed without delay – a measure which made a powerful contribution to the expansion of the traffic." [19] Four companies operated transatlantic freight services during the summer season, 1949:

• Pan American operated DC-4 cargo planes on a New York/Gander/Shannon/London/Brussels route , extended to Istanbul and the Middle East;

• TWA operated DC-4 cargo planes in a New York/Gander/Shannon/Paris/Geneva/Rome/Athens link, extended to Cairo and the Middle East (Dhahran);

• BOAC continued until 27th September to operate a freight connection between Great Britain and Canada, using Liberator bombers;

• KLM inaugurated its Amsterdam/New York freight service in June 1948. It operated three times per fortnight on "a DC-4, which carries 7,000 kilograms of freight in 20 hours between the Old and the New Worlds", and boasted one feature of note: the presence on board of a "freight courier". "This attendant, who was part of the crew, prepared the necessary documents during the flight, and sent telegrams to the next landing point in order to ensure that the freight for onward transit was immediately transhipped to other planes." [20] Hence KLM, which only possessed a limited national market, based its activity on transit traffic, which it obtained from all the countries in the world. It could apply to its own situation the boast of Joost Van Den Vondel to Queen Marie de Médici in 1639: "We, the people of Amsterdam, will go anywhere, where there is money to be made." [21]

Alongside these four scheduled airlines, respectable members of IATA, an American outsider tried to make its way: the Seaboard and Western Company, created in 1946 by brothers Arthur and Raymond Norden. It put on its first transatlantic flight on 10th May 1947 with an aircraft named "Airtrader", bound for Luxembourg. The CAB provided it with its letter of registration on 8th July 1947, conferring upon it a hybrid legal status, somewhere between that of a charter company and that of a scheduled carrier, which did not prevent it from operating almost regular connections between the United States and Switzerland from 1948 onwards.

Since it was not a member of IATA, at least at the outset, Seaboard was free to use rates, which were different from those of the Association. It did not hold back, and inspired spirited recriminations from airlines, who were unaccustomed to this kind of competition, judged unseemly in a well ordered world. It supplied its own rate structure defined by a very simple system of weight breaks which favoured the groupage of small consignments and the loading of large shipments. This kind of commercial policy, which was much appreciated by consolidators and freight agents, would have enjoyed even greater success if it had been accompanied by a better quality of service.

Trade by air between the United States and Latin America
Immediately after the war, the trade of the United States carried by air was mainly in a north-south direction. Traffic coming from and going to Central and South America represented 76% of the total. The Miami-Havana route was the main artery for freight traffic, with 19 scheduled cargo flights per week! (see table opposite).

Except for some connections with the Caribbean areas, which were served by a number of small charter companies, Latin America remained the preferential theatre of operations for Pan Am, more in the case of freight than passengers. In fact it operated a number of cargo lines on DC-4s or C-46s from Miami, New York, Houston, New Orleans and Panama to the majority of the countries in Latin America.

4 PROBLEMS OF A YOUNG INDUSTRY

By 1950, commercial aviation seemed to have entered definitively into the age of airfreight, the "Air Cargo Age", as the Americans call it. Traffic increased three-fold in three years, and all the analysts agreed in predicting a very rosy future for this

US external trade carried by air in 1947

	Exports		Imports	
	Tons	%	Tons	%
Canada	870	4	940	19
Central America	10,770	54.5	3,110	62.5
(of which Cuba)	(4,685)	(23)	(1,600)	(32)
South America	5,060	25	270	5
Europe	2,190	11	520	11
Asia	790	4	70	1
Australia	100	0.5	20	0.5
Africa	250	1	30	1
Total	20,030	100	4,960	100

Source: Bureau of the Census

young industry. However certain questions still needed to be answered:

Question one – what rate of growth?
It was a period of great enthusiasm. The question was not whether air transport as such was going to expand. It was rather a question of evaluating, while trying to keep one's feet firmly on the ground, just how far the expansion could go.
Sir William Hildred, who was well able to combine economic realism with grand visions of the future, got carried away by his downright passion for airfreight when he wrote:

> "Without suggesting that in the foreseeable future aircraft will ever move the millions of tonnes of primary products, coal, iron, wheat, wool, cereals, I confidently predict that, in the next few years, air transport can carry a thousand times as much freight as it does now, if there is sufficient reduction in rates. And I am equally confident that this reduction will be attained." [22]

Fifty years later, Sir William's forecasts still had not been fulfilled.

Question two – what is the role of charter transport?
The existence of many small charter lines alongside the scheduled companies looked very much like a break with the principle of "safe and orderly growth". For the scheduled airlines members of IATA, the competition from these charter companies was all the more irritating because they were so small. They were buzzing with activity, which was rather disconcerting, and they were often run by war veterans whom one had to treat with a certain respect, and finally, they offered rates, which were below those fixed by IATA (which was certainly their greatest crime).

The problem therefore arose as to what role, and what natural markets these charter companies could occupy in a world dominated by the scheduled air lines. There was a whole branch of literature devoted to the "tramp aircraft", similar to "tramp steamers", but this ignored the fact that the latter were the fruit of the freedom of the seas, which is quite the opposite of the freedoms of the air (in the plural). In reality, facts would

soon prove that the most reliable future for a charter company was for it to become a scheduled airline.

Question three – how can traffic flows be balanced?
In general, passenger traffic is a two-way traffic. Freight traffic is only one way, with few exceptions (exhibition equipment, machinery for repair). While travellers make return journeys, goods are on a one-way ticket: this illustrates the problem of balancing traffic flows according to direction.

"A major problem exists for air carriers: that of return freight", as one reads in the June 1948 issue of "Aviation Marchande". And what is meant by "return freight"? "It is the freight which, on a given route, is the most difficult to find". At the time, people talked of return freight because Europe was dominant in comparison to Africa and Asia, and North America was dominant in comparison with all the other continents: for European and American commentators in the years 1948–1950 the problem was truly one of return freight. The fantastic economic explosion of Asia, and the cultivation of out of season horticultural and agricultural products in Africa, have since reversed the problem.

Question four – how can the obstacles to the development of airfreight be removed?
In 1950, the obstacles were mainly on the ground. They were caused by the airports, Customs and the airlines themselves. There were few airports which committed to the necessary investment for building freight terminals and providing the necessary handling equipment. On the other hand, the world in 1950 was still bristling with tariff barriers and all kinds of quantity and quality checks, which limited and slowed down the movement of goods and people. At the instigation of the ICAO, many actions were initiated in order to facilitate international trade by reducing administrative formalities. In Europe, certain Customs Administrations made arrangements to give airfreight

the benefit of quick and preferential treatment. And finally, the airlines themselves did not always confer the required degree of consideration and attention on a new activity which, in the minds of some individuals, was not regarded as such a noble aim as carrying passengers.

Question five – how could airfreight operations be made profitable?
With a mixture of pride and relief, the Director General of IATA declared at the end of 1952: "At last we are more or less self sufficient." [23] Taken across the board, the air carriers had for the first time in their history achieved the financial break-even point. They appeared to be no longer dependent on any system of subsidies, official or hidden.

It is in this context that we must review the question of the profitability of freight activities. In reality, the global problem of freight profitability (transport in the holds of passenger aircraft and possibly in cargo planes) was not yet appreciated by the airlines. Airfreight was still too young. Nor did they yet possess the indispensable tools of analytical accounting.

On the other hand, all the operators of freighters knew how difficult it was to balance the books whether they were scheduled airlines or charter operations. The one thing that was missing was a machine specifically designed for the civilian transport of goods and mail. The question of profitability raised the problem of the cargo aircraft itself.

Seaboard Western Lockheed L-1049 Constellation freighter.
Air Cargo News UK

3 THE PROBLEM OF THE CARGO AIRCRAFT

Many studies were dedicated to the "problem of the cargo aircraft," [1] immediately after the war. They sought to define the technical and economic characteristics for an ideal civilian aircraft, with the aim of convincing the aeronautical industry of the advantages of taking up the manufacture of an aircraft with these specifications. This reasoning resulted from two findings:

1. The extraordinary development of military transport and the rapid expansion of airfreight can only be explained by the massive and widespread usage of fleets of "all-cargo" aircraft.

   The results recorded in the United States only serve to corroborate this first observation. Thus, in 1949, cargo aircraft carried 83% of the traffic and brought in 73% of the revenues for airfreight. The scheduled airlines, which were principally orientated towards passengers, only carried 23% of their goods traffic in the holds of their passenger aircraft. Whether one looked at the 16 scheduled airlines, or the four certified all-cargo companies, the conclusion remained the same: the future of airfreight lay in the cargo aircraft.

2. Except in a few cases, none of the cargo aircraft then in service had been designed for civilian goods transport: they were either passenger or "mixed" aeroplanes which had been more or less converted, or military aircraft which had not been very well adapted.

Every day, operators in the United States, Europe, Africa or elsewhere were confronted with technical questions or economic difficulties arising from the unsuitability of the equipment. As a result, they came naturally to the conclusion that their problems could only be solved by an aircraft, which was specially designed at drawing board stage for transporting freight. They had raised the "cargo aircraft problem", which has two aspects: technical and economic.

I THE TECHNICAL CHARACTERISTICS OF THE IDEAL CARGO AIRCRAFT [2]

These can be grouped around two central points, depending on whether they affect the architecture of the aeroplane or its internal arrangements.

Architectural features
These concern principally the fuselage, the floor and the doors.

• The fuselage
For aerodynamic reasons, the cross-section of the fuselage is normally circular or ellipsoid. This results in a curvature of the walls, which is unfavourable to an optimum use of the internal space for parcels or containers, which generally have rectangular forms. This means that the usable volume of a hold is different from its theoretical volume.

The ideal fuselage for freight should have an internal cross-section, which is as near as possible to being consistently quadrilateral, so that the hold inside has the shape of an elongated rectangular box. Rectangular, because this is the only form which allows the complete utilisation for freight consisting of packages of standard dimensions. Consistent, because a hold which has a changing internal cross-section can make it much more difficult to prepare the loading plans.

The maximum height of the hold was often estimated as being somewhere between 2 metres and 2.5 metres. In reality, experience had since shown that a height of 3 metres is altogether reasonable, providing precautions are taken to avoid crushing of parcels placed in the lower positions.

• The floor
Ideally, the floor of a cargo aircraft should be low-lying, horizontal and sturdy.

If the height above the ground is not more than about 1.2 metres, the cargo aircraft is independent: it can be loaded and unloaded using only its own handling equipment (loading ramps, winching systems). In the contrary case, the floor is too high, and the aircraft becomes "dependant" unless special measures are taken: it relies on the presence of more or less specialised handling equipment being available on a given airport. This is why aircraft, which were designed for freight generally correspond to this requirement (Bristol 170, Bréguet, "twin deck" 763), in contrast to modified passenger planes (Douglas DC-4, DC-6 and Lockheed L-1049) or cargo aircraft derived from passenger versions (which is the case with the majority of modern cargo aircraft).

One does not have to be an aeronautics engineer to understand quite easily that the option of the low-lying horizontal

ABOVE Bristol 170 Freighter.
RAF Museum

LEFT RAF Blackburn Beverley.
RAF Museum

It could reach 4,000 kilograms in certain conditions for military cargo planes (Lockheed C-130 Hercules).

• The doors

The larger the dimensions of the main door, the easier the loading operations. The speed and ease of loading reduces handling costs, which are an important part of the operating costs, and reduce the time on the ground, thereby allowing a proportionate increase in the average daily utilisation of the aircraft. There are two methods of loading: axial (length-wise) and lateral (from the side).

Axial loading is better for getting bulky packages (machines, pipes, and vehicles) on board. It is normal in military cargo aircraft. This solution appears in several forms, depending on whether loading is carried out from the front (Bristol 170, NC211 Cormoran, Carvair, Douglas C-124 Globemaster, Boeing 747F), or from the rear, which is the most usual case (Bréguet Two-deck, Short Belfast, Blackburn Beverley, Lockheed C-130 Hercules and C-141 Starlifter, CL-44 Canadair, Noratlas, the Franco-German military transport plane Transall C-160, or the Russian cargo aircraft Antonov An-12 or An-26).

The giant planes such as the American Lockheed C-5A Galaxy and the Russian An-124 Ruslan are fitted with axial doors at both ends of the fuselage to permit simultaneous loading and unloading. With regard to the opening techniques, the door may open in two halves, or on hinges on one side, or rise upwards.

Lateral loading, via a large cargo door generally fitted in the left side of the fuselage, is the most usual form, particularly for

deck, chosen for the majority of military, American, Russian, British or French cargo aircraft, is accompanied by the location of the wings in an elevated position.

This is the only arrangement which achieves sufficient space above the ground to accommodate the rotation of the propellers or the attachment of the jet engines.

If it cannot be low lying, the floor must at least be horizontal. On the planes which had a "classic undercarriage" with a tail wheel (Douglas DC-3-C-47 and Curtiss Commando C-46) the slope of the hold floor made loading and unloading operations particularly heavy work.

Every aircraft is subject to loading limitations, in order to avoid damaging its structure. These are especially important for cargo aircraft, which are called upon to carry heavy loads. There are several kinds of loading limitations. We will mention only two: the area load limitation, "expressed in kilograms per square metre (or lb/sq ft) of hold floor, and the linear limitation "expressed in kilograms per metre (pound per inch) of fuselage length". The former is intended to avoid permanent deformations of the floor, and the latter to prevent deformations of the fuselage.

The average strength per square metre for civilian cargo aircraft in the 1950s was in the order of 800–1,000 kilograms.

civilian cargo aircraft. In fact, this has been the case with converted passenger aircraft and cargo versions derived from passenger machines (Douglas DC-6, DC-HF or Boeing B707F). We could mention one exception: that of the Carvair, a modified version of the Douglas DC-4, in which the pilot's cabin was moved above the hold, which allowed an axial opening with a side-hinged door at the front of the aircraft.

Later, the Boeing B747F was to introduce an original solution by combining axial loading from the front with lateral loading.

Internal arrangements

The arrangements and equipment inside cargo aircraft fulfil two requirements: to divide up the consignments – according to unloading point, or other criteria – and to provide firm anchorage for the packages so as to ensure the stability and safety of the aircraft by preventing the cargo from shifting during flights. At the time when the decks of cargo aircraft had not yet been designed to take equipment for pallets or containers the problem of the fixing of the cargo inside the plane took a different form, according to whether the hold was not provided with any sort of partitions, or, on the contrary, was equipped with movable partitions. [3]

"In the most frequent case, that of an undivided hold, one had the benefit of a vast open space allowing the most varied loading combinations" including particularly bulky or irregularly shaped consignments (machines, aircraft engines, ship's propeller shafts etc).

The solution with movable partitions in the hold, which was usual in the United States during the 1950s, was particularly advisable for consignments made up of small and medium-sized packages as it makes it easier to put them in place, sort and unload them. "Depending on its dimensions the aircraft may be provided with two lines of compartments installed on either side of a central gangway (eg the Sky Freighters of American Airlines) or in a single line along a corridor on one side (eg the Cargoliners of United Airlines). The partitions are made of a metal grill stretched across aluminium or wooden frames, positioned perpendicularly to the longitudinal axis of the aircraft. These frames, spaced at approximately two-metre intervals, are moveable. The cargo, located in the compartments which are thus formed, is kept in place by means of an array of belts interlaced to form a net, fixed to the frame and to the floor." [4] The problems of tying down the consignments inside cargo aircraft are of vital importance. Several serious accidents have been caused by cargo which has come loose. Special precautions must be taken in order to ensure that the load remains stable during acceleration or deceleration phases, or turbulence, since faulty tie-down can cause a lot of changes in the balance of the aircraft with respect to its centre of gravity. It is necessary to be twice as vigilant when the aircraft is almost empty.

"There should be numerous anchorage points on the floor and on the walls. In practice, anchoring points 50 centimetres apart and spread across the floor and over the side walls of the hold provide an excellent arrangement." [4] Cargo is tied down by means of ropes, straps, belts provided with loops and hooks at their ends, and by means of nets. In a hold loaded with bulk cargo, without partitions or bins, nets made of webbing straps and fitted with rings to attach them to the tie-down points provide the most efficient method for spreading and dividing the load.

A lot of nonsense has been talked and written on the subjects of pressurisation, ventilation and heating in the main hold in cargo aircraft. On the pretext of reducing operation costs, some people have recommended the construction of cargo aircraft, which would be neither heated, pressurised nor ventilated. This Ebenezer Scrooge doctrine of cargo aircraft, for which no one has ever been able to show convincing profit advantages, shows a serious ignorance of the extreme diversity in the types of goods transported by air. Many of them do in fact require normal equipment for ventilation, heating and pressurisation: animals, flowers, various types of fruit and vegetables, some chemical and pharmaceutical products etc. Contrary to what some, often well-intentioned souls, have thought, cargo aircraft are by no means second-class machines.

2 ECONOMIC ASPECTS OF FREIGHT OPERATIONS

Before looking at the various elements of expenditure, which make up the operating costs of a cargo flight, we ought to review some of the fundamental facts which determine the profitability of operations.

Critical factors in the economics of cargo aircraft

We will concentrate on the three major factors:

• The heterogeneous nature of the supply of airfreight

The operator of cargo aircraft is not developing in a homogeneous environment. He is in charge of his overall costs but, except in a few cases, he cannot control the unit price he receives.

The airfreight supply is characterised essentially by its heterogeneity, consisting partly of residual capacities in the holds of passenger aircraft and partly of the capacities of "all-cargo" planes. It consists of one single, entirely independent, activity – cargo business – and of one "by-product" – passenger activity, without this description in any way implying a negative connotation. After the first few post-war years had elapsed, the capacities in the holds of passenger aircraft easily dominated in the totality of world freight capacity: "in 1960, approximately 19% of international traffic, and one third of the scheduled world freight traffic were carried by cargo-only services and the rest on passenger services." [5]

The result of this is that the operators of passenger aircraft have a strong influence in the determination of freight rates. And in this field they have a margin of freedom, which the "all-cargo" airlines do not possess. If they wish, they can introduce into their economic approach an element of marginal costing which the cargo operator, who is forced to balance his expenses exclusively with his freight income, can not allow. Fortunately, in practice the full consequences of this rather disturbing observation are largely attenuated by three considerations: that very many cargo lines are exploited by "passenger" or "mixed" airlines; that the cargo companies concentrate on specific market niches; and that the operation of cargo services does bring particular commercial advantages.

• Average daily utilisation

A plane on the ground represents dead capital. Its operating costs are therefore partially dependent upon its annual daily average utilisation.

Planes are forced to stay on the ground on at least two occasions: for programmed maintenance work, and for landings to load and unload, the duration of which depends very much on the speed of the handling operations.

TOP LEFT **Front-loading Bristol 170 Freighter.**
Air France Museum

TOP RIGHT **Example of rear loading of a car into a Bréguet Deux Ponts 763 destined for Algiers.**

ABOVE **RAF Short Belfast C1.** *RAF Museum*

But there are many other elements which affect the daily average utilisation: the programme structure (the number of stops per route, the frequency, and the average length per flight section), curfew problems with many airports, inevitable technical faults, and finally, the concern with fulfilling the needs of the market and the expectation of the clients with regard to days and hours of operation.

For all these reasons an annual utilisation of between 5,000 and 5,700 flying hours represents an ambitious but realistic objective for a long-haul cargo aircraft. The quality of the operating programme is an essential precondition for the profitability of a cargo fleet.

• Load factor
Although the idea of a load factor seems relatively simple for passenger activities – it is the ratio between the number of people transported and the number of seats available – it is complex when applied to freight. There are several ways of calculating it, depending on whether one considers it by weight or by volume, and whether one uses the theoretical or the actual volume. In one case, the maximum payload may be reached when half of the volume is still empty. In another, with the same aircraft, the space available is completely full, while half of the possible weight is not utilised. Which data should be used for calculating the load factor? Weight or volume? Or a mixture of the two? Traditionally, in the air transport industry weight is the preferred index, since rates are expressed in units of weight modified with correction factors reflecting the volume.

Since all kinds of goods are defined by their specific density, the relationship between the volume available and the payload is a fundamental characteristic for any mode of transport. Each mode of transport follows particular rules according to the natural environment in which it takes place (water, air or the surface of the ground) and its method and power of propulsion. Bearing in mind all the above considerations, and with a large degree of simplification, one can say that shipping is a mode which carries large weights and low volumes, while air transport on the contrary is a means of transport with low weights and high volumes. This is why pricing or rating approaches are so different. From the economic and commercial point of view, a cargo aircraft can be defined by way of three characteristics: payload, volume, and the ratio between these two figures. Experience shows that a cargo aircraft has an increasing probability of being profitable if its weight/volume ratio reaches the average density of the products transported, and if the operator is able to achieve almost simultaneously a full utilisation of weight and volume capacities. Depending on different periods and sectors of operation, the average density of airfreight is between 5 and 7dm³/kg, which equals a weight of between 140 and 200kg/m³.

The make-up of operating costs
The classic distinction is between direct costs – or "air" costs – and indirect costs or "ground" costs. The addition of these two costs gives the total cost or the full operating cost. This can then be expressed by flying hour, by flight, or by unit carried: gross tonnes or tonne kilometres offered or transported.

The direct costs are the total costs attributable to the operation of an aircraft. They include the depreciation and the insurance of the aircraft, maintenance, the flight crew, fuel and the payments due for the use of the infrastructure along the route and on the ground.

These items of expense are identical for passenger planes and cargo planes except for one important difference: the crew is exclusively technical on the latter, but technical and commercial on the former.

Independently of the price of these production factors, the level of direct costs depends substantially on two elements: the tonnage of the aircraft and the length of the sectors flown. The unit operating costs per available tonne-kilometres become lower as the tonnages of the aircraft become higher and the length of the sectors flown becomes greater. In the latter case, the effect of differences in average speed combines with the necessity to spread the

airport costs over a greater or lesser distance, since these constitute the largest proportion of indirect costs.

Indirect costs include all the costs, which do not contribute directly to operations in the air. These are essentially the costs on the ground, which are particularly significant for freight activities, due to their proportion of the total operating cost. A study of the International Civil Aviation Organisation published in 1971 showed that "the level of ground costs and indirect costs is almost equal to the level of direct costs",[6] on long-haul freight services.

The ground costs for airfreight refer to four distinct activities:

• Commercial activity: distribution, sales, publicity, bookings;
• Accounting and financial operations: invoicing and collection of payments, payment of expenses, inter-company invoicing;
• Ground processing of parcels and documents: reception and delivery, sorting and stocking;
• Loading and unloading of cargo planes and holds of passenger planes.

This group of operations represents the major area of concern for freight operators for two reasons: it could represent an

ABOVE RIGHT **British United Carvair.**
Air Cargo News UK

RIGHT **Transall C-160 belonging to the Federal German Air Force.**
MAP

area for extremely large savings, and it contains the key to quality of service.

3 VINDICATION OF THE CARGO AIRCRAFT

The cargo aircraft is an irreplaceable tool for the development of airfreight. For the client, it presents a whole range of advantages, which can be grouped under four headings:

1. The cargo aircraft offers certain and guaranteed capacities. The capacities available in the holds of passenger aircraft are to some extent residual capacities. An unexpected increase in the number of passengers or last-minute baggage can mean that some of the freight traffic has to be unloaded.

2. The cargo aircraft allows the operator to adjust the characteristics of the operation to the specific needs of the freight clientele (days and timetables, itineraries).

3. The loading facilities on cargo aircraft (door dimensions) allow the loading of heavy and bulky units (machines, engines, tubes in long lengths, helicopters).

4. The absence of passengers enables the transportation of products, which are prohibited on board passenger aircraft (chemical products, perfumes in large batches etc.)

For all these reasons, carriers equipped with cargo aircraft have always had the highest rankings among the air carriers.

TOP LEFT Lockheed C-130 Hercules.
MAP

ABOVE LEFT Nord 2501 Noratlas of the Federal German Air Force.
MAP

LEFT Air China Antonov An-12.
Air Cargo News UK

4 AIRFREIGHT AND THE COLD WAR

"When the war ended, the tremendous relief of the peoples of the world was accompanied by a strange illusion. They believed that things would return to normal. But history never repeats itself." [1] Instead of the peace, which was so yearned for, the "Cold War" set in. The disagreements between the Allies, which had already become evident immediately after the Yalta Conference before the end of the war, intensified until they produced a situation characterised by multiple forms of local confrontation: the Cold War. This exhibited phases of crisis (the Berlin blockade of 1948–1949, the Korean War in 1950–1953) and periods of remission. However in general, international tension remained at such a pitch that it maintained permanently very large requirements – actual or potential – for the transportation by air of military supplies.

1 THE BERLIN BLOCKADE: THE LARGEST AIRLIFT IN HISTORY (JUNE 1948-AUGUST 1949)

The origins and commencement of the blockade
Since 1945, Germany had been divided into four occupied zones: American, British and French in the west and Soviet in the east. Although it was situated in the Soviet sector, Berlin as the ancient capital of the Reich was also divided into four sectors. The communication routes joining the western sectors of Berlin to the occupied zones in the west of the country therefore had to cross the Soviet zone. All the geographical prerequisites were therefore in place, which would make the question of services to Berlin a factor of paramount strategic importance if a serious crisis were to arise between the former allies. Dissatisfied with western policies towards Germany, the Russians seized the entry into circulation of the new currency, the "Deutsche Mark", in the western zones, as a pretext for increasing pressure and trying to evict the western powers from Berlin. On 24th June 1948, they banned all surface transport of persons or goods between Berlin and the western occupied zones: only the air routes remained open.

This was the beginning of the Berlin Blockade. It was to be the first major Soviet failure, since the British and the Americans decided to invest all their strength in the "Battle for Berlin" to put a stop to Russian expansionism in Europe. For its part, France, to all practical purposes, did not take part in the Berlin airlift because the restricted air transport capacities of its air force were tied up in Indo-China, and because of the determined opposition of its very powerful Communist party.

The elements of the problem
Once the Soviets had thrown down the gauntlet, the British and the Americans set themselves a dual objective: not only to supply the Berlin population with a minimum number of calories, but also to sustain economic activity by supplying industry with the necessary energy and raw materials.

When the blockade started, the stocks of food in the western sectors, which had a population of 2.1 million inhabitants, were not particularly high: flour for 17 days, powdered milk for 26 days, and 42 days' worth of potatoes. The Western Powers had been taken by surprise. The initial daily requirements, corresponding to the daily delivery for all kinds of products in the three western sectors amounted to 13,000 tonnes. This figure was far above the capacity of any airlift. They therefore made every possible effort to reduce the average tonnage, which was indispensable for the survival of Berlin's population and industry. Finally, the "vital minimum tonnage", which still required great sacrifice on the part of the civilian population, was fixed at 4,500 tonnes/day: "this was the lowest level compatible with safeguarding public health and employment".

What infrastructure did the Anglo-American forces possess on the ground and in the air, in order to supply these irreducible requirements? According to the agreement between the four Occupying Powers, Berlin was connected with the three Western-occupied zones by means of three "air corridors", each 20 miles wide. They joined Berlin with Hamburg, and Hannover in the British zone, and Frankfurt in the American zone. They converged on two Berlin airports with limited reception capacity: Tempelhof, the large pre-war airport situated right in the centre of the city, in the American sector, and Gatow, a former military airport near Lake Havel, in the British sector. The success of the airlift rested entirely on these three narrow, invisible roads – that insubstantial bridge of air, in the words of the British Air Ministry. [2]

The start-up of the Berlin airlift
With a solemn affirmation of their determination, the British and American powers launched the airlift less than 48 hours

**Working during the Berlin Airlift —
Avro Lancastrians of Flight Refuelling
Ltd.**
RAF Museum

Most of the pilots were Second World War veterans and a former "Hump" campaigner, Major General William H. Tunner, took over the unified command of the American and British forces from October 1948. As for motivation, this was remarkable at all levels: the determination of the British and American politicians, the self sacrifice of the pilots, of whom 60 were to die, and the total devotion of the tens of thousands of German and Baltic labourers involved in the handling operations at both ends of the "Air Bridge".

after the blockade had been announced, using whatever means they had available at the time:

• On 26th June, it was the 61 Transport Unit of the US Air Force that carried 80 tonnes of milk, flour and medicines from Wiesbaden to Tempelhof;

• On 28th June the Royal Air Force entered the fray: a Dakota (DC-3) loaded with flour took off from the base at Wunstorf, near Hannover, destined for Gatow.

History's greatest airlift had begun. Like any military operation, it had a code name: "Operation Vittles" for the Americans and "Operation Plainforce" for the British.

The first reinforcements were quick to arrive: a group of 35 C-54s (military version of the DC-4) left Alaska on 28th June, while two squadrons of RAF Sunderland flying boats landed on the lake at Finkewerder near Hamburg on 5th July and immediately began their return trips to Lake Havel in the British sector of Berlin. At the end of June, 160 machines of the USAF and 100 of the RAF were taking part in the airlift.

The inevitable teething troubles were quickly solved, and traffic expanded very quickly: the daily objective of 4,500 tonnes were reached on 12th August (4,742 tonnes in 707 flights) and the minimum monthly target was exceeded in the month of September. To win the contest, there was only one more enemy to defeat: "General Winter".

Development of traffic in the Berlin Airlift

Months	Tons by month	Tons by day
June 1948	1,404	-
July 1948	69,006	2,236
August 1948	119,003	3,970
September 1948	139,623	4,650
October 1948	147,000	4,740

The success factors

As in any enterprise of this scope in a period of crisis, it was the human factors which made the difference. The Berlin Airlift was first and foremost a victory won by the experience of some and the motivation of all.

Although they never all flew at the same time, 621 aircraft took part in the airlift: 441 for the US Air Force and 147 for the Royal Air Force and 104 from British charter companies, which carried 146,980 tonnes. Whereas from October 1948 onwards the USAF depended on a uniform fleet of 300 C-54s, the British brought in a multifarious line-up, for the most part consisting of former bombers converted into freight aircraft (Avro Yorks and Avro Lancastrians, developed from the Lancaster bomber, and Handley Page Haltons, derived from Halifax bombers).

The British civil airlines took an important part in the Berlin Airlift, making 21,921 flights and carrying 146,980 tonnes amongst them, the charter airlines representing about 85% of the total. The first charter aircraft flying to Berlin with a complete load of fuel was a Flight Refuelling Ltd's Avro Lancastrian on 27th June. Apart from Flight Refuelling Ltd, the most active private charter companies were Bond Aero Services Ltd, Skyways Ltd, Airflight Ltd and Eagle Aviation Ltd, and the Lancastrian Aircraft Corporation and British South American Airways Corporation made further contributions.

In order to avoid absolute congestion in the air corridors and the Berlin airports, they endeavoured to develop ground infrastructure and to employ the most sophisticated air navigation support systems. On several occasions the reception capacity of the Berlin airports was increased, with the opening of new runways in Tempelhof and Gatow, and construction of the Tegel airport in the French sector in a record time of three months. The installation of new radar equipment, and the general employment of the GCA (Ground Control Approach) systems during landing enabled them at the same time to master the inclemencies of winter 1948–49 and to increase traffic volumes, which reached the record level of 171,952 tonnes in January 1949 and 152,218 tonnes in February. "General Winter" was defeated.

Apart from this, it was only by the unbending application of extremely rigorous procedures for loading and unloading the aircraft that they were able to achieve an ongoing optimum utilisation of men and equipment, day and night.

The Berlin airlift operated like a gigantic piece of clockwork. Let us hear what the British reported, hot off the press:

"The operation was so timed that at the precise moment that the aircraft came to rest and stilled its propellers the first lorry was in position to back up against its door. This was a somewhat tricky operation since a backing lorry could easily damage an aircraft and put it out of service. So a regular 'chock drill' was worked out. There was rarely the slightest mishap.

"The German labourers then swarmed into the aircraft and pulled its load onto the lorry. Once the first vehicle was full, it gave place to the second. If the load were coal, two women sweepers followed to brush out spillings and sweep them together; and two men with a handtruck went from aircraft to aircraft, gleaning. Even an ounce of coal was precious in Berlin.

"Directly the two unloading lorries had driven off, a third was ready to take their place, to fill the aircraft with the 'back-load'.

"Then the aircraft's crew pushed aside their empty coffee-cups in the wooden Malcolm Club, walked across the runway to be given their manifest of cargo, and took the aircraft back to its home airfield.

"Stated like this, the loading and unloading sounds simple. In essence it had to be, of course. Imagine not one aircraft but 10 arriving in half an hour; 30 lorries and gangs moving across the apron in criss-cross pattern; 100 tonnes of freight, every ounce of it valuable, to be extracted from awkward holds, and a small amount reloaded. Imagine the same thing being repeated in the next half–hour and the next, and the next, throughout day and night. Remember the occasional arrival of some particularly difficult load – a bulky piece of machinery, say, lashed to wooden spars, or heavy sheets of metal that could only just be manoeuvred though an aircraft's door.

"The organisation, to work at all, had to be perfect. And it was." [3]

Victory and overall assessment of the Berlin Airlift
From April 1949, traffic reached new heights, and then a summit, which reached a series of ever increasing plateaus: 235,000 tonnes in April, 250,000 in May, and 240,000 in June. A daily average of 8,000 tonnes!

The record traffic for a single day was achieved on 16th April 1949: 12,940 tonnes – 1,398 flights! It was on Easter Day. General Tunner had felt that victory was in his grasp. He wanted to have some fun and make an impact on the population of Berlin, which had weathered the storm, and to score a hit against the Soviet authorities who were getting increasingly upset. So he organised what he called his "Easter Parade" – with the results already quoted above.

From then on, the end was not long in coming. Diplomatic contacts between the Americans and the Russians at the beginning of February came to a conclusion at the beginning of May: the siege of Berlin was lifted on 12th May 1949. But that was no reason for the airlift to stop. It continued at a sustained rhythm, until ground communications were fully re-established, so that Berlin could maintain its considerable stocks of foodstuffs. It only reached its final conclusion on 30th September.

In total , 2,325,000 tonnes of goods were carried to Berlin in 15 months via the airlift. Three groups of products made up this enormous volume of traffic: coal (64% of the tonnage), foodstuffs (26%) and industrial products (10%). The rather surprising predominance of coal resulted from the resolve of the Western Allies to maintain a certain degree of industrial activity in Berlin: they therefore had to carry coal by plane in order to produce electrical energy and keep production companies operating as far as possible.

Certain ungenerous commentators have considered that the Berlin Airlift, in spite of it being a technical success, was of no interest at all for commercial airfreight.

One could make the same remark about all military or humanitarian airlifts, since by definition they are set up to deal with exceptional situations. This kind of remark is rather short sighted. Such airlifts demonstrate to the public the potential for mass air transport at a particular time. They represent an incredible publicity coup for airfreight, and can lead companies to make innovative decisions on how to use it. In the final analysis, the Berlin Airlift remains a supreme lesson in logistics – the art, which was military in origin, of controlling and harmoniously combining the displacement in space and time of a significant number of moving elements.

2 THE IMPACT OF MILITARY TRANSPORT AVIATION ON AIRFREIGHT: THE UNITED STATES EXAMPLE

During the Cold War period, the dominant nations, whose influence and activities extended throughout the world, had an enormous need for the rapid transport of military equipment. The United States and the Soviet Union were both in this position. However there was a difference in style: Whereas the United States published quantities of information and figures, even about such a sensitive topic, the Soviet Union, paralysed by an immoderate concern with secrecy, practised an "Iron Curtain" policy. This is why we shall examine the question of the inter-relationship between military and civil transport in airfreight, using the example of the United States. American commentators are unanimous in considering that military air transport exerted a consistent influence on airfreight in general: "Military airlift requirements and capabilities have played a significant role in the development of the commercial air cargo industry" [4] and "The military charters programme has been a very important facet of the airline cargo picture." [5]

The organisation of military transport aviation in the United States
We have now entered the kingdom of acronyms: ATC; NATS; MATS; MAC; CRAF. In fact this is all very simple, and is more or less self-explanatory.

During the Second World War, all military air transport activities were grouped together within two organisations: The Air Transport Command (ATC) for the Army and the Naval Air Transport Service (NATS) for the Navy. After the end of the war, a reorganisation was carried out on 1st June 1948 (some days before the beginning of the Berlin blockade): the ATC and NATS were replaced by a new entity, the Military Air Transport Service (MATS), which was in charge of all Strategic Airlift Operations.

Hardly had it been set up, than MATS had to organise two major strategic transport operations, although they were very different in nature: the Berlin Airlift, followed by the Pacific Airlift during the Korean War. The first was a transport operation involving massive quantities of civilian supplies over short distances (around 250 miles). The second was a military transport operation over very long distances (over 6,250 miles), carrying personnel and equipment (80,000 tonnes of freight and 214,000 soldiers in one direction and 66,536 injured personnel on the return).

There was a further reorganisation in 1966: realising the increasing importance of the "transport function" in military organisation, Congress decided to replace MATS by an organisation situated at the highest level of the US Air Force hierarchy: the Military Airlift Command (MAC), which in 1970 possessed a fleet of 750 transport aircraft with which to carry out all of its missions. In certain particularly urgent situations, it was possible that this purely military fleet was inadequate: in such cases the President of the United States could call upon the resources of the CRAF.

The Civil Reserve Air Fleet (CRAF) was created in 1952 during the Korean War, and was a strategic reserve fleet, made up of commercial aircraft normally used by airlines. In 1972, there was a total of 431 aircraft, of which 322 were long-haul machines.

The participation of the American airlines in this reserve fleet, which involved a certain number of restrictions, occurred on a voluntary basis. In reality, relations between the airlines and the US Airforce were more ambiguous, and less unilateral than would appear:

"Under CRAF, participating air carriers voluntarily commit aircraft and personnel to support defence when DOD airlift requirements exceed the capability of the USAF. [6] In return, USAF ensures that CRAF participants receive airlift contracts with the DOD." [7] What did all this mean?

The impact of military activities on the cargo airlines

Military contracts represented a very important part of the activities and the income of American cargo companies during the 1960s, due to a combination of three factors:

• The realignment of the main thrust of American strategy to the benefit of conventional forces, in spite of the nuclear deterrent remaining at the heart of defence policy: "this development increased to a significant extent the demand for air transport." [8]

• The redefinition of the operating methods of MATS. As time went by, MATS became almost a proper airline, with scheduled services which frequently mirrored the services of commercial companies. In 1960, it was instructed by the Department of Defence to limit its own activities and to transfer the operation of regular links by contract to the airlines, within a framework of calls to tender. The portion of MATS activities provided by civilian carriers went from 27% in 1959 to 55% in 1963. The "charter programme" of MATS was of special importance to "all-cargo" companies:

The proportion of MATS traffic in the total sales income of American cargo airlines

Companies	1962	1965
Flying Tiger	72%	56%
Slick Airways	100%	80%
Seaboard	51%	56%
Riddle (Airlift)	85%	56%

The author of a major airfreight study which appeared in 1972 writes as follows: "The sudden growth in contract airlift caused

a number of problems: the size of the programme and the promise of further expansion caused MATS to gain a considerable amount of influence over the civil carriers." [9]

The American involvement in Vietnam

After the commencement of the war in 1965, this involvement reached its height in April 1969, and then was regularly reduced between July 1969 and May 1972 under the Presidency of Richard Nixon.

Naturally, Military Airlift Command followed the development of the conflict, and its brutal variations were reflected in the fluctuations in traffic in the Vietnam Airlift. In 1967 it registered a record average monthly level of 42,000 tonnes of freight and 65,000 passengers carried to South East Asia. Even more than before, MAC had to use the resources of civilian carriers to clear traffic flows of such magnitudes. However, its usual suppliers – the all-cargo carriers and supplemental airlines – could not cope. So MAC appealed to the services of the large American scheduled airlines, which up till then had played little part in military activities: Pan American took up an active role and Continental made a fleet of 14 Boeing 707C aircraft available for MAC's requirements.

The disengagement of the Americans from Vietnam, and a degree of abatement in the Cold War at the end of the 1960s, brought about a spectacular fall in the amount of military cargo and passenger contracts. This was the beginning of a tough period of readaption for the cargo and charter companies, which did not all live to tell the tale. In order to understand the scope of the problem, let us follow the development of the proportion of military income in the turnover of Flying Tiger: 51% in 1962; 56% in 1965; 51% in 1969; 8% in 1977. By this stage, Flying Tiger had become a normal civilian carrier.

In spite of this radical contraction of activity MAC remained one of the leading actors on the world stage for the transport of goods during the 1970s (based on its own military aircraft and civilian aircraft for all types of contract): it had a traffic of over 900,000 tonnes in 1970 and 700,000 in 1971.

The influence of military transport on civilian carriers

Immediately after the Second World War, civilian carriers had no other choice than to use the cargo aircraft available on the market. These were either military versions of civilian planes (C-47 for the DC-3 and C-54 for the DC-4) or civilian versions of military planes (conversions of the British Halifax and Lancaster bombers). In both cases, the Forces and civilian companies operated the same fleets. It was therefore possible to deduce that a standardisation between civilian and military transport fleets was well under way, but there was only one remaining step, which some imprudently took. They paid scant regard to the specific military requirements, the chief of which is described by an expert:

"Over the ten or fifteen years which followed the end of the War the need for rear loading doors for easier supply drops or for loading and unloading vehicles became a fundamental part of specification for military transport." [10]

If this was the most important specification, it was not the only one. We should also note particularly high floor strength, reinforced landing gear and engines that were sufficiently powerful to permit rapid take-offs and landings on poor quality runways.

USAF C-47 aircraft at Tempelhof airport during the Berlin Airlift.
RAF Museum

The main types of strategic transport aircraft which followed the C-54 in the American Forces all fulfilled these different requirements in varying forms. We will mention them in chronological order:

• C-124 Globemaster, built by Douglas from 1950 onwards (it should be noted that in this case the axial loading doors were not situated at the rear, but at the front);

• C-141 Starlifter manufactured by Lockheed, the first strategic military transport aircraft with jet engines, offering a payload of 30–43 tonnes. After coming into operation in 1965, it became the workhorse of the Vietnam Airlift;

• C5A Galaxy manufactured by Lockheed; "the gigantic C-5 Transport, with tremendous payload capability" [11] (over 100 tonnes). It went into service in 1969 and played a decisive role in the airlift between the United States and Israel during the Yom Kippur War (22,395 tonnes of military aid despatched within a few days over an average distance of 7,750 miles).

None of these types of aircraft, whatever their advantages, was regularly operated by civilian carriers. Looked at from this point of view, the influence of the US Air Force on the equipment of the civilian airlines was extremely limited: military aircraft for the Forces, and civilian aircraft for civilians. Before closing this section, we should mention tactical military transport, in direct contact with the front, which is outside the framework of this book. Two aircraft stand out, which were very different from one another:

• The C-119 Flying Boxcar made by Fairchild: this was a high-winged two-engine plane with a twin boom specifically designed for transporting military equipment, and made its first flight in 1944 in a version which was originally called C-82 Packet. "It was practically built around an oblong box-shaped hold of square cross section" and carried out innumerable missions during the wars in Korea and Indo-China;

• The C-130 Hercules from Lockheed, "a legend in its own time". [12] It was put into service in 1951 and is still being made today. It was the battle horse of tactical transport aviation during the Vietnam War. It was produced in numerous different versions for particular missions, frequently updated, and went through several size increases. It is a high-winged cargo aircraft with four engines (four Allison T56-A15 turboprops each rated at 4,910hp) with a basic payload of about 20 tonnes. The main loading door was at the rear, consisting of two horizontal panels, of which one could be lowered to serve as a ramp. We shall have reason to return to this extraordinary "aeronautical phenomenon" because, uniquely among the strategic and tactical transport aircraft of the US Air Force, it was ordered in limited quantity by some civilian airlines.

Logistics: a military art

No sooner had the war ended than the US AF devoted attention to solving its own logistical problems. With sound logic, it envisaged the prospect of making maximum utilisation of airfreight, and developed various study and research programmes concerning the reduction of the weight of packaging, the equipment of freight terminals, standardisation of equipment and stock reduction.

"The Air Force is a big believer in using airlift to cut down on warehouse inventory costs… to eliminate or greatly lessen the size of its stockpiles" within its bases in the United States and abroad. In order to reduce the average waiting time between ordering a component and its delivery, it adopted a system called Logistic Airlift, abbreviated to Logair, in 1954.

Logair was a vast air network run by the US Air Force connecting the principal airbases within the United States. It was entirely operated by private carriers working under contract and by 1970 Logair had become the largest all-cargo system in the United States, consisting of four transcontinental services and 11 feeder lines. It connected 46 bases, eight ports of embarkation to foreign countries, two naval air stations and five general store locations. In 1972 Logair handled 170,000 tonnes.

The Navy had an equivalent system for its own requirements. It was called Quicktrans and carried approximately 40,000 tonnes in 1972. As with Logair, it was run by supplemental charter companies under contract.

The sheer mass of military charter contracts on behalf of MAC, Logair and Quick Trans gives a true indication of the degree of overlap between civilian and military activities in American air transport during the years 1950–1970.

There is another logistics field in which the US Air Force played a decisive role: that of the standardisation of equipment and of loading units for air transport, pallets and containers. One of the people responsible for logistics services in the Air Force wrote in 1955: "We look forward to the day when we will be able to handle the majority of our cargo from producer to consumer without the necessity of ever breaking the shipment below the pallet unit load" and further, "the different forms of pallets and containers must be manufactured according to a Standard Module." [13]

RIGHT **Map of Logair and Quicktrans military transport networks.**

BELOW **Air Rescue Service Fairchild C-82 Packet.**
MAP

BOTTOM **US Marines Fairchild C-119 Flying Boxcar.**
MAP

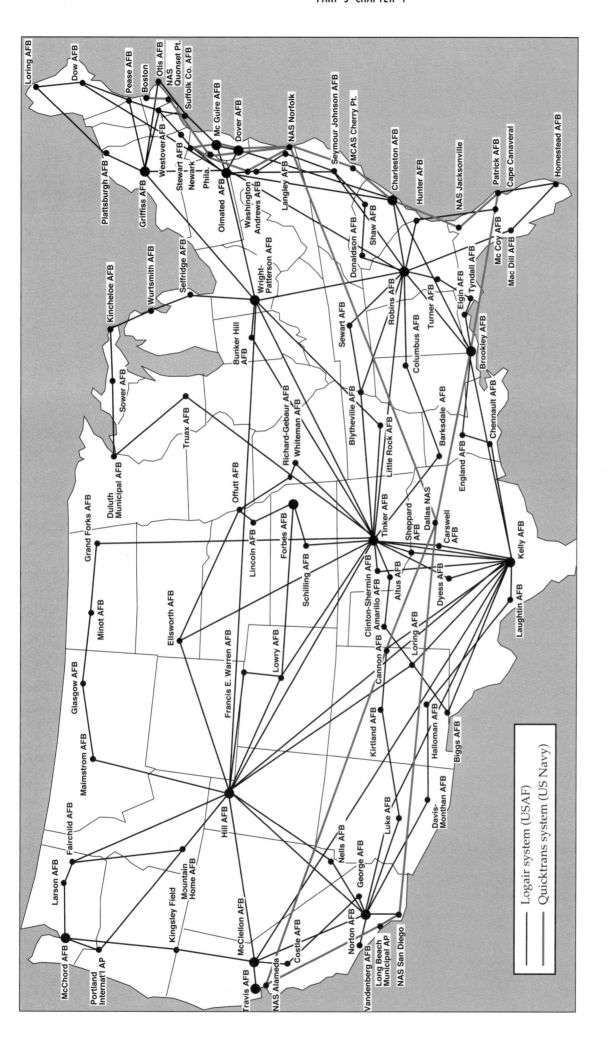

LEFT **RAF Lockheed Hercules C1.**
RAF Museum

BELOW **US Air Force Lockheed C-141 Starlifter.**
MAP

OPPOSITE PAGE, ABOVE **US Air Force Lockheed C-5A Galaxy.**
MAP

OPPOSITE PAGE, BELOW **US Air Force Douglas C-124 Globemaster.**
MAP

5 COMMERCIAL REGULATIONS GOVERNING AIRFREIGHT

We will examine the two main branches of commercial infrastructure: distribution and tariffs.

I THE ESTABLISHMENT OF A DISTRIBUTION NETWORK

The setting up of an efficient distribution network is the primary commercial concern of any enterprise producing goods or services. Transport companies are even less likely to escape this requirement, since they have the dangerous characteristic of generating product, which cannot be stocked.

What type of distribution should be adopted? Distribution through the company's own offices or via intermediaries? Via exclusive or non-exclusive agents? The airlines developed an original solution to these classic questions by providing themselves with a common and universal sales network.

Registered IATA cargo agents
From 1945, one of IATA's priorities had been to organise a world-wide distribution system, common to all airlines. Work proceeded at a pace. The working group which had the job of going up the outline of a complete statute regarding sales agents for the airlines held its first meeting in London in January 1946. The final text, entitled "Sales agency resolution " was adopted in 1947.

The philosophy of this fundamental text can be summarised in the form of three conditions:

1. The agencies belonging to the network, travel agencies (approved passenger sales agents) for passengers and freight forwarders (registered cargo agents) for freight are linked to IATA through a contract (eg Standard IATA Cargo Agency Agreement), which is identical in all countries of the world, and identical for all carriers. This demonstrates the dual wish for standardisation and universality, common to all international organisations after the war.

2. The Agencies belonging to the system, known as registered agencies, retain their complete financial independence.

3. The IATA airlines entrust their sales development to this collective network of registered agents, but without renouncing the use of their own sales offices if required.

It was as though the car manufacturers from all over the world had decided to entrust their sales activities to a single world network of dealers who offered their entire production range to the clients. This gave exceptional ease of access and freedom of choice, offset by the consideration that according to the IATA perspective, as an analogy, all manufacturers making cars of the same cylinder capacity would charge strictly identical prices. Indeed, the Director General of IATA wrote: "It is proper to say that the shop door of the IATA certified travel agent in the remotest town of the smallest country has already become the gateway of the world." [1] This still applies today.

• The 1947 regulation concerning registered agents
With the exception of one or two details, this was common to passengers and freight. This has led freight specialists to say that the regulations regarding registered freight agents were based on those for registered travel agents.

The regulation was put into practice by local and regional Boards headed by an Agency Committee, whose principal task was to draw up and permanently update the list of agencies approved by the Association. In 1954, these numbered 12,000 (passenger and cargo activities together). [2]

It was up to the would-be member to complete the application procedures. Usually, the applicant would be a forwarding agent for land transport and or shipping, who wished to extend his range of services to include air transport. Less frequently it would be a new company targeted exclusively at airfreight (Emery in the United States, Aérofret or TTA in France).

The first task of the candidate wishing to be registered was to find a sponsor, among the airlines. This was generally an easy task, since one could always find an airline who would be "interested" in supporting the candidature, even if doubtful, of an agent, since he would become at the same time a future client. The candidate had to submit a standard form of application and received visits from one or more investigators who were members of the local Airline Investigation Board or AIB, which submitted the applicant's file to the Secretary of the Regional Agency Committee for a decision.

What criteria did the IATA authorities use as a base for granting, refusing or deferring their agreement which would be demonstrated by the candidate's enrolment onto the cargo agency list, and the signature of the IATA Cargo Agency Agreement?

Although it was hardly finished with the war, the air transport industry was aware of the decisive role it had played in the outcome of the conflict, and knew that it was destined for enormous growth. It needed commercial promotion: salesmen. The registered agents would be first and foremost "sales agents": their candidature was judged in the light of this objective. All other criteria (financial situation, physical amenities) were secondary. Once approved, the agent was obliged to conduct himself as a representative and sales agent for all the IATA airlines. In practice, even if only as a result of personal relationships and preferences, which always played a substantial role in airfreight activities, preferential relationships were soon built up with particular airlines.

In return for these commercial activities, what rights did registered agents receive? Essentially, a fixed commission of 5% on sales, and travel facilities (reduced rate tickets in a quantity depending on turnover).

Another category of agents featured on the list established by the Secretariat of the Agency Committee: General Sales Agents. These were exclusive representatives for a specified territory, acting for one airline, which did not wish to set up its own commercial organisation. The general sales agent was bound by a contract to the airline whose interest he represented. Like the airline itself, the general sales agent promoted the common distribution network, for the benefit of his principal.

• The consolidation problem: agents, consolidators or both?
The IATA regulation applying to registered cargo agents only recognises individual consignments (one consignment = one airway bill). It ignores the question of consolidation. As we shall see later, this situation is the exact opposite of what was going on in domestic American transportation. However, the IATA airlines were soon confronted with the reality of consolidation becoming an unavoidable practice as soon as there is a tariff structure which includes a minimum charge and a sliding scale of rates depending on weight breaks.

The IATA Bulletin for December 1953 gave a good definition of a consolidator:

"The consolidator/airfreight forwarder has been defined as:

a) "One who assembles or who provides for assembly in single consignments goods delivered to him by the general public; and

b) Assumes responsibility to the general public for the transport of such goods from the point of receipt by him or his agent to point of delivery by him or his agent; and

c) Quotes for this service his own rates which may be different from the rates fixed by the carrier."

Taking advantage of the sliding scale of rates according to the weight breaks, the consolidator is in a position to offer, at least for small- and medium-size consignments, rates below those published by the carrier. Hence the official rate structure of the

carriers co-exists on the market side-by-side with the price structures of the consolidators. This sometimes presents the carrier with a delicate situation.

The consolidator uses two categories of transportation document: the Master Airway Bill – MAWB – for the consolidated consignment in his dealings with the airlines, and an internal House Airway Bill – HAWB – in his dealings with his clients, in order to cover each of their part consignments.

The practice of consolidation raised a host of questions within IATA, which gave rise to heated debates:

• Should they regulate the relationship between the carrier and the consolidator?

• Should a commission be paid to the consolidators who were already getting paid by buying wholesale and selling retail?

• Should they accept or ban the consolidator offering his client prices lower than those published by the airlines themselves?

No agreement could be reached between supporters and opponents of consolidation. For the former, consolidation represents an added-value product, which meets the economic need of the carriers, whose task it makes easier, especially when goods are pre-packed on loading units, and of the individual consignors, for whom it reduces the invoice amount. For the latter group, this practice had the effect of delaying consignments, which had to wait for the despatch date of the consolidated load – rarely a daily service – and of drawing a sort of opaque curtain between the prime users and the carriers. It happened that the carriers did not even know what prices were charged on their services, in cases where the consolidators were not obliged to file their price lists.

At all events, the consolidators, by allowing their main clients to benefit from "special deal" seasonal or annual rates, had managed to fill out the main gap in the IATA rate system: the lack of rates for loyalty or for regular repeat business for large users.

The reform of the cargo agency programme of 1968 solved the question for once and for all, even if it did not calm everyone's feelings: the new regulation applied to all agents acting as professional middlemen of freight transport, whether or not they were involved in consolidation.

• The reform of 1968
The agency programme of 1947 had placed the accent on the development of sales. The reform of 1968, which ratified the differentiation between regulations for passengers and freight, emphasised the correct fulfilment of all the physical and documentary procedures, which are combined in processing airfreight, and which determine the quality of service.

This new spirit in the regulations was expressed in a powerful concept, which unfortunately is too frequently underestimated by the airlines: the promotion of airfreight is inseparable from the quality of service.

The IATA resolution of 1968 introduced a new concept: that of a "consignment ready for carriage". The approval of agents was thereafter dependent on their ability to deliver to the airlines consignments "ready for carriage". Let us look at the conditions necessary for a consignment to qualify in this respect (IATA Resolution 608):

• The airway bill shall be issued properly, accurate and complete in all respects;

• All documents for each consignment shall be completed and/or checked;

• The contents of each consignment shall be properly packed;

• All packages of each consignment shall be marked in accordance with IATA regulations (the AWB number, the destination airport and the total number of packages) and finally, if necessary, the very restrictive regulations concerning the transport of "restricted articles" or "dangerous goods" should be scrupulously applied; the shipper's certification, duly signed and completed, as set forth in the IATA Restricted Articles Regulation shall be provided by the shipper or his authorised agent.

It was only under these conditions that the registered agent could make an effective contribution to the quality of the overall handling process, and consequently to the further development of airfreight.

This change of direction was not by chance. It corresponded to a change in the scale of airfreight arising from the operation of jet cargo aircraft with a capacity of 35 tonnes, and the imminent introduction into service of wide-bodied aircraft.

Registered ATAF agents

"The same reasons which caused the international airlines to gather together within IATA in order to co-ordinate their actions in the field of international transportation caused the Compagnie Nationale Air France and the private airlines operating air services within the French Union [3] to collaborate in the same spirit within the framework of the ATAF... To some extent, the ATAF was the IATA of the French Union." [4]

After its creation in 1950, the Agreement for Co-operation between Air Carriers within the French Union (l'Accord de coopération entre transporteurs aériens de l'Union Française) was rapidly modified to become the Association of French Air Transporters (Association des Transporteurs Aériens Français) and then, after the independence of countries and territories belonging to the French Union, the Air Transport Association for the Franc Area (l'Association du transport aérien de la zone franc).

On the model of IATA, the ATAF organised within the framework of its geographical area, a specific distribution network responsible for the promotion and sale of airfreight within the French Union, and later within the franc zone.

In practice, the majority of French forwarding agents were accepted both by IATA and ATAF. This is why in Paris in 1954, out of a total of 70 registered offices, there were six offices registered only with ATAF, eight offices exclusively with IATA and 56 offices which held both IATA and ATAF registrations. Only the ATAF agents were entitled to use the rates of that association.

The American distribution network: the airfreight forwarders

The forwarder or freight forwarder is a classic part of the domestic American transport scene. He is a freight agent who also carries out consolidation.

The idea of the Air Freight Forwarder came to the fore in the United States at the beginning of the 1940s as airfreight was emerging. Since the land forwarders were regulated by the powerful Interstate Commerce Commission (ICC) the question arose as to which authority would govern the new Air Freight Forwarders (AFF). As one might expect, the Civil Aeronautics Board asserted its competence in 1942 by establishing a typically American legal concept, that of the "Indirect air carrier". This meant that although the Airfreight Forwarders were not expressly mentioned in the Civil Aeronautics Act of 1938, they were subject to regulation by the CAB in their role as indirect air carriers. [5] As such, they were only allowed to carry out their activities after having been authorised by means of a Letter of Registration which was divided into two categories: Interstate or Domestic Air Freight Forwarders, and International Air Freight Forwarders.

The CAB started by legitimising the existence of airfreight forwarders, concluding that the services of Air Freight Forwarders fulfilled a demand, which had been sufficiently proven to justify, in the public interest, the authorisation of airfreight forwarding operations for a period of five years.

Referring to this statement of principle, the CAB provided regulations for freight forwarders in 1948 [6] and obliged them to file their "rates", [7] to make quarterly statistical reports and to respect the very strict rules for invoicing to the airlines (identical in spirit to those binding on the registered agents of IATA or ATAF). Even if the CAB submitted the profession to strict rules, it nevertheless sought to make it not too difficult to join, considering that it was important to maintain liberty of access to freight forwarding activities. The question of establishing whether the services of a particular air forwarder correspond to the requirements of the public should be left to the opinion of the clients themselves.

When applying these rules, the CAB always remained faithful to its doctrine, and increased the number of Airfreight Forwarders from 57 in 1949 to 292 in 1972 (of whom 172 carried out both domestic and international activities), and regularly widened the circle of professions entitled to receive a Letter of Registration (road transport operators in 1967 and 1969, railway companies in 1970 and removal firms in 1972).

The Air Freight Forwarder fulfils four main tasks: pick-up and delivery door to door; weighing and ticketing packages; producing the transport documentation; consolidation of small consignments. According to the American concept, the Airfreight Forwarder is above all a consolidator. Grouping consignments is essential to his activity: it is the base of his profit and his economic justification. He does not receive commission and must earn his remuneration by offering to the public value-added products (collection and delivery, insurance and consolidation). In such conditions, the direct services provided by the airlines remain extremely competitive for all large consignments. This is why the proportion of business through Airfreight Forwarders [8] within the domestic American market remains below 50% (25% in 1965, 43% in 1971) whereas that of the IATA agents in international traffic considerably exceeds this proportion

Offices operated by the airlines themselves

IATA did not recognise the old maxim from French law: "*Donner et retenir ne vaut*" – "you can't give with one hand and take back with the other". At the same time as it gave its registered agents the job of obtaining and carrying out sales, the airlines retained the possibility of fulfilling these operations through their own offices. They reserved the possibility of maintaining a group of "direct clients" in parallel with those handled through the forwarders, who felt this activity by the airlines to be a kind of unfair competition (unless it was really a threat!).

In the years 1955–1960, the airlines were still achieving 15 to 30% of their international sales via their own offices. The great migration towards the airports was only just beginning, and their own freight offices, along with those of many forwarders, were established in city centres, in veritable "cargo districts". This was the case in New York, London or Paris.

Paris provides a typical example. Out of 70 registered offices [9] there were:

• 6 in the Second Arrondissement (the district around Halles, before they were transferred to Rungis);

• 13 in the Eighth Arrondissement (where a number of shipping agents are to be found);

• 32 in the Ninth and Tenth Arrondissements, which seems to be the historical district for transport activities, as witnessed by the street names: Rue des Petites Écuries ("Little Mews" Street); Rue de la Douane ("Customs House" Street); Rue des Messageries ("Parcel Service" or "Messenger" Street). Since the 19th century, companies in transportation, customs clearance and freight forwarding had worked alongside many kinds of industrial and commercial activities (clothing industry, the fur trade, the press, caterers etc…) In 1955 there were over 50 transport and forwarding companies established there. It was a working class quarter, teeming with people, full of life and buzzing with activity, providing a home for the freight agencies of most airlines: Air France at Fauborg Poissonnière; BEA, C/O Hernu Péron at 13, Rue de Nancy; KLM at 10, Rue de Chabrol; Pan American at 3, Cité d'Hauteville; Sabena at 37, Rue Caumartin, and TWA at 1 Bis, Rue de Paradis.

Little by little, these districts were hit by traffic congestion, and were deserted by the transportation and forwarding professions. Everyone who worked there remembers them with certain nostalgia.

2 RATING SYSTEMS FOR AIRFREIGHT – GENERAL PRINCIPLES

For any mode of transport, rate systems are based on simple principles, even though their application may be complex. They can be separated into two families, according to whether their authors were inspired by the theory of "cost of service provided" or that of "value of service rendered". Airfreight systems borrowed from both schools to a variable degree, depending on geographic areas, various time periods and the carriers concerned.

A priori it would appear obvious to try to establish the level and structure of the rates as a function of the costs incurred by the airline in giving a particular service.

However, once this healthy principle of transport economics has been stated, the difficulties begin. First of all, the cost of a service is a more complex notion than one would think. Its precise evaluation for a certain type of traffic on a given route

requires the application of numerous cost allocation formulae for which the calculations can often raise serious problems. The factors to be taken into account are indeed multifarious. In addition to the nature of the traffic (bulk or containerised), the total distance and the average sector length, and the size of the consignments plays a decisive role. All the studies show that the cost per kilogram transported decreases rapidly as a function of the increase in the unit weight of the consignments, up to a certain limit, above or beyond which rate reductions have no further economic foundation and may only be justified by commercial reasons.

On the other hand, the theory of the cost of service presupposes an in-depth knowledge of the real operating costs. In the domain of airfreight, it must be admitted that knowledge of costs frequently leaves something to be desired, due to the great variety of the supply. If the average cost for the freight transported in a cargo aircraft is easy to establish, this is not the case for freight carried in the holds of passenger planes. How is one to evaluate with precision, and incontrovertibly, the price of a by-product which is partly of a residual nature? In practice, all methods have been applied and defended, from the most restrictive – the total cost method – to the most liberal – based on pure marginal cost. After one has taken into consideration all the expense elements on the ground and in flight, allocated proportionally to the volumes concerned inside the plane, divided according to passenger and freight activities, and after only making a direct charge for specific direct costs on the ground, how can one possibly establish rate structures based on the cost of service?

This economic principle results in a simple rate structure based on the size of consignments taken by weight and volume, without looking at the nature of the goods transported. The rate scale is based on the cost price, and cross-subsidising between the rate levels is limited.

The theory of the value of service has been charmingly defined as "a polite way of saying that the carriers should charge what the traffic will bear." [10] It is based on the idea that any category of goods possesses its own "profit contribution potential", which is essentially dependant on its value. This is the old Anglo-Saxon principle of "What the traffic can bear", which is the foundation of the traditional rate policies of the shipping conferences and the rail companies. "Rich" goods can support high rates and "poor" goods, low rates. The average income is the result of a general cross-subsidy between very different rate levels.

Although the first theory may satisfy a certain idea of "economic truth", the second favours a certain kind of "economic justice" since the rich support the poor. Which leads to a rate system based on the nature of the products. Although it is attractive, it generally results in rate structures with a complexity which risks disappearing into infinity, and may give rise to all kinds of frauds and false declarations, since the rate levels can vary greatly depending on how the nature of essentially similar goods is declared. Having dealt with the economical and philosophical foundations, cargo rates present two fundamental characteristics, which distinguish them from passenger fares:

• They are directional: passenger fares apply to a return journey, while freight rates are one way. What is more, they are usually markedly directional, that is to say that on a given stretch they vary according to the imbalance of the traffic;

• They vary according to distance, but are independent of the chosen itinerary: this means that a 1,000kg Paris/New York consignment will always pay the same price, whether it is carried on a direct flight, or via Tokyo or San Diego (to give rather absurd examples). This rule made an important contribution to the development of transit traffic.

IATA rates

Now we are coming to the most controversial role of IATA: that of the tariff regulator. In the IATA system, all international rates are worked out, discussed and adopted unanimously by the member companies, then approved by Governments and published. They then become legally binding. All the airlines serving on the same connection apply identical rates: there is no rate competition. Any violation of this rule becomes the object of an enquiry and may be sanctioned by means of fines, which can reach very high amounts. But it would be a great error to reduce the role of IATA to that of a policeman.

Between 1945 and 1975, the Association was able to give proof of a considerable spirit of adaptation and innovation in order to bring out the best benefit from the new possibilities offered by technological progress. From the outset, it had the ambition of constructing a world rating system, which would integrate harmoniously all the rates in force, so that a consignment, using a single transport document established on a "once and for always" basis, could be sent anywhere in the world, successively employing the services of any member airline.

"Originally, IATA fixed freight rates simply by referring to the passenger fares. A passenger with his 20–30 kilograms of baggage allowance was considered to weigh an average of 100 kilograms, and so it was accepted that the basic rate for freight should be one hundredth of the passenger fare. Later, this ratio was reduced to 1:125. Experience was to prove that this concept was not appropriate. It was not justifiable to try to establish a constant relationship between tariffs applicable to two kinds of traffic with altogether different characteristics, and where the evolution of each was subject to completely different factors. This led IATA to separate the passenger fares from the cargo rates." [11]

Until the introduction of rates for unit loads (pallets and containers) at the end of the 1960s the freight rating structure of IATA contained two rate categories: general rates and specific rates.

• General Commodity Rates or GCR

There are in existence general commodity rates, open to all kinds of goods, on all international connections served by one or more IATA airlines.

The general rates consist of a basic rate applicable to consignments of 0 to 45kg (or 100lb) and sliding scale rates depending on break points by weight. There is always a break point above 45kg accompanied by a rate reduction of 25%. This two-level scale (- and +45kg) represents the initial and traditional rate structure of IATA. It was only very slowly enriched by the introduction of higher weight break points as a result of increases in capacity. Its surprising longevity is the reflection of the reservations of many carriers concerning this type of rate.

• Specific commodity rates or SCR

Until the end of the 1960s the essence of IATA creativity in rate

matters expressed itself in specific rates for different kinds of goods. A specific rate (or Co–rate in professional jargon) is a rate reserved for a precise category of products for a specific connection, and for a minimum weight.

From then on, the imagination had free range, whether regarding goods, connections, weight breakpoints or the percentage reductions calculated in relation to the basic rates, since, according to the logic of the doctrine of the value of service, it is a matter of developing case by case a tailor-made rate appropriate for promoting a new kind of traffic at a rate which can be tolerated by the goods concerned, and which is optimum for the carrier.

The IATA Traffic Conference, which met in Nice in 1949, decided to create Commodity Rate Boards, with the task of studying, drafting and adopting the increasingly numerous rate proposals submitted by the airlines. Confronted with the blossoming of these specific rates, IATA very soon felt the need for a standard goods classification.

At the conclusion of various changes, the following nomenclature was adopted, which divides all goods into 10 main categories.

Specific commodity rate nomenclature

Item numbering	Group description
0001-0999	Edible animal and vegetable products
1000–1999	Live animals and inedible animal and vegetable products
2000-2999	Textiles, fibres and manufactures
3000-3999	Metals and manufactures, excluding machinery, vehicles and electrical equipment
4000-4999	Machinery, vehicles and electrical equipment
5000-5999	Non-metallic minerals and manufactures
6000-6999	Chemicals and related products
7000-7999	Paper, rubber, wool and manufactures
8000-8999	Scientific, professional and precision instruments
9000-9999	Miscellaneous

An increasingly detailed numbering system within each group allows the required degree of precision to be selected.

Here is an example of a specific tariff in force in 1960:

• Paris/London – SCR 2102 – Cloth, exclusively in bales, bolts or pieces, not further processed or manufactured.

Weight breaks	Rate per kilo	Percentage reduction
> 45kg	48 FFR	51%
> 100kg	40 FFR	59%
> 250kg	35 FFR	64%

Throughout the whole of the first stage in the development of airfreight, until the introduction of wide-bodied aircraft, specific rates played a decisive role.

These are the main features of the IATA rate system. Moreover, in order to avoid a certain number of economic abuses, freedom in setting general and specific rates was limited by three safeguards:

• Minimum charges: Whatever the actual weight of a consignment, the sum charged by the carrier may not go below a certain minimum amount;

• Class rates: As a result of their very particular characteristics, certain goods are not allowed for the application of specific rates. In relation to the base rates, they are always increased by a multiplication factor (eg live animals, human remains, gold ingots), or by reduction factors (eg newspapers);

• The volumetric trigger: The rate per kilo is subject to an increase when the relationship between the weight and the volume of a consignment passes a certain threshold. Depending on the geographical sectors and the times, this evolved between 6 and 9dcm^3 per kilo. But whatever the actual figure, the volume limitations in airfreight, compared with other modes of transport, are extremely liberal. Due to of its physical characteristics, air transport favours high volume goods: weight counts far more than volume, which is the opposite of marine transport.

Modified according to these three limitations, the IATA rating system would appear at first sight to be complete, capable of development, and well balanced between the theories of service cost and service value. In reality it possessed two serious deficiencies: there was no provision for "large consignments" and above all offered no incentive for "regular customers". It was an ad hoc system, prone to kickbacks. And whether one is for or against contractual systems, it is commercially unrealistic not to recognise the buying power of large regular customers.

The ATAF rating system
Misjudged by many, and suspected by some of being merely a reincarnation of French neo-colonialism, the ATAF has borne the brunt of many criticisms. Nevertheless, it is the only professional co-operative organisation, which has managed to develop a balanced rate system able to preserve the individual interests of the clients (regular user contracts), of the forwarders (groupage rates) and of the carriers (profitability). The general outline of the ATAF system was devised by the Commercial Department of Air France just after the war, in order to promote traffic between France and North Africa, and was later applied to long-haul services within the French Union, with the support of the companies, Air France, UAT and TAI.

Compared with the tariff framework of IATA, that of ATAF possesses three characteristics – one could even say three advantages:

• A scale with a much wider range of weight break points.
At a time when the IATA structure only included two bands of below and above 45kg, the ATAF offered a band of +500kg, modified by a reduction of 40% for North Africa and "French Sub-Saharan (AEF = French Equatorial Africa, AOF = French West Africa).

• Contract rates for regular shippers.
These discounts for regular shippers, which were initiated for connections between France and North Africa in 1948, were extended, subject to appropriate conditions, to users and freight forwarders who undertook, contractually, to receive or send a certain minimum monthly or annual volume of traffic. This meant that there were export and import contracts.

In 1950, Air France offered the following contract conditions for regular shippers:

Min monthly deliveries	"Regular shipper" discounts	
	France/Algeria/ Tunisia	France/Morocco
1,000kg	30%	30%
2,000kg	50%	40%

At the same time, ATAF approved freight agents could take advantage of regular user discounts of up to 40%.

This policy of contract rates underwent a remarkable expansion on long-haul services to Africa, from the 1960s onwards under the influence of UAT (which later became UTA after taking over TAI) and Air Afrique. Naturally, freight-forwarding contracts were converted into consolidation contracts. It was the intelligent co-existence between less than half a dozen consolidation contracts and a few "large shipper" contracts made with large trading or oil companies, which assured the remarkable development of airfreight to French West Africa.

These two families of contracts must be linked with a third: the group of foodstuff exporters.

• Very innovative rates applied to the "empty" freight direction (south/north).
The problem of return loads had always presented itself in a very extreme manner for the ATAF services running north/south: they were full on the outbound, and empty on the inbound sector. By introducing a particularly attractive rate policy, the ATAF airlines managed to create new forms of traffic (eg french beans from Senegal or Burkina Faso, or mangoes from Mali), or to transfer existing products from sea freight to airfreight (early fruit and vegetables from North Africa, pineapples from the Ivory Coast). In the context of innovatory rates we should mention "campaign" rates, which are fixed for a whole production season after agreement with the professionals concerned, and rates index-linked to the quoted prices for the goods transported. This sophisticated technique was used for services leaving North Africa in order to maximise air traffic by varying the rate levels in proportion to the prices of the merchandise in the wholesale markets in Paris.

Domestic rates
IATA only legislates for international trade. Domestic rates are subject to the jurisdiction of the relevant national air authorities.

In 1950, as today, one domestic market dominated all the others together: that of the United States. What was the structure of the American domestic rates? Once again, we will only highlight the particularities in comparison with the IATA system, limiting our study to the period before 1970:

1. A structure orientated towards general rates rather than specific rates.
It is thanks to this particular characteristic that the American Air Freight Forwarders immediately turned towards consolidation: the rate structure favoured it. Not that specific rates were entirely absent; but they were to be found mostly on the low-load-factor sectors, and only

applied to a limited number of products (perishables). By comparison, general rates were always being extended by new weight breaks, as capacities increased. Thus, in 1968, in addition to rates for under and over 100lb, there were breaks for 1,000, 2,000, 3,000, 5,000 and 10,000lb, and even 35,000lb for a small number of markets.

2. Deferred rates.

    Deferred rates appeared at a very early stage in the American rating nomenclature. These are especially low rates applying to consignments, which have no priority and are loaded as space becomes available. At least that is the theory. In practice, everything depends on the filling coefficient on that sector: either it is low, and the deferred freight is loaded without waiting; or else it is excellent, so that the deferred freight which has to be despatched some time or other, ends up by becoming urgent. It is an abuse of the system. Although they present an attractive formula for filling planes, rates involving deferred rates are generally tricky to put into practice. Moreover, deferred freight eventually ends up by taking over storage space in the freight terminals. Finally, it appears to us that there is a basic contradiction between the raison d'être for airfreight – speed – and the notion of deferred freight.

3. Assembly and distribution rates.

    These refer to special products, services for assembly and distribution, carried out on a large scale by domestic companies within the United States. The assembly service consists of physically regrouping consignments arriving in a town from several shippers to deliver them in a single load to a single addressee. On the other hand, the distribution service consists in accepting at departure a single load from a single shipper and breaking it up on arrival into a number of despatches to be delivered to two or more addressees situated in the same area. In both cases, the airline carries out a consolidation operation, with its usual advantages, for the benefit of the addressee or the shipper, in return for the payment of a charge.

The combinability of cargo rates

When we look at this proliferation of rates, one question immediately presents itself: is it possible to combine these different rates so as to arrive at the most advantageous formula, or is such combination forbidden? Naturally IATA got things organised and set up some rules. It is only possible to combine two rates on condition that three principles are respected, in the interest of the carriers:

Rule 1: Where a through rate is published, any combination resulting in a lower rate of the same type is prohibited (the type of the rate, when an international rate is combined with a domestic one, is always determined by the type of the international rate).

Rule 2: It is not permitted to combine two international specific commodity rates, for the reason that such rates are offered to the public for very specific traffics supposed to move from one particular point to another particular one.

Rule 3: For the same reason, the combination of an international specific commodity rate with an international general cargo rate is not allowed.

Hence, in the international field, the combinability of cargo rates is limited. On the other hand, it is widely permitted between domestic and international rates.

6 THE GREAT LEAP FORWARD OF THE 1960s

"The Jet Age" and "Container Era" were two abrupt changes, which broke with all previous developments and revolutionised airfreight, raising it to a new plateau in its evolution: the industrial stage.

Within a few years, the advent of jet propulsion – The Jet Age as the Americans call it – completely revolutionised air transport. Sensing the magnitude of the phenomenon, the Director General of IATA wrote in 1956: "We are rapidly approaching the Jet Age. The approach of this new era has stirred the imagination; its repercussions on the community of nations and individual men and women will be tremendous." [1] Four years later, Sir William was in a position to indicate the scale of the change: "Re-equipment of the industry goes on at a fantastic rate. At the end of 1958, IATA members had taken delivery of 14 jets. ... and the total at the end of 1962 should be approximately 600." [2]

The name of Pan American Airways remains closely linked with the history of jet transport: on 13th October 1955 it placed an order for a fleet of 44 aircraft (23 Boeing B707s and 21 Douglas DC-8s), unleashing an unprecedented buying boom among its competitors. But first come first served and on 26th October 1958, Pan Am opened the first regular jet service across the North Atlantic between New York and Paris.

Although the above is historically true, it is unjust and does not give the full picture, since it omits two predecessors: the first, the De Havilland 106 Comet 1, struck by misfortune, and the second, the Soviet Tupolev 104.

The Comet 1 was a sleek-lined aircraft of great elegance, with its jet engines incorporated into the thickness of the wings. It had entered into commercial service on 2nd May 1952 on BOAC's routes, and was introduced on the Dakar route in December 1952 by the young French private airline UAT. It was fitted with 36–44 seats, and flew at a speed of 500mph at an altitude of 30,000 to 40,000ft. As a result of a series of spectacular accidents it had to be taken out of service. It was a typical passenger aircraft, built for the needs of a particularly busy clientele, but we should honour its memory for one reason in particular: in fact, it was initially designed as a transatlantic postal aircraft, carrying only six passengers and the mail.

1 FIRST PERIOD: CONSEQUENCES OF THE INTRODUCTION OF JET PASSENGER AIRCRAFT

The doubling of available freight capacity
Between 1960 and 1962 the freight transport capacity of the scheduled airlines increased more than twofold. The two components of capacity – the holds of passenger aircraft and the payload of cargo aircraft – increased in equal proportions.

The possibilities for the new passenger jets to carry goods underwent a tremendous expansion as a result of the cumulative interplay of three factors. The volume of the holds increased from around 20m^3 (Douglas DC-7: 18m^3, Lockheed L-1049G: 19m^3) to 40m^3 and over (Douglas DC-8: 39m^3, Boeing 707-20: 48m^3). The load made available by jet aircraft was at once higher and more reliable than on the piston-engined passenger planes which had recently been put into service: except when weather conditions were unfavourable, they ensured a capacity of 4–5 tonnes or more. And then the final factor: the cruising speed leapt from 300 to 550–550mph. The joint influence of all these three elements – volume, payload and speed – explains why the replacement of a piston-engined Douglas DC-7 by a jet-powered Douglas DC-8 resulted in a quadrupling of the freight capacity.

From another angle, the modernisation of the passenger fleets happened so fast that it very quickly presented the problem of what to do with several hundred piston aircraft in perfect condition. What about turning them into cargo aircraft? In its annual report of 1960 IATA suggested two possibilities: "It is estimated that there will be a surplus in the industry of anywhere from 1,200 to 1,800 piston-engined aircraft by the end of 1961. The disposal of these machines, many of them not yet fully depreciated, is itself a problem of great magnitude. Some can be converted to all-cargo... Others can be used on charters."

Many piston-engined aircraft would be transformed into cargo planes, accentuating even further the subordination of freight activities to passenger transport: not only was the vast majority of the goods traffic carried in the holds of passenger aircraft, but even the cargo aircraft themselves were former passenger aircraft which had been converted! Airfreight was not an autonomous activity, but was in a state of fundamental dependency.

The Douglas DC-7 and Lockheed L-1049 were the aircraft which were most often converted for cargo transport. As an example, we will take Air France.

In 1960, Air France decided to convert two Lockheed L-1049Gs into cargo versions, by making such changes as were absolutely necessary. In the classic manner, these concerned three areas: the door, the floor and the internal fittings.

• Installation of a cargo door
This was positioned on the left-hand side of the fuselage at the rear, and was 2.63 metres wide by 1.87 metres high. It was operated by a manual hydraulic bolt, and opened upwards and outwards.

• Floor reinforcement
In order to take heavy loads with a density per square metre far above that of passengers, the cabin floor had to be strengthened. It was covered entirely in metal, using sections of profiled laminate, in which were embedded three rows of tie rings and four fixing rails for seats (for possible accompanying personnel in the case of transport of horses, exceptional works of art or military freight). The floor strength was increased to $970kg/m^2$, and the linear strength varied between 445 and 770kg, depending on the fuselage zone.

• Interior fittings in the cabin
The walls were covered in glass-fibre panels, so as to protect the windows, which were retained. The cabin was divided into six loading zones with respect to their influence on the aircraft's trim. It was divided into 10 compartments, produced by fitting transversal partitions or rows of anchoring points to give volumes of 6.9 to $8.1m^3$. A passageway 0.8m in width was arranged on the left-hand side, providing access for the crew to the rear of the cabin.

With a load of 15 tonnes for a usable volume of $97m^3$ ($78m^3$ inside the cabin; $29m^3$ in the hold) the first converted L-1040D went in service on the Paris–New York route in spring 1961.

The table below gives a picture of the world long-haul fleet developed. [3] In view of this surge of capacity, how would the airlines react?

Adaptation to the growth in capacity
This took two forms: One progressive, the other coercive.

• The first method of adaptation : rate reductions
With the massive increase in capacity and the reduction in unit costs brought by jet aircraft, one policy came to the fore: reduce and readjust the rates, exploit the rate flexibility to its maximum, and push promotion campaigns so as to make a real breakthrough in the transportation market, and an appreciable increase in sales. Although the airlines agreed on the analysis, they differed on how to apply it. And once again, within the specialist committees of IATA, there was a clash between the proponents of the two rating schools: the supporters of general cargo rates, versus those of Specific Commodity Rates. Of course, the North Atlantic, as the dominant sector of the market, became the preferred battlefield. After a confrontation of truly Homeric proportions, richly rumbustious, and after the intervention of the CAB, the airlines at last managed to reach an agreement. Through force of circumstance, it had to be a compromise agreement, but this is a good illustration of IATA's ability to adapt and of its powers of innovation during those halcyon days. Sir William was not mistaken about the historical consequences of the consensus. He wrote that the Montreal Traffic Conference had reached a decision, which would have long-term consequences when it introduced a new simplified rate structure for the North Atlantic, with the aim of encouraging large volume consignments. Although at that point it was too early to predict the results of the new structure, it represented a definite break with the past, and a bolder plan for the future. It involved the recognition that freight could no longer be considered simply as a by-product of passenger operations. [4]

Let us see what major innovations were introduced by this new rate grid, which entered into force on 1st September 1961 after being approved by all the Governments (see table at top of page 213). They were:

1   An overall reduction in general and specific rates;

2   For general rates: the introduction of new weight breaks up to 7,500kg;

3   For specific rates: simplification by means of re-grouping and eliminating less productive rates, and introduction of higher weight breaks for products representing the largest potential for expansion.

• Second method of adaptation: the sharpening of sanctions
The over-capacity in all areas was the dominant feature of world air transport at the time of the Annual General Meeting of IATA in Dublin in September 1962. How should the airlines, subjected to market pressures, but obliged to respect their undertakings

Development of the number of cargo planes in service

Type	Situation as at 1.1.60			Situation as at 31.12.61		
	Number	Unit capacity	Total capacity	Number	Unit capacity	Total capacity
Lockheed L-1049	50	15t	750t	59	15t	885t
Lockheed L-1649	-	-	-	7	15.2t	106t
Douglas DC-6	37	12.8t	474t	37	12.8t	474t
Douglas DC-7	-	-	-	49	15.2t	745t
Total	87		1,224t	152		2,210t
Growth				+75%		+80%

Development of the structure of general cargo rates (GCR)

In US cents/kg Weight breaks only	London/New York [5]		New York/London [5]	
	Before 11.9.61	After 1.9.61	Before 1.9.61	After 1.9.61
0/45kg	280	220	280	220
45/100kg	212	152	212	152
100/250kg	212	110	212	110
250/500kg	212	90	212	90
500/1,000kg	183	79	183	79
1,000/7,500kg		73		73
>7,500kg		68		

Development of the number of special commodity rates

	Before 1.9.1961	After 1.9.1961
London/New York	50	18
New York/London	45	12

regarding rates (which had been jointly adopted and approved by their Governments) react in order to avoid the spread of hidden kickbacks and other forms of "malpractices" that had already been witnessed in the area of freight transport? Should they apply the law of supply and demand, by reducing capacity and officially reducing rates or, just the opposite, improve control and impose heavier sanctions on any infractions of the unanimously reached decisions? Undoubtedly, ideas of public service and "orderly growth" were once more strongly favoured than the principles of the market economy in the hearts of the senior figures of the air transport industry present in Dublin. It would be better to solemnly reaffirm the commitments they had made, and to harden the monetary sanctions, than to give way to market forces. What was more, the credibility of the Institution was at stake.

And all the Presidents and Managing Directors of the airlines stood up and promised, each more solemnly than the next man, to respect the rating decisions and regulations of the Association. Were they convinced? Of course. Were they unanimous? Almost.

Two or three did allow themselves to point out that overcapacity was the basic reason for the doubtful application for the official rates. The person who gave the clearest message in this

Flying Tiger Line CL-44 at Burbank Airport, California. Turnaround time for a full load of 65,000lbs was 45 minutes.
Air Cargo News UK

respect, and this should not surprise us, was the representative of the only IATA member scheduled cargo company, Seaboard World Airlines (SBW). Mr Jackson of SBW said that it was the law of supply and demand which determined the climate in which the "malpractices" would prosper or perish. To a considerable extent, supply was controlled by a few large companies. Demand was a function of the price of a product. If the price was too high, demand dropped, and the climate became favourable for "undesirable practices". Mr Jackson considered that the Executive Committee would have to look at this problem more closely. At the same time he confirmed that his company would apply the decisions of the Traffic Conferences.

When it came down to practicalities, what was the impact of what has often been called "the Dublin Oath"? It undoubtedly induced a better application of the official rate levels, and a reduction in discounts of all kinds. To use the language of the transport companies, it succeeded in bringing about a temporary "clean-up" of the market.

2 THE PROPELLER-TURBINE INTERLUDE [6]

The first jet cargo aircraft went into service fours years after 26th October 1958, the date of the first Pan Am jet transatlantic passenger service. In the meantime, two cargo aircraft fitted with turboprop engines had come onto the scene: one long-haul aircraft – the Canadair CL-44, and one medium-haul plane – the Argosy series 100 manufactured by Armstrong-Whitworth.

The Canadair CL-44D: the first modern cargo aircraft
The CL-44D was, first of all, a very innovative cargo plane, with its swing tail and unit load devices. But above all, it became the "flight element in an Integrated Air Cargo System". From now on, the cargo aircraft would constitute the essential link in a whole transport chain, which closely combined the air transport component with the ground-based handling and loading equipment. The aircraft gained reliability and speed of handling, but lost autonomy.

As a long- and medium-range transport aircraft, developed from the "Bristol Britannia" passenger machine, the CL-44D was fitted with four Rolls-Royce Tyne 12 second-generation turboprop engines, each of over 6,50hp, driving four-bladed De Havilland propellers. It was not a purpose-built cargo plane. On the contrary, it could be used as a passenger, cargo or mixed version, and quickly transformed from one version to another, hence its name, the "Trivalent" aircraft. [7] It had the following physical characteristics:

• wing span: 43.40m; length: 41.70m; height: 11.20m;

• maximum weight at take off; 92,500kg;

• payload: approximately 28,000kg;

• theoretical volume: 205m³ (of which, main hold: 156m³).

The CL-44D possessed two unique features:

• A swing tail, which offered the best possible facilities for loading the main hold, which was 26.61m long, 3.40m wide and 2.08m high;

• a novel loading and unloading system consisting of two parts: onboard and ground based.

• Onboard
Whereas up to that time cargo aircraft had mostly been bulk loaded by hand, the CL-44D is a "unitised" plane – that is to say that the packages, instead of being loaded individually into the plane, are previously arranged on pallets fitted with retention nets, or inside containers. The main floor is equipped with 10 slide pallets made of a plywood panel with aluminium alloy sheets bonded to the top and bottom surfaces mounted on skids. Provision is made within the main cargo compartment for the tie-down of palletised or containerised loads. The floor of the compartment is fitted with Nylatron rubbing strips to facilitate the movement of the Canadair slide pallets. Internal winching is provided by a chain and cable system running down either side of the compartment.

• On the ground
The pallets are transported from the terminal to the plane on special dollies and pallet carriers, fitted with rollers, arranged so as to continually support the panels, which are too thin to bear the weight of their load. A lift vehicle (loader) which itself is fitted with rollers forms the link between the pallet carrier (low level) and the floor of the plane (upper level). The last, optional, component of the Canadair Integrated Air Cargo System is a specially equipped cargo terminal situated at the edge of the freighter parking area, including a stocking facility, unit load devices on several levels, and lightweight equipment on the ground (roller conveyors) for the horizontal movement of pallets and containers.

In total, 39 CL-44 Canadairs were manufactured between 1959 and 1966:

• 12 CL-44-6 Yukon built for the Canadian Air Force, whose order allowed them to start the manufacturing programme. These planes were fitted with two large forward and aft doors, and did not have the swing tail;

• 23 CL-44D4s, with swing tail, which were initially purchased by three American cargo airlines: Flying Tiger, Seaboard and Slick Airways. These machines then passed into the hands of a number of cargo charter companies. Some are still in use. One or two of them were modified and lengthened. Under the name of "Sky Monster" they were adapted to carry very bulky or outsize loads;

• 4 CL-44Js, the stretched "all passenger" version ordered by the Icelandic company Lofleidir for its Luxembourg/New York economy service.

Flying Tiger took the Canadair CL-44D into service in spring 1961 and gave it a glowing tribute, describing it as: "The first and only all-cargo aircraft which makes no compromises. It is indispensable to the development of airfreight." In order to put it to the best possible advantage, Flying Tiger introduced a new tariff on its American routes on 16th October 1961, based on the operating costs of the CL-44 and using a goods classification system divided into seven categories of articles depending on their density. The CL-44D had many good points, but had

RIGHT **Flying Tigers CL-44.**
MAP

BELOW RIGHT **BEA AW Argosy.**
British Airways Museum

BOTTOM RIGHT **AW Argosy.**
British Airways Museum

two intrinsic faults: its palletisation system was not up to scratch, and its operating costs were higher than those of the future jet cargo planes, which were just coming onto the scene.

The Armstrong Whitworth "Argosy" series 100
This plane was designed from the beginning for goods transport, including vehicles, and came into service with the American company Riddle Airways in December 1960, and then with the Cargo Division of British European Airways (BEA) in 1961.

It had many of the features of the ideal cargo aircraft: a very low floor, at truck height; great ease of loading and unloading thanks to large doors fore and aft; standard pallet equipment; and finally a good weight/volume ratio. On paper, the Argosy was a remarkable medium-range cargo aircraft.

But in practice it had one insuperable defect; it was not profitable. It needed a load factor of about 95% to break even. Several factors contributed to the poor economic performance: the payload was low (10,400kg) for a four-engine plane; the aerodynamics were poor due to the positioning of the cargo doors at the two ends of the fuselage; and the lack of commonality [8] with other types of aircraft in service meant that specialist technical crews had to be formed, and individualised maintenance systems organised.

This last factor is of fundamental importance. It partly accounts for the limited success of the CL-44D. Unless it wants considerably to increase its operating cost, no mixed airline, which operates passenger and cargo services at the same time, can afford to introduce into its fleet some examples of a

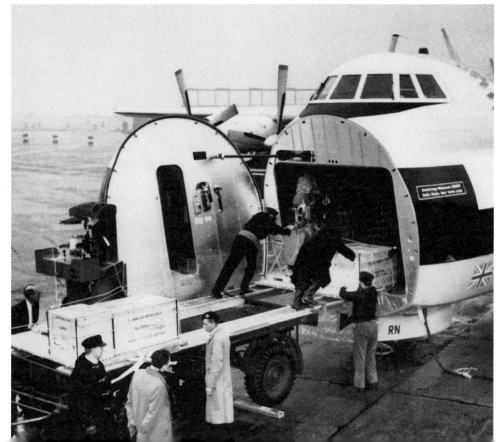

Air France B707-320C at Paris Orly airport.
Air France

Comparison of B707-320C and DC-8-55 [9]

	707-320C	DC-8F-55
• Dimensions		
Wingspan	44.41m	43.40m
Length	46.61m	45.94m
Height	12.94m	13.10m
Sill	3.07m	3.35m
Engines	4 jet engines	4 jet engines
• Max load		
MTOW	150,200kg	148,800kg
MLW	112,000kg	108,900kg
MZFW	104,000kg	101,600kg
Max payload	40,000kg	38,500kg
• Cargo cabin		
Length	30.81m	30.35m
Width	3.25m	3.25m
• Cargo Door		
Location	Front left	Front left
Width	3.40m	3.55m
Height	2.31m	2.15m
• Cargo cabin equipment		
Number of pallets	13	13
Dimensions of pallets	2.24m x 3.18m	12 – 2.24m x 3.18m
		1 – 2.24m x 2.74m
	2.24m x 2.74m	13 2.24m x 2.74m
Max wt per pallet	3,500/4,410kg	3,070/4,690kg
	(According to position)	
• Volume of holds	48m³	40m³
• Handling/loading	pallet-moving equipment + lifting platform	

particular aircraft – however remarkable it may be – if it has no commonality with its passenger machines, which are far larger in number.

3 THE SECOND PERIOD: THE ARRIVAL OF CARGO JETS

"We believe this aeroplane heralds the beginning of a new chapter in the amazingly swift growth of world wide air cargo."

This was the press release with which Pan American World Airways opened the era of jet cargo aviation on 3rd June 1963, when the first Boeing 707-320C went into service in the North Atlantic.

Two lords of the air enter the fray: the Boeing 707-320C and the Douglas DC-8F Jet Trader
In 1962, the airlines began the process of modernising their cargo fleet. They placed orders for the cargo versions of their passenger aircraft, thus supporting the commonality between their cargo and passenger machines. They entered this road with prudence, even circumspection. They did not order pure freighters, without windows, but the convertible versions of the Boeing 707 and the Douglas DC-8, each of which made a great play on adaptability. After its opening fanfare, the Pan Am press release stressed: "Convertibility of the entire upper deck compartment to all – passenger or all-cargo configuration or combinations of the two. ... This new air plane is a further development of the Boeing 707-320B turbofan Intercontinental. Major innovations, besides the forward cargo door, includes strengthening of general structure components, especially in the landing gear and main cabin floor to accommodate heavier loads."

We find the same prudent approach with Douglas. On unveiling its DC-8F "Jet Trader" version in February 1962, Douglas emphasised its great flexibility of utilisation: "The DC-F offers various loading possibilities: passengers, mixed or freight. Ten different positions are provided for the mobile partition which, in the mixed version, separates the freight hold from the passenger cabin."

These two types of aircraft, which were very similar to one another, were to dominate the long-haul freight market for over 10 years. In addition to their own particular features, they had two points of similarity with the Canadair CL-44D: the elimination of manual loading of loose cargo in favour of loading on "unit load devices" (pallets or containers) and integration into a ground-based freight handling system. With the introduction of these modern aircraft, new and expensive (due to their special features, convertible or all-cargo versions were more expensive than the passenger versions), which in addition required considerable investment on the ground (handling machinery and equipment for the freight terminals), freight activities finally entered a new category. No longer a relatively low-cost trade, it became a capital-intensive industrial activity. Fortunately, Freight Managers still had two weighty arguments for convincing their Directors to buy the cargo aircraft of the future: their flexibility of adaptation, and their operating costs.

Because of the devaluation of currencies and the optimism of manufacturers, it is always very difficult to get objective measures and compare the direct operating costs of different aircraft. Under all the usual reservations, and based on information published by the ICAO, we can get some idea of the following orders of magnitude:

Development of direct costs per produced unit (ATK)*

Type of aeroplane	Index
DC-4	100
DC-6/L-1049	50/70
DC-8F/B707-320C	30

* Available tonne/kilometres

Taking advantage of their adaptability, several companies operated combi versions of these aircraft. A greater or lesser proportion for passengers or freight was carried on the main deck, according to the position of the main partition. We could mention Braniff, operating between the United States and South America, Northwest headed for Japan, with a variable layout taking four–nine pallets, or again, on the North Atlantic, Aer Lingus or Lufthansa. KLM is indisputably the company which made greatest use of this solution, for destinations in America, Asia or Africa, changing the number of pallets according to the seasonality of the goods traffic.

Whereas Boeing encountered major technical difficulties in producing further developments of the 320D version, Douglas carried out a very successful modular "stretching" policy for its DC-8-50 version, which gave rise to a series called the DC-8-60. Among the convertible versions of this series, one should mention the DC-8-63F, equipped for 18 pallets, thanks to an elongation of the fuselage which increased cabin volume by around 40%, and provided a payload of 45 tonnes over a distance of 3,125 miles.

Medium-haul jet cargo aircraft

During the period under consideration, these aircraft never dominated the cargo markets as decisively as did their long haul brothers. This was less to do with the presence of the Argosy, the success of which was very limited, than with the persistent usage of old aircraft such as the Douglas DC-4 and the Curtiss C-46, and the conversion into cargo versions of turboprop passenger aircraft produced after 1959: the Lockheed Electra and the Vickers Armstrong Vanguard (re-christened "Merchantman" for the occasion).

The cargo version of these two aircraft showed great similarities regarding their payload (15 tonnes for the former and 17–18 tonnes for the latter) and their basic equipment (8 pallets 88in x 125in or 88 x 108in).

The convertible versions of the medium-haul Douglas DC-9s and Boeing B727s and B737s came off the production lines between 1966 and 1971. They were capable of quite a variety of adaptations for mixed use depending on the position of the separating partition. In their "all-cargo" version they lay in a fairly narrow range of load capacity from 15 to 20 tonnes. Naturally, they were all fitted for standard pallets transferable to long-haul cargo planes (eg eight pallets 88in x 108in for the

BEA Vickers Vanguard.
RAF Museum

DC-9-33AF

Europe freighter

Serving the European and inter-Scandinavian network

Douglas DC-9 Cargo). The Caravelle, the archetype of the two-engined medium-range passenger jet, which entered in service in 1959, also existed in a mixed version. This started work on 21st September 1967 with Air Afrique, who used it on its domestic network.

A new type of medium-range convertible aircraft appeared in 1966: the "Quick Change". From 1965 to 1970 the two American manufacturers devoted considerable efforts to promoting this solution which is altogether an attractive and innovative approach. Douglas presented the DC-9QC, Boeing the B727QC or the B737QC.

A "Quick change" plane (or QC for short) is a creature with two faces: the day face – "all-passengers", and the night face – "all-cargo". In these planes, the idea of palletisation

ABOVE **Lufthansa Boeing B737-300QC can be changed from a passenger to a cargo aircraft in 75 minutes.** *Lufthansa*

LEFT **This photograph showing the loading of an SAS DC-9-33AF cargo aircraft illustrtaes well the different types of load – igloos, pallets etc..** *SAS Cargo* is pushed to its ultimate limit: even the passenger seats, like the packages are palletised. Or more precisely, they are mounted on pallets. Hence, in order to change the version, it is only necessary to take out the pallets to which the seats are fixed, and to replace them with the freight pallets. And vice versa to change back. This extreme adaptability meant that QC planes led a "double life" [10] as a passenger plane by day and a cargo plane by night.

The advantages of the QC are obvious: an increased daily turnaround frequency, which permits annual depreciation to be spread over the largest number of flying hours, and the establishment of complete commonality between cargo and passenger fleets. The Quick Change solution was quite a craze for a while in Europe (Alitalia, Lufthansa, Aer Lingus etc) and in the United States, where United Airlines and TWA operated fleets of 36 and 35 QC aircraft respectively at the beginning of the 1970s. In the United States, there was even a case of two different companies joining forces to operate a QC machine together on the Miami/New York route: one as a passenger version by day (National Airlines), the other as the cargo version by night (Airlift, a supplemental carrier). It is lucky that they both operated from the same base!

As always in such situations, one would be justified in asking: if this system has so many advantages, why has it not been adopted by all companies? There are a number of reasons: not all companies operate medium-haul cargo services; the limits on night flights for certain airports restrict the utilisation of the cargo version; QC aircraft are heavier and more expensive; and the continual change routine ends up by causing a lot of wear and tear to the passenger equipment.

For these reasons the Quick Change solution was gradually abandoned. (Until it made a reappearance recently.)

4 CONTAINERS AND UNIT LOAD DEVICES

The so called "Container Revolution" was a movement with universal impact, which started at the beginning of the 1950s, and involved transporting an ever increasing proportion of goods of ever increasing variety in standardised "boxes" which could be transferred from one mode of transport to another. It was initiated in the United States by a road haulier, who had gone over to shipping – Malcolm MacLean – and a venerable shipping company, which had specialised in routes between California and the Hawaiian Islands – Matson Navigation Co., and began by influencing, and later inundating, all modes of transport, whether by sea, rail, road or air. In spite of this, the permanent concern with standardisation left each transport mode with certain specific characteristics. Hence, out of the panoply of unit-load devices, which are involved in this evolution, air transport favoured pallets and igloos in preference to containers, in contrast to its competitors in sea and rail transport, who gave the dominant position to the container.

The necessity of standardisation
The standardisation of boxes is an absolute condition for the successive use of the same container for different modes of transport, which is the definition of inter-modality. The word "container" was in common use well before the 1960s. At that time it designated a whole multitude of containers of very different dimensions, volumes and forms, which did not have a single common denominator, but which reflected an identical aspi-

ration: to assemble packages into intermediate boxes in order to facilitate and speed up handling operations. It was a kind of "super package".

Everything changed with the standardisation of the containers: "Container technology is a transportation technology and not a sophisticated form of packaging." [11] The work of standardisation was carried out by Technical Committee 104 of the International Standards Organisation (ISO), which took on the task of defining containers and lifting equipment.

• Definition of a container
"*A container is understood to be a transport device:*

a) Of a permanent nature and therefore resilient enough to allow repeated use;
b) Specially designed to facilitate the transport of goods without breaking down loads, between one or several means of transport;
c) Fitted with devices which make it easy to handle, particularly during trans-shipment from one means of transport to another;
d) Designed for ease of filling and emptying;
e) Having a volume of at least 1 cubic metre".

• Dimensions of containers
This definition is sufficiently broad to authorise the existence of a very wide range of containers. However the "Container Revolution" which was accomplished by shipping companies was achieved through the generalised utilisation of "large ISO containers".

This refers to rectangular box-shaped containers with a standardised cross section of 8ft x 8ft (2.44m x 2.44m), and having lengths varying between 5 and 40ft. In practice, the predominant lengths for containers are 10, 20, 30 and 40ft (3, 6, 9 and 12m respectively).

• Handling of containers
Some container ships today carry more than 6,000 "20ft equivalent" boxes, piled six or more high. Under these conditions, marine containers must have two principal qualities. First of all, physical strength, so that they can be stacked to a considerable height without any risk of crushing. Next comes the ease of attaching lifting gear, so as to speed up handling operations within the port and improve the turnaround time for the ships. For these reasons, the large "ISO containers" are boxes made of thick sheet steel, strong but heavy, and provided on all four corners with devices to permit lifting by means of hooks, shackles or spreaders with twist locks. Such standardised top-corner pieces are an essential feature of the large ISO containers, which are lifted vertically.

Adaptation of containers for air transport

• Historical review
Containerisation in its original sense, ie a pre-packaging of goods on non-standard loading devices for the purpose of easier handling, had been a concern of the airlines for many years. If we consider only more recent examples, BOAC and Seaboard carried out tests in 1956 and 1957 using corrugated cardboard containers to transport clothing and removals, while American Airlines ordered freight containers in 1958 to equip

its DC-6 cargo aircraft.

We have also seen that the Canadair CL-44 was the first unitised cargo plane. However, air containerisation only adopted its own particular features with the entry into service of the convertible versions of the B707 and the DC-8.

• Technical aspects of air containerisation

An aircraft is a long empty "cigar-tube" covered with a thin aluminium skin. This elementary observation results in several distinctive features:

1. Payload is a rare commodity. Hence, air containers must be as light as possible in order to reduce the "dead weight" – the tare – to a strict minimum. This imperative requirement for lightness has three consequences:

- Unit load devices (ULDs) are fragile (principally made of aluminium), expensive to buy and costly to maintain;
- Unit load devices are so light that they cannot support the load they contain without a serious risk of distortion. They must constantly rest and/or be moved on systems equipped with multiple rollers, which are sufficiently close together to avoid deformations of the metal. This means that air containers are handled in a horizontal plane, whereas marine containers are handled vertically;
- Pallets with nets, and igloos, which are lighter, are often preferred to containers. In the context of air transport, one should talk of "unitisation" rather than "containerisation". Igloos, which are a hybrid between pallets and containers, are a particular product used by air carriers. The term "igloo" applies to a rigid shell without a floor, which is fixed over a pallet and closed off with a net. Its weight is somewhere between that of a pallet and that of a container.

2. Due to the varying height curve along the aircraft within the main hold of various kinds of long- and medium-haul cargo planes, the standard dimensions for aircraft loading devices before the Boeing 747F came onto the scene, were restricted to two sizes. Two standard base sizes were recognised: 88in x 108in (2.2m x 2.74m) and 88in x 125in (2.24m x 3.18m) with "lengths" or "breadths" not differentiated, since, depending on the aircraft and the way it is fitted out, the same pallet can be loaded either cross-wise or length-wise.

3. In order to ensure the optimal interchangeability for the loading devices between the different kinds of aircraft, IATA succeeded in completing a remarkable work of standardisation. For this purpose it created a Container Board in 1963, which was later to become the Unit Load Device Technical Board. Its activity consisted principally in defining the standards, registering the units corresponding to these standards, and assigning them an identification code (IC Code).

• Commercial aspects of air containerisation

At the same time, unit load devices are rating assessment mechanisms and marketing tools.

• Unitisation and rating

Once aircraft are obliged to be equipped with loading devices, it is within the carriers' interest to transfer to some other person, the client or the forwarding agent, the job of filling the igloo the container, or the pallet. In turn, in order to achieve this, the clients or forwarding agents must have an advantage in doing so. Whatever the rate incentives accepted, the appearance of standard unit loading devices, (or ULDs) introduces a new factor into the principles for setting rates: that of a differential for unitisation. From this point on, there were rates for freight handed over in bulk, and lower rates for freight delivered on loading units, since part of the handling work had already been done.

We shall not go into detail about a field which is technically very complex. Suffice it to say that there are two main approaches, depending on whether one merely gives a discount to the person delivering a unitised consignment (the rating scales not being modified in other respects) or whether one introduces more innovative principles.

• Unitisation and marketing

How could unitisation, which is a technical obligation and an economic necessity, be turned into a sales pitch? The IATA Traffic Conference held in Athens in 1969 approached the problem by adopting the principle, revolutionary for its time, of charging a fixed price per ULD, whatever the category of goods carried: a rate system known as (FAK Freight All Kinds).

The principle is simple: the client pays a fixed price for a certain unit, within the limits of a maximum load known as the "pivot weight", below which he pays the fixed charge. Above it, he pays a very advantageous price per kilo for every additional kilo loaded, up to the physical weight-carrying limit of the unit. This rate only applies if the unit is delivered ready for carriage, and collected in the same state at its destination.

Freight forwarders and/or clients therefore must obtain the necessary equipment so that they can themselves carry out the unitisation of the loads.

The Athens Conference introduced this novel concept on quite a number of long-haul sectors. Because of this two-level rate system, unitisation became a tremendous incentive to develop consolidation, and to look for new high-density business. In the event, although this concept was very revolutionary, its introduction proceeded cautiously, as a result of delicate compromises within IATA. This is why the level of many commodity special rates remained below those for unit load devices. The rating theory was seductive, and far ahead of the ideas of the time, but the conditions under which it was applied were inconsistent with the logic of the system. It was not surprising that the clientele at large (customers and freight forwarders) were far from enthusiastic about the reform.

A TALE OF TWO DECADES 1950–1970: ENTHUSIASM, DECEPTION AND CRUEL REALITIES

The technology of the Jet Age marked a sharp division between the two decades. The first – 1950–1960 – was characterised by low growth rates in a general atmosphere of questioning about the real future of airfreight; the second – 1960–1970 – was marked by rapid expansion and renewed enthusiasm, though tempered by a worsening economic results.

The first decade had started with fanfares, resulting from over-confidence in spectacular expansion, and was destined to produce bitter disillusionment. The example was set at the highest level. Sir William Hildred drew up a veritable credo regarding the transport of goods by air when he wrote in 1948:

> "Cargo transport has developed phenomenally. On some routes it already accounts for almost as much payload as passengers and a number of lines are regularly operating all-cargo schedules, and this is only the small beginning of the air cargo story."

Confidence in an unlimited future for airfreight was not just the view of a few hundred former war pilots who were having difficulty getting back into civilian life, it was expressed by the highest authorities in civil aviation. Contrary to all expectations, it was not the cargo business, but passenger traffic which first entered the era of mass transportation.[1] Freight became a "sleeping giant". The arrival on the scene of jet aircraft had brought about the technological break which freight had needed in order to fulfil the premature hopes which had been placed on it. Whereas one commentator painted a sober picture of "the renewal of airfreight",[2] Sir William, once again expressing the incorrigible optimism of an airfreight enthusiast, when he talked of the future of air services having no relationship with the situation at the time, since jet aircraft would offer totally new possibilities. If he did not expect that they would transport cement, minerals, wheat or locomotives, they would handle all the rest, goods like whisky, tractors, fragile or perishable products for which they were already the market leaders.

I GENERAL TRENDS

Four main trends can be seen: the rather jerky growth of traffic; the regular decline of the proportion of domestic traffic; the collapse of American supremacy; and the spectacular growth of all-cargo services.

The uneven expansion of traffic
Before the introduction of jet aircraft, freight traffic was growing less rapidly than passenger traffic. The arrival of jet aircraft reversed this trend.

Average annual growth rate by type of activity (in percent)

Activity Period	Passengers	Freight	Mail
1950/1960	+14.5	+10.2	+11.8
1960/1970	+13.5	+17.8	+15.8

Due to the ups and downs in traffic growth , the proportion of freight within the physical activity of the airlines remained stable for the 20 years under consideration: 22.1% in 1950 and in 1970.

The constant decline in the proportion of domestic traffic
In 1950, domestic traffic represented two thirds of world traffic. This situation reflected the power of American commercial aviation, the role of airfreight in exploiting the resources of certain new nations (Canada, South America) and the low level of international trade. Under the dual effect of the resumption of international trade, and advances in surface transportation, the relative proportion of domestic traffic started an inexorable process of decline, which was to continue until the present day.

International and domestic traffic growth

Years	Int	%	Domestic	%	Total	%
1950	265	34	505	66	770	100
1955	440	35	800	65	1,240	100
1960	930	46	1,110	54	2,040	100
1965	2,500	52	2,300	48	4,800	100
1970	6,430	61	4,100	39	10,560	100

Source: ICAO

Breakdown by region of international airfreight traffic on scheduled flights (in percent)

	North America	Europe	Asia	South America	Oceania	Africa	Middle East	Total
1951	45.8	39.4	4.4	3.4	4.6	1.4	1.0	100
1960	36.7	44.6	4.3	3.9	4.4	2.5	3.6	100
1965	34.7	45.7	5.6	4.0	3.4	3.8	2.8	100
1970	32.4	44.2	8.3	4.9	2.7	3.2	4.3	100

Source: ICAO

Note: This table does not follow the development of all traffic within the major geographical sectors, but of the traffic carried by companies having their registered offices in the zone stated

The decline of American domination

Air transport is one of the most obvious aspects of America's crushing supremacy in the post-war world. In whatever field, passengers, goods or mail, more than 50% of the world traffic was carried by the American flag between 1945 and 1970. This domination arises out of the enormous American internal market, and its size continued to increase within the world total for domestic traffic.

It is just the contrary with international traffic, where the American banner visibly loses ground. Although Pan American was the leading international airline throughout this period, the percentage of the United States' international traffic fell from 39% in 1950 to 24% in 1970. This fall-back in American dominance was the result of the boom in the European economies after 1950, the growth in momentum of the Asian airlines after 1960, and the emergence of the Middle East. (See table above.)

The growth in power of all-cargo services

The proportion of cargo flights in the activities of scheduled carriers made strong and continuous progress. It grew from 6% in 1951 to 19% in 1960 and 40% in 1970. The development of cargo flights, and more precisely of charter cargo flights, received a strong impulse from the Baltic Exchange. This British institution has been very active from 1949 to 1975 in the City of London. To fix charters either as a supplier – the airline – or as the customer – the shipper – this would have to be arranged through the Air Brokers Association of the Baltic Exchange. The brokers were all shipping companies with air charter departments. A shipper had to appoint a Baltic Exchange broker to approach another such broker representing the airline to be used.

The better named brokers included names such as Instone which employed as its principal broker one of the more colourful characters on The Baltic Exchange the Frenchman, Gaston Levy-Tilley, Furness Withy, Brokalloyd, Clarkair, Escombe McGrath, Hunting Gibson, Bahe Behrend, Lambert Brothers, Atlas Air and ASA Aeroservices.

An owner or airline's broker took 2½% commission, while a charterer or shipper's broker took 5%. A broker could be both an airline and a shipper's broker.

Apart from the national carriers, such as KLM and Air India, all the cargo charter airlines from both Britain and abroad were used.

We shall not review each of the world's geographical sectors as this book could not accommodate all the information. We will concentrate on a few representative samples of the various types of activity but we will not re-visit the American domestic market, which was adequately dealt with in chapter 1 of this section.

2 THE HALCYON DAYS OF THE NORTH ATLANTIC

For over 50 years, the North Atlantic was the primary route for air transport. And as far as freight was concerned, things were never better than in the 1970s.

The first impression is one of extraordinary vitality, demonstrated by an average annual growth rate of above 20% from 1955 to 1970, reaching around 29% for the 10 years 1955–1965. On two occasions traffic even showed short-lived but impressive periods of acceleration between 1958 and 1960 (from 25,000 to 47,000 tonnes) and between 1966 and 1969

Development of North Atlantic freight traffic (in tonnes)

	North America/ Europe	Europe/North America	Total	Traffic on Cargo flights in percent
1951	3,980	3,703	7,683	17.8%
1955	5,474	7,706	13,180	26.6%
1960	21,908	24,941	46,849	43.5%
1965	88,254	74,600	162,854	46.9%
1970	196,438	214,522	410,960	60.2%

Trade by air of United States/Canada with Europe

Year 1970 in tonnes	Exports by air	Imports by air	Proportion of exports in the total
United States	181,000	176,000	50.8%
Canada	14,000	38,000	27.6%

Source: US Bureau of the Census

(from 201,000 to 249,000 tonnes). Within 20 years, traffic grew from 6,000 tonnes in 1950 to over 410,000 tonnes in 1970.

In 1970, the North Atlantic represented approximately 50% of international traffic world-wide (see table above.). [3]

The second impression is that one is witnessing the establishment of a complete air transport system, integrating the frequency of passenger flights with the capacities of the cargo flights. It is a phenomenon unique in the world, the proportion of traffic carried on cargo-only flights hit the 50% mark in 1966 and reached 60% in 1970. Here one can see the effect of the massive introduction of converted passenger aircraft in the 1960s, followed by the introduction of jet cargo planes from 1962 onwards.

The third impression is that of a remarkable balance in the two directions of the traffic. During the cumulative period 1955–1970, traffic leaving Europe was 50.35% of the total, and that leaving North America was 49.65%. However this overall picture disguises two types of imbalance: in time and in space.

Imbalances in time were limited, and varied according to the development of trade. On the other hand, imbalances in space, from country to country, were both permanent and profound: they reflected the structure of external trade affecting the nations of North America or of Europe.

The table above underlines the contrast between a very highly developed industrial economy and the situation of a "new country", where exports still consist for the most part of agricultural and mineral products not suitable for air transport.

Analysis of the trade by air between the USA and certain European countries leads to observations along the same lines. They confirm that airfreight, once it has achieved a certain maturity, is the mirror of economic geography and an accurate barometer of external trade (see table below).

The fourth impression is of the narrow range of product categories sent by air. A superficial analysis of the customs statistics could lead one to think that trade by air shows great variety. It is true that almost every type of goods is carried by plane, but often in minuscule quantities. In reality, even on the North Atlantic, a sector particularly suitable for air transport, traffic consists of a limited number of types of goods, all belonging to the category for manufactured products of a certain value, the only exception being perishable goods.

If one looks at exports by air from Western Europe to the United States in 1970, three major product categories make up nearly 60% of the traffic: textile products and footwear (32%), machinery (18%) and electrical equipment (8%). In the opposite direction the situation is very similar, since machinery (in particular computers), electrical equipment and transport equipment represent over half of the exports by air from the United States to Western Europe.

The last and final impression is characterised by a feeling of uncertainty on how to answer the question: what is the position of airfreight within total transatlantic trade? Insignificant or important? Both are true, depending on whether one considers the tonnage (0.42%) or the value (21%).

3 OPENING UP AFRICA

In October 1963 Air France would carry its millionth postal package within the next few weeks. The General Management of the PTT and the Directors of the national airline intended to celebrate the event. It only remained to find the recipient and the contents for this millionth airmail parcel. The recipient was an old medical doctor from Alsace, Albert Schweitzer, winner of the Nobel Peace Prize. For over 40

Trade by air of United States with Western Europe

Year 1970 in tonnes	Exports by air	Imports by air	Portion of exports in the total
France	27,140	14,550	64.9%
Germany	35,380	34,590	50.7%
Italy	15,920	36,450	30.4%
United Kingdom	51,770	31,700	62.1%

Source: US Bureau of the Census

LEFT **Transport of sheep by Air Dakar.**
Photo Artis Dakar

RIGHT **Loading a Citroen "Deux Chevaux" onto an Air France aircraft bound from Douala to Yaoundé.**
Air France Museum

are called "mixed cargo aircraft", capable of transporting goods and second or third class passengers in variable proportions. [7] In particular, there were the Douglas DC-4s, which were specially modified with a cargo door at the rear. Since we cannot examine the whole diversity of the African continent, let us look at a few examples.

years he had been fighting against leprosy in his hospital in Lambarene, [4] lost in the heart of the equatorial jungle. The contents were 10 boxes, each containing 500 tablets of medication for combating leprosy. Doctor Albert Schweitzer, when he first contacted a representative of Air France in Libreville, had only dared to request a single box:

> "It was just that our supplies of this medication have run out and we would be most interested in receiving some by the fastest means. I trust that a box of 500 tablets, which would already be of considerable service to us, would not be too heavy for an air parcel." [5]

The millionth airmail parcel was sent from Orly on 2nd December 1953. How could one provide a more symbolic illustration of the power of air transport for breaking the isolation of African countries, lacking in surface transport?

Everyone who was interested in Africa at the beginning of the 1950s – geographers, administrators, politicians – made the same observation: "... surface transport is inadequate for meeting the needs of the African economy, and in most regions, this economy is still too rudimentary to be able to finance the extension of the railways and roads which would be needed." [6] How would air transport be able to break this vicious circle?

Post-war Africa did experience a phase of economic prosperity though the most clear-sighted observers already recognised its undoubtedly temporary character. In the context of the short-lived riches, due to the increase in the prices of numerous raw materials and to the investment of the colonial powers in the fields of agriculture and mining, all the regions of sub-Saharan Africa experienced a veritable boom in regional air transportation. One is struck by the density of the colonial air networks. In 1954, the local networks of Air France served 75 airports in Western and Equatorial Africa and 38 in Madagascar. For its part, Sabena flew to 32 locations in the Belgian Congo. The demand for goods transport on these African regional lines was sufficiently permanent for them to be operated with what

How the aircraft created new markets: beef from Chad
Within French Equatorial Africa, the herding of animals was concentrated on the high plateaus, far removed from the tsetse fly. This is why "... Chad, along with North Cameroon, made up one enormous ranch, providing meat to the whole of the former French Equatorial Africa, and even Congo Kinshasa." [8] However there are 600 to 1,000 miles between the production area and the centres of consumption (Brazzaville, Pointe Noire, Leopoldville-Kinshasa etc).

Until 1948, the herds migrated along roads, or via the waterways, depending on the season. Overcome by the heat and exhausted by the journey, the beasts lost a lot of weight, and the quality of the meat suffered. The General Administration of French Equatorial Africa decided to change the supply system for the meat in April 1948: from then on, the animals would be slaughtered at the production sites and transported by Douglas DC-3 cargo planes to Brazzaville. In 1950, the traffic was in the order of 100 tonnes/month (one DC-3 left for Fort Lamy [9] every day at 04.50 hours in the morning, the "freshest part of the day". In 1954, scheduled services operating with mixed cargo planes connected Fort Lamy and Mundu (North Cameroon) with Duala and Brazzaville. Cold stores with a capacity of 14 pallets of fresh meat were built at Fort Lamy airport : the traffic reached 4,500 tonnes in 1960 and then evened out at about this figure. The aeroplane had increased the traffic tenfold.

"Steamer-aeroplane" transport or the birth of "sea-air" freight
Transport by "steamer-aeroplane" or "mixed mode transport" arose from a very simple comparison: in order to transport goods between France and landlocked regions of Africa, which were situated 600 miles or more from the coastal ports, freight transport by sea and land was slow and cheap, and airfreight was fast but expensive. Why not try to combine the advantages of both, by operating the fastest boats (steamers and banana boats) between France and the African ports and using air transportation out to the landlocked regions of Chad, Ubangi

and Upper Cameroon or the Niger Basin? This solution was introduced in 1951 by the airline UAT, a subsidiary of La Compagnie Maritime des Chargeurs Réunis, and taken into full-scale operation by Air France.

This "mixed mode transport" or "steamer-aeroplane" proved to be a good compromise. It ensured a transit time of around 30 days to reach the towns of the African interior, compared with three months or more by sea and land. The goods were covered by a single document from end to end of the journey (a mixed transport consignment note) and the fixed rate per kilo combined all transport operations to the final destination.

This form of transport prospered until long-haul cargo jet services were introduced between France and Africa in 1966. The resultant reduction of almost 50% in the unit operating costs allowed the introduction of a new rate structure which allowed direct flights to capture a proportion of the "steamer-aeroplane" traffic.

4 DOMESTIC TRANSPORT IN CANADA

"Air transport is a fundamental factor in the prodigious expansion of the Canadian economy." [10] In Canada, domestic transport took on many different forms, depending on whether it was a question of "aviation by the main airlines" (Trans Canada Airlines and Canadian Pacific Airlines), or "bush aviation", regional transportation for the public (Trans Air, Nordair, Quebecair, etc) or even charter operations.

Charter operations
Commencing in 1952, considerable demands for air transport were brought about by large construction projects (iron ore mining equipment for Ungava-Labrador, construction and aluminium works for Kitimat, British Columbia, powerful hydro-electric plants in Quebec) and the construction of lines of military radar installations in the far north (especially the Dew Line, designed to provide warning against Soviet air attacks). Following a classic phasing scheme, work proceeded in four stages in which passengers and goods were inseparably associated:

1. Site preparation period: light aircraft transport personnel and equipment (Cessna 180).

2. Transport of surveying and research equipment in aircraft with a carrying capacity of 700 to 1,200kg (Otters, Norsemen).

3. Completion of construction programme: use of wide-bodied aircraft (DC-3, DC-4, C-54).

4. Construction completed and production underway: regular mixed services for passengers, goods and mail.

These charter operations, linked with the fulfilment of major mining, hydroelectric or military projects, obviously varied greatly from one year to the next. The traffic increased from 28,000 tonnes in 1954 to 79,000 tonnes in 1955, to reach 111,000 tonnes in 1956, and then fell to 58,000 tonnes in 1958. The contribution of air transport was particularly valuable in the opening up of the Ungava-Labrador Mine. [11] In 1884, a Canadian geologist discovered one of the world's largest deposits of magnetic haematite on the Labrador plateau, northwest of Quebec. The deposit of Ungava-Labrador, which formed a strip of over 600 miles in length and 50 miles in width, had to wait more than 50 years before it was exploited, due to the " particular hostility of the environment: until recent times the only means of transport were by canoe in summer and dog sled in winter". For a period of some 10 years between 1936 and 1948, the Labrador Mining and Exploration Company carried out the systematic mapping and evaluation of the deposit. Even in this preliminary stage, the contribution of the aeroplane was absolutely crucial: the prospecting teams and all their equipment were carried to the various working sites by sea-planes, which landed on the innumerable lakes of the region. The results from the prospecting work were positive: there was a deposit of economically exploitable ore located 340 miles from the port of Sept Iles, on the northern side of the St. Lawrence River. The workings of the deposit required the construction of a railway line linking the port with the centre of the

The development of imports and exports by air between the United States and the Asian countries of the Pacific Rim (in tonnes)

	1964	1970	1975
Exports by air			
to Japan	3,430	20,700	35,450
to the other countries	1,770	15,920	30,835
Total	5,200	36,620	66,285
Imports by air			
from Japan	3,900	23,975	51,230
from the other countries	1,830	30,720	103,000
Total	5,730	54,695	154,230
Exports and Imports			
Japan	7,330	44,675	86,680
other countries	3,600	46,640	133,835
Total	10,930	91,315	220,515

Source: US Bureau of the Census

mining district, where the township of Schefferville would be constructed.

As soon as the decision to start the workings was reached, an air company was set up, Hollinger Ungava Transport Ltd. Its aircraft were to play a decisive role in transporting the men who built the railroad and in carrying the materials necessary to keep pace with the progress of the work.

In spite of the rigours of the climate (the thermometer fell below -50°C!), the construction work was finished in record time, thanks to a judicious use of all available means of transport, "from dog sleds to canoes towing rafts, via tractors, to trucks pulling trailers on skids". But above all "this task would have been much more difficult and infinitely slower without the gigantic airlift. It proved the marvellous effectiveness of air transport in opening up isolated regions totally lacking in means of surface transport." As with the railroad, the dam for the provision of energy to the mining district was constructed through the employment of an airlift. "Every man, every machine, every piece of equipment, every gallon of fuel, every pound of food was, almost without exception, transported by plane from Mont Joli or Sept Iles to various landing strips which were constructed as work progressed, along the path of the railway." In total, between 1950 and 1954, during the course of the work, 5,753 flights were made, carrying 41,370 passengers, and 18,000 tonnes of supplies, almost entirely in Douglas DC-3s.

5 THE EMERGENCE OF ASIA AND THE IRRESISTIBLE ASCENDANCE OF THE PACIFIC

Until 1965, the North Pacific remained only a secondary air sector in comparison with the North Atlantic. Between 1965 and 1970, traffic developed explosively and went on growing. Between 1964 and 1975, over a period of 11 years, American exports by air to Asian companies bordering the Pacific grew by 26% per year, while air imports from these countries increased by over 30% annually. The changes were even more

spectacular if one only looks at the four famous "Tiger Economies": Korea, Hong Kong, Taiwan and Singapore. The airfreight traffic between the United States and these four countries literally soared from 1,864 tonnes in 1964 to 113,670 tonnes in 1975! So far as trade by air between the United States and Japan was concerned, this showed a continuous and better balanced growth, from 7,330 tonnes in 1964 to 44,675 tonnes in 1970 and 86,680 tonnes in 1975. Under these conditions, the relative importance of the North Pacific in comparison to the North Atlantic, expressed in gross tonnes, progressed rapidly: 22.2% in 1970 to 38.5% in 1975.

Elsewhere, the developing trade by air between Europe and Asia was reflected in the opening of new cargo routes. Up to the end of the 1960s, the only all-cargo links between Europe and Asia were between Hong Kong and Great Britain.

The first cargo flight between Europe and Japan was inaugurated on 1st April 1969. This was a weekly Frankfurt/Paris/Tokyo service by a B707C operated on a joint, triangular basis between Air France, Japan Airlines and Lufthansa. The pressure of traffic was such that a second service followed on 5th March 1970, and then a third on 1st November of the same year. The first cargo flight between Europe and Korea was launched on 6th October 1973 between Paris and Seoul, by Air France and Korean Airlines.

The Asian-Pacific region in total went through a formidable expansion for goods sent by air: between 1964 and 1973, over a period of 10 years, the freight traffic of the Asian airlines increased on average by 26% per year, and traffic through the Asian airports by 27%.

Asia was threatening the supremacy of the North Atlantic, and was challenging all the established airfreight rankings.

6 AN UNUSUAL SERVICE: A CROSS CHANNEL AIR-FERRY FOR ACCOMPANIED CARS

Is it freight or passenger traffic? Neither one thing, nor the other: a mixed service combining automobiles and passengers.

British tourists eager to discover the Continent loaded their vehicles onto a specially adapted aircraft (with large doors opening in the front section of the plane, and loading ramps) and collected them at the other side of the Channel.

The cross-Channel service for accompanied vehicles was launched on 14 July 1948 between Lympne in England and Le Touquet in France, by the British private airline Silver City Airways, flying a Bristol Freighter aircraft. This new service rapidly proved to be a success: it fulfiled a need at a time when British tourists were rediscovering the Continent after the privations of the war, and when sea transport was not competitive. Silver City opened other routes to Calais and Ostende – the main competitor to Le Touquet – and also between Southampton and Cherbourg.

But Silver City became the victim of its own success: in 1954 it was purchased by the mighty Peninsula and Oriental Steam Navigation Company (P & O). With the help of the financial muscle of this new shareholder, the car ferry activities assumed new dimensions.

1 Opening of a "Vehicle ferry terminal" or "Ferryfield" near Lydd (which replaced Lympne).
2 Extension of the car ferry formula to other links between England and Ireland.
3 Introduction of a new type of cargo aircraft, the Bristol 170 MK 32.

The success was such that it attracted the competition. A new British company, Air Charter, opened routes from Southend to Calais and Ostende. Then the small French airline Air Transport took a share of the traffic between Lydd and Le Touquet in association with Silver City which celebrated its 100,000th cross Channel flight in July 1957.

The "car ferry" service reached its peak during the years 1955/1965, reaching a figure of 100,000 cars per year. During the summer months (the traffic was very seasonal) the airport at Le Touquet was extremely busy, with 64,000 vehicles passing through during 1962, or more than 60 flights per day through Lydd in July–August 1965. The number of aircraft movements were reaching their operational limit. They had to find an aircraft with larger capacity – it was to be the Carvair, a converted Douglas DC-4 (with a swing nose door at the front and the pilot's cockpit above the freight cabin) capable of carrying five average sized cars. The Carvair was introduced in 1963 by Channel Air Bridge, which had taken over Air Charter in 1960, to become British United Air Ferries soon afterwards, and then British Air Ferries.

The year 1964 was marked by an important event, which presaged a new era with the reorganisation of the British operating airlines: British Air Ferries bought up the car ferry activities of Silver City. But the end was in sight with the appearance of new sea transport technologies (roll on/roll off ferries and Hovercraft) which were much more competitive. From 1965 onwards traffic declined, and then collapsed in 1970. British Air Ferries was sold and entered a period of severe financial difficulties. The Lydd–Le Touquet service was closed on 1 October 1970. Subsequently, cars were taken across the Channel by boat or by rail via the Channel Tunnel. Nevertheless the cross-Channel car ferry services still represent a noteworthy success for air transport: over a million cars were carried by air between Great Britain and the Continent.

8 THE POST, OR THE ABANDONED BRIDE

The growing number of chapters concentrated on freight give us insight into a new situation: the Post is no longer the chief concern of the airlines. After making such an enormous contribution to the birth of commercial aviation, it was pushed into second place by goods traffic, not to mention passengers. It was abandoned, wrongly so, if one considers its development potential and its contribution to the net profit of the carriers, but for one very simple reason: "Whereas in 1938 the revenues obtained from the mail still represented around 50% of the total, they only stood at 9% in 1951, 5% in 1960, 4% in 1970 and 2% in 1975."

Comparative development of mail and freight traffic
World scheduled traffic
(in millions RTK)

	Freight	Mail	Total (cargo)	Total mail
1938	12	36	53	68%
1946	120	100	220	45%
1950	770	200	970	21%
1960	2,160	610	2,770	22%
1970	10,460	2,750	13,210	21%

Source: ICAO

This collapse was the culmination of a pincer movement: on the one side, the extraordinary expansion of both passenger and goods traffic, and the marked fall in mail average unit revenue on the other.

Nevertheless, postal traffic also experienced a phase of strong growth. From 1950 until 1970, its development paralleled that of freight traffic, with annual average rates of expansion of 12% from 1950 to 1960, and of 17% between 1960 and 1970.

The relative reduction of postal income between 1951 and 1970 therefore results from the reduction of the income per unit by two thirds, due to the decline in rates, and the change in the make-up of traffic. Expressed in American cents per revenue tonne kilometre carried, it fell from 67.5 in 1951 to 22.7 in 1970, getting much closer to the level freight unit revenue.

1 INTERNATIONAL AIRMAIL

International airmail developed at the same pace as domestic mail (+15% per year between 1950 and 1970) made up almost half of the world's traffic: 45% in 1950 and 48% in 1970. It was transported "almost exclusively on scheduled passenger services" [1] which in 1961 took on an average postal load of 380kg. As in the case of passengers or goods, the North Atlantic was the busiest international route, responsible for a quarter of international mail, with a traffic volume of 16,000 tonnes in 1960 and almost 47,000 tonnes in 1970.

Development of relationships between the Post and the airlines
The Congresses of the Universal Postal Union, of which the most important were those of Paris in 1947 and Brussels in 1952, punctuated the relationships between the Post and the airlines. Neither the extreme courtesy of tone, nor the mutual respect of the delegates from both camps, were sufficient to paper over the fundamental differences which separated IATA and UPU immediately after the war. On the one hand, the airlines, worried about their uncertain financial situation and still under the influence of the generous pre-war postal payments, could not accept with good grace to pass on generously to the Postal Administrations the financial benefits which had resulted from technical progress. All the more so, since the airlines suspected them of not totally passing on the rate reductions regarding the lower levels of airmail surcharges paid by the end user. For their part, the Post Offices were not at all keen to continue acting as the providers of indirect subsidies, and suspecting they had been previously "taken to the cleaners", now wished to be treated rather as demanding clients, fully aware of their full value, than as bountiful administrations.

The crucial problem regarding the basis of the airlines' rates of remuneration lay at the heart of all their discussions: should the postal rate reflect the cost of transport, or take into account the value of the service? And when the postal authorities repeatedly demanded that the level of airmail rates should be harmonised with the operating costs of the most efficient aircraft, IATA replied that "the rates charged by the operators for the carriage of mail were not out of line with normal rate-making practice, which took into consideration the value of the service to the user". [2]

Development of revenue of scheduled air carriers of ICAO member states
(In current US cents per RTK)

1. Changes in percentage of each type of revenue from scheduled services

Income source	1951	1955	1960	1965	1970	1975	1980
Passengers	78.3	81.6	84.9	85.0	85.6	85.8	86.4
Freight	12.6	11.8	9.9	10.4	10.6	12.0	11.7
Mail	9.1	6.6	5.2	4.6	3.8	2.2	1.9
Total	100	100	100	100	100	100	100

2. Changes in unit sales revenue by income source

Income source	1951	1955	1960	1965	1970	1975	1980
Passengers	42.9	43.6	44.8	42.4	40.8	58.0	83.0
Freight	23.4	26.2	22.9	18.2	16.7	24.1	35.2
Mail	67.5	51.4	43.2	36.7	22.7	32.1	47.2

Source: ICAO

In 1947, the Paris Congress made a great contribution to maintaining the airlines in their illusions. In fact, it met their wishes on a number of points:

• by establishing a semi-official line of communication between IATA and the Executive and Liaison Commission of the UPU – which had just been created by the Congress;

• by accepting remuneration rates in accordance with the wishes of IATA;

• by recommending that the amount of air surcharges should be a direct function of the air transport rates: "this is of particular importance to operators, since it means that any reduction in the rates paid to them will be passed on to the public automatically and will, therefore, result in a greater volume of mail" [3];

• by ruling that correspondence transported by plane for distances of up to 2,000km [1,250 miles] on European and related services, would be exempt from surcharge.

This was a fundamental new trend expressing "a general tendency among the Post Offices and the airlines to accept progressively the whole of the mail for carriage without surcharge. [4] The French Postal Service took a leading role in this change, and decided by stages to abolish air surcharges for North Africa (12th June 1945), for the totality of its Overseas Territories and Departments (10th January 1949) and then for Europe, following the recommendations of the Paris Congress (9th May 1950).

Alongside these decisions, which were likely to maintain the airlines in a false sense of security, delegates at the Paris Congress adopted several recommendations, which better expressed their fundamental views:

1. "Rates of air transportation charges are unacceptably high". With the benefit of hindsight, the tariff agreement of the Paris Congress was rather surprising. Since it had not succeeded in abolishing the geographical distinction between "ordinary services" and "extraordinary services" it substituted them with the concept of Category A services ("European and other services whose operational costs are similar"), and Category B ("services whose maintenance involves greater expense").

Taking the lead from IATA, the Congress retained the rate of 3 gold francs per kilometric tonne for Category A services and 6 gold francs for those of Category B. This was absurd from an economic point of view, since the rates were modified in contradiction to the movement in unit costs, since unit costs fall with increasing distance! When voicing its recommendation, Congress took the opportunity of formulating its wishes: 2 gold francs instead of 3 and 5 francs instead of 6.

It also specified that the rates adopted should be the upper limit, and several delegates could not restrain themselves from remarking that airlines allowed, on a bilateral basis, negotiations for charges below the official rates.

2. *"Air transportation charges should always be proportioned, in a just and equitable manner, to the rates charged by air carriers for the transportation of passengers. For correspondence other than letters, postcards, money and collection orders, as well as for postal subscriptions (LC, or first class post), the charges should not exceed the rates required by the airlines for the transport of similar goods (AO or second class post)."*

In October 1947, a UPU Observer at the Annual General Meeting of IATA, underlined the "paramount importance" which the Congress placed upon the creation of a second class of airmail in order to "promote the development of the press and advertising of trade and industries". One can see how the change was taking shape: replacing a differentiation of postal rates according to distance – which was very much open to criticism in the way it was structured – by a distinction according to the items carried (LC, from the French "Lettres, Cartes Postales"- "letters and cards", and AO, from the French "Autres Objets" – "other objects/items").

In other words, the UPU delegates requested the airlines:

1. to charge second class mail (printed matter, business papers, newspapers, samples) all AO category at the same rate as now applied to the carriage of freight by air;
2. to adjust the transportation charges for the first class mail (letters, post cards, money orders) or LC category to the fares applicable to passengers.

3. *"The Executive and Liaison Commission is directed to contact the International Civil Aviation Organisation with a view to making arrangements with the airlines in order that they undertake definitively to grant absolute priority to postal despatches."*

Although at first sight this is a legitimate wish, it is noted that the idea of priority for airmail can only be justified by a high level of remuneration, and that any attack on remuneration rates will necessarily endanger the question of priority.

In consequence, various contacts were made from 1948 to 1952 between IATA and the Executive and Liaison Commission of the UPU, in order to attempt to develop a common position. To put it correctly, it was more a question of discussions than negotiations, since the Congress had sovereignty in remuneration matters. However, it seems that a kind of consensus was arrived at, which maintained the status quo for LC and introduced rates of 1.50 francs for AO and 1 franc for newspapers.

What happened in fact? Were the IATA representatives deluding themselves or did the Congress repudiate the views of the members of the Executive and Liaison Commission? At all events, it came as a severe blow when the Brussels Congress, irritated by the claims of IATA, finally imposed its own view:

• The abolition of Categories A and B in favour of a single rate of 3 gold francs per tonne kilometre for LC mail. Instead, however, as a temporary measure, a rate of 4 gold francs was allowed for services corresponding to the former "Category B services".

• The introduction (which was only rubber stamping an already widespread practice) of two new postal categories: for AO (Other Objects) at 1.25 francs and newspapers at 1 franc.

On a more technical note, the Congress simplified the accounting provisions applying to airmail and, for the first time, regulated the conditions for the use of airmail letters (pre-printed forms/aerograms).

For the leaders of IATA, the Brussels remuneration decisions were interpreted as an imposition of brute force by the UPU Congress. "To say that this vote came as a shock is to make an understatement." [5] More than the content, it was the manner in which the decision was reached that aroused indignation: "It is necessary to emphasise that this vote was unilateral, it was reached without discussion or negotiation with your representatives." The wound still had not closed by 1956, when Sir William once more put a coruscating pen to paper, but not without a certain logic: "This is a very strange situation: the user of the service sets the rate without the transporter having any say in the matter at all."

Once the anger had subsided, they returned to the road of "amicable contacts". Both sides stuck to their positions on a matter of principle, but technological progress, by reducing unit costs and bringing massive increases in capacity, made it easier for views to converge. In 1961, IATA expressed satisfaction about "the harmonious exchanges with the UPU". The Tokyo Congress in 1969 took two major decisions, which were in line with the views of the Association:

1. "The elimination of the last traces of the Extraordinary Services by abolishing the famous 'temporary arrangement' established by the Brussels Congress. Rate changes according to the nature of the postal items (LC or AO) replace the distance-dependent rate (medium-haul or long-haul): 3 gold francs for LC and 1 gold franc for AO.
2. "The maximum utilisation of airborne post for transporting mail"- which was to be referred to, in a terrible expression, as: "maximalisation".

Even in 1947, the Director General of the French Post observed that "the aeroplane is increasingly becoming the normal and current means of transport for mail". One of the delegates at the Vienna Congress [6] in 1964 noted that "as the years go by, there is an increasingly dominant tendency to regard the aircraft as the normal and usual means for the carriage of mail". The Tokyo Congress made the decisive step and set up as a guiding principle: "the use of the aeroplane as the normal means of carrying mail". [7]

Development of rate for the transport of international airmail
(in gold francs per RTK)

Categories	Paris Congress 1947	Brussels Congress 1952	Tokyo Congress 1969
1. for services			
Services Category A	3	3	-
Services Category B	6	4	-
2. Postal classification			
L.C.	-		3
A.O.	-	1.25	1
Newspapers	-	1.00	

The adoption of this principle opened a new chapter in relationships between the Post and the airlines. For their part, the airlines undertook "studies regarding the transport by air of surface mail", which showed that the penetration of the postal market by air transport was only 50% for LC and 10% for AO.

"Our overall objective is to attract towards air transport the majority of mail which is currently moved by surface, through the application of rate levels which are acceptable to the public, viable for the Postal Administrations, and profitable for the airlines." [8]

This outlined a good area of common ground in terms of studies and measures taken, with view to the 1970s and beyond.

2 DOMESTIC AIRMAIL

Domestic airmail was an altogether different context. Here, the Universal Postal Union no longer had any competence. Universal rulings were replaced by bilateral relationships between Post Offices and airlines within the conditions applying in each state.

The United States: the use of scheduled airlines

During the years 1950–1970 the United States, with the extent of its territory and the intensity of its exchanges of correspondence, the density of its air network and its unequalled airmail tradition, represented over 80% of domestic airmail within the entire membership of the ICAO. [9]

Two decisions, one taken by the CAB and the other by Congress at the beginning of the 1950s, enabled a rapid clarification of the legal framework for relations between the Post and the airlines:

1. The CAB, on 19th September 1951, made an unmistakable pronouncement in favour of the theory of cost of transport in contrast to that of the value of service: "Accordingly, the future service rate for the period on and after 1st January 1951 will be based upon the cost of mail of the big four carriers [10] for the year 1950." [11]

2. From 1949 onwards, the Congress adopted a group of measures in order to make an explicit separation between remuneration for postal services and the allocation of subsidies. This movement, was implemented in 1949 by the Representative John F. Kennedy, who wished to determine the true profitability of domestic air transport and to introduce more rigorous public accounting principles. On 1st October 1953 it resulted in the transfer from the Post to the CAB of that part of postal remunerations which might be considered as a subsidy.

From then on, subsidies were allocated as such, to the benefit of local airlines and helicopter services. For their part, the major airlines were no longer in receipt of subsidies which were disguised through "adjustments" in the postal remuneration, as American Airlines emphasised strongly in its annual report for 1950: "American receives no subsidy for carrying mail. The US Post Office Department pays American almost exactly the same rate per pound-mile for mail that the company charges for carrying passengers."

Even before these decisions had been taken formally, the Postmaster General had received in his office a document dated 15th March 1946 entitled: "The Future of airmail transportation". [12]

Outlining the development perspectives in the new technological context after the war, it put its finger on three essential points:

• the long-distance transport of first class mail (LC): although this was the market for the future "neither the Department nor the air carriers are presently equipped to handle the volume of non-local first-class and airmail combined by air";

• the rate for remunerating the airlines: "It appears inconceivable that the transportation of mail should cost more than other kinds of traffic" (freight and passengers);

• the carriage of mail on exclusive charter flights which "could be operated on schedules best meeting the needs of the postal service."

The American Post Office did not follow up this last recommendation for many years, due to the influence in Washington of the "lobby" on behalf of the large airlines. During the period under consideration, the Post Office frequently took advantage of the services of scheduled airlines, which at the time operated a certain number of night flights, for both airfreight and passengers. In particular between the East Coast and the West Coast.

Thanks to the supply of an enormous volume of capacity operated by regular carriers, the Post was able to increase its domestic traffic 15-fold between 1950 and 1970. In 1970, it reached a total of 1,165 billion tonne kilometres, corresponding to 85% of the total of domestic airmail, and 44% of the world's airmail.

The invention of jet aircraft provided an opportunity for the CAB to reaffirm its doctrine – "the mail rate should be based entirely on the cost of providing the service, including a fair profit" [13] and of declaring a new rate reduction which caused a fresh spurt of growth in surcharge airmail. On the other hand, in 1965 the US Post Office started to transfer to airmail increasing quantities of non-surcharged first class mail. Since it was loaded on the basis of space available in the holds of passenger aircraft, it paid a rate which was over 50% lower than that for true airmail. At this time in 1968, the tonnage of non-surcharged mail exceeded that of surcharged airmail.

Under these circumstances, the average unit revenue paid by the Post to the American airlines showed a fall of 48% between 1958 and 1968, and the proportion of postal income within the turnover of the carriers kept on reducing, until it reached a figure around 2%. Nevertheless, even in 1970, "the Postal Service is the nation's largest single shipper" [14] in providing 165 million dollars of income for the airlines.

At the beginning of the 1970s, came various signs that times were changing:

1. The elimination of several hundred night flights by scheduled airlines in 1970/71 due to the economic crisis. The Post found itself in a tricky situation, and had to reconsider the possibility of operating means of transport exclusively for its own use. Until then, the only exception to the rule of using the capacity on scheduled flights for carrying mail had been the chartering, authorised by the CAB, of night-time air taxis to ensure service to a large number of small communities.

2. The efforts by the Post to escape the tariff supervision of the CAB. It tried to replace the system in force by a procedure involving calls to tender in order to encourage competition between airlines. In 1971, the Post had to back down in front of the CAB which was still all-powerful, but it had succeeded in mapping out a road for the future.

3. The first experiment at "Express Mail" was launched in 1970. These were the beginnings of a movement of which no one foresaw the future magnitude.

4. The increased emphasis on the policy of sending non-surcharged, first class post by air, alongside surcharged airmail. This situation, which was becoming more and more bizarre, reached a logical conclusion in 1977 with the elimination of "airmail" as a postal category. From then on, the postal service normally used air transport to carry first class (LC) mail over long distances.

India: the early introduction of a postal network
The Indian Postal Service carried out a particularly interesting experiment with an airmail night service between 1949 and 1951. Indian Night Air Mail, which was launched on 30th January 1949, was operated by a fleet of four Douglas DC-3s. The network was started up with two daily services (Delhi/Madras and Bombay/Calcutta) which crossed at around midnight in Nagpur in the centre of the country, for the transfer of mail sent from the main economic centres. Although it was initially reserved for surcharged mail, the service was opened up to first class deliveries on 1st April 1949. The traffic at that time was around 6 tonnes per day. The airlines were paid by the Post on the basis of the freight rate increased by 25%.

Europe: night airmail services
In Europe, with its shorter distances and efficient means of surface transport, the problem of carrying domestic mail by air did not arise on a continental scale, but in the more limited context of each constituent country. In these circumstances, air transport could only make an impression if it absolutely fulfilled the following conditions: "complete reliability, whatever the weather; accuracy of timetables; connections provided exclusively at night within determined time bands; and finally an acceptable cost within the framework of a single rate charged over the whole of the territory".[15] The scene was set, with emphasis on the particularly European characteristics of airmail: whereas the American Post surcharged the "air mail" up to 1977, and used capacities available on scheduled airlines, the European postal services carried ordinary mail without surcharge using chartered aircraft operating at night for their exclusive use. They all were trying to reach the same objective: that a letter posted at the end of the afternoon on day one at any point in the territory could be delivered to its addressee with the first delivery on day two. Only the aeroplane, integrated into a system, which would closely link it with other transport methods, could allow this performance level to be achieved on a permanent basis.

The particular geographical characteristics of Europe and its varied means of terrestrial transport led European postal administrations to develop different systems for night-time airmail networks. We can differentiate between networks operating through one or more hubs, and systems based on point-to-point flights.[16]

• Single hub network systems
In Germany the night air postal system started up on 1st September 1961. It was operated by Lufthansa on behalf of the Postal Administration and, in 1975, linked the airports of Bremen, Frankfurt am Main, Hamburg, Hannover, Cologne/Bonn, Munich, Nuremberg and Stuttgart. The mail was transferred at Frankfurt, which was the hub of the network. The first flights left at 22.55 hours, and the last landed at 02.35 hours: the whole operation, including flights and the transfer of the mail only took 3 hours 40 minutes. For these postal services, Lufthansa used the aircraft which had been put into service for its daytime flights: Boeing 737 passenger and QC aircraft and Boeing 727-200s carrying between 8 and 15.8 tonnes of mail. Berlin West was connected to the network via a Pan American cargo flight. In 1970, traffic amounted to 32,500 tonnes, rising to 37,200 tonnes in 1975.

In Italy the night flights started much later, on 11th October 1974. As in Germany, the Postal Administration excluded the possibility of operating its own fleet, which was considered too expensive. The network, consisting of 14 night flights – of which 13 crossed at Rome Fiumicino Airport – was operated by Alitalia and Itavia, using DC-9, Caravelle, DC-6B, Viscount, Fokker 27 and Dart Herald aircraft. In 1975, traffic amounted to between 40 and 50 tonnes per day.

Spain started operating its first night airmail service in 1954 between Madrid and Barcelona, for the carriage of non-surcharged letters and postcards.

In 1975, Spain had a night post network connecting Madrid with Barcelona, Valencia, Palma, Seville and Malaga. The airline Aviaco carried out the flights on behalf of the Postal Administration. It made six flights per night from Monday to Saturday, and the schedules were so designed that all the flights crossed at Madrid for transhipment of the mail. Aviaco operated one Caravelle, one DC-9 and one Fokker 27. As a particularly Spanish feature, these machines were also used for transporting newspapers.

Sweden started its night service in 1958 using chartered cargo planes on the Malmö/Stockholm and Stockholm/Göteborg/Stockholm services at the request of businesses, who were unhappy with only having the existing rail connections. In 1975, the network consisted of five services operated five times a week from Monday to Friday, all passing via Stockholm, so as to offer the maximum number of connecting flights:

Stockholm/Malmö/Stockholm
Stockholm/Visby (on the island of Gotland)/Stockholm
Stockholm/Umea/Lulea/Umea/Stockholm
Stockholm/Carlstat/Borlänge
Stockholm/Carlstat/Borlänge/Stockholm.

By operating this network, the Swedish Administration learned a general lesson: "the best solution is arrived at when all the methods of transport, rail, road and air, are used in harmonious combination". Night flights are only one link in a chain, an essential component in a wider system.

• Multi-hub network systems
France, "where postal aviation by night is the direct descendant of the famous Aéropostale",[17] provides the most notable example. We'll come back to it later.

Let us now consider Czechoslovakia, "where the geographic and economic structure, particularly with regard to the decentralised location of the two largest cities, Prague and Bratislava, caused the postal administration to set up a night air network which, in combination with post trains and postal trucks, solved a number of problems for the postal service."[18]

In the Five-Year Plan for 1951 – this was still a socialist economy – the Czechoslovak Post was given the objective of distributing LC mail and urgent post packages on a next-day service, as long as they were posted before a certain cut-off time on the previous evening. This was impossible to achieve with "rapid" trains travelling at 35mph, and requiring 20 hours to cross the country from east to west. Nor were day-time passenger flights the appropriate tool. Only the night-time postal flights could provide the answer.

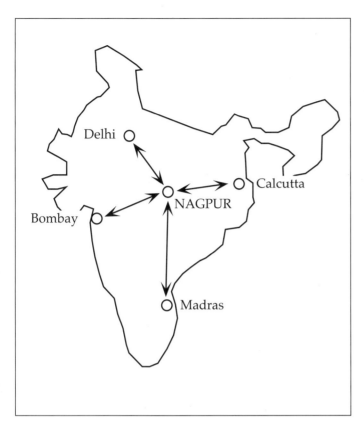

LEFT **Origins of the Indian night post network – 1949-1951**

BELOW **Night airmail network in the Federal Republic of Germany in 1977.**
Union Postale, 1/1977

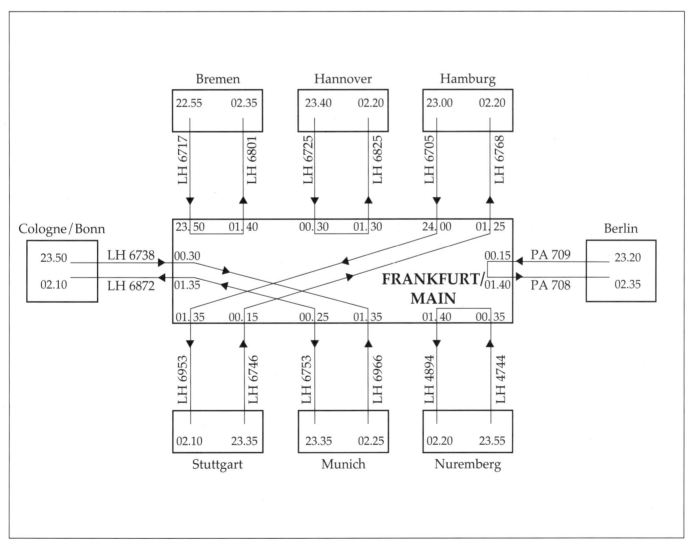

The first night postal service was opened in 1952: Bratislava/Brno/Prague/Pilzen (410 miles) on a DC-3. This service was not entirely satisfactory, even though it brought some improvement. Apart from during the winter months with their high rate of interruptions, the objective was only achieved in 1954, by operating two postal services from Monday to Saturday:

• Prague/Brno/Zvolen (in Slovakia);

• Prague/Bratislava/Kosice (in Slovakia).

The unusual feature of these services, which were operated by the airline CSA using Ilyushin Il-14s, carrying a maximum of 3 tonnes, lay in the equipment on board the aircraft, which were fitted out as mobile sorting offices, similar to the special postal trains (which were limited to distances below 150 miles) or postal trucks.

• Point-to-point flights
These serve two or more localities, without a link between the different services: they do not form a network. This type of night postal flight has been operated by Denmark (Copenhagen/Billund), Great Britain (London/Belfast or Manchester/Belfast), Greece, Norway and Yugoslavia.

France: "la Postale de nuit"
It will be recalled that, as before the war, France had invested in domestic postal aviation, first of all by day (and hence doomed to failure) and later by night in 1939.

After the Armistice of June 1940, "Didier Daurat obtained from the Directorate of Post and Civil Aviation the authorisation for the renewed provision of postal air services." [19] On 5th September 1940, two circular postal routes were launched. The first left from Vichy at 17.15 hours for Limoges, Bergerac, Clermont-Ferrand, Saint-Etienne, Grenoble and Lyons, and returned to Vichy at 13.10 hours. It set off again at 13.20 hours on the same route, but this time in the reverse direction, returning at 18.55 hours. The second service left Toulouse at 7 o'clock in the morning and flew via Agen, Pau, Perpignan, Montpellier, Nîmes, Nice and Marseilles, where the plane arrived at 13.05 hours. Another plane, leaving Marseilles at 12.40 hours, made the whole journey in the reverse direction, landing in Toulouse at 18.45 hours. [19] These were all day-time flights due to the ban on night flights decreed by the German authorities. The service finally stopped on 8th November 1942 after a rather chaotic period of operation.

However, in 1943 the Director for Post initiated a study for a "plan for serving the whole of the territory through an air postal network complementing the road and rail network, with a view to ensuring intercommunication for all post offices during the night." [20] This resulted in a project for a network consisting of nine routes serving 20 stations, using aircraft with a commercial speed of 200mph, and a payload of 2,500 to 3,000kg. Once Liberation came, everything was ready – at least on paper – to get things moving. Thanks to the continuity assured by some of the officials in the Department for Post and Civil Aviation, the re-launch was remarkably fast, in spite of innumerable obstacles.

"A reduced network" [21] was set up during the course of summer 1945. It operated during the daytime between 06.00 and 12.00 hours, and enabled "the interlinking of the airports served in order to supply mail for the second afternoon delivery in the large towns." [22] It linked Paris with 10 provincial cities and carried an average of 500,000 items of mail per day, but did not fulfil the requirements of the Post. These were simply stated: "To establish an entirely autonomous system of night postal aviation, freed from limitations arising from the transport of passengers." Didier Daurat and Raymond Vanier took the matter in hand.

In order to fulfil the requirement for the operational autonomy of the Post, a specialist domestic airmail department, which was later known as the "Centre d'Exploitation Postal Métropolitain" (CEPM) was created within Air France. For the public at large, with its sense of occasion, this unprepossessing administrative acronym was soon replaced by a title which was synonymous with total technical success: the "Postale de Nuit" ("The Night Mail").

The first services were opened leaving from Le Bourget in 1945 and 1946: the Paris/Bordeaux/Toulouse/Pau service on 26th October 1945, followed by the Paris/Lyons/Marseilles/Nice service on 2nd July 1946.

The operations encountered numerous difficulties. The "chosen" aircraft, Ju52, did not fulfil the required specifications regarding speed and payload. The airports were not properly equipped for night landings in bad weather, particularly with respect to landing lights. The Civil Aviation administration in charge sometimes showed what was felt to be excessive caution, and imposed certain hotly contested operational restrictions. In spite of these obstacles, the tenacity of the men who were in charge and the self sacrifice of the crews – some losing their lives on the services – were to enable (at the cost of limited investment in ground equipment) pioneering techniques for zero visibility flying to be developed, with almost perfect success, including during thick fog:

> *"Our crews are the only ones in the world to take off every night, whatever the weather, and whatever the visibility. On occasions when others give up, the men of the Postale carry out their unsung tasks and nothing can stop their daily round."* [22] *"We were the only ones in commercial aviation throughout the world to prove by our results that the densest of fogs cannot prevent a landing."* [23]

One Paris daily newspaper, always eager for an eye-catching headline, wrote "No fogs for Air France's Postale de Nuit".

On the basis of the almost perfect reliability established in 1949, the Post expanded the network. Without going into too much detail we will mention one or two significant phases:

• 1953: opening of the third service, Paris/Lyons/Montpellier/Toulouse, which "marked the debut of a network: it was no longer a question of merely ensuring rapid communications between Paris and distant provinces, but of achieving every night the key objective: that of interlinking all the landing points."

• 1961: for its 15th anniversary, the Postale chalked up a reliability ratio of 99.76%, a good example of tight cooperation between the Post, Air France and the Department of Civil Aviation.

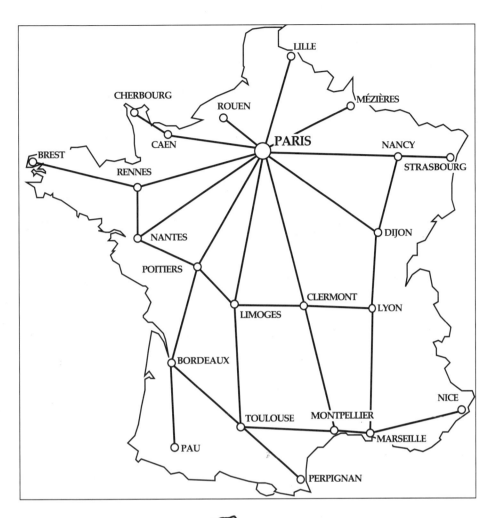

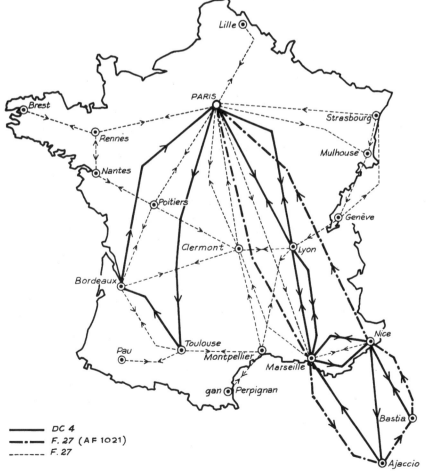

ABOVE LEFT **Project for an air postal network for Metropolitan France.**
Source: Revue des PTT, No 1, May-June 1946

LEFT **French internal night mail 1st March 1971.**
Source: Air France-La Documentation française

235

LEFT Air France DC-3 freighter.
Air France

BELOW DC-3 on the Air France night mail, c. 1950.
Air France

BOTTOM Air France Transall C-160 on domestic airmail network.
Air France

BELOW RIGHT Loading an Air France Transall at night — the containers are lined up and waiting by the side.
Air France

• 1962: development of two-way links between the air postal services and the post buses, which were specially equipped for sorting mail en route (examples: Poitiers/Saintes-Narbonne/Montpellier).

• 1966: the inauguration of the first transversal service, from province to province (Strasbourg/Mulhouse/Geneva/Lyons). Decentralisation had made its appearance.

Elsewhere another important development occurred on 4th October 1964: the Postale de Nuit was transferred from Le Bourget to Orly at the request of the Post.

At the same time, the network went on growing, and traffic developed: from 1,346 tonnes in 1946 it grew to 2,650 tonnes in 1950, reaching 32,406 tonnes in 1970 and 42,750 tonnes in 1975.[24] This was a result not only of the network but also of the fleet.

The fleet had been modernised at the same time as traffic had grown. The slow but untiring Ju52s had been replaced from 1948 onwards by DC-3s, which were faster, had wider bodies and consumed less fuel. Then the DC-4s supplemented the DC-3s on the main traffic arteries. In 1968/69 a fleet of 12 Fokker 27-500s progressively replaced the DC-3s, which in their turn had become too slow and expensive to maintain. The problem of the replacement of the DC-4s became critical from 1969: after eliminating the Caravelle 10R, which was too noisy for night flights, and the Lockheed Hercules, which was well-suited but American, the choice fell on the Franco-German Transall C-160 aircraft, introduced on 10th August 1972.

This was a Franco-German military transport plane and provided the Postale with additional load capacity (13.5 tonnes against 8 tonnes for the DC-4), an increase of speed (280mph) and the benefit of containerisation. For carrying mail it was equipped with 26 containers of almost 3m³ capacity, supported on two guide rails and locked in place in the hold by means of a system of bolts.

In 1970, the Metropolitan postal network, or the "Postale de Nuit", consisted of 11 routes (see map) including three transversal services Strasbourg/Mulhouse/Geneva/Lyons/Clermont-Ferrand/Bordeaux; Rennes/Nantes/Poitiers/Clermont; Toulouse/Montpellier/Lyons. The fleet consisted of 12 Fokker 27s and seven Douglas DC-4s.

There was a daily flight schedule, except for the night from Saturday to Sunday. The 20 towns served were all interconnected by a system of multi-hub connections (Paris, Lyons, Clermont, Montpellier etc). The reliability was almost absolute, and the stopover times were reduced to the bare minimum (in the order of 15 minutes) and the arrival and departure times for the connecting flights were extremely tight. In a word, it was a remarkable piece of timekeeping, and a fine logistical and technological success.

The size attained by the network and the acuteness of the economic problems (renewal of the fleet) led the Post and Air France to redefine their relationship. A new Convention between Air France and the French Post Office (PTT) was signed on 2nd January 1969, replacing that of 1947. It strengthened the presence of the Post in the operations of the CEPM. It established the principle that the Post should finance and supply the aircraft and spare parts, and that Air France should charge the Post with its personnel costs for flight crews, maintenance and operating staff on the basis of expenses actually incurred "with neither profit nor loss".

The activities of the Postale reached their first peak in the years 1976–1978 with a traffic approaching 48,000 tonnes, prior to the expansion of motorway services and the introduction of the first TGV postal train – even the Postale de Nuit was not immune to competition.

TOP **Air France Fokker F-27 mail aircraft.**
MAP

ABOVE **Air France DC-4, "Ciel de Bretagne".**
Air France

Part Six
The Time of the
Great Upheaval:
1970–1980

Throughout the decade 1970–1980 there was a constant series of doubts and upheavals, profound transformations and decisive developments. We will look at a few dates to guide us through the maze:

• 22nd January 1970: Pan American Airways opened the era of wide-bodied jets – or jumbos – by carrying out the first commercial flight of a Boeing 747 across the North Atlantic.

• 14th November 1970: the USSR joined the ICAO, ending 25 years of sullen non-co-operation.

• 15th August 1971: President Nixon announced the end of the convertibility of the dollar into gold, upsetting the Bretton Woods monetary system and opening the way for the introduction of floating exchange rates.

• 19th April 1972: Lufthansa introduced the Boeing 747 Freighter on the Frankfurt/New York service, crossing the psychological barrier of 100 tonnes available capacity.

• 1972: Fred Smith, at that time one of the world's greatest entrepreneurs, began running an air taxi company specialising in the carriage of small parcels, operating out of Memphis,

Tennessee. Working on totally new principles, "Federal Express" would completely change the airfreight industry.

• 1973–1979: Two oil crises, resulting from confrontations between Middle Eastern states, ended the era of cheap energy and sketched out a new map for the world economy.

• December 1973: IATA published a first global study on the future role and contribution of information technology to the airfreight industry. The transport of goods was becoming inextricably linked with the transmission of information.

• 21st January 1976: Air France and British Airways ushered in the supersonic age, the former with a flight to Rio, and the latter to Bahrain.

• 24th October 1978: The Airline Deregulation Act came into force, providing the United States with the legal instrument for deregulating air transport, which was begun on 9th November 1977 for all-cargo operations.

• July 1979: the European Commission in Brussels published a memorandum on air transport which, in spirit and general import, extended to Europe the overall principles of the great wave of liberalisation which had arisen in the United States.

Even if it was not fully abolished, "the safe and orderly growth" desired by the founding fathers in the Chicago Convention of 1944, was replaced by a strong though uneven development, shaken by numerous crises, and within an ever more challenged and uncertain institutional and regulatory framework. During this crucial decade, those changes and developments which emerged, or were imposed, would forge the general features of the world at the end of the 20th century and the beginning of the 21st century. To take up the foreboding phraseology of the singer-songwriter, it was indeed a time of "great upheaval".

Lufthansa Cargo B747-200F.
Lufthansa

1 THE END OF STABILITY AND CERTAINTY: A TIME OF CRISES

Without fear of contradiction, one can apply to air transport the words of a marine shipping expert in 1979: "Thirty years ago, the shipping world was still in a state of health ... The Bretton Woods Agreement guaranteed fixed exchange rates between the main currencies. Shipping conferences were solid organisations. This has all changed, and it seems to us that, these days, the commercial operations of the shipping companies are like sailing through thick fog without radar." [1] Within a few years, the stable and reassuring world of continuous growth and written regulations had been replaced by a disconcerting environment of intermittent growth, subjected to the implicit laws of market economics, which are not recorded in any international treaty. The former linear development gave way to progress interrupted by crises. Even more serious and disconcerting, those clear groupings, which lulled many into greater security by creating an impression that they belonged to a finite world, were replaced by vague and ill-defined organisations which challenged the well-established demarcations and traditional categories. This is how the airlines could begin to act as freight forwarders, while freight forwarders operated powerful cargo fleets, charter companies offered scheduled services and vice versa, whilst the Post, under threat in its noblest activity, urgent letters, threw itself into the express parcels business. The content of the most dependable of categories became uncertain. One could no longer even rely on the meaning of words!

1 THE TIME OF CRISES: THE ECONOMIC CRISIS

No one foresaw the economic downturn at the beginning of the 1970s, neither the OECD economists, nor the IATA experts. On the contrary, these latter, comforted by the forecasts of the former, were predicting an acceleration in the growth and development of traffic: based on a growth rate of almost 10% a year for international trade, they forecast an average annual expansion rate of 20% for airfreight traffic during the decade 1970–1980. Freight traffic was set to grow from 11 to 66 billion tonne kilometres between 1970 and 1980. [2] In reality, traffic actually reached a volume of 29 billion tonne kilometres in 1980: a reduction of 56% against the forecast made 10 years before.

One cannot blame the IATA forecasters. They were only showing their unshakeable faith in the continuation of growth which had already endured for the previous 25 years, [3] and expressed so forcibly by the experts of the OECD.

This new economic phase began in 1970, but did not reveal itself in the form of a general crisis, nor even of a recession, since traffic continued to grow on average by 10% a year between 1970 and 1980. Instead, it was defined by an anarchic succession of expansions, stagnations and resumptions of growth, varying from country to country and year to year, as is demonstrated in the following extracts from IATA Annual Reports, and other studies:

• July 1971: "The profound crisis in air cargo transport continued throughout the year 1971" (Air France, internal document);

• September 1972: The American journal, "Cargo Airlift" evoked the "slump in airfreight" and spoke of "a recession psychology";

• November 1973: "The OECD countries experienced a strong economic growth in 1972" (IATA, Annual Report, November 1973);

• November 1975: " (Following the first oil crisis) the 1974–1975 economic recession has become the most severe in the post-war period" (IATA Annual Report, 6th October 1975);

• February 1976: "During the last two or three years, the ailing international economy has been trying to catch its second wind ... it seems to be a kind of wasting disease" (IATA Bulletin, 1976, No 8);

• November 1976: IATA Annual Report for November 1976 reports "the end of the recession" and "a pronounced turn-round which started in mid–1975";

• November 1977: "1976 was a year of rapid growth in world trade";

• November 1979: "For the third year in succession, the financial results of the airlines have improved";

• October 1981: As the result of the "world recession" caused by the second oil crisis, "the airlines have registered their worst financial results since the end of the war" (IATA, Annual Report, 1981).

Thus the world had entered into a period of economic instability, which was globally described as a "crisis", consisting of an often rapid and violent succession of growth and recession periods, that were either caused, maintained or worsened by the oil crises (see Chapter 3) and the widespread currency instability.

2 A TIME OF UNSTABLE CURRENCIES: MONETARY CRISES AND FLOATING EXCHANGE RATES

In order to promote international trade, the post-war organisers had conceived of a system of stable exchange rates. Based on a fixed relationship between the ancient security for currencies – gold – and the unit of currency of the great victor nation – the dollar – it assumed that the dollar could be converted into gold at the rate of $35 for 1 ounce of gold. From that point, the various currencies were defined according to a fixed relationship with the dollar, which could only be modified by solemn decisions, as devaluations or revaluations from case to case. The system depended more on confidence in the dollar than in gold, since the level of gold stocks in the American Federal Reserve Bank was far from allowing the real conversion into gold of the ever increasing volumes of dollars in circulation throughout the world. It was a decline in confidence towards American power which would bring about increasing pressure on the dollar and trigger Richard Nixon's historic decision.

But the principle of stable parities based on the convertibility of the dollar did not suddenly shift to that of flexible exchange rates. Matters proceeded "in three successive stages: first with the abandonment of the convertibility of the dollar into gold in August 1971 – then devaluations within a system of fixed exchange rates – and finally the decision to allow fully floating currency rates" [4] from 1976 onwards. This development is only one illustration, among others, of the transformation from a well-regulated, stable and reassuring world to a world of instability and bewilderment.

In the field of freight transportation, the adoption of a floating exchange rate system brought about two sets of consequences, affecting rates and the commercial situation.

Tariff consequences: the search for an ideal unit of account
In order to appreciate the full extent of the problem, one should recall that international air transport rates throughout the world were fixed, depending on the geographical zones, either in pounds sterling or in American dollars. Then they were converted into local currency: for example, the Paris/Chicago rates or fares would be expressed in French francs, but only by way of conversion of a tariff calculated in dollars, converted at a fixed exchange rate.

In this new monetary context, the two basic currencies were affected. The American dollar was devalued on two occasions, in December 1971 and then in February 1973, and the pound sterling was floated in summer 1972.

Before trying to rebuild a universal rate system based on a stable unit of value, it was necessary to do some fire-fighting and make provisional arrangements which would enable the maintenance of the real tariff levels previous to the monetary manipulations. Hence, in 1972–1973, IATA held a series of conferences known as Currency Tariff Conferences which resulted in the introduction of currency surcharges for the countries whose currencies had been devalued, or currency discounts for countries whose currencies had been revalued.

The solution adopted, although dependent on a certain sleight of hand, was ingenious. It consisted of freezing the conversion rates, which had existed before the crisis (thereafter known as the IATA conversion rates), and applying a collection of currency adjustment factors designed to correct the currency fluctuations which had arisen in the meantime. Ingenious though it was, the system could not be anything more than provisional. In the event, it was threatened by its increasing complexity due to the proliferation of surcharges and discount factors linked with the fluctuations of the currencies, in comparison with the former units of account. But provisional solutions sometimes have a long life: this one lasted 12 years.

Nevertheless, IATA immediately set out in search of "a new IATA unit of value (IUV) which would be stable, practical and worthy of confidence". [5] They thought they had found a solution in 1975 with special drawing rights (SDR) of the International Monetary Fund, but the solution met with opposition from a number of Governments. The temporary system "based on fictional values in terms of dollars and sterling" was becoming increasingly complex and incomprehensible, and it was therefore decided to abandon the over-ambitious idea of a universal unit of value, in favour of local currencies.

The IATA Conference of May 1983 adopted the new formula for currency regulation suitable for freight activities.

This new formula came into force on 1st August 1984 and involved:

• abandoning the basic currencies and replacing them by local currencies (or by the American dollar at market rates in the case of currencies which were too unstable);

• the introduction of a system of automatic rate adjustments, specified in local currencies, in cases where such currencies would fluctuate by more or less than 3% with respect to Special Drawing Rights during a period of over 20 consecutive days.

Commercial consequences: would airfreight profit from the currency fluctuations?
Currency fluctuations have obvious effects on international trade in goods, and consequently on the volume of airfreight. From this point of view, the development of trade by air between the United States and France during the years 1980–1988 offers a particularly striking example of the close correlation between monetary fluctuations and variations in goods traffic (see graphs opposite).

One can see very well that the United States made massive increases in its imports by air from France when the dollar was increasing in value against the franc; an increase of 117% in the exchange rate between 1980 and 1985 led to a growth of airborne traffic of 140% in the same period.

On the other hand, one can see that it is much more difficult for the United States to sell to France when the franc is depreciating against the dollar: a reduction of 54% in the value of the franc from 1980 to 1985 corresponds to a 36% decrease

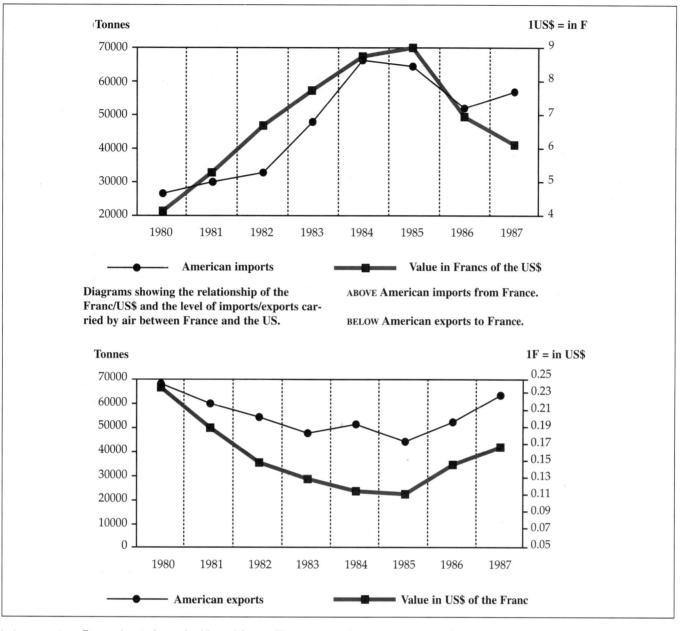

Tonnes

1US$ = in F

| | 1980 | 1981 | 1982 | 1983 | 1984 | 1985 | 1986 | 1987 |

— American imports   ■ Value in Francs of the US$

Diagrams showing the relationship of the Franc/US$ and the level of imports/exports carried by air between France and the US.

ABOVE **American imports from France.**

BELOW **American exports to France.**

Tonnes

1F = in US$

| | 1980 | 1981 | 1982 | 1983 | 1984 | 1985 | 1986 | 1987 |

— American exports   ■ Value in US$ of the Franc

in imports into France by air from the United States. They were re-established again by 44% between 1985 and 1987 when the franc revalued against the dollar by 49%.

What is more, during periods of strong monetary fluctuations, the aircraft becomes an irreplaceable means for rapid adaptation to the violent but often temporary swings in the market. It enables one to fulfil orders more speedily and to get goods out into the market before one's competitors. It enjoys a frequently observed amplifying effect, which is only restricted by the economic necessity of putting an upper limit on the capacities dedicated to satisfying an exceptional, one-way demand.

3 THE CRISIS IN AIR TRANSPORT

The economic, monetary and oil-dependent quakes which shook the years 1970 to 1980 would have easily sufficed to provoke a crisis in air transportation. But these general causes were supplemented by specific factors working to destabilise air traffic. Thus IATA noted in its 1975 Annual Report: "The regulatory framework for international transport envisioned at Chicago and Bermuda, while appropriate for its time, has become increasingly inadequate to deal with modern-day political, economic and social change."

Factors peculiar to the air transport crisis
Three main factors contributed to triggering the crisis in air transportation: the problem of the co-existence of scheduled services and charter flights, the incessant interventions of the American CAB, and certain malfunctions within IATA.

• The problem of the co-existence of scheduled services and charter flights

Although it rarely reached dramatic proportions in the freight market, this was a major problem in passenger transport for more than 10 years. Whereas in world freight, non-scheduled flights (or "charters") never exceeded 10% of the world activity, in 1975 they represented about half of the Europe-Mediterranean passenger traffic, and about 30% on the key sector of the North Atlantic. From then on, the co-existence of two different marketing methods, one of which – charters – benefited from a much wider pricing flexibility, became the major stumbling block in air transportation. In an attempt to overcome it, IATA, supported by certain Civil Aviation

Authorities, tried with limited success to define a global, co-ordinated system for determining capacities for use both in scheduled services and for charters.

The IATA position arose from the idea that there are not two distinct markets, one for charters and the other for scheduled flights, but a single market consisting of "all potential air passengers". Although this might be to some extent defensible with respect to passengers, the "single market principle " does not correspond to the realities of freight activities. Alongside continuous traffic streams, which require the commitment of scheduled capacity, there must indeed exist a specific market for individual deals, either one-off or in series, appropriate for chartering techniques. There are many examples during the 1970–1980 period: the exceptional transport of several thousand tonnes of coffee between Entebbe and Djibouti during the summer of 1977, following a sudden increase in prices; food aid operations for the benefit of various African regions; or entire flights of cattle between Canada and Iran, or of racing cars and tyres for the Formula I Grand Prix races. That a number of airlines specialised in this kind of traffic represented the best proof of the existence of this market.

• The incessant interventions of the American CAB

No civil aviation organisation has made such use – and abuse – of its authority in approving rates adopted by airlines in IATA, than the Civil Aeronautics Board of the United States, whose prerogatives in tariff matters were further extended by a law of 1972. Its constant interventions, its increasingly pernickety demands for economic justification, its repeated rejections of rates and its increasingly energetic suspicions with regard to anti-trust exemptions made a considerable contribution to the seizing-up of the "IATA rate-making machinery" which was having ever greater difficulty in functioning at all. Out of innumerable cases we would mention a few significant freight examples:

- In 1972, it rejected the rates for the North and Central Pacific for the reason that "the rate increases are not justified or in accordance with public interest".

- In 1973, it stipulated the requirement that, prior to any decision, the airlines supply "economic documentation justifying all tariff measures". Since the documentation submitted was never judged to be either complete or in line with an excessive degree of formality, the CAB incessantly postponed its decisions. Whether deliberately or not, the system was slowly reaching suffocation point.

- In 1975, instead of continuing to take ad-hoc decisions, without any overall vision, the CAB published a statement in which it clearly dictated its "tariff requirements". The rates put forward for its approval had to be "economically justified" and "established in line with the full cost of providing the service" in contrast to marginal costs. The rate structures would have to put increasing emphasis on general cargo rates and rates per container, with specific cargo rates being limited to a few categories of goods and reserved for high weight breaks. In addition, "the Board has reserved a 60-day period within which to act on submitted IATA resolutions. Such a period does not begin, however, until all documentation including full (economic) justification is received from each affected US carrier". Finally, the

CAB stated that "the Board intends to adhere stringently to these conditions and apply them to all IATA Conference agreements". This document is of major significance. Over and above the repeated declaration of a certain kind of imperialism, it carries within it a condemnation of the multilateral fixing of rates, which is replaced by an affirmation of the authority of the country of origin.

- In 1978, continuing its work of undermining the regulatory edifice, the CAB expressed its disapproval of the principle of a fixed level of 5% for the commission paid to the IATA registered cargo agents, and decided that the rates adopted should no longer be considered as minima (which had been the rule) but as maxima.

• IATA malfunctions

The resignation from IATA in 1971 of the American cargo airline Seaboard was an indicator of the extreme difficulty of designing a freight rate structure which would be acceptable to all members of the Association. It demonstrated the increasingly glaring incompatibility between the unanimity rule and the growing differences of the freight policies of the airlines. How could it be possible to reach unanimous agreement between airlines operating cargo aircraft with over 100 tonnes capacity and those which only offer the capacity available in the restricted holds of narrow-bodied passenger aircraft?

In fact, it was not so much a deadlock situation as one would think, for various reasons. Firstly, IATA made efforts to loosen up its operating rules, without going so far as to deny the unanimity rule (by attempting to achieve restricted agreements, sub-dividing Traffic Conferences into more limited and homogeneous geographical areas etc).

Secondly, whatever people might say, in the 1970s IATA was still demonstrating considerable skill in rate innovations, whether in relation to the introduction of rates for containers, without considering the type of goods transported (freight of all kinds, or FAK rates), or the introduction of rates for high weight breaks (30 tonnes) so as to permit the carriage on scheduled flights of large consignments which were incorrectly known as "charters".

Finally, there was a trend which first made an appearance and then expanded, consisting in superimposing upon general IATA agreements (for example those valid for the whole of the North Atlantic) bilateral agreements between individual countries, limited to a specific rate category. These bilateral agreements were negotiated by Governments at the instigation of their national airlines, and served to break the multilateral harmony (often a façade) and replace it by a succession of bilateral agreements, which better fulfilled individual requirements.

At the very last, we should mention numerous violations of the official tariff regulations (the famous malpractices in British and US terminology). Although they were widely practised, they remained obscure and difficult to prove until the moment when certain airlines (Air France in particular) had the courage to officially advertise the rate which was actually applied. They constituted a necessary safety valve in a coercive system. Tariff liberalisation, by making official the rates which were actually used, resulted in a significant reduction in questionable and in some cases frankly reprehensible practices in the ways in which they were operated.

Tradewinds CL-44.
MAP

Britain, which at that time possessed a number of very enterprising cargo-charter companies. This opened hitherto unheard-of prospects for charter companies on both sides to operate across the North Atlantic, whether as full charters, cattle charters, or even split charters. The British airlines Tradewinds Airways and IAS Cargo Airlines were the first to benefit.

• The denunciation of the Bermuda Agreement
Since they considered that the problems of capacity and rates could not be solved within the framework of the Bermuda Agreement, the British decided to withdraw from it on 20th June 1976, having no compunction in challenging one of the principal tenets of international civil aviation:

> "*This is a crucial event in the history of air transport as it has been since the Second World War: a thunderbolt, but descending from skies which for some time have not been altogether blue. Nothing can better emphasise the seriousness and the depth of the present upheavals, which are reflected in the challenge against this agreement.*" [6]

Or again: "The inevitable explosion finally occurred where it was most to be expected, that is to say on the world's busiest route, the North Atlantic." [7]

After bitter negotiations, which were dragged out until the last possible moment – the cancellation of the Bermuda agreement only took effect one year after its notification – the two parties arrived at a new agreement, known as Bermuda II, on 23rd July 1977. We will not go into detail about this new agreement, but, like Bermuda I, it achieved a skillful balance between the British, who obtained a certain degree of satisfaction regarding the control of capacity, and the Americans, who only succeeded by dint of strict limitations in establishing the principle of multiple designation for airlines operating on a determined route (in contrast to the classic theory of single designation). Nevertheless, the bilateral "Bermuda II Agreement" is of the utmost significance. Breaking with the doctrine of zero discrimination, it embodied two route structures, one for passenger services and the other for cargo services. It opened the way to similar arrangements in numerous later bilateral agreements. In addition, it retained for cargo services the benefit of more liberal clauses than those for passenger services, thus confirming the trend which has already been observed, that freight, which is a highly technical field, and subject to little media attention, acts as an ideal test case for new liberal doctrines (eg flexibility clause). [8]

Moreover, the "Bermuda II Agreement" has a "cargo charter" Appendix which was introduced at the request of Great

4 THE INSTABILITY OF TRADITIONAL ORGANISATIONS – THE CATEGORY CRISIS AND THE ERA OF HYBRIDS

In a world which had been organised to ensure "the safe and orderly growth of international civil aviation", every business unit had its own place and well-defined functions and boundaries. There was no overlap between categories, and any exceptions only served to confirm the rule.

The decade 1970–1980 called this simple and reassuring system to question. Not only were the most certain of values – the Bermuda Agreement, the convertibility of the dollar and then the gold franc of the UPU – razed to the ground, but the best established distinctions between scheduled airlines and charter companies, between airlines, freight forwarders and clients, between freight forwarders, airlines and post offices, were radically reviewed, to such an extent that boundaries were blurred and words began to lose their meanings. In a few cases, rigid classifications softened to give rise to hybrid organisations, integrating numbers of activities which had previously been compartmentalised.

• Airlines and freight forwarders encroach on one another's territories
The traditional scheme of things in which customers produced, freight forwarders processed the shipments and airlines transported goods were confronted with change from all sides: the airlines bought freight forwarders, while the freight agents got involved in running cargo airlines on their own account.

Among the first, Air France discreetly purchased in 1973 a minority share in the capital of one of the chief freight forwarders in France. Its objective was less to increase market share than to get to know from the inside how a large group operated and arrived at its prices. The experience was disappointing all round: the airline considered that it received inadequate payback, and the freight forwarder complained about not receiving any privileges. The marriage, always courteous but void of passion, was dissolved a dozen years later, with the same discretion.

In 1979, taking advantage of a change in the IATA regulations concerning the ownership of registered agencies, SAS bought the Swedish number one (Olson & Wright) while

Swissair bought 27% of the capital in Jacky Maeder, the main airfreight forwarder on the Swiss market. When carrying out the purchase Swissair took care to point out that it was only taking up a minority investment, and that it would continue in the market place to respect the rules of commercial neutrality. The investment must have been a good one since in 1988 Swissair bought up the major shares which were held by two subsidiaries of the Union de Banque Suisse, and became the main shareholder in Jacky Maeder, to the tune of over 98%.

The movement whereby airlines took up controlling interests in freight forwarders did not go much further, since experience frequently showed that it was very difficult indeed to maintain privileged relationships with an in-house forwarder, without spoiling relationships with the profession as a whole. The game was just not worth the candle.

On the other hand, the large freight forwarders started operating with their own private transportation, either by chartering capacity for a start-up period or by purchasing their own fleets and becoming airlines, while, of course, maintaining their role as freight forwarders. This movement started in the United States, but the freight forwarders entered the airline business less for pleasure than out of sheer necessity. The American freight forwarders had an absolute requirement for night cargo capacity, particularly on domestic services. Within a few years (1973–1984) the American domestic airlines got rid of their cargo fleets and closed all their freight services, usually operated at night, and the principal forwarders, with a gun at their heads, had no other choice than to take the place of the failing airlines which, in the heat of the moment, had perhaps not appreciated the full implications of their decisions. It is always dangerous to produce your own competitors. This is how Emery Airborne, Burlington or Air Express International became airlines.

In Europe, the movement stayed at a much more limited level, particularly due to the policies of Air France and Lufthansa in building up all-cargo networks. Nevertheless, there were a number of examples of in-house transport operations carried out by European freight agents on international long-haul services, using aircraft hired from charter companies: such as Danzas bound for Venezuela or Charlotte (the large textile centre in North Carolina), Pandair on the North Atlantic or Panalpina going to Nigeria during the oil boom.

• The integrators or the challenge to traditional functions
In the United States, at the beginning of the 1970s, a group of new operators emerged: the integrators. As specialists in the express transport of small parcels door to door, they shook to the core the traditional division of competencies between the client, the freight forwarder and the airline. They provided the client with a complete range of services from his door to that of the recipient, integrating in a single offer services which had been hitherto divided between the airfreight forwarders and the airlines. These were the integrators who forged a single service out of two relatively watertight categories. They pushed their challenge against traditional organisations still further by attacking certain types of postal traffic, and managed to spirit away some business from the Post and the airlines. They shook up airfreight and airmail to such an extent that we will later look at their activities at length.

"The hybridisation of air services" [9]
The Chicago Convention envisaged the coexistence of "scheduled international air services" (Article 6) and "aircraft not engaged in scheduled international air services" (Article 5) but it defined neither. After considering the legal position long and hard, the ICAO experts proposed a definition for scheduled flights: scheduled air services are understood to be a series of flights open to the public in return for payment (the method by which they are marketed is a major criterion) and carried out "according to a regular timetable the regularity of which is of a clearly systematic character".

In contrast to the scheduled services, charter flights are individual flights carried out in response to a specific, temporary demand, sold in its entirety by the carrier to a sole and single client, known as the charterer.

This is the traditional concept of charter flights covered by the IATA regulations. In fact, IATA went no further in defining charter flights than did the ICAO, but it did regulate the freight transport activity in very strict terms in its Resolution 045a. The IATA member companies are free to use or provide charter services on condition that they fulfil three essential requirements:

• "a member (of IATA) may perform air transportation by chartering the entire weight/volume capacity of an aircraft … the charterer shall be charged for the entire payload of the aircraft, regardless of the space or available weight to be utilised by him";

• "The charter agreement shall be made only with one person for its own use".

• "Each charter agreement shall be put in writing and signed prior to operation".

On the other hand, the freight charter rates are not regulated by IATA, and result from free negotiations between the charterer and the carrier. Such rates were not published, except initially in the United States where the CAB demanded that charter rates should be registered by type of aircraft, and possibly by day of the week and by nature of goods carried, and expressed in dollars per statute mile.

IATA's major concern, which was to be progressively demolished, was to establish a clear distinction between scheduled flights and charter flights, so that regulations applying to the former could not be evaded by the latter. This question was to occupy the CAB and certain European administrations, which had become attracted by liberal ideas from the mid–1970s.

At this point in the story, it is necessary, in order to understand the events that follow, to master one or two additional technical concepts:

• On-route and off-route charters
An off-route charter is a charter flight carried out on a route on which the charter company does not normally operate. For Air France a Lyons/Minneapolis charter flight is off route. On the other hand, a Paris/New York charter would be on route because the airline operates a scheduled Paris/New York service. This charter operation can be carried out in two ways: either by putting on an extra aircraft, or by using a regular scheduled flight for the purpose. In such cases the flight is known as a "decommercialised" or "blocked-off charter".

• Full charter, part charter and split charter

Only full charters conform to the IATA regulations, which require that the charterer takes the whole of the capacity on the chartered aircraft.

Part charter is a practice, which consists in selling only part of the capacity on the aircraft to the charterer. This procedure is very widely used by all the scheduled airlines operating wide-bodied cargo aircraft in order to get into the market for large consignments in competition with the charter companies.

Split charter is a formula, which consists of splitting the capacity of a chartered aircraft into a number of lots, of a minimum size fixed in advance by the carrier, or more generally by the Civil Aviation Authorities. What the limits are, is an important question, since the higher the number of splits, the more the presentation resembles that for scheduled flights.

• Single charters and series charters

A single charter is one which is not repeated (eg a single lot of 100 tonnes from Stuttgart to Bombay). Series charters are a succession of charter flights carried out during a specific period in order to fulfil a demand of a temporarily repetitive nature, or which would exceed the load capacity of a single aircraft. The question arises: at what point does a series of "charter flights" carried out over a long period, one or several times a week, between two fixed points, become a scheduled service?

• True charters; so-called charters and large shipments

Even if we are convinced that there is a true market for chartering alongside the scheduled market, its real size is much lower than what is usually referred to as the "charter market". The reason is that, alongside the "true charter" market consisting of consignments which really do have a need to take over the whole of the capacity of an aircraft between two points, there exists an enormous "false charter" market consisting of clients who have available large consignments and are looking for an attractive rate, rather than an actual chartering operation with all the risks which that might entail. What these clients are looking for is that their consignments can take advantage of a "charter rate" (by definition the most favourable rate in the opinion of the public), but that they are loaded on scheduled flights, combining the competitiveness of the former with the dependability of the latter. And so we come to the awkward question: where does a "large consignment" begin?

One should keep the above technical concepts in mind when attempting to understand the subsequent course of events in the United States and in Europe.

In the United States, the CAB regulations were always more liberal than the IATA regulations with respect to charters. Before liberalisation became fully effective, the CAB had admitted the principle, subject to numerous restrictions, of chartering by freight forwarders and of split charters in their most elementary form (the idea of joint chartering limited to two participants or joint loading). From the mid 1970s, the policy of the CAB consisted in removing the various hurdles set up by itself against the free exercise of practices which it had recognised in principle, to the benefit of cargo airlines and supplemental carriers.

In 1977, after a long and detailed investigation known as the Airfreight Forwarders Charters Investigation, the CAB decided to make a significant extension to the rights of freight forwarders so that they could carry out charters for their own requirements (put bluntly, for the carriage of goods of which they were not the owners). Such a development could only reinforce the identity of the American Airfreight Forwarders as "indirect carriers". In 1979, the CAB completely liberalised the practice of split chartering, by eliminating the concept of a minimum size of consignment and the maximum number of charterers. Was there still any distinction between scheduled flights and charter flights?

With regard to part charters, the CAB proposed that they could be loaded without restriction on scheduled flights.

In Europe, the regulatory problem which arose was that of split charters. At the beginning of the 1970s, several charter cargo airlines began to operate regular "charter flights" out of Great Britain, The Netherlands, Luxembourg and later Germany, to destinations in Asia (Hong Kong), the Middle East (Dubai) and Africa (Nairobi, Lagos etc). The regulation of split charters varied from country to country: very liberal in The Netherlands and Luxembourg; more restrictive in Great Britain. As in the United States, but showing greater prudence, the civil aviation authorities started out on the road towards easing the restrictions, whether in terms of the number of authorised charter flights, the minimum size of consignments, or the maximum number of charterers on the same aircraft.

Thus they arrived at a situation in which the charter airlines (such as Cargolux, Tradewinds, German Cargo Services) operated a kind of "regular charter services" marketed according to standards which increasingly resembled those of the scheduled airlines, whilst the scheduled airlines operated, without compunction and on a large scale, a formula of part charters. One can well understand why the Director General of IATA wrote in the 1974 Annual Report: "The traditional distinction between scheduled services and so-called non-scheduled flights has been overtaken by events. It is artificial and there is no longer any sense in it." What happened to the good old days with their inviolable classifications?

2 THE ERA OF WIDE-BODIED AND SUPERSONIC AIRCRAFT

With the Jumbo and Concorde, air transportation entered a new phase in its development: that of wide-bodied aircraft, capable of carrying 500 passengers or over 100 tonnes of goods, and that of supersonic flight at over 1,200 mph.

I THE WIDE-BODIED AMERICAN PASSENGER AIRCRAFT: GODSEND OR MENACE TO THE FREIGHT TRANSPORT INDUSTRY?

In March 1966 the Board of Directors of Boeing decided to start the construction of a new four-engined long-haul aircraft of large capacity. A few weeks later, Pan American World Airways announced that it had ordered 25 Boeing 747 aircraft. It thus opened the era of wide-bodied jets, which commenced on 22nd January 1970 with a flight between New York and London.

For the first time in aviation history, progress no longer took the form of an increase in speed:"… it is through its fuselage diameter of 6.10m as against 3.55m for the Boeing 707, that the B747 introduces a change of magnitude." [1]

Speeding up their own their pace, Douglas and Lockheed brought out two three-engined, wide-bodied medium-haul aircraft, the Douglas DC-10 and the Lockheed 1011, soon to be followed by the long-haul versions. Although these two machines were slightly narrower than the Boeing 747, the width of the fuselage became the characteristic feature of these wide-bodied aircraft, distinguishing them from the first generation jets. For the passengers, they brought comfort and a sense of space into the cabin. For luggage and freight they brought volume and load unitisation.

The holds of these wide-bodied aircraft consist of three elements: two unitised lower compartments below the main deck (one forward hold and one aft hold) and a compartment for bulk items stowed in the main deck, in the rear part of the fuselage. These offer a much larger volume than the holds in narrow-bodied craft: 128m³ for a B747, against 48m³ for a B707 (a factor of 2.7). The unitisation of the holds became necessary for two reasons: economic – to speed up the turnround times of the planes by reducing stopover periods; and commercial – to reduce the average time taken to deliver luggage to the passengers. It only remained for the three manufacturers, under insistent pressure from future users, to define the characteristics of a common, standard container which would be interchangeable between all wide-bodied aircraft. This standard container, known under various code references depending on the nomenclatures (LD3, AKE, A1 etc) is used universally for the transport of luggage and goods. It is a box with a base of 154cm x 156cm and 163cm high, with a volume of 4.5m³ and a payload of around 700kg with good quality cargo. This container has one special feature: one wall is slanted at an angle virtually half way up one of the sides, giving it an unusual shape, but fitting perfectly to the outline of the lower hold, but a priori making it unsuitable for a rational loading of the cargo.

Independently of this container, which was originally designed for transporting luggage, the hold of wide-bodied aircraft can accept a wide variety of load units. The basic arrangement used varies depending on the number of passengers and the commercial policies for passenger and freight operated by the carrier. As an example, for the B747, with a combination of luggage containers (C) and palettes of 88in x 125in (2.24m x 3.18m) (P), depending on the characteristics of the route served (number of intermediate stopovers), one can have a range of configurations from 18C/4P to 10C/7P, including the solution 12C/6P shown ;eft.

In the case illustrated, the cargo capacity of a B747 passenger aircraft is between 14 and 18 tonnes, which is approximately half that of an all-cargo B707C. Although remaining a by-product of the passenger activity, freight traffic takes on such importance in the sales figures that it becomes an essential component in the profitability of wide-bodied passenger aircraft. Confronted with this

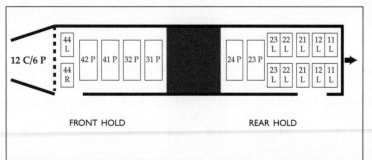

12 C/6 P

| 44 L / 44 R | 42 P | 41 P | 32 P | 31 P | | 24 P | 23 P | 23 22 21 12 11 L / 23 22 21 12 11 L |

FRONT HOLD   REAR HOLD

AKE baggage and cargo container.
Air France

Since the commercial innovations did not bear fruit, some carriers went over to making dramatic withdrawals of night cargo operations, in the hope of filling their daytime freight capacity. Emery Airfreight, as the leading American forwarder, clearly outlined the implications of this policy in its annual report for 1975:

"From 1946, when the company began doing business, until 1973, we relied almost exclusively on the major airlines for moving freight. As these carriers grew in size and stature, we prospered along with them. The transition to the jumbo jets, however, could well prove to be a turning point in our relationship with the major airlines. While the B747, the DC-10 and the L-1011 added dramatically to both passenger and freight capacity, they contributed indirectly to a sharp deterioration in service during evening and night hours – the time most critical to the airfreight industry. In order to insure continuity of service to our customers, we have had to redirect our activities, resulting in a sharp increase in the use of charter aircraft, commuter and air taxi carriers, at the expense of the major carriers."

problem, the airlines adopted two techniques: commercial imaginativeness, and reducing their cargo flight programmes.

The question arose in a more extreme form in the domestic American market, where freight traffic was in essence transported by night on cargo aircraft. The American airlines, at a time when their economic position was worsening, had to respond to a the challenge of how to fill the enormous daytime freight capacities. "The next few years will see a major concentration of effort by airline freight marketing officials to devise a formula to fill the cavernous but still largely empty bellies of their wide-body jets with revenue-producing freight... This represents a move into a new market philosophy for airfreight – that of a daylight market as opposed to the traditional night-time market." [2] (J. B. Gebhardt, Director of Cargo Sales and Services for United Airlines.)

All the airlines pounced on this new market sector which had to be developed at all cost. In September 1971 TWA introduced a special day rate for LD3 containers. It was the first to introduce daylight rates, which are US domestic rates only and are based on a flat charge for containers presented to the airline terminal between specific times, generally 4am and 4pm.

This was of no interest to the freight forwarders who were looking for night cargo capacity, but was aimed directly at the shippers of high-density products, since the price was the same whatever the weight loaded (within the limits of the technical strength of the container). The results were disappointing. Few freight agents associated themselves with this promotional action by the airlines, while many clients emphasised the difficulties in loading and handling LD3 containers, on which the campaign was too exclusively based. The average cargo load for B747s belonging to the American domestic airlines did not exceed 3.6 tonnes in 1972.

On the international long-haul routes, the introduction of the new wide-bodied passenger aircraft also resulted in reductions in cargo frequencies, which varied according to the airline and the sector. The North Atlantic provides a perfect example of this development.

Development of freight traffic of IATA airlines over the North Atlantic Total of both directions (in tonnes)

	Total Traffic	Traffic on cargo flights	Cargo flights Total in %
1969	429,000	268,000	62.4%
1970	411,000	247,000	60.0%
1975	615,000	327,000	53.1%
1980	860,000	386,000	44.9%

Source: IATA Statistics

An Air France press release of 27th October 1971 [3] illustrates the cargo capabilities of the B747 passenger aircraft:

"The advantages of a door-to-door service for cargo have been confirmed after Air France has provided a major American manufacturer with a daily delivery, from Chicago to Paris, of the most urgent spare parts needed in the maintenance of its brand of earth-moving equipment used in France. The company's European centre, based at Ris Orangis, gets a list of its requirements for urgent components every morning. At mid-day, the order is sent by telex to the

giant warehouse at Broadview near Chicago. The time difference also works in favour of the system, as it is then 6 o'clock in the morning on the shores of Lake Michigan. At 7 o'clock a team of data entry staff input the order onto the computer and the components are selected. At 10.30, the goods, which have been taken out of stock, labelled, and invoiced, are packed and then loaded on site into a container provided by Air France.

"The container is fitted with a customs seal and loaded into a lorry, to be taken to Chicago Airport, where it is delivered, with documentation, to the Air France cargo service. It is then 13.30 hours. The container is added to the consignment waiting to be loaded onto the next flight for Paris.

"The aircraft, a giant Boeing 747, takes off at 17.20 hours and arrives on the following day at Orly at 08.55 hours … The container is unloaded, put on a lorry and delivered directly to the depot at Ris Orangis: the consignment goes through on-site customs formalities and is immediately made available to clients.

"Less than 24 hours have passed between the establishment of the order and its delivery."

2 THE BOEING 747 CARGO AIRCRAFT

The birth of a new aircraft version

Is the Boeing B747 passenger aircraft a cargo plane, which has lost its way, or is the B747 cargo aircraft a modified passenger machine? Let us listen to a design engineer who wrote in 1974: [4] "The design came into being in late 1965-early 1966 at about the height of enthusiasm in the US for a supersonic transport. Within Boeing it was argued that the introduction of a new four-engined sub-sonic transport made sense, but that cargo as well as passenger usage must be considered from the beginning. For, if the supersonic transport did survive its initial development period, and a successful passenger carrier resulted, the 747 role could become largely a cargo carrier. There, both the high pilot compartment – to accommodate nose-loading of 8ft x 8ft containers on the main deck – and the fuselage size which could accommodate two 8ft x 8ft containers side by side, became fundamental characteristics of the design."

It would no doubt be going too far to make the claim that the B747 was primarily designed for the needs of cargo. But cargo requirements were incorporated right from the drawing board stage.

In which the forerunner is not the one expected

At the beginning of 1968, within the space of a few weeks, the orders for the B747 cargo and convertible aircraft fell from around 30 to a mere half dozen. It was particularly the large American airlines who withdrew. What was happening? "Had the Boeing 747 arrived too early for cargo?" asked the Institut du Transport Aérien. IATA noted "that the airlines now seem less interested in the cargo version of the 747". Airlines were unsettled by the increase in the tare weight of the versions concerned, whilst others wanted time to examine in more detail a civilian version of the C-5A military transport aircraft proposed by Lockheed.

In the end it was Lufthansa who had the privilege of opening a new chapter in the history of airfreight, when it flew the first Boeing 747F (F = Freighter) between Frankfurt and New York on 19th April 1972.

Characteristics of the B747F

There is no doubt that with its upward-pivoting nose, which opens up the whole of the main deck, its side door of over three metres in height and its payload of 114 tonnes, the B747F is a superb cargo aircraft. Although it retains the general dimensions of the passenger version, it is distinguished by three key elements:

• **The upward-pivoting nose-door**
This is the most distinctive feature. The upward displacement of the entire nose section of the aircraft gives the best possibilities for loading machines and all items of cargo with extended length. However, surprisingly, Boeing proposed at an early stage a cargo version without the nose door, fitted with only a single side door. This version was preferred by American Airlines and Flying Tiger, who no doubt considered that the additional cost of the nose door was not compensated by a sufficiently large competitive advantage.

• **The main cargo deck**
This is 56m long and 6m wide. Its basic offer consists of: either 28 positions for pallets 96in x 125in (2.44m x 3.18m) or 88in x 125in (2.24m x 3.18m) loaded in two rows side by side, plus a 29th position placed at an angle at the rear of the aircraft (known as position T), or 32 positions for pallets 88in x 108in (2.24m x 2.74m) plus a 33rd pallet in position T.

Working on this basis, the operators can obtain innumerable combinations by mixing pallets, igloos and containers, which can be up to 40ft (12.16m) in length.

In addition to the arrangements on the main deck, it has nine positions in the lower hold, which can take either pallets or containers with a base of 88in or 96in x 125in (2.24m or 2.44m x 3.1m) with a height not exceeding 1.60m, plus the capacity of the rear hold for bulk items (22.5m³). The ceiling height of the main deck is not uniform, due to the positioning of the cockpit above the main cabin. The eight foremost positions have a height limitation of 2.44m or 8ft, whilst the following positions can be increased to 3m, providing that they are only loaded via the side door which is 3.10m x 3.05m.

• **The in-floor equipment on the main deck**
The loading and unloading operations on this aircraft need only a reduced number of personnel, because the movement of the pallets and containers is entirely automated, using rollers between guide rails. The ULDs are moved by means of large rubber-rimmed wheels, driven by electric motors and operated by remote control – known as PDU (Power Drive Units).

The illusion of intermodality

In the minds of its designers, one of the main advantages of the B747F would be its ability to transport containers of the same dimensions as sea containers: 8 x 8ft in cross section (2.44m x 2.44m) by 10, 20 or 40ft in length (3.04m , 6.08m or 12.16m). "These containers are designed to be intermodal with surface transportation." The great wild goose chase had begun for intermodality!

At the risk of disappointing transport theorists, it must be admitted that there has been an almost complete failure in this area. Sea containers are almost never transported by plane, while so-called "intermodal" aircraft containers are even less likely to be carried on ships.

ABOVE Loading a car through the side door of a Lufthansa B747-200F.
Lufthansa

LEFT Lufthansa inaugurated the operation of the Boeing 747F on 19 April 1972 between Frankfurt and New York.
Lufthansa

BELOW Pan Am Cargo Boeing 747 freighter.

ABOVE A Lufthansa B747-200F demonstrates its capacity by showing its load of 72 Volkswagen "beetles" in 1972.
Lufthansa

LEFT 20-foot pallet in the hold of a B747F.

BELOW RIGHT In Manchester Martinair DC-10F freighter loads the world's most valuable car, a Rolls Royce "Silver Ghost" (1907 vintage), bound for Hong Kong.
Air Cargo News UK

BOTTOM RIGHT Martinair Holland, DC-10 freighter.
MAP

FAR RIGHT DC-10-30CF with 30 x 88" x 108" (2.24 x 2.74m) pallets

The reason for the failure is quite simple: a B747F entirely equipped with "intermodal" air containers would be carrying a "dead weight" of 14.5 tonnes, compared with 4.7 tonnes when carrying only pallets and 8.5 tonnes with a mixed arrangement of pallets and igloos. Intermodal transport between air and sea, or vice versa, will only be possible when containers have been built which are sufficiently light to be transported by air without excessive loss of payload, but which are sufficiently strong to be stacked vertically to the considerable heights required by the container ships.

We should also add that units of 20 or 40ft appear to correspond to the characteristics of sea consignments, whereas 10ft containers seem more suitable to those of air consignments.

A new commercial and economic dimension

The B747F brought commercial and economic benefits. Helmuth Klumpp, who, as Director of Lufthansa's cargo division, made a major contribution to his company's decision to take the aircraft, provided a good definition of the commercial advantages of the B747F during the B747 Cargo Marketing Meeting in Seattle in 1974: "The B747F has attracted heavier and bulkier shipments which simply could not have been transported before its operation. The 747F is unique in a lot of ways. Among others, it can take 75 Volkswagens."

As to the economic advantages, these were nicely summed up in an internal Air France report from 1975: "The respective capacities of the B747F and the B707C are in the order of 90 tonnes and 30 tonnes over comparable routes, giving a ratio of 3 to 1. Under the same conditions their costs are in the order of 2 to 1. Economically, the B747F sets a new standard for the industry."

3 THE DOUGLAS DC-10 FREIGHTER

Although it receives less media attention than the B747F, the cargo version of the DC-10 passenger aircraft, the DC-10CF convertible or the DC-10F all-cargo version, is none the less a first rate machine for freight transportation, offering a payload of around 70-74 tonnes. Its success alongside the B747F has constantly reminded us that, for freight as well as for passengers, the "frequency effect" has gained ground over the "capacity effect". "This provides the ideal compromise between aircraft such as the smaller DC-8 and the Boeing 707 and the biggest of them all, the Boeing 747F" (Martinair Freight, July 1976).

The Douglas DC-10CF is more of a classic aircraft than the B747F. Loading is carried out exclusively via the side door, and it cannot accept rectangular containers of 8ft cross section (2.44m) because the ceiling height in the cabin is limited to 2.23m. In other respects, it can cope with the rest of the range of aircraft unit load devices, and its payload of 70 tonnes is better suited to many markets than the 114 tonnes of the B747F.

The main deck of the DC-10CF is, like that of the B747F, capable of various equipment configurations. We will only mention the main ones:

• 22 pallets of 88in x 125in (2.24m x 3.18m) installed in two lines of 11 pallets arranged lengthwise;

• 30 pallets of 88in x 108in (2.24m x 2.74m) installed in two lines of 15 pallets arranged with their longest axis across the aircraft. (See diagram bottom right.) Since the cross-section of the cabin changes, the outer dimensions of the pallets must be adjusted to the variable ceiling height, which makes it more complex to rearrange loads.

4 THE "COMBI" VERSIONS OF THE WIDE-BODIED PASSENGER AIRCRAFT

It was in 1974 that Boeing proposed the definitive version of the B747 Combi. The characteristic features of this aircraft are a large cargo door located at the rear left side of the fuselage, and the installation in the aft half of the cabin of a floor similar to that of the 747F. There are two possible configurations, depending on whether the rear cargo section is equipped for six pallets (plus a seventh in the T position) or for 12 pallets (plus a 13th in T position).

This Combi aircraft can be described as two machines in one: forward it is a passenger aircraft with (typically) 210 to 260 seats, and at the rear and in the hold it is a cargo plane with 13 to 19 pallet positions plus a bulk cargo compartment, accommodating a total of 35 to 50 tonnes.

A number of European, African and Asian companies decided to equip themselves with this type of machine. In Europe, Air France, Lufthansa and KLM were to become its principal users. KLM became its champion, and based its entire cargo policy on

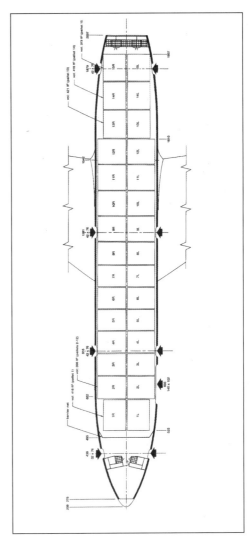

Although with many advantages, the "Combi solution" is not without its limitations.

Flexibility is one of its virtues since the main deck can be equipped for six to 12 cargo pallets. However, in view of the time required, this version cannot be reconfigured from one day to the next, nor even from one week to the next, even though passenger demand and freight demand change in relation to one another. As a general rule, the equipment is only reconfigured according to the IATA seasons (winter season from 1st November to 31st March, and summer season from 1st April to 31st October). On the other hand, even if it does represent two aircraft in one, the Combi aircraft remains above all a passenger machine. Consequently, the regulations applying to the transport of goods still apply as for a passenger aircraft: Combi aircraft are not authorised to carry dangerous goods in the "CAO" (Cargo Aircraft Only) class, which are for carriage exclusively on cargo aircraft.

5 AIRBUS: THE END OF THE AMERICAN HEGEMONY AND THE REVOLUTION IN MEDIUM-HAUL FREIGHT

It might be useful to recall four key dates:

• 26th September 1967: signature of a Protocol of Agreement between Germany, France and Great Britain for "the joint construction of a large-capacity aircraft for short- and medium-haul journeys."

• 18th December 1970: foundation of Airbus Industrie, in the form of an economic interest group according to French commercial law with its headquarters in Toulouse.

• 28th October 1972: maiden flight of Airbus A300, the first aircraft manufactured by the economic interest group Airbus Industrie.

• 23rd May 1974: Air France inaugurates the first Airbus commercial flight on the Paris/London route with an Airbus A300B2, a medium-haul, twin-engined aircraft with an average capacity of 270 passengers.

This put an end to the American hegemony in aircraft production, and marked the beginning of intense competition between Europe and the United States, which would gradually extend to cover the whole range of civil aircraft as the production of Airbus Industrie diversified.

The Airbus A300 is a wide-bodied aircraft with an outside width of up to 5.64m. First of

all in Europe and then worldwide, it did for medium-haul airfreight what the B747 had done for long-haul freight in terms of capacity and unitisation. By adopting the ULD dimensions of the American manufacturers, which had become a universal standard, Airbus "allowed carriers to make a direct exchange of containers between long-haul operations and regional medium-haul flights, thus reducing the handling costs and giving a new impulse to the airfreight market, already in rapid expansion." [5]

The Airbus A300, both in the B2 (short- and medium-haul) and in the B4 (medium- and long-haul) versions has three holds: one unitised hold forward and one unitised hold aft, equipped with an automatic loading system, and one bulk cargo compartment situated at the rear. The equipment in the holds varies according to different criteria (route, commercial policy etc), but the version with eight LD3-type containers and four 88in x 125in pallets is undoubtedly the most common.

The introduction of the Airbus made the European airlines re-examine their freight policies from two points of view: reduction of all-cargo services and the development of transit traffic. By bringing regular, frequent and unitised capacity onto the scene, the Airbus A300 made it possible to eliminate all-cargo services of doubtful profitability, which in any case were hard hit by the increase in fuel costs. By making it easier to carry out transit operations, it encouraged operating companies to strengthen their policy for sixth freedom traffic [6] and contributed to the overall growth in traffic through improvements in service and by intensifying competition.

Although, Airbus passenger aircraft met with exceptionally rapid success, the breakthrough was slow in coming for the convertible and cargo models. It was not until 1991, when Federal Express ordered a fleet of 25 A300-600F cargo aircraft, with a payload of 51-55 tonnes, that things really got moving. This was

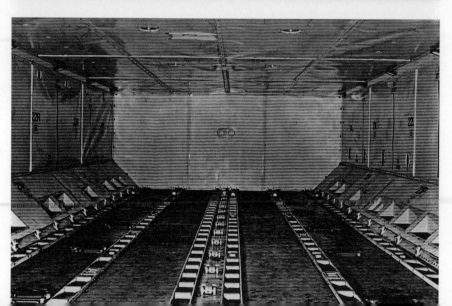

ABOVE RIGHT **Hapag Lloyd Airbus A300-C4-203.** *MAP*

RIGHT **The bellyhold of the Airbus A300.** *Airbus*

in spite of the fact that the A300F (all-cargo) and the A300C (convertible) versions had been offered from the outset.

The first A300C4-200 convertible, fitted with a side cargo door of 3.58m x 2.56m, left the factory in November 1979 and was taken into service by the German charter airline Hapag Lloyd in 1980. The first A310 convertible (the A310 differs from the A300 in having a shorter fuselage) was delivered to the Dutch charter airline Martinair in 1984. The convertible versions were indeed well suited to the needs of charter companies which, depending on the season, used them for passengers or freight. "The Airbus A310-203C has proved to be a great aircraft, especially for carrying bulky freight" (Martinair).

6 SUPERSONIC AIRCRAFT

Supersonic aircraft are too sleek and streamlined to carry cargo in any significant quantity. However, in addition to Air France and British Airways using the hold of Concorde to carry express freight, supersonic aircraft and air cargo have had a closer relationship than one would imagine.

In Russia, the Tupolev 144, following the usual practice for Soviet manufacturers, initially made a long series of test flights, carrying nothing but mail, between Moscow and Vladivostok during summer 1975 and then between Moscow and Alma Ata for nearly two years, from December 1975 to October 1977. The Tupolev 144 was made available for passenger traffic on 1st November 1977, but withdrawn on 1st June 1978.

On the Anglo-French side, a number of Concordes were nearly converted into cargo machines for carrying express documents and parcels. Fred Smith, the founder-President of Federal Express, carried out very far-reaching negotiations in this direction with the French and British Authorities and airlines from 1980 to 1984.

At the time, Federal Express was only operating a domestic American route structure, but had already made the decision to set up in Europe, and to establish a transatlantic link between its two networks, the existing American one and the future European one. Fred Smith was attracted by the publicity value of the operation, and was apparently convinced of its profitability. He made overtures to the British and the French with a view to establishing a transatlantic cargo connection, operated with converted Concordes, under the Federal Express flag. This service would have joined New York on the one side with Prestwick, Shannon, London or Paris on the other, according to a timetable of the following type:

| 20.00 hours | Europe | 05.00 hours |
| 17.45 hours | New York | 20.00 hours |

Although the negotiations reached an advanced stage, the deal was never done, mainly because guarantees given by the Governments concerned were considered to be inadequate:

"The reason we didn't, is because we couldn't get the assurance of the British and French Governments that they would continue the certificate of the Concorde through the 1980s. We couldn't of course run the risk of having the certificate being pulled and not being able to amortise our investment." [7]

We will probably have to await the appearance of a new generation of aircraft before cargo becomes a significant factor in supersonic transport.

ABOVE **Air France Concorde at Toulouse.**
Airbus

BELOW **German Cargo Services B707F on the apron at Hong Kong. The company is Lufthansa's subsidiary cargo charter airline.** *Lufthansa*

3 THE OIL CRISES: THE END OF CHEAP ENERGY

Two oil crises, in 1973-74 and 1980-81, stand out in the decade 1970–1980, and led to a sea of troubles. From then on, any rise in the fevered temperature of the Middle East would be accompanied by tension in the oil market, symbolised by soaring prices. The price per barrel, which was $3 in September 1973, reached $34 in January 1980. It was the end of the era of cheap energy.

On 29th November 1973, Pierre Donatien Cot, the Managing Director of Air France, observed that "We have become engaged in an irreversible movement, which means that we will never again see petrol at $2 per barrel."

1 "THE OIL CRISIS DESCENDS UPON THE WORLD" [1]

On 15th September 1960, Saudi Arabia, Iraq, Iran, Kuwait and Venezuela created the "Organisation of Oil-Exporting Countries" or OPEC. The countries belonging to the organisation first attempted to obtain an increase in the dues paid by the oil companies, and then attempted to take control of production. After the increase in royalties and the take-over of production, an increase in the price for oil products would, in the view of the shrewdest observers, represent the next natural step:" One may predict that the negotiations currently under way with a view to a more active participation of the group of OPEC countries within the oil companies will result in a new increase in fuel prices." [2] The Yom Kippur war, which broke out on Saturday 6th October 1973, sparked off the first "oil shock". This was the first time that the Arab oil-producing countries had used it as a weapon. Initially, the Gulf States increased the price of a barrel of oil from $3.001 to $5.119. Then, at the Teheran Conference in the month of December, the OPEC members imposed a price of $11.15.

The regime change in Iran provided the conditions for the "Second Oil Crisis" in 1980–1981. Oil prices recorded another spectacular hike and leapt from $12 to $34 per barrel. But from 1983 onwards, a reduction in consumption led to a fall in prices, which varied between $10 and $20 per barrel from 1983 to 1990.

The invasion of Kuwait by Saddam Hussein on 2nd August 1990 caused the "Third Oil Crisis" and "a price hike of up to

$40 per barrel at the beginning of 1991". [3] After the end of the war, prices fell again very quickly to levels of around $15-$20. Oil had therefore become one of the raw materials most sensitive to international tensions.

These days, after air transport has recorded an enormous expansion since the first oil crisis (with passenger traffic increasing by a factor of four and goods traffic by a factor of five between 1973 and 1996) it is difficult to imagine the violence of the impact which shook the industry in the years between 1973 and 1975 – a violence which was such that everyone felt it was the beginning of a new era:

"The past year (1973) which was dominated and turned upside down by the difficulties with oil, visibly represents a point of no return both in the field of air transport policy and in the commercial operations of the airlines." [4]

2 ADAPTATION

Adaptations were made in three main areas: rates, consumption and aircraft design.

Rate increases

IATA called a number of special rate conferences, which found it all the easier to adopt rate increases since the economic justification was glaringly obvious, and all the airlines were affected. The increases took the form of uniform percentage rises applied to all the rates. The actual tariff structure was not affected.

In general, because of the escalating prices of jet fuel, one conference would never have been enough. It was necessary to initiate several waves of increases in an attempt to keep track of the changes in costs. After the second petrol crisis, six tariff conferences decreed six series of increases, numbered from "Fuel 1" to "Fuel 6" between March 1979 and October 1980.

At that time, the rate situation for freight had reached a situation of extreme complexity: the "fuel surcharges" which were not approved by all Governments at the same time, were joined by the "exchange rate adjustments" already referred to and by "rate revaluations" which were justified by the rate of inflation. All these changes were calculated on the basis of rates, which were always expressed in theoretical non-devalued base currencies which no longer meant anything to anyone apart from a few specialists. Things were moving nearer and nearer to a world of Kafka.

In an attempt at rationalisation, IATA adopted an "automatic rate adjustment system" in 1980 to take account of the changes in the prices of jet fuel according to the following principles:

• increase of 1 to 3%: automatic increase;

• increase of 4 to 6%: application of an increase following a vote by correspondence;

• increase above 6%: convocation of a rate conference.

Simple as it was, the above formula could only upset certain Governments, who, due to the influence of the automatic adjustments, were deprived of their right to interfere. Furthermore, it took no account of individual situations, as was stressed by the American CAB:

> "The Board has decided it cannot find that the uniform industry increase in all fares and rates would be in the public interest. We will give favourable consideration to individual carrier tariff filings proposing increases warranted by the carrier's experienced fuel cost escalation."

The principal complaint that one could make against the fuel surcharges would be less against the principle, which was economically undeniable, than against the way in which they were applied, more often than not unidirectional. The way that they were included, pure and simply, into freight rates, often seemed like a kind of turnstile which could not be reversed, even in cases where temporary increases were followed by appreciable reductions in oil prices.

In retrospect, the proposition made by one airline in August 1990, during the third oil crisis, for the adoption of a surcharge, which would not be integrated into the cargo rates and not subject to commission, opened the way to satisfactory further progress.

Reductions in consumption
These took two forms. One under duress – the results of rationing; and the other voluntary – resulting from a series of decisions aimed at reducing fuel consumption.

• Reductions under duress: interruptions of supply and rationing
"The cost of airlines' life blood – fuel – has soared alarmingly while supplies have been restricted." [5] The United States, one of the first countries to be affected by the 1973 crisis, adopted a system of fuel rationing placed under the care of the CAB. These arrangements, which turned out to be very cumbersome in practice, did not prevent the cancellation of 400,000 flights in 1974. Outside the United States, many flights were cancelled, but the other countries involved were affected in very different ways, depending on their geographical situation and their political attitudes. The second and third oil crises were accompanied by much less severe restrictions.

In the field of cargo, the application of these rationing policies sometimes caused serious tensions within airlines which were too prone to cancel cargo flights rather than passenger flights, in the erroneous belief that parcels cannot speak.

• Voluntary reductions: fuel economies
Each energy crisis gave rise to a hue and cry by airlines in search of fuel economies. The many actions included:

– engine operating procedures, from starting to shut-down, including take-off thrust;
– speed selections and use of auto-throttle;
– actions related to climb and descent procedures, take-off and landing flap settings;
– the definition of the route, cruising speed and altitude to give minimum consumption; and
– the adoption, as far as possible, of more economical procedures for climbing to and descending from cruising altitude.

Two methods, applicable to all types of aircraft, are of particular interest to cargo flights:

– improved flight planning techniques, including more accurate calculations of fuel reserves and calculations relating to different alternative airports;
– research of an optimal balance. A balanced condition, as aft as possible, within the allowed limits, provides fuel savings which may be more than 1% of consumption.

Finally, the increase in fuel prices rekindled the debate concerning the equipment in the hold and on the main deck of cargo planes: "The wisdom of using containers should be re-examined." [6] Containers mean weight, and therefore extra fuel. In the search for weight reductions and fuel economies, the container came under threat more than ever before from the lighter and better adapted solutions such as pallets and igloos: "We have to return to the ultra light load units of the 1960s." [6] And this was a real blow for inter-modal containers, which were at least twice as heavy as the classic air containers.

Developments in aircraft design
At first, those airlines with the means to do so speeded up the modernisation of their fleets. This worked in favour of wide-bodied aircraft, with lower fuel consumption per unit than in the case of the B707s or DC-8s, and of aircraft fitted with third-generation engines (consumption reduced by 25% compared with the first generation). This consideration speeded up orders for wide-bodied aircraft. Air France represents a typical case.

In the second phase, the aircraft producers set about designing a range of aircraft which used less fuel, with lower noise and pollution levels, placing economic and ecological concerns above technical performance. Their investigations centred on four main areas:

• aerodynamics (wing with high aspect ratio and super-critical profile);

• structural engineering (use of new aluminium alloys and composite materials in order to reduce the ratio between structural weight and payload, so reducing consumption);

• avionics (an integrated computer network allowing an optimisation of flight characteristics);

• and finally the engines (significant improvement in specific fuel consumption and reduction in noise levels).

The aircraft of the generation at present in use are the result of such research, including the A320/321 and the A330/340 from Airbus, the B757/767 and 747-400 and the B737 series 300/400 from Boeing and the MD11 from McDonnell Douglas (now Boeing).

In response to the same considerations, a "re-engining" of 110 Douglas DC-8-60s by Cammacorp between 1980 and 1983, using SNECMA/General Electric CSM 56 jet engines, gave a new lease of life to these cargo aircraft by providing a 23% reduction in fuel consumption. Among others, Cammacorp's clients featured Lufthansa's charter subsidiary (German Cargo Services), Air Canada and the American small parcels carrier, UPS Airlines. Although it was expensive, the conversion of DC-8-60s into DC-8-70s (the series reference given to the re-engined DC-8) was an economic success for those companies which were able to carry the cost. The DC-8-73CF, a lengthened version with a maximum payload of 47,990kg on 18 pallets, remains one of the best cargo aircraft of its generation.

Development of the share of fuel costs in airline cost structure
This very revealing index (see chart below, source: ICAO) is a combination between the increased importance of the fuel bill and the variations in other cost factors together with economies made in fuel consumption and the introduction of more modern aircraft. It can be seen that after a period of very rapid increases (see graph below), which were particularly pronounced between 1974 and 1985, it returned to a level similar to that observed before the first oil crisis.

3 THE OPERATIONAL CONSEQUENCES OF THE OIL CRISES

Airfreight services were challenged, road transport links reinforced, and charter companies came under threat.

A tough time for cargo
The tripling of the oil price was a fatal blow to many cargo routes, where the cost of jet fuel could represent over 35% of operating costs. [7] In the United States, the majority of cargo services were losing money in the years 1969–1972, under the combined effects of the massive entry onto the market of capacity in the holds of wide-bodied passenger aircraft, and of a severe economic recession. The escalation in fuel prices made the situation even worse. In view of this financial haemorrhage, the major American airlines, one after another, adopted the same policies over a period of a dozen years: closure of loss-making cargo networks, and re-alignment towards the sale of day-time capacity in passenger aircraft. They themselves were therefore responsible for opening up the yawning chasm into which the express parcel carriers and the Airfreight Forwarders, deprived of night-time capacity, were then cast.

In 1973, Delta Airlines withdrew its cargo flights. In the same year Continental Airlines followed suit. In 1975 it was the turn of Eastern Airlines to take the plunge. In 1978 TWA drew a line under its domestic freight operations, through not having been able to modernise in time its large cargo fleet of gas-guzzling B707s.

Finally, after putting up a brave resistance, it was the turn of the two giants United and American. In 1971, United was top dog in the freight market. It operated the largest cargo network in the United States, with a unified long-haul fleet of 15 DC-8Fs, and an impressive medium-haul fleet of 36 Quick Change B727s operated as the night cargo version – a total of over 50 aircraft. Although they remained profitable until 1968, both

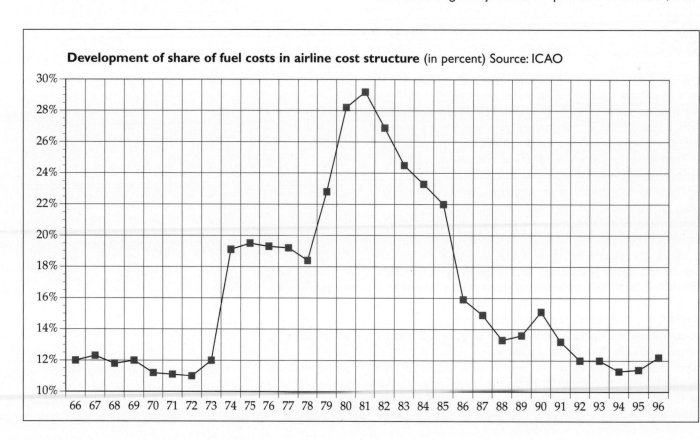

Development of share of fuel costs in airline cost structure (in percent) Source: ICAO

American Airlines B747 freighter.

parts of the all-cargo activities went into the red in 1969. Compared with the fast and often brutal reactions of other American companies confronted with this type of situation, United showed remarkable patience. It exhausted all other solutions before resorting to surgery: it reduced in stages the number of B727QCs operated as the night cargo version, optimised the turnround times of its fleet of DC-8Fs, and launched a top-of-the-range product known as "Priority Service" to distinguish it from regular freight. It was then confronted with the most difficult question of all: how to fill the holds of its passenger aircraft at prices resulting from the new rate concessions, without further undermining the economics of its cargo flights? In the absence of a satisfactory answer, United Airlines threw in the towel in 1984.

Then American, which in 1974 was in a similar position to that of United, chose the modernisation route: it bought three B747Fs (with single-side loading door) to replace some of its ageing B707s, with their high fuel consumption. Until 1981, it operated the B747Fs on the principal sectors, and 707Cs on the feeder routes.

When the second oil crisis broke, American decided to keep its too costly B707 cargo aircraft on the ground. Once again, it favoured modernisation and carried out a far-reaching reorganisation of its cargo network: it increased its fleet of B747Fs from three to six, developed road transport services, sub-contracted the operation of its feeder services and created a system of hubs. The feeder routes were operated by two "supplemental" airlines, Transamerica and Southern Air Transport using Hercules L100-30 aircraft, a civilian version of the C-130 military machine. Transamerica operated between Boston and Chicago and Southern Air Transport flew between

Port au Prince, Santo Domingo and San Juan, linking up with the B747Fs of American Airlines. [8]

Unfortunately the system was too expensive. American Airlines in its turn abandoned cargo operations in 1984.

We still have not finished living out the dramatic consequences of these abandonments. They eased the task of the new express freight carriers, and forced the most dynamic of the domestic Airfreight Forwarders, eager to maintain the quality of the products they offered their clientele, to set up for themselves night freight capacity which the scheduled airlines were no longer providing. When one takes a closer look at things, the breakdown of the barriers between freight forwarders and carriers resulted more from the weakness of the former than the ambition of the latter. For proof of this, one has only to look at the annual reports of the Emery Air Freight Corporation.

Emery, which had been founded in 1946 as an airfreight specialist , was now the world's leading forwarder for airfreight, whether in terms of volume of activities or quality of service. It was one of the largest clients of the airlines, particularly of the American ones, but when these were unable to provide night-time all-cargo services it was forced to change its purchasing policy:

• Annual Report 1974: "In 1973 and through most of last year we found that the only way to provide our customers overnight airfreight services to the Eastern and Central areas of the US was to charter four Electra airplanes to serve the triangle running from Ohio to New England and to the South Central states" (p.5).

• Annual Report 1976: In the course of the three previous years, the quadrupling of the fuel price and the appearance of wide-bodied jets had had a dramatic effect on the operations of airlines. This was particularly the case at night, when they

Flying Tigers B747F.

wanted to shift their consignments. In order to remedy the situation Emery decided to change up a gear, and introduced Emery Air Force on 14th September 1976. This in-house airfreight system included a whole variety of cargo planes, from DC-8s carrying 30 tonnes to Beechcraft 18s, carrying 1,100kg.

• Annual Report 1977: "The aircraft charter element of Emery Air Force consisting of 16 aircraft, including two DC-8s, four Lockheed Electras, four Convair 580s and a variety of small planes, remained basically unchanged during the year, although the number of cities served by this private airline grew from 21 to 26." New developments would follow thick and fast!

In Europe, the oil crisis had a disastrous impact on medium-haul cargo links. Companies like Air France, which in 1970 had begun to question the justification for its European cargo operations, took the opportunity to speed up its withdrawal. British European Airways, which at that time operated Europe's densest cargo network, reduced its fleet of Merchantmen from nine aircraft to four on 1st May 1975. It closed a series of routes to Brussels, Paris, Zurich, Vienna and Hamburg… but this was only the first stage in shutting down the network completely, and was followed by a campaign to fill the hold capacities offered by its passenger aircraft. As for Lufthansa, it abandoned its domestic cargo flights and stopped the night services of its fleet of B727QCs.

The rise in fuel prices brought about very varied repercussions for the long-haul cargo operations. Some airlines speeded up the process of modernising their fleets, going over to the most economical aircraft, such as the B747F, the re-engined DC-8F or the DC-10CF. That was the policy of Air France, Japan Airlines or Lufthansa. Other airlines followed the North American example and abolished their long-haul cargo services. This was the case with Swissair, British Airways and even KLM.

In the long series of abdications by the largest airlines, KLM plays an altogether special role. The decision to close down its transatlantic cargo services, which had been opened in 1948, had a shattering effect in view of KLM's previous long-term commitment to freight. It sowed doubt in the minds of the managements of several airlines, who became uneasy at seeing such a redoubtable competitor change its strategy so radically. In fact, this was not so much a renunciation as a new policy,

based on the acquisition and optimum utilisation of a large fleet of Boeing B747 Combis. This aircraft had become KLM's workhorse, and at all levels and for all types of service was regarded as a true passenger aircraft, doubling as a full-blooded cargo machine. Or vice versa. This operation was underpinned by a close integration between passenger and freight activities during the programme definition stage, and by the very large degree of autonomy granted to the two functions concerning their organisational and commercial policies. This is what KLM called "The Combi philosophy". [9]

At the end of each of the first two oil shocks, a number of cargo services disappeared. For long-haul requirements, they were replaced by the capacity available in the holds of wide-bodied passenger aircraft, and for medium-haul operations in the United States and Europe they were replaced by road connections.

Trucks take the strain

In Europe, new kinds of road services replaced the air cargo services, which began to be abolished in 1970. The road links had been created for pre- or post-shipment of transit traffic between one airport and another. Hence Air France operated a Düsseldorf/Paris service to bring freight from German customers to Paris by truck, for onward shipment to Brazil, Japan or Canada, or the same service in the opposite direction. These new types of services were known as "surface air transport", "road services" or sometimes "truck flights", or more simply "ARS" (Air Route Services) or RFS (Road Feeder Services). The last name is perhaps most accurate: it expresses the idea of road services used as feeders to supply long-haul passenger or cargo flights.

Until 1973, a rather restrictive IATA regulation limited the involvement of a surface transport method (generally road) to cover the first section of a long-haul route. It was only possible to substitute an air section by a surface section within the context of a transport document and rate established end-to-end (for example from Düsseldorf to Sao Paulo) if one of the six following conditions was fulfilled:

1. Lack of available cargo space on the air carrier's services;
2. Size of the consignment is such that it cannot be accommodated on the type of aircraft operated by the carrier;
3. The air carrier refuses to accept the consignment;
4. Carriage on the air carrier's service will delay its arrival at the connecting point or the final destination;
5. Carriage on the air carrier's services cannot be accomplished within 24 hours of acceptance;
6. Carriage of the consignment on the air carrier's services will result in a missed connection.

Such a restrictive regulation was not appropriate for a continent as small as Europe, once a large part of the available cargo services had been abolished, and the freight capacities on long-haul flights had been considerably increased as a result of the introduction of wide-bodied aircraft. As always happens in such cases, the regulation was cheerfully broken. The only thing to do was to change the regulation. This happened in the IATA Conference of 1973, which completely liberalised the practice of "substitution" within Europe, inside a zone including Germany, Austria, Belgium, Denmark, France, Luxembourg, The Netherlands and Switzerland.

Three companies, British European Airways, Air France and KLM, were the pioneers of "truck-flights" in Europe. BEA, tired of the structurally determined losses of its domestic cargo services, closed the operation, and on 1st December 1969 opened a "truck network" consisting of three services out of London (to Manchester, Birmingham and Bristol) and two out of Manchester (to Liverpool and Teesside). For its part KLM launched an international Amsterdam/Antwerp/Brussels truck route in 1970. Finally, Air France, learning from BEA's example, but wishing to offer a quality service to its clients in the provinces, posed the following question in 1970:

"The continuation of considerable losses appears intolerable and raises the problem as to whether it is really the vocation of the aeroplane – other than mixed versions – to carry freight on connections of 200 [125 miles] to 500km [300 miles], and whether fast ground communications, which would be less expensive and just as regular, could not replace it." [10]

As the reply was positive, Air France started setting up a domestic road network on 1st January 1971 and opened seven routes in succession:

• 1st January 1971: Lyons/Paris return and Marseilles/Paris return

• April 1971: Mulhouse/Paris return and Strasbourg/Paris return

• 1st May 1971: Lille/Paris return

• 1st October 1971: Toulouse/Paris (Service operated by rail with a road carrier in a combined piggy-back system, due to inadequate road infrastructure.)

• 1st November 1978: Bordeaux/Paris

This service pattern did not change until the introduction of wide-bodied Airbus aircraft by Air Inter. As road services offered transport and transit times which were too long for small consignments, the problem was solved by using palletised capacity available on the last passenger flight of each day.

All these road connections shared certain common characteristics which distinguished them from previous solutions. They were now scheduled services, operating according to a published timetable and provided with a "flight number". They were not operated by the airlines themselves, but by road transport companies under contract, who used vehicles, which had been specially modified for handling airline loading units (floors fitted with rollers and an anchoring system). From every point of view – price levels, handling procedures, consignment documents and follow up system – they were integrated into the airfreight operation. To take up the picturesque expression of a road transporter, [11] they really did operate as "planes without wings". Thus a new mode of operation was born, intimately combining road and air transport. Within a few years this integrated solution would meet with extraordinary success, to such an extent that it became the cornerstone of the European airfreight system. From its modest origins it expanded in three areas: technical, operational and geographical.

From a technical point of view the first lorries, which were superficially modified to transport 2.24m-wide pallets gave way to increasingly sophisticated specialised vehicles.

These new versions could take the whole variety of units in service, up to 2.44m wide and 3.02m high. The trucks were equipped with rollers which were originally fixed, then retractable, and the floor was covered with a non-slip surface. Particular configurations had been designed to carry certain categories of goods: air-ride suspension for computers, various types of scientific equipment or aircraft engines; and controlled temperature systems for perishable products etc. In addition, there was a complete range of equipment from a truck able to carry three pallets, up to a trailer for five pallets.

From an operational viewpoint, the solution of the "truck-flights" formula at several European airports (Roissy, Amsterdam, Frankfurt, Luxembourg etc) enabled connecting hubs to be organised between trucks and aircraft, based on the American hub & spoke system, [12] gaining access to all the flexibility of road transport, and permitting rapid reaction to the needs of the market. It benefited greatly from the improvements in the European motorway network and provided the only means of carrying out pickups and deliveries of large consignments door to door, either by means of supplementary services or at the expense of slight detours. Like any formula, it had its weak points, but these were secondary in comparison to its advantages. Trucks are certainly slower than aeroplanes, but they are much more economical. With some over-simplification we can say that aeroplanes should carry small consignments on inter-continental transit; trucks (with few exceptions) should carry consignments of a pallet or more. With regard to the quality of transport, a smooth flow of operations on the ground requires perfect palletisation techniques. If this is not ensured, particularly in the case of journeys outside the motorways, goods can pile up against the walls of the truck, under the effects of vibration from the road, and unloading deformed pallets can be a long and difficult process.

From a geographical point of view, the period 1970–1990 saw expansion in various directions:

LEFT **The alliance of the truck and the aircraft.** *Air France Document*

RIGHT **Map of Nigeria.** *Source: ITA, Blue Study, 1975/2 "Transport, the key to development in Nigeria"*

BELOW RIGHT **Loading a Tradewinds B707 freighter.**

• Europe was quickly covered with a close network of "feeder flights" using surface transport. It is no exaggeration to say that from 1980, airfreight was being carried by road throughout the length and breadth of Europe. Air France and KLM, whose performance figures were visibly better than the potential of their domestic markets, were among the companies which used "surface flights" on the largest scale.

As an example, in 1987, Air France provided a regular service to 50 European cities, several times per week or per day, carrying out 400 truck movements per week, and transporting over 150,000 tonnes per year.

• The United States was slower in taking up private road feeder services for two basic reasons. The first was negative, and resulted from very restrictive road transport regulations, which were only dismantled after 1980. The second, which was positive, was the presence of a venerable institution: Air Cargo Inc. This was a kind of co-operative, founded in 1946 and jointly owned by a large number of scheduled airlines. From the time of its creation, its principal mission was precisely to organise deliveries and pick ups at the client's door, and pre- or post- flight connections, through negotiating contracts with road hauliers.

• Finally, the other major providers of airfreight set up similar services: Brazil, Japan, China etc.

In 1981, one professional summarised the position as follows: "At the present time, the pre-flight transportation by road for goods for carriage by air seems irreplaceable." [13]

Charter companies under threat
Whereas the first oil shock was favourable to charter companies, we shall see that the second had a negative impact.

In seven years the situation had completely reversed, for three major reasons:

1. The massive increase in freight capacity offered by scheduled airlines.
2. The desire of these companies to re-launch a commercial offensive against the charter carriers.
3. The obsolescence of the equipment owned by the majority of charter companies.

Under these conditions, a massacre of the charter companies ensued, especially among the British ones, whose low equity funding did not allow them to modernise. Within a few years, IAS Cargo Airlines, Transmeridian Air Cargo, British Air Cargo and Tradewinds disappeared from the scene, one after the other. The same happened with the Swiss Transvalair and the American Saturn Airways. A reorganisation of the charter market was observed, favouring certain continental European companies, which were in better financial shape (Martinair in Holland and Cargolux in Luxembourg), as well as scheduled carriers who were increasingly managing to free themselves from their regulatory scruples. The latter might have said that the market had been "cleaned up".

4 COMMERCIAL CONSEQUENCES OF THE OIL SHOCKS

Whereas a vast number of countries suffered from the steep rise in oil prices, the oil producing countries witnessed an unprecedented boom.

Nigeria
An enormous country about 600 miles long on each side, a federal republic, Nigeria had just emerged from a terrible civil war and at the beginning of the 1970s was the state with the largest population in Africa. It had a considerable need for all kinds of investment.

At the time, it was largely agricultural, but within a few years the country transformed itself into an oil-producing economy. Production, which was located in the Niger Delta on either side of Port Harcourt, between Bonny and Forcados, grew from 13 million tonnes in 1965, to 54 in 1970 and to 100 in 1973.

The oil revenues went up by a factor of eight between 1970 and 1974. On 1st April 1975, Nigeria launched an ambitious Five-Year Plan, of which the main objectives were to develop refining capacity, to start up the process of industrialisation (cement works, car assembly plant) and to modernise transport and telecommunications.

There was an explosion in the imports of investment goods. The transport infrastructure, which was very defective, soon became saturated, and Nigeria was close to suffocation. The congestion at the Port of Lagos-Apapa illustrates most dramatically the paralysis which was threatening the Nigerian economy: because of the lack of adequate quayside capacity, and of means of dispersal into the interior, ships had to lie off-shore for several weeks or even several months before being unloaded. So importers turned in droves to airfreight. Within

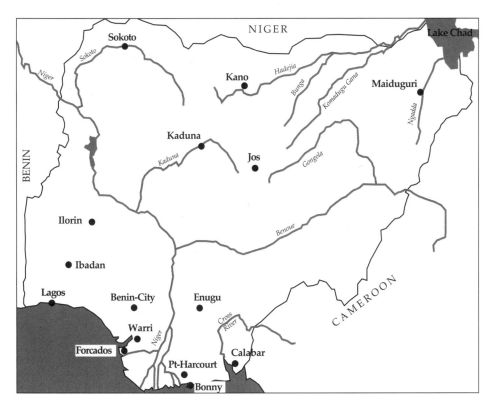

flights landed every day at Lagos airport, where they accounted for the majority of the business.

Sometimes they were full charters, but more often they were split charters, against which the IATA companies raised violent objections. This caused Antoine d'Aymery, the fiery Director for Freight and Mail at UTA, to say: "The charter companies have come storming onto this route and are charging crazy prices." Nevertheless, UTA, which was the leading scheduled airline to Nigeria, increased its frequency from one to three DC-8 cargo aircraft per week, and introduced a B747F into Lagos airport in 1979.

From a logistical point of view, the most interesting industrial traffic on the cargo links to Nigeria was the supply of cars in knocked-down form to the Volkswagen assembly lines near Lagos in the south, and of Peugeot at Kaduna (near Kano) in the north.

five years, goods traffic in the principal airports underwent a spectacular transformation (In tonnes):

	Lagos	Kano
1972	5,505	880
1977	66,000	55 000

A gigantic new market had opened up for the air companies. All the European charter companies supplied Nigeria. When traffic was at its peak in the years 1975–1977, half a dozen charter

Main charter companies serving Nigeria

Departure airport	Company
London	IAS Cargo Airlines
	TAC: Transmeridian Air Cargo
	Tradewinds
Frankfurt	GCS: German Cargo Services
	(Charter Subsidiary of Lufthansa)
Luxembourg	Cargolux, in close collaboration with

Swiss forwarding agent Panalpina
Madrid   Aviaco
Basel   Balair

• The Volkswagen example

In order to supply its assembly plant in Lagos, built near the port at Apapa, Volkswagen of Nigeria Ltd used to import about 14 500m³ of parts per month – one third from Germany and two thirds from Brazil. The siting of the Volkswagen factory was theoretically perfect, but in practice the port was completely blocked by congestion and the ships could not be unloaded. To resolve its problem Volkswagen called upon an unusual form of air/sea transport: helicopters.

Every month ships arrived from Santos and Hamburg. They anchored out at sea, and the containers were unloaded onto barges, which were towed to a point 1.25 miles from the factory. Since there was absolutely no possibility for them to get to a quay for unloading, a Bell 214 "Big Lifter" operated a relay service between the barge and the factory, carrying rather more than 2 tonnes on each voyage. During the first year of operation, from August 1976 to August 1977, this system enabled the transport of 36,000 tonnes, and reduced the average unloading time from more than six weeks to a fortnight.

At a somewhat later date, a similar helicopter service was used in the Port of Hodeida in the Yemen.

• The example of Peugeot

This is the only example of a large-scale civilian commercial airlift: more than 130,000 tonnes in five years. It was an exemplary operation – which became a text book case in logistics. It was minutely described by the Managing Director of GEFCO, a subsidiary company of Peugeot, which acted as a public carrier and transport broker, that had been made responsible for the operation. [14] Perhaps we should let him speak for himself:

"In the first phase, it was a question of regularly transporting the components for assembling 80 cars per day of types 404 and 504, ie roughly 20,000 cars per year, or, if you prefer, somewhat over 20,000 tonnes.

"I would like to draw particular attention to the word 'regularly'.

"In fact, the supply of an assembly line requires an almost absolute regularity, in the absence of which any consistent manufacture becomes impossible, especially since, at a distance of 6,000km [3,750 miles], it is difficult to arrange emergency supplies.

"We quickly saw that the real difficulties began with the arrival at Apapa, which is the industrial port for Lagos.

"Even while we were doing the first investigations on this problem, the Port of Apapa had almost reached saturation point.

"Subsequently, the situation got even worse, since in October 1975, the 300 ships which were lying off Lagos were subject to waiting periods of over three months...

"The question was, how to transport cases, packed for ocean transport, representing a volume of over 150,000m³ per year, in the best conditions for transit time and safety, from Lagos to Kaduna.

"The town of Kaduna lies in the interior of the territory, around 900km [562.5 miles] north of Lagos, and had been chosen by the Nigerian authorities. One could envisage two means of transport between the Port of Apapa and the Kaduna site: rail and road. Nigerian Railways were very supportive, but their ability to absorb this amount of traffic also depended on a development of their infrastructure.

"We examined the possibility of undertaking transportation by truck, although the road was long, sometimes narrow, and difficult for trucks transporting extremely large cases.

"There were so many uncertainties and adverse aspects, which we felt to be factors capable of putting the supply of the assembly factory at risk, that we were prompted to examine whether other means might be employed, and this is how we were brought to look at air transport.

"What were the main groups of problems that we needed to resolve with UTA on the one hand, and with the technical services of Sochaux on the other?

"The first thing was to find the characteristics of the components to be transported, in the knowledge that knocked-down vehicles include heavy mechanical components, which are sometimes quite fragile, as well as upholstery parts which are light and deformable. Each type of component has its own density resulting from its dimensions and weight, and the average density of the whole assembly of parts, once calculated, enabled us to determine how to use the capacity offered by different types of aeroplanes.

"Once we knew the number of pallets available on board a certain aircraft, we used the experimental method, that is to say numerous palletisation tests in the factory, in order to define the number and type of constituent parts that could be loaded onto each pallet, so as to ensure that everything could be got onboard.

"In order to achieve this, it was necessary to overthrow all previous conceptions of load preparation, in order to adapt it for the great novelty of transport by air, which eventually meant the almost total absence of packaging.

"In order to give an idea of the effort which had to be made in this load preparation study, I can tell you that the packing for a single lot of 24 model 504 cars by sea required the use of 30 cases, with a volume of 170m³ and a gross weight of 37,700kg.

"The same batch by air was prepared in 10 pallets with a volume of 130m³, and a gross weight of 27,900kg, including chocks.

"It therefore saved 24% in volume and 26% in the weight transported.

"The weight of the pallets was between 1,400 and 4,700kg, depending on the type of components loaded onto each type.

"The second series of problems lay in the operational study for the different possible airports, at each end of the transport route. Both in France and in Nigeria, several airports might have been used.

"The choice fell on Lyons-Satolas and Kano, which had runways with the necessary characteristics. Both points were at some distance from the factories, so that it was necessary to arrange surface transport from Sochaux to Lyons-Satolas and from Kano to Kaduna. Because railway transport was impossible, since the airports had no rail connections, a road solution was adopted. It led us to adopt vehicles fitted with handling equipment which enabled the loading of different types of pallets (roller conveyors).

ABOVE **Air Afrique DC-8.**

"Thirdly, it was necessary to do a thorough study on the economics of different types of cargo planes on the market – DC-8-55, DC-8-63, DC-10, B747 – in order to estimate their costs, so as to compare them with those of sea transport.

"These studies, which were carried out together with the commercial and technical departments of UTA, led us to consider the DC-8-63F as the aircraft best suited to our needs for the first stage.

"Since the technical situation was accepted both by Peugeot and by UTA, it remained to work out financial estimates for the operation.

"And in the event, the cost of air transport in itself proved to be considerably above the cost for surface transport.

"However, it is not only a question of comparing the rates that apply to aircraft or ships, but to compare the totality of the elements which contribute to the cost of distribution, of which the freight rates are only one component. One has to add the transportation times, and the amount of capital tied up during these periods. One should also consider the turnover of the stocks, which determines their size, and also the direct and indirect costs of packing and the insurance premiums, which are lower for air transport than the marine rates.

"However, what really made it possible to adopt this system was the saving made in financing stock during the whole period of the transportation chain, due to the success of load preparation and packaging.

"We estimated that between leaving Sochaux and arriving at Kaduna the sea route would involve a minimum transit period of two and a half to three months, which might occasionally extend to six months. Accordingly, the stock in the factory would have had to be at least two months, or even three months of production, which meant that in total, with the stock in transit, and the factory stock, five to six months of production would have been tied up in stocks.

"With the air transport solution, the all-inclusive transport time was one week when working to a definitive rhythm and the factory had only to hold two or three weeks of stock, hence any emergency deliveries could be made almost immediately.

"It is possible to estimate the savings in stocks tied up at a minimum of four months production – 16 weeks or 80 working days.

"At a rate of 80 cars/day, this represents 6,400 vehicles, or a frozen investment, including both costs and freight, in the order of 125 million francs.

"The reduction in finance costs which we were able to enter in our final accounts amounted to roughly 800F per vehicle transported, for an annual production of 18,000 vehicles...

"... so the deal was struck between GEFCO and UTA: on 12th May 1975 the first DC-8-55F flight left Lyons-Satolas bound for Kano."

This integrated logistics system, which ensured highly efficient operations for handling, stocking and pallet loading, immediately proved to be a remarkable success. The air transport resources kept pace with the production build-up in the Kaduna factory: the 13-pallet DC-8-55Fs were replaced by DC-8-63F aircraft which took 18 pallets, and the number of weekly flights was raised to 17. But after the decision was made to raise the daily output from 160 to 180 cars, the DC-8 aircraft, even in its lengthened version, was no longer suitable. A B747F took its place on 16th October 1978. This machine, with the registration number GPAN, [15] was noteworthy for two unusual features: its gross payload, which was increased to 128 tonnes after its manufacturer had obtained a special certificate; and its livery, in which the name of the client – GEFCO – was combined with that of the carrier, UTA.

The growth of traffic was impressive: 2,500 tonnes in 1975, 18,000 in 1976, 29,000 in 1977 and 40,000 in 1978.

"This airlift, since it is indeed one, marks an important development in the transportation of goods, and proves that the cargo aircraft has, at last, won its spurs in noble combat.

"In the general scheme of things airlifts have been associated with memories of war (Berlin, Vietnam) or of famine (Sahel). But this time aviation has served the interests of economic growth, by bringing industrial countries nearer to those in the course of development. This was a turning point in commercial aviation, and for our part, we are glad to have been involved as promoters and participants. [16]

On 15th September 1979, the Lyons/Kano airlift hit the headlines: "Nigerian Government demands end of Peugeot–UTA airlift." [17] If we just look at the "transport" aspects of the question, the position of the Nigerians can be explained by two considerations:

• Difficulties in agreeing with UTA on an operating solution which would permit an equitable share in activities and above all in profits;

• The modernisation of the infrastructure within Nigeria: the Port of Lagos had been expanded, and was no longer overloaded; the Lagos/Kaduna railway line had been renovated. In addition, the Nigerian National Shipping Line was short of business.

The decision of the Nigerians was irrevocable. After four years and 10 months of operation, the Lyons/Kano airlift closed down in March 1980 with an eloquent record of success:

	Number of flights	Tonnes
Nigerian Airways	227	10,000
UTA	2,140	120,000
Total	2,367	130,000

A little over a year after the termination of the airlift, one could read in the press: "The sea link has replaced the airlift without any problems." [18] It was a tough lesson in humility.

Middle East

The Middle Eastern oil states are made up of two categories. The history of one group has been disturbed by violent events (Iraq, Iran, Kuwait), while the development of the other countries has benefited from political stability and peace (the states of the Arab peninsula). A detailed review of the air imports into the countries of the first group, by year and by country of origin, might provide the subject for a lesson in diplomatic history, whether "official" or actual, but it would go beyond the limits of this work. We will therefore concentrate on the second group. These are the countries, of which the economy, infrastructure, population and even the landscape have undergone a complete metamorphosis due to the increase in oil revenues. Although the revenues later dropped off, these countries managed to convert the boom of those "crazy years" into lasting economic prosperity, as can be seen from the table below, which traces the cumulative development of air imports into the states of the Arab peninsula, coming from five countries (Germany, United States, France, Great Britain and The Netherlands) between 1970 and 1985.

All the countries of the Middle East found themselves in the same situation in 1975, with a surge in imports, and congestion on all communication routes.

The sea routes, which had been the traditional transport method, were close to suffocation point: the time lost at anchor off Jeddah often reached 100 days! The ports were blocked, and so companies turned to surface transportation: rail and road. There are two rail links between Europe and the Middle East: one northern route via the former USSR and one southern route via Turkey. Both routes rapidly became overloaded in their turn and it could take three to six weeks to reach Syria or Iran, with frequent damage to the cargo.

It was then that road transport underwent an extraordinary development: the roads linking Western Europe to the Middle East in 1974–1978 witnessed some of the finest passages in road transport history. A whole folklore grew up around these routes which crossed Yugoslavia, Bulgaria and Turkey. During each journey, the lorry driver, who was very much dependant on his own resources, had the opportunity to

---

Development of imports by air of the states of the Arabian peninsula
(In tonnes)

	Saudi Arabia	United Arab Emirates	Bahrain Oman-Qatar, Yemen	Total
1970	3,650	2,500	1,250	7,400
1975	24,100	16,100	9,500	49,700
1980	50,000	23,000	15,000	88,000
1985	62,500	27,100	32,400	122,000

RIGHT **TMA of Lebanon DC-4.**
Air Cargo News UK

BELOW RIGHT **TMA (Trans Mediterranean Airways) Avro York.**
MAP

BOTTOM RIGHT **TMA of Lebanon B707-320C.**
MAP

rediscover the truth in the old saying: "The Orient begins at Vienna". There were innumerable obstacles: the permanent risk of accidents on the narrow crowded roads, the passage through villages teeming with activity, the crossing of dangerous snowed-up winter passes in Turkey, long and complicated customs formalities to get across each frontier, the lack of lay-bys or simply somewhere to stay en route.

The average transit times, if the idea of an average still had any meaning, were – depending on the season – between 9 and 20 days to Iraq and Iran, and 20 to 30 days to Saudi Arabia and the Emirates. Overcrowded roads, blocked-up railways, strangled ports – but the airways were free, so long as the airports themselves were not congested! Three features characterise the rapid expansion of the air transport of goods from Europe and the United States to the Middle East during the years 1974–1980:

• The break-up of the old transport system between Europe and the Middle East
Previously, Beirut had been the hub between Europe and the Middle East, and the Lebanese airlines had profited greatly from the situation. Trans Mediterranean Airways (TMA) had certainly done so for freight. It had been set up in 1953 by Munir Abu Haidar to provide supplies of fresh foodstuffs for the expatriate personnel of the almighty Aramco on its various exploration and operating sites in Saudi Arabia. He had started off with two York cargo planes (the civilian development of the British Lancaster bomber), and had then bought a number of DC-4s, after obtaining from the Lebanese authorities permission to operate scheduled cargo lines in 1959.

When the first oil crisis broke in 1973, TMA became a large cargo company: it operated a fleet consisting of seven B707-320Cs and a few old DC-6s. It flew to the United States, Europe, Japan and the whole of the Middle East, and even provided a "round the world" cargo service, and its legendary "rate flexibility" did not stop it belonging to the establishment of the IATA airlines. To a large extent, Beirut was a "compulsory stop" between Europe and the countries of the Middle East, which lay to the east and the southeast.

From about 1975, Beirut lost its function as "port of entry" to the Middle East, under the three-fold effect of expanding traffic (which justified direct flights to the final destination); the calling into question of Beirut's traditional role by the oil states, and the disturbances in Lebanon, which forced TMA to leave Beirut and take refuge in the Gulf.

Among all the European airlines, Air France, under the dynamic leadership of its Freight Director Jean Rispal, was best able to take advantage of the new economic structure in the region. In order to keep up with, or even anticipate, the rise in traffic volume, Air France successively opened direct cargo services from Paris to all the main centres of the Middle East, flying B707Cs and then B747Fs.

• The pre-eminent role of chartering
Chartering in general, not only that carried out by charter companies, represented a considerable proportion of the traffic. We again meet the same airlines that were involved in Nigeria. The Middle East was a kaleidoscope of countries, all with very different regulations. Some of them were very restrictive regarding charter companies (Saudi Arabia, Iran) while others were more open (Iraq, Kuwait) or even positively welcoming (Dubai, Sharjah, Abu Dhabi).
Dubai, with its past as a maritime and commercial centre, its very liberal policies and its speedy and efficient customs procedures, which had the edge on those in force in most other countries of the region, very quickly asserted itself as the great caravanserai of air transport. All the charter airlines in Europe met up there and engaged in split chartering.
However, full charter services, either individually or in a series of a few tens or even hundreds of flights, were also one of the typical features of this incredible time, when aircraft were used to transport sacks of cement and steel tubes, or even entire orchards or palaces. Although sometimes operated by charter airlines, these flights were often carried out by scheduled airlines (Saudia, Lufthansa, Air France), using their own or hired aircraft.

• The diversity of goods carried
During the years 1975/1980, all imaginable products were carried by air: the richness and diversity of the market seemed to be limitless !
First of all came all the items which were connected with oil exploration or production, from the most sensitive equipment – measuring instruments – to the heaviest types of product – valves, tubing of all sizes, and even oil pipes. The traffic reached its highest levels between Houston, the main world centre for oil equipment, and all the oil-producing countries.
Next came an enormous variety of investment goods and industrial products connected with the modernisation of the infrastructure (ports, airports, telecommunication networks) and the construction of the first industrial projects (electricity generating stations, petro-chemical complexes, seawater desalination plants). Then, as the major initial projects were completed, the supply of spare parts gradually took over.
Within the framework of a strict urban planning regime, whole towns arose in the desert or were totally transformed: Jeddah, Riyadh, Abu Dhabi, Dubai, Muscat, etc … The oil revenues were so abundant, and there was such a thirst for building, in the face of such crying need, that the authorities hastened to turn their dreams into realities in the shortest

possible time. It was only the frequent and often irrational use of airfreight that allowed work to be completed on time, avoiding the often punitive penalties for delay: there were even charter flights to deliver street lighting equipment or slabs of fibre-reinforced cement…
Arabia is also a region where royal families lead luxurious lifestyles. The European construction industry was engaged in building sumptuous palaces. More than for any other type of building work, it was necessary to adhere to the agreed completion dates, and marble slabs and mosaic tiles all arrived by air.
Along with wealth, oil brought to these sovereigns of the desert, who had been born in tents, the most valuable of commodities: water. They cultivated gardens and planted orchards of imported trees. The largest contracts were won by a French company, Établissements Delbard, who supplied several million fruit trees to Iran and Saudi Arabia in the years 1975–1980. Packed with bare roots, in bundles of 25, weighing about 10 kilos, the plants were transported by the planeload to their destinations.
The affluence of the local population, and the introduction of large numbers of expatriates, created an important market for consumer goods in countries which produced nothing – except for oil! Several European freight agents built up groupage services for clothing, perfumes, photographic goods and hi-fi or white goods. Spare parts for cars and lorries, mostly German or Japanese, were among the most regular products transported and were therefore the most coveted by the airlines. Even expensive luxury cars were delivered by air.
The expatriate population along with the affluent locals were also partial to fresh foodstuffs. Thousands of tonnes of perishable goods were flown in: vegetables and mangoes from India and Pakistan and grapes from Cyprus. Fresh meat from Eastern Europe and Australia (mutton, with Halal certification went on sale in the butchers' shops in Dubai and Abu Dhabi less than 24 hours after being slaughtered in Melbourne). No souk of the Orient, however rich, could ever have rivalled the variety of products transported by plane!
We will end this list with a mention of the programme for distributing food rations to the school children of Saudi Arabia. In response to an idea of King Faisal in 1971, "The School Feeding Programme" got under way in 1976. It consisted in providing each child every day with a cardboard box containing a ration of food (biscuits, figs, condensed milk, orange juice). After a detailed logistics study, a solution combining sea and road transport was finally adopted, based on a supply centre in Cyprus. As was often the case, air transport was only employed during the start-up phase of the operation, and later after the launch to overcome possible breakdowns in surface transport. Between December 1976 and November 1977, Air France transported nearly 5,000 tonnes of food rations pre-packed by a large French food company, sent from Paris Orly and Lyons-Satolas to Dhahran and Jeddah. No souk of the Orient, however rich, could ever have rivalled the variety of product transported by plane.

4 THE EXPRESS EXPLOSION

The ever-punctual and indefatigable "pioneer of overnight, courier-accompanied package-delivery, as every man in the street will tell you, is Santa Claus"! [1] To judge by the number of companies, that exist today, specialising in the express transport of all kinds of documents and parcels, he should be proud of his offspring.

Express parcel services, which originated in the United States and have spread throughout the world, were not born in the 1970s. However, since then they have acquired such energy that they have become one of the major events in commercial aviation and in transport history towards the end of the 20th century.

I "EXPRESS IS IN THE AIR..."

Around 1970, in various sectors of the economy, one could observe a desire for new fast transport techniques, arising from the failure of traditional systems.

Market pressures

At the end of the 1960s, the world was undergoing rapid transformation. International trade was developing at a sustained rhythm, and multinational companies were becoming increasingly important.

Together with the new phenomenon of industrial relocations, such developments generated hitherto unknown requirements for fast communications of all types: information, documents, goods.

At the same time, "service industries" moved to top position in world economic activity. The international expansion of banks and financial institutions, insurance companies, design offices, consultancy companies and advertising agencies produced increasing floods of business papers, contracts, quotations for tenders etc.

The "micro-processor revolution" was building up at the same time, creating additional demand for urgent consignments of computer components and data processing material.

Finally, the introduction of new methods of managing the flow of manufactured goods ("just in time", or "zero stock techniques") made production more dependent than ever on the regularity and reliability of incoming and outgoing trans-portation. The breaking down of unitised loads into smaller lots, resulting from the practice of continuous supply, and the miniaturisation of many products also served to increase the number of small consignments, and to produce the extremely rapid development of a time-sensitive market.

First reactions

This market need precipitated a myriad initiatives, some of them very original. Three Californian students, during the summer of 1968, found an enjoyable way of making some pocket money – carrying business papers between San Francisco and Hawaii, and delivering them directly into the hands of their addressees. "Air tickets and incidental expenses were of course paid by the sender, for whom a few hundred dollars was small beer, compared with the importance of the consignments – bills of lading for sea freight, documentary credits, samples – which the Californian postal services did not treat with sufficient care to meet their demands. Business was so good that, at the end of the vacation, the three college boys decided to continue the work on their own account. At the beginning of 1969 they founded their own private courier business." [2] All that was needed was a name. They decided to take the initials of their family names, and since they were called Dalsey, Hillblom and Lynn, that made "DHL".

They had just founded the archetype of a new kind of enterprise for the rapid transportation of business documents and small parcels from door-to-door: international couriers. Originally, the operating principle depended on sending bags full of documents and parcels in the holds of passenger aircraft accompanied by a courier travelling in the passenger cabin on a normal airline ticket.

Without taking up such revolutionary solutions, traditional operators tried to respond to this development of the market by launching new products, which were frequently ill-adapted to the demand.

The American Post Office, far from taking a partisan view of things, reacted quickly to the needs of the market by proposing in 1970 a new service called Express Mail. This was a fast postal service with special delivery, but with no provision for collection from the sender. The items had to be taken to Post Office counters, and not all offices were open for this new service.

Looking at the airlines, one sees a positive blossoming of schemes: in July 1972, 15 domestic American airlines offered accelerated services for small packages – SPS or small package services. A year later there were 18. The Sales Manager of Western Airlines Cargo gave the following opinion on the situation: "There is a whole new market in the time-critical items and the market demands a premium service" [3] The "small package service" is an extremely efficient airport/airport service: the consignments (up to 25 or 3kg) are taken to the passenger check-in desks up to 10 minutes before the departure of the plane, and are picked up from the luggage delivery conveyors (the procedures are very simple, since this is domestic transportation and there are no customs formalities). If the package is not loaded on the intended flight, the sender automatically receives a reduction of up to 50%.

The Delta Airlines Cargo Manager pointed out that this was "the fastest growing segment" of the market, and his opposite number in Alaska Airlines considered that "the SPS – Small Package Service – fills a previously severe need in the total transport chain." [4] Whatever the service was called (AA Priority Parcel Service for American Airlines, Sprint for Eastern Airlines, etc) the pick-up and delivery services were left up to the customers. But the market wanted an "end-to-end" or "door-to-door" service.

For its part, in 1971 IATA studied a revolutionary proposal from Air France concerning experimental door-to-door cargo transportation in Europe, offering the customers "an all-in, door-to-door rate for consignments of a minimum of 200kg delivered in containers to the airlines by the air cargo agents". It is a pity that this proposal, which had the merit of introducing the idea of door-to-door rates into the IATA regulations, did not receive a more favourable reception. It might have given the traditional airlines and freight agents, at the cost of some far-reaching changes, and of a serious commitment by all concerned, a coherent door-to-door express transport system. But the IATA companies missed their opportunity. Express freight, in its current form, was born in the United States outside their circle.

2 THE UNITED STATES: FERTILE GROUND

The express revolution fulfilling a growing market need, resulted from a whole bundle of mutually dependent causes.

First cause: an old American tradition
The force of history was the fundamental cause. Express freight services lay at the heart of American history in the 19th century, tied up with the race to the West, the Gold Rush and the Native Americans. It became part of folklore. The modern express services were a return to America's roots and can be traced back over 150 years.

In 1850, at the time of the Gold Rush, Plumas County, in the north of California, was a wooded and mountainous country, lacking safe roads and covered in a thick layer of snow for many months of the year. The local chronicle [5] reported:

"The express lines were quite an institution in the pioneer days. It was several years before any Post Offices were established in the country or any mail service inaugurated and the people had to depend upon the Express for all postal accommodation… Letters, newspapers, small parcels and gold dust

were the articles carried by the express men, the postal business being the most important and the most remunerative."

Like the pilots of the US Airmail or those of Aéropostale, the messengers "got through" in any weather:

"During the Winter of 1852–53 the express men had a hard time of it on the road from Bidwell, being compelled to leave their mules at Teavine and fight their way on foot through the snow. At that time snow shoes were unknown here and the luckless messenger had to plunge and flounder through the deep snow as best he could."

It was a great advance in 1858, when dog sledges were introduced:

"On the sledge was a small chest in which were carried the US mail (a Post Office having been established two years before at Quincy)."

This is how the express messengers and the American Post supported one another.

Express was also the story of Bill Cody – better known under the name of Buffalo Bill – who at the age of 14 carried important packages for the house of Russel, Majors & Waddel. This was the Pony Express, whose young riders, no more than 18 years old, went from the town of Saint-Joseph, Missouri to Sacramento, California, galloping like the wind across prairies, mountains and deserts in 10 days to spread the great news: "Lincoln elected". In total of 35,000 letters were delivered by the Pony Express [6] between April 1860 and October 1861.

But starting on 4th March 1839, express deliveries would take on a new guise, which they would keep for over a century: an activity closely linked with the legend and the industry of the railroads. At the outset, the conductors on the trains had carried out small errands for individuals living in the localities they passed through. In its new form, express grew from the separation of the two functions: that of the conductor and that of the agent carrying transactions between individuals and businessmen, ensuring the rapid despatch of small packages, newspapers and even letters and commercial orders. On 4th March 1839, a locomotive driver from the Boston & Worcester Railway, William F. Harnden, took a big step. He founded his own company, "The Cheney & Co's Express", and started the first "express service" between New York and Boston. He inspired many emulators, and express services enjoyed considerable success, which went hand in hand with the construction of the world's largest rail network. The Post reacted, and on 3rd March 1845 an Act of Congress prohibited the conveyance of inter-city letters by independent mail and express companies, becoming effective on 1st July 1845. Always obedient, Harden published a notice: "Letters are not taken on any terms." [7]

After a phase of intense proliferation, a regrouping soon followed. Three companies came to dominate the express industry during the second half of the 19th century: Adams in the east of America, Southern Express in the south and Wells Fargo, the most famous, in the west. This last was founded in 1852 by Henry Wells and William Fargo, co-founders of the American Express Company – and it played an active role in opening up the West, and developed banking activities in parallel with those of express carrier. It defined itself as "Banker and Express Company".

Thus, express became deeply anchored in the history of the United States. So much so that express men "soon earned a reputation for efficiency and integrity that was actually described in the proverbial phrase "with the promptness and fidelity of an express man". It is significant that the express services of today include a number of features of those express services at the end of the 19th century. [8]

• Day and night transport on board passenger trains;

• The emphasis on three inseparable key criteria: speed, safety of the consignments and reliability of the service;

• "Automatic" collection of the consignments at the door. In 1915, an advertisement of the Wells Fargo & Co Express explained that it was enough to hang out a Wells Fargo placard at the door of a shop to have one of the company's vehicles pass automatically to collect the consignment! That was even easier than using telephone, which not everyone had installed at that time;

• Direct "point-to-point" distribution, ie from the manufacturer to the retailer, short-circuiting the usual chain of intermediate warehouses;

• The scale of the resources and the magnitude of the traffic: in 1895, 40,000 express agencies covering the whole country transferred over 100 million packages of goods, and 20 million consignments of bank notes and coinage.

To take up the words of the President of the Adams Express Company: "The express had then become a recognised necessity in the commercial and industrial transactions in the country." [9]

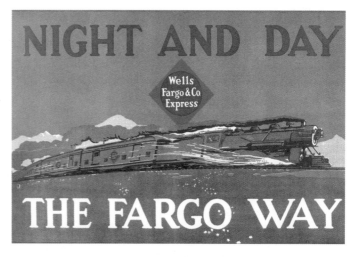

Two posters advertising the advantages of Fargo & Co express service and night and day business services.

Second cause: the closure of the Air Express service of the REA (Railway Express Agency)

It will be recalled that from 1927 onwards, the United States had built up an original system of express transport by plane, which featured a generalisation of the offer on the part of the airlines, and an exclusive marketing system.

In 1969, the REA entered a period of turbulence, and was sold off by the railway companies when it began losing money. In 1970, it turned to the CAB to re-negotiate rules for splitting the income with the airlines. The CAB granted a provisional uplift of the remuneration to the Agency in September 1970, but at the same time it set in motion one of the large investigations which were its forte. The investigation would last several years, and was known as the Air Express Investigation Case.

This initiative spelled danger for the REA, which was monopolistic in character, at a time when the first premonitory signs of deregulation were beginning to become apparent. Proclaiming that "free competition stimulates the development of airfreight operations", the CAB decided that the exclusivity which the REA had enjoyed up till then was not in the public interest, and fixed the date of 30th June 1974 to bring to an end the Air Express Service as it had existed in the United States since 1927. It added: "The time has come to create a solid basis for an excellent service for small consignments." [10] Air Express

left the scene just at the moment when new forms of express transport were emerging. This was not by mere coincidence, for nature abhors a vacuum and it was very rapidly filled. As Emery Air Freight emphasised, the cancellation of the Air Express contract with the airlines would prove to be of great importance. [11]

Third cause: weaknesses of the Post and the airlines

It might be thought that the seeds of the new express services would not have germinated so easily if the Post and the airlines had been able to maintain a high standard in their quality of service. We might recall that in 1920, an air parcel collected in Paris at 11.00 hours was delivered in London at 17.00 hours. And we might reflect on the fact that the "petite poste" organised by M. De Chamousset in Paris on 1st January 1769 provided nine deliveries per day! In the beginning, the services of the Post and the airlines were similar to an express service. By 1970, this was no longer the case…

In the United States, the postal service often performed badly: "Today, on impulse, I conducted a private study of the morning's airmail originating west of the Mississippi (my office is in New York). Fully 90% took five days or more to deliver. Even taking into consideration the fact that a holiday intervened, this record in the age of air transport, is atrocious." [12]

Among the airlines, the situation was far from satisfactory. Too often, consignments spent an amount of time on the ground, in the warehouses of the carriers and or freight agents, which was incompatible with the very nature of airfreight. In addition, the general practice of consolidation resulted in many cases in an excessive slowing down of the shipment of small consignments, which benefited from the largest rate reduction for the sender, and at the same time generated the maximum of profit for the forwarder.

3 THE DETONATOR: FRED SMITH AND FEDERAL EXPRESS

The story of Frederick W. Smith, the founder of Federal Express, is that of one of the greatest American entrepreneurs of the second half of the 20th century.

"There is no denying Smith's role as father of a new industry. By starting his express-transportation business in 1971, he ignited an explosion of demand that continues to shoot off new business sparks." [13] Twenty-five years later, in 1997, Federal Express had a turnover of $11.5 billion (73% on the domestic American market and 27% on international markets), transported 2.7 million express packages and documents per day, employed a fleet of 584 aircraft and 38,500 vehicles, used an extremely efficient computer system connected to nearly 700,000 customers and employed 108,000 people world-wide. [14]

Fred Smith came from a business background in Memphis, Tennessee, where his father owned a bus company called Dixie Greyhound. Like Juan Trippe, he went to Yale University. There he wrote a thesis, which only received a mediocre mark, describing the outline of a new system for the express door-to-door transport of small packages. Then he served with the Marines in Vietnam, an experience that was to affect him profoundly. On his return, since he had a certain amount of capital, he founded the Federal Express Corporation in 1971 with the intention of putting into practice the revolutionary ideas which he had developed in his academic thesis. After two market studies carried out by external companies had confirmed the dissatisfaction of the customers, and the existence of a potential market, he started operations on

17th April 1973. According to Fred Smith's vision (and vision is a term which features frequently in his vocabulary), this new system for the express transport of packages is both an operational concept and a commercial product.

• The operating concept depended on three principles:

1. The use of a single hub facility, located in Memphis, Tennessee. This is the famous hub-and-spoke system, in which all the aircraft converge upon a single connecting hub during the night. In fact, "the reduction in transit times is achieved by an intensive utilisation of night transport". [15]

This system was used in the United States by road transport companies and by United Parcel Service (UPS), and partly operated in Europe in the night transport network of some Post Offices (Germany, France). It had never been applied in such a stringent manner as by Federal Express.

In this example of the concept, the aircraft leave their home airports during the evening and head towards Memphis for a gigantic night-time rendezvous, which reaches a peak between 01.00 and 04.00 hours in the morning. The planes hardly have time to touch down before they are unloaded. The packages are sorted and assigned to a flight according to their final destination. The reloaded planes take off before 04.00 hours in the morning back to their original airport, so that the packages can be delivered to their addressees during the course of that morning.

On the face of it, the concept seems nonsensical, since a package collected in the evening in New York for delivery to Boston on the following morning has to travel via Memphis! In reality, the single-hub concept presents numerous advantages: it allows a maximum number of towns to be served with a minimum number of aircraft, it reduces the heavy ground investment by concentrating it at a single point, and improves productivity and makes it easier to follow up individual consignments.

The choice of Memphis as the single hub was not for sentimental reasons, but for objective considerations – its central location, the quality of the climate, and the particularly favourable terms of business granted by the airport authorities.

2. The execution of all operations – on the ground as in the air – entirely by Federal Express, "from the shippers dock to the consignee's door"

Federal Express advertisement.

May, 1973.
The small package airline comes to your rescue.

Until now, the man who had to ship or receive small packages in a hurry lived at the mercy of the system.

So we created a system just for him.

Federal Express is an airline designed from the ground up just for the door-to-door delivery of small packages.

Most important, it's so fast, so reliable, so cheap, it's going to change your whole way of doing business. Overnight.

Our flights now cover 30 major cities. Soon, we'll be serving 90% of the U.S. To get the details on this revolutionary new system, and find out if it's now serving your area, simply call us, toll free, at (800) 238-5560.

Now it costs less to ship packages faster.

In contrast to classic systems, which break up the transport chain between several operators (road carriers, freight forwarders, airlines), Federal Express carries out all these operations itself, whether on the ground or in the air. It integrates all the means and all the operations of transportation: it is an integrator. At the same time it is also a road transport company, a freight forwarder and an airline. It shook up and transcended all categories. It worried the competition in every category because it escaped categorisation.

Thus it was that Fred Smith and his colleagues started looking for a small jet aircraft which could be converted into a cargo plane. They were limited in their choice because they wished to avoid getting involved in the long, costly and uncertain procedures of the CAB which were necessary to obtain a Certificate of Public Convenience and Necessity. It so happened that in September 1972, the CAB decided to exempt from formalities operators of aircraft having a payload of less than 7,500lb, which the CAB classed in the category of "air taxis". So the choice fell upon the Mystère Falcon 20 manufactured by Marcel Dassault-Bréguet, which perfectly fulfilled the required specification with a payload after conversion of 6,060lb or 2,760kg. Thus, with a fleet of 32 French aircraft, Fred Smith prepared to revolutionise air transportation. In contrast to his competitors, he was not dependent on the frequencies and the timetables of the scheduled American airlines, which were known to be growing increasingly unhappy with cargo operations.

3. The limitation of parcel unit weights and dimensions.
The packages handled had to correspond to certain physical standards – not over 50lb (23kg) and a maximum developed sum of the three dimensions of 108in (274cm). This desire for standardisation, which was also reflected in the offer of standardised containers to the customers, was a product of the need for simplification and automation in the handling operations in the central Memphis hub. The system, choreographed like a kind of nightly ballet, could only function if the hub ground-equipment in Memphis was capable of ingesting and sorting within a very short period of time an increasingly spectacular number of parcels.

• The commercial product was upgraded as time went by, but its original concept changed little, defined by three fundamental characteristics: it is door-to-door, guaranteed, with end to end traceability:

1. Door-to-door, ie from the sender's to the recipient's premises.
This means that the rates are simple and all-inclusive, covering pick-up, transport and delivery. The two variables are the weight and the destination.

2 Guaranteed.
The products are "time definite" (TD). If the delivery time is not achieved, the sender is reimbursed (principle of money back guarantee). "Express" implies that the delivery is "fast". However the speed of delivery can be modified according to the requirements of the customer or the nature of the goods. This is why express is not a monolithic product which only offers a single speed of shipment. It is designed less according to the concept of speed, which is always relative, if not subjective, than to a "guaranteed delivery time or date", which opens up the way for a whole range of products which are more or less urgent, but for which the door-to-door transit time is always guaranteed.

At the beginning, Federal Express proposed two systems. The first was an express service called Priority One – Overnight Air Service, with delivery to the addressee before midday on the working day following the day of collection. The second was a fast service called Standard Air Service, with guaranteed delivery on the second working day following that of collection.

3. End-to-end traceability.
Every sender is a worrier. To be reassured, he needs to know that his parcel has arrived. And to that end he receives, in return for the consignment he sent, a document called, in express jargon, a POD [16] signed by the addressee and showing the time of delivery.

This was the new product, which Federal Express was preparing to launch after a sustained publicity campaign addressed directly at the shippers. The first few weeks of operation were difficult and Fred Smith, at the age of 29, was confronted with a severe financial crisis. He managed to resolve the situation towards the end of 1973 by gathering together a substantial amount of capital in New York, and obtaining sufficient credit from his bankers. From that moment on, he was destined for success, as the figures prove, and his first profits came rolling in during 1976.

Development of key indicators in Federal Express activity

	1975	1980	1985
Income (million dollars)	43.5	415.4	2016.0
Net profit (or loss)	(11.5)	37.7	76.1
Ratio 2/1 (in percent)		9.1%	3.8%
Number of packages/day	11,100	68,022	406,049
Average weight of package (kg)	5.1	4.45	2.54

Source: Annual reports of Federal Express

Such a rate of development was not possible without changing the initial operating system or modifying the product. Competition was quick to show itself, and it became necessary to react. The development of traffic quickly raised the question of whether it was justified to have only a single handling centre. At first, the answer was to construct a super hub with an area of 54,000m^2 which in 1983 was capable of sorting over 300,000 packages every night, and later by introducing a greater degree of automation, involving early use of leading-edge data processing technology (bar codes, scanners). At the same time, overwhelmed by success, and implicitly accepting the limitations of a system that depended on a single centre, they began to implement various procedures to lighten the load at the Memphis centre (eg truck connections when the distance was compatible with the guaranteed service). After that, there was nothing to do but to open other hubs, at Newark (New Jersey), Indianapolis (Indiana) and Oakland (California).

With deregulation in 1977, there came a profound change in operations: by freeing up the capacities of both of Federal Express and of its competitors, it paved the way for an explosion of express traffic in all its forms.

Fed Ex B727.

miles around the airports, the Carrier Motor Act of 1980 enabled economic access to almost the whole of the American market (98% of the population). Finally, the de facto loosening of the conditions under which the postal monopoly was applied made it easier to sell products designed for documents and business mail, which competed directly with the Post (for example Overnight Letter Service).

Once it had ensured coverage of its home market, and obtained long-haul aircraft, Federal Express was able to go on to a new phase in its expansion: the international market. It set up its European operating centre in Brussels and started a Memphis/Brussels connection via London on 15th June 1985. As for the products, they had in the meantime become much more varied and sophisticated.

The deregulation of air services in 1977 eliminated the restrictions which had limited the payload of Federal Express aircraft to 7,500lb. Aware of the perspectives which were opening up, Fred Smith soon bought Boeing 727-100s and then wide-bodied DC-10s, spreading anxiety and consternation among the airlines, who now understood the extent of his ambitions. This is how he started a fleet policy, which was essentially based (up to the recent past) on buying and converting second-hand passenger aircraft.

The deregulation of road transport brought additional operational flexibility. By cancelling the rule, which limited the zone for home collections and deliveries to a radius of 25-50

The weight limits were continuously pushed higher (from 50 to 70 and then 150lb per package) whereas the "envelopes" containing documents completed the array of small parcels. These changes were of great importance: they widened the "areas of competition" between Federal Express and the classic airlines on the one hand, and with the Post on the other. As for the latest delivery times, they were brought forward from

12.00 hours to 10.30 hours for the overnight product. The introduction in 1981 of a computer system called Cosmos, and the timely employment of bar code technology, made considerable improvements to the information available to the customers. Thanks to data entry at the stage of collection or delivery by the driver/delivery person, the customer was now in a position to follow the progress of his consignment step by step in real time, since in practice, the item always remained in the possession of the integrator.

However, Fred Smith did not sweep the board of his competitors. Due to his over-ambitious view of the future, he committed two major strategic errors, which cost the company hundreds of millions of dollars: the launching of a system of electronic document transmission (called zapmail), a few years before fax machines invaded the market, and the premature organisation of a European transport network, underestimating the idiosyncrasies of the continent. But nobody's perfect!

4 THE EXPRESS EXPLOSION

The success of Federal Express in the field of small parcels, and of DHL for documents and business papers, encouraged many operators, airlines, forwarding agents and specialist companies to follow this new trend, enticed by the potential of a promising market and seduced by the attraction of high unit revenue – which sometimes proved illusory in economic terms. Express services spread like wild fire, promoted by three categories of operators: specialist companies, (international) couriers and the airlines. The specialist companies devoted all or an important part of their activities to the express transport of small packages. As well as several large American operators, one giant Australian company emerged, whilst medium-sized French or European players managed to establish a niche by means of specialisation in a particular market segment and a prudent policy of international market development.

In the United States, Purolator Courier was the first to take up the challenge. This was a company, which specialised in transporting bank documents and commercial packages and started up its express overnight service on 27th September 1976, working from its hub in Columbus, Ohio. In 1983 it carried over eight million parcels in a fleet of 110 chartered aircraft. On first sight the figures are impressive but they are modest when compared with the company's global traffic (only 10%), and above all when compared with the results of Federal Express. In 1984, Purolator started a policy of acquisition and of operating with its own cargo fleet. It rapidly learned to its cost that building up an integrated system for express freight needs heavy investment, and that the high unit revenue does not equate with profits in a field where economies of scale, which can be spectacular, count for everything. This was all the more so, because, with the help of the competition, the unit revenue declined. Purolator couldn't stand the heat and it was absorbed by Emery in April 1987.

In 1970 the Emery Air Freight Corporation was the benchmark for American Airfreight Forwarders, on the domestic and the international markets, whether for service quality, traffic volume or financial stability. Emery offered its customers a door-to-door service using passenger flights and the night cargo network of the large American domestic airlines. When the latter abandoned their cargo business Emery was hard hit, and immediately recognised the new danger which had emerged: "a new competitive element came to the fore in 1974. A Memphis-based air carrier, Federal Express Corp, operating under an air taxi authority, very heavily financed with venture capital, commenced operations in 1973. As of year-end 1974, they are said to be operating some 33 Jet Falcons between some 75 cities." [17]

Feeling threatened to the very core of its activities, Emery immediately followed in Federal Express's footsteps and on 2nd October 1978 launched Emery Express, a network based in

FAR LEFT **Fed Ex network in 1980.** *Source: Federal Express*

LEFT **Emery express network in 1978.**

ABOVE Burlington Air Express "stretch" DC-8 landing at Los Angeles International Airport. The engines have been "hush-kitted" to meet FAA noise regulations.

BELOW Emery Worldwide DC-8 cargo aircraft operating daily from Manchester International UK to its hub in Dayton, Ohio.
Air Cargo News UK

BOTTOM UPS was one of the two biggest players in the 1980s.

Dayton-Ohio, using dedicated air and road transport facilities.

After a period of experimentation, Emery defined its commercial strategy in January 1982: it did not subject its express product to any weight limitation, thus distinguishing itself from all the competition. But this ambitious policy proved expensive and the financial results deteriorated. Emery was forced to grow in order to achieve the economies of scale, which would allow it to reduce its unit costs. It was against this background that Emery absorbed the ailing Purolator in order to achieve "a critical mass". This was not the first time that a company imagined it would improve its situation by taking over a lame duck! As the financial chasm became ever wider, Emery was in turn taken over by Consolidated Freightways. Express is a killer industry!

Happily, other companies were more fortunate. Still in the United States, Airborne Freight Corp., a freight forwarder, converted to become an integrated carrier in 1980 and adopted the trade name Airborne Express in 1985. With its own hub airport in Wilmington, Ohio, Airborne managed to play the right cards in this extremely competitive market by adopting a proven fleet policy, putting the accent on high value-added products (like Sky Courier) and by achieving a clever balance between the functions of integrator on the domestic market and freight forwarder on the international market.

Another American freight forwarder, Burlington, originally developed out of the railway company Burlington Northern, also dived into the market for the express transport of small parcels on a D+1 (overnight) basis in 1980. With an original approach, Burlington Air Express, the operating unit in charge of the new product, possessed a fleet of special trucks and its own installations at the airports, but it did not own any planes. Therein lay the difference. Going against the general trend, the President of Burlington Northern Airfreight decided to depend exclusively on the services of all the regular carriers. The service was not without success and it was only later that Burlington brought its own private aircraft into service.

The year 1982 deserves a special note in the history of express freight, due to the entry on stage of a real heavyweight: United Parcel Service, abbreviated to UPS.

UPS, founded in Seattle in 1907, was a giant in true United States' style. It dominated the market for the delivery of small packages, without competitors other than the American Post. [18]

A few figures will give an idea of its size. In 1984, UPS transported 1.9 billion packages by surface transport (7.8 million per day!) and 56.6 million by air (ie 220,000 per day). It possessed a fleet of 62,000 vehicles and its 85,000 truck drivers, all members of the International Brotherhood of Teamsters, called automatically every day on the 680,000 customers to make pick-ups, whether they had been called or not. The physical side of the operation was combined with exceptional financial stability due to a very high rate of profitability (around 8% after tax), and a particular capital structure: UPS is a "private" company in the American sense of the term (ie not quoted on the stock exchange) and its shares are held by the management and those in retirement.

For several years, UPS had developed an air transport product for delivering packages on D+2, known as Blue Label Air, but the D+1 products were entirely outside the area of concern for UPS, who were accustomed to compete against the surface mail of the Post. However the day came when a study showed that a large number of customers were attracted by the new D+1 services of its competitors. Once its decision was taken in principle, UPS had no choice but to strike hard and fast:

• 21st September 1982: Launch of air operations from the hub in Louisville, Kentucky, with a fleet of 24 B727 QCs.

• 1985: UPS operates a fleet of 152 aircraft, including six 747Fs, serving 300 locations.

• 1985: UPS sets up in Europe and commences a policy of acquiring road transport companies. Establishes its European hub at Cologne airport.

• 1987: UPS serves as the trial company for launching the cargo version of the Boeing B757 known as the "Package Freighter". It places a firm order for 20 aircraft and takes out an option on a further 15. Until then, the integrators had tended to buy passenger aircraft, which had been fully depreciated, and then converted them into cargo versions.

• 1990: UPS opens its line Anchorage-Hong Kong line.

A gigantic battle then ensued between two superpowers: Federal Express and UPS.

But the spread of express services was not a solely American phenomenon. In a number of countries, particularly in Australia and Europe, companies were converted or founded in order to profit from this new heaven-sent opportunity.

In Europe by the late 1970s courier material was still carried as accompanied baggage on scheduled passenger flights by couriers working for companies such as DHL, Airport Courier Services, Skypak, David Martin, World Courier, IML, Gelco, Purolator and others. However, the scheduled passenger flights only commenced operating from about or just before 7.00am and ceased flying in the evening, with the result that with the absence of night services, documents could not be collected from shippers late in the afternoon and guaranteed delivery elsewhere in

ABOVE **Elan Merchantman "Agamemnon".**

BELOW **XP Express Parcels F-27 "Monique".**

BOTTOM **TAT Express F-27.**
MAP

ABOVE LEFT DHL Convair 580 and B727.
Malcolm Nason

LEFT European Expedite Convair 580.
Paul Duffy

ABOVE United Parcel Service B747.
Air Cargo News UK

ABOVE RIGHT Airjet F-27.
MAP

RIGHT Elan "The Overnight Delivery System", A.W. Argosy.

BELOW Loading a United Parcel Service B727.

Europe, before mid-day on the next day. The only way in which such a service could be achieved, as was being practised by Federal Express in the United States, was for special cargo flights to operate at night.

The first two such services to operate in Europe were started in August 1979 by World Courier and Skypak. Skypak, an Australian company contracted with Air Foyle to provide a Piper Aztec aircraft operating five nights a week between Luton and Brussels carrying up to 400 kilos of documents and parcels accompanied by an on-board courier before the days of aviation liberalisation. The service ended in 1981 following the acquisition of Skypak by IPEC, another European door-to-door overnight trucking company. (Founded and led by the Australian entrepreneur, Gordon Barton. IPEC was a direct competitor of XP Express Parcels.) Not long afterwards, TNT, another rapidly expanding Australian transportation group, under the leadership of Sir Peter Abeles, acquired Skypak from IPEC and then went on to acquire IPEC itself.

Apart from its Skypak courier division which continued to charter light aircraft to carry courier material overnight (such as between Aberdeen and East Midlands airports in the UK), TNT UK and TNT-IPEC remained exclusively road transport integrators.

However, by October 1985, with the onset of increasing competition in terms of speed delivery, TNT-IPEC decided that it could only offer its customers the speed of delivery which they were demanding by setting up two overnight air routes. In November 1985 TNT-IPEC contracted with Air Foyle to provide two Herald cargo aircraft to operate nightly between Birmingham and Hanover, and Birmingham and Nuremberg. By the autumn of 1986 these were replaced initially by a BAC-111-475 freighter and then by a Boeing 737-200QC. (This operated four nights a week Dublin/Birmingham/Nuremberg/Hanover/Birmingham/Dublin. However, this was only an interim move as by this time Sir Peter Abeles had decided to open up a European network based upon a major new hub and spoke air network in Cologne and was particularly attracted to the British Aerospace 146 freighter conversion aircraft owing to its extreme quietness.

Consequently TNT placed options with British Aerospace for up to 72 of the cargo variant of the BAe 146 aircraft — the Quiet Trader or QT. However, TNT was an Australian company and could not consequently, own and control a European airline. The way to get around the problem was to select European airlines owning air operators' certificates and licenses granted by their own authorities to operate the BAe 146 aircraft within Europe on TNT's behalf. The first airline selected was Air Foyle — which started flights on 5th May 1987 and operated up to ten aircraft — followed by Pan Air of Spain, Mistral Air of Italy, Euralair of France, Malmo Aviation of Sweden, Malev of Hungary and NFD of Germany. By using a multiplicity of national operators TNT was before the advent of European liberalisation able to "mix and match" available traffic rights to optimise the carrying capacity and destinations serviced by its network.

In 1996 TNT was acquired by the Dutch Post Office, KPN, thereby removing much of the rationale of having its aircraft managed by European operators when TNT itself had become European. So, by the summer of 2000 TNT had formed its own airline in Belgium, TNT Airways, having already transferred its hub from Cologne to Liège.

France didn't stay on the outside for long, and gave birth to Jet Services and TAT Express. Jet Services was created in Lyons in 1973 to deliver small packages and documents throughout France in less than 12 hours, profiting from the night-time. Thanks to the energy of its two founder Directors (Roger Caille and Michel Garcia) and in spite of certain obstacles from the Post, the company was able to develop sufficiently by 1981 to create an air transport subsidiary, Air Jet. Flying two Fokker 27 cargo aircraft, it made nightly connections between Paris, Lyons and Marseilles. It was then possible, with some care, to move to the next stage of development: international business, with its immediate European neighbours and the United States/Canada.

TAT Express was set up by Michel Marchais in 1976, following a study mission to Memphis, and provided door-to-door transport within France for packages between 5 and 50kg, within a 24-hour transit time. TAT Express, ever anxious to avoid all possible conflicts with the French Post, occupied very precise market niches: industrial packages, and distribution for mail order companies. By 1984, TAT Express was combining road with air transport in the form of Fokker 27s, via three airport hubs – Belfort, Paris Orly, and Montpellier, which were fed by the regional road links. In 1985 it engaged in a development of major importance by collaborating with the Post to create a postal express service in France, and with Air France to set up a joint subsidiary for express parcels, known as Sodexi.

The scheduled airlines could not avoid becoming part of a groundswell which became increasingly powerful, affecting postal traffic as well as freight, concerned with consignments of increasing unit weight. According to all the predictions, this market would enjoy almost limitless growth, thanks to the creation of ever novel spin-off markets.

Within a dozen or so years, nearly all the scheduled airlines had created their own express products. In the United States, TWA launched its Next Flight Out Service in 1975, whilst United Airlines offered United Express. Even Seaboard World, notorious for its preference for large consignments and consolidation, launched an express product called Speed Way Service! The Commuter Airlines, small local companies, were not to be outdone and also offered express products, connecting up with regional and national airlines, and often gave their products snappy titles: Bar Harbour Airlines marketed "Zip Ship" and Rio Airways promoted "Rio Rapid". In Europe, Swissair became the pioneer. In November 1977 it introduced its SPEX (Swissair Parcel Express) formula for destinations in the USA, working in collaboration with Federal Express. The packages were picked up from 15 European cities and carried by Swissair to Boston, where they were taken over by Federal Express for delivery throughout the country. Swissair gradually expanded this airport-door express product to almost all the countries in which it operated.

Little by little, in different forms, all the European airlines organised express services: Worldspeed, for KLM, Airporte for the domestic French airline Air Inter, and Air France Express for Air France. Other companies used more unusual methods, which were often doomed to failure.

The Scandinavian airline SAS, whose ambition outstripped its means, set up in Cologne with two DC-9 cargo aircraft on 3rd December 1985. This express network combined road and air transport, and was called Air de Cologne, or A de C . This network was supposed to cover the whole of Europe, and its management invoked the vision of a European Federal Express. All in vain! In March 1988 TNT took over Air de Cologne, which had made heavy losses.

In order to combat the integrators, the scheduled airlines realised that they would have to do something extra: to offer a true "door-to-door" express product alongside their traditional "airport to airport" or "airport to door" products. They all moved in the same direction, but along different routes. In 1982, Lufthansa launched a product called C+d door-to-door Express cargo, working together with the German forwarding agent Schenker, while Air France extended its range of express services in 1986 with a product called "Domicile Express" run in association with TAT Express. Neither company had much success with these products.

These various attempts, which were costly both in time and money, soon demonstrated a merciless lesson: you cannot improvise integrated transportation. Express is a profession in itself, quite distinct from traditional airfreight. It does not only require specific resources and particular procedures, but a different mental approach.

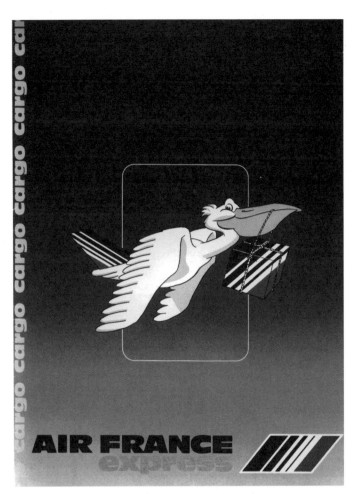

RIGHT **In 1984 Air France launched its classic airport to airport express product, called Air France Express.**

BELOW **Air de Cologne Lockheed Electra on charter from Fred Olsens Flyselskap.**

5 ECOLOGY, CONSUMERISM AND PUBLIC OPINION

Safeguarding the environment and consumer protection took on a restrictive power in our field of interest during the decade 1970–1980. Under the driving force of these two movements, a group of measures was first adopted and then systematically strengthened, which constituted a web of constraints that bore down on the transport companies. Nevertheless, up to the present time, these new constraints have not hindered the expansion of airfreight. However if they became more burdensome, they are likely to call into question or to slow down the development of certain forms of activity.

I AIRFREIGHT AND THE ENVIRONMENT

The IATA Annual Report for 1970 stated that ecological problems were becoming an ever more acute preoccupation within our highly industrial society. This observation, which today affects the whole of air transport, is of greater concern to freight and mail activities than to passenger transport. In at least three areas – noise, land encroachment and movements of heavy vehicles – there is a risk of conflict between the expansion of traffic and a reasonable concern for environmental protection.

Noise

In 1975, the French Institute for Air Transport noted that: "There has been a considerable escalation in the fight against noise on airports." It appears that for several reasons cargo flights are more susceptible than passenger flights when it comes to measures taken to protect people near airports from the effects of noise:

• Freight and mail are night activities par excellence. In every country, every shipper, would like to hand over his correspondence or parcels to the carrier at the end of one day for delivery at in the morning or during the course of the following day;

• Express freight, which had been expanding constantly for the last 25 years, is the archetypal night-time activity. Moreover, its operational technology, using a central connecting hub, generates a large number of night-time take-offs and landings;

• Cargo charter airlines frequently suffer from a serious degree of under capitalisation. They often use converted passenger aircraft which belong to older production series and are fitted with engines which generate more noise and pollution than those that are installed in the latest aircraft. The methods for combating noise take two main forms: the first concerns the noise levels of the aircraft, while the second affects the operating rules for the airports.

• The reduction of aircraft noise levels

A large number of measures have been defined and adopted in order to reduce the nuisance arising from noise: by ICAO on a world scale (Annex 16 of the Convention) at the end of the 1960s; by ECAC (European Civil Aviation Commission) and the European Commission (Directive of 20th December 1979); and finally by the various Aeronautical Administrations (Regulation "FAR36" of the American FAA).

For new aircraft, it is sufficient to make their certification dependent on a certain noise level. In passing, it may be noted that the fuel cost increases, which caused airlines to introduce aircraft that were more economical and therefore generated less noise and less pollution, unwittingly contributed to the fulfilment of the ecological objectives.

It was in order to meet the noise requirements of the most demanding of airports, that the British manufacturer British Aerospace brought out in 1986 a medium-haul cargo aircraft which was particularly silent: the BAe 146QT Quiet Trader. This aircraft, which was a freight version of the four-engine passenger jet BAe 146, provided a payload of 11-13 tonnes according to the version, divided on six or seven pallets of 2.24m x 2.74m (88in x 108in) on the main deck. The first user was the Australian small packages carrier TNT, which used it to equip its European night network based in Cologne in support of its Overnight Express Service (13 aircraft operating in 1990). British Aerospace based its whole sales argument on the aircraft's noise level: "The 146QT's low noise operation is absolutely fundamental to its commercial viability and profit potential. The enormous potential of the overnight freight and package market can only be realised by the use of aircraft that can be operated 24 hours a day without infringing environmental constraints. That is the bottom line and is what the 146 – as no other aircraft – offers."

With regard to aircraft already in operation, the ICAO's policy consisted in defining increasingly demanding standards, and

British Aerospace 146QT, the Quiet Trader.

in progressively forcing the operating companies to conform to them. In this context, all aircraft were divided into three "chapters" corresponding to three noise levels and three phases of action:

- "Chapter I", corresponding to "FAR 36 Stage I", referred to the oldest jet cargo planes, Boeing 707 and DC-8. These were either submitted to acoustic engineering modifications, or were banned from flying in the United States after 1985. At greater or lesser time intervals, other countries adopted or began to adopt similar measures;

- "Chapter II", equivalent to "FAR36 Stage 2", includes Boeing 727, the older types of B747, B737 and DC-10, and also the DC-9 aircraft;

- "Chapter III" conforms to "FAR36 Stage 3" and covers all the then recent aircraft, in particular the Airbus fleet, fitted with quieter engines and producing less pollution. Since the aircraft according to Chapter I had been eliminated or adapted, the next phase consisted in reducing the noise levels of all the aircraft in Chapter II to bring them into line with the Chapter III standard before

1st April 2002. There were three methods to achieve this: new engines, adaptation or elimination.

*To re-engine an aircraft the old engines have to be removed and replaced with modern engines. This is the most efficient, but also the most expensive, solution. It is therefore restricted to aircraft, that still have sufficient potential flying hours available to amortise a high investment. The oldest example, which was already mentioned, was the re-engining project for a hundred DC-8s, many of which were the convertible or cargo version, when Cammacorp fitted them with CFM56 SNECMA/General Electric engines. The American express parcel carrier UPS soon afterwards carried out an exemplary modernisation campaign. After buying a fleet of over 40 medium-haul Boeing 727-100 aircraft at a low price, it decided in 1990 to re-engine them completely with Rolls-Royce, Tay 651 engines with a noise level appreciably lower than the minimum for stage III. A UPS executive commented as follows regarding his company's choice: "We launched the B727 QF or Quiet Freighter (as now known) because it makes good business sense and offers environmental benefits. We want customers to know that their shipments are moving on aircraft that will always be welcomed at any airport in the world." [1] The modification and re-engining programme for the B727-100 fleet was completed at the beginning of 1997. The following information appeared in the trade press: [2] "All UPS jets now fulfil the requirements of stage III. Hence UPS is setting a good example, since the regulation will only become compulsory in the United States in three years' time, on 31st December 1999. ... In addition, fuel consumption has been reduced by 18% and exhaust gases by 22%."

The moral that environmental protection had become an important factor in a company's brand image had become a good sales argument.

*The modification of engines in service by means of noise reduction equipment (hush kits) was by far the most widespread practice. Although this method increased operating costs, with some additional fuel consumption, it only required limited investment.

Some hundreds of cargo aircraft of various types (B727, B737, DC-8, DC-9) had already been modified by 1988, and such modifications continued, particularly in the United States. There were various types of noise reduction equipment on the market. Federal Express worked together with engine builders Pratt & Whitney to develop a special unit enabling the B727 cargo to fulfil the stage III requirements.

* Elimination is the last ditch solution for aircraft which can no longer be modified, or which are at the end of their useful lives, or (in the case of small charter companies) if the operator has insufficient financial means. It is perhaps regrettable that a more energetic anti-noise policy did not achieve a faster rationalisation of the world cargo fleet.

• The tightening of airport operating rules.
The most effective way of guaranteeing the sleep of people living near large airports is to restrict or ban completely takeoffs and landings for all or part of the night. This is the "noise-ban" system exercised by many of the world's airports. This system basically penalises cargo flights and freight activities, since passenger aircraft try to avoid night-time schedules.

Noise-ban policies can take very different forms, depending whether it is a matter of a complete noise ban – the airport is closed to all aircraft between 23.00 hours and 0500 or 06.00 hours in the morning; a selective noise ban – for example the airport is only open for domestic postal flights; or a noise ban as an incentive – where the airport is only open to aircraft conforming to Chapter 3.

Whatever the details, NASA considers that the problem of noise around airports will become more acute. [3] We will mention a few examples relating to airfreight:

- Brussels National was the leading European airport for express freight. The Belgian authorities had attracted specialist carriers at a time when new facilities with excess capacity were available to the carriers.

Some years later, in 1988, "with aims not entirely disassociated from ulterior motives of an electoral nature, the new Minister for Communications, Jean–Luc de Haene, who was the Member for the constituency which contained Brussels National, declared war against the disturbers of the nocturnal peace, which were the express parcel companies. Not because he wished them to decamp to other climes, but because he was determined not to accept any additional operators." [4]

- Cologne was the second European airport for express freight. In May 1995, ecologists (the Green Party) became members of the Coalition Government in the State of Rhineland-Westphalia. The principal operator took fright. Without awaiting the imposition of intolerable restrictions (it was mooted that night flights would be banned from 2002 onwards) TNT decided to transfer its activities to the airport of Liège in the Walloon part of Belgium (30 flights per night, 300 tonnes of parcels and documents). Why Liège? It had a good geographical location within Europe, of course, but above all, it had given a promise not to restrict night flights until the year 2015.

- Strasbourg was petitioned by DHL in 1996 as a site for its night operations hub. Under pressure from environmentalists and people living near the airport, Strasbourg rejected DHL's offer and decided to put its quality of life and environment first, in spite of a notable rate of unemployment.

Under such conditions, one can better understand the concerns of express parcel carriers who considered that "there is no acceptable solution for replacing night-time operations".

Airport land encroachment
The cargo areas of large airports occupy enormous surface areas. They include Customs and various administrative services, the offices and warehouses of the freight forwarders, the freight terminals of the airlines, installations for support and maintenance companies, and sometimes even some types of intermodal operations. The absence of available land is often an obstacle for the development of freight activities. When this occurs, as in Hong Kong, it is necessary to build upwards, or, as in Frankfurt and London, to transfer outside the airport area all or part of the warehouses for freight agents.

From this point of view, Roissy Airport possesses a tremendous advantage which makes it one of the largest airports for post and goods transported in the 21st century: space.

Road traffic
In reality, airfreight is a bi-modal transport involving air and road. This is why all large airports generate an intense amount of activity on the roads. In addition to vehicles collecting and delivering goods door-to-door, and providing a shuttle service between the warehouses of the customers and the premises of the freight forwarders, the 1970s added many "road feeder services" for the airlines. Hence, cargo airports must be directly linked to the motorway network and possess vast parking areas.

In Europe, the strengthening of bans on heavy vehicles and the tightening-up of certain technical limitations (maximum

length of truck and trailer combinations) are likely to put serious pressure on the freight activities of the largest airlines. They may therefore turn towards alternative rail solutions, which have up to the present merely been the subject of limited trials (eg. between Switzerland and Holland) and are far from offering the operational flexibility of road transport.

2 AIRFREIGHT AND CONSUMERISM

In its annual report of 1970, IATA observed that in the rapidly changing environment in which air transport was operating, it was becoming the object of increasing interest from consumers and consumer associations. [5] There was in particular an increased desire for participation in decision-making, and a strong demand for fair compensation in case of damage.

Desire for participation: representation for agents and shippers
We are not in the field of consumer goods. The "consumers" are in this case transport professionals in export or import. Their aspirations to official recognition and their concern for participation were recognised and confirmed by IATA in its major work of self-analysis in 1978, when it invited third parties (other than the airlines themselves) to present their views at all meetings for rate co-ordination. Any person or organisation would be able to obtain a copy of the agenda and to submit written proposals or present his/its views orally. In this way, IATA believed that travel agents, freight agents, passengers, people sending goods and consumer organisations would all have the possibility of making their positions known. [6]

The FIATA Airfreight Institute [7] was officially recognised by IATA in 1970 as the sole representative of Registered Agents (freight forwarders) worldwide. In this role, it expressed the grievances of the agents, and made suggestions and proposals. In 1979 IATA expressed satisfaction regarding its good relationship with FIATA: "Cooperation with FIATA has developed in a manner which should prove satisfactory to both parties." This was shown within the IATA-FIATA Consultative Council, which dealt with all matters of joint interest (including the delicate problem of how to develop the form and content of the Cargo Agency Agreement). Echoing these older appreciative remarks from IATA, the FIATA Airfreight Institute underlined in 1996 "the spirit of co-operation between commercial partners," [8] in spite of some inevitable points of disagreement.

The IATA/FIATA Air Cargo Training Programme was the area in which the co-operation between the two organisations proved most fruitful.

More recently, a working group combining airlines and freight forwarders was created, on the initiative of IATA, in the form of an IATA interest group called "Cargo 2000" for the purpose of "improving the efficiency of all parties involved in the sector for the benefit of all".

On the side of the shippers, the pioneering role was assumed by the International Chamber of Commerce – ICC – founded in 1919. Its "Commission on Air Transport", which was a specialised branch of the Transport Users' Commission, has been speaking out for half a century on behalf of the shippers as customers, and trying to obtain more flexibility in all the regulations. Its persistent activity has shown what degree of convergence there exists between the consumerist trend and the tendency towards liberalisation.

At the end of a conference on airfreight organised by the ICC in February 1976, the Commission on Air Transport once again

TNT Airbus A300B4F.
TNT

emphasised the need for a "dialogue between shippers, airlines and freight agents". Not without some bitterness it observed: "Since 1967, some progress has been noted in the establishment of a dialogue, although the progress has not been significant."

Towards the end of the 1970s, things began to move rapidly. First of all there was a change of tone. The Shippers' Associations became more aggressive: "The shippers show their teeth", "Le Journal pour le Transport International" of Basel pertinently reported. Then the users of air transport appeared as a body, getting together to gain recognition and make their views known. European Air Shippers Councils (or EASC) which have a different legal form and affiliation in each country, appear within or in parallel to the European Shippers' Councils (or ESC) which dealt with marine business.

> *"The activities of the EASC were particularly on a political level with the Commission of the Communities in the context of measures for liberalising air transport, and with the IATA organisation. The EASC supervised attentively any authorisations for agreements, which might be granted to the airlines. Another topic on their agenda was the question of air transportation of dangerous materials, in order to work out regulations which would not be excessively restrictive."* [9]

As in the case of marine transport, the Air Shippers' Councils gathered together in a European Federation, which tried sway in Brussels in favour of its very liberal ideas. In September 1998 it published a White Paper for shippers entitled: "Airfreight 2000 and beyond".

The requirements for just compensation: from the Warsaw Convention to the Montreal Convention

One may recall the conditions under which the Warsaw Convention was drawn up. In order to support the development of air transport, which was still in its infancy, the authors of the Convention had set up a system of liabilities which was quite advantageous to the carriers. A presumption of liability was stated, but was subject to upper limits, and modified by several possible reasons for exoneration.

As soon as the war ended, voices were heard requesting a revision of the Warsaw Convention to make it more favourable to users, particularly with regard to the upper limits of liability, in order to take into account the developments in aircraft technology. In addition, it had become apparent that "the possibility

offered to the carrier to escape the presumption of liability by proving that he had taken all necessary measures to avoid damage was more theoretical than actual" [10] due to the difficulty of proof. Between 1955 and 1975 four documents signed in The Hague in 1955, Montreal in 1956, Guatemala City in 1971 and Montreal in 1975 amended the text of the Warsaw Convention.

This collection of documents – the Warsaw Convention and related agreements – gave way to a new Convention which was worked out during an international conference on air law organised by ICAO and signed in Montreal on 28th May 1999. It entered into force on 4th November 2003, 60 days after the registration of the 30th ratification document (by the US) with ICAO.

This new Montreal Convention "achieved a delicate equilibrium between the interests and needs of all the partners in international civil aviation", according to the President of the Council of ICAO. One should rather say "a new equilibrium". In fact, "the Montreal Convention is no longer a convention for airlines. It is a Convention for consumers/passengers." [11] The preamble to the Convention, even if it does not have the force of law, provides a good illustration of this development:

> *"THE STATES PARTIES TO THIS CONVENTION, RECOGNIS-ING the importance of ensuring protection of the interests of consumers in international carriage by air and the need for equitable compensation based on the principle of restitution."*

In order to keep to essentials, we will examine four major modifications:

1. Documentation relating to the carriage of cargo
The first paragraph of Article 4 stipulates as follows: "In respect of the carriage of cargo, an air waybill shall be delivered." This was the traditional arrangement inherited from the Warsaw Convention. But the second paragraph of the same article introduces a very far-reaching element of flexibility: "Any other means which preserves a record of the carriage to be performed may be substituted for the delivery of an air waybill." This clause is of crucial importance: it makes the use of electronic air waybills legal and official and opens the path to "a paperless world".

We should also note that Article 5 (Contents of air waybill) makes considerable simplifications in the number of headings compared with the old Article 8 of the Warsaw Convention.

2. Liability of the carrier
Article 18 establishes the principle of the objective or "automatic" responsibility of the carrier.

"The carrier is liable for damage sustained in the event of the destruction or loss or damage to cargo upon condition only that the event that caused the damage so sustained took place during the carriage by air."

The carrier is no longer only assumed to be responsible for the damage incurred. He is "automatically" responsible due to the sole fact that the damage occurred during transportation. Under this legal system, the reasons for exoneration open to the carrier must be few in number and clearly indicated. This is the purpose of Paragraph 2 of Article 18:

"However, the carrier is not liable if and to the extent it proves that the destruction, or loss of, or damage to, the cargo resulted from one or more of the following:

a) Inherent defect, quality or vice of that cargo;
b) Defective packing;
c) An act of War or an armed conflict;
d) An act of public authority carried out in connection with the entry, exit or transit of the cargo."

Moreover, this new system of liability, which on the whole is more severe for the carrier, and therefore more favourable to the consumer, is also applied to surface transport if this is used in substitution by the air carrier:

"the drafters of the Montreal Convention specifically provided that if a carrier substitutes surface (truck) carriage for a segment of the carriage contracted for under the air waybill, the Convention governs that transportation and the carrier's liability." [12]

3. Liability limits
The Montreal Convention retains the concept of a limit of liability. However, it replaces the gold franc, which had become increasingly esoteric, by the SDR of the International Monetary Fund (IMF) Article 22, Paragraph 3:

"In the carriage of cargo, the liability of the carrier in case of destruction, loss, damage or delay is limited to a sum of 17 Special Drawing Rights per kilogram, unless the consignor has made, at the time when the package was handed over to the carrier, a special declaration of interest in delivery at destination and has paid a supplementary sum if the case so requires."

But a carrier is able to stipulate a higher liability limit, or even no limit at all.

4. Arbitration clause
"With regard to the transportation of goods, the Montreal Convention provides for arbitration arrangements between professionals, which should permit faster resolution of certain disputes." [13]

Article 34 – Arbitration
"1. The parties to the contract of carriage for cargo may stipulate that any dispute relating to the liability of the carrier under this convention shall be settled by arbitration."

This clause reflects two facts: that freight transport is a business between "professionals"; and that the "carriers" and the "consumers" will henceforth be placed on an equal footing.

3 AIRFREIGHT AND PUBLIC OPINION

Airfreight, a technical and logistical activity carried out in a restricted professional environment, is in itself of little interest to the media, except for certain spectacular operations. However, some categories of product cannot remain unimportant to the public at large, either because they give rise to fear – dangerous goods – or because they touch their feelings – live animals. In these areas, and one could add others, public opinion, with the never-failing support of the media, exercises a kind of control over various aspects of airfreight activities, which is often justified, but which is sometimes onerous.

Transport of dangerous goods
These are sometimes referred to as restricted articles and sometimes as dangerous goods. Suffice it to say that the transportation of various categories of goods, irrespective of the methods used, are subject to increasingly demanding regulations resulting from the potential risks that they present to the crews, the passengers of mixed aircraft, the ground staff of airlines and freight forwarders and the general public in case of air accidents.

This is why IATA very soon became concerned about the transportation of such goods. In 1952 it published a detailed list

The transport of racehorses by air always requires special care..

of restricted articles accompanied by explanatory notes concerning packaging and transportation. The first edition of the "IATA Dangerous Goods Regulations Manual" was published in 1953 ("IATA Regulations relating to the carriage of restricted articles" 1st edition, 1953). Since then it has regularly been updated by "The Restricted Articles Working Group", which has since become the "IATA Dangerous Goods Board", one of the most important parts of the Association. In 1962 IATA introduced into the regulations a differentiation between mixed flights carrying freight and passengers, and cargo flights, which only transport freight. The latter then benefited from a more favourable treatment, without, of course, affecting the safety requirements; but the IATA member airlines were thenceforth able to transport much larger quantities of chemical products and other hazardous materials in their all-cargo aircraft." [14] However concerned the IATA experts were to fulfil the recommendations of specialised international organisations – the United Nations Committee on the Transportation of Dangerous Goods and the International Atomic Energy Authority – it might appear unusual that the regulation for air transport came from the airlines themselves. Once public opinion had been aroused on this matter, following a number of incidents and accidents caused by faulty packaging of dangerous goods, ICAO took things in hand.

Following very prolonged labours, ICAO published the new regulations for the air transport of dangerous goods in 1982. It constitutes Annex 18 to the Chicago Convention and came into force on 1st January 1983. The "IATA Dangerous Goods Regulations Manual" has therefore become a kind of practical working document relating to Annex 18 and its Technical Instructions. Four key concepts, which correspond to four stages in the process of handling consignments, allow us to summarise regulations which are extremely complex in detail:

1. Classification – All goods considered to be dangerous are divided into nine hazard classes defined by the Experts' Committee of the United Nations:

1. Explosives;
2. Gasses;
3. Flammable liquids;
4. Flammable solids;
5. Oxidising substances and organic peroxides;
6. Toxic, poisonous and infectious substances;
7. Radioactive materials;
8. Corrosives;
9. Miscellaneous dangerous goods.

The first thing to do is precisely to define the nature of the product to be transported, so as to classify it properly. This is sometimes a difficult task.

2. Packaging – labelling

The quality of the packaging is the best guarantee of safety. Since 1991, the packaging has to be certified in conformity with UN standards. Each parcel must be labelled in accordance with the hazard class or division to which the goods transported are assigned.

3. Acceptance

The acceptance of consignments of restricted articles represents an enormous amount of work for the airlines which are responsible for verifying that the regulations are applied (classification, packing/labelling, maximum quantities by parcel or by consignment depending on whether the goods are to be carried in a passenger plane or on a cargo aircraft). The acceptance of consignments of radioactive products (generally for medical use) are subject to particularly rigorous procedures.

The airline inspection is carried out according to an essential document: the Shipper's Declaration for Dangerous Goods.

This declaration acts as the identity card for the goods. It must be filled out in English by the customer himself and not by his freight agent. The shipper confirms his criminal liability in case of false declaration.

4. Loading

It is up to the carrier to respect scrupulously the instructions and precautions for loading: rules concerning the incompatibility of dangerous goods with respect to one another; direction in which parcels are loaded/stowed; details of palletisation.

The transport of restricted articles, a preferred field of activity for the co-operation between IATA and FIATA, has become the subject of a great deal of attention. Considerable progress was made during the 1990s, on the part of the shippers, the freight agents and the airlines themselves. However, this is clearly an area which demands the highest degree of vigilance.

Transport of live animals

Live animals were also subject to special regulations, involving a rather similar process to that for Restricted Articles. The regulations have been progressively developed and finalised by IATA experts within the Live Animals Board, which since 1968 has been regularly updating and publishing the "IATA Live Animals Regulations Manual". Detailed and binding regulations are all the more necessary, since abuses can easily be committed and public opinion in some countries is particularly vigilant when it comes to the conditions under which live animals are transported. The term "regulation" covers a series of measures and prohibitions for the purpose of guaranteeing that animals are transported under appropriate conditions. (For "humane" one might almost write "human"!)

Many animals have no need of special legal protection. They are of such high value, or they are transported under such special conditions, that they are the object of every care by their owners and by the carriers. This is the case with race horses, breeding stock, chicks or exotic fish.

However, there are other species which need the concern of the legislators, since they are threatened with extinction (CITES Convention, 1973) or may simply be the subject of a very profitable trade (tropical birds, small pets, etc.). Unless the airlines maintain vigilance in every part of their networks, they can at any moment be associated with the transportation of animals in lamentable circumstances (overcrowded cages, fatalities on take-off, etc.). The indignation of public opinion represents the most effective means of protection in this respect, at least where image-conscious airlines are concerned.

In this field, the European Union has adopted very strict rules, which demonstrate an active concern for the humane treatment of animals. Nowadays, at the large European freight airports (Frankfurt, Amsterdam, Roissy, etc.) there are even full-scale "animal hotels".

6 THE OMNIPRESENT COMPUTER

The first applications of computing techniques to airfreight go back to the end of the 1950s. IATA mentioned the topic in its annual report of September 1960. Electronic data processing (EDP) soon became the only means for achieving speed of transport, quality of service and cost control within an activity characterised by the complexity of its processes – determined by the inertia of the goods, the diversity of products and the multitude of regulations, the close interdependence of the operational commercial and accounting aspects, and by the sheer volume of data.

However, the general introduction of independent (closed loop) computer systems owned by the airlines, the freight forwarders or others involved in the transport chain quickly showed their limitations. In the event, there evolved data handling processes which resulted from the juxtaposition of very powerful systems, but which had no means of inter-communication, apart from traditional manual processes, which were error prone, time consuming and expensive. The idea then emerged, without prejudging the question of technical feasibility, of interconnecting the independent systems in order to build up a vast unified network, joining all the links in the airfreight chain, from shipper to consignee.

1 A DREAM TOO SOON

In 1970, IATA found to its disappointment that airlines were continuing to look for their own solutions to the challenges posed by cargo operations, and that there was very little or even no collaboration at all in critical sectors such as administrative procedures and exchanges of information. In order to remedy the situation, the Association decided in 1972 to create a special group for studying the problem, the Cargo Automation Research Team, or CART.

The report published by CART in December 1973 was the first detailed and coherent attempt to develop a "conceptual international air cargo information exchange scheme". In accordance with the universalist ideals of IATA, it sought to define the operating rules for a complete system of data exchange, uniting all the participants and allowing them to follow the transportation of the consignment end to end, an idea which the integrators have exploited with the success that we have already seen.

Without going into excessive detail, we should emphasise how much this project was ahead of its time, in spite of the sarcastic remarks with which it was greeted. The report began by recording two basic truths:

1. "The fundamental service advantage of airfreight is speed", but
2. "Much of this (time) is being lost on the ground" in cargo agents' warehouses and in airlines' cargo terminals, since on average, a consignment spends 90% of its total transit time on the ground.

How could these untenable working times be reduced, to provide the customers with better service? The report explained: "... by the expanded use of electronic data processing and the co-ordinated implementation of an integrated computer network" [1] for the airfreight industry. What would be the requirements? Standard data elements and a set of standard messages.

What system was proposed? The report outlined that "... the ultimate scheme would have a number of manufacturers/shippers, forwarders, consolidators, carriers, deconsolidators, brokers, Customs and consignees in a local area connected to a host system. Each host system, envisaged to service the industry, would be linked to the other systems via the existing but extended ...communications networks." [2] Just imagine the practical operation of such a system! A forwarder collects the consignment from the consignor and takes it to his warehouse. He then feeds in the data concerning the consignment into a terminal connected to the regional host system. This then distributes the data to the parties concerned. It sends to the Customs the information necessary for preparing the export authorisation. The forwarder then hands in the consignment at the desk of the airline. Once the goods have been taken over, the host computer receives the data and at an appropriate time generates the load list, and then the cargo manifest. Whilst the plane is in the air, the host would transmit all the information to the destination and to the regional downline computer. Once the data has been received, this computer would then transmit them electronically to Customs, the airline and to the freight agent of the consignee, so they can prepare their various activities before the physical arrival of the goods.

This was a very attractive plan in theory, but in the eyes of most of the airlines it was too futuristic, since it corresponded neither to the status of their own equipment nor to the state of development of data processing technology. History has shown that it was first necessary to pass via a phase of individual systems, before being able to envisage interfaces.

However, the project was not altogether a Utopian dream since it drew its inspiration directly from a community system, which united Customs, airlines and freight agents and which entered operation on 1st September 1971 at London Airport, known as LACES or London Airport Cargo EDP Scheme. [3] LACES, which was modified and refined a number of times, had originally been an automatic system for processing import consignments data. "The object of LACES is to make available to agents, airlines and HM Customs an integrated system for the inventory control of packages and the clearance of goods imported to London Airport" (LACES Brochure – NDPS). Although in the first instance it had been set up in the interests of efficiency by HM Customs & Excise, the project had closely involved representatives of the airlines, [4] freight agents, banks and the Customs. It had resulted in the introduction of a system operated by the National Data Processing Service, linking these different categories of participants, and covering, from the outset, two types of function. The first function corresponded to the specific needs of Customs & Excise, with a view to accelerating the Customs procedures for consignments by eliminating manual declarations and by providing automatic customs duty and excise calculations. The second function was related to a series of operations carried out by the airlines (tally on arrival, warehouse management, daily inventory report, transfers to cargo agents), for which computerisation resulted in an appreciable improvement in quality, and in manpower reductions.

2 CLOSED LOOP SYSTEMS

Since they had not been able to agree on a plan for general interfacing, which proved to be too ambitious, the airlines, freight agents and even certain customs authorities developed autonomous data processing systems, designed to fulfil their own needs. In the 1970s, all the major airlines had computer

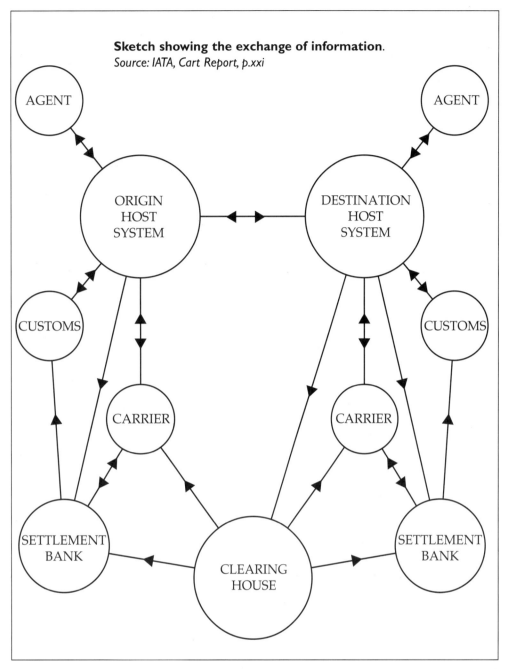

Sketch showing the exchange of information.
Source: IATA, Cart Report, p.xxi

systems for freight. It was very unusual for them to include at the outset global solutions covering the totality of functions in the business. Companies often utilised several systems, with the risk of errors which always arise from multiple data input: one system for commercial and accounting functions (bookings, shipment tracing and invoicing); and another for managing the freight warehouses. The total cost of the introduction of these systems, over and above the initial price of the central processors, was destined to increase as a function of the number of stations connected.

To a large degree, the freight computer systems came from two families, associated with two manufacturers.

The IBM P04, (or "FAST") family had been developed by Alitalia and was sold to a number of airlines, which subjected it to far-reaching modifications, depending on the functions upon which they wished to concentrate (Swissair, KLM, British Airways, etc). When it was introduced in 1973, the P04 system provided flight cargo capacity management, instant aircraft space availability control, and carried out shipment reservations. It recorded in memory the number of the airway bill and all the details of the consignment, following its movement throughout the network. Alitalia, which should be regarded as the great pioneer in the field of computerisation of airfreight, continued improving and refining P04, which had in the meantime been renamed FAST.

The family of USAS-Cargo systems, which appeared later, was marketed directly by the producer, Sperry-Univac (UNISYS). Sabena, Cathay Pacific, Northwest, Lufthansa, Qantas and Air France were among its purchasers, and all made an appreciable contribution to the further development of the original version.

In 1971, Air France had introduced a system called SAFO – "Système Automatique Fret Orly" – providing the main functions of capacity management and processing of the consignments in the automated Orly freight terminal. To replace SAFO, which had become overloaded and too limited (it had remained a "Parisian" solution), Air France decided in favour of USAS-Cargo in October 1983.

Seven years later, in 1990, the situation had changed markedly. Over 80 stations were linked in the network of Air France Cargo, and USAS-Cargo (which had been re-christened Pelican) had reached a certain degree of maturity resulting from numerous and important adaptations. Its field of application covered five principal areas:

1. Booking and space control.

2. Single entry capture of the commercial and financial data, allowing the automatic calculation of rates and destination charges, issuance of airway bills and transmission necessary for the management of customer accounts.

3. Warehouse handling of export and transit consignments at shipment level (acceptance of the consignment, intermediate storage and/or palletisation) and at flight preparation level (warehouse handling, follow-up of shipments assigned to a flight, issuance of cargo manifest).

4. Handling of consignments on arrival (automatic printout of notices of arrivals and interline transfer manifests, and delivery to consignee with issuance of an import invoice).

5. Tracing: permanent memorisation of all the shipment's movements, enabling knowledge of the exact location of a shipment, at any time and at any point on the network, or permitting tracing back through the consignment's history.

Thus Air France reaped the benefits of the "systems approach" which it had taken: integration of all aspects of freight activity, single entry of the data, and the possibility of dialogue with the freight agents or Customs.

Alongside these two large families of systems, some companies preferred to develop their own solutions. The most original was certainly the system named CHAMP belonging to CARGOLUX. It was designed from the outset as a tool for checking and evaluating the revenues received, consignment by consignment, and flight by flight. It was above all a commercial and economic management tool, for the purpose of systematically investigating the profitability of each flight.

The forwarders, for their part, began in the 1970s to install more or less high-performance systems, but which were extremely varied and heterogeneous in nature, from the integrated worldwide system for some multinationals, to the simplest programmes for personal computers. The most usual functions offered were: automatic production of master AWBs, flight invoicing, warehouse management and, for the best equipped, the tracking of consignments. Emery Airfreight was the first international freight forwarder to design and develop a system for exchanging information linking its various sites, based on the establishment of a world telecommunications network using all existing technologies (cable, satellite etc.). Its EMCON System (Emery Control) was launched in 1970 and by 1975 was already linking 100 offices throughout the world, allowing them to provide customers with "a quality of information which up to that time had been without equal". As the Managing Director of Danzas in France remarked a few years later: "The customer will increasingly choose a carrier on the basis of his data processing competencies. We should therefore be as good at data processing as at transportation." [5]

During the same period the Customs Authorities also introduced systems exclusively for Customs purposes without any other possible form of data link except the installation of terminals in the offices of the transport companies and freight agents acting as customs agents. This was the case with Sofia in France, Alfa in Germany and CEPACS in Canada.

Within a period of 15 years, from 1970 to 1985, the airlines, freight agents and Customs Authorities had acquired in-house computer systems. The physical transportation of goods could no longer be envisaged without an invisible and parallel transfer of information. It is impossible to have a continuous flow of shipments without an automatic flow of data.

3 DIALOGUES BETWEEN SYSTEMS

At the beginning of the 1980s, the airlines, which up till then had had considerable reservations about projects for interfaces and/or community systems, began to change their attitude. Little by little they realised the usefulness, and appreciated the necessity, of having some kind of dialogue between systems that could interact with one another. Several factors may explain this strategic attitude change on the part of the carriers:

1. The level attained by the computer systems: all the large companies by 1980–1985 possessed complete freight systems. They were therefore able to devote their resources to establishing links with the outside world.

2. The continual activity of IATA in promoting solutions for community systems, introduced under its tutelage. One can read in a small publication issued in 1984:

"No company in the air cargo industry can act in isolation since the very nature of the business is that several interests, if not many, are involved in every shipment. Just as the physical goods are passed from hand to hand, so the information concerning those goods is passed from person to person. IATA is extremely interested in developing the framework within which this information can be passed by electronic means." [6]

To this end it developed very broad systems permitting the intercommunication, on a regional basis, of systems which were very different from one another, and belonging to all interested parties: airlines, freight agents, Customs, airports etc. At first they were called SIF (Standard Interchange Facility),[7] and then CCS (Cargo Community System). The CCSs were essentially designed as "connection boxes" linking the computer systems of the participants and managed by them. They had a strong local or national connotation.

3. Initiatives by airports: Some airports decided to encourage the creation of a community system on their own host computer in order to accelerate the flow of goods through the improved circulation of information. The best example, among many failed attempts, is the Cargonaut system at Amsterdam.

4. The appearance of a new language: EDI, Electronic Data Interchange. IATA accomplished a considerable task over a period of more than 30 years, in defining and applying a system of specific standard messages known as Cargo-IMP (for "Cargo Interchange Message Procedures") designed to facilitate the exchange of information between airlines and between airlines and freight agents. However, these messages were no longer suitable as soon as computer systems were opened to give access beyond that restricted circle (to be extended out to consignors and consignees). The solution to the problem was reached in 1986 with the adoption, within the framework of the United Nations, of a new universal language: UN-EDIFACT, or "EDI for Administration, Commerce and Transport". EDIFACT is a standardised language for the transfer of structured information between computers and can be used in the fields of administration, commerce and transport.

5. Competition from integrators. Free of the carrier/forwarder distinction, and having invested enormous sums in developing very elaborate computer systems, the integrators were, at the beginning of the 1980s, in a position to offer their customers the possibility of permanent real time tracking of their consignments, and later to propose the installation of terminals on their own premises. In this field, as in others, the integrators imposed their quality standards upon the whole market.

6. Pressure from international freight forwarders. To respond to competition from the integrators, the international forwarders had to offer an identical service to their customers. Always of an anxious nature, the customer had to be kept constantly informed. However in this area, the freight forwarders were dependent on the carriers: they therefore had to collect the information from the airline data banks, requiring interfaces to be established from system to system.

"... The period of time that a product is in the hands of the carrier is traditionally known to the forwarder as the 'black hole'. We have an urgent need to fill the 'black hole,'"[8] as one of the world's leading forwarders declared in 1992. One could not be more explicit!

In fact, the data exchange between airline and freight agent was better balanced than would appear from the above stricture. If the freight agents needed the airlines, the airlines also needed the agents, who held within their own databases numerous pieces of information which, if transferred automatically, would avoid the carriers having to get involved in expensive data capture operations (particularly for establishing the AWBs).

So the time was ripe to proceed to systems interfacing. But how was it to be done, and what direction should be taken? Would it be driven by IATA, a computer service company or a group of airlines?

To cut a confusing and eventful story short, suffice it to say that a group of four airlines, representing 20% of the international freight market – Air France, Cathay, Japan Airlines and Lufthansa – managed to gain a pre-eminent position in the field of interfacing freight systems using their "Traxon" products created between 1990 and 1993. Traxon is a global information system for the airfreight industry, comprising a network of data-processing services and telecommunications organised around a connection box installed near Frankfurt and composed of three host platforms situated in Europe, Asia and America. It offers market coverage unequalled anywhere else in the world, due to the support of its founding airlines and a clever policy of good relations and contacts with other common cargo-CCS systems established in a number of countries. The communications which it provides between the participating airlines (33 airlines connected to Traxon plus 44 "status only" airlines) and the freight agents who are linked to the system – over 5,000 offices – are concerned with shipment (tracing/tracking), shipment booking, and airway bill data transmission (a field in which there is still much to do) but, whatever function is under consideration.

Traxon is no longer the only system on the market that connects customers/freight forwarders and airlines. Its principal competitors are Tradivision and Sintegra.

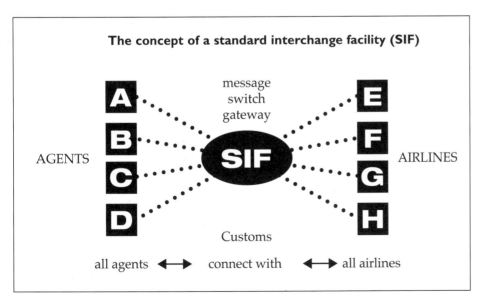

The concept of a standard interchange facility (SIF)

message switch gateway

AGENTS   SIF   AIRLINES

Customs

all agents ⟷ connect with ⟷ all airlines

7
THE TIDE OF LIBERALISATION

Air deregulation in its various forms was only one aspect of a much larger movement which was triggered in the telecommunications field in the United States by a decision of the Supreme Court in the Carterfone Case in 1968. Starting out from the United States, which at that time was one of the most regulated countries in the world, the liberal movement spread out across many countries with different intensity, and successively affected various sectors: financial services, telecommunications, transport etc.

As one commentator noted in 1976: [1] "Deregulation is a negative term: 'opening up' would better describe the spirit of the reform. Opening up the closed sectors which had been rigorously protected like private hunting grounds; opening up conditions and ways for entrepreneurs to participate in the markets; opening up the competition; opening the rates, and finally, throwing wide the doors of the procedural prisons."

In some French circles, it is considered that the deregulation of air transport was a devilish theory concocted by a few malevolent American academics. One would perhaps do better to ask whether the re-emergence of liberal doctrines had its natural origins in the undeniable economic success of the Free World between 1950 and 1970. This success logically caused some men of ideas to ask if the arsenal of regulatory conditions adopted to deal with the consequences of the 1929 slump and the Second World War, was still justified. Considered from this point of view, deregulation can be seen paradoxically as the fruit of the remarkable success of "orderly development".

I DEREGULATION OF THE AIR – AND ITS LIMITS

Airfreight: the test-bed for deregulation
The first attempts at providing the "freight-only services" with a more liberal legal framework than that of general air law, go back to the mid–1950s. The conference of the European Civil Aviation Commission held in Strasbourg in 1954 recommended: "that the States invited as full members of the Conference should afford a favourable reception to the request, which would be presented to them in the name of European carriers wishing to adopt indirect routings for the purpose of operating services limited to freight transport to and from points situated within Europe." [2] Although this recommendation was not put into effect due to

reservations expressed by certain states, it was repeated on several further occasions at later conferences of ECAC. It quite correctly draws attention to the idea of "an indirect itinerary": since freight traffic, in contrast to passenger traffic, is by definition one way, and is therefore often out of balance, the technique of indirect itineraries is the only possibility for optimising the overall load factor by allowing the homeward routes to be different from the outward routes. This is reflected in practice by the operation of "circular" freight routes of the Paris/Dhahran/Bombay/Paris type which links the fully-loaded Paris/Dhahran and Bombay/Paris sections. This practice enjoyed considerable growth under the name of "flexibility". The achievement of flexibility is in many cases an unavoidable prerequisite for profitable freight operations.

On a broader scale, the publication in Great Britain of the "Edwards Report" in 1969 reflects the way people's minds were changing. While continuing to remain in the camp of "orderly competition", it strongly emphasises the benefits of a competitive environment:

"We believe that competition is the most efficient way of guaranteeing that the travelling public receives an appropriate and comfortable service, with sufficient capacity, and to allow it to benefit from the advantages of technical progress, and finally, perhaps most importantly, to offer the choice of several carriers." [3]

These few examples illustrate the slow spread of the concept of liberalisation in air transport. However it was necessary to wait until the beginning of the 1970s before the movement, constructed within the academic community and relayed by consumer associations, emerged onto the American political scene. In 1974, President Gerald Ford, a Republican, requested Congress to nominate a commission for the purpose of examining the powers of the Regulatory Agencies, while Senator Edward Kennedy, a Democrat, launched a vast enquiry, brilliantly orchestrated, concerning the policies and practices of the CAB.

The two sides ended up with identical conclusions: domestic American air transport was suffering from excessive regulation, whether regarding market access, choice of routes and frequencies or the establishment of rates and fares.

Deregulation was on its way, with the support of the American political class, but where was it to begin?

Among the American airlines, the cargo-only air carriers were the most enthusiastic about the idea of lightening or even eliminating the regulatory barriers erected by the CAB in order to protect the freight incomes of mixed airlines. In particular, Federal Express and Flying Tiger saw this policy in the perspective of free development of their activities. The legislators gave in to pressure from the freight-only carriers and freight activities were the first to be deregulated:

"Congress decided to unleash the domestic airfreight industry and let the force of free competition determine the future of the industry. The enactment of P.L. 95.163 on November 9, 1977 [by President James Carter] removed virtually all CAB authority over the US domestic all-cargo and combination airfreight operations. In future the CAB was not to control airfreight rates or conditions of service unless the proposed rates or rules were considered to be unjustly discriminatory, prejudicial or predatory. Furthermore, a new class of air carrier [domestic operators of all-cargo aircraft] was created." [4]

One year later, on 24th October 1978, President Carter signed the Airline Deregulation Act, which extended the deregulation measures to cover the whole of American commercial aviation. Once again, freight had led the way!

The CAB seemed suddenly to be infected by a kind of "liberal pruritis", and, not to be outdone, decided on its own authority to apply the spirit of Public Law 95-163 to the airfreight forwarders. The conditions for approval became extremely liberal, and the number of airfreight forwarders in the United States jumped from around 300 in 1976 to more than 1,200 in 1979! The domestic deregulation of air transport in the United States came to its conclusion on 31st December 1984 with the winding up of the CAB, the residual functions of which were to a large extent taken over by the Department of Transport.

Difficulties in exporting domestic deregulation
For the Americans, the deregulation of air transport was from the beginning considered as an export product. In his speech of 21st August 1978 President Carter, in advance of the law which liberalised the airlines, declared himself firmly in favour of an international open sky policy, which would consist in extending the liberal principles practised within the United States to cover bilateral air agreements.

It was only the American cargo airlines who adhered immediately to this open skies policy, of which the "Statement of US International air cargo policy" [5] published on 10th May 1989 by the Department of Transportation (DOT) lists the seven key points:

1. Freedom of carrier entry: "The US seeks unrestricted entry into international air cargo markets for all types of US cargo operators."

2. Routing flexibility: "The US seeks maximum international routing flexibility for US carriers so that they can serve intermediate and beyond points freely and efficiently utilise their hubs in the US and abroad. Increased routing flexibility expands cargo opportunities, and in some cases may be critical to the viability of a cargo operation."

3. Pricing freedom: "The US seeks to establish regimes that permit airline management, maximum flexibility in the setting of prices."

4. Elimination of restrictions on frequency and capacity.

5. Efficient ground-side environment: "The areas that US aviation authorities examine closely are (i) the rights of an airline to perform its own ground handling and to offer ground handling services to the airlines; (ii) the availability of adequate warehouse facilities; (iii) the efficiency of the (customs) clearance process.

6. Broad intermodal rights: "To move cargo by truck or other service means intermodal rights have become particularly critical as air cargo systems have evolved to include door-to-door services."

7. Elimination of discriminatory practices.

How would it be possible to pass from a liberal declaration of intention to flying it in practice? In international air transport, there is only one possible solution: bilateral negotiations between sovereign states. Ideally, the increasing number of signatures of bilateral "open sky" agreements should have quickly resulted, by way of so many reciprocal arrangements, in the establishment of a kind of vast multilateral structure, within which freight-only services could have benefited from a regime of almost complete freedom, providing they observed the technical regulations in force – a regime comparable to the freedom of the seas.

What happened in fact? Two short quotations will explain the limits of international deregulation far better than a long treatise.

• January 1987: "Deregulation is catching." [6] But that was in the era of illusions.

• August 1997: "It's still a bilateral world." [7]

So what was the situation at the end of the 20th century?
On the one hand the United States did not manage to convince all its partners of the virtues of "open skies" agreements, although many agreements of this type were signed, particularly with Asian and European countries. On 18th June 1998, France negotiated and signed a progressive air agreement which was described as an "Open skies-like pact" [8] which ended at the beginning of 2002 with an "Amendment to the agreement of 1998" ratifying a culmination of the liberalisation process. Other countries as important as Great Britain and Japan stayed on the sidelines, not to mention more or less the whole of Africa, the Middle East and South America. In all these cases, the extension of traffic rights continued to give rise to very close-fought discussions, of which the negotiations between the United States and Japan regarding all-freight services present a good example.

On the other hand, outside their dealings with the United States, the large majority of nations remained attached to the traditional principles of bilateral agreements (strict definition of routes and in many cases predetermination of capacities). The countries which practised an open skies policy (United Arab Emirates) or which came out in favour of a very liberal policy on traffic rights (United States, Singapore, The Netherlands, Luxembourg, Belgium etc) remained a minority.

For the most part, we are still in a world of bilateral relations, with two vast liberalised domestic zones: the United States and Europe.

The liberalisation of air transport within Europe

A degree of ambiguity in the Treaty of Rome relating to marine and air transport contributed to delays in starting the process of internal deregulation of air transport within Europe. The uncertainty on this matter was ended through a decision of the European Court of Justice in April 1974, stating that air and marine transport should, like other modes of transport, be subject to the general conditions of the Treaty concerning free circulation and competition rules.

After its initiation through the Memorandum on Air Transport within Europe, published by the Commission in July 1979, the progressive evolution towards establishing a European regime of freedom of the air was only completed in 1997. It affects mixed services as well as freight-only services, and scheduled flights as well as charter flights. European deregulation (which of course only concerns flights inside Europe) is very similar in content to the American deregulation scheme. It establishes legal conditions characterised by freedom of market access for airlines from the European Union, freedom of access to intra-community routes, (third, fourth and fifth freedom services), the establishment of capacity related to market needs, and freedom in the pricing of rates and fares.

2 RATE DEREGULATION AND HOW IT WENT TOO FAR

IATA always exercised a dual function: that of rate regulation and that of harmonising services and procedures in all areas of commercial aviation. Whilst this second function was always greeted with general approval, the first was often criticised and even vilified.

Malfunctions of the multilateral rate-making system

"The IATA Traffic Conferences must reach unanimous agreement so that every airline, large or small, can exercise a right of veto." This sentence, which expresses the essence of the IATA rate philosophy, also shows up its strengths and weaknesses. The rule of unanimity was a sign of respect for the small airlines. It was also the only way to devise and apply the coherent universal multilateral rate system in which the first Directors of IATA believed. At the same time, it is easy to see the dangers in the rule of unanimity. A single airline can block the whole system and decisions taken are never likely to be more than compromise solutions, which all too often favour carriers with high unit costs.

The smooth operation of the IATA system depends on two conditions: that the airlines are developing in a sufficiently homogeneous world, and that they share a minimum number of ideas about rates. So this was why the conjunction of three events, which occurred in the early years of the decade 1970–1980 (introduction of wide-bodied aircraft, the onset of the oil crisis, and the increase of competition from passenger charters), unleashed tensions of such intensity that they forced the airlines to take divergent individual decisions.

With regard to freight, the crisis came to a head in the number one sector – the North Atlantic. Over-capacity induced the

major airlines to show much ingenuity in finding traffic. Such imaginative ideas were more individualist than collective, and led to the introduction of innovative rate structures which varied according to the countries and the carriers involved (high weight-break rates, multi-pallet rates, contract rates etc). The noble multilateral edifice was beginning to crumble, and give way to bilateral rate agreements (since the Governments retained their powers of approving the rates), and even to unilateral situations, whether in fact or in law, resulting from the initiative of an individual carrier, generally supported by his national civil aviation authority.

The "IATA machinery" seemed completely paralysed, for both passengers and freight. It was then, that IATA, with the triple objective of answering the bitterest criticisms, finding a solution to its own malfunctions, and satisfying the CAB (which was threatening to abolish its anti-trust exemption), decided to bring about its own reformation.

The IATA reforms of 1978

These reforms can be summarised under four headings:

1. The functions of the Association were henceforth divided into two parts:

   • "Trade Association" activities, which included all the non-competitional aspects of IATA (technical, legal, medical and financial questions, along with standardisation of procedures);

   • "Rate co-ordination activities", covering rate negotiations and the remuneration of the sales network.

   These two different functions corresponded to the two types of membership: each member company necessarily belonged to the "Trade Association" section, but had the possibility of not belonging to the "Rate co-ordination" section. In this field there was additional freedom for airlines to participate in the co-ordination of passenger fares and/or freight rates.

2. Associations of consumers or shippers could express their opinions during the opening of Traffic Conferences.

3. Several technical arrangements were introduced in order to render the mechanisms for rate setting more flexible and to adapt them to market fluctuations.

4. The department responsible for supervising the application of rate systems, which was a symbol of the repressive function of IATA, adopted a role, which was more preventive than punitive.

The 1978 reforms, which realigned IATA nearer its mission as a trade association, helped to perpetuate its existence and strengthen its influence.

From multilateral rates to individual quotations

The reform of IATA did nothing to slow down the dismantling of the freight rating system. More precisely, after having been fossilised, it was replaced in the market place by a whole series of rates and practices which varied immensely between countries and companies, and even between customers and consignments. Within a few years, the universal multilateral system was replaced by a fragmented rate structure, whether bilateral or unilateral.

Of course, "rating frauds", ie the deliberate misuse of the rate structures in force, had always existed. Even in December 1956, IATA noted in its Bulletin: "Freight rate agreements are being broken on a fairly wide scale." Freight was always the naughty boy in the class, when it came to respecting official rates, but at the time, the fraud consisted, more often than not, in allowing a freight agent or customer to benefit from a reduction calculated on the basis of a rate that was still considered as an immutable edict. From 1975 onwards, this situation changed completely. The unofficial rates, known as "market rates", which were completely disassociated from the official structure, appeared and spread through certain major sectors (North Atlantic, Europe/Middle East, Europe/Asia) to such an extent that they eventually covered the majority and then almost the whole of the traffic. This development reached its culmination when: 1. large customers put out calls for tender in due and proper legal form, for the annual transport of their freight requirements, and 2. more and more airlines increased their number of ad hoc "quotations" for supposedly large-scale consignments.

By around 1985–1990 a point had been reached where at least five rate categories existed side by side:

• An IATA reference structure which was still chiefly used for calculating the pro-rata costs for consignments transported via services of a number of carriers (determination of the proportion of income due to each company);

• So called "market" rates, which were official or unofficial from case to case, reflecting the rate concepts of each airline;

• Rates granted to certain large customers, resulting from tenders or confidential negotiations;

• Specific quotations, varying from day to day according to the available capacity or modified according to the size or nature of the consignment;

• Charter rates.

This was not the law of the jungle, however, but simply the law of supply and demand coloured by the buying power of a few customers, which experience showed not to be in strict proportion to the traffic they provided. Nevertheless, once this degree of deregulation had arisen, people began to imagine a controlling authority whose task would be solely to ensure, on a permanent basis, that the airfreight rates would be:

1. Published: as a token of transparency in rate matters, this minimum requirement could only be satisfied by means of publication of all the rates on the market, at least one month before they entered into force.

2. Non-discriminatory: it was only the fact of being compelled to register all contractual rate scales with an unquestioned authority, which would ensure confidentiality, that would oblige the airlines to respect certain objective criteria and avoid a drift towards using rates cobbled together from customer to customer.

3. Non-predatory: in theory, any rate which is below the marginal cost of production should be considered as anti-economic or predatory. In reality it is difficult to see how dumping rates could be avoided in an activity which favours the idea of average unit revenue over that of an intrinsic rate level, and in which the great variety of supply (cargo-only planes and the bellies of passenger aircraft) makes it impossible to use the idea of marginal cost of production.

Whatever the chances of introducing a certain amount of discipline, one thing has probably been established for good: air rates will no never again be the result of co-operative decisions, approved by Governments. The only airlines to survive will be those capable of generating an adequate profit level by offering a competitive price-quality relationship.

8 AIRFREIGHT IN THE SOVIET UNION: FROM ZENITH TO COLLAPSE

The history of the development of airfreight in the Soviet Union, from the end of the Great Patriotic War to the creation of the Community of Independent States in December 1999, is so specific to that country that it requires a separate chapter. While it remains so untypical during its development, its final phase illustrates almost to the point of caricature the realities of a world "changed utterly".

The entry of the USSR into membership of the ICAO on 14th November 1970 did not really constitute a break with tradition. Rather, it was one stage in the long process of normalisation in aeronautical relations between East and West, of which the opening of the Moscow/New York service in summer 1968 had been a symbolic manifestation.[1]

At the time when the USSR became the 120th member state of the ICAO, its air traffic was considerable. Aeroflot, which enjoyed a quasi monopoly in all fields of airborne activities, was the world's leading aviation company, with proportions of total traffic amounting to 17% for passengers, 10% for mail and 13% for freight (see table on page 295 showing development of USSR and CIS freight traffic 1970–95). One can recognise two periods in this 50-year span of history: one phase of reconstruction and development (1945–80), followed, 1980–95, by a phase of mummification of the collectivist system, which resulted in the implosion of the Communist regime and the collapse of the air network.

I FIRST PERIOD – RECONSTRUCTION AND EXPANSION (1945–1980)

Although it is difficult to make an accurate comparison between the Soviet figures, which do not always distinguish between mail and goods, and those of the ICAO, it seems that USSR freight traffic experienced rapid growth between 1950 and 1970, but was very soon to reach a stage of lower growth in the decade 1970–80.

Comparative development of freight traffic for USSR and ICAO (average annual variations in percent)

Periods	USSR	ICAO
1950–1960	+15.0%	+10.2%
1960–1970	+12.2%	+17.0%
1970–1980	+4.9%	+9.8%

Expressed in gross tonnes, the freight traffic sent by air in the USSR rose from 150,000 tonnes in 1950 to 546,000 in 1960, and then to 1,516,000 tonnes in 1970 and approximately 2,500,000 in 1980.

Cargo aircraft

In the mid–1960s, Aeroflot's scheduled cargo network was operated by three types of aircraft: the Lisunov Li-2, developed from the Douglas DC-3; the Ilyushin Il-14, a sort of modernised and rejuvenated Lisunov; and the Antonov An-12. A fourth aircraft type, the Antonov An-22, was introduced in 1968 and used principally for charter flights in Siberia and the northern regions.

The An-12 and An-22 were originally designed for military purposes and then adapted for civilian use, and in spite of their considerable difference in size shared a number of common points: high wings, rear loading ramp and non-pressurised main cabin. In addition, both could manage on primitively prepared landing strips.

The Antonov An-12 is the cargo version of the An-10. It made its first flight in 1958 and became the standard transport machine for the Soviet Air Force before being introduced into service with Aeroflot in 1965, particularly for flying the Siberian routes (see map of Aeroflot cargo network in 1966). The An-12 is a four-engined turboprop aircraft with a maximum payload of 20 tonnes and a normal operating load of around 12-15 tonnes, with a volume of 97m³ (dimensions of main hold: 13.50m x 3.50m x 2.61m). The later arrival of a powerful fleet of An-12Bs marked a further stage in development of the aircraft.

The Antonov An-22 made its maiden flight on 27th February 1965 and went into service in 1968. In its day, this aircraft, powered by four turboprop engines, was the largest in the world and illustrates a certain propensity towards gigantism in the Antonov Design Bureau. It is a heavy cargo aircraft, adapted for carrying bulky loads with high unit weights, and was particularly well suited for work in opening up Siberia – in addition to its military capabilities. It was named Antus (from the name of the giant in Greek mythology who regained his strength every time he touched the ground), it offered a payload of 80 tonnes and its cabin, with a length of 33 metres, was characterised by a square cross-section of 4.40m x 4.40m. On 26th October 1967, it carried a record load of 100,444.6kg. Like

Development of USSR and CIS freight traffic from 1970 to 1995
(in million RTK)

	International Flights			Domestic Flights			Total		
	World	USSR	Share in %	World	USSR	Share in %	World	USSR	Share in %
1970	6,380	80	1.3	5,640	1,480	26.2	12,020	1,560	13.0
1975	11,470	170	1.5	7,730	1,940	25.0	19,200	2,110	11.0
1980	20,260	260	1.3	9,120	2,250	24.6	29,380	2,510	8.5
1985	29,380	200	0.7	10,430	2,480	23.8	39,810	2,680	6.7
1990	46,230	390	0.8	12,480	2,155	17.3	58,800	2,545	4.3
1995	70,320	595	0.8	12,800	385	3.0	83,120	980	1.2

Source: ICAO

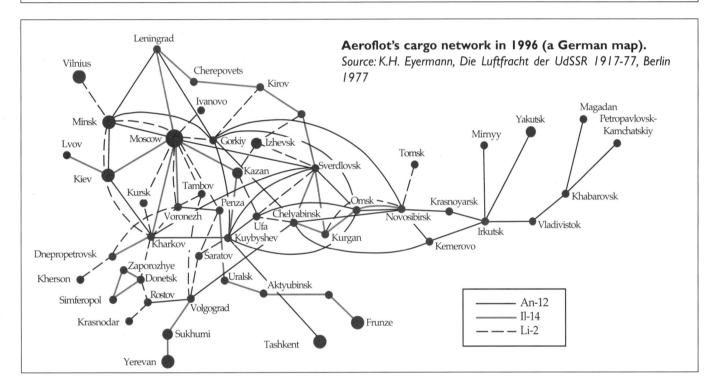

Aeroflot's cargo network in 1996 (a German map).
Source: K.H. Eyermann, Die Luftfracht der UdSSR 1917-77, Berlin 1977

other Soviet cargo aircraft, it was not palletised and its crew consisted of no fewer than eight people.

This was an aircraft destined for special missions, rather than to operate scheduled services which are under pressure to produce economic results.

The situation in 1975 [2]

What was the future of airfreight in the USSR in 1975? The picture is of an immense empire turned in on itself, with domestic traffic taking up over 92% of total activities, and of a powerful economy generating traffic of over two million tonnes. However, here as elsewhere, these figures should not give rise to any illusions: only a very small proportion of total goods transported was sent by plane – 0.04% – although its contribution to the opening up of certain regions was irreplaceable. There was a high proportion of charter activity: it reached 35% and went on growing due to the implementation of major development projects in parts of the country without communication routes (Siberia, the Urals) (see table "Development of USSR domestic freight traffic by region").

Soviet economists distinguished between two categories of cargo services:

1. Those linking up with points served by railways (Group I)
2. Those which link points without railway connections (Group II)

Traffic developed more rapidly in the second category of links (see table below: Development of airfreight traffic by link category).

Development of USSR domestic freight traffic by region: 1965–1975 (in thousand gross tonnes)

	1965		1975	
Regions	Traffic	%	Traffic	%
European USSR	461	48.1	775	37.1
Siberia and the Urals	229	23.9	808	38.8
Far East	174	18.2	371	17.7
Asia and Kazakhstan	94	9.8	137	6.5
Total	958	100	2091	100

Malev Il-18 freighter.

Development of airfreight traffic by link category
(in thousand gross tonnes)

	Gross Traffic			Breakdown in %	
	Group I	Group II	Total	Group I	Group II
1965	565	394	958	59	41
1970	785	751	751	51	49
1975	858	1,233	2,091	41	59

The type of goods carried varied according to the two categories, but industrial products always made up the majority of traffic: 85% for routes in the first group and 60% for those of the second, on which food products (fruit, vegetables etc) made up 30%. In total, 40% of traffic was carried on cargo flights, and 60% in the holds of passenger planes.

Let us now examine the criteria determining whether a certain consignment or traffic flow would be sent by air. In the absence of motivation of a capitalist nature, "The central planning organisations will compare all the alternatives and will arrive at a conclusion regarding the type of transport to be chosen for a particular connection: as a result, competition – assuming that we could use such a term in its proper sense – ceases at the project stage, and that choice is accepted, which is the most rational for the country as a whole." [3] Airfreight is only one element, mostly predetermined, in the "unified transport network" or "Edinaya Transportnaia Systema", in which all modes of transport are integrated.

2 SECOND PERIOD – STAGNATION AND COLLAPSE (1980–1995)

Domestic freight traffic, which continued to represent over 90% of the total, started to stagnate from 1980 onwards. According to figures communicated to ICAO, it moved from 2,250 revenue tonne kilometres in 1980 to 2,155 millions in 1990. Nevertheless, the aeronautical industry continued to supply valuable items of equipment, well suited to the specific economic features of the Soviet regime.

Cargo aircraft production
Out of a rich and varied aircraft production, we will concentrate on three types: heavy helicopters, the Ilyushin Il-76 TD, and the giant cargo aircraft Antonov An-124 Ruslan.

• Heavy helicopters
The USSR held a unique position in this field "having developed a range of heavy helicopters from 12-50 tonnes which have practically no equivalent in the West". [4] Several factors contributed to this situation: the geographical peculiarities of the country, the distribution of the inhabited sectors and of the natural resources, the interests brought to bear by the army, and finally, the presence of two first-class aircraft designers, Nicolas Kamov and Mikhail Mil. Each of them produced a range of aircraft, from the Ka-15 to the K-Max by the former, and the Mi-1 to the Mi-26 by the latter. Most of these helicopters exist in a cargo version. However, the Mi-8 and the Ka-26, in addition to the Mi-6, the Mi-10 and the Mi-26 heavy helicopters, were the ones which were most frequently used for carrying goods and for airborne missions (construction, electric power lines in inaccessible areas, laying pipelines for gas or oil in marshy regions, or in regions without means of communication, etc.).

The Mi-6 was the first of the giant helicopters: "the Mi-6 is truly enormous". [5] It was as long as a Douglas DC-9, and made available a payload of 12 tonnes carried in the cabin and 9 tonnes for suspended loads. Commissioned by Aeroflot in 1961, its production fulfilled a requirement for transporting trucks, tracked vehicles, boring equipment and other heavy loads. The Mi-6 was followed in 1967 by the Mi-8 (load 2 tonnes) and by the Mi-10, a sort of gigantic flying crane with a similar lifting capacity to the Mi-6, capable of carrying a bus beneath its fuselage.

The whole of this range of helicopters was exploited intensively by Aeroflot in various regions of the USSR between 1975

LEFT A Mil-10 heavy helicopter ready for take off with a 28-seat bus at Le Bourget, Paris, 18 June 1965.
John Stroud

BELOW LEFT Aeroflot Mil-26 heavy helicopter.
MAP

BOTTOM LEFT Aeroflot Il-76.
Air Cargo News UK

of this project, which was called "Baikal-Amur-Magistral", or BAM, extended into the decade of 1980–1990. It brought a considerable fleet of cargo aircraft into action, concentrated on six main logistics centres, including heavy helicopters for transport and air lifting operations.

• The Ilyushin Il-76 cargo aircraft

This four-engined jet aircraft entered into service in the Aeroflot fleet in 1976, and was part of the series of Soviet cargo aircraft already described, designed for both military and civil use. It was designed for transporting heavy and oversized equipment over inhospitable terrain, and possessed a high level of autonomy regarding ground handling (rear loading ramp, interior winches). It has a pressurised cabin, which is equipped with very thick non-standard pallets which are not suitable for optimum exploitation of the theoretical payload in the case of

and 1990, particularly on the occasion of three major projects:

- the laying of a pipeline 1,000 miles in length between north-western Siberia and the Urals (Urengoi/Chelyabinsk) between 1975 and 1980;

- the drilling and bringing into production of one of the world's largest oil fields in the Tyumen region of western Siberia (the operation used hundreds of Mi-8 and Mi-6 helicopters);

- the construction in central and eastern Siberia of a 2,200-mile-long railway line running parallel to and northwards of the Trans-Siberian railway. It was started in 1974, but fell very much behind the original production schedule, and the construction

normal freight (40-45 tonnes on a conventional runway and 33 tonnes on an earth landing strip). The Il-76, with its long-haul version known as Il-76 TD, rapidly became – and remains to this day – the workhorse for air transport in Siberia, for which its characteristics are ideally suited.

• The Antonov An-124 Ruslan

This is the world's largest aircraft used for commercial purposes. It is impressive from all perspectives: payload (120–150 tonnes according to the circumstances); cargo cabin dimensions (length 36.48m; width 6.05m; maximum height: 4.40m); the makeup of the crew (14 people, including handling and loading specialists); and loading technology (front and rear ramps permitting simultaneous loading and

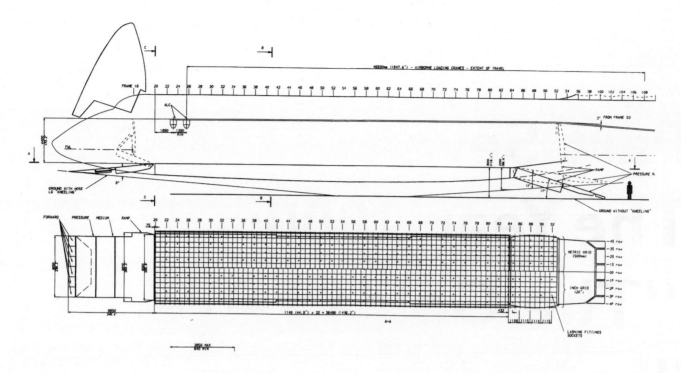

ABOVE The An-124 Ruslan's enormous cargo space.

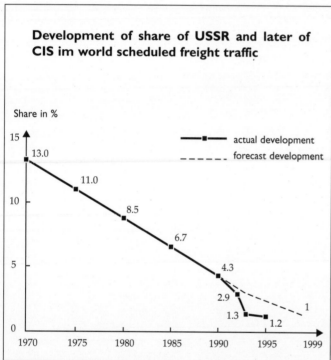

Development of share of USSR and later of CIS im world scheduled freight traffic

A collapse programmed far in advance

The stagnation in airfreight, as a symbol of the progressive decay of the USSR economy, started a long time before the dissolution of the Communist regime. It went back to the 1970s, and was revealed by a regular and constant decline of the share of the Soviet flag in world traffic, which fell from 13% in 1970 to 4.3% in 1990. As is shown by the graph below, the end of the Soviet Union only speeded up a process which had started some 20 years before: it merely brought forward by about six years, from 1993 to perhaps 1999, the apparently unavoidable reduction of the Soviet flag's market share to about 1%.

The upheaval of the whole of the Soviet air transport world following the political disruption was no less profound, as is shown in the small table below:

Development of scheduled freight traffic: 1980–1995
(in thousand RTK)

	International Traffic	Domestic Traffic	Total Traffic
1980	260	2,250	2,510
1995	595	385	980
1995/1980	+128%	-83%	61%

Total international traffic took over the major share (60%) whereas internal traffic fell by over 80%. Such a spectacular collapse gives food for thought. It may have had multiple causes: the reduction in economic activity, the disappearance of traffic linked with propaganda purposes (political literature or press), or the failure to communicate certain figures to the ICAO. However, one cannot avoid questioning the veracity of certain official statistics from the years 1970–1990.

unloading as for the American heavy military cargo aircraft Lockheed C-5A).

Under these conditions (see sketch at top) "the entire width and height of the fuselage are available for cargo access. There are no restrictions caused by either the nose or tail cargo doors... A unique feature of Ruslan is the overhead travelling cranes. Providing a lift capacity of up to 37 tonnes, these allow heavy cargoes to be loaded with minimum preparation and without the use of special airport loading equipment." [6]

It is not surprising that the An-124 features in the "Guinness Book of Records 1996" thanks to the loading by Antonov Airlines in partnership with the British charter company Air Foyle, of a single item weighing 124 tonnes taken from Düsseldorf to Delhi on 22nd September 1993. The Ruslan is the charter aircraft par excellence.

Part Seven
The Year 2000:
"The Golden Age
Illusion"

Title of a book by Professors Michael J. Webber & David L. Rigby, which appeared in 1996.

1 AIRFREIGHT: A PANORAMIC VIEW

The last year of the second Millennium appears now to have been now particularly economically vibrant. International trade, airline traffic and the volume of business for the freight forwarders had never previously reached such levels. From every point of view, the year 2000 was a record year, the culmination of a tremendous movement of expansion which, within 30 years, in spite of numerous crises, brought about a 12-fold increase in world cargo traffic. Although the figures in this section of the book only relate to the year 2000, that the trends within the industry and the policies in different sectors, which straddle the end of the 20th century and the start of the 21st century, have subsequently taken a different turn. However, since it is the role of history to assess events according to criteria valid at the time, we have been careful not to allow future events to colour our analysis of the state of play in 2000.

AIRFREIGHT – A PANORAMIC VIEW

Although it may seem surprising, there are no official statistics enabling a direct evaluation of world airfreight traffic, due to the absence of figures for Taiwan (whose airlines hold over 5% of the market) and to the distortion arising from the different publication dates of the data for scheduled traffic and charter traffic. It is therefore necessary to reassemble the puzzle.

The world traffic in airfreight for the year 2000 reached almost 37 million tonnes, corresponding to 137 billion RTK.

I COMPOSITION OF TRAFFIC

These figures include both scheduled traffic and charter traffic, along with humanitarian missions, private carriage and common carriage, and express freight and traditional traffic.

Scheduled and charter traffic
Scheduled flight traffic represents over 90% of world traffic, and this percentage is tending to grow at the expense of charter traffic. Seventy-five percent of charter traffic is operated by scheduled airlines and 25% by charter airlines. Hence the scheduled carriers account for almost 98% of the world traffic in goods. The cargo charter companies do not hold a dominant

position except in two particular fields – the market for over-sized shipments and humanitarian freight.

Humanitarian freight
These missions, which are often a valuable source of income for carriers, take very varied forms. First of all there is the "all comers" market – small and medium shipments of medicines, clothing and blankets, school supplies or condensed milk, sent directly by innumerable charitable associations, often with religious affiliations, to Africa, South East Asia and Latin America. For this type of mission, the airlines frequently agree special pricing conditions, which may extend to working free of charge.

Then there is the flow of regular transportation of large-volume shipments originating with the specialist agencies of the United Nations (UNICEF, The International Committee of the Red Cross [ICRC], World Food Programme [WFP] and the World Health Organisation [WHO]) and from the best organised of the NGOs (CARITAS, the Lutheran Churches, CARE, Médecins Sans Frontières etc). These organisations are well-informed about transport problems. They normally use the services of one or several cargo agents who seek competitive quotes from various carriers to obtain the lowest rates.

Finally, there is ad hoc traffic associated with the occurrence of natural catastrophes (for instance, earthquakes in Armenia or Mexico, a volcanic eruption in the Philippines or a cyclone in Honduras) and the airlifts established to prevent or limit major humanitarian catastrophes (eg famines in Africa, or the consequences of war in Cambodia, Angola or Afghanistan). Two critical factors then hold sway: urgency and an ability to work in airports which are often badly equipped, or even on primitive landing strips situated as near as possible to the location of the disaster. Since the scheduled airlines are not equipped for this kind of activity, such challenges remain an area reserved to the operators of extremely robust cargo aircraft of military origin, capable of operating on rudimentary airstrips and/or having a large degree of autonomy regarding loading and unloading operations. This is the case with certain cargo charter companies (Air Foyle Heavy Lift, Volga-Dnepr Airlines etc) and a small number of national air forces operating Lockheed C-130 Hercules, Transall, Antonov An-124 Ilyushin Il-76 and C-17 aircraft.

World Freight Traffic in the Year 2000

	Freight in gross Tonnes (Millions)	Freight in RTK (Billions)	Mail in RTK (Billions)	Cargo in RTK (Billions)
Scheduled traffic ICAO				
International	18,8	101,08	2,66	103,74
Domestic	11,4	16,50	3,37	16,87
TOTAL	30,2	117,58	6,03	123,61
Taiwan Airlines International	1,2	7,69		7,69
Non Scheduled traffic				
International	1,0	4,80		4,80
Domestic	4.5	7,40		7,40
TOTAL	5,5	12,20		12,20
World traffic				
International	21,0	113,57	2,66	116,23
Domestic	15,9	23,90	3,37	27,27
TOTAL	36,9	137,47	6,03	143,50

Source: ICAO (except for Taiwanese Airlines)

Here we come to one of the central characteristics of humanitarian operations. Although they are civil in nature, they frequently require the involvement of military transportation facilities. One of the latest examples was the passage of the hurricane "Mitch", which devastated Honduras in November 1998. At the request of the Agency for International Development, which is attached to the Department of State, the US Airforce brought out an imposing fleet of cargo aircraft and heavy helicopters to go to the aid of the population and to carry out initial repair operations. [1]

This proves that there are common links between humanitarian and military operations – a similarity, which is sometimes exploited by the armed forces' commanders of certain countries in order to obtain additional transportation equipment.

We cannot leave the field of humanitarian transportation without mentioning "Aviation sans Frontières", or ASF, an association founded in 1980 by three Air France pilots, "which today unites all people working in transportation, in the air, on the ground, hostesses, stewards, mechanics, pilots etc… who wish to give some of their time in alleviating the suffering of others. Its vocation is to put the aircraft at the disposition of humanitarian organisations in order to assist them in solving their transport problems – foodstuffs, medicines, medical personnel." [1]

Private carriage and common carriage
In contrast to road transport, air transportation has always had a very limited application for private carriage. Airbus Industrie is at the present time the best example of this. With its production centres located throughout Europe and its assembly factories situated in Toulouse and later also in Hamburg, Airbus Industrie was confronted at the outset by tricky logistical problems. For 25 years from 1972–1998 it transported large-dimension components (wings, fuselage sections) in Super Guppies. The Super Guppy was a Boeing C-97 Strato-Cruiser modified according to the requirements of NASA (for the transportation of rockets). It was in the form of an enormous shortened cigar, offering a volume of 1,100m³ for a payload of only 24 tonnes.

In 1996 the Super Guppy was replaced by an "in-house" aircraft, the A300-600ST (for Super Transporter), known as the Beluga, due to its profile resembling that of a white whale. It was developed from an A300-600F and offers an impressive volume of 1,400m³ (compared with a volume of 780m³ for a B747-400F) and a load of 45 tonnes. It carries whole aircraft sections between the production factories and the assembly centres in Germany, France and Britain. It is a perfect example of the use of air transport as part of an integrated logistics chain. In addition, the Belugas carry out transport missions on behalf of third parties.

Boeing is soon likely to follow Airbus. In February 2004 Boeing engineers announced that they have come up with a novel way to get the large fuselage and wing structures of the B7E7 Dreamliner into special 747-400 freighters that will haul the assemblies to Everett from Japan, Europe and the United States for final assembly. The aft fuselage of the huge jumbo jet will swing open like a gate to allow loading of the 7E7 composite structures. Boeing stated that only two such aircraft would be required initially, but that a third could be added later. Given the light weight of the B7E7 composite structures, the beefed up floor of the B747-400 freighter is not needed, so it is likely that used B747-400 passenger jets will be modified.

Express traffic versus traditional traffic
Express traffic originated in the 1970s. By contrast, "classic" or "traditional" traffic refers to airport-to-airport transportation, whether carried out by integrators or by "traditional" airlines, preferring the old established shipper/freight agent/air carrier triangular relationship.

ABOVE AND ABOVE RIGHT Two views of the C-97 Super Guppy
operated by Airbus.
RAF Museum

Postal and military traffic

Postal and military traffic is not included in the world airfreight figures. Airmail is included in a set of independent statistics and will be treated in Chapter Five of this part of the book. In peacetime, military traffic transported by scheduled civil airlines is of limited scope. It usually consists of demonstration equipment.

In periods of crisis, military traffic can assume considerable dimensions. This is the case in the United States where the Air Mobility Command of the US Airforce has powers to charter, to any extent necessary, the cargo (or passenger) capacities of American carriers belonging to the Civil Reserve Air fleet (CRAF). These military contracts, which are awarded exclusively to US airlines, can represent a very valuable competitive advantage when commercial goods traffic is decreasing. In addition, the enormous amounts of capacity needed to satisfy an

essentially one-way military requirement may completely destabilise an already fragile market. This phenomenon was observed during the first Gulf War in 1990–1991.

The first Gulf War at the end of 1990–early 1991 was the occasion for a gigantic logistical deployment between the United States and the Arabian Peninsula: "The supply effort of the Gulf War had few parallels in history – in several aspects it exceeded the logistics achievements of such famous events as the Berlin Airlift and Normandy Overlord." [2] Within a few weeks, over 500,000 men, 560,000 tonnes of equipment (armaments, vehicles, equipment, provisions) and 40,000 tonnes of mail were transported by air (along with 2.3 million tonnes by sea). The success of this enormous operation, which played an essential role in the result of the conflict, depended on four key factors:

• Unity of logistical command, conferred upon Lieutenant General William "Gus" Pagonis at the head of the US Army's 22nd Support Command with 12,000 men, directly attached to General Schwarzkopf.

• Complete supremacy in the air (the primary importance of this factor always tends to be under-estimated by commentators).

• The employment, probably for the first time, of EDI

**Development of scheduled Domestic Traffic in the principal markets 1990-2000
(in million RTK – Revenue Tonne Kilometres)**

Country	Rank 2000	2000 Traffic	1990 Traffic	Average Annual Growth %
United States	1	11,175	7,260	+4.4%
P.R. China	2	1,571	285	+18.5%
Japan	3	827	610	+3.0%
Brazil	4	451	390	+ 1.7%
Russia	5	347	2,167	n.s.
Australia	6	313	92	+13.0%
France	7	298	195	+4.4%
Total		16,500	12,480	+2.9%
Total excluding Russia		16,153	10,313	+4.4%

Source: ICAO

ABOVE **UN marked helicopter being loaded into a Beluga.**

ABOVE LEFT **Airbus Beluga Super Transporter.**
Airbus

technology between fighting units and the military depots in the United States, to speed up supplies.

• The employment of a powerful transport fleet, for the most part consisting of Lockheed C-5A cargo aircraft with a payload of 120 tonnes each.

The motto of the 22nd Support Command, "Good logistics is combat power", deserves to be remembered by many civilian enterprises.

2 CHARACTERISTICS OF THE AIRFREIGHT MARKET

A satisfying vitality
The continuous expansion of traffic in airfreight has not failed in over 50 years. Admittedly the average yearly growth has declined, but growth has been sustained, consistently around 8% per year from 1980 to 2000 for international traffic and around 7.1% for total traffic.

Development in growth of scheduled traffic

Period	Domestic traffic	International traffic	Total
1950–60	+8.2%	+13.5%	+10.2%
1960–70	+14.2%	+21.5%	+17.8%
1970–980	+2.9%	+12.2%	+9.4%
1980–90	+4.9%	+8.2%	+7.1%
1990–2000	+2.9%	+8.1%	+7.1%

Source: ICAO

The factors which explain this development can be grouped under three major headings:

1. The growth of international trade, which has been speeded up by the globalisation of the economy, the re-localisation of production facilities and changes in consumer behaviour;

2. Progress in aeronautical technology, which is reflected in continuous reductions in rates expressed at constant value, and finally;

3. Developments in the methods of managing the physical flow of goods.

An increasingly international activity
From being a means of domestic transport, just after the Second World War, when international trade was at its lowest level and the power of the United States was at its height, the aircraft has become, as far as goods are concerned, a chiefly international means of transport. Domestic traffic represents no more than 14% of the kilometric traffic, although this is still 38% of the gross traffic. This difference in the figures is explained by the difference in the average distances travelled 3,360 miles for international traffic, compared with 904 miles for domestic traffic.

The aircraft is becoming increasingly a means of long-haul, international transportation. Only the development of express freight in Europe would be capable of slowing down this tendency.

With almost 70% of world domestic traffic, the United States retains complete supremacy in this field, illustrating the vitality of its economy and the size of its territory. In spite of its undeniable maturity, the American domestic market has continued to develop at a rate of over 4% per annum during the period 1990-2000. Although the market was formerly in the hands of the major airlines and a few cargo airlines (Flying Tiger), it is now controlled to an extent of over 80% by integrators (Federal Express, UPS, DHL) and by integrated freight forwarders (BAX Global, Emery, Airborne) who have specialised in the carriage of industrial products with guaranteed delivery times, without weight restrictions.

We should not leave the field of North American domestic traffic without reference to a very specific activity: the freight-only or combined air services in Alaska and in the Canadian far north. There, in particularly hostile climatic conditions, some specialised companies (Lynden Air Cargo, Northern Air Cargo founded in 1956), along with Alaska Airlines, ensure the survival of communities that are cut off from the world for all or part of the year, relying on such robust aircraft as Lockheed L-100-30 Hercules, or such venerable aircraft as the Douglas DC-6 (later replaced by B727 and B737 Combi and cargo aircraft). "There isn't anything we don't carry", to use the words of a Manager at Northern Air Cargo. [3] The situation is even more extreme for the islands of the Canadian Arctic (Banks,

Melville, Cornwallis, along with the station at Resolute): here the aircraft really is the "survival link". [4] This is one of the regions in the world where, in spite of the very high level of technology, one can still find that pioneer spirit which left such a mark on the early days of air transport.

China has shown spectacular development in its domestic traffic, which increased five-fold in 10 years. This market offers the strongest potential for the future, and in the long term could catch up the American market. On a shorter time scale, the start-up and ongoing works on gigantic projects at the beginning of the 21st century (a 2,625-mile gas pipeline from the Tarim Basin to the Port of Shanghai, Three Gorges Dam and the diversion of the waters of the Yangtse towards Beijing etc) are likely to generate enormous quantities of freight charter activities resulting from the inadequacies in the land-based infrastructure.

The Japanese domestic market takes third place in the world rankings, with a gross traffic of 930,000 tonnes in 2000. The spread of the population and of economic activity throughout a chain of islands is a factor which is very favourable to airfreight, in spite of the quality and the intensity of the marine connections between the islands. The principal traffic artery connects Tokyo-Haneda with Sapporo-Chitose on the island of Hokkaido.

Brazil is ranked in fourth place with a domestic traffic of around 350,000 tonnes. The main connection links the economic capital of Sao Paulo with Manaus in the heart of Amazonia.

A tried and tested multi-modal link – the sea-air traffic
The aircraft is never an isolated means of transport. It is preceded and followed by more or less complex operations for pick-up and onward delivery. It is always part of a chain. Air transport is essentially and necessarily multi-modal. The association of air and road links is widespread and goes back many years. The conjunction of air and rail, which was highly developed between the two world wars and then almost abandoned, seems now to have a new lease of life in spite of its qualitative limitations.

The integration between air and sea has also experienced a renewal of interest since the 1960s. This "sea-air" traffic, to take up the expression used by one forwarding agent: "Gives you a 50% reduction on the time by sea with a 50% reduction on the rate for airfreight."

"Sea-air" traffic consists essentially of traffic flows leaving Asia (Japan, South Korea, Taiwan, China and India) for destinations in Europe, South America and Africa. The vast majority consists of textile products, toys and electronic equipment.

Air Canada can claim to have initiated the modern version of "sea-air" traffic when in the 1960s it was looking for a source of supply to fill its capacity in the easterly direction, leaving Vancouver as well as Montreal and Toronto. In 1965 Air Canada launched a "Sea-air Service" specially designed to promote a new product – the combined "sea-air" transport linking by sea the ports of Yokohama and Vancouver, then by road or by air Vancouver to the East coast, and finally by air from Montreal or Toronto to Europe. This product was so successful with the carriage of substantial tonnages of Japanese photographic equipment that the American ports of Seattle, then Los Angeles and San Francisco rushed in to compete with Vancouver. This "historical route" for sea-air traffic, connecting Japan and then Korea with Europe, then entered a period of stagnation, if not decline (the Japanese traffic stood at around 45,000 tonnes), due to competition from new routes via Singapore and the United Arab Emirates (UAE) – Dubai and Sharjah.

The competition from Singapore started in 1986. As a very active centre for sea and air transit, this city-state gained a position for itself within the streams of "sea-air traffic" for which it was geographically best placed: towards Europe from Taiwan and towards Australia from the Far East and India.

The main competitor to the North Pacific route for combined transport is now Dubai. Exploiting to a maximum the abundance and quality of its port and airport installations (Port Rashid and Djebel Ali) and its airports, the simplicity of its administrative formalities, the frequency of its sea connections and the rapidity of transit times between ship and aircraft (up to four hours!), Dubai has won a strong position in sea-air traffic coming from the Far East (mainland China and Taiwan) and from the Indian sub-continent (India and Sri Lanka) for destinations in Europe, Africa and the former states of the USSR.

RIGHT A humorous vision but very expressive of sea-air traffic. From Port Rashid Authority publicity, 1991.

FAR RIGHT KLM Boeing 747-400F. *KLM*

Its most redoubtable competitor in this field is none other than the neighbouring airport of Sharjah.

Korean Air launched a new service from China in collaboration with its parent company, the Hanjin Shipping Company, at the end of the 1990s. Named the "Sky-Bridge Service", "it originates in China-Tianjin, Shanghai, Qingdao, Dalian, Weihai by sea to reach the gateway seaports of Pusan or Inchon in Korea. From there it moves on bonded transport to Seoul-Inchon or Pusan International Airport to be connected to any of our flights to major cities in the world. This multi–modal service opens a new pattern of transportation by combining land, sea and air." [5]

Although a good sea-air journey does not exceed 15 days between Asia and Europe, the future of this formula is still open to question, since it is squeezed between straightforward shipping by sea (the quality of service of which is improving) and normal air transport (the rates of which are decreasing). This is especially true because, although we are dealing with multimodal transport, there can be no question of "inter-modal transport" since the marine containers are not transferred onto the aircraft but are opened up so that the goods can be then reloaded onto aircraft pallets. Let us leave the last word to "Cargo Vision", the excellent publication of KLM Cargo:

"As a transport mode for consignments which cannot support long transit delays, and as a half-way house between direct airfreight and direct sea freight from Asia, sea-air is likely to remain a useful alternative option. But will it really take off again?" [6]

The express freight explosion
The irresistible rise of express traffic for mail and goods is one of the major trends in transport history in 1970. This revolution (which began in the United States and which has had consequences comparable those of containerisation and the applica-

tion of information technology) is associated with the names of a few individuals: Frederick W. Smith, the charismatic founder of Federal Express, and the family names which are masked by the initials DHL (Dalsey, Hillblom and Lynn). Although it began with air transport carried out by couriers and integrators (those hybrids which unite the functions of carriers and freight agents), the express revolution has expanded widely into road transport.

Due to lack of statistics outside the United States it is extremely difficult to evaluate the share of express traffic within global air traffic. This is all the more difficult because in this field it would be necessary to consider three sets of data: the number of shipments – considerable for express traffic due to the low unit weight of the consignments; gross traffic and kilometric traffic.

Furthermore, this evaluation requires a clearly agreed definition of the term "express freight". There is a lot of confusion caused by "traditional" or "classic" – ie non-integrated – airlines who tend to designate as "express" any form of accelerated carriage, even if this does not have specified or guaranteed delivery times ("TD products" or time-definite products). This leads to a confusion between express traffic in the strict sense of the word and express traffic in a wider sense.

• In the strict sense, express is a product with three characteristics: rapid transport door-to-door; a commitment to a time of delivery accompanied by the promise of a refund (Money Back clause); and finally, documentation accompanying the consignment providing a proof of delivery or POD signed by the addressee and returned to the sender. These products are generally subject to weight limitations.

• By extension, and often erroneously, certain airlines have launched "express" products which are nothing more than solutions for "first class freight" from airport to airport, characterised by reduced times for acceptance and delivery and a

formal undertaking that the consignment will be loaded on a particular flight or with a guaranteed delivery period. These products, which are a partial response to the challenge raised by the integrators, do not appear to us to fulfil the strict definition of express traffic since they fail to meet some of the specific requirements.

This being the case, how can one express the share of express traffic in the strict sense of the word in proportion to the total international air traffic? In terms of kilometric traffic, the big "express companies" (Fedex, UPS, DHL, TNT) produced around 8% of world traffic in year 2000 in RTK. But this percentage is not representative of the share of express in total international traffic, for at least three reasons:

1. The "integrators" also transport "classic" freight.
2. They use "classic" companies for part of their services.
3. The "classic" airlines carry a modest quantity of truly express freight as part of their own services. Taking into account all these factors, one can evaluate the share of the express traffic at between 10% and 12% in international traffic (in RTK and around 8-20% in world total market (in RTK).

The complete discrepancy between the values and the weights transported

When one considers the tonnages carried, the share of airfreight in total freight transported appears to be negligible. If one looks at the value of goods transported, its role appears to be essential. Marginal yet fundamental, essential though negligible – these are the principal characteristics of airfreight, if they were to be stated, the best expression of its uniqueness.

Once again, a short table illustrates the point:

Development of the share of air transport in the external trade of the United States – 1970–2000

Year	Export		Import	
	Value	Weight	Value	Weight
1970	13.9%	0.18%	8.6%	0.10%
1980	20.3%	0.25%	11.7%	0.13%
1990	28.1%	0.40%	18.2%	0.32%
2000	36.4%	0.80%	25.3%	0.45%

Source: US Bureau of the Census

Can the example of the United States be considered as representative? In all the cases, these statistics confirm a general rule, which can be deduced from the American statistics: airfreight represents approximately 1% by weight and 25% by value in world international trade.

3 FREIGHT SUPPLY AND THE CARGO FLEET

The varied nature of the freight offer is the fundamental difference between passenger activities and freight activities, and has crucial implications. If there are no problems arising from the dimensions or compatibility of goods, they can equally well be transported in the holds of mixed planes chiefly designed for passengers, or on board all-cargo aircraft. In the year 2000, freight traffic was divided in more or less equal parts, 50/50, between the holds of passenger planes and cargo aircraft.

If we only take into consideration jet aircraft with a payload of over 10 tonnes/20,000lb, the world cargo fleet has also developed:

Date	Number of aircraft	Change
1.1.1998	1,370	
1.1.1999	1,470	+100
1.1.2000	1,550	+80
1.1.2001	1,620	+70

This picture is not complete: it does not include the many low-capacity feeder aircraft, Russian cargo aircraft, or other categories. Generally speaking, cargo aircraft can be classed in seven categories. [7]

• First category: wide-bodied aircraft with a payload of above 65 tonnes (140,000lb) (373 aircraft).

These are the wide-bodied aircraft in the Boeing B747F and McDonnell Douglas DC-10 and MD-11F families and form the main framework of the intercontinental cargo network. They are the workhorses of the traditional airlines.

The Boeing 747 freighter is the most numerous (240 aircraft). This is a very diverse fleet. In the year 2000, one could still find a few very old B747-100Fs, mainly operating in the United States. The B747-200F or converted models still had the lion's share, although many of them were beginning to show obvious signs of ageing.

The B747-400Fs, launched at the end of 1993 and still in production 10 years later, only form a quarter of the group. They are operated by the American wet-lessor Atlas Air, Cargolux Airline and a group of six Asian companies (Singapore Airlines, China Airlines, Cathay Pacific, Korean Air, Asian Air and Eva Air). These latter companies own the majority of the world fleet of this aircraft, which has the highest performance on the market.

Compared with its ancestor, the B747-200F, the B747-400F has several characteristics designed to limit fuel consumption and reduce operating costs: improved aerodynamics (winglets), advanced jet engines which are cleaner and use less fuel, reduction of dead weight through the use of new materials, and electronic flight deck equipment and related systems permitting the plane to be flown by two people. The result is a lower unit cost, a greater flying range under full load, and an additional volume of 20m³ (obtained by means of an extra pallet at the front of the main deck and another one in the rear hold).

In the year 2000 Boeing proposed a new version, the B747-400ERF (Extended Range Freighter), which offers an additional 40% on the operating range at full load (5,625 miles against 4,000 miles with 112 net tonnes). This machine, which was put into service by Air France at the end of the year 2002, is proving to be extremely economical over long distances.

There are fewer aircraft of the Douglas DC-10 cargo family in use (130 units approximately). Fedex, which operates a sizeable fleet of aircraft of this ageing type, launched an ambitious plan for the conversion and complete modernisation of the passenger fleets of United Airlines and American Airlines in 1996, in order to convert them into DC-10 Cargo aircraft flown with a two-person crew. The newest model in this family is the MD-11-Freighter.

The MD-11F is one of the " New Generation" modern cargo aircraft. It was introduced by Fedex in May 1991 and is the aircraft which occupies the market niche for 80/90 tonnes, carrying 26 pallets on the main deck, in comparison with the B747-400F which occupies the niche for 100/120 tonnes. Hence, these two aircraft complement rather than compete with one another. No doubt this is why, after its purchase of McDonnell Douglas, Boeing's decision to cease producing the MD-11F in the year 2000 met with so much criticism from customer airlines, particularly from Lufthansa Cargo. The main airlines operating these aircraft are Federal Express (42 aircraft – "it has always been our vision that the MD-11F would be the backbone of our express freight and network", as Gill Mook, Senior VP, recounted), [8] Lufthansa Cargo (14) Eva Air (5) and Martinair (6).

• Second category: wide-bodied aircraft with a payload of 30-65 tonnes (70,000–140,000lb) (278 aircraft).

This is essentially the domain of the American and European integrators, who operate 90% of these aircraft which are well suited to their needs for long- and medium-haul flights. Airbus has carved out the major share of the market in this category with 168 aircraft out of 278, thanks to its wide range of machines of 40-55 tonnes capacity, consisting of converted passenger aircraft (A300B4, A310-200) and cargo aircraft such as the A300-600F.

The A300-600 Freighter is a New Generation cargo aircraft which entered into service in 1994. It offers a payload of over 50 tonnes for a range of 1,875 miles. The standard configuration of the main deck has 15 pallets (nine pallets 88/96in x 125in + six pallets 88in x125in). This plane was specially adapted to suit the specific needs of the integrators (with containers and pallets) and is used both by UPS (90 units delivered or on order by 2008) and Federal Express (39 units in operation).

Boeing has a presence in this category, with its cargo version of the B767 operated by Federal Express and Airborne Express (ABX Air), which has made it the main machine in its fleet.

• Third category: Narrow-bodied aircraft with a payload of between 27 and 55 tonnes (60,000 to 120,000lb).

With the exception of the B757-200PF, this category consists of very old first-generation cargo jets. The B707 has become the noisy and pollution-prone aircraft of the poor countries of Africa, South America and the Middle East. On the other hand, DC-8s are still used in the United States, because their noise levels have been reduced either by fitting hush kits or because they have been re-engined (for instance, the fleet of DC8-71F and 73F aircraft operated by UPS and

TOP **Cargolux Boeing 747-400F.**
Cargolux

BELOW **Cargolux B747-400F loading.**
Cargolux

BOTTOM **Lufthansa Cargo Boeing MD-11F.**
Lufthansa

America. It consists for the most part of older converted B727s fitted with hush kits, and of even older DC-9s, which in the United States still form the basis of the medium-haul fleets of the integrators.

Among the more recent aircraft types, responding to current environmental concerns, are the BAe 146QT, which for many years was the workhorse of TNT, and the latest B737s (such as the 15 B737QCs operated by Europe Air Post, the air transport subsidiary of the French Post Office).

• Fifth category: feeder or taxi aircraft with a payload of less than 10 tonnes (22,000lb) Although this is a large family – some 400 members – its exact size is difficult to determine precisely, due to the overlap between passenger and freight (express) among a number of companies which have specialised in operating this type of aircraft. Among those most frequently encountered, we should mention the Cessna 208B Super Cargomaster, the Fairchild Expediter, the Short 330 and 360, the Raytheon Beech 1900 and 199, the Fokker 27 500/600 and the cargo versions of the ATR 42 and 72. These single-engine or twin-engine planes have a dual function: that of air taxis and of feeder aircraft to supply the routes served by the North American and European integrators. The latter have ceased to operate this type of aircraft and have handed over this class of operation to companies with whom they have contrac-

Air Transport International – ATI – on behalf of the freight agent/integrator Bax Global).

The B757-200PF (Package Freighter,) specially equipped for express traffic, was for many years exclusive to UPS who ordered 20 units in 1986, and who by the year 2000 was operating a fleet of 75 machines. DHL introduced this type of aircraft on its European network more recently with the acquisition of 34 ex British Airways B757 aircraft which were converted to freighters by Boeing and designated B757SF.

• Fourth category: narrow-bodied aircraft with a payload of 10-27 tonnes (from 22,000 to 46,000lb) (656 aircraft).

This is the largest category (40% of the world jet cargo market) and almost 70% of this group are based in North

tual links (eg Mountain Air Cargo or West Air for Fedex, and Danish Air Transport or Boston-Maine Airways for DHL).

• Sixth category: CIS aircraft.

These are turbojets originally designed for military use, and present some common features derived from their original purpose: a very low floor and an inclined rear ramp offering great ease of loading and unloading; high volumes but using non-standard pallets; the possibility of access to airports or even landing strips with very primitive infrastructure (earth runways); noisy gas-guzzling engines; a large number of crew members.

The range of machines involved is very large, since it goes from the Antonov 26 and 32 with payloads of 5.6 and 6.7

tonnes respectively, the Antonov 12 (a veteran) with 18 tonnes, and the Il-76TD, particularly well suited for humanitarian operations for the United Nations and its specialised agencies. Finally, we should mention the entry into commercial charter operation, after being grounded for many years, of the "world's largest sky bird": [9] the Antonov An-225 Mryia, which was initially designed to transport on its back the Russian space shuttle Buran. This aircraft, powered by six jet engines, offers up to 250 tonnes of payload and its internal dimensions are truly impressive: 43m x 6.4m x 4.4m (141ft x 21ft x 14.4ft). In addition, it can carry a variety of externally mounted loads on the upper surface of the fuselage. Antonov Design Bureau certified its sole example of this aircraft type for commercial use in 2001 and it entered service with Antonov Airlines at the end of that year. Since then it has achieved almost 200 world records, including the carriage in testing of a payload of 253 tonnes consisting of five main battle tanks, and will continue to set new standards for air cargo. A second An-225 which was partially manufactured some years ago is likely to be completed and to enter service during the next few years. It is a unique monster – for transporting monsters! But the Antonov 124 remains the unquestionable workhorse for outsize and very heavy cargoes, in particular for relief and military operations which have experienced a strong demand due to the situations in Afghanistan and in Iraq. The Antonov An-124 was introduced to the worldwide commercial cargo market for outsize and very heavy cargoes in the summer of 1989 by the Antonov Design Bureau of Kiev.

The An-124-100 M variant is now being developed. This version will operate with a cockpit crew reduced from six to four and with normal payload increased from 120 to 150 tonnes and maximum take-off weight increased from 392 to 420 tonnes. The aircraft's range will increase by 10 to 15% and the useable airfield elevation increased to 2,600 metres. There will be reinforcement of the nose structure and undercarriage to allow loading of heavier items while the overhead crane capacity will be increased to 40 tonnes. There will be improved equipment component lives, better braking systems and crew areas. The majority of innovations arise from the improved T engines which now have greater reliability and higher power output for takeoff at higher weights and greater elevations. At the Paris Air Show in 2003 Antonov announced the An-124-300 which will have a stretched fuselage and dramatically longer range.

• Seventh category: other cargo aircraft.
Here, with nostalgic affection, one finds that 14 DC-3s and 13 DC-6 Cargo aircraft were still flying in the USA in 2000, that the Lockheed Electra was still going the distance in spite of its great age, or that the Lockheed Hercules continues with ease to justify its title of the "indestructible cargo plane" – a flying legend. In the UK a fleet of DC-6, DC-3 and Lockheed Electra cargo aircraft are in 2004 still being operated with commercial success by Air Atlantique and sister company Atlantic Airlines.

4 THE GEOGRAPHIC ORIGINS OF TRAFFIC

For the last 50 years, the ICAO has been grouping the traffic of airlines according to the location of their head offices, summarised by major region and flag.

International traffic by region
Whatever political and economic developments occurred in the second half of the 20th century, the share of the dominant regions – North America, Asia and Europe – never varied from between 85% and 90%.

Region-by-region analysis:

LEFT Mine clearance equipment for Angola being loaded aboard an Air Foyle An-124. *Air Foyle*

BELOW AND RIGHT Four views of Volga-Dnepr An-124s taking on outsize cargoes. *Volga-Dnepr*

ABOVE LEFT **HeavyLift CL-44 Conroy Guppy departs Stansted.**
HeavyLift

BELOW, FAR LEFT **In its specially constructed cage in the Sonora Desert is the giant 20-tonne 200-year old cactus transported by Antonov/Air Foyle An-124 from Mexico to EXPO '92 in Seville.**
Air Foyle

BELOW LEFT **The plane takes the plane—Air Foyle Antonov An-124 "Ruslan" loading a Ju52 aircraft.**
Air Foyle

ABOVE **Airbus A300-600 Super Trnsporter gorging on another large load.** *Airbus*

BELOW **The enormous six-engined Antonov An-225.**
Antonov

ABOVE Vehicles are loaded onto an Antonov Airlines An-225 at Kabul, Afghanistan.
Antonov Airlines

LEFT Trucks secured inside an Antonov Airlines An-225.
Antonov Airlines

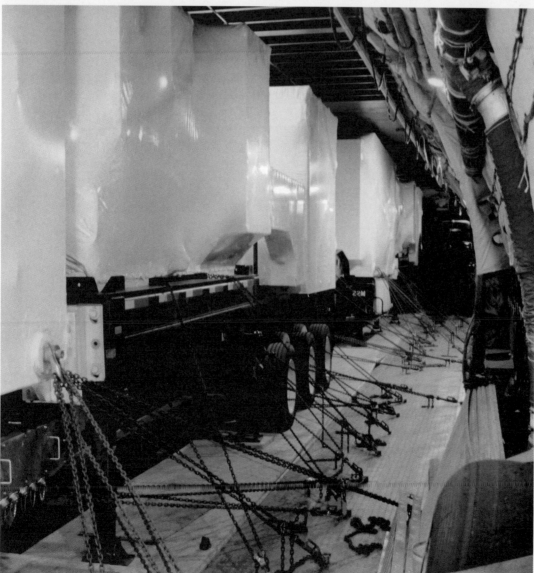

LEFT Antonov Airlines'
An-22 freighter, the
world's largest turboprop
in service.
Malcolm Nason

BELOW Another view of a
Volga-Dnepr An-124.
Volga-Dnepr

• Europe: The share of traffic held by European airlines, which was above 40% between 1951 and 1980, fell to 33% in the year 2000, due to the sudden growth of Asian airlines and a certain amount of new activity on the part of American companies (international development of Federal Express and UPS). In view of the growth demonstrated by these two groups, it might be asked whether Europe will be able to maintain its position.

• Africa: The transition to independence did not change anything, in spite of a slight improvement in the years between 1970 and 1980.

• Middle East: After reaching a figure of 6.5% in 1980, after the first oil shock, the Middle Eastern airlines saw their share of traffic reduced to 4.4% in 2000 under the dual effect of the collapse of oil revenues and the fading of the performance of the Israeli flag.

• Asian Pacific Area: The last decades have seen spectacular progress from the Asian flags, from 8.6% in 1960 to 36.1% in the year 2000, which was successively carried along by the extraordinary development of Japan, and then by the trio South Korea/Hong Kong/Taiwan, and currently by China. This has been the major change in the last 40 years.

• North America: The deep and constant loss of market share by the United States is the other essential characteristic of the last 50 years. The contribution of the North American airlines has declined from 42.3% to 17.6%. Things came unstuck between 1970 and 1980, coinciding with the decision of the "majors" to abandon operating their cargo fleets. Since 1995, a new tendency has appeared, linked with international expansion of Fedex and UPS. The US market share has jumped from 17.6% in 1995 to 20.2% in 2000.

• Latin America: The already weak share of carriers from this continent is tending to diminish, due to the chaotic economic situation in many countries.

Traffic by country
The classification by flag has exhibited significant changes, even since 1990: the collapse of the states of the former Soviet Union, the great leap forward for China and the Gulf States, the sudden growth of the Asian flags (South Korea, Taiwan and Singapore), and the reduction of certain European flags, particularly Great Britain and France.

5 THE MAJOR ARTERIES OF AIRFREIGHT

Ignoring domestic markets, among which it is appropriate to include intra-European traffic, the world airfreight network in the year 2000 consisted (to use some earthbound terminology) of three large motorways running east/west with traffic reaching or exceeding 2.5 million tonnes each, of one gigantic intra-Asiatic boulevard running northeast/southwest carrying over 4 million tonnes, and of three north/south avenues carrying traffic of between 0.5 and 1 million tonnes.

ABOVE LEFT **Antonov An-225 with five main battle tanks — a record breaking load.**

LEFT **Train takes the plane or the plane takes the train? Antonov Airlines An-124-100 loading a diesel locomotive and in the process taking another world record: 148 tonnes from London, Ontario to Dublin, Ireland.**

ABOVE RIGHT **Air Atlantique DC-3.**
Air Atlantique

RIGHT **Atlantic Airlines Lockheed Electra.**
Air Atlantique

Airfreight "motorways"

• North Atlantic (2.9 million tonnes)
Chiefly fed by trade between Europe and North America, the traffic on this primary route is augmented by all or part of the airborne trade between the United States and Canada on the one hand, and the Middle East, the Indian sub-continent and Africa on the other.

The air transport market between Europe and North America, which was the first to reach a state of maturity, is composed of an extremely varied range of products. Investment goods and industrial products (telecommunications equipment, professional electronics, automobile and aeronautical equipment etc) fly side by side in both directions with consumer products (top-of-the-range textiles, perfumes, consumer electronics etc), and finished products are carried with perishable goods (French cheese, Belgian chicory, Spanish grapes, Italian chestnuts or Dutch tomatoes leaving Europe, and Canadian lobsters, limes from Florida, Californian strawberries and asparagus, or Mexican strawberries and exotic fruits, exported from North America).

Here as elsewhere, airfreight is a good barometer of changes in economic geography: in the United States one sees strong growth in traffic from the states of the "New South" (Alabama, Georgia and North and South Carolina) and the states which have benefited from the most recent expansion in the electronics industries (Texas, New Mexico, Arizona, Utah). Although it has been described as "mature" for over 20 years, the airfreight market of the United States has continued to show a remarkable degree of health, achieving growth rates of above 7% between 1980 and 2000. It is by far the world's largest airfreight market, since over one tonne in three originates in, or is being sent to, the United States. Traffic with Europe represents 36% of exports and 35% of imports.

• North and Central Pacific (2.5 million tonnes)
Expressed in kilometric tonnes, the trans-Pacific air traffic between North America and Asia represents the leading freight market in the world, due to the distances involved. The traffic shows a lack of balance in favour of the Asia to North America direction, due to massive American imports of textiles from China and electronic goods coming from Taiwan, along with sea-air traffic between Japan and Canada.

Japan remains by far the leading market on the trans-Pacific route with a share of over 33% of traffic. Reflecting accurately the high degree of development of the Japanese economy, the structure of airborne trade between the United States and Japan is very similar to that of transatlantic traffic in its variety and the value of goods exchanged.

• Links between Europe and Asia (2.6 million tonnes)
This section includes relationships and markets of very different characters.

Between Europe and the Far East, one finds the same distinctions as the trade between the United States and Asia, corresponding to different stages of development, varying from Japan, with its very diversified structure of trade, to the "Tiger Economies" (South Korea, Hong Kong, Taiwan and Singapore) whose airborne exports consist of electrical equipment and textile products, and finally to China and the newest emerging countries (Vietnam and Indonesia) where the export traffic consists essentially of clothing articles (textiles, footwear). However, the reality is more complex than the statistics can show. Hence, Thailand has gained a major position for perishable products (fruit and tropical vegetables), Singapore is associated with electronic components, optical goods and orchids, while Malaysia specialises in electronics.

A similar complexity applies to goods leaving Europe: consumer goods, chemical products and industrial equipment are all jostling for position bound for Japan, whereas investment goods win by a large margin en route for Korea, China or Taiwan.

India occupies a particular position within Asia. Air transport is responsible for an appreciable share of Indian external trade, with market shares by value of over 30% for exports and over 25% for imports. This market of almost 560,000 tonnes, adding both directions together, remains under the close control of Indian freight agents, who have grouped themselves into a very active association, the Air Cargo Association of India, or ACAI. Among its members we should mention East-West Travel and Trade, Lemuir Air Express and Continental Carriers. Whereas the composition of air imports is straightforward (almost exclusively investment goods), the export side is much more diversified. Apart from traditional industries which dominate the market (textile articles leaving from Bombay, Delhi and Madras, leather goods from Madras, and local craft goods) there are perish-

Analysis by region of international freight traffic on scheduled flights (in percent)

Region	1951	1960	1970	1980	1990	1995	2000
Europe	42.5%	44.6%	44.1%	41.1%	37.8%	33.6%	33.3%
Africa	1.3%	2.6%	3.2%	3.5%	2.4%	2.0%	2.0%
Middle East	1.0%	3.6%	4.3%	6.5%	5.1%	5.4%	4.4%
Asia/Pacific	8.8%	8.6%	11.0%	24.9%	32.1%	36.8%	36.1%
North America	42.9%	36.7%	32.4%	19.0%	17.9%	17.6%	20.2%
Latin America	3.5%	3.9%	5.0%	5.0%	4.7%	4.6%	3.7%
Total	100%	100%	100%	100%	100%	100%	100%

Source: ICAO

Development of the United States airfreight market

	1970	1980	1990	2000
Exports	403,350	1,008,000	1,532,700	2,800,000
Average annual change		+9.5%	+4.2%	+6.1%
Imports	281,680	610,800	1,666,000	3,645,000
Average annual change		+8.0%	+10.5%	+8.0%
Total	685,030	1,618,800	3,198,700	6,445,000
Average annual change		+9.0%	+7.0%	+7.2%

Source: US Bureau of the Census

able goods bound for the Middle East (all sorts of fruits and vegetables) and for Europe (mangoes), chemical and industrial products out of Bombay, and high-tech products exported from Bangalore (aerospace, telecommunications satellites, computer equipment). Due to its diversity and its highly individual nature, the Indian market is one of the most interesting in Asia.

The Middle East is divided into several groups of markets, each with its own distinctive characteristics: markets based purely on oil (Saudi Arabia, Kuwait), markets combining oil with a function as a commercial and air communications hub (United Arab Emirates), Mediterranean markets (Lebanon, Syria, Jordan) and, finally, the Israeli market.

The Israeli market for airfreight exceeds 250,000 tonnes. The exports are a showcase for agricultural know how (flowers and fruit) and for industrial technologies in which Israel has a leading position (electronics, scientific instruments, aeronautics).

The great inter-Asiatic boulevard (over 4 million tonnes)
This route links all the markets of the Far East in a wide diagonal band running northeast/southwest, on both sides of an axis from Tokyo to Singapore. This is the main freight highway

Ranking of the 12 leading countries' scheduled flights (in million RTK)

Country	Total Traffic 2000 Rank	Traffic	1990 Rank	International Traffic 2000 Rank	Traffic	1990 Rank
United States	1	30,131	1	1	18,951	1
China (1)	2	8,760	17	5	7,289	21
Japan	3	8,549	2	2	7,718	2
Korea	4	7,774	7	3	7,630	6
Taiwan (2)	5	7,692	n/a	3	7,650	n/a
Germany	6	7,128	3	6	7,109	3
The Netherlands (3)	7	6,609	8	7	6,609	7
Singapore	8	6,005	9	8	6,005	8
France	9	5,227	3	10	4,939	4
Great Britain (4)	10	5,161	5	9	5,155	5
Luxembourg	11	3,533	n/a	11	5,533	n/a
Gulf States	12	2,038	31	12	2,038	30
Canada	15	1,806	10	17	1,520	11
CIS/USSR	20	1,041	6	25	694	24

(1) Including Hong Kong and Macao which were not part of China in 1990
(2) Although it does not appear in the ICAO or the IATA statistics, Taiwan occupies the fifth rank in the world with its companies China Airlines and Eva Air.
(3) Including the results of Martinair
(4) Hong Kong was a Crown Colony in 1990.

Source: ICAOC and additional information

of the world, the expansion of which goes back to the mid–1970s.

Its development is connected with the blossoming of the Asian economies, with the dispersal in several countries of complementary production centres belonging to the same enterprise, and more recently with the relocation and implantation of numerous Japanese factories into South East Asia. In addition to traffic in electronic components and industrial products, there are enormous markets in this zone for perishable goods, exported from Thailand (fruit and vegetables), Indonesia, Australia and New Zealand (seafood, fresh meat, fruit) or from Taiwan, destined for Singapore, Hong Kong and Japan.

In this zone two markets predominate: Hong Kong, the gateway to China whose trade with Asia provides over 50% of total activity, and Japan.

Since 1960, the airport and market centre of Hong Kong has fulfilled three functions which have each come to the fore during three development phases, partially overlapping:

1. The function as a manufacturing centre from 1960–1980: the flow of exports, basically composed of local products (textiles and toys, and later electrical and electronic goods), represented 60% to 70% of the total traffic.

2. The function as a transit hub from 1970 to 1990/1995: transit traffic to and from Japan, Korea, Taiwan and later China, complemented and reinforced local production, which was slowing down due to the increases in the costs of labour and which was obliged to re-orientate itself towards high-tech products.

3. The function as a gateway to China, from 1990/1995: over 80% of the present-day traffic comes from the enormous industrial concentration around the mouth of the Pearl River and the thin coastal district extending from Guangzhou to Shanghai (textiles, electronics, toys and games). Transit traffic is in strong decline as a proportion of total traffic, due to the increase in the number of direct flights from Taipei, and the reduction of market rates for flights leaving Japan. Local traffic is concentrated on a few high value-added products (high-tech).

Whatever period we look at, the Hong Kong market has for over 40 years demonstrated average annual growth rates which are consistently in double digits. The year 2000 was particularly outstanding, with a growth of over 13% in exports as well as imports, and total traffic of 2,237,000 tonnes. The table (top) indicates that exports permanently exceed imports, in spite of a long-term effort to re-establish the balance, and shows the predominance of traffic flows within Asia.

Japan (see table above), which stands as a benchmark, is a high-technology market on the export side (1,110,510 tonnes), and an importer of consumer goods, electronic components

Geographical Analysis of Traffic Through Hong Kong in 2000

Geographical Area	Imports Traffic	Share in %	Exports Traffic	Share in %
Trans-Pacific	282,000	21.9	79,000	8.3
Europe	254,000	19.7	198,000	20.7
Asia/Pacific/Middle East	749,000	58.4	675,000	71.0
Total	1,285,000	100.0	952,000	100.0

Analysis of Japanese external trade in 2000 (in tonnes)

Geographical Area	Exports Traffic	Share in %	Imports Traffic	Share in %
Transpacific	277,050	25.0	324,651	24.0
Europe	194,006	17.5	251,241	18.5
Asia/Pacific/Middle East	639,474	57.5	777,878	57.5
Total	1,110,510	100.0	1,353,770	100.0

and industrial products (1,353,770 tonnes). With the total of 2,464,280 tonnes it occupies second place in the world behind the United States.

Neither a certain maturity of the market, nor the high value of the yen, nor a policy of relocation of Japanese industry was able to prevent a strong resurgence of exports after a period of decline in 1990–1995.

The vitality of Japanese exports, reflects an extraordinary capacity for technological innovation (average annual growth rate of 8.6% for 20 years), and shows a strong trend in their geographical structure as the share of Asian destinations went up from 46.3% in 1980 to 57.5% in the year 2000.

Imports show the same geographical trends in the market. At an average expansion rate of 12%, they underwent a more rapid, though more irregular, development than exports. By the year 2000, they had exceeded export levels for over 10 years (55% of the total).

This growth in the total of external trade transported by air in a nation where the gross industrial product has been stagnant for several years is explained in part by the constant increase in the rate of penetration of air transport, promoted by the remarkable quality of the Japanese airfreight industry.

Development of the share of air transport in Japanese external trade (in value billions of yen)

Year	Exports Total	By Air	% Air	Imports Total	By Air	% Air
1980	29,832	2,492	8.48	31,995	2,725	8.51
1985	41,955	4,350	10.36	30,084	4,126	13.71
1990	41,456	6,687	16.13	33,855	7,743	22.90
1995	41,580	10,145	24.42	31,549	8,417	26.67
2000	51,654	17,926	34.70	40,938	12,708	31.04

Source: Japanese Rate Association

The North/South Avenues

• North America/South America (0.7 million tonnes)
This particular route was opened up by Pan American Airways at the end of the 1920s. Since that time it has always remained one of the major airfreight axes.

It is slightly out of balance in favour of the south/north direction (55% of the total traffic) due to the level of the tonnages of perishable products imported by the United States: fish from Chile, tropical fruit from Brazil and Costa Rica, but above all flowers from Colombia (over one hundred thousand tonnes per year). Alongside these traditional exports, the development of new traffic can be observed, signs of the growing industrialisation of the South American states (textiles from Colombia or Peru, engineering products and electrical equipment from Brazil, computers from Argentina). In the north/south direction the traffic is composed mostly of spare parts and industrial investment goods.

In contrast to what happened in Asia, the internal traffic in South America has remained very limited. However, it looks likely that the creation of Mercosur will give rise to new flows of trade by air.

• Europe/South America (0.5 million tonnes)
The structure of trade by air between these two continents is similar to that between North and South America, with an increasing proportion of manufactured products coming from South America.

Brazil is the leading market, with a traffic to and from Europe of 90 000 tonnes in 1995.

• Europe/Africa (approximately one million tonnes)
The air traffic between Europe and Africa is very typical of the world north/south trade: mainly industrial goods outbound, and perishable goods inbound. The diversification and growth of African exports of perishable products has led to a reverse of the traditional imbalance in traffic to the advantage of the south/north direction: one need only mention French beans from Morocco, Senegal Kenya or Ethiopia, mangoes from Mali, grapes and plums from South Africa, pineapples from the Ivory Coast, apricots from Tunisia, aubergines from Egypt and tens of thousands of tonnes of flowers from Zimbabwe or Kenya.

The island of Mauritius, off the southeast coast of Africa, is a special case. Its airborne trade of around 40,000 tonnes is closely linked with the existence of and activities in its duty free zone which is more based on its customs status than its geographical location. The chief activities are geared towards tex-

ABOVE **Today, Korean Airlines is the world's second airline in international freight.**
Korean Airlines

tile production (woollen pullovers, shirts) destined for markets in North America and Europe. Although sea transport takes the majority of traffic, airfreight is used either at the request of the consignee, to fulfil sales requirements, or at the initiative of the manufacturer in case of production delays or for certain top of the range articles. As always happens with textiles, the traffic is seasonal, with two peaks corresponding to the build-up of the winter and summer collections in Europe. The increase in the cost of labour brought about by the success of this manufacturing activity, partly operated by Mauritians and partly by Chinese, has led to two consequences: the installation of production workshops in Madagascar, and the re-direction of production towards higher quality goods, both tendencies favouring airfreight.

The Republic of South Africa, for its part, has considerably broadened the range of its exports by air: in addition to traditional perishable goods (fruit from the Cape area, sea food from the Cape and neighbouring Namibia), some tens of thousands of tonnes of automobile components and equipment are currently being sent by air, principally to Germany.

2 THE CUSTOMERS

"The customer decides our fate"
By customer we mean the primary user of airfreight. This can be the shipper and/or the consignee, depending on the influence of the one and or the other in the decision process regarding the mode of transport.

I THE CHOICE OF AIR TRANSPORT
The decision to use air transport for carrying goods results from a combination of the advantages offered by aircraft and the wishes of the customers.

Characteristics of aircraft
With regard to the goods carried, the aircraft is a method of transport which presents four major techno-economic characteristics.

- Speed
  It is a truism to say that an aircraft is fast. To assess this advantage properly, the undeniable superiority of an aircraft's speed must be put into context. The total transit time, door-to-door, is more important than the intrinsic speed of the means of carriage as such, and other means of surface transport have made great progress in the last 30 years, with the acceleration of sea transport and the extension of the motorway network. To sum up, the advantage of speed increases as the distance travelled increases.

- Safety
  Because an aircraft is vulnerable, "this delicate machine which is the aircraft requires that those who load and unload it do so with a degree of precautions and meticulousness which benefit the goods." [1]

- Availability of volume
  An aircraft is a "large lightweight cigar". It is supported by the air, while its competitors rest on water or on the ground. In comparison, an aircraft cannot carry large loads but has a superiority in terms of volume. Since charge structures are merely a reflection of the physical characteristics of each mode of transport, it follows that the aircraft is, in

general, the most competitive means of transporting high-volume products (densities 4 – 7).
- Cost
  Cargo rates for aircraft are high. Undoubtedly, there are cases when air rates are less expensive than surface rates: for small consignments, goods with high volumes or high values …but in general, airfreight is still distinctly more expensive than its competitors on land or sea.

These four fundamental characteristics, arising from the physical nature of the means of transport, make the case for using airfreight in the following categories:

Characteristics of the aircraft as a means of transport
Airfreight is particularly suited for:

Speed	Perishable products and goods
	Urgent shipments
Safety	Easily damaged goods
Generous on volume	High-volume products
Expensive	Goods of a certain unit value combining: high labour content and/or high-technological content

Customer motivation
All studies agree [2] that the customers, whether shippers or consignees, use air transport for three main reasons: speed of transport, quality of carriage and reduction of stocks.

• Speed of transport
The need for speed in all its forms is the main reason for using airfreight transport. It arises from a number of constraints, which can be grouped into three main categories:

* First category: physical perishability of the goods
This category includes numerous varieties of exotic fruits, fruit and vegetables sold out of season (strawberries, cherries, French beans etc), cut flowers and live animals (chicks, race horses, breeding stock, or laboratory animals) but also certain radioactive products for medical use. In all these cases air transport enables sales to reach distant markets

that are either inaccessible using surface transport or where it would be too slow, and allows the distribution of products which have retained all their freshness.

* Second category: restricted commercial life of products
An increasing range of products comes under this heading, as a result of the shortening of product life cycles. This includes not only fashion articles, but all kinds of novelties in the field of electronics, photography or media. In this case the aircraft allows an increase in sales volume through the rapid distribution of new products, while following and sometimes even anticipating the whims of the customer.

* Third category: fulfilling commercial commitments
Here we are talking of air transport as an ambulance service: it catches up on manufacturing delays, avoids delay penalties and enables the speedy repair of a manufacturing facility or a ship.

• Quality of carriage
The idea of quality of service is one reason for using airfreight, on which customers insist more than ever, due to the increasing use of modern techniques of managing the physical flow of goods. What is meant by "quality of carriage" with regard to air transport? It is the situation created by the combination of multiple factors: the high frequency and regularity of operation, the quality of handling and the low occurrence of damage, simplicity of formalities and quality of information.
One French customer recently stated:

> "For us, air transport is becoming increasingly important. Firstly the high value of some of our products justifies the use of air transport. And our customers are always wanting faster reaction times. In addition, air transport often allows us to overcome the disadvantages of sea transport. For us, airfreight means 'zero failure' and as a result, it plays a major part in our approach to quality." [3]

This high quality environment of air transport is particularly suitable for certain types of products, such as medical equipment. Throughout the world, for long distances, x-ray equipment, scanners, all the highly-developed detection and examination instruments are transported by air as a matter of course.

• Reduction of stocks
Although reduction of stocks is not the reason which is most often quoted, it is one of the most important. The Director of the spare parts distribution centre of a large American automotive producer in Singapore observed some years ago:

> "by value, approximately 40% of incoming and 30% of outgoing material is sent by air. What is the reason, when airfreight is generally known to be more expensive?
>
> "The decision to use air or sea transport depends directly on our largest investment, our stock. Our principal challenge is to maintain an optimum stock level, which allows us at the same time to satisfy demand and limit our investment. This is why airfreight plays such an important role."

This role is doubly important: in terms of quality and of cost.

2 THE PARADOX OF AIRFREIGHT

The whole commercial dilemma of airfreight can be summed up in a single question: "How can one convert a high price of transport into an advantageous cost of distribution?"

Behind this question lies the Total Distribution Cost Concept, so dear to the British and the Americans. By this they understand a long and difficult economic and commercial analysis, from which it is assumed that is possible to demonstrate objectively the commercial and financial advantages of using airfreight on a large scale. This ambitious process has consumed a lot of ink, and has disappointed more than one airline manager. Without being a cure-all, the good old formula of complete cost of distribution, somewhat revised and corrected, still seems to us to be the only serious method for marketing airfreight. To avoid miscalculations, it should be carried out with regard to two basic principles:

1. A study should be made at the level of each company, because each company represents a special case;
2. It should involve all the divisions in the business, and should be supported by the General Manager.

Let us carry out this process in its four successive stages, from the simplest to the most complex:

Stage one – packing and insurance
Good packing is expensive and represents a not inconsiderable element in the price of distribution for a product. Being fast and safe, air transport permits considerable economies under this cost heading, replacing wooden cases, which are still frequently used in surface transport, by cheaper and lighter packaging (corrugated cardboard boxes, jute sacks, and cans and drums for chemicals and pharmaceutical products). The simplification of air packaging is at its most radical when transporting machine tools, engines, large computers or helicopters: they are simply placed on a pallet without special protection and covered with plastic foil, or sometimes provided with a cover of see-through plastic over a rudimentary framework. Since air transport is preceded and/or followed by land transport, it is of course necessary to take account of the quality of transport on the surface section, particularly in developing countries.

Air transport is also secure. Damage to goods is rare compared with other modes of transport as airports are areas under observation, within which theft is less prevalent than elsewhere. For the two above reasons, the rates for air insurance premiums are attractive.

Hence, under the two cost headings of packing and insurance, savings tend to compensate in part for the higher rates for airfreight.

Stage two – level and costs of stocks
This is the area in which airfreight brings the most decisive economic advantage compared with its competitors. Provided it is planned and integrated into the distribution policy – this condition is absolutely essential – the regular use of air transport should be reflected in a reduction in stock levels and in the costs of financing capital tied up in goods. Thanks to the combination of frequent services, fast flights and regular connections, airfreight guarantees that the manufacturer or trader has sufficient security of supply to justify a more or less

significant stock reduction, without taking excessive risks. In fact, to some extent, stocks only exist as a safety factor, " the buffer between supply and demand".

A proper use of airfreight should bring about reduction of stocks at three points: with the manufacturer, with the consignee of his products (reduction of both basic stock and minimum security stock) and during transport (reduction of stock in circulation due to the physical effects of air transport's speed).

The reduction, and even the quasi elimination of stocks, do not only lead to a parallel reduction in financial costs. They generate additional savings in two interrelated areas: warehousing costs (cost of surface area used, lighting, heating, security, management etc) and the cost of depreciation.

Stage three – airfreight as a commercial tool
Here we leave the quantitative field, dealing with the numerical equation between the cost increases (airfreight rates) and the cost decreases (packing, insurance, and above all financial costs), to consider a more dynamic concept of the consequences of airfreight.

What are its effects on the level of sales, the degree of customer satisfaction and the commercial image of the company? "Airfreight is a modern marketing tool." [4] Thanks to airfreight, products are available quicker and in a state of freshness which was hitherto unheard of: retailers can deal with sudden increases in orders and adapt to fluctuations in demand; manufacturers are in a better position to satisfy delivery deadlines. Airfreight increases sales, raises the quality of service and upgrades the image of the company using it.

Stage four – airfreight: the instrument of a new distribution policy
The distribution cycle of a product depends on a method of transport. The adoption of a very specific transport method, the aircraft, must logically lead to a fundamental review of the traditional distribution process for the products concerned. All experiences and all studies have led to the conclusion that it is impossible to use all the benefits of airfreight on a large scale without reassessing from top to bottom the whole supply chain, with a view to modifying and simplifying it. Current practice tends not only to consider the distribution of finished products but to integrate the totality of physical operations, from the initiation of the manufacturing process through to the after-sales service for the customer. At this stage, the concept of the supply chain replaces that of cost of distribution. Airfreight becomes one of the major components in the very complicated logistics chain on which depend the operations of the big names in electronics, the automotive industry and the chemical/pharmaceutical industry. Its use then becomes regular, programmed and fully integrated. Like airmail, it becomes everyday usage.

Once one reaches this stage – although it is not possible for airfreight to have the advantage in every detail – it will become clear that the sum of the advantages brought about by the regular use of air transport considerably outweighs the initial obstacle of the difference in rates. One phrase sums it up: "You pay more and you get more." [5]

3 CUSTOMER EXPECTATIONS

The essential task of airlines and freight agents is to fulfil customer expectations. Their fate depends on it.

What are these expectations? They have been the object of recent studies in the United States and Europe, which led to similar conclusions. Customer put two expectations very much at the top of their preoccupations:

• Reliability: that is to say the fulfilment of undertakings concerning transport, reservations and delivery times. Dependability is more important than speed whenever the use of air transport is programmed;

• Information: that is to say the possibility of being continuously informed about the whereabouts of goods, and the issue of immediate notification of some interruption in transport.

A large French customer underlines these concerns:

"… it is essential that the airline should not only respect the flight reservations made, without splitting up the batches handed over to it, but that it should inform us at the earliest possibility if it happens… we require our service-providers to give us transparent, speedy and reliable information about the progress of our deliveries." [6]

This does not mean that airfreight customers regard speed of transport and the price of the service as secondary factors. It goes without saying that the speed of the aircraft and the free negotiation of rates are part of the deal.

The future belongs to those carriers and forwarders – not to mention the integrators – who are able to supply their customers speed at an appropriate price, with dependable scheduling and information.

4 THE CATEGORIES OF GOODS

Bearing in mind the characteristics of aircraft and the expectations of customers – firms, exporters, importers – we can review the categories of goods which are most usually transported by air.

Some people, swept along by their faith in air transportation, have not hesitated to declare: "The aircraft can transport anything, anywhere." "Anywhere", perhaps, but " anything" certainly not!

Admittedly, it may happen that in certain exceptional circumstances, without significant economic consequences, almost any category of goods can be sent by air. However, in practice, airfreight deals with two categories of merchandise: perishable goods and manufactured products. The aircraft is not the way to transport oil or coal, minerals or cement or construction materials, wood pulp, rubber, steel or metallurgical materials, or fertilisers, basic chemical products, cereals, oil seeds, sugar or coffee…

Category One – perishable products
Some perishable products have a limited life, and thus require rapid transport. These goods "of a perishable nature" include fruit, flowers or various pharmaceutical products. By contrast, others are not perishable in themselves, but only because of how they are used: they are "perishable by use" such as newspapers and magazines, articles meant for exhibitions, and the majority of express traffic (correspondence and business documents, spare parts, etc).

ABOVE **Loading cattle into an Air Canada Cargo hold.**

LEFT **BOAC elephant freighter.**
British Airways Museum

Since it is impossible to mention everything, it will suffice to summarise below live animals, consumer goods, flowers and, as an example of a product "perishable by intended purpose", *Le Beaujolais Nouveau*.

• Live animals
These were among the first airline passengers: KLM is proud of having taken a cow on board a Fokker biplane in 1920! All the animals in Noah's Ark have been airfreight customers, and conditions for carrying them have been specified in great detail by IATA.

Horses have been loyal passengers since the day in 1924 when the champion race horse "Phantom" was hoisted with great difficulty aboard an aircraft, to take it from Paris to London. These days, treated with great consideration, they travel in stalls mounted on pallets, accompanied by their groom. All kinds of horses travel by air: race horses (between Europe and America or Asia, or between Australasia and the race courses of Hong Kong, Tokyo or Singapore); horses for jumping trials and dressage contests (Olympic Games); yearlings for the Deauville sales; the mounts of France's Republican Guard, or

Canada's Royal Mounted Police on the occasion of prestige visits abroad; Argentinean polo ponies destined for Europe, the United States or the Middle East; thoroughbreds; or breeding stock (such as horses from Brittany for Japan). Every year, there are thousands of horses, often rather nervously, travelling by air.

Livestock is an entirely different market, that can take two different forms depending on whether one is considering animals separately or as a group.

Cattle and calves are the most commonly transported animals, for the purpose of regenerating or building up herds, from Canada and the United States, from Holland, Denmark or France, to Africa, the Middle East or South America. Cattle stalls can take five head of cattle at 500kg each, whereas stalls for animals such as goats, sheep and pigs, with intermediate floors, permit the loading of about 50 head at 40kg each, on two or three levels. In all these cases, proper water proofing of the stalls is essential, so that animal waste does not corrode the floor of the plane.

Sometimes a whole herd of animals is carried by charter aircraft. From 120 to 220 animals can be sent on a B747 freighter, which is thus transformed into a "flying cattle truck". These

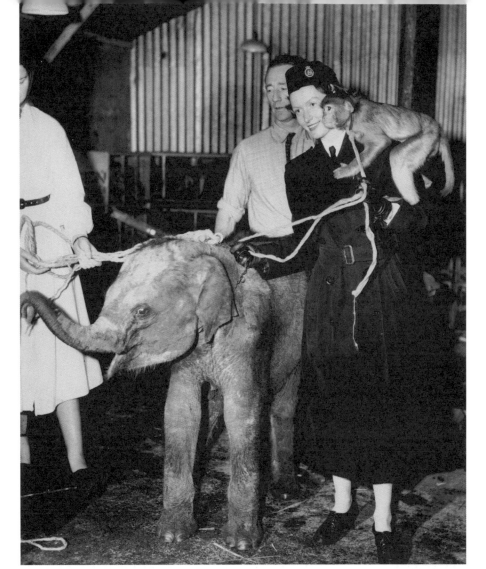

LEFT Grooms keep a careful eye on horses in a B747 bound for Australia. Dehydration over long flights is a particular risk and reegular watering is essential. *Air Cargo News UK*

INSET LEFT Black rhinoceros about to be shipped aboard a Northwest Orient B747 freighter from Houston to Seoul, Korea. *Air Cargo News UK*

BELOW LEFT Cattle on a Martinair freighter. *Air Cargo News UK*

RIGHT Livestock by air in the 1960s. *British Airways Museum*

BELOW Otter post! *Air Cargo News UK*

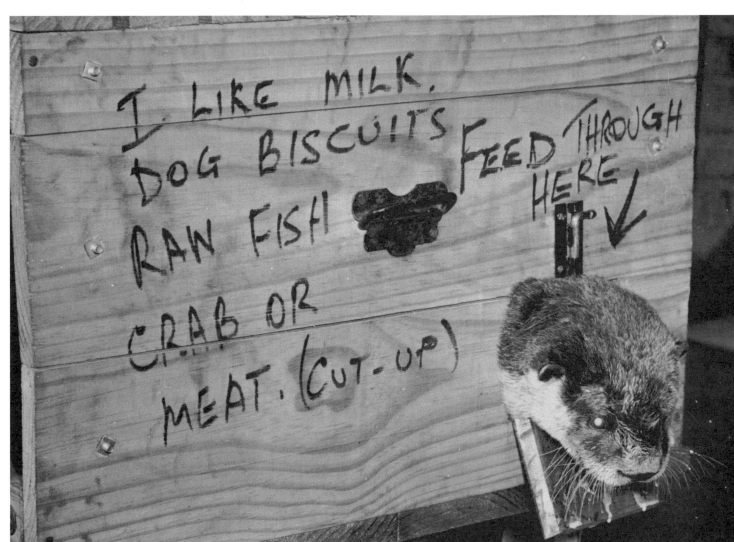

animals give off considerable amounts of heat and carbon dioxide, so that it is necessary to pay great attention to the ventilation of the main deck and the holds, particularly during stopovers.

"Day-old" chicks are an exclusive preserve for airfreight over long distances. After hatching, day-old chicks can live for 72 hours without eating or drinking. Based on this time window, their journey is the subject of rigorous planning, from the hatchery to the final destination. This is the archetypal "time sensitive" product, extremely vulnerable, demanding excellent ventilation while remaining sensitive to draughts and cold. The chicks are placed in specially designed boxes (50-100 chicks per box); these boxes are loaded on pallets so that the air can circulate liberally between them, and then firmly tied down to avoid any risk of crushing, which would be fatal. The transport of day-old chicks requires faultless know-how; which explains why producers select airlines principally according to their quality of service and only secondarily on the basis of price (which amounts to between 10 and 20% of the final selling price).

Through the Franco-American company Hubbard-Isa, France is the one of the few large producers of day-old chicks. They are exported to Africa and the Middle East, and are generally transported in the holds of passenger aircraft. Occasionally, the size of orders calls for the use of charter aircraft. The Dutch airline Martinair has made a speciality of this kind of traffic.

Conditions for the transport of exotic animals are strictly regulated by IATA (minimum cage dimensions) due to the numerous abuses to which this kind of animal trade has been subject.

Without any claim to exhaustiveness, traffic includes giraffes, tigers, lions, antelopes and zebras from Africa, bound for all the zoos in the world; tropical birds, very sought-after in the European and Japanese markets, but which certain airlines will no longer carry under pressure from nature conservation organisations; tropical fish, a speciality of Singapore, transported in water-filled plastic containers to Europe, Japan and the United States; and laboratory animals, the transport of which gives rise to frequent demonstrations.

• Perishable food products

These form a major component of the air cargo market with world traffic of several million tonnes. Thanks to its speed, airfreight is synonymous with freshness for the consumer, with added-value for food industry professionals. However, the goods which can benefit are the most perishable, and top of the range products alone are capable of absorbing the cost of air transport in the price to be passed on to the consumer.

Exotic and out-of-season fruit and vegetables

These goods, which were formerly only available at the counters of a few luxury food shops, have invaded the shelves of all the supermarkets in Europe, Japan and North America. The most important traffic streams come from Africa (Kenya, Senegal, South Africa, Egypt, and Morocco, bound for Europe and the Middle East), South America (Brazil, Chile, Argentina and Peru towards North America and Europe), from Israel to Europe, from Australia and New Zealand to Japan and Hong Kong, from Thailand to Europe, Hong Kong and Singapore, and from India and Pakistan towards the Middle East. Confronted with this multiplicity of traffic we will take only a few particularly significant examples.

We should mention French beans as an example of an out-of-season vegetable, and, as an example of exotic fruits, those from Thailand:

• French or green beans represent the principal flow of "perishable" traffic between Africa and Europe: more than 30,000 tonnes are flown per year from Kenya, Senegal, Burkina Faso, Egypt, Ethiopia, Morocco, Zimbabwe and Zambia. There are two kinds of green beans: thin or very thin "string" beans, principally coming from Kenya and Morocco into the French market, and the mange-tout type of green bean known as "bobby", exported from Senegal, Egypt, Ethiopia and Zambia to Great Britain, Germany and The Netherlands. Due to the marked seasonality of this product (February-May), exporters often run into acute situations of under-capacity, which are all the more difficult to resolve since green beans (and other vegetables such as aubergines or peppers) enjoy rates which are lower than those applied to other products competing for capacity (flowers from Kenya, sea food from Senegal and Morocco).

• Exotic fruits have invaded the markets in rich temperate countries: mangoes and papayas from India, Mali, Peru and Brazil, or limes from Brazil, Mexico or the Caribbean.

Thailand is the paradise for exotic fruits, exported in tens of thousands of tonnes. In addition to the traditional Asian markets, with resident communities of well-off Chinese (Hong Kong, Singapore, Taiwan), there are new openings in the United Sates and Europe, where Thai exporters (often native Chinese) supply fruits and vegetables to Thai, Chinese and Vietnamese restaurants and food stores. Japan has become a more recent market. Among the numerous Thai fruits (mangustan, rambutan, sapote, longan), one is worthy particular attention: the durian. It has a peculiarity which struck the Abbot de Choisy, who wrote in his "Journal of a voyage to Siam" published in 1686: "While lying off Bantam, I ate a durian; it smells quite badly, and does not seem very good to me. All those who have lived for some time in the Indies say that if I ate of it four times, I would find it the best of all the fruits in the world." And indeed, those who enjoy it consider it to be the "king of fruits" although it does smell very bad. There is an apocryphal story on this subject: a Cathay Pacific captain landed his B747 freighter in Bangkok after flying from Hong Kong to take on 50 tonnes of durians and a large load of pigs. At the last minute, the pigs did a "no show". It was said that they refused to fly with the durians! It is hardly surprising that the author himself experienced some difficulties with discontented passengers when carrying a load of 30 tonnes of durians on the main deck of a B747 Combi, flying between Bangkok and Hong Kong…

Alongside these exotic fruits, there are many fruits traded out of season: strawberries from Mexico, Israel or California bound for Europe and Japan, red berries (raspberries, redcurrants etc.) from Chile for Europe and North America, cherries from the Chile and the northwest US (Washington and Oregon) for Japan (over 700,000 20lb boxes during the season), grapes and peaches from South Africa, as well as melons.

Seafood

The speed of airfreight allows seafood – fish, crustaceans, shellfish – to be eaten fresh at a distance of several thousand miles from the place where they were caught. In order to maintain the cold chain, temperature-controlled refrigerated containers

are used, or alternatively, polystyrene boxes together with crushed ice or dry ice.

First of all, there are the regular shipments of fresh food to the importing companies throughout the year. We should mention three of the main supply routes:

1. From Chile and Ecuador to the United States (over 50,000 tonnes) and Europe (Spain is the largest market);
2. From Southern Africa (Namibia, the Republic of South Africa, and Reunion for products from the Kerguelen Islands) to Europe and more particularly Spain (the airport of Vitoria in the Basque country has earned the title of "Hub of the fish trade");
3. From Senegal, Mauritania and Morocco towards France, Italy, Spain and Greece (over 4,000 tonnes to this destination alone) and even to Hong Kong (shark fins).

Then come the traffic flows dedicated to specific products: lobsters from Canada, prawns and scampi from Ecuador and Central America, Madagascar, Senegal and Morocco. And finally, there is the trade in salmon and tuna.

Fresh salmon caught in Scotland, Alaska and above all in Norway is distributed over long distances by air. Since its commencement in the 1960s, salmon farming at the mouths of the fjords has taken on almost industrial proportions in Norway. Exports to Europe are made in refrigerated lorries, while exports to North America and Asia – Japan and Hong Kong – favour air transport (approximately 50,000 tonnes per year). In spite of the seasonal variations, this is a year-round trade. It takes between 48 and 72 hours for Norwegian salmon to leave their home farm and arrive on the plate of the Japanese consumer.

Once fresh tuna is caught, it is rushed by plane towards a single destination: Japan. The Japanese customers, with their high purchasing power and pronounced appetite for fresh tuna, is prepared to pay a very high price. But this is subject to one absolute condition: impeccable quality, which requires first class transport. In view of the seasonal nature of the fisheries, the Japanese importers, in order to satisfy their market during the whole of the year, take their pick of all the oceans of the Earth: first of all from the Pacific (Indonesia, and the islands of Guam, Saipan and Palau), but also the Mediterranean (Spain, France, Tunisia, Italy, Turkey), the waters off Oman, and from the Atlantic Ocean (Bay of Biscay, which is developing a kind of "quasi-fish farming" of tuna).

Fresh meat

This is not so much trade in fresh meat as in seafood. However, of this trade one should note horse meat from Canada and the Mid-West, imported by France and Belgium, beef from Australia to Europe, Asia and the Middle East, and from Argentina, Uruguay and Brazil to Europe (particularly Switzerland), or lamb or mutton from Australia and New Zealand to the Middle East, Hong Kong and Singapore.

"Added value" perishable goods

While the traffic flows for "primary" perishable products mentioned so far generally flow south/north, the flows of "processed" perishable goods which include a higher added value tend to go from east to west or west to east. This is a very wide range of food products: cheese, charcuterie, prepared meat dishes ready for consumption, and even certain types of fruit and vegetables (especially those produced by The

HeavyLift CL-44 Conroy Guppy loading giraffe.
Air Cargo News UK

Netherlands). These products are destined for the shelves of European supermarkets in the Middle East, to certain countries of Africa, in the Indian Ocean or even in Asia, and to high-quality grocery stores in the United States, Japan or Hong Kong. They are also supplied to European restaurants – particularly French – all over the world. France (approximately 18,000 tonnes), The Netherlands (with a much higher tonnage), Italy and Germany are the main suppliers of this kind of product.

• Flowers

What could be more fragile and perishable than a cut flower? Over 300,000 tonnes of flowers are transported by air every year. Around 5 to 6 billion carnations, roses, chrysanthemums and orchids – one flower for every human being on the planet!

There are three great flows of floral air traffic in the world: departing from Colombia and Ecuador, from Kenya and Zimbabwe, and finally from Israel, for destinations in the major centres of consumption where a hard climate is coupled with strong purchasing power: the United States, northern Europe (Germany, Scandinavia, Great Britain) and, to a lesser extent, Japan.

In addition to these major routes, with bouquets of roses, carnations or pom pom chrysanthemums, there is a more limited and specialised traffic: anthuriums from the island of Mauritius, porcelain roses from the West Indies, roses from Morocco, orchids from Thailand and Singapore, and tulips and other flowers from Holland (around 12,000 tonnes exported to the United States and the Far East).

Holland maintains its position as the international hub for the trade in flowers. Tens of thousands of tonnes of flowers from Israel, Africa, Colombia and Ecuador arrive via several European airports (Frankfurt, Amsterdam, Roissy-Charles de Gaulle, Luxembourg, Liège etc) to converge upon the flower centre of Alsmeer, where they are sold at the reverse bidding auctions. The Dutch, who have been masters in horticulture for centuries, have now become traders without equal. Acting as buyers for flowers arriving from everywhere, they re-export them to all the countries in the world, after having added their professional expertise (composition of bouquets, packaging and presentation of flowers) along with their commercial know-how.

Since it is impossible to say everything about so perfumed a market, we will restrict our comments to Colombia (although one could have equally well mentioned Ecuador, the newest entrant). Colombian flowers are a real "success story". The first commercial greenhouse in Colombia was built in 1964 in the "Sabana de Bogota". The first exports to the United States started in 1968, and to Europe in 1975. Production – under plastic tunnels – is still mostly concentrated in the "Sabana de Bogota" within a radius of 40 miles from the airport. The advantage lies in the favourable physical conditions in the area: an altitude of 1,500 to 2,500 metres, an equatorial location, which brings moisture and light, and an extremely fertile soil. This is combined with the human activities which favour this kind of activity: the existence of a class of Colombian entrepreneurs, the local development of agricultural engineers, and the presence of a cheap and abundant labour force.

The producers, of which there are many, work with export companies, in which they often own shares. They join together within the Colombian Association of Flower Exporters or Assocolflores, a powerful economic lobbying force, for the purpose of protecting the profession and searching for outlets.

The main flowers produced are carnations, chrysanthemums and roses. Since the 1980s, one has observed efforts at diversification, with the appearance of new varieties of flowers, including statices (sea lavender), gerberas, alstromerias and miniature carnations.

The flowers are cut at the precise moment they open, when they are almost still in bud. They are cut in the morning to avoid dehydration, and packed in standardised cardboard boxes of 105 x 52 x 17cm with an average weight of 20kg for carnations (approximately 350 blooms) and 15kg for roses. This is a traffic with quite a good density, since 2,600 to 3,000kg per pallet are loaded on the upper deck, or 1,800 to 2,000kg per pallet on the lower deck. The combination of these average loads with profitable rates means that cut flowers are a traffic with a high profit contribution for the carriers (the same applies to exports from Kenya or Ecuador). But this is a market which is strongly seasonal, with a low season from May to November and a high season from November to May, and peaks of extreme activity for All Saints Day, the year-end festivities, Mother's Day and, the top of the bill, St Valentine's Day. This is the time when every available cargo aircraft, loaded with flowers, converges on the great markets in Europe and the United States/Canada: 85% of Colombian production is aimed at North America, while about 15% goes to Europe and even to the Middle East.

• Products perishable because of their intended purpose – the example of "Beaujolais Nouveau".

"Le Beaujolais Nouveau est arrivé!" In order for this ritual phrase, synonymous with high spirits and good humour, to ring out at the same moment in Paris, Osaka, Chicago and Hong Kong, a veritable "logistics miracle" must occur. In fact, it is necessary to send within a very short period – 4 to 5 days – some ten thousand tonnes or about nine million bottles, of Beaujolais Nouveau, bound for dozens of countries, in particular the United States and Canada, Hong Kong and Japan (the leading market with over 4,000 tonnes sent by air), French overseas territories etc…

The reason for such a demanding operation is that the marketing of Beaujolais Nouveau is governed by three key dates:

1. The start of consumption at midnight on the third Thursday in November,
2. The commencement of air shipments on the preceding Friday at 22.00 hours,
3. The stocking of bottles on the premises of authorised freight agents for palletisation from 31st October.

The "Beaujolais Nouveau campaign", as it is called by the airlines and freight agents, is therefore strictly limited in time. From the first minute allowed on the Friday evening, at 22.00 hours, a flood of lorries, loaded with bottles, leaves the wine cellars or warehouses of the freight forwarders to fill all the capacity available in aircraft holds on scheduled or chartered freighters, leaving for Japan or Hong Kong, from Lyons-Saint Exupéry and all the major airports in Europe. The objective is that throughout the world, at midnight on the Thursday, the Beaujolais Nouveau can be celebrated at the same instant. As one of the freight agents have said: "There is no question of arriving at the destination before the fateful moment, and it is absolutely unthinkable to arrive late."

Beaujolais Nouveau is not perishable in itself. But every year, around 15th-20th November, it becomes "critical". Once the moment of madness has passed, sea transport takes over again.

Category two: manufactured products
These can be grouped into four large families:
• First family: textiles, footwear and leather goods
Only top-of-the-range articles are regularly transported by air. Air cargo is relied on for more ordinary merchandise only sporadically when fashion collections are being put in place, or for coping with unexpected surges in demand. Traffic in textiles – and this is a difficulty – show very marked seasonal fluctuations corresponding to the winter and summer collections. However, there is a tendency to increase the number of collections in an attempt to even out the seasonal variations.

The largest traffic flows originate in low-wage economies: China and the Indian sub-continent for textiles, Brazil and Latin America for footwear. The former exporters of these kinds of products, South Korea, Hong Kong and Taiwan, now specialise in electronics. One can also observe the opening of new markets with exports from Africa (Madagascar, the Republic of South Africa), South America (Colombia) and the Caribbean region (Costa Rica, Dominican Republic).

In addition to this trade from low-wage economies to industrialised countries, which makes up the vast majority of air shipments for textiles, there are regular shipments on a scheduled basis carrying considerable tonnages of high-quality articles exported by countries known for their creativity and quality of workmanship (Italy, France, Spain, Britain etc). Here we are dealing with knitwear and clothing, footwear, travel goods and fancy leather articles transported to the countries with high purchasing power in North America and Asia (Japan, Hong Kong, Singapore etc). Benneton and Louis Vuitton are amongst the largest customers for airfreight.

• Second Family: Chemical products
Air transport merely touches this highly diversified category of products. It concentrates on a few commodities which are most appropriate in view of their physical (limited lifetime) or economic characteristics (high average value). Many such products, which are considered dangerous, are subject to special regulations and can only be loaded in large quantities on freighters.

Among the products of this family most frequently sent by air, we can mention perfumes and cosmetics (one of France's main exports to Asia and North America, with over 40,000 tonnes), and pharmaceutical products and vaccines. The large pharmaceutical companies from Basel (Novartis, Roche) are the leading customers for airfreight in Switzerland, although not so much for finished products as for the base chemicals used to manufacture medicines. A manager from the Franco-German company Aventis recently stated: "The high value of our products fully justifies using airfreight." For its part, Pasteur-Mérieux sends the main part of its vaccines by air: "Our products have all the characteristics appropriate to airfreight: high added-value, an urgent need on the part of the importers, and difficulties in conservation."

• Third family: Electrical, electronic, "high-tech" and optical goods
Telephone and telecommunications equipment, radar installations, medical equipment (x-ray machines etc) are transported on a large scale by air. This is why companies such as Alcatel, Thalès, Siemens, Philips, Nortel, Ericsson and General Electric are among the most loyal airline customers. But today, electronics and "high-tech" goods for both consumers and businesses are the principal drivers of expansion in this family of goods, particularly for the countries of Asia and the United States. For consumer goods, airfreight is normally used only for articles at the very top of the range, or for new products, to provide rapid market saturation (for example the Walkman when it was first launched, and more recently, the Sony Play Station II). The largest traffic flows carry industrial products (components, semi-conductors, integrated circuits) manufactured in the Far East and incorporated into the supply chains of the biggest names in electronics and computers.

One example is Agilent Technologies. With factories in Singapore and Malaysia (Penang), it manufactures a very wide range of semi-conductors (2,500 products) for the computer and telecommunications industry. Its customers are names such as Alcatel, Compaq, IBM and Hewlett Packard. Every evening the total production is sent by air, because "the product life cycles are extremely short in the semi-conductor industry." [7]

• Fourth Family: Machines, engines, automotive components
This is a vast and varied category, in which air transport's rate penetration remains low. However, trade in these products between industrialised countries or to developing countries reaches such levels that it provides considerable tonnages for airfreight, particularly in the automotive industry, aircraft manufacturing or precision engineering.

The automotive industry is the main customer, with permanent requirements for the distribution of certain types of spare parts and, less frequently, for the partial supply of assembly lines. There are also temporary requirements, sometimes ad hoc or sometimes on a scheduled basis, for dealing with stock shortages, catching up with production after industrial action, or to fulfil demand which exceeds forecasts (new model launches). All the principal car manufacturers are among the leading customers of airlines: Fiat, Renault, PSA, Ford, General Motors, Toyota, Volvo, BMW, Volkswagen or Mercedes.

The aircraft manufacturing industry employs lightweight, value-added materials and components that are well suited to air transport. There is a close connection between air transport and the functioning of assembly lines (all avionics equipment), and in the engine manufacturing process, as in the case of the SNECMA/General Electric alliance. Supplying airlines with spare parts, which at one time was carried out by in-house services, is now being increasingly outsourced to specialised forwarders offering "aviation logistics services", such as SDV, KN, Shenker, Danzas, and Bax Global.

An example of precision mechanics is surgical instruments. Most are manufactured manually in northwestern Pakistan, in the region of Sialkot. The airfreight traffic generated is sufficiently unusual to be noted. Metal pieces are flown in to Sialkot and the surgical instruments made from them are flown out. This is Pakistan's main export, along with carpets and textiles, and the dense traffic provokes ferocious rate competition among the airlines.

3 THE AIRLINES

From the outset, the statistics show one fundamental conclusion: the share of cargo revenue (freight + mail), within the total commercial income of the airlines, on a world-wide basis, has decreased appreciably since 1950, falling from 21.7% in 1951 to 15.1% in 1960 and 12% in 2000. Since 1970, it has been more or less static between 12 and 14%.

One can see that this negative development is explained by the relative decline of airmail revenue. However, at the same time, the proportion of freight income has not managed to make real progress in spite of the tremendous increases in traffic, since it has been outweighed by the expansion of passenger traffic and the continuous erosion of average freight yield per RTK. This crucial observation, which contradicts many accepted ideas, and throws cold water on many a fulsome press release, lies at the heart of the problems of airfreight. It means that there is no future for companies unable to reduce their unit costs and to add value to their products.

I TYPES OF AIRLINES

Almost all airlines carry goods, but in this field the airlines exhibit extreme diversity. However, they can be divided into categories using two determining factors:

• Whether or not they operate "cargo-only" flights:
On the one hand there are companies which only offer capacity in the holds of their passenger aircraft (these are the belly carriers), and on the other hand there are airlines for whom cargo aircraft provide a variable proportion of their supply (these are the cargo carriers and the passenger airlines).

• Whether or not they integrate activities as freight agents and carriers:
On the one hand there are the integrators, and on the other hand the "traditional" or "classic" airlines.

On the basis of the interaction of these two criteria, it is possible to describe four categories of airlines as identified below:

First category: traditional, cargo-only airlines (12% of world traffic in 2000)

In this category, there are scheduled carriers and charter carriers.

• Cargo charter airlines
This group has seen its activities decline rapidly from the end of the 1970s, under the threefold effect of the introduction of wide-bodied cargo aircraft by the scheduled airlines, the deregulation of rates and the decrease in specific markets following the end of the oil boom. Though often spectacular, the cargo charter market is somewhat restricted (consignments with exceptional dimensions and or weights, humanitarian missions, urgent operations following natural catastrophes etc).

But this business needs specially modified aircraft, usually of military origin, made in the United States (Lockheed Hercules) and above all in Russia and Ukraine (Ilyushin Il-76 and Antonov An-124).

This very specialised market is in the hands of a small number of operators who in particular fly the Antonov 124: Polet Cargo Airlines, Volga-Dnepr Airlines, which was linked to the carrier HeavyLift up to the end of the year 2000, and Antonov Airlines, the commercial aircraft operating division of the Antonov Design Bureau, which has been associated with the British company Air Foyle since 1989. After having been competitors for many years, these two British charter companies joined forces under the aegis of Christopher Foyle in a joint venture which created Air Foyle Heavylift in the middle of 2001. Air Foyle Heavylift, trading as Antonov Airlines, is now the Western partner and worldwide sales and managing agent of Antonov Design Bureau.

Antonov, like the other major aircraft design bureaux, was a state enterprise of the Soviet Union. With resources from the centre declining, Antonov's visionary leader and general designer, Piotr Balabuev, realised that for the Antonov Design Bureau to survive and to continue to design and build new aircraft types, it would need to generate its own independent source of revenue by becoming a commercial operator of the An-124 in the worldwide charter market.

Following unsuccessful attempts to obtain the necessary permissions, it finally succeeded following a personal visit to

| Development of income by category of traffic (world-wide) in % | | | | | |
Year	Passengers	Mail	Freight	Freight + mail = cargo	Total
1951	78.3%	9.1%	12.6%	21.7%	100%
1960	84.9%	5.2%	9.9%	15.1%	100%
1970	85.6%	3.8%	10.6%	14.4%	100%
1980	86.4%	1.9%	11.7%	13.6%	100%
1990	88.1%	1.3%	10.6%	11.9%	100%
1995	87.0%	1.1%	11.1%	12.2%	100%
1999	86.5%	0.8%	12.7%	13.5%	100%

from Aviant, the Kiev production factory.

As the commercial industrial market became increasingly accustomed to the An-124's potential, the aircraft has performed a large number of flights with a variety of unusual loads ranging from live ostrich and giraffe to tunnel boring machines, and from sections of the Ariane V space rocket to a 20-tonne, 64ft high, 200-year old cactus plant and most of the yachts for the Americas Cup races in different parts of the world over the years.

In the industrial market, a number of world records have been achieved. These have included:

Antonov in Kiev in March 1989 by President Gorbachev. Initially, Antonov commenced operations in July 1989 with two An-124 aircraft and over the years this grew to a fleet of eight, complemented by the An-225 in 2001 as well as An-22 and An-12 turbo-prop aircraft.

The arrival of such a large aircraft as the An-124 in the air cargo charter market place added a new dimension. It took time for the appreciation of the availability of so much additional large size and weight-bearing potential to be digested by the marketplace. Initially, growth was slow, but kick-started by the first Gulf War in 1990-91, the aircraft really came into its own.

Seeking to emulate Antonov's pioneering success, Volga Dnepr, based in Ulyanovsk Russia, commenced commercial operations in the autumn of 2001 having formed a joint venture with another British cargo airline, HeavyLift Cargo Airlines.

In the early 1990s, Antonov and HeavyLift Volga Dnepr were joined by more An-124 operators, four of them Russian: Ayaks, Rossia, Titan and Polet, Antonov Airtrack of Ukraine and Air Sofia of Bulgaria, but all of these except for Polet had disappeared by 1999. In addition, more recently, two aircraft were acquired by the Libyan government and at the end of 2003, the government of Abu Dhabi purchased the last new An-124-100

An-124 — heaviest single piece of a generator of 135.2 tonnes from Düsseldorf to New Delhi for Siemens.

An-124 — heaviest commercial load of 148 tonnes including a 109 tonne railway locomotive from London, Ontario to Dublin, Ireland.

An-225 — For Kühne & Nagel a transformer weighing 145 tonnes, plus further equipment, making a total payload of 170 tonnes, from Linz in Austria to Phoenix, Arizona, USA.

The An-124 has also been intensively used by the United Nations to support a number of its peace keeping operations around the world by moving heavy equipment for the military of the participating countries from such countries to the UN area of operation. These have included: First Gulf War, Rwanda, Angola, Sierra Leone, Belgian Congo, East Timor, Somalia, Mozambique and Liberia.

One of two Bell 212 helicopters being loaded on to the HeavyLift Conroy Guppy for Brisbane.
HeavyLift

LEFT **Heavylift Belfast SC5.** *Air Cargo News UK*

BELOW LEFT **Il-76TD and Lockheed Hercules L100-3D on charter to Oil Spill Response.** *Air Foyle*

RIGHT **MNG Cargo Airlines A300-B4 freighter.** *Malcolm Nason*

BELOW **Air Atlantique DC-6.** *Air Atlantique*

The aircraft has also been increasingly used by the defence ministries of various countries to assist in the moving of equipment and materials starting with the first Gulf War in 1990-91, the war against the Taliban in 2002-03 and the Second Iraq War in 2003-04. Revenues from three civil An-124 fleets are now in excess of US$ 450 million per annum with 22 of the An-124-100 in commercial service.

Heavylift Cargo Airlines (originally TAC Heavylift) was founded in 1978 – the same year as Air Foyle – by the Cunard Steamship Company and a second shareholder, to utilise a fleet of six Short Belfast aircraft which had belonged to the Royal Air Force. The aircraft had been decommissioned in 1975 and converted into cargo planes. "Designed to give Transport Command a world-wide military airlift capability, including remote airfields where ground support is minimal", the Belfast, fitted with four turboprop engines, has proved to be well suited to transporting consignments falling outside the usual formats. With a pay-load 50% higher than that of the Lockheed Hercules (36,500kg/ 80,500lb), a volume of 338m³ (11,350cu ft) and a main hold of impressive dimensions (27.43m x 5.00m x 4.06m or 90ft x 13ft 4 in x 16ft 1in), the Belfast became irreplaceable when carrying the Ariane rocket out to Kourou (French Guyana). Heavylift Cargo had the foresight at the outset to remain within its market segment – transporting outsized cargoes – and diversify its fleet with this in mind, by taking into service a CL-44 Guppy, and then making a joint venture with Volga-Dnepr. However, a number of changes in shareholders, ill-fated attempts at diversification, and, finally, the termination of the collaboration with Volga-Dnepr got the better of Heavylift.

There is no very clear boundary between ad hoc charter cargo airlines, contract charter cargo airlines and scheduled cargo airlines. Frequently, the same companies operate two or all three types of flight, even if one or other activity makes up the major portion of its traffic.

Channel Express, a British company based in Bournemouth in Dorset, and led by Philip Meeson, operates a cargo fleet consisting of Airbus A300B4s, Lockheed Electras and Fokker 27s. It used to operate a fleet of Handley Page Dart Herald turbo prop aircraft. For many years it operated scheduled flights carrying newspapers and parcels for integrators and returning with fresh flowers from the Channel Islands. This business has since deceased significantly due to better roll on/off ferries. Today, Channel Express's main activities consist of a major contract for the British Post Office won by a joint venture company formed with Titan Airways, called Postal Air Network, to provide eight Boeing B737s and five BAe 146s, while its Airbus A300B4 freighters are operated for UPS and TNT.

Titan Airways of London Stansted Airport was established in 1998 primarily to assist with the demand to move parts for the automotive industry. Titan operates a fleet of BAe 146-200 QC & QT and Boeing B737-300F aircraft and specialises in rapid response charter in addition to their joint venture postal contract with Channel Express.

Other ad hoc and contract cargo charter airlines worth a mention are:

Air Atlantique of Coventry with its fleet of DC-3 and DC-6 freighters and its sister company Atlantic Airlines operating the largest fleet in the world remaining of Lockheed Electra, eight in number.

Emerald Airways of LIverpool with a fleet of 14 BAe 748s, one ATP, ten SD-360s and one SD-330 cargo aircraft on contract and charter services throughout Europe for Royal Mail and express parcel carriers, as well as scheduled cargo services to the Isle of Man.

African International Airways operating two DC-8-54Fs and two DC-8-62Fs was formed in 1985 by two historical personalities of the air cargo industry, Alan Stocks and Bernard Keay, as an all cargo carrier flying charters between Africa and Europe together with sub-services for scheduled airlines such as Alitalia. Originally registered in Swaziland and now in South Africa, its commercial office is in the UK.

Air Contractors (Ireland) a Belgian/South African consortium based in Ireland operating a fleet of A300B4s, one Lockheed Hercules and a fleet of smaller turbo prop aircraft. In addition to ad hoc work the Hercules is based at Bournemouth Airport on 24-hour standby for Oil Spill Response while the other aircraft are principally operated for integrators, previously DHL but now mainly Federal Express.

BAC Express of Horley, UK was founded in 1994 and operates a fleet of F-27 and SD-360 cargo aircraft on ad hoc and contract charter work.

Centurion Air Cargo of Miami, Florida emerged following the end of Challenge Air Cargo in 2001. Challenge had been led for many years by Bill Spohrer, a well known personality in the air cargo industry and former President of TIACA. UPS bought the name, trademark and the Latin American routes of Challenge Air Cargo. The aircraft were not included in the UPS takeover and Challenge's owner Peter Ulrich retained three DC-10-40 freighters and the FAA operating certificate and renamed it Centurion Air Cargo specialising in ACMI "wet lease" contracts.

Evergreen International Airlines of McMinville, Oregon founded and led by one of the well known characters of the industry, Del Smith, operates a fleet of B747 and DC-9 freighters principally on contract charters, ACMI "wet leases" for other carriers and military contracts for the US MAC.

Star Air of Copenhagen Denmark operates a fleet of B727s and B757s in Europe for the integrator UPS.

MK Airlines registered in Ghana is led by its owner and CEO Mike Kruger and is based in the UK. Operates a fleet of B747-200s and DC-8 cargo aircraft on worldwide charters but principally on contract for the Swiss forwarder Panalpina/ASB Air Cargo.

Kitty Hawk Air Cargo of Dallas, operate a fleet of B727s and DC-9s on contract to consolidators and integrators.

Kalitta Air of Ypsilanti, Michigan led by another colourful American cargo airline entrepreneur, Connie Kalitta, operates a fleet of 11 B747s principally on ad hoc and contract charter for the US postal service, MAC, integrators and freight forwarders.

Two growing Icelandic cargo operators are:
Bluebird Cargo founded in 2000 and led by its CEO ex Cargolux executive Thor Kjartansson. Bluebird operates a fleet of four B737-300 and one B757-200 PCF freighters on scheduled services, contract charters for integrators to and from Iceland and within Europe and Scandinavia, and

Islandsflug which operates a fleet of Airbus A-310s, A-300s and B737s on "wet lease" contracts worldwide.

Southern Air of Columbus, Ohio, operates a fleet of B747 freighters on charters and ACMI "wet lease" contracts.

WDL Aviation of Mülheim-Essen, Germany, was founded in 1956 and in addition to operating its own airships and BAe 146 passenger aircraft operates a fleet of 16 F-27 freighters on contracts for the integrators Deutsche Post and ad hoc charters for th automotive and other industries.

Transafrik International of Sao Tomé have for years been operating B727s and Lockheed L-100 Hercules aircraft on contracts and charters in Angola and other parts of Africa.

World Airways of Atlanta, Hartsfield, Virginia, founded in 1948 and purchased in 1950 by another aviation character Ed Daley, who died in 1984 aged 61. World successfully overcame its financial difficulties in the 1980s and today operates a fleet of MD-11s and DC-10-30s, principally on contract flying for the cargo industry and the military and ACMI "wet leasing" for other airlines.

Other contract cargo airlines include Air Transport International (ATI) operating DC-8s, and Amerijet International of Fort Lauderdale, Florida, and Capital Cargo International of Orlando, Florida operating B727s on contracts and ACMI "wet leases".

Mention was made earlier of the Russian rear ramp loading aircraft such as the Il-76, An-12, An-26 and An-32 aircraft. There are a number of airlines in the CIS and eastern Europe operating such aircraft and the more noteworthy of these include: from Russia, Atran-Aviatrans and Atlant-Soyuz of

Moscow and Volga-Dnepr of Ulyanovsk, from Ukraine, Antonov Airlines, Khors Aircompany, Ukrainian Cargo Airways and Volare Aircompany of Kiev, Avialeasing Aviation Company as well as Uzbekistan Airways of Tashkent, Turkmenistan Airways of Ashkhabad, Air Sofia and Vega Airlines of Sofia, Bulgaria and Inversia of Riga, Latvia.

As far as agents are concerned, the charter market, which demands both technical know-how and 100% availability, is controlled by a very small number of charter brokers, such as Transvalair in France (who claim to "deal with everything which the scheduled airlines cannot carry"), Chapman Freeborn ("whose core business is to negotiate air charter contracts on a global scale" and which boasts 46 branches in 18 countries) and Air Charter Service in the UK.

At the risk of straying into the field of specialised aerial work cargo charter airlines have sometimes won contracts to provide aircraft on 24 hour, seven day a week standby in the event of a major oil spill disaster anywhere in the world. One of the more important contracts is let in this field by Oil Spill Response Limited, a company owned by the principal oil companies of the world. For many years HeavyLift Cargo Airlines held this contract with Il-76 and Hercules aircraft and in the mid-1990s it was held by Air Foyle who provided one Hercules to perform aerial spraying to counter oil pollutants and one Il-76 to transport the heavy equipment. Today this contract is held by Air Contractors (Ireland) while Atlantic Airlines with its Lockheed Electras holds the contract let by the Marine Coastguard Agency (MCA) of the UK.

We cannot leave the field of air charter without mentioning air taxis. The operating companies are rarely all-cargo airlines. They are most often generalists who offer a range of narrow-bodied aircraft, with pay loads from 400 to 2,000kg. These are the "flying fire fighters" of the airfreight world, and provide "tailor made" services, with extreme urgency being the decisive characteristic. In the United States, air taxi companies have a particular role: they have a share in the public service of the US Postal Authority in order to reach the most remote communities.

• Scheduled Cargo Airlines
As just mentioned many cargo airlines undertake both charter work (ad hoc and contract) as well as scheduled services. As examples we can mention a number of scheduled cargo airlines:

Tampa Airlines is a Colombian company, which was founded in Medellin in 1973. It operates a fleet of five DC-8–71s and in addition to its General Cargo activities, it has specialised in transporting flowers to Miami. The Dutch Martinair purchased 40% of its capital in 1996.

Cargo Airlines – CAL – is an Israeli cargo airline founded in 1976 by agricultural co-operatives to promote exports of flowers, fruits and vegetables to Europe by air. It operates two Boeing B747–200C aircraft, flying to Europe (Liège and Amsterdam) as well as the United States.

Coyne Airways, a British company based in London, founded and led by Larry Coyne, a former president of TIACA, is probably unique in being a non-asset based airline. It operates regular scheduled charter flights from Europe to various countries in the Caspian and central Asian region, the Gulf States, Afghanistan and

ABOVE **Polar Air Cargo B747.** *MAP*

BELOW **American International Lockheed L1011 Tristar.** *Malcom Nason*

ABOVE RIGHT **Cathay Pacific B747-400 freighter landing at Hong Kong.** *Malcolm Nason*

BELOW RIGHT **Varig DC-10 freighter.** *Air Cargo News UK*

performer of this group. Cargolux, based at Luxembourg Airport, was founded in 1970 by Loftleider Islandic, Luxair, the Swedish shipping line Salen Shipping, and five Luxembourg banks. After being initially confined to charter flights, due to a lack of traffic rights, it managed, with the support of its Government and the benefit of a certain degree of liberalisation, to build up a world-wide network of scheduled cargo flights to all five continents, particularly to the West Coast of the United States, Australia and South America. One of the advantages of Cargolux is the young age and homogeneous structure of its fleet: 11 B747-400Fs in the year 2000 (a 12th machine was delivered in 2002). Its marketing policy is clear and consistent, straightforwardly aimed at the freight forwarders: "We are the company for freight forwarders."

For many years it maintained a special association with the Swiss freight agent Panalpina (of whom more later). The capital structure of Cargolux presents one peculiar feature, which is potentially a source of uncertainty. The former Swissair group, which had bought a 24.5% share from Lufthansa,

Iraq as well as from Seoul to Sakhalin. It operates its flights primarily with aircraft "wet leased" from CIS carriers.

Also worth a mention is DAS Air Cargo (the British air cargo market is certainly varied!), owned by Captain and Mrs J. C. Roy, who run a fleet of five DC-10-30Fs to 20 or so destinations in Africa and the Middle East.

MNG Cargo Airlines of Istanbul, Turkey was founded in 1997. It operates Airbus A300B4, A300C4 and A300F4 freighters on scheduled flights as well as on "wet lease" for major freight forwarders and other airlines. It also provides ad hoc charter services.

Alongside these medium-sized companies there are a few big-league players: the American Polar Air Cargo (with an imposing but assorted fleet of 18 B747Fs of different types), the Japanese Nippon Cargo Airlines (where the prestigious attendees at the board meetings include, in addition to All Nippon Airways, all the major names in Japanese insurance, freight forwarding and shipping), and the Luxembourg company Cargolux.

With a carried traffic of 3.5 billion kilometric tonnes, Cargolux, 14th in the overall world rankings, is the star

owns 33.7% of the Cargolux capital. The failure of the Swissair charter group should logically lead to a redistribution of the shares, which would end something which has always looked like a marriage of fish and fowl!

Second category: passenger-only airlines (14% of world traffic)
These companies run no cargo flights at all. This does not mean that they do not carry freight; they still have their hold capacity, which allows them to take 14% of the world market, more than the traditional cargo airlines. In this group can be found most of the American "majors" (with the remarkable exception of North West). The share of freight of their commercial income is very low: from 2% to 4%.

Third category: mixed "cargo-passenger" airlines (50% of world traffic)
These companies operate passenger services and cargo services simultaneously. They hold a leading position on the market, since they fill eight of the 10 top places in the world rankings. And justifiably so, since they offer to their customer the widest range of services, combining the advantages of destinations and frequencies supplied by passenger services with the benefits of power and specialisation of a cargo network. They form a very

diverse group, with the proportion of traffic on cargo flights varying between less than 20% to over 80% according to the company. It is therefore appropriate to distinguish between two sub groups.

• First Sub Group: Mixed companies carrying half or more of their traffic on cargo flights (39% of world traffic)

Here, the ranking (see table above right) is not a question of size; this criterion allows us to evaluate the degree of commitment of these airlines in favour of their freight activities, with respect to investment and strategic orientation. Thus it is that El Al, which is 36th in the overall world traffic ranking, is catapulted up to the top of this group, to join Korean Airlines, which is third in the world ranking. The Taiwanese airlines (China Airlines and Eva Air) and Martinair also make their appearance.

The companies from Taiwan, which are conspicuous by their absence from international statistics, collectively line up a fleet of 16 B747-400Fs, two B747-200Fs and nine MD-11Fs, with which they distribute world-wide the high-tech products in which Taiwan has specialised. Airfreight brings in over 40% of their sales income.

The Dutch company Martinair was founded in 1958 by Martin Schröder, and is one of the most unusual and interesting companies in the business. Martinair is owned in equal shares by Nedlloyd and KLM, and is active right across the board: for passengers and freight, scheduled flights (for cargo) and charter flights (for cargo and passengers). Its fleet is made up partly of convertible B747-200Cs and MD-11CFs, which are operated in summer as the passenger version and in winter as the cargo version, in addition to cargo-only aircraft. Flexibility and adaptability are its main qualities. Its cargo network resembles, though on a smaller scale, that of Cargolux and presents the same strong points. Although the programme of cargo operations is very

Ranking according to percentage of traffic on cargo flights

Airline (mil RTK)	Traffic% in cargo international	Ranking for traffic
Korean Airlines	6,461	81	3
El Al	886	81	36
Lufthansa Cargo	7,115	64	2
Air France	4,980	56	6
Singapore Airlines	6,020	55	5
Saudi Arabian Airlines	1,000	55	37
Alitalia	1,743	53	23
Cathay Pacific	4,108	53	10
Japan Airlines	4,607	51	7
Aeroflot	629	51	-
China Airlines	4,133	>50	9
Eva Air	3,558	>50	13
Martinair	2,355	>50	18

advanced, it does in reality consist of scheduled flights, whatever the legal trappings, which have a share of over 80%. Some disappointing experiences in the passenger field led Martinair in 2000/2001 to reinforce the proportion of cargo flights in its overall activities.

• Second Sub Group: Mixed companies making 15% to 50% of their traffic in cargo flights (19% of world traffic)

Here, the field is led by companies in the 40-48% band, including Lan Chile (48%), Ethiopian Airlines (46%), Air China (44%), North West (43%) and Varig (42%).

Loading a Martinair B747F.

companies who have re-entered the cargo market after ceasing to operate in-house cargo flights after the oil shocks.

Fourth category: the airlines belonging to the integrators (16% of the world market).

The function of the integrators goes far beyond that of a simple airline, since – by definition – they integrate a whole series of ground operations, and extend to running increasingly complex transport systems, which closely combine air and surface transportation (road, and no doubt rail in the near future, at least in Europe).

However, every integrator owns an airline for its exclusive use. Hence, there is Fedex Express for Fedex, TNT Airways for TNT, UPS Airlines for UPS and European Air Transport in Europe for DHL. These companies covered 16% of the total world market, but only 8% of the international market in the year 2000: this difference shows the extent of the great superiority of the integrators in the enormous domestic American market. The integrators and their airlines should be split into two groups: on the one side, DHL and TNT, "the European postal integrators", which we will consider along with the Post (chapter five), and on the other side there are Fedex and UPS, or "the independent American integrators".

Up to the present time (2003) the express business has been dominated by two giants, Fedex and UPS, who, having built up their power base in America, are continuing to develop an international network, anchored on a number of hubs. They vie with each other in spite of their differences – Fedex ever flamboyant and communications-orientated, like its boss and founder, and UPS the taciturn but frighteningly efficient giant from Atlanta.

"Fedex is one of the largest transportation companies in the world. Our business strategy is to offer a portfolio of transportation services through our independently operated business units." [1] Here we can find an illustration of the modern trend towards "one-stop shopping". To this end, Fedex combines several units, with the principal ones being Fedex Express – the historical core business and "the world's largest express transportation company" – and two important ground transport operations, Fedex Ground, "North Americas second largest small package ground carrier", and

Lan Chile is an excellent example of a medium-sized company with a strong involvement in freight operations due to the determination of its boss Enrique Cueto. Benefiting from the liberalisation of air transport in South America, he provided his company with a uniform fleet of newer cargo aircraft (B767-300Fs carrying pay loads of 35 tonnes over a range of 3,750 miles). This aircraft is well suited to the characteristics of its routes to Miami and Europe, and puts Lan Chile, of which 44% of the sales revenue came from freight activities in the year 2000, at the top of the list of South American airlines. The acquisition of the Brazilian cargo company ABSA in December 2001 has given Lan Chile access to new markets in Argentina and Brazil.

North West is the "American exception". It is the only passenger airline to operate a powerful cargo network, chiefly centred on the Pacific. Cargo accounts for 8% of its sales revenue. Its one problem is how to renew an ageing fleet of 12 B747-200Fs.

Next comes a group of companies who carry about 20% of their traffic on cargo services. China Southern, Egyptair, Emirates and SAS, as well as British Airways and KLM, two

Fedex Freight, "the US market leader of next - day and second-day regional, less-than-truck-load freight services". When it bought Caliber Systems in 1997, followed by American Freightways, the fourth largest parcel company in the United States at the end of the year 2000, Fedex made a two-fold strategic decision: in favour of a ground transportation system to complement and double the capacity of its air network, and in favour of its domestic market (although continuing to develop the international market). Following these acquisitions and the general expansion of business, its international sector in 2002 barely represented 20% (compared with 15% for UPS).

The fleet of Fedex Express (numbering 324 aircraft, not counting feeder aircraft operated by sub contractor airlines) is made up of Airbus A300-600Fs and A310-200Fs, ageing Boeing B727-100s and -200Fs, and aircraft in the family DC-10/MD-11Fs. The fleet is soon to be supplemented with ATR 42s converted into cargo versions. At the same time Fedex has placed a firm order for 10 A380Fs, with a payload of 150 tonnes, to be delivered between 2008 and 2011, and has taken an option on a further 10 aircraft.

While Memphis remains the super-hub of the network, the increasing number of domestic and international services and the growth of traffic (over 3 million packages per day, of which 90% are for the domestic market) have brought about the need to create other strategic platforms: Paris, Dubai, Subic Bay and Anchorage in the international network, and Newark, Miami, Oakland and Indianapolis on the domestic network, along with a new hub in the design stage at Greensboro-North Carolina (Piedmont Triad International Airport planned for 2006).

Throughout all these strategic orientations and this mass of investments, the objectives of Fedex remain clear: in the overall domestic market to grow market share at the expense of UPS, and in the international sphere to be able to serve 90% of the world market in 24/48 hours. Let us leave the last word to George Bush, the 41st President of the United States: "Like many people I really don't remember 'life before Fedex'. The advent of overnight delivery services revolutionised not only the business world but also how we lived our lives."

United Parcel Service or "Big Brown" [2] is, by far, the world's leading ground carrier for small packages, with an average daily traffic of 13.6 million packages. Unlike Fedex, domestic activities remain very much at the forefront (over 80%), in spite of investments approved for building up an international network, which came into the black for the first time in 1998.

ABOVE Federal Express DC-10F.
Malcolm Nason

BELOW Lynden Air Cargo Lockheed Hercules L-100.
Malcolm Nason

BOTTOM Gemini Air Cargo DC-10-30F.
MAP

LEFT Airborne Express B767F.
Malcolm Nason

BELOW LEFT UPS DC-8 loading.
Air Cargo News UK

postal "Conglomerates".

Fifth category: the "phantom airlines" or the "contract carriers"

There is indeed a fifth category of airlines: airlines which are merely phantoms – or almost so – from a point of view of traffic statistics, but which nevertheless make their presence felt on the market. These companies have specialised in the rental of "turn key" cargo aircraft for periods of one to two years, which may be increased to up to five years on the base of ACMI contracts (Aircraft, Crew, Maintenance, Insurance). It is no longer necessary to own aircraft, nor even to operate them oneself, in order to have access to a cargo network. This is a recent phenomenon, born in the 1990s, and experiencing tremendous growth up to the year 2000. It explains the return to fashion for cargo-only operations – with no investments and minimum risk – among airlines, which had abandoned them years before.

In addition to the previously described variety of American and European cargo charter airlines and which include ACMI work in their repertoire, the two big American players in this field which stand out are: Atlas Air and Gemini Air Cargo. Atlas Air was founded in 1992 by Michael Chowdry, who was a combination of dynamism, charisma and professionalism. With Chowdry in the driving seat, Atlas Air, responding to market needs, underwent an extraordinary expansion, to the extent of putting into service a fleet of 26 Boeing B747Fs. According to the catchy and very accurate catch-phrase of its founder, Atlas Air appeared at that time to be "the airlines' airline", always complementary but never in competition. However, with the tragic loss of Michael Chowdry in January 2001 and the almost simultaneous reversal of its growth, the company entered into a period of serious financial turbulence from which it had not emerged by December 2003. Nothing has enabled it to regain its stability: neither the opening of its own air services – at the risk of entering into direct competition with its airline customers – nor the purchase of Polar Air Cargo, bringing its impressive fleet of 19 B747Fs of all types, nor even the "musical chairs" played by the directors. Atlas finally entered Chapter 11 bankruptcy protection on 13th January 2004.

Gemini Air Cargo came onto the scene like Atlas's twin, born in 1996. Although these two contract carriers are competitors, they are above all complementary to one another. Where Atlas Air only offers units of 100/120 tonnes, Gemini specialises in units of 70/80 tonnes, with a fleet of eight converted DC-10 – 30F aircraft, and four MD-11Fs.

Turnover of Fedex and UPS, year 2000 in billions of US dollars

	FEDEX	UPS
International	4.1	4.2
Domestic	12.5	24.0
Logistics & Other	1.6	1.6
Total revenue	18.2	29.8

Like Fedex or DHL, UPS is looking to diversify its product range – placing the emphasis on its logistics solutions – and to extend its international air network with an eye on "one-stop shopping". Pursuing both domestic development and external growth, since the year 2000 UPS purchased the airline Challenge Air Cargo, flying out to South America from Miami; Fritz Companies, an ocean and airfreight forwarder, and a major "customs broker"; the financial services activities of First International Bancorp; and the network "Mail Boxes etc.".

The fleet of UPS Airlines, the air transport company of UPS, owns 227 aircraft. Its composition is different from that of Fedex: no DC-10F/MD-11s, one of the work horses of Fedex, but DC-8 series 70 aircraft, fitted with new engines, and 70 Boeing B757-200TFs. These two warring brothers have one thing in common: the importance given to the Airbus A300-600F, of which UPS has ordered or taken out options for 90 units! The development of the UPS international air network crossed a decisive point at the end of 2000, with the grant of traffic rights for China. The principal hubs for UPS Airlines are Cologne in Europe, Taipei and Clark (in the Philippines, formerly Clark Air Force Base) in Asia, and Miami and Louisville in the United States.

Based on their power arising from an 80% share of the American domestic market, Fedex and United Parcel Service, each one with its own very different style, are currently the only two integrators of global stature to confront the European

A third significant player has entered the arena: Air Atlanta Icelandic, based in Reykjavik. Offering B747-200Fs – generally owned by lessors – on an ACMI basis, this new contract carrier may add to Atlas Air's difficulties.

A special type of "phantom airline" is the one that does not buy or lease aircraft on its own account and at its own risk but, instead, operates and manages with its crews on its own certificates and licence aircraft owned by other principals. Examples of this mentioned elsewhere included primarily Air Foyle of the UK and a number of other European airlines such as Euralair of Paris, Panair of Madrid and others which operated aircraft owned by TNT for TNT at TNT's risk, and Ryan International Airlines of Wichita USA, which operates various cargo aircraft including B727s and DC-9s for their different owners which include integrators such as UPS and Emery and the United States Postal Service.

2 COMPANY RANKINGS

The 37 airlines which each have traffic exceeding the symbolic hurdle of one billion RTK transported in the year 2000 represented over 90% of world total scheduled traffic. Among these are 13 Asian companies, 10 each from Europe and North America, two from South America and two from the Middle East. Looking at type of activity, they divide into seven cargo airlines and 30 mixed airlines.

Only Fedex Express crossed the threshold of 10 billion RTK. The next four companies have over five billion RTK: Lufthansa Cargo, coming in an extremely creditable second, Korean Air, which occupies a remarkable place in the international field, United Parcel Service, thanks to its domestic traffic, and Singapore Airlines. Air France only misses being in this leading bunch by a hair's breadth.

Lufthansa Cargo AG
Lufthansa converted its cargo division into a 100% subsidiary company on 1st January 1995. Under the courageous and warm-hearted, firm and yet sometimes rather rough-handed management of Wilhelm Althen, followed by the more rounded style of his successor Jean- Peter Jansen, Lufthansa Cargo AG established itself solidly at the top of the international world rankings. To a journalist who asked him about the advantages of making Lufthansa Cargo an independent subsidiary, Wilhelm Althen replied: "My only disappointment is that it took 20 years to persuade my colleagues that we could never succeed as the unloved child of the passenger parent." This statement is no doubt exaggerated, as is often the case with Wilhelm, but was the founding father of the new company.

Among the strengths of Lufthansa Cargo, we should mention:

1. A fleet of 14 MD-11Fs which has proved to be highly efficient economically.
2. A marketing policy launched in 1998, based on the idea of "time definite" or "TD products".
3. The establishment of a new type of working relationship with a limited number of "preferred cargo Agents", within the framework of a "Business Partnership Programme" which was also introduced in 1998.
4. Its leadership of a cargo alliance, restricted to a small number of airlines: Japan Airlines, SAS and Singapore Airlines Cargo.
5. A particular kind of relationship with the "new DHL",

which on the one hand acted as a supplier of capacity on the European network, replacing the B737QC aircraft previously operated by Lufthansa on its own cargo network, and on the other hand had become Lufthansa's leading customer. This relationship presents Lufthansa with a trump card but also creates some problems: one could envisage the establishment of financial links between Deutsche Post and Lufthansa Cargo, or other members of the New Global Cargo alliance, which would lead to the creation of the world's leading transport group. Beginning in 2004, Lufthansa and DHL have signed a five-year commercial agreement to share five MD-11F's capacity on international routes.

Korean Air
This Korean company operated its first cargo flight over the North Pacific, destined for Los Angeles, in 1971, and in October 1973 opened its first cargo service to Europe, bound for Paris, in association with Air France. Thirty years later, it occupies the second place in the international rankings. This exceptional position is a tribute to the enormous economic effort which Korea has made since 1970. It is all the more remarkable because Korean Air is not the only Korean airline: Asiana is placed 14th on the list.

Korean Air Cargo operates a fleet of 16 cargo aircraft, made up of B747Fs and MD-11Fs, which carries almost 80% of its freight traffic. Freight provides 34% of the airline's revenue. The recent opening of a new airport at Inchon–Seoul puts the company in an excellent position to draw maximum benefit from the expanding Chinese market, with feeder services by air or by ship (Sea-Air Solution together with the shipping group Hanjin, known as the Sky Bridge Service). Korean Air is a member of the Sky Team Cargo alliance.

Singapore Airlines Cargo
Created in 1972, at the same time as the city-state, the economic success of which it symbolises, Singapore Airlines did not take delivery of its first cargo aircraft until 1989. Ten years later it was operating a uniform and modern fleet of 10 B747-400Fs, and freight represented a quarter of the company's revenue in the year 2000. The Cargo Division of Singapore Airlines was, like that of Lufthansa, converted into a subsidiary in July 2001.

Air France
To a considerable degree, Air France owes its current position, unique for a French company in the international transportation field, to the remarkable efforts of Jean Rispal, its first Freight Director. The strategy of Air France Cargo was defined by its present Director, Marc Boudier, and was finally established in November 2000. It is based on five key practices:

1. the segmentation of its products, placing particular emphasis on Express and the supply chain;
2. the alliance Sky Team Cargo;
3. partnerships with freight forwarders;
4. fleet modernisation, with partial replacement of ageing B747-200Fs by B747-400ERFs on long-haul sectors;
5. quality of service through IT systems and permanent on-ground process adjustments.

RANKING OF AIRLINES WITH FREIGHT TRAFFIC EXCEEDING I BILLION RTK IN 2000
Scheduled Traffic (in million RTK)

INTERNATIONAL			DOMESTIC			TOTAL TRAFFIC		
Rank	Airline	Traffic	Rank	Airline	Traffic	Rank	Airline	Traffic
1	Lufthansa	7,096	1	Fedex	6,353	1	Fedex	10,809
2	Korean A.L.	6,357	2	UPS	4,144	2	Lufthansa	7,115
3	Singapore A.L.	6,020	3	Emery	1,300	3	Korean	6,461
4	Air France	4,968	4	United A.L.	917	4	UPS	6,318
5	British Airways	4,555	5	NorthWest A.L.	825	5	Air France	6,020
6	Fedex	4,656	6	Kitty Hawk	761	6	Singapore A.W.	4,980
7	Japan A.L.	4,321	7	DHL A.W.	672	7	Japan	4,607
8	China A.L.	4,133	8	American A.L.	614	8	British Airways	4,564
9	Cathay Pacific	4,108	9	Delta A.L.	570	9	China	4,133
10	KLM	3,964	10	China Southern	422	10	Cathay Pacific	4,108
11	Eva Air	3,558	11	ATI/BAX	422	11	KLM	3,964
12	Cargolux	3,523	12	All Nippon	403	12	United	3,694
13	United A.L.	2,777	13	Japan A.L.	286	13	Eva Air	3,558
14	Asiana	2,598	14	Varig	236	14	Cargolux	3,523
15	North West A.L.	2,409	15	Air Canada	195	15	Northwest	3,234
16	Martinair	2,355	16	Tradewinds	171	16	American	2,780
17	Nippon Cargo	2,186	17	China Eastern	169	17	Asiana	2,598
18	UPS	2,174	18	Lynden	168	18	Martinair	2,355
19	American A.L.	2,166	19	Air China	165	19	Nippon Cargo	2,186
20	Swissair	1,930	20	Japan A.L.	140	20	Delta	2,095
21	Malayasia	1,812	21	China S.W.	132	21	Swissair	1,932
22	Alitalia	1,734	22	Shanghai A.L.	109	22	Malaysia	1,868
23	Thai Airways	1,678	23	Korean	104	23	Alitalia	1,743
24	Polar	1,659	24	Southwest A.L	101	24	Thai Airways	1,713
25	Qantas	1,531	25	Alaska	98	25	Qantas	1,619
26	Delta A.L.	1,525	26	VASP	76	26	Air China	1,618
27	Air China	1,453	27	TWA	69	27	Polar	1,603
28	Emirates	1,288	28	Transbrazil	69	28	Emery	1,580
29	Lan Chile	1,260	29	US Airways	68	29	Al Nippon	1,523
30	All Nippon	1,121	30	Indian A.L.	67	30	Lan Chile	1,307
31	Air Canada	1,074	31	Hainan A.L.	67	31	Emirates	1,288
32	Virgin	1,016	32	Garuda	63	32	Air Canada	1,269
33	Varig	976	33	Xiamen A.L.	63	33	DHL/EAT	1,250
34	Continental	959	34	China N.W.	62	34	Varig	1,211
35	Saudi Arabia	918	35	China N.	62	35	Continental	1,079
							Virgin	1,016
							Saudi Arabia	1,000

3 ISSUES FACING THE AIRLINES

We shall limit ourselves to considering four major questions, which all point to a dual objective: the profitability of the freight activity and of cargo flights in particular, and the defence of market share against competition from integrators and postal conglomerates.

Question one: what is the right fleet policy?
This is the overriding priority in this series of questions. It breaks down into three stages, which can only be achieved if each stage is accomplished in turn.

• I Cargo or no cargo?
Up to the end of the 1970s, most airlines of any importance operated cargo aircraft. Then the first oil crisis came, and many American and European airlines halted their cargo-only activities. Since the beginning of the 1990s, we have witnessed a return to favour for cargo flights, resulting from the good

health of the market, and the reduction of belly capacity due to the increase in passenger load factors. So all-cargo operations are once again in fashion. Once the decision to operate cargo flights is taken, what is the next step?

• 2 Owning freighter aircraft or ACMI contracts?
Chartering has always been a way of dealing with temporary situations. However, since 1992/93 a new practice has been emerging: the outsourcing by the airlines of all or part of their cargo network through long-term, "wet leasing contracts". This solution has the major advantage of minimising the investment of the lessee. Admittedly, he must bear the profit margin of the wet lessor, in addition to an annual depreciation rate, and in practice this solution also brings the negative effect of making the operating programme more rigid. This is why the airlines, when they avail themselves of the charter option, do not normally enter into long-term charter contracts, except for a fraction of their operations.

For the portion of freight operated in-house, there is one final question.

• 3 New cargo aircraft or converted ex-passenger machines?
The basic issues are straightforward: the cargo versions of new aircraft are expensive, their profitability is always finely balanced and the financial resources of the airlines are limited. On the other hand, a number of passenger aircraft, even after a several years in operation, still offer a sufficient number of flying hours to provide economic justification for the relatively limited expense of converting them into cargo versions. If one adds that the range of new cargo aircraft is relatively limited, and that the integrators – the main users – are forced to run profitable operations with a very low number of flying hours per year, then all the conditions are in place to sustain the continuation of the practice of converting of former passenger aircraft into cargo aircraft, which as been the trend of more than the last 10 years.

The conversion market, which is estimated at between 80 and 120 units per year over a period of 20 years, is regarded as being much more reliable, since it can involve an increasing variety of aircraft – B727, B737, B767, B757 (DHL has just signed an agreement with Boeing for converting 34 units), B747-200, and quite recently, B747-400 passenger and Combi versions. Airbus is not lagging behind with conversion programmes for the A300B2/B24, A300-600 and A310-200/300. A new conversion programme was launched during the year 2000 by the consortium ATR for the models ATR 42 and ATR 72: the cargo versions will offer a payload of 5.8 tonnes and 8.2 tonnes and will be introduced by DHL on its African network (Nigeria).

In spite of all their advantages, these converted planes are still second-hand models, even though they may represent an excellent deal. By comparison with a brand-new Boeing 747-400F or an Airbus A300-600F, they have two drawbacks: higher operating costs and lower reliability. But, in order to opt for new aircraft, the airline concerned must have the financial means to do so.

Question two: what should the capacity management policy be?
Like the previous question, this can also be broken down into three stages.

• 1 Optimisation of the load factor
Whatever the mode of transport, the load factor is a more complex concept for freight than for passengers. While a passenger is a single unit to be matched up with an empty seat, a tonne of freight, depending on its volume, size, or other characteristics, may present physical aspects, or pose regulatory problems in totally different ways. These need to be borne in mind when making capacity reservations, whether by telephone fax or e-mail.

For freight as for passengers, carriers are confronted with the consequences of "no-shows" and the effects of provisional bookings. The search for an optimum use of capacity always involves a systematic practice of over-booking. Hence, the first stage in managing the supply consists of booking reliability. This process can take different forms: simply making continual follow-ups, the application of downward correction factors to reservations made by customers known not to honour their commitments, or financial penalties in case large consignments fail to be delivered.

The commercial practice of Blocked Space Agreements, or BSA, has been in continuous development over several years. The customer, generally a freight forwarder, pays for a guaranteed capacity on a predetermined route, for a given period, and takes the risk of filling the capacity. This takes care of the double concern of ensuring the reliability of bookings – at a negotiated price – for the airline, and securing capacity, in exchange for the transfer of risk, for the freight agent.

• 2 Yield management
The maximisation of global income is to an equal extent a function of the rate levels applied to different consignments and of the load factor. This has given rise to the idea of managing freight capacity using forecasting methods inspired by those which have been applied to passenger flights for a good many years. Arriving later on the scene, managers of freight flights do not yet have such a sophisticated battery of computerised tools as their colleagues, but several airlines, led by American Airlines and Air France, have made considerable progress in this field. Only by the application of these techniques of yield and revenue management, which require the real-time processing of a considerable mass of information, can airlines gain the few percent of additional income that can make the difference between profit and loss.

The segmentation of the capacity offered is the first part of the process. Initially, part of the total capacity is allocated to scheduled traffic, which has been the subject of annual or bi-annual rate/capacity negotiations, and to high margin traffic (express, mail). The new methods for optimising yields would then be applied to the proportion of the capacity that has not been otherwise allocated (generally between 40 and 60%).

It is on this second portion, even more than on the first, that the management process is carried out, to optimise revenue rather than load factor. To this end, it is necessary to "anticipate the demand from the customers, rate category by rate category, flight by flight, in order to ensure that at any particular moment the capacity utilisation of the plane has been achieved under the best rate conditions, giving preference to the demand providing the best revenue, in terms of global revenue and not merely unit revenue. It is therefore a process of calculated risk assessment, which is reiterated, right up to the flight departure. This means that revenue becomes the primary criterion in accepting freight consignments, whereas capacity management becomes a question of forecasting in order to reserve space for the consignments with the highest yield expected on the flight." (Quotation from Air France Cargo internal document: "*Les clés du yield management fret*" – "Keys to airfreight yield management".)

However, and this is fundamental, revenue management can only properly bear fruit if it is integrated into the whole decision chain throughout the freight activity. There must be a constant search for consistency between revenue management and the establishment of the general level of the supply, the fixing of the sales targets and the content of the marketing strategy. Revenue management is a strict discipline that is as demanding on the airline as on the customer.

• 3 Cost and revenue management, or profit optimisation
The ultimate aim is to maximise the operating margin. This requires, in addition to a good command of the techniques of revenue management, a detailed knowledge of unit costs according to the nature of the products and services. It should be based on a reliable analytical accounting system, available in very few airlines. According to this approach, it is not at all evident that certain so-called "value added" products will automatically be the most profitable.

Whatever the degree of sophistication in the techniques used, there is still one essential question to answer: what should be given priority, management for the short term or management for the long term? The answer would appear to be obvious, although its application requires a considerable amount of self-control: "to maintain goodwill and build relationships, a company should take the long term perspective." [3]

Question three: which marketing policy?
This question has replaced the question from the 1990s: "What should be the strategy for express products?" It is a sign that traditional airlines, realising that they could not seriously challenge the integrators on their own territory, have widened their response to cover the totality of the market, by attempting to provide their customers with a complete range of products and services. Market segmentation, which forms the basis for a segmentation of the capacity offered, is the major feature of current freight marketing policies.

Not all airlines have achieved the same degree of awareness. Some companies are continuing to practice a rather rudimentary form of "global marketing", contenting themselves with combining good service quality with competitive rates. The financial results of such airlines – all-cargo and Asian carriers– prove that this conservative policy has by no means lost all its merits. However, to an increasing extent, airlines are practising "segmented marketing" in an attempt to define a complete range of services covering all the needs of the air transportation market. This is certainly the case for the integrators (such as Fedex Express, with its products "Fedex International Priority", "Fedex International First" and "Fedex International Priority Freight") as well as for traditional airlines, amongst whom one can recognise two types of approach, that practised by Lufthansa and that by Air France.

In 1998 Lufthansa, launched and then continued to add to, a complete range of services (segmentation according to delivery times) and products (segmentation according to the characteristics of the goods: live animals, high value consignments, clothes on hangers, dangerous materials etc.) based on the idea of "time definite" (TD) or "guaranteed" delivery. From a logical viewpoint, there is no longer any reason to supply the customer with a booking confirmation showing a flight number, since the airline commits to a date/precise hand-over time for the goods. Lufthansa proposed three levels of service, corresponding to three transit times, with, naturally, three rate levels. This demonstrates a perfect coherence between marketing, pricing and revenue management: "The time definite services td.Pro, td.X and td.Flash guarantee precisely defined time frames beginning with the latest acceptance time (LAT) at the departure point and ending with the time of availability (TOA) at the destination point." The range of "products" (time-definite service packages) is constructed according to the same pattern: Cool/td, Fresh/td, Safe/td, Care/td, etc.

Companies such as KLM (with Select 100, 300 and 700) and Japan Airlines (with J Speed, J Freight, J Special) have adopted similar tactics.

Air France launched its new marketing policies two years after Lufthansa, in January 2000. It was at once more traditional and more innovative. More traditional, apparently, because it gave preference to the practice of making bookings for a specific flight/date. More innovative, because it was more complete. The Air France range was built up around four complementary offers known as Equation (express services), Variation (specific offers for specific goods: livestock, perishables, artworks, "outsize" etc), Dimension (based on an offer suitable for freight forwarders who require a reliable airport-to-airport service for their consolidators), and finally Cohesion or "the Tripartite Integration Agreement". This is the truly original item in the Air France array.

Cohesion is an integrated service, designed to fulfil the needs of companies who work on "just in time" logistics chains, and who are regular airfreight customers in conjunction with their freight forwarders, without limitations of tonnage or volume. This service is embodied in a written tripartite contract between the customer, the forwarder and the airline, specifying the reciprocal undertakings of each party. It covers the totality of the transport chain and both assumes and implies a new kind of partnership between the three parties. Air France commits to capacities and delivery times, a stable rate level and individualised tracking of the consignments 24 hours a day with a provision for giving out warnings if things go wrong; the customer commits himself to quantified flows of goods in terms of tonnages and volumes, while the freight agent commits to providing a particular content and quality of service. Cohesion is probably the most competitive response of a traditional airline to the challenge from the integrators, at the same time paying homage to their influence. It is also an example of tripartite customer relationship management in the field of services.

Question four: what e-business policy?
Because, in the customer's mind, the transfer of information is as important as the physical movement of his goods, information technology has become the nervous system for transport and logistics operations. What are the main requirements from the market? Three stand out:

• Tracing and tracking consignments along the total length of the transport chain from door-to-door;

• Access to capacity through e-booking;
• Systematic assessment of quality standard compliance by developing a benchmark transport plan and introducing a warning system.

E-booking is an urgent requirement from freight agents in order to reduce the time spent in communicating by telephone and fax. This is all the more important, since in contrast to passenger operations, they have almost nothing to fear from the practice of direct "on-line booking" between customers and airlines. Since the end of 2000 there have existed platforms for electronic booking or "virtual market places" within the airfreight industry. The earliest and the largest is GF – X (Global Freight Exchange). Amongst the shareholders are Air France, American Airlines, British Airways, Lufthansa Cargo and Swiss Cargo, along with Deutsche Post and the forwarders Panalpina. The participating companies recently decided to intensify their efforts to promote this market place by providing access for the whole of their products to freight agents using them. The purpose is to speed up the expansion of electronic trading in the field of airfreight because of the considerable advantages it brings for all concerned – both airlines and freight agents – in terms of speed and costs.

Air Charter Exchange, an electronic market place for the air cargo charter market was founded by the air charter broker David Burnett in 2000. It is based on a platform built by SITA to enable major freight airlines and agents to provide and match up their respective availability and requirements.

Over and above these advantages, information technology can prove to be a very effective means for promoting the development of "customer loyalty" or even that of "customer dependency" (at least to a certain extent). The best example is the Powership Programme or the Fedex Ship Manager Programme from Federal Express. Over 70% of traffic volume is handled by means of electronic equipment installed free of charge by the integrator on the premises of his major customers (electronic weighing scale, micro computer with modem, bar code scanner and a laser printer). Naturally, it is the customer himself who operates the system. He is assured of the quality of service, but he is also "bound to the company." [4]

4 STRATEGIC PERSPECTIVES

Alliances and their role

One thing is clear: alliances between airlines were not founded to satisfy requirements of the freight sector, but they do present opportunities to the managers in charge of freight!

Out of all the alliances which either exist or in the making, either wilting or blooming, at least two seem destined for a future in freight: Star Alliance and Sky Team.

Apart from its seniority and its good global coverage, Star Alliance is strengthened by its two freight heavyweights: Lufthansa Cargo and Singapore Airlines. It carries 21% of world international traffic. As there are airlines in this alliance for whom freight is not an overriding concern, within the main group a kind of "Star Alliance Cargo" has formed, limited to three companies: Lufthansa, Singapore Airlines, Scandinavian Airlines. Known as New Global Cargo, discussions started in April 2000 and it was created in October 2001. It proposes to unify the cargo

The pallet sorting building at the Air France cargo terminal, Roissy-Charles de Gaulle. The roof is made of metal beams covered with fabric.
Air France

networks, harmonise data processing systems (as yet unconfirmed whether simple interfaces or single system) and to establish common marketing, sales and freight handling on the ground. The process kicked-off at the end of 2001 with the launch of harmonised express products under the brand "WOW".

The three founder companies of New Global Cargo have one feature in common: they are all autonomous, wholly owned subsidiaries of their parent companies. Indeed, after the formation of Lufthansa Cargo AG, SAS Cargo was created on 1st June 2001 and SIA Cargo a month later on 1st July. Although the formation of independent freight subsidiaries is not a sine qua non for the success of a cargo alliance, one must admit it brings about a certain flexibility of movement, and opens the way to numerous possible developments: equity swaps, mergers, the creation of holding companies, or reciprocal shareholdings in freight agents and/or logistics companies. However, Japan Airlines, which is still only thinking about creating a subsidiary for its cargo activities, entered the WOW alliance mid-2002.

A further and very symbolic step was made in 2003, leading towards a degree of integration, the boundaries of which still have to be defined: the painting of the first aircraft of Lufthansa Cargo in the livery of WOW.

Sky Team also has two cargo heavyweights: Korean Air and Air France, alongside Delta, Aeromexico, CSA and Alitalia. The alliance's cargo arm, called Sky Team Cargo, was launched in September 2000 "to give shippers open access to a global network, to offer them a range of harmonised products and quality standards for sales and service, to ensure perfect co-ordination of shipments and deliveries to all Sky Team destinations, thanks to an integrated information system." Unlike New Global Cargo, which is limited to four carriers, Sky Team Cargo includes all the airlines in the Sky Team Alliance. This approach is more consistent with the spirit of a true

351

alliance and covers a larger area, but is no doubt more difficult to operate, owing to the number of members and the differences between them. Until now, this inconvenience does not appear to have been too problematical; it has even become a source of strength. Sky Team Cargo has made progress in a number of areas: definition of product range (the Air France range has been adopted by the alliance), common policies in the area of ground operations (idea of the "one roof policy"), intelligence technology (co-ordination and interfaces between existing systems) and sales (concept of a "single point of contact"). The most spectacular advance has been in the United States with the creation of a joint sales and marketing company for the international airfreight services of alliance members. This joint venture, which recently received anti-trust immunity, is a critical step, since it emphasises the name Sky Team Cargo over the separate identities of the members, even if at this stage, each one is operating under its own name.

Naturally, the take over of KLM – a prestigious freight carrier – by Air France, announced on 30th September 2003, will strengthen Sky Team Cargo considerably, and will open up new vistas, as long as a suitable balance can be achieved between integrating the systems and equipment, and respecting the individual personalities of both airlines.

But whether it is WOW, Sky Team Cargo or some other alliance, we are only at the beginning. All bets are still open regarding the future scope and intensity of cargo alliances.

The regulatory framework
On the whole, the regulatory framework within which air transportation continues to evolve, is still that established by the Chicago Convention of 1947, which, it will be recalled, set up the principle of "orderly (ie regulated) growth". This regulatory framework certainly did not prevent the explosive expansion of air transport, but it no longer fully corresponds to the needs of the present-day world, especially as cargo flights have always benefited from more flexible practices and arrangements. In particular, criticisms have been levelled at the regulation of traffic rights in the context of bilateral agreements, at the "national ownership rules", which in most countries limit foreign participation in the capital of domestic airlines, and at the obstacles to "wet leasing" of aircraft (with crew).

The wave of liberalisation has only affected air transportation, whether cargo or passenger, in three well defined sectors: in the United States (Air Cargo Act of 1977 and Air Deregulation Act of 1978); in Europe (European Air Liberalisation Packages of 1988, 1990 and 1993), and in relations between the United States and other countries ("open sky" air agreements). This is why a number of public and private organisations have produced studies on, or are campaigning for, the general liberalisation of air transportation. The question is no longer "whether" to liberalise but "how" and at what pace, in order to build up the global cargo network best suited to the needs of the market.

• ICAO devoted a conference in March 2003 to the theme of liberalisation. It is logical that ICAO remains convinced that air transportation can be made more flexible within the context of the bilateral system, by liberalising the traditional "nationality clauses".
• The Directorate for Science, Technology and Industry of the OECD has, since 1997, been producing a number of works "on

the liberalisation of air cargo transportation" and held various seminars on the subject in 2000 and 2002. "Convinced of the need for regulatory reform", the Secretariat of the OECD proposed two approaches: one, in the form of a "Protocol regarding bilateral agreements" in force, and the other, which is more ambitious, in the form of a "Multilateral agreement for the liberalisation of airfreight services".

• The European Commission in Brussels, on 5th June 2003, received a mandate from the Ministers of Transport to negotiate with the United States regarding a multilateral air agreement leading to a single deregulated air space over the USA/Europe, leading towards a "Trans-Atlantic Common Aviation Area".

Alongside these public organisations, two private bodies are militating for the deregulation of airfreight throughout the world: the ICC and TIACA.

• The International Chamber of Commerce – ICC – wrote in a statement published in the year 2000: "The ICC is in favour of a freer exchange of air services throughout the world... There are many paths to liberalisation. Regional approaches, for example, can be pursued in parallel with further bilateral reforms or in conjunction with lead sectors such as cargo".

• The International Air Cargo Association (TIACA), originated in 1960 as a Committee of the Society of Automotive Engineers (SAA) of the USA for the purpose of organising a biennial air cargo conference and exhibition, the International Air Cargo Forum, the first of which was held in Atlanta, Georgia in 1962.

After 1990 TIACA separated from SAE and, once independent, was registered first in Luxembourg and then in the Cayman Islands but with its General Secreteriat and administration located in Miami, Florida where in 2003 it was finally registered. TIACA "is the only inter-professional and inter-disciplinary organisation representing all sectors in the airfreight industry" – customers, forwarders, carriers, aircraft manufacturers, airports. [5]

In the "TIACA Manifesto", published in 1998, the Association clearly defined its objectives:

"Its major role is to identify issues critical to the industry and its future growth, formulate industry positions which support the advancement of the industry... TIACA must take the lead in communicating those positions to Governmental, regulatory and other policy-making institutions. It should encourage the removal of barriers to trade, especially air cargo..."

In short, it should become "the catalyst for change". There is every sign that traffic and operating rights (ground handling, customs, inter-modality) are indeed a "critical issue", but, while there is consensus on the necessity of a regulatory reform, those concerned are still far from agreeing on its content and speed of implementation, even though it is probable that air cargo will be used as the "lead sector" for a global policy on liberalisation of air transport. [6]

4 THE CARGO AGENTS

The IATA agency programme celebrated its 50th anniversary in 1997. After making some adjustments of limited practical consequence, it is still the cornerstone in the distribution network of the airlines and the cargo agents still remain committed to it. The airlines still hand over the distribution of their services to a common network, consisting of registered agents, who represent all IATA airlines in general but none in particular. In 1995, there were 4,420 registered cargo agents in the world. [1]

Whether they are called cargo agents, or organisateurs de transport, Spediteure, freight forwarders or middle men, cargo agents have never occupied such a decisive position in determining the choice of transport. And never have they represented such a high proportion of the freight revenues of the airlines: approximately 90%. [2]

1 THE STATUS OF REGISTERED AGENTS: PERMANENCE AND EVOLUTION

The enduring nature of the network of registered agents bears witness to its solidity as an institution. While holding on to essentials, IATA has, with some skill, succeeded in developing the regulation of the agencies so as to adapt to regional peculiarities and to stay in line with liberalisation changes.

The first danger signals naturally came from the United States, where in 1978, the CAB disapproved of the principle of fixed commission rates (at 5%) paid by IATA airlines to their registered agents, thus opening the door to a system of free negotiation. Some years later, the cancellation of the anti-trust immunity regarding the status of agencies led to the disappearance of the Agency Programme in the United States. However, in 1984, the airlines replaced it with an organisation which was legally independent of IATA – the Cargo Network System or CNS – that establishes and updates the list of air cargo agents who are endorsed "according to variable criteria depending on the airlines". In the absence of any collective agreement and selection criteria for approval, the number of air cargo agents in the United States is impressive: 1,242 in 1985, 1,377 in 1995, and 1,393 in 2000.

The revision of the Agency Programme was undertaken at the end of 1980s in association with the agents themselves, through the intermediary of FIATA's Air Freight Institute, and led to the adoption in 1990 of a collection of new resolutions (Nos 801,803 and 805) which entered into force in 1991. The content of resolution 805, which is reserved to member countries of the European Union, is particularly interesting.

It responds to the requirements from the Brussels Commission which insisted on three conditions before providing an exemption to the terms of the Treaty of Rome regarding competition:

1. Elimination of fixed commission rates
   Competition between carriers extends to the remuneration of Registered Agents. This condition, which reflects a real break in ideology, did not in fact trigger a "commission war", which was hoped for by some and feared by others.

2. Relaxation of conditions for registration
   Registration is retained. This point is essential in the eyes of airlines as well as of the agents. Although liberalised, access to the profession remains subject to several criteria:

   - operational: the presence of two qualified persons who have completed professional training courses, at each location which is entitled to hand over to airlines freight "ready for carriage". This fundamental concept is preserved;

   - financial: since other conditions had been relaxed, the examination of the financial position of the registration candidate takes on a particular importance;

   - commercial: the applicant should operate in the country under review at least one office for the purpose of promoting or selling international airfreight services. On the other hand, the concept of "agent productivity", which had been introduced in order to question the registration of agents whose productivity was judged to be inadequate, was removed;

   - ethical: the applicant must not have rendered himself guilty of any "voluntary violation" of the financial regulations in force.

It appears that the application of this regulation, which was intended to ease the conditions for access, has indeed resulted in a moderate acceleration in the increase of the number of registered agents.

Growth in the number of registered agents

	1985	1990	1995	2000
Germany	124	157	191	215
France	145	158	177	198
Italy	190	201	211	264
United Kingdom	190	210	225	234

3. The institution of an arbitration procedure
    Any candidate or registered agent who considers that he has been harmed by a decision of the IATA Agency Administration can henceforth benefit from an arbitration procedure, if he so wishes.

Such were the modifications, which allowed the Agency Programme to be adapted to the new competition rules. Beyond these amendments, various people have, since the end of the 1980s, spoken out in favour of a far-reaching reform in the status of registered agents, incorporating the changes which have occurred since the last reform in 1968. As a sign of our modern times, it rapidly became apparent that this new status could only be the culmination of a common and joint action between the airlines and the agents. It became the subject for the "IATA-FIATA Consultative Council" for many a long year.

After having considered the most radical of reforms, all parties ended up by recognising the merits of the existing institutional and relationship framework, as defined in the "IATA Cargo Agency Programme" and the "Cargo Accounts Settlement System" (CASS).

In order to reinforce what had already had been achieved, while profoundly transforming its underlying philosophy, they retained the powerful idea of the Airfreight Partnership, "a concept of a shared industry distribution system, that, whilst maintaining the option of a Cargo Agency Programme, introduces the feature of an alliance between carriers and airfreight forwarders acting as a team of equals." [3]

The European Air Cargo Programme, introduced in 2003, represents the first application of this new framework to the Airfreight Partnership. It is an "Air Cargo Distribution System designed jointly by IATA and FIATA". It includes a "joint council" responsible for the proper functioning of the EACP. The chief novelty in this agreement is the introduction of the concept of an airfreight forwarder alongside the traditional role of the agent. The "agent represents the carrier"; "...acts on behalf of the carrier..."; "issues airway bills with the shippers name".

By contrast, the airfreight forwarder "issues airway bills on a principal to principal basis" and the two parties, the carrier and the airfreight forwarder, "recognise that they are jointly to provide an integrated service to the shipper, and the forwarder acts as if it were a customer of the carrier". This agreement marks an important stage in the relationship between carriers and intermediaries. It is a step in the right direction, even if it still falls short of a declaration of intent to provide a true "integrated service".

2 THE CASS: A NEW TYPE OF RELATIONSHIP BETWEEN AIRLINES AND AGENTS

The CASS – Cargo Accounts Settlement System – is a centralised system for the settlement of freight accounts operating within the frame work of IATA. This system was designed "to simplify the reporting systems for sales accounting, as well as the settlement of amounts due to the airlines, reducing costs by the central utilisation of data processing technology". [4]

In practice, the registered agents take receipt of the amounts due from the senders and then transfer them to the airlines. Some airlines require that the agents submit a sales report. Others send their own invoices to their agents. A very high number of transfers of funds are caused by these procedures, since every airline works with several agents and each agent works with several airlines. This is the origin of the idea for simplifying the total of these administrative and accounting activities by centralising all the financial dealings between the airlines and their agents via a single "Settlement Office". The Settlement Office carries out all the operations on the basis of copies of the airway bills presented by the agents or the airlines. The outcome of this is that the agent pays to the Office

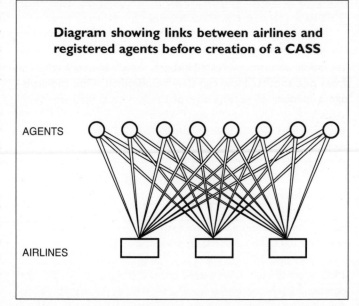

Diagram showing links between airlines and registered agents before creation of a CASS

AGENTS

AIRLINES

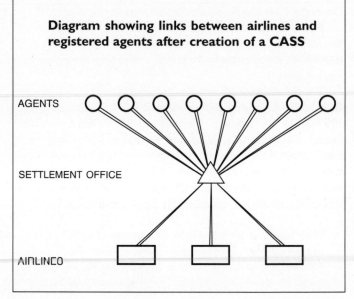

Diagram showing links between airlines and registered agents after creation of a CASS

AGENTS

SETTLEMENT OFFICE

AIRLINES

an amount corresponding to the sums he owes to the whole group of airlines with which he has worked, while the Office pays to each company in a single payment, an amount representing the totality of the sums due to them from all the registered agents during the period concerned. This results in a tremendous simplification of the financial dealings between the agents and companies.

The first CASS was launched in Japan in 1974 as a pilot project. Systems for the centralised settlement of freight accounts were then introduced in Australia, Canada, the United States, in most of the countries of Europe, and in other markets (Argentina, South Africa, Philippines, etc). In the year 2000 34 countries each had a CASS, representing 64% of global invoice value. It is probable that all the freight markets will be covered by a CASS within a few years, due to the advantages of the system, in spite of some its restrictions.

Beyond the simplification which it brings, the application of a centralised settlement system introduces a new type of relationship between agents and companies, which has lost its former financial preoccupations (payment delays) and is now entirely concentrated on commercial matters.
The CASS is a great success story for IATA.

3 TYPES OF AIR CARGO AGENTS

Air cargo agents constitute a world which is in perpetual evolution, consisting of organisations, which are very different from one another. How can they be classified? One can envisage a number of criteria: age of the business, legal or capital structure, or even turnover, nationality, fields of activity or exclusiveness in dealing with airfreight. Space precludes us from examining each criterion individually but we can look at two of them: age of the business and field of activity.

Age of the business
Agents dealing solely with air transport are necessarily quite young companies, created after the Second World War. There was one exception, Air Express International, which for many years was one of the leaders in airfreight. Founded in Miami in 1935, it could compliment itself on having been one of the first companies to send goods via Pan American Airways to South America, and via the Zeppelin Luft Reederei across the North Atlantic, but AEI has now left the scene, taken over by Deutsche Post and absorbed into Danzas in the year 2000.

However, air cargo agents are more usually specialised departments or divisions of multi-modal freight forwarders, in land or sea transport, and these were sometimes founded over a century ago.

The Swiss freight forwarders enjoy considerable longevity: Goth Logistik Services AG celebrated its 125th anniversary in 1995, Jacky Maeder was founded on 30th December 1882 (under the name of J. Wild) and Panalpina, which later took over J. Maeder, can trace its origins back to 1895, with the foundation of the company Hans im Obersteg, situated in Basel (as were Goth and Jacky Maeder). The undisputed prize should go to Danzas, which has described its origins as follows:

"The history of Danzas begins at Waterloo (in 1815). This was when one Marie Mathieu Nicolas Louis Danzas, a French sub-lieutenant in the 13th Light Cavalry Regiment, following his de-mobilisation, took up employment with Michel

L'Evêque, Etablissement de Commission et d'Exploitation, in Saint-Louis" (just across from Basel)." [5]

Although Danzas could trace its history back to Waterloo, the story ended sadly in 2003. After it had been purchased by Deutsche Post in December 1998 and taken over Air Express International in 2000, Danzas lost its identity within DHL, which had become wholly owned by Deutsche Post World Net.

In Germany, Kühne & Nagel celebrated its centenary in 1990: it was on 1st July 1890 that August Kühne and Friedrich Nagel founded a little office in the Hanseatic town of Bremen. In Britain the leading cargo agent, MSAS Cargo International, belonged to the Ocean Group until the first half of 2000. The origins of the latter go back to the establishment in 1865 of the shipping company Blue Funnel Line. In Scandinavia the group Bilspedition markets airfreight under the trade mark "Wilson", the name of a British business man, J. W. Wilson, who in Göteborg in 1843 founded a trading company, which Bilspedition purchased in 1983.

Then there is the Japanese Nippon Express, a world beater in all categories, commonly known as "Nittsu". It can trace its origins to companies transporting express mail which were part of the state-run company Riki-un Moto Kaisha at the beginning of the Meiji era in 1872.

France does not need to play second fiddle – far from it. The Bolloré Group currently incorporates two of France's most venerable freight agencies: SCAC, founded on 17th November 1885, which is the main member of the Transport Commission of the SDV Group (SCAC Delmas Vieljeux), and Mory. The name of Mory disappeared from the list of IATA registered agents when the company's air transport branch was absorbed by Saga Air Transport, which itself had been controlled by the Bolloré Group since 1997. The activities of the Mory Company go back to the first years of the 19th century, when Nicolas Toussaint Mory, established at Calais, became a "Commissioner of the London Post Office for the reception and despatch of newspapers". [6] After such a succession of prestigious names, the French company André Chenue, an IATA Registered Agent specialising in the transport and packing of works of art, seems rather insignificant. However, this company can proudly claim to be the most venerable of all the registered agencies in the world. Its origins go back to the second half of the 18th century. It was established in the Rue des Petits Champs in Paris, and at that time, under the same name, held the title of "Layetier – Emballeur de le Maison du Roi" (box-maker and packager to the King).

Beside these respectable enterprises, there are a lot of energetic young companies! Air transit does indeed have the advantage of not requiring a large start-up investment, providing one knows how to limit one's ambitions and work 25 hours per day. This is why one regularly sees all sorts of "cowboys" – full of energy and enthusiasm, but whose financial stability leaves something to be desired. "They are a thorn in the flesh for the big cargo agencies. These companies resent that, after having been trained by them, the reprobates left them, taking the customer list." [7] It is encouraging to find that some of them, after a merciless natural selection process, have managed to assert themselves and climb to top positions. This was the case with Bernard Toudic, who created TTA – Tous Transports Aériens – in 1965, and turned it into one of the finest French companies in airfreight forwarding, now belonging to the SDV Group. A more

Reproduction of etching, "Box maker and packer to the Royal Household".

recent example is Peter J. Rose, who founded Expeditors International in Seattle in 1981. After opening with seven employees and six offices (three in the United States and three in Taiwan), Expeditors International, some 20 years later, has reached 10th place in the world rankings for cargo agents — some performance!

Field of activity
This is the real criterion by which air cargo agents should be classified. They can be divided into six categories:

• 1 Large multinational agents
These fulfil three conditions: an establishment in each of the main markets on all five continents, a turnover in excess of $500 million (even if there is some degree of arbitrariness in fixing such a cut-off point), and finally, and this is the major condition for belonging to this group, the achievement of a significant proportion of their activities (ideally over 50%) outside their national markets.

There are less than a dozen businesses in this category ; these include:

- Swiss-German air cargo agents Danzas (absorbed into DHL in 2003) and Kühne & Nagel whose boss Klaus Michael Kühne is one of the great personalities in this profession.
- German cargo agent, Schenker, which was taken over in 2002 by Deutsche Bundesbahn.
- British cargo agent, Excel, which was formed in the first half of 2000 out of a merger between Ocean Group and National Freight Consortium (its two brands, MSAS and Exel Logistics, gave rise to Exel, which is very strongly represented in Asia).
- the Swiss company, Panalpina, which is sufficiently unusual for us to consider again later.

- American cargo agents Bax Global (whose origins go back to 1972 when Burlington Northern Railroad decided to get involved in airfreight), EGL Eagle Global Logistics (the dynamic Texan logistics service provider which took over the Circle International Group at the end of 2000), Emery (it has been a leading company but underwent a number of trials and tribulations in 2001, when it stopped operating its domestic air network, only to be taken over by the new organisation Menlo World-wide) and, finally, Expeditors.
- Japanese companies, Nippon Express and Kintetsu (an offspring of Japanese Railways). These two Japanese firms have difficulty in fulfilling the third condition, since they only achieve 30% and 36% respectively of their air transport activities outside Japan.

• 2 Medium-sized multinationals and the largest national cargo agents.
In terms of revenue, these are in the range of $100–$500 million, with 13 agents, ranking from 13th to 24th position, enter this category.

Some of them have international operations nearly as extensive as those of the major multinationals and/or earn most of their revenue in foreign markets. This is the case for US firms Arthur Fritz (now part of UPS), Geologistics, UTI and Airborne, as well as the European companies Hellmann (Germany), SDV -SCAC Delmas Vieljeux (France), ABX (Belgium), and DHL, which is an IATA registered agent in many countries. Others, like Japan's Yusen Hankyu, NNR and Nissin, or Italy's JAS, have high revenues but do not satisfy either of the other two conditions.

• 3 National cargo agents
The companies in this group have revenues of several tens of millions of dollars and their operations are exclusively or primarily in a national market, of which they control a substantial share. Examples are Gebrüder Weiss in Austria, Paloff Eretz Israel, in Israel and Road Air BV in The Netherlands.

• 4 Specialised Cargo Agents
Some cargo agents operate in niche markets. Specialising in one product category or, more rarely, one geographic segment, they are able to supply high-quality services and shield themselves from predators, at least for a time. Cargo carried includes horses (Hypavia), films, newspapers and other media (Aérofret, Higgs), or even perishable goods (fruit, vegetables, flowers etc). The forwarding of such products is handled by specialised companies in the producer countries (Israel, Norway, Australia, South Africa), or by separate departments of the major cargo agents (Danzas, KN, SDV, Hellman etc).

•5 The Integrated Forwarders
There are integrated forwarders, just as there are integrated carriers. By choice or by necessity, they have decided to provide themselves, in varying ways, all or part of the transport capacity they need.

In the United States, due to the withdrawal of the "majors" from cargo transport, and the increase in power of Federal Express during the 1970s, a number of forwarders were forced to operate their own domestic cargo services in order to keep their customers. They created their own "in-house" airlines so as to offer express services (Airborne) and a range of time-definite, or TD, services, designed for industrial products, without restrictions of weight or volume. These companies operate interlinked private networks on the hub and spoke principle, based on the main platforms for connecting flights: Toledo for Bax Global, Wilmington for Airborne, Dayton for Emery.

With the fall-off in domestic traffic from autumn 2000, these in-house airlines, generally operated with ageing aircraft, became a source of technical problems and financial worries: Bax Global had to trim its sails, Emery was called upon by the FAA to end its in-house service, while Airborne fell into the hands of Deutsche Post AG.

The European and Japanese forwarders who were not confronted with the same problems as their American counterparts have, on the whole, retained the traditional division of labour between airlines and cargo agents. The few contradictions to this principle are of limited significance, with one exception: Panalpina.

How should Panalpina be defined? Is it a sea and airfreight consolidator? An IATA Registered Agent? The "NVOCC [8] of airfreight"? There would some truth in each, but there is no doubt that it is a success story under the inspired leadership of Gerhard Fischer. Panalpina is by far the forwarder which makes greatest usage of charter capacity. Everything started during the first oil crisis, when there was a lack of capacity for Nigeria . In order to overcome this situation Panalpina created a subsidiary, Air Sea Broker, or ASB, which specialised in marine and air charters. One therefore finds ASB was founded for the same compelling reasons as those which created Emery Air Force: the inability of scheduled airlines to provide the necessary capacity.

Since then, Panalpina seems to have been dominated by a dual obsession: a "palletisation culture" and "capacity control". To overcome this permanent preoccupation, Panalpina has developed a formula, which is more flexible and less risky than that of the American "integrated forwarders". It is based on two components:

- a simple reservation of capacity, in the form of annual allocations, or the confirmed purchase of guaranteed capacity in the form of "blocked space agreements", otherwise known as BSA, from "friendly airlines";

- and the chartering of cargo aircraft for exclusive use under annual or multi-year contracts.

Panalpina is not an airline and certainly has no intention of becoming one. [9] There nevertheless exists a Panalpina World Cargo Network based in Luxembourg, arising from its long-standing and close (though today less preferential) ties with the carrier Cargolux. Some routes on this network, especially numerous to the Americas and Africa, have been given colourful names, such as "Dixie Jet" for the daily B747-400F connection between Luxembourg and Huntsville (Alabama), or the "Panalpina Rainbow" for the twice-weekly service to Johannesburg.

This original concept, which combines "all the advantages of a full- freighter forwarder product with the services of a first-class carrier" (and which succeeds in making the competing airlines nervous), has definitely contributed greatly to Panalpina's growth over the past 20 years. It is not, however, without financial risks during periods of recession or shrinking

yields. The integrated forwarder then finds itself in the same position as the cargo carriers and, like them, deplores the competition from the "belly carriers".

• 6 Others

There are thousands of other forwarders, whose revenues range from several thousand to several million dollars. With IATA's liberalisation of the conditions of entry to the profession, the world of airfreight forwarding is more active than ever, with a few major companies jostling for position, and a very large number of small- and medium-sized companies that will not survive, unless they succeed in designing tailor-made products for their customers.

4 MARKET STRUCTURE

Each year IATA publishes the total turnover achieved by registered agents with the member airlines of the Association, country by country and agent by agent. The figures should be taken with a very large pinch of salt. In fact, the turnovers of the registered agents are greatly influenced by the rate levels of the different markets, and exchange rate fluctuations, since all revenues in local currencies are converted into dollars. Also, in certain countries (Japan) the agents persist in declaring theoretical revenues that are very far from the "market rates" actually charged, thereby introducing an important distortion factor working in their favour.

In view of these uncertainties, it is not possible to plot reliable trends. However, in spite of their imperfections, these statistics allow us to make some cautious comparisons between markets.

In the year 2000, the airfreight market was a concentrated market, with the 10 leading multinational agents (out of a total of over 5,000 agents) holding 36% of the international global market. The agents in the first two categories (24 in total) hold over half: 52%.

The market is not merely concentrated – it is becoming increasingly concentrated: the 10 leading agents who held 36% of the market in the year 2000 only had 30% in 1990 and 25% in 1985. That is an increase in share of 50% in 15 years.

At the same time as the market is becoming more concentrated, it is globalising. That is to say, the power of the multinational forwarders is becoming more pronounced, at the expense of domestic forwarders, although certain countries (Israel, Pakistan, Saudi Arabia, Norway or India) are bucking this general trend.

5 THE ISSUES FACING CARGO AGENTS

Internal issues: what type of growth?
"Size is an absolute must. In our industry we are extremely focused on economies of scale. This means that through size, a very large potential for synergies can be exploited." [10] Growth is merely the way to achieve the desired scale effect, with the aim of lowering unit costs and, more important, acquiring the ability to respond to three market trends:

• Outsourcing of transport and distribution activities by companies. The following comes from the Nippon Express brochure "Quick and Powerful" (1999): "In this era of slimmer management structures, many organisations seek to outsource their distribution activities. To meet these needs, Nippon Express uses advanced information technologies to provide links with our business partners and ensure efficient operations through supply chain management."

• Supply Chain Management. The American integrated forwarder BAX Global states plainly: "As a leading provider of international freight transportation and supply chain management BAX Global enables its customers to quickly and flexibly enter new global markets." (The Pittston Company 2000 Annual Report, p. IX.)

• One-Stop Shopping. As Danzas puts it: "The key to success for a provider of logistics services is to cover every one of the needs related to supply chain management by offering a One-Stop Shopping service." (Danzas 2000 . P.3.)

• While everyone agrees on the reasons for growing a company, there are different opinions on the way to do it. Some give priority to internal growth and set up new operations; others expand through mergers and acquisitions. There is no single model. "The Danzas Group (since being taken over by Deutsche Post AG) has grown to become a world leader in logistics solutions through a series of acquisitions made over the course of the past two years." (Danzas 2000 Annual Report, p.3.)

Panalpina is very satisfied with its internal growth, but does not rule out making acquisitions: "Our proven strategy of organic growth will continue to guarantee our corporate success, without precluding the possibility of new acquisitions to complement our palette of services." (Panalpina Annual Report 2000, p.7.)

Expeditors has built its success on a policy of internal growth: "We firmly believe that our controlled organic style of growth really pays off for our customers, vendors and employees… Our industry continues to see major consolidations and acquisitions…this has afforded us tremendous opportunities to secure new offices and personnel." (Expeditors 2000 Annual Report.)

What is the explanation for this favouring of internal growth? Experience shows that many mergers and acquisitions fail because the expected synergies do not materialise or because the revenues of the new entity are less than those of the two companies which merged. Or even worse, because of both.

Nevertheless, there are examples of successful mergers. The French forwarder SDV is a good illustration. A relatively recent name in the international freight forwarding business, SDV appeared on the scene in 1991 when a number of brands and businesses – SCAC, TTA (Tous Transports Aériens), Transcap plus 30 other companies of all sizes – were brought together in the Bolloré group. There were risks in this enterprise: how could brands, which were so solid and so rich in tradition as these, be developed into the new SDV Group without losing their customers or their best employees? By advancing one step at a time, by pooling all the cost centres and by showing infinite caution and respect towards the trademarks. Daniel Delva gave a remarkable demonstration of the superiority of progressive integration over mergers at a forced pace.[11]

External issues
These are more complex, since they involve relationships with customers, integrators and airlines.
• Relationships with customers

Customers vary widely. Firstly, there are major customers, called "key accounts". To simplify their operations, these large companies are reducing the number of suppliers, transport companies and forwarders they use, which is why the idea of "one-stop shopping" is so important. In its most extreme form, it presumes a truly "win–win" partnership between the shipper and the freight forwarder.

There are also the many small and medium-sized enterprises, "SMEs". Though they often go unmentioned, they rely on a particular marketing approach, and are all the more important because their traffic allows the achievement of profit margins which much higher than those of the largest users.

• Relations with integrators
With regard to the integrators, the large multinational cargo agents have passed from a feeling of fear, which was widespread in the 1980s, to an attitude of reasoned acceptance, although in the meantime, the integrators have siphoned off a significant proportion of the small consignments, which form the most natural and most profitable part of their consolidations.

What brought about this change of attitude? It is partly due to the practical experience, that the very standardised products offered by the integrators do not fulfil all the needs of international trade. To achieve this, even the integrators would have to modify and enrich their product range. But then they lose part of their specificity, and then would have to fight with the same weapons as everyone else. However, the main reason for this change of attitude is the in-depth modification of the forwarder's role, which started 20 years ago but which accelerated and became better focused in the last 10 years, is that there is a big difference between the cargo agent of former times and today's integrated logistics services provider, delivering a whole range of value-added services to his customers.

At the same time, the "one-stop shopping" strategy called for co-operation between integrators and forwarders, since neither the latter nor the former can claim to provide the totality of logistics services alone. The head-on clash of the 1990s has given way to a less clear-cut situation, in which the adversaries recognise that they are in some ways complementary, though they have not gone so far as to split roles.

Nevertheless, it would be wrong to imagine that the times of confrontation have passed: the recent purchase of the American forwarder Fritz Companies by UPS, the rapid expansion of UPS Logistics and the emphasis placed by TNT Express World Wide on logistics products and solutions, all give out unmistakable signals. There is no fixed and recognised boundary between integrators on the one side and cargo agents and traditional carriers on the other. But the contest seems more equally balanced, above all since, due to relationships reflecting a new spirit, cargo agents and airlines are managing to develop hitherto undreamed of forms of integration.

• Relations with airlines
In the real sense of the expression, cargo agents are "middlemen" between the shipper and the carrier. Theirs is a delicate and ambiguous position, particularly because in the air transport market they are at the same time agents for the airline and representatives of the shippers.

The difficulties really arise because the agent/airline relationship is in reality a ménage à trois of customer, agent and airline. Each party knows everything about the other, and their

Distribution of world freight turnover in 2000 – all registered agents
(in million $US)

Geographical area	Turnover	Share of total	Chief countries
America excluding United States	738	2.7%	1. Canada 138
			2. Brazil 115
			3. Chile 90
United States	3,157	11.6%	
Europe/Africa/Middle East	6,534	24.1%	1. Germany 1,049
			2. Italy 857
			3. Great Britain 528
			4. France 415
			5. Netherlands 346
			6. Spain 316
			7. Switzerland 210
			8. Ireland 190
Asia/Australasia	16,718	61.6%	1. Japan 6,882
			2. Hong Kong 3,505
			3. Singapore 1,656
			4. Taiwan 936
			5. Thailand 737
			6. India 616
			7. Korea 580
			8. Australia 372
TOTAL	27,147	100%	

Source: IATA

In fact, Emery inspired few rivals, and became an object lesson in the fact that a prestigious cargo agent, with an exceptional reputation, could go to rack and ruin by becoming a carrier. With its back to the wall, and losing over a million dollars per day, it were bought up by Consolidated Freight Ways, a giant American road carrier. The new president of Emery World-wide declared in 1994: "I have no intention of operating international air services as long as the commercial carriers provide me adequate capacity." [12]

In the last few years, despite some minor upheavals, with tempers cooled, the protagonists have been moving towards new forms of partnership, initiated by the largest forwarders:

"The whole of the SDV Group is pursuing a clearly declared policy of partnership towards the airlines", Hubert De Saint-Simon declared in 1997. [13] A short time previously, Klaus Geissler, the Director of the Air Transport Department of Schenker, had expressed himself in the same terms: "Airlines and forwarders depend on each other…forwarders and airlines are building long-term partnerships on a mutual understanding of each other's core competence." [14]

mutual grievances can serve only to feed suspicion.

Cargo agents, particularly the consolidators, take the carriers to task for not treating them as customers, not offering them attractive rate structures, and not always providing a satisfactory quality of service.

The airlines retort that the agents are looking after the interests of shippers to too great an extent, and are contributing to the erosion of revenue units by constantly trying to put airlines in competition with each other.

However, it is the relationship with the "primary" or "end" users (importers or exporters), which forms the main problem area, or at least the most sensitive one. The agents accuse the airlines of maintaining commercial contacts with the commercial accounts. They accuse them of illogically competing against their own distribution network. On the other hand, the airlines cannot accept being deprived of direct contact with their customers, even if it is only a question of better identifying their needs and anticipating market trends. Relations between agents and airlines once again became strained in the period 1975–1980, when some cargo agents decided to operate their own air services, either using their own means of transport, or through chartering.

Emery Airfreight played a major role in this development. In consequence of the abandonment of cargo services by the American airlines, Emery (after setting itself up with a powerful fleet, known as the Emery Air Force, based at Dayton) entered a new phase in 1985 when it began operating transatlantic and trans-Pacific cargo services. Would it catch on?

Airline/forwarder partnerships take on various forms: institutional, commercial or technical. At the institutional – and almost theoretical – level the European Air Cargo Programme introduces the revolutionary concept of the airfreight forwarder. For the first time the cargo agent is no longer considered as the middle man, but as the customer. With regard to commercial partnerships, we have already considered the contribution made by the Cohesion product from Air France, which no doubt goes furthest towards a contractual embodiment for a triangular customer-cargo agent-carrier partnership. With the same general idea, Lufthansa had launched in January 1998 a "Business Partnership Programme" with a number of selected forwarders. On this occasion, a senior manager of the airline noted: "Companies will need to offer integrated systems if they are to survive future competition." Finally, information technology provides an indispensable field of co-operation between agents and airlines, in the interest of a common quality management policy. Paradoxically, it is the integrators who have made the greatest contribution to this promising development. They are the only ones who are in control of and responsible for the whole transport chain, whereas it is normally fragmented between forwarders and traditional carriers, so that the integrators are best placed to offer – and to guarantee – to their customers a high quality of service, supported by the systematic use of cutting-edge technologies. The carriers and forwarders, concerned about the competition from the integrators (which was increasingly spreading outside their original market of small, urgent consignments), came under pressure from their customers and had no other choice than to start out on integrated policies to ensure quality of service. The first initiatives came from the airports (Aéroports de Paris was one of the forerunners) and the shippers' associations. The European Air Shippers' Council did a great deal of work in defining standards and key performance indicators needed to measure and compare the level of quality among the various participants in the transport chain (known as benchmarking).

However, things really got moving in spring 1997 with the creation of an "IATA Interest Group" known as Cargo 2000, made up of a number of the most important cargo agents and carriers – although it remained open to everyone. Cargo 2000 promoted a project on a "quality management system" which would be common to all participants. This design for a common system was based on a master operating plan, which outlined three phases:

1 Carriage airport to airport;
2 Transport door-to-door;
3 Identification of packages.

Phase one is well under way and several participants received certification in 2002/2003. For each consignment, it introduces the concept of a "route map". In case of deviations from this map, the system automatically issues warnings, following the establishment of check points. Phases two and three are less advanced, and their introduction will require considerable effort and investment.

Cargo 2000 is the most promising area of activity, which could lead to a kind of virtual integration between the carriers and the airfreight forwarders.

6 FORWARDERS AND E-COMMERCE

Everybody is gearing up for e-commerce, starting with the integrators. Fedex is providing its customers with software (Fedex Ship API and Fedex Track API) to facilitate "the passage from the virtual world to the real world". Not to be outdone, United Parcel Services has created a specialised subsidiary called "UPS e-Ventures".

The largest airfreight forwarders have also jumped onto the e-commerce band-wagon: "Kühne & Nagel Management Board has established a central e-commerce development unit." (K&N 2000 Annual Report, p. 20). Or, again: "Danzas is determined to become a market leader in the field of e-commerce"; or "E-Commerce will have a great future, even if the initial euphoria has somewhat died down… however, to be successful in e-commerce it is necessary to have logistics processes that meet the requirements of the internet trade." (Stinnes Logistics – parent company of Schenker – 2000 Annual Report, p.16.)

The last phrase is crucial. As an Austrian forwarder recently said: "Without logistics, there is no e-commerce." (JTI, No 25/2001.)

Despite recent disappointments, there is no doubt that e-commerce has all the qualities to be one of the major freight markets in the future. Particularly for those integrators and Postal Authorities who have made the best preparations.

**Air Ecosse
Datapost
Bandeirante.**

THE POST

The Post is bearing the full brunt of competition from companies with express products, and from the repercussions of the liberalisation movement. Its traffic is being threatened and its monopoly challenged at a time when the explosive growth of telecommunications systems and means of data transfer are already causing a slow-down in the exchange of correspondence. The questioning of the traditional position of the Post is expressed in the radical reduction in the growth rates of airmail traffic observed over the course of the last 30 years:

Development of World Airmail Traffic (in billion RTK)

	International Traffic	Domestic Traffic	Total Traffic
1970	1,380	1,706	3,086
1980	1,510	2,170	3,680
1990	2,180	3,200	5,380
1995	2,370	3,230	5,600
2000	2,670	3,380	6,050

Annual Average change in percent

	International Traffic	Domestic Traffic	Total Traffic
1980/70	+0.9	+2.5	+1.8
1990/80	+3.7	+4.0	+3.9
1995/90	+2.0	+0.1	+0.9
2000/95	+2.5	+0.9	+1.6

Source: ICAO

1 INTERNATIONAL AIRMAIL
This represented 44% of world traffic in 2000.

Maximisation of traffic
It will be recalled that the Tokyo Conference of the Universal Postal Union in 1969 had established the principle of "using the aircraft as a normal means for the transport of mail". This declaration had permitted the opening of a new and more relaxed chapter in the history of the relations between the UPU and IATA. They no longer spoke solely about remuneration. They

fixed a common objective as motivation: the maximum utilisation of the airways for the transport of mail. The theme of maximisation was taken up again by the Rio Congress in 1979, during which the Commission for airmail decided "to reconstitute the IATA/UPU Contact Committee", to give it the job of "studying what measures should be taken to promote the institution of systems for maximising the use of air transport".

The question put to the experts from IATA and UPU was easy to formulate: how could all or part of the mail, which had hitherto been sent by surface means, be transferred to air transport? This is the origin of the acronym SAL (Surface Air Lifted) which is universally used to designate this new category of mail carried by air.

It was recognised that SAL Mail could not be the subject of a universal regulation due to the extreme diversity of situations. Instead, bilateral negotiations were permitted between the Post Offices and their national airlines or other carriers. With more or less speed according to the philosophy of the Postal Administrations and the attitude of the airlines, there appeared a second-class airmail, the conditions for which did not fall within the regulatory frame work of the Universal Postal Union. For the user it is characterised by slower transit times but at lower rate levels (reduction or elimination of the air surcharge), and for the carrier by the alignment of his levels of remuneration according to those for airfreight.

The airmail of former times has thus given way to a two-speed system of airmail: one "priority" mail – the true airmail – and one "economy" mail – with deferred delivery. A fear, shared by the Post and the airlines, that part of the priority mail would shift over towards the economy service, which, in fact, had been designed to take over from the former sea mail, led different operators to evolve special handling procedures so as to differentiate clearly between the two products.

Although it might be possible to see a certain internal contradiction between the utilisation of air-mail, and the practice of deferred despatch, it must be admitted that the development of the SAL service enabled a slow expansion of airmail to be maintained. The example of the Swiss Post, which introduced the doctrine of "maximum utilisation of air transport" from 1976, enables us to measure the impact of this policy. Under the constraints of available capacity, the operating difficulties it encountered, and its own financial problems, the Swiss Postal Authority very gradually increased the volume of surface mail (AO) transferred to air transport from 925 tonnes in 1976 to 4,178 tonnes in 1985. [1] Contrary to some fears expressed, the growth of the SAL service was mostly achieved at the expense of sea mail rather than priority mail. However, in spite of the success of deferred mail, priority mail continues to make up the majority of traffic and above all to provide airlines with the largest part of their postal income.

The development of priority mail: regulation and rating practices

The Tokyo Conference had eliminated the distinction between category A services (short- and medium-haul) and Category B services (long-haul), giving way to a distinction based on the postal categories of the items transported (LC and AO).

With a concern for simplification, the Rio Conference in 1979 decided to standardise the remuneration to air carriers by adopting for the 1981–1986 period a uniform rate of 1.74 gold francs per kilometric tonne transported, independently of the content of the item posted. The Conference then decided to abandon the gold franc, an increasingly esoteric monetary unit, to replace it by SDRs (Special Drawing Rights on the International Monetary Fund) at a rate of 0.439 SDR/TKT in August 2003.

At the time, the uniform rate of 1.74 gold francs appeared reasonable to all the parties concerned, whether representing the Postal Authorities or the carriers.

One might have hoped that the era of rate confrontations had come to an end, but that would have been to ignore two factors: the second oil crisis of 1979, which pushed up airline operating costs, and the resolute will of the UPU, from which it has not moved, that it should never again permit an increase in the official rate of remuneration. Today, the attitude of the UPU seems all the more defensible, since the revenue unit for mail (excluding SAL services) have remained visibly above the revenue unit for freight, and because the official rate established by the UPU is, in many cases, nothing more than a reference – as is the case with the IATA airfreight rates.

The liberalisation movement began to effect the postal world towards the end of the 1970s. Although cases of privatisation remain extremely rare, there are many Postal Administrations whose legal status has been changed to allow them to obtain administrative and financial autonomy. In many countries, the Post Offices were converted into public companies, which were responsible for managing the businesses. This brought about a profound change in the relationships with their suppliers: the courteous exchanges between a Postal Administration and its national airline(s) was replaced by the more usual kind of customer/supplier dialogue. However, one should not generalise in this area as all possible combinations of factors arise. Some administrations remain extremely conservative and concerned to respect the spirit and the letter of the decisions of the Universal Postal Union (as in the case of Japan); others content themselves with negotiating confidential rate concessions with their traditional carriers; and yet more – increasingly numerous in North America and Europe – deal as a matter of principle through bidding for tender: every year the Post renegotiates the conditions for carrying its traffic. At this stage of deregulation, there is no longer even any reference to official rate level.

The Post has been exposed to tough competition from international couriers, but at the same time has been released from some of the restrictions which had limited its freedom (though some social constraints still remain) and henceforth behaves like a demanding business organisation. It wants to have its cake and eat it in terms of the prices and the service. The contracts between Postal Administrations and airlines generally have two parts, one, quite brief, dealing with rate conditions, and the other, more lengthy, containing the details of the handling of the mail on the ground, the kind of information to be provided to the postal services and the quality standards to be fulfilled. The Post has understood that it can only fight on equal terms with its competitors if it can both reduce its costs and improve the quality of its products.

This is something that has been well understood by the European and American Postal Authorities who are members of the International Post Corporation, based in Brussels. "With the help of state-of-the-art transponder technology" [2] IPC has set up a system for performance monitoring using "test-letters containing special transponders". Over a million such test letters are put into circulation every year within the European Union and North America, and the percentage of letters delivered "within three days of posting" increased substantially between 1994 and 2001.

Remail

Remail is an old technique, invented in The Netherlands (by the airline KLM and its partner the Dutch Post Office) during the 1950s. What does it involve? "The mechanism of remail is simple: a non-postal enterprise offers its services at very competitive prices to large customers of a post office, collects their mail and transports it to another Postal Administration which agrees, in return for payment, to inject the mail as if it was its own, into the network of its partners, the other recipient postal authorities." [3]

In fact, in its original form, remail was not concerned with correspondence but with American publications, from publishers of magazines, periodicals and catalogues, for delivery to Europe. In this case, which is practised on a very large scale, the publisher hands over his publications without labels or addresses to a "non-postal enterprise" known as a remailer. He produces the address labels for the recipients, either directly on the item or on a plastic envelope, sorts and assembles the labelled publications by country of destination and delivers them to an air carrier (for example KLM on the Chicago/Amsterdam route), under the conditions applying to freight and not as mail. On arrival, the Postal Authority who receives this "consolidated freight" (because this is what it is) extracts the items, and distributes or re-despatches them, this time as mail. Thanks to this technique, which for many years remained the prerogative of KLM and the Dutch Post Office, the American magazine publishers, for their issues sold by subscription to Europe and beyond, can profit from rates which are very much below those for airmail end to end, but for a quality of service which is far above that of surface mail. This is a text-book example, which very closely resembles that of sea–air traffic.

For many years, in spite of its attractions, this practice, operated by KLM/the Dutch Post Office, remained limited to one geographical sector – the North Atlantic – and to one category of products – periodical publications.

The main reason is that this practice infringes the letter, and to an even greater degree, the spirit of the UPU regulations. This is why the majority of Post Offices in North America as well as in Europe resisted it for so long, believing remail to be a "challenge against the Post Offices".

That was the case until, as everywhere else, the liberalisation movement took effect, and the legal barriers began to weaken. The large-scale expansion in remailing started in the 1980s, and was practised more energetically in the 1990s.

1. The field of application widened to include actual correspondence (large volumes of business mail or corporate remail), although periodicals, catalogues and miscellaneous publications (for example company annual reports) still constitute the major part of a traffic amounting to several tens of thousands of tonnes.

2. The geographical spread of remailing has reached the entire globe, although the North Atlantic remains the principal market.

3. Little by little, a number of Post Offices, particularly in Europe, have entered the remailing field, following in the footsteps of the Dutch Post Office and later (between 1975 and 1980) of the express carriers and the international couriers (in particular TNT Skypak with its Mail Fast service at the beginning of the 1980s).

4. Remailing techniques have become increasingly liberalised, that is to say increasingly remote from the UPU principles. The European Post Offices have opened offices in countries of publication (USA) and have bought remailers in Europe and the United States. It has even reached a stage where the publications are stamped directly in the USA for remailing routes, and cross the North Atlantic or other oceans, under postal documentation (CN 38 which replaced the famous AV7), but, of course, still charged at freight rates!

2 DOMESTIC AIRMAIL

This represented 56% of the world airmail traffic in the year 2000 (a percentage which had been stable for 30 years). The gross tonnages of domestic mail, which vary according to population, size, economic activity and the postal policies of different countries, often reach very large totals: over 1,200,000 tonnes in the United States, almost 170,000 tonnes in Japan, 150,000 tonnes in Germany and 60,000 tonnes in Brazil.

Domestic airmail is generally transported in one of three ways: in the holds of scheduled passenger planes; via a "dedicated" network operated by or on behalf of the Post; or under a mixed solution using both techniques. We will consider four examples.

Japan: transport in the holds of passenger aircraft
The Japanese domestic airmail market reached 166,000 tonnes in the year 2000. Over the previous 10 years it had varied between 160,000 and 173,000 tonnes (the level reached in 1991 and 2001). There is no domestic postal network. Mail is carried on board the passenger planes of the domestic airlines. This is certainly the most economical formula, since it does not require the involvement of any specific investment.

France: transport via a domestic airmail network
The airmail network set up in France at the end of the Second World War, and constantly updated since then, appeared to have reached its limits by 1990:

- insufficient capacity;
- ageing fleets in need of replacement;
- the direction of the round trips did not permit sufficient time for mail sorting operations in the Paris region;
- the Post considered that it did not have sufficient power to make decisions within the Centre d'Exploitation Postal (Postal Operations Centre).

A complete reorganisation would be necessary if the Post wished to "remain long term the main across-the-board operator for mail in France, particularly in the sectors of urgent mail and express parcels". After long negotiations between the Post, the Air France Group and TAT, the principle of semi-dependent subsidiaries for Postal aviation was established, and a new French domestic airmail network came into being in 1991. Compared with the proceeding system, it is characterised by an unusual legal/financial solution, the introduction of a new type of aircraft, and the complete reorganisation of operational structures.

From a legal point of view, a distinction was introduced between the financial structure and the operating structure. As a result, two companies were created:

- The Société Financière Aéropostale, or SFA, a subsidiary of the French Post Office, for the purpose of financing the aircraft.

- The Société d'Exploitation Aéropostale, or SEA, a joint subsidiary of the French Post Office, the Air France Group and TAT, with the purpose of operating the aircraft and the network.

With regard to the fleet, the objective was to reduce the unit costs without endangering the very high quality of service. The adoption of the B737-300 Quick-Change removed both these preoccupations. In its night cargo version, its containerised capacity (15 to 18 tonnes for 110m^3) and its cruising speed (560mph on the Paris/Montpellier route) fulfilled the requirements of the Post. The additional benefit of operating it in its passenger version by day on routes of the Air France Group allowed an increased average daily utilisation of the aircraft, and reduced the unit cost.

From an operational point of view, the new Postal air network had the following characteristics:

- constructed around two hubs: Roissy-Charles de Gaulle (15 services operated with B737s and F27s) and Lyons-Satolas (seven routes served by F27s);

- the reversal of the direction of the delivery rounds: the aircraft, which for the most part were based in the provinces, converged on the hubs during the night, freeing up additional time for sorting the mail in areas of high traffic density.

What was known as "La Nouvelle Aéropostale", referring to its legendary predecessor, functioned for a period of 10 years from 1991 to 2001. It did well in fulfilling its mission: with annual traffic of the order of 120,000 tonnes (normal mail, Chronopost express parcels and newspapers) and almost one and a half million passengers, it offered a very good coverage of the postal territory and an exceptional quality of operations, but it only lasted 10 years. Apart from technical and commercial problems associated with the constraints of operating the network with Quick-Change aircraft, the true cause lay in the absence of in any real "team spirit" between the French Post and Air France.

After Air France relinquished its 50% share in the Société d'Exploitation Aéropostale (excluding the brand "Aéropostale", of which it remained the owner) the French Post Office formed a new 100% subsidiary, la Société Europe Airpost, which in 2001 commenced operating the domestic postal network with a lower cost base. The fleet was changed (wide-bodied Airbus A300B4, B737 Cargo and Quick Change aircraft), the network rearranged around the hub at Roissy-Charles de Gaulle and the legs to Marseilles and Toulouse, and a number of other flights were discontinued in summer 2003 to reduce night-time disturbance. Europe Air Post is now on an even keel, and is attempting to develop additional daytime traffic (passengers, express freight and heavy freight) in support of its night-time postal activities, which have absolute priority, five nights per week – and there lies the nub of the problem.

United States: the mixed solution

The United States alone accounts for 75% of the world's domestic airmail traffic.

The American Postal Authority uses three different methods of air transport to carry its mail: scheduled airlines; air taxis to reach the more distant locations; and a private network. The normal airmail without surcharge (first class mail: LC) is basically carried on the regular passenger services of the major American airlines. In 2000, they transported around 1,130,000 tonnes of mail, which corresponds to 2.3 billion kilometric tonnes, equivalent to an average distance of about 1,250 miles. In 1993, the mail represented 35% of the traffic, but 42% of the revenue from cargo holds in these companies; the difference between these two percentages expresses the cost of priority given the Post, which the American postal community refers to as "the mail boarding priority premium". Three companies, American, Delta and United, received two thirds of the domestic postal traffic, which in 1995 accounted for 1.5% of the commercial income for all American airlines together.

The Airline Deregulation Act of 1978 brought about a profound change in the relationship between the Post and the airlines. Previously, postal rates had been fixed by the CAB. Subsequently, they were fixed by the Postal Authority itself, taking into account the market prices for airfreight, increased by the mail boarding priority premium. The prices paid by the Post consist of two elements: one fixed element, covering the cost of ground handling, and one variable element, covering the cost of air transport.

Relationships between the Post and the scheduled airlines has, since 1979, been regulated by a uniform system contract known as ASYS (Air System Contracts): "under this system the Postal Service determined a fair rate of payment and airlines were obligated, by contract, to board mail on any flight chosen by the Postal Routing Instructions, after passengers and their baggage" (but before freight).

Since the rates fixed by the Postal Service are identical for all carriers on a particular route, "competition comes into play with respect to the level of performance". This is why the Postal Service introduced a Performance Measurement System. It is stated, among other things, that "the Postal Service requires a high level of on-time performance for all mail tendered to and delivered by contractors... Therefore, the Postal

Tupolev Tu-204C on contract to TNT.
Air Rep

Service expects the contractor to perform at a minimum level of 98% on-time delivery for all mail tendered." (USPS air contract No ASYS – 94-01 Part 3 – section H. §11 Performance a/.) However, the passenger flights of the scheduled airlines cannot fully meet the needs of the American Postal Service. On the one hand, the general introduction of the hub and spoke system has reduced the quality of service by increasing the number of indirect transit routes. On the other hand, the flights of the scheduled airlines are in essence day-time flights, which may be suitable for ordinary airmail (the average transport time for first class mail is between three and five days) but they could never meet the needs of priority mail and even less those of express mail. The latter is transported through a "dedicated" airmail network, the " Eagle Air Network", which carries 300/350 tonnes per night, ie approximately 100,000 tonnes per year. In the land of free enterprise, this in-house postal network is not operated by the US Postal Service but by a private airline, which is generally chosen following a bidding process. For many years the American Postal Service worked with Emery World-wide Airlines (EWA), which operated out of Indianapolis with a fleet of 29 aircraft painted in the USPS livery and serving 46 cities every night.

After various trials and tribulations, USPS terminated the two contracts with Emery for the carriage of priority mail and express mail. Then, at the end of the year 2000 it negotiated directly with Fedex a very far-reaching agreement for a period of seven years, which came into force in August 2001. Under this contract, which has a total value of $6.3 billion (almost $1 billion per year) the American Postal Service entrusts to Fedex the responsibility for the transport of Priority Mail and Express Mail and entitles it to install over 10,000 drop boxes at postal outlets in return for a rental fee. From the end of August 2001 this mega-contract mobilised 42 DC-10F flights per day, with departures from Memphis, four times per week (Tuesday, Wednesday, Thursday and Sunday). In a full year, the traffic reaches something in the order of 300,000 tonnes.

Although it is difficult to imagine it happening in the American context, a close association between a private com-

pany – Fedex – and a public organisation – the US Postal Service – in such a competitive sector, raises the question as to whether the USPS-Fedex agreement will not further open the way towards a strategic alliance, rather than just straightforward co-operation.

Great Britain: a changing policy
As in France and Germany, Royal Mail is contracted to deliver first class mail on the next working day following posting. To reach this target a certain amount of mail has to be air lifted. As a rule, road is used for distances of up to around 150 miles, rail has traditionally been used for middle distances and longer distance mails, over 300 miles, tend to be flown.

In the long and rather complicated story of domestic air mail in the United Kingdom we will consider two main phases.

• Phase one: Spokes on Speke and the East Midlands Network
To improve the basic quality of service, mainly around the edges of the country, Royal Mail introduced on the 2nd July 1979 a hub and spoke air network located at Liverpool's Speke Airport. The so-called "spokes on Speke" was born. This chartered air mail network featured flights from Aberdeen, Belfast, Bournemouth, Bristol, Cardiff, East Midlands, Edinburgh, Exeter, Glasgow, Inverness, London (Gatwick), Lydd, Norwich and Stansted airports. A variety of aircraft were used to operate this network, mainly in the 1,500–3,000kg payload range. Flights would take off from the most distant points up to around 23:00hrs each weeknight arriving in Speke around midnight and depart from 01:00 onwards.

Airmail traffic increased due to the better quality of service, so a complementary network alongside Speke was launched in October 1983 with East Midlands Airport as its hub. This new hub was connected with van services and the train-based Travelling Post Office network (TPO).

• Phase two: Skynet
With mail volumes continuing to grow, it seemed that in the beginning of the 1990s, that this two-hub formula was no longer workable. A new system, called Skynet started operating on 28th September 1992. It was based on eight "peripheral hubs" located in Liverpool, East Midlands, Belfast, Bristol, Edinburgh, London (Gatwick), Newcastle, and Stansted. This organisation enabled the use of larger aircraft in the range of

3,500–6,000kg.

As with the two first arrangements, this system quickly reached its own limits. What was needed was a further radical review of the network over all the major transport modes— road, rail and air — and a new product specification (single daily delivery). The first phase of the consequent inland air mail network with containerised aircraft was introduced in January 2004.

3 COMPETITION FROM EXPRESS AND INTERNATIONAL COURIERS

The vocabulary of the "Union Postale", a journal which has been published monthly for over a century in Bern by the Universal Postal Union, has been constantly enriched with new words since 1975. Where it was once merely a question of "mechanisation", "codification", and "automation", new concepts are appearing and taking over with ever greater insistence: international couriers, competition, the end of postal monopoly, accelerated mail, express. The Post is finding that it is not the only operator in its field.

International couriers emerged at the end of the 1960s with success, firstly for domestic traffic (in the United States and Australia), and then for international traffic. When the major operators of express small parcel services extended their activities to deal in "envelopes" (large standardised cardboard envelopes, capable of containing all kinds of documents and business papers) the Post became aware of the danger. For the first time it had to face up to competition – quality competition.

In 1976, the Canadian Post courageously observed: "The parcel services were the first to offer fast deliveries at very interesting prices. They are in a phase of fast development, partly due to the fast strikes called by postal employees." [4]

How did the postal services react? How did they respond to this challenge from new companies who claimed to represent the virtues of the free economy in the face of state monopolies? Thanks to different timetables and approaches, which varied from country to country, the reaction of the Postal Authorities proceeded in four phases, some of which overlapped:

• 1 The legalist response or the reaffirmation of the law
The Post brandished the weapon of law. It appealed to the sacred texts guaranteeing its monopoly since deepest antiquity, by virtue of a royal prerogative of which it had always been the unchallenged representative.

In an article which appeared in 1981, [5] the French Post Office recalled that the legal establishment of the Postal monopoly was confirmed by two decrees from the Privy Council issued on 18th June and 29th November 1681 at the request of Lazare Patin, Farmer-General of His Majesty's Post. The decree forbade any person "to undertake the transportation of any correspondence other than the way bills for merchandise which they shall carry, such being open and not sealed."

The postal monopoly was later defined in article L.1. of the "Law on Post and Telecommunications" in the following terms: "The transportation of letters as well as packages and papers not exceeding the weight of one kilogram is exclusively the responsibility of the Post and Telecommunications Administration."

In this early period, the Post was intent on having its monopoly respected: "…instructions have been issued to the officials in charge of the Postal Service, requesting them to seek out any carriers who habitually infringe the regulations concerning the postal monopoly, and to report all infractions committed." [6] At the same time, the Post reconsidered the situation and arrived at a new justification for its monopoly – both social and economical:

> "*the Postal monopoly is justified by the duties and obligations inherent in the nature of the Administration of the PTT as a public service… In order that the price of the Postal Service be maintained at a reasonable level for the generality of users, it is necessary that, by means of cross-subsidising, the costs for very unprofitable traffic, such as that for rural areas, should be compensated by the receipts from profitable traffic.*"

• 2 Compromises or the law amended

Since the services offered by the international couriers responded to new requirements in commerce, the Post had to admit that a mere reminder as to the law was not enough. And so they considered amendments to the regulations in order to limit and accommodate the postal monopoly. Gradually (and, in Europe, occasionally under pressure from the authorities in Brussels), compromise solutions were reached, which recognised the activities of the new competitors in law and in fact, subject to the fulfilment of two conditions: the urgency of the items transported, and the levying of a charge per object which would be X times more than the value of the normal postage charge. This was a way of recognising the economic justification for express services.

Could the Post remain a mere spectator to this?

• 3 The intelligent response, or the commercial counter-offensive

Once they had got over their surprise and indignation, the Postal Authorities went over to the counter-attack by launching their own express products and services for mail and small parcels. They took up the challenge: "The organisation of ultra-fast services represents a real challenge for the Post in a period of profound changes in the world of communications." [7]
The first examples go back to the beginning of the 1970s: Express Mail in the United States (1970), Datapost in Great Britain (launched in 1970) and Postadex in France (1972).

Datapost has been one of the most rapid and rewarding of the postal counter attacks. Launched by the British Royal Mail as early as March 1970 as a separate product and organisation, Datapost was originally tailored to carry pouches of computer disks and data. Soon it was extended to include business from financial institutions and then large department stores, but exclusively as a "contract only" guaranteed overnight delivery service.

Using first rail and road transport inside a so-called "golden triangle" in England, this express next day product was then extended to other areas using regular Royal Mail flights, such as to/from Belfast and Edinburgh.

By the end of the 1970s, it appeared that the only way to meet the customers' needs was to operate a network of regular and dedicated air charter services. On 4th June 1979 Datapost started its first dedicated air service (or DAS) by chartering a Bandeirante aircraft from Air Ecosse (see photo page 360) to operate to and from Edinburgh while its second service to and from Belfast, started on 1st November 1979 operated by a Navajo chartered from Air Foyle.

Once a long term strategy on air charter had been agreed, between 1979 and 1986 other services were added to/from

Glasgow, Bristol, Exeter, Cardiff, Manchester and Newcastle. In 1986 Datapost created two alternating centres, the first at Luton airport and the second at Manchester airport. Initially limited to domestic traffic, these services were later extended progressively to a certain number of international routes within the framework of bilateral agreements made between Postal Administrations. It slowly became apparent that there was a need for a certain degree of harmonisation, at least at a formal level, between these various express products, developed on the initiative of each administration, in the absence of any official standardisation.

A Postal conference was called in the Hague in 1977, and it was decided that accelerated mail services would retain, in each country, their particular name, but would henceforth be referred to on a global scale by a common commercial denomination: Express Mail Service or EMS.

• 4 EMS, or the limitations of a universal response

The French Post Office created quite a stir at the end of 1985 when it joined with TAT Express, the small parcel specialist, to found a private limited company: the Société Française de Messagerie Internationale, or SFMI. By separating off its express transport activity as a subsidiary, the Post released itself from the constraints which were holding it back. The alliance with a private company gave it the flexibility that it lacked.

On 1st January 1986, SFMI launched the Chronopost Service, which brought to the market a whole range of products both domestic and international. Guy Meynié, the Chief Executive of SFMI, put his cards on the table:

> "*Chronopost is already the concern of every postal employee, and we must now mobilise operating staff and commercial people, carriers and distributors. This is our response, employing imagination, flexibility and responsibility against a new challenge, a challenge which all involved in the Postal Services are prepared to meet.*" [8]

The French Post had found a battle cry.

Relying solely on its own organisation for successfully dealing with domestic traffic, for international traffic the French Post Office is obliged to use the services of foreign Post Offices. In reality, Chronopost has to depend on the international network for accelerated mail: the EMS – Express Mail Service. Therein lies the problem… because, in spite of its logo adopted by all Postal Services, EMS is much more a collection of bilateral agreements than a proper network. Whereas its competitors have completely integrated their services, EMS has to make do with drawing them together under a common name and symbol. Thus, in the EMS network, in which many Post Offices continue to believe, the best businesses have to work in harness with the mediocre. This disparity is the main weakness of the system, as the Assistant Director General of the Swiss Post Office so courteously put it: "The co-operation with other Postal Administrations within the framework of the Universal Postal Union frequently leaves something to be desired." [9] The officials of the UPU are fully aware of the problems. At each of their conferences they try to make a further step towards harmonisation of services; improvement of the quality of service; and the extension of the EMS network. At the Washington Conference of 1989, they adopted "…an outline agreement for regulating the EMS, formalising and strengthening the service, while retaining the necessary flexibility."

In 1994, the Seoul Conference, "…established the fundamental EMS service principles, taking care to avoid excessive regulation…" This is an ambiguous declaration, which expresses at the same time a wish to make progress, and an inability to find common solutions.

In comparison with its competitors, EMS suffers from two weaknesses: the absence of any hierarchical authority over the Postal Administrations which constitute its membership, and the dependency in certain countries on inefficient administrations to carry out delivery operations. As a result, EMS is developing slower than its private competitors. The official publication of the UPU, "L'Union Postale", reported on the position, without the least complacency: "Despite a number of positive developments, EMS finds itself today at a cross roads of survival in an increasingly competitive market." [10]

In an attempt at "reversing the alarming tendency of EMS services to lose ground", the Postal Operation Council of the UPU created an independent co-operative in 1998. "An EMS co-operative has been established in 1999 with the main objective of harmonising the product offering, setting measurable standards, regular performance monitoring, training programmes." [11]

The EMS co-operative numbered over 110 countries in 2002. Will it manage to save the EMS system? At the present time, this looks probable, but this will not worry the large express companies in the least. This is why the most dynamic and ambitious Postal Authorities have taken another route.

4 THE COUNTER ATTACK FROM THE POST

It started in two phases. In the first phase, the response was limited and inadequate. In the second phase, the counter attack was devastating, and, with the exception of the two American giants Fedex and UPS, pole-axed the whole of the express business.

– Phase One: GDEW, or the failure of a limited response
The inadequacies of the EMS network account for the fact that several Post Offices, both European and North American, made regular attempts from 1986 onwards to find more effective solutions within restricted groups. In 1986, seven European Administrations had joined forces to create "a European Express Postal Network" based on Brussels airport. In 1987, the initial group was expanded, and 21 national postal services created the group IPC-Unipost (International Post Corporation) in order to harmonise commercial practices, set joint quality standards and design common data processing tools.

Unipost and the postal hub in Brussels stayed under the banner of EMS within the UPU. Some Postal administrations began to distance themselves from the EMS/UPU but they had not yet crossed the Rubicon.

This happened at the beginning of 1992 when the Postal Administrations of Sweden, Germany, The Netherlands, France and Canada, considering that progress within Unipost was far too slow, decided to go it alone. They joined up with the European branch of the Australian giant TNT, one of the world's leaders in door-to-door express transport for documents and small parcels. The "Band of Five" and TNT founded a joint venture, with share holdings on an equal 50/50 basis, which was called Global Delivery Express World-wide – GDEW for short. The news hit the postal world like a bomb, and provoked retal-

iatory measures on the part of certain Post Offices (Japan in particular). This alliance between the Post Office and TNT was not well received by traditionalist Post Offices, nor was it welcomed by the airlines concerned, who witnessed the transfer of considerable tonnages of accelerated mail onto TNT aircraft. In support of the effort, Aéropostale opened a night cargo service connecting its Roissy hub to that of TNT in Cologne.

At last, the member Post Offices of the GDEW possessed identical and reliable international express products: the Skypak products of TNT.

However, whether the commercial game plan had not been sufficiently well defined from the start (so that in France, Chronopost marketed Skypak products, but TNT retained its own organisation) or because the partners had disagreed about the wider strategic considerations, the contract lasted no longer than four years. During 1996, the Dutch partner took back sole control of GD Net BV, the financial organisation which held 50% of GD Express World-wide, operating under the brand of TNT Express World-wide.

• 2 The battle of the Post Offices [12]
If, in the 1990s, anyone had written that the old European Postal Administrations would have swallowed up TNT and DHL in a single mouthful, along with many others of less stature, he would have been considered an utter lunatic. Nevertheless, it only needed a little freedom, and the total or partial privatisation of some of these venerable institutions, for them to absorb their enemies and suddenly confront one another in the battle to carry express mail and parcels B2B [13] and B2C [14] in Europe and the rest of the world.

Hostilities between both the European Post Offices themselves and the Post Office and integrators broke out at the end of 1996 when the Dutch Post Office, KPN, purchased TNT and created the holding company TNT Post Group (TPG).

The German Post Office Deutsche Post AG did not take long to retaliate, and bought a 22.5% share in DHL on 1st July 1998 and made no secret of its intention, in the long term, of turning DHL into a 100% subsidiary. This was achieved in 2003. There then followed a positive buying frenzy on the part of the various Post Offices – not only the Dutch and the Germans, but also the British (German Parcel in 1999 and the French companies Crie and Expand in 2000), and the French (TAT Express in 1994, Jet World-wide in 1998 and DPD-Deutsche Packet Dienst in stages between 1998 and 2000).

But it rapidly became clear that the game was over, and only the German Post, with DHL, and the Dutch Post, with TNT, had gained a world infrastructure and a global future. The other European Postal Services were reduced to a European destiny by making alliances with one or other of the "Band of Four" (Fedex, UPS, TNT Post Group or Deutsche Post) for intercontinental traffic.

The French Post Office, whose "Parcels and Logistics" activity was reorganised within the GeoPost Group, made a productive decision to concentrate on the European parcel market, operated through two networks, express and fast. It now owns quality brands in France (Chronopost, Tatex etc), Germany (DPD) and Great Britain (Parceline and Interlink) and has concluded agreements with Postal Authorities in Spain, Portugal, Italy and Sweden. At this stage, one could ask three questions:

TOP **TNT B737-300F.** *TNT*

ABOVE **TNT B727 awaits loading.** *TNT*

LEFT **TNT's first BAe146-200QT operated by Air Foyle from May 1987.** *Air Foyle*

1 Has this dispersal of brands belonging to the French Post Office become a handicap in the face of the media power of the "Big Four".

2 Is the legal status of the French Post Office a major obstacle, if not a prohibitive factor preventing freedom?

3 Could it be that the commercial alliance signed with Fedex in September 2000 and automatically renewable until 1st January 2006, is both proof of wisdom and a sign of weakness in the heart of Europe?

According to this agreement, the express products of Chronopost International gain access to the whole of the Fedex network, and are transported by Fedex in Europe, whereas the French Post takes care of the collection and delivery of Fedex parcels in France (except for Paris) and in Belgium.

Looking at the British Post Office, its prospects seem equally limited after the failure of Consignia. However, the alliance signed at the beginning of 2002 with TPG (the majority partner) and Singapore Post could nevertheless give the British Post Office access to world markets.

The remaining champions Deutsche Post and the TNT Post Group have continued to battle in pursuit of their world-wide ambitions, and in a few years have succeeded in founding new business.

These are a kind of "Postal Conglomerate" business made up of three sections: two traditional sections, mail and financial services, and one new section, transport and logistics.

TNT Express World-wide is strongly established in Europe and Asia, particularly in China and Australia. It has chosen to place the accent on contract logistics (warehousing and distribution) in the framework of agreements with the world's largest firms, as a complement to its express transport activities: "TPG, the logistics giant of the future". To that end, it continues to favour all forms of external growth, for example the purchase of CTI Logistix in the United States, the take-over of Jet Service in France and a 50% share in the Danish DFDS Transport Logistics. Since 1998 the hub of TNT Airways has been based in Belgium at Liège-Bierset, and every night it flies to 55 European airports using its own fleet of BAe 146QTs, B737-300Fs and Airbus A300B4 freighters, supplemented by chartered aircraft (such as the Tupolev Tu-204 120C). However, as one would imagine from the way in which the logistics function has developed, the large majority of European traffic is transported by road, pending the introduction of sufficiently fast freight trains. The recent introduction of B747-400Fs into the fleet reflects the new international ambitions of TNT Express World-wide, nourished by the numerous postal agreements signed by the mother company and by the success of the logistics activities.

The power of Deutsche Post AG is on an altogether different scale to that of the TNT Post Group, as is shown by the table below for the year 2000:

Comparison of TNT Post Group and Deutsche Post AG

Units = Billion Euros

	TNT Post Group		Deutsche Post AG	
Turnover	10.9		26	
Of Which: Post	4.5		11.7	
Express	4.2	6.4	6.0	14.3
Logistics	2.2		8.3	
Profit	0.5		1.5	

Since 1998, Deutsche Post has led the way in external growth through acquisition in the fields of express air transport (DHL International purchased in stages between 1998 and 2002) and of freight forwarding and logistics. Amongst others, we should mention (without giving an exhaustive list) Ducros Services Rapides in France, Securicor in Great Britain, MIT in Italy, Global Mail and Yellowstone in the United States, Guipuzcoana in Spain, Nedlloyd Transport in Europe, not forgetting Danzas which, in its own right, took over the Swedish company ASG and the world leader in airfreight forwarding, the American company Air Express International. That is not the end of it, since in 2003 Deutsche Post purchased the ground-based activities of the American integrator Airborne: "A strategic acquisition which should help to make Deutsche Post World Net one of the major players in the vast express market in the United States, while at the same time making it the world number one in logistics." This declaration by President Klaus Zumwinkel stresses clearly Deutsche Post's ambitions. In only five years, Deutsche Post has managed to build up two business sectors, on a European on a world-wide scale:

• A complete logistics and freight forwarding network covering rail, road, sea and air, along with warehousing, supply chain and distribution. All these functions are now grouped within a single entity, DHL, divided into four divisions: DHL Express, DHL Freight, DHL Danzas Air and Ocean and DHL Solutions (Logistics).

• An air express network operated by a number of DHL companies, with DHL Aeroexpress in Panama, DHL Air UK based in East Midlands Airport operating a fleet of 14 Boeing B757 – 200SFs, DHL Airways [15] in the United States with its hub in Cincinnati/Kentucky, DHL de Guatemala, DHL International in Bahrain and European Air Transport in Brussels, along with subsidiaries and associated companies in Africa. In Asia DHL set up a hub in Hong Kong and acquired a 40% participation in the cargo airline Air Hong Kong, a subsidiary of Cathay Pacific. To service the north Pacific sector, it has entered into an agreement with Northwest, which operates on its behalf several flights per week out of Cincinnati, while on the North Atlantic its flights are operated by Gemini Air Cargo.

In conclusion: "DHL International could be the first company to truly combine express and traditional air cargo." [16] Being at the same time a large cargo airline and a major purchaser of capacity from traditional airlines, DHL and its parent company Deutsche Post AG provide a brilliant illustration of the prediction made 10 years ago: "The Post: from partner to competitor." [17]

6 THE AIRPORTS

Airports are the necessary interfaces between goods and aircraft. They are also assembly points within strictly controlled and defined territorial boundaries, used by all those involved in airfreight (usually excepting the end users): the airlines, the service and handling companies, road carriers, freight forwarders, the Post and all the Government departments (Customs, Health, Agriculture etc). Administrative procedures, are generally considered to be an obstacle to the development of airfreight, which is very sensitive to anything which compromises its chief advantage, speed. This is why ICAO, via its "Standards and Recommended Practices on Facilitation" (Annexe 9 to the Convention on International Civil Aviation) has been labouring for over 50 years to simplify all the regulations which tend to slow down the transit of passengers and merchandise through the airports. For their part, the national and international bodies representing couriers and express carriers have been fighting energetically for over 20 years with national and international Customs Authorities (the Customs Co-operation Council, later World Customs Organisation) to obtain procedures suited to their particular needs.

Generally speaking, Customs formalities at airports have been considerably simplified, through the computerisation of operations, the introduction of new procedures ("Point of Origin Clearance", for example), and above all through changes in mentality. Unfortunately, the situation varies considerably between continents and individual countries: while we are sometimes approaching "a paperless world" (particularly in Europe), there are too many Latin American, Asian and African countries that are still applying administrative and Customs procedures at airports which are incompatible with the nature of airfreight. This gave rise to the colourful title of a specialist review: "Avoiding the Hurdles of Latin American Customs Clearance". [1]

I AIRPORT CLASSIFICATION

I All-cargo airports

Just as there are all-cargo aircraft, there are all-cargo airports. They are few in number and, in some cases, may have some limited passenger activity. This is why they are sometimes called by the generic term "industrial airports", [2] because some of them possess industrial parks and Free zones.

All-cargo airports are generally decommissioned air bases, formerly belonging to the US Air Force in the United States and NATO in Europe. They are situated away from large conurbations – an essential factor with respect to noise and pollution – and possess one or more large runways, with vast areas of available space. Where such suitable air bases exist, local politicians have often tried to have them converted into cargo airports accompanied by logistics and/or industrial parks: "The closure of dozens of US military bases has left local communities scrambling to make up the economic losses." [3] In the event, the conversion of these former military bases has often proved difficult. Nevertheless there are a few successful examples.

In the United States, the integrated forwarder Airborne Freight Corp. owns an airline – Airborne Express – operating a fleet of around 100 aircraft. It is based in Wilmington-Ohio, on a former base converted into an industrial park and private airport. No doubt due to its central geographical position, the state of Ohio can congratulate itself on having a second example of a successful reconversion: that of Rickenbaker Air-Industrial Park, near Columbus, where traffic reached 96,000 tonnes in the year 2000.

But the most spectacular success story of a cargo airport is that of Alliance Airport near Fort Worth-Texas. Owned by the Perot Group, it is presented as "the first pure industrial airport in the Western hemisphere" and in the year 2000 achieved traffic of 242,000 tonnes, a growth of almost 50% over the previous year.

In the Philippines, the former US Navy base at Subic Bay has become the Asian hub for Fedex and, with its international traffic of 600,000 tonnes, it features among the world's 20 leading airports, whilst Clark has become the main Asian hub for UPS.

In Germany, Hahn Air Force base, located 75 miles from Frankfurt, in the Palatinate, became Hahn Flughafen in 1994. Frankfurt International Airport acquired a majority shareholding in 1998. Airfreight (70,000 tonnes) and passenger charters are its two main activities.

In France, Chateauroux-Déols, a "logistics and multi-modal site in the heart of Europe" that presents itself as "the all-cargo airport of Paris", has worked hard to promote itself for several years. While a stronger emphasis on logistics has brought overall growth, airfreight traffic remains a modest 2,000 tonnes. The Europort de Vatry, near Châlons in Champagne, did not open until 21st January 2000. Well-positioned between Paris, Brussels and Luxembourg, it claims to be primarily a "major logistics centre" and a "tri-modal traffic hub (air-rail-road) with an international airport reserved exclusively for cargo aircraft". After a very slow start, airlines are beginning to base their cargo flights there.

When all is said and done, these cargo airports are well suited to the all-cargo airlines and the express carriers, which can use them for all their operations, that are largely nocturnal. On the other hand, they do not match the essential requirements of the "mixed" airlines. The splitting-up of operations, between one airport for passenger flights and another for freight, would be madness from a commercial viewpoint, since the strength of these airlines lies precisely in the integration and synergy of capacities and frequencies between cargo and passenger flights.

2 Hub airports of express freight operators
Airports chosen as hubs or sub-hubs by express freight companies must fulfil three conditions:

1. to be open 24 hours per day, with no restrictions on night-time operations;
2. to possess the necessary space and infrastructure to handle many aircraft simultaneously;
3. to be situated near the economic centre of the region or country served.

This last condition explains why major hubs are located in very specific areas:

• in Europe, in the central northwestern part of the continent, with airports at Brussels (DHL), Cologne (UPS), Liège (TNT) and Paris-Charles de Gaulle (Fedex Express);

• in Asia, within a triangle bounded by Hong Kong (DHL and TNT), Taiwan (UPS), and the Philippines (Fedex Express and UPS).

• in the United States, within a tight rectangular area encompassing Indiana, Ohio and Kentucky, with Emery at Dayton (Ohio), DHL in Cincinnati (Ohio), the US Postal Service Eagle Hub at Indianapolis (Indiana), UPS at Louisville (Kentucky) and Airborne Express at Wilmington (Ohio). Only Fedex Express is somewhat on the sidelines in Memphis, for reasons of history. At all events, as a result of their success, the main integrators (Fedex Express and UPS) have had to replicate their central hub and open several subsidiary hubs to prevent over-loading of the main hub (Anchorage, Oakland, Miami, Newark and Indianapolis, for Fedex Express).

3 Major inter-continental traffic platforms
These exercise influence far beyond their immediate economic zone and fulfil additional functions in logistics and distribution. Their traffic is made up, in widely varying proportions, of domestic, regional, inter-continental and transit freight. Except for one or two cases, their traffic exceeds one million tonnes. The following airports are indisputably among the world's main interchange platforms:

• in Europe: London (Heathrow/Gatwick/Stansted), Paris (Roissy-CDG/Orly) Frankfurt and Amsterdam;
• in Asia: Tokyo, Hong Kong, Seoul and Singapore;
• in the Middle East: Dubai;

Geographical concentration of the hubs of express freight operators in the United States.

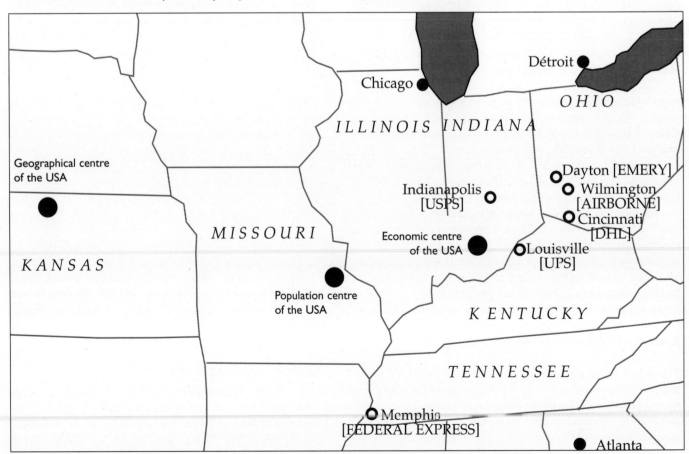

• in North America: New York (Kennedy/Newark/La Guardia), Miami, Chicago, and Los Angeles.

These are immediately followed by other key airports, which, although they do not fulfil all the criteria for inclusion among the great world traffic hubs, nevertheless stand out among their peers. This second group includes:

• in Europe: Brussels and Luxembourg;
• in Asia: Bangkok and Taipei;
• in North America: Dallas, Atlanta and San Francisco.

4 National and regional airports
The airports of Latin America, Africa and the Middle East (excepting Dubai and perhaps Sharjah) and the Indian sub-continent fall into this category for two reasons: the political and economic barriers which continue to divide these continents, and the rigidity of Customs regulations, which restrict or exclude transit traffic.

In the United States, some airports in this group handle very high tonnages, consisting essentially of domestic freight and postal traffic (Boston, Philadelphia, Denver etc).

In Europe, the majority of international airports fall into this category (Madrid, Milan, Copenhagen, Stockholm, Rome etc) along with all regional airports. Some of them are specialised, such as Ostend in Belgium (charter flights and traffic for Africa), Billund in Denmark (express traffic and charter flights for cattle transport), or Vitoria International Airport in Spain (import of fish from Southern Africa, and from South America).

5 Airport conurbations
In fact, this is less a category of airports than of geographical areas within specified boundaries, inside which are established several airports which may or may not have institutional links with one another (in contrast to multi-airport systems – cf. Section 2 ,"Airport Rankings"). There are three which are worth mentioning: San Francisco Bay, the United Arab Emirates and the Pearl River Delta in China.

The "San Francisco Bay area, a square 50 miles long by 25 miles wide, with the actual bay at its centre, is home to three sizeable freight airports: San Francisco (868,000 tonnes), Oakland (685,000 tonnes) and San Jose (148,000 tonnes), a total of 1,700,000 tonnes per annum.

In the UAE, the airports of Dubai and Sharjah, located 12 miles apart but in different Emirates, have a combined total of around one million tonnes per annum.

The best example of an airport conurbation is found at the mouth of the Pearl River in China. Concentrated within an area approximately 100miles long by 60 miles wide are concentrated the new airports of Chek Lap Kok/Hong Kong, Macao and Shenzhen, as well as the airport of Guangzhou, which in total handle almost three million tonnes per annum. This gateway to China is one of the world's largest sea/air multi-modal centres.

2 AIRPORT RANKINGS (see tables on page 375)

The world traffic through airports surveyed by the ACI [4] for the year 2000 amounted to 73.3 million tonnes: the airports of North America (31.8million tonnes), Asia (20.4million tonnes) and Europe (14.2million tonnes) represent 90.7% of the total; those of Latin America, Africa and the Middle East, 9.3%. The

ranking can be done in two ways: either by individual airports or by multi-airport systems.

In the second approach, which seems better to reflect the geographic and economic realities, the various airports serving the same conurbation are gathered under a single heading. This is the case with New York (with JFK, La Guardia and Newark), Los Angeles (with Ontario and Los Angeles International), Tokyo (with Narita and Haneda), London (with Heathrow, Gatwick and Stansted), Paris (with Orly and Roissy-Charles de Gaulle), Shanghai, Sao Paulo…The various airports within the same multi-airport system are generally managed by the same authority.

We shall restrict ourselves to a few observations regarding the table concerning the 25 leading multi-airport systems.

1. Only the New York airport system approached the 3 million tonne level. New York is successfully defending its position at the top of the world ranking, in spite of all the criticisms to which it has been subject in the past. It remains at the top of the list of American Customs Offices, with respect to the value of exports and imports by air, and the introduction of a Fedex express hub at Newark has added a new dimension.

2. Five cities exceed 2 million tonnes (New York, Tokyo, Los Angeles, Memphis, and Hong Kong) with London following close behind. The ranking of Memphis reflects the size of Fedex Express. However, it also illustrates the observation that the principal of operating a hub-and-spoke system has the consequence of doubling the traffic statistics for the number of tonnes handled via the hub. This remark also applies to Anchorage, Louisville, Indianapolis, Oakland, Subic Bay and, to a lesser extent, New York, Paris and Miami.

3. The 18 airport systems with over a million tonnes represent 45% of the world airport traffic. Among them feature eight American cities, six Asian cities and four European cities. Since we cannot describe each in detail, we will take Miami as an example. Miami occupies a particular position. It is above all the gateway airport to South and Central America for flights originating in North America, Europe and Asia. It is an extremely busy airport, served by many domestic airlines alongside the major operators, and one can see every possible type of cargo aircraft there. Furthermore, it is an airport which advertises itself remarkably well: "Bridge to the Americas, Miami today is a key link in the world's traffic lanes, opening the Golden Door for air cargo moving between the United States and Europe and all points in Latin America." [5]

4. Indianapolis, which was the main centre of activities for the US Postal Service in 2000, was by far the leading postal airport in the world, with a traffic of 400,000 tonnes. This is followed in order by New York (291,000 tonnes), Atlanta (238,000 tonnes), Dallas (234,000 tonnes), Los Angeles (223,000 tonnes) and Paris (213,000 tonnes), which is the leading non-American postal airport.

3 AIRPORT OPERATIONS

Recent trends
We shall consider changes which have occurred in three areas:
1 The approaching end of the monopolies. Although with some

Ranking of the top 35 individual airports in 2000 (in thousands of tonnes/ Source: Airports Council International)

International Freight			Total Freight			Cargo (Freight and Mail)		
Rank	Airport	Traffic	Rank	Airport	Traffic	Rank	Airport	Traffic
1	Hong Kong	2,240	1	Memphis	2,452	1	Memphis	2,489
2	Tokyo-Narita	1,875	2	Hong Kong	2,240	2	Hong Kong	2,268
3	Singapore	1,682	3	Tokyo-Narita	1,885	3	Los Angeles	2,038
4	Seoul	1,597	4	Seoul	1,852	4	Tokyo-Narita	1,932
5	Frankfurt	1,519	5	Los Angeles	1,815	5	Seoul	1,874
6	Anchorage	1,493	6	Anchorage	1,804	6	New York-JFK	1,817
7	Paris-CDG	1,384	7	New York-JFK	1,690	7	Anchorage	1,804
8	London-LHR	1,298	8	Singapore	1,682	8	Frankfurt	1,709
9	New York-JFK	1,275	9	Frankfurt	1,573	9	Singapore	1,705
10	Amsterdam	1,222	10	Miami	1,557	10	Miami	1,642
11	Taipei	1,196	11	Louisville	1,519	11	Paris-CDG	1,610
12	Los Angeles	911	12	Paris-CDG	1,410	12	Louisville	1,519
13	Osaka Int'l	890	13	London-LHR	1,307	13	Chicago	1,468
14	Bangkok	820	14	Chicago	1,293	14	London-LHR	1,402
15	Chicago	728	15	Amsterdam	1,222	15	Amsterdam	1,267
16	Brussels	676	16	Taipei	1,196	16	Taipei	1,209
17	Subic Bay	629	17	N/York-Newark	970	17	Indianapolis	1,165
18	Dubai	562	18	Osaka Int'l	966	18	N/York-Newark	1,082
19	Luxembourg	500	19	Bangkok	865	19	Osaka Int'l	1,000
20	Kuala Lumpur	479	20	Indianapolis	761	20	Dallas	904
21	Sharjah	475	21	San Francisco	692	21	Atlanta	894
22	San Francisco	430	22	Brussels	676	22	San Francisco	869
23	Sydney	401	23	Dallas	670	23	Bangkok	868
24	Cologne	394	24	Dayton	667	24	Dayton	832
25	Zurich	382	25	Atlanta	655	25	Brussels	687

Ranking of the top 25 multi-airport systems in 2000 (in thousands of tonnes/ Source: Airports Council International)

International Freight			Total Freight			Cargo (Freight and Mail)		
Rank	Airport	Traffic	Rank	Airport	Traffic	Rank	Airport	Traffic
1	Hong Kong	2,240	1	New York	2,678	1	New York	2,970
2	Tokyo	1,907	2	Tokyo	2,542	2	Tokyo	2,702
3	London-LHR	1,811	3	Memphis	2,452	3	Los Angeles	2,502
4	Singapore	1,682	4	Los Angeles	2,259	4	Memphis	2,489
5	Seoul	1,597	5	Hong Kong	2,240	5	Hong Kong	2,268
6	Frankfurt	1,519	6	Seoul	1,852	6	London	1,959
7	New York	1,497	7	London	1,831	7	Seoul	1,874
8	Anchorage	1,493	8	Anchorage	1,804	8	Anchorage	1,804
9	Paris	1,481	9	Singapore	1,682	9	Paris	1,730
10	Amsterdam	1,222	10	Frankfurt	1,573	10	Frankfurt	1,709
11	Taipei	1,196	11	Miami	1,557	11	Singapore	1,705
12	Los Angeles	911	12	Louisville	1,519	12	Miami	1,642
13	Osaka	890	13	Paris	1,517	13	Louisville	1,519
14	Bangkok	820	14	Chicago	1,293	14	Chicago	1,468
15	Chicago	728	15	Amsterdam	1,222	15	Amsterdam	1,267
16	Brussels	676	16	Taipei	1,196	16	Taipei	1,209
17	Subic Bay	629	17	Osaka	1,113	17	Osaka	1,169
18	Dubai	562	18	Bangkok	865	18	Indianapolis	1,165
19	Luxembourg	500	19	Indianapolis	761	19	Dallas	904
20	Kuala Lumpur	479	20	San Francisco	692	20	Atlanta	894
21	Sharjah	475	21	Shanghai	683	21	San Francisco	869
22	San Francisco	430	22	Brussels	676	22	Bangkok	868
23	Shanghai	426	23	Dallas	670	23	Dayton	832
24	Sydney	401	24	Dayton	667	24	Shanghai	708
25	Cologne	394	25	Atlanta	655	25	Brussels	687

delay, the liberalisation wave has also affected airport operating methods. "The private sector is increasingly present in airports", stated the "Journal of the ICAO" in April 2000. It is in Europe that this development has been most marked, following the publication by the European Union on 15th October 1996 of its "Directive on the Liberalisation of Ground Handling Services", which opened the way to competition in airport operations. Its application brought about the disappearance of numerous monopolies for the ground handling of freight (handling in warehouses, loading and unloading of aircraft). This liberalisation movement is not limited to Europe. Hence the opening of the new Hong Kong Airport in 1998 was an opportunity for ending the monopoly of HACTL (Hong Kong Air Cargo Terminals Ltd), and for introducing a second cargo handling company in the form of AATC (Asia Airfreight Terminal Company). In the same way the Government of Taiwan ended the freight handling monopoly at Taipei Airport in 1998.

2 The introduction of synergies. The formation of alliances and the appearance of co-operations between airports are very recent phenomena.

In 1999, Aéroport de Paris, made two agreements with Liège – the TNT hub – and Chateauroux airport. The objective of Aéroport de Paris was to set up in the medium term a network of complementary hubs, which in future would be linked by TGV high-speed freight trains and capable of working with all kinds of traffic.

More immediate objectives were achieved by Pantares, a joint venture set up in 2000 by FAG (Flughafen Frankfurt/Main AG) and the Schiphol Group (Amsterdam), which recorded an important success in 2001. In association with domestic companies, it signed a contract for the construction and operation of a logistics and distribution centre in the Chek Lap Kok airport in Hong Kong, under the name of Tradeport Hong Kong. Pantares is said to have the ambition of creating a world network of Tradeport Logistics Centres.

3 The time for logistics ambitions
The large airports are no longer satisfied with their traditional functions in handling /warehousing freight. They are beginning to transform themselves into complete logistics platforms, offering transport by air, road and, in the future, rail – at least in Europe – and integrating transport, stocking and distribution activities. The cargo zones are generally too restricted to house all these functions, which require vast surface areas and extend way beyond the airport boundaries. Thus, enormous air logistics "nebulae" are growing up in the neighbourhoods of the main airports.

Cargo zones and "cargo villages"
Most airports possess "cargo zones" which are more or less separate from other areas. Most are on a very modest scale, with a few offices and a "shed-style" warehouse, but the main airports have vast, well-identified cargo zones, which are directly connected to the surrounding motorway network (rail connections are very rare). The airports with sufficiently large cargo zones house the whole of freight and mail activities within the airport boundaries (as in Roissy-Charles de Gaulle). Otherwise, where space is at a premium, forwarders are obliged to set up outside the airport off-airport facilities (as in Frankfurt or London Heathrow).

For about 20 years, there has been a process bringing increased diversification and complexity to airport cargo zones. In addition to cargo terminals, new buildings have appeared: "dedicated" terminals for express freight, special installations for perishable goods in order to provide a high level of health standards (meat, sea food etc) or animal hotels. In this field, KLM is one of the pioneers:

"The first animal hotel opened at Schiphol in the 1950s, to provide temporary accommodation for live animals awaiting export shipment or import clearance. After its latest and most complete refurbishment in 1995, the animal hotel now covers an area of 1500m²." [6]

The "cargo village" concept is a type of cargo zone. It can be described more closely as "an organised grouping, in a single location, of all the freight forwarders and airlines, generally on the initiative of the airport authorities". The cargo village of Dubai, which was opened on 28th July 1991, is the most sophisticated example. As with all the Arabian oil monarchies, a strong desire for central planning is evident, generating efficiency and with a suitable architectural expression. The Dubai Cargo Village, managed by a single organisation, the Dubai National Air Travel Agency or DNATA, acted quickly and decisively, comparable to HATCL in Hong Kong. From the outset, the village consisted of a main building of 25,000m², containing the warehouses and stocking areas, along with a building for the freight forwarders and airlines. Since its opening, several extensions and improvements have been made: the opening of a special freight terminal for the Emirates Airline (managed by DNATA who has the handling monopoly), the introduction in 1992 of new computer systems (Cargo Activity Management Information System) "to monitor service quality at all levels", then, in 1998, the commencement of an enormous programme for extending the cargo handling and preparation areas, ending with the commissioning of a "mega cargo terminal", an "international flower centre" and an "express and mail centre", all operated by DNATA Cargo.

Cargo terminals
One can attempt to classify these according to two criteria: the type of management, and the stocking and handling systems.

1 Management methods
In airports, one finds three main ways of running cargo terminals. Historically, the first two management styles were more usually practised, and later, with the increase in traffic, the third method tended to come to the fore, provided the necessary funds were available.

- Public cargo terminals
  These are financed and constructed by the airport authorities. The airlines, and any freight forwarders who wish to do so, can rent space privately. The terminal operators can on their own behalf carry out documentary and physical operations for freight handling.

- Private cargo terminals managed by third parties
  This solution is generally adopted by airports that wish to hand over the operating monopoly to an organisation, which they control, or to the national airline. In any case, the

airport authority finances and constructs the facilities. However, in the first case the airport authority operates the cargo terminal itself (eg Milan). In the second case it hands over responsibility for fitting out and managing the terminal to the national airline (Swiss Air benefited from this type of solution for many years in Geneva and Zurich).

Today, this solution is criticised on all sides, because it transfers prerogatives, judged to be unacceptable, to national airlines or management organisations, which enjoy a monopoly. However, it does present one plus-point, particularly advantageous when space is restricted, in that it makes best use of the available space. The example of Hong Kong airport is informative in this respect.

Airfreight operations got under way in Hong Kong in the 1960s. The airlines had small, private storage areas within the old passenger terminal which had been "converted" into a cargo hall. No one was happy: the working areas were not large enough and shipments often had to be prepared outside, even in the rainy season. As the situation became insupportable the colony's Government decided to take the matter in hand. After considering the very small amount of space available at Kai Tak airport, and the prospects for the growth of traffic, it came down in favour of a cargo terminal under third-party management, open to all the operators. It handed over the management of this new cargo terminal, which was opened in 1976, to a company

specially created for the purpose, in which the colony only retained a 10% holding: HACTL – Hong Kong Air Cargo Terminals Ltd. Due to the growth of traffic, HACTL opened a second terminal in 1984. These terminals function according to two principles: vertical storage of ULDs, owing to the lack of space available on the ground, and sophisticated handling techniques with specialised transfer vehicles. From the point of view of the operators, this solution gives good results: an excellent quality of service at a competitive price.

• Private cargo terminals (for operation by individual companies) Today this is the most usual solution, wherever adequate surface area is available. In the large airports, the main airlines occupy private premises or cargo terminals, which they operate on their own behalf or via a sub contractor. In other cases they use a service provider (a handling company).

Within the last 40 years, the airline freight terminals have developed from sheds in wood or corrugated iron, to terminals with several thousand square metres on the ground, equipped with extremely sophisticated stocking and

The multi-level container storage system at SuperTerminal 1, Hong Kong Kai Tak, provides over 3,500 storage positions and is designed to maximize speed and efficiency.
"Super Terminal One" brochure published by HACTL

handling systems, making use of mechanical handling and automated operating systems.

2 Storage and handling systems

This is the criterion with the greatest influence on structural requirements, since it determines the choice of architecture and the overall design of the terminal. At the risk of over-simplification, one can contrast freight handling systems built along a horizontal plane with integrated handling systems along a vertical plane. We will take as examples the two cargo terminals which best illustrate the two solutions: the Air France terminal G1 XL at Roissy-Charles de Gaulle and the HACTL Super Terminal One at Chek Lap Kok airport.

- Whether we look at the old Kai Tak airport or the new facilities at Chek Lap Kok, space is always in short supply in Hong Kong.

    The solution adopted for operating the freight area of the new Chek Lap Kok airport was inspired by the system successfully used at Kai Tak. It is based on the operation by HACTL of a giant cargo terminal known as Super Terminal One, and introduces an element of freedom and competition with AATC.

    Super Terminal One has a capacity of 2.6 million tonnes, and has a total surface area of 247,000m², distributed on seven levels, not including the Express Centre which has a total area of 46,000m². Beyond its imposing dimensions, the most characteristic feature of Super Terminal One is its "vertical, integrated freight handling system". The two facilities for stocking containers and pallets have a capacity of 3,500 units distributed over 11 levels, whilst the two facilities for stocking consignments have a capacity of 10,000 storage bins on 21 levels at a height of 36 metres.

- The Air France cargo terminal at Roissy-Charles de Gaulle, known as G1XL is the opposite of the Super Terminal One at Chek Lap Kok.

    Roissy is an enormous airport with a cargo zone amongst the largest in the world. Thus, Air France has made the choice of a single level facility: it uses a "horizontal" handling structure in order to provide an optimum fluidity of operations. The premises cover a surface of 107,000m², providing a handling capacity of around one million tonnes. After its opening in 1977 it has been considerably expanded, and its processes underwent complete revisions in 1995 and 1998. Its unique feature is the existence of two complementary buildings – the cargo dock and the freight hall – situated on either side of a road under Customs supervision.

    The cargo dock measures 190m x 149m. This is the section of the terminal dedicated to handling cargo aircraft (four parking positions). Its function is based on three principles: the continuous loading/unloading of B747Fs via an elevated ramp, the assembly of pallets and containers in the dock in the order in which they will be loaded onto the plane, and separate handling facilities for exceptional loads (greater than or equal to 20ft).

    The freight hall from the outset was designed for easy expansion. Highly developed technological solutions are employed, such as the electronic labelling of pallets, driverless pallet transporters guided by underground copper

cables, a specialist storage stack for small parcels, and the computer system which controls all the physical movements in the terminal.

    A final extension is under construction, which is planned to increase the surface area by 15% and permit a capacity increase of 40%. This will bring the capacity to almost 1.5 million tonnes by 2004, following process modifications.

4 AIRPORT PROBLEMS

These can be summarised in two key words: security and the environment.

Security

The Lockerbie disaster on 21st December 1988, and the reappearance of terrorist threats after the Gulf War of 1990 /1991 have already put security to the forefront among the pre-occupations of air transport: "alongside with operational safety, security is a top priority for ICAO".[7] At that time, the member states of the ICAO adopted, in the form of Annexe 17 (Security) to the Convention, a body of measures to forestall the risks from terrorism:

> "*Standard 4.3.8 Establish measures to ensure that cargo, courier and express parcels and mail intended for carriage on passenger flights are subjected to appropriate security controls.*
>
>   "*Standard 4.3.9 Each Contracting State shall establish measures to ensure that operators do not accept consignments of cargo, courier and express parcels, or mail for carriage on passenger flights unless the security of such consignment is accounted for by a Regulated Agent or such consignments are subject to other security controls to meet the requirements of 4.3.8.*" (Annexe 17. International Standards and Recommended Practices – Security – 6th edition. March 1997.)

It is therefore the responsibility of each contracting state to adopt the regulatory measures necessary for applying these standards on its territory.

In France, Law No. 96-151 of 2nd February 1996 subscribes to these general conditions. It inserts into Book II of the "Code de l'Aviation Civile" (Law on Civil Aviation) Article L321 – 7, which stipulates:

> "*As a precaution in order to ensure the security of flights, air carriers must use the services of a 'known shipper' for the despatch of freight or postal packages for the purpose of transporting them.*"

Moreover, "specific security procedures which could entail visits undertaken by regulated agents" are planned if necessary.

All the regulatory measures adopted by the various states are based on two fundamental concepts identified by the ICAO: that of "Regulated Agent" and that of "known consignor" or "known shipper":

- A "Regulated Agent, is an agent, freight forwarder or any other entity who conducts business with an operator and provides security controls that are accepted or required by the appropriate authority in respect of cargo."

- A "known shipper", is a shipper who has established business relations with a Regulated Agent or an aircraft operator on agreed criteria relating to the security of his cargo.

The designation of "known shipper" is reserved for organisations which undertake to observe a certain number of rules. [8]

1 "The consignor undertakes to prepare its consignments in secure premises."
2 "The consignor undertakes to employ in the preparation of consignments only identified persons, possessing the required skills."
3 "The consignor certifies that all measures have been taken to avoid its consignments containing any explosive device or any object liable to compromise the security of the cargo."
4 "The consignor undertakes to protect the consignments, or cause them to be protected from any unlawful interference during their preparation, storage and transport."

The spirit of this regulation therefore lies in distinguishing clearly between "known shippers" who accept subjecting themselves to a whole system of rigorous security procedures, and "unknown shippers", whose consignments must be systematically inspected (and therefore if necessary delayed) at the time of their registration. The idea is to closely link and invoke the responsibilities of all parties involved: customers shipping the goods, freight forwarders, and airlines, in such a manner that security really does become "the responsibility of everyone" and that the transport chain becomes completely secure.

Thus, although they were not perfect, these effective security measures had already been in force for a number of years when other events further occurred which changed security from a priority to an "absolute imperative".

The environment
Environmental pressure groups have never been so powerful and influential as at the present time, particularly in Europe. The general population and public opinion have never been so sensitive to nuisances caused by airports, whether in terms of noise levels, night flights or infrastructure.

In all such fields, the tendency is to adopt regulatory measures, which are becoming increasingly severe and restrictive. With regard to noise, the recent disagreement between Europe and the United States is significant. Under pressure from people living around airports, the European authorities attempted to resist unilaterally the operation of cargo aircraft fitted with hushkits. The fact that all these aircraft were of American manufacture, aroused the fury of the United States at their potential ban as their noise levels did fall unquestionably within – although only just, and that is the problem – Chapter 3. After a period of tension, the matter was brought to a natural conclusion within the ICAO in October 2001. The decisions reached mark an important new stage towards the reduction of maximum allowable noise levels, with the introduction of a new Chapter 4, which comes into force in 2006.

In the meantime, noise-sensitive airports may from case to case issue more restrictive conditions than the Chapter 3 standard, and, to a certain extent anticipate the conditions of the new Chapter 4. With regard to night flights, the operating restrictions in force at numerous airports have been strengthened during the last few years. The newest of these, issued in June 2003 affect the airport of Roissy-Charles de Gaulle.

It is the integrators who are the most threatened by these noise bans. However, the recent climb-down by the Belgian authorities, confronted by DHL in Brussels and TNT in Liège, shows that opposing parties are still searching for an acceptable compromise between safeguarding economic activities around the large airport complexes, and the legitimate concerns of their neighbours.

With regard to airport infrastructure, it looks as though Asian countries were the only ones capable of building new large-scale hub airports: Inchon for Seoul, Pudong for Shanghai and Chek Lap Kok for Hong Kong, not counting Kuala Lumpur and Osaka, with Bangkok and Guanzou planned for the near future.

There is such a large contrast between these hyper-active countries and the rest of the world that it leads to some startling comparisons: in March 2000, an American journal ran the article: [9] "In Hong Kong there is still room to expand" and in September 2001, as though in echo, a British journal [10] entitled its article on the difficulties of developing airports in the United States: "The battle to expand"!

One thing seems likely: it will be the Asian countries which boast the world's largest cargo airports in the first half of the 21st century.

5 COMPETITION BETWEEN AIRPORTS

Should we perhaps be talking of "hub wars?" [11] However one puts it, there is no doubt that "fierce battles were waged" [12] between the large airport hubs – and some smaller ones.

Competition between airports depends on a number of factors, which can be classified under four main headings.

1 the level of airport fees, attendance charges and property rentals.
2 the quality of services offered by all the links in the transportation chain.
3 the existence of further land reserves within the boundaries of the airport or inits immediate vicinity.
4 Regulations applying to night flights.

Competition is particularly fierce in Western Europe due to the geographical proximity of the airports, the concentration of markets and the density of terrestrial communication networks. The three main protagonists, Amsterdam, Frankfurt and Paris each possess their own advantages.

Amsterdam
Schiphol Airport is a symbol of continuity (it has been operating since 1920) and of quiet efficiency, whether in quality of handling or in the excellence of its connections with the nearby road, rail or sea networks. It represents one of the elements of the image which the Netherlands have been cultivating for several centuries: that of a merchant nation, a "gateway to Europe" and an international distribution centre.

Frankfurt

Restricted in its development for many years due to lack of space, in 1994 Frankfurt received a tremendous boost with the transfer of 329 acres from the American Rhein-Main military airbase. The construction on this site of a new "Cargo City South" will increase its handling capacity to almost three million tonnes by 2010. The purchase of a controlling interest in the airport of Hahn opens up new perspectives for Fraport to carry out a co-ordinated expansion of freight activities between the two locations.

Paris

Roissy-Charles de Gaulle owns an asset which is particularly valuable in Europe – space and more space – with a freight area which could be expanded to over 1,730 acres. Forming a vast U it concentrates on a single site all of the participants in the airfreight process around the cargo aircraft parking bays. Among the buildings within this zone, the Freight Forwarder Terminal, which was inaugurated in 1974 when the airport was opened, is worthy of special mention. This building with a footprint of 269,098ft^2 is run by SOGAFRO (Société de la Gare de Fret de Roissy) and was entirely financed by over 60 freight forwarders. It represents "the world's first collective effort to build a freight terminal" on the part of the freight forwarders. The choice of Roissy by Fedex for the establishment of it European hub – which was opened in June 1999 – represents an undeniable success for the Paris Airport Authority. During the coming years it will be interesting to follow the impact of the agreement between Air France and KLM regarding the development of relations, and synergies between the airports of Roissy and Schiphol

It would be wrong to consider only Paris, Frankfurt and Amsterdam when looking at competition between airports in Continental Europe. At least three other airports, Brussels, Luxembourg and Cologne – not to mention Liège – possess important advantages. In future, the question of the regulation or even the prohibition of night flights threatens to become an important factor in competition between airports.

Finally, the Continent cannot ignore the London hub. In fact London, with Heathrow, Gatwick and Stansted is the principal European airport complex, ahead of Paris, Frankfurt and Amsterdam. Admittedly, cargo frequencies are less numerous than in the large Continental airports, but the capacities of the "belly carriers" from all over the world, flying via London, are so large that they enable it to maintain its European leadership. This position would clearly not be possible without the brilliant world fifth ranking of British Airways, won in spite of its reduced cargo fleet, by means of an optimum utilisation of the hold capacities of its passenger aircraft.

Outside Europe, Asia is the continent where competition between airports will be at its fiercest in the coming years.

In the north-east of the continent, the new airport of Seoul-Inchon, opened in April 2001, makes no secret of its ambitions regarding the Chinese and Japanese markets. The opening stages between 2005 and 2020 of a vast customs-free zone will enable it to offer a very large range of services. In the centre, competition looks like being particularly aggressive between Hong Kong and Shanghai, both possessing relatively new airports.

In the south-west, the construction of the new Bangkok airport will renew competition against Singapore, which up to the present time has been able to maintain its superiority. Finally, in the UAE States, Dubai and Sharjah will continue to confront one other, to the greater benefit of their clients!

7 THE PEOPLE

"There are no riches other than men."
Jean Bodin, 16th century French economist

It is the human factor which constitutes the main richness of airfreight activities. With its multitudes of trades, it resembles a chain in which every link is unique. This is why all the professions in freight transport have the same dignity, since they have the same importance, whether sales rep or warehouse man, accountant or commercial clerk, loading supervisor or route planner, truck driver or aircraft pilot.

A cargo sales rep has an exciting job. He is generally enthusiastic – he has the good fortune to be in direct contact with markets, to feel their pulse and anticipate how they will develop.

Like all cargo jobs in freight, sales solicitation needs a solid technical background. It goes without saying that the cargo sales rep must have a detailed knowledge of the commercial regulations, but above all he needs to master the physical transportation conditions, according to the nature of the goods, the volume of the consignment or the characteristics of the aircraft. He is not, as some might say, just selling empty air. He has to propose to his customer a solution that is technically well thought-out and commercially attractive. "You can't leave anything to chance. This work leaves no room for improvisation", said the manager in charge of the "Live animals and perishable products", at Air France Cargo. [1]

But technical know-how is not enough. It must be backed up by a continual personal availability. "This job means that I just have to make myself available. If a customer wants me to be present in the middle of the night to accept a big load, I'll be there. My presence reassures them. It's all to do with building customer loyalty." [1] The American forwarder, Expeditors International, says the same thing: "Communication is not just electronic. The staff of Expeditors are always available to give their customer personal attention. That's what makes the difference." [2]

Rate deregulation and the establishment of direct computer links with the forwarders has brought a profound change to the work and the role of a reservations clerk. He has become increasingly an information provider and a salesman, constantly asked to negotiate special rate conditions.

The role of route manager is crucial; he is responsible for yield management. His business acumen, his fine understanding of traffic flows and the particular details of each customer, his gift of anticipating market fluctuations, and his ability of reconciling economic concerns with commercial considerations, determine the financial results of a flight, the profitability of the route and the satisfaction of the customer. The exercise of this profession requires the employment of extremely sophisticated computer techniques, combining a considerable number of parameters. However, in every case, indispensable as they are, they can only be an aid to decision-making. The main thing is to have a keen mind.

There are those who consider personnel in charge of dealing with customer complaints and the settlement of claims as mere administrators or "legal eagles". They could not be more mistaken! They are front-line sales staff. One customer may be lost due to the bad investigation or sluggish handling of a minor complaint. The loyalty of another may be won by settling a dispute quickly, with some commercial "nous".

Cargo warehouses, especially in the large terminals, are a different world, very much standardised and strongly unionised. There, you can feel that the traffic is alive, with its rhythms and surges. Warehouses experience intense last-minute rushes during peaks of activity, in late afternoon and evening for cargo inwards, and in the very early morning for deliveries. Here one can best understand that freight traffic is a nocturnal activity, like airmail or express, and for the same reason: for the customer, night eliminates time. Warehouse staff work in teams, on rotating shifts, day and night.

Automation and computers have transformed the work. Overall, they have enriched the individual tasks. More than ever, the warehouse staff have to combine physical tasks – made less onerous by handling equipment – with thought and initiative. Under these conditions, they play a decisive role in two key areas: quality of service and profitability.

The number of claims with customers is largely dependant on the good work of the warehouse man. Careful handling avoids damage. The meticulous and complete covering of pallets with plastic foil prevents damp in case of bad weather during loading and/or unloading operations. Proper securing of the parcels will ensure that the packaging is not harmed. The protection of the goods from damage depends on people respecting loading instructions ("top", "bottom", etc). And one could go on...

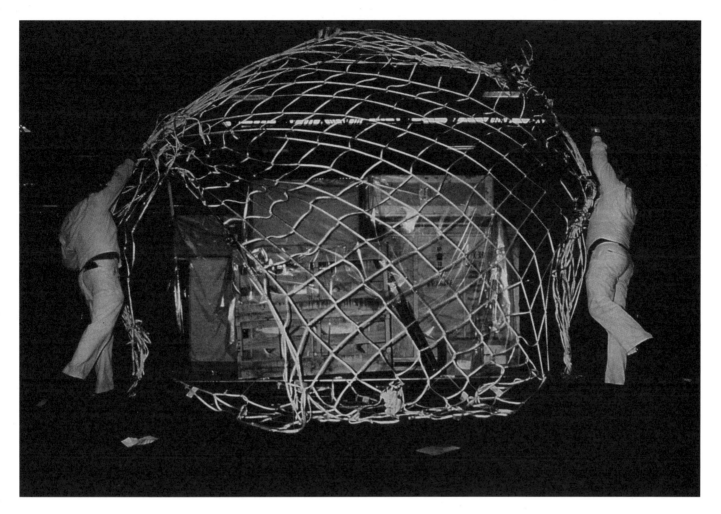

Beauty of professional know-how. Two cargo handlers load a net over a pallet.
Air France

The contribution of the warehouse men and their managers to the profitability of freight activities is no less important. The profitability of a cargo flight depends in part on the load factor. This frequently depends on the way in which pallets and containers have been loaded, and, if required, filled up during transit. Whereas an efficient team can load 3000kg of freight onto a pallet, by dint of their experience, intelligence, shrewdness and conscientiousness as professionals, a mediocre team will only manage to load 2,500 or 2,700kg. In the first case the flight makes a profit. In the second, it's in the red.

From these few examples, one can see that the warehouse is a highly professional area, in which people are usually proud of their knowledge and competence.

Near the warehouse, just at the exit or the entrance, are the loaders. It is their particular job to carry out all the tricky loading and unloading operations, in the case of oversized consignments or ones with exceptional unit weight. This is work for professionals, who can combine technology and experience with a certain amount of intuition.

Naturally, the freighter crews are also part of this great family. In all-cargo airlines, they only fly this type of aircraft, by definition. In the other airlines, they are most often generalists. Due to a concern with optimising shift plans: they will fly either passenger or cargo versions of the same type of aircraft, but it should be noted that flight crews often have a preference for cargo flights. By their attitude, they can also make a large contribution to the profitability of cargo operations, when they accept without demur an unforeseen refuelling stop to increase the payload, or a last-minute change to the flight plan to meet the requirements of a customer.

Nor should we forget the truck drivers without whom airfreight, which is in essence bi-modal, could not exist. Although they rarely belong to the airline personnel, they help to achieve the overall transport times between the shipper and the consignor, especially when, as in Europe or the United States, air carriers entrust them with pre- and or post-flight shipments of over 600 miles.

Computing is now an omnipresent factor in the carriage of goods. Computer specialists also play a key role within the freight team. The ideal is to have both computing qualifications and cargo experience.

Finance and accounting staff are also valuable team members, and the functions they fulfil have changed as centralised CASS invoicing systems are becoming more widespread. Yet in some circumstances, they must, as in the past, understand how to combine the indispensable financial disciplines with a commercial regard for the customer. These two concerns are sometimes difficult to reconcile. Financial vigilance is especially advisable in mail business, where a straightforward application of the UPU accounting regulations would lead to unacceptable payment delays.

So it is that many trades and professions contribute to freight transport in all its aspects. It is a continuous process, in which the least hiccup can cause a complete breakdown. For it to proceed harmoniously, it requires the cohesion and solidarity of various categories of personnel. At station level, this finds expression in the Cargo Teams so popular with the Americans, and which are often driven by a powerful "esprit de corps" emanating from a feeling of being different and from a collective pride.

Some people still think that freight is a men's world, perhaps even macho. These days, nothing could be further from the truth. Although the male predominance has traditionally been overwhelming in handling operations, women are gaining an increasing place in all other roles in the freight business, including aircraft loading. Today, we are witnessing a growing tendency for more women to be employed in commercial positions, and some women are even beginning to hold posts as regional directors.

The introduction of women in the recruitment of the airfreight business is by no means a recent phenomenon. It goes back to the earliest days of commercial aviation, as is shown by the example of Thérèse Christ in France. With an indefinable mixture of freshness of spirit, feigned naiveté, and unshakeable faith in future of air transportation, she recounted:

"You want me to tell you about my memories of the long years I spent in the service of air cargo. I am happy to do so, though in a rather higgledy-piggledy manner, just as you might take out of a big basket full of toys the ones which filled your childhood with wonder and magic, and which then gradually took over your working life. It was in 1922, with Messageries Aériennes (there's a name to conjure with) that I first made contact with freight operations ... The set-up was rather rudimentary, but the employees were multi-talented and full of confidence in the future. Because of the meagre capacities available on the first aircraft at that time, we had to use up the tonnage left over after loading urgent mail, diplomatic bags, the passengers and their luggage. Every passenger had to be weighed and it caused a lot of ironic smiles when a lady passenger tipped the scales at around 80kg..." [3]

She continues with two anecdotes, the first regarding Josephine Baker:

"She was a loyal passenger on our services, and always travelled with a lot of luggage, and, together with other artists, played a role in the creation of freight rates, because the costs of excess baggage were charged at the rate of 1% of the passenger fare per kilogram, and it is likely that we would have lost their business. But I was always surprised that a singer such as Josephine Baker, who got by wearing a few centimetres of hardly visible gauze or a belt of bananas, needed such a large amount of luggage."

Then regarding a consignment of gold:

"Right at the beginning of the operation of the Paris/London route, there was an incident involving a consignment of gold ingots on its way to London. The cargo holds of the aircraft gave way under the weight of several bullion boxes, and they ended up burying themselves in a field of potatoes in the Département of Oise. The pilot had to come down immediately on an emergency landing strip near Beauvais, and was able to recover them, thanks to the conscientiousness of the field's owner, who did not realise what manna had fallen to him from heaven."

In 1933, Madame Christ entered into the Freight Service of Air France at the time of its foundation, and after the war took over the management of the Paris Agency located at the Carrefour de Chateaudun. She left Air France in 1962, at the end of a career lasting 40 years, entirely devoted to airfreight.

You can leave the freight business, but you never forget it.

Part Eight
Beyond 2000:
9/11 An Act of War

"Be not afraid."

(The Gospel According to St Mark, 16.6)
Address of Pope John II Paris, 21st August 1997
for the World Youth Days (*"Journées Mondiales de la Jeunesse"*)

11th September 2001 shook the world. The destruction of the twin towers of the World Trade Centre in New York and the unthinkable fire at the Pentagon humiliated the United States and, for an instant, cast doubt on their absolute supremacy.

On 12th September, wounded to the quick, the Americans realised more clearly than other peoples, numbed with shock, that the world had been changed forever. There was now a new scale of values. Time, the evaluation of which had been the driving force behind the development of air transport, was no longer the reference standard. Security had become the absolute value. Whether willingly or not, the world will have to live for a long time under the shadow of the anti-terrorist battle as conceived by the world's only "hyper-power".

1 SECURITY: THE "ABSOLUTE IMPERATIVE"

It is no longer possible to write: "Cargo security can be viable only if its effect on operations and cost is reasonable." [1] Cargo security now has absolute priority.

On 7th December 2001 the council of ICAO adopted Amendment Number 10 to Annex 17 of the Convention. The member states undertook to strengthen the security measures on airports. In February 2002, ICAO called a "High Level Ministerial Meeting" in Montreal to elaborate the "Aviation Security Plan of Action".

For its part, the European Community "is given a mandate to develop EU legislation on aviation security". On the basis of this mandate, it drafted EU regulation 2320/2002, the force of which is "mandatory". Regulation 2320/2002 provides that "each Member State shall adopt a national civil aviation programme in order to ensure the application of the common standards referred to in regulation 2320/2002". In pursuit of these various requirements, a number of measures were adopted in order to apply more strictly the principle of "known shipper" and to strengthen and systematise the physical inspection of goods (screening etc) and to restrict conditions of access to freight terminals. This is why Lufthansa Cargo AG, when it moved into its new cargo terminal at New York JFK airport, Cargo Building 23, in July 2003, adopted a "state-of-the-art security technology":

"Digital cameras with 200m functions are directed at every square inch of the facility. Specially encoded magnetic cards only give employees access to places they are really supposed to be. Regiscope cameras compile photo identification cards of all persons who pick-up freight, before they are allowed to enter the building." [2]

2 THE BREAKDOWN OF EXPANSION

During the year 2000 Boeing and Airbus had published their long-term traffic forecast (2000-2019). Boeing was predicting an average annual growth in freight traffic of 6.4% and Airbus of 5.7%. The first years of the 21st century were far from confirming these forecasts, since the traffic in the year 2003 hardly differed from that in the year 2000. But the events of 11th September are not sufficient to explain this hiatus. Naturally, they made things worse, but the crisis pre-dated 9/11. It had hit the American market and its airlines in autumn 2000 with respect to domestic traffic, and in February 2001 in international activities. The Asian airlines had been affected during the winter of 2000/2001, and the European airlines in spring 2001. The attacks of 11th September only served to aggravate and prolong the crisis.

However, this global outlook of an industry which had been failing for three years, should not obscure certain developments, which have taken place, both regarding the flags of carrier nations and the airlines.

With regard to the countries, changes were clearly limited. Rankings for total traffic remain stable. Singapore went up a place at the expense of The Netherlands. In international traffic, China passed from fifth to second place, while Japan fell back from second to fifth place. However, though the total amount of traffic did not increase, four flags showed strong growth: China (+23%), Singapore (+13%), Luxembourg (+18%) and the Gulf States (UAE +35%).

If we look at the airlines, while traffic on a global level showed few signs of life, we should highlight the strong expansion of Fedex (+20%) Cargolux (+18%) and several Asian carriers (Eva Air +16%, Cathay Pacific +16%, Singapore Airlines +12%).

The real growth came from Emirates Airlines (+52%!), jumping from 31st to 20th place in the world rankings, whilst LAN Chile moved from 30th to 26th place.

Civilian traffic remained static, but there was an explosion in military transport during the wars in Afghanistan and Iraq. Since the end of the year 2001 an almost permanent airlift has linked the United States with various airfields situated near, or directly within, the theatres of operation, via US Airforce bases in Germany (Rhein-Main and Ramstein) for C-17s and in Spain for the C-5 "Galaxies". It would appear that the years 2002/3 provided a triple lesson regarding these two campaigns:

1. Although the traffic for Afghanistan exceeded 500,000 tonnes, supplies by air during the Iraq war stayed below those during the Gulf War of 1991. Various logistical innovations were introduced in order to avoid the build-up of equipment, which had occurred during 1990–1991.

2. The C-17 Globemaster III, which had first seen military service in Bosnia and Kosovo in 1995–1996, has become the airlift work-horse of the US transportation command, after the C-141 Starlifter underwent a planned withdrawal due to age and fatigue, and following the reduction of the C-5 Galaxy fleet. "The C-17 is a cross between a strategic air lifter and a tactical air lifter that can operate into austere airfields." [3]

   It made its maiden flight in September 1991 and offers a payload of 70/75 tonnes over distances in excess of 3,000 miles.

   The C-17 fleet of the US Air Force, which initially consisted of 120 aircraft, was increased to 180 units, and could well end up at over 220 aircraft.

3. Bearing the mind the limitations of the US military aircraft fleet and the first successes of Unmanned Air Vehicles (UAVs), the US Airforce is considering starting design work for an Unmanned Air Logistics Vehicle with a payload of 45 to 75 tonnes.

3 A LEAP INTO THE FUTURE: THE YEAR 2025

This is not meant to be a scientific preview based on the application of the latest econometric techniques, nor a futurological study, which could only be made by a multi-disciplinary team, but simply represents one possible scenario amongst many others. Imagine we are in the year 2025.

Development of freight traffic by country 2000–2002 (on scheduled flights)
(in million RTK)

Country	TOTAL WORLD TRAFFIC 2000	2002	02/00%	Ranking 00	02	INTERNATIONAL TRAFFIC 2000	2002	02/00 %	Ranking 00	02
United States	30,131	29,070	-4	1	1	18,950	18,9461	=	1	1
China	8,760	10,756	+23	2	2	7,289	8,739	+20	1	1
Japan	8,549	8,162	-5	3	3	7,718	7,335	-5	2	5
Korea	7,774	7,919	+2	4	4	7,630	7,769	+2	3	4
Taiwan	7,692	7,878	+2	5	5	7,650	7,878	+2	3	3
Germany	7,128	7,196	+1	6	6	7,109	7,181	+1	6	6
Singapore	6,005	6,772	+13	8	7	6,005	6,772	+13	8	7
Netherlands	6,609	6,669	+1	7	8	6,609	6,669	+	7	8
France	5,227	4,997	-4	9	9	4,934	4,775	-3	10	10
Great Britain	5,161	4,941	-4	10	10	5,155	4,937	-4	9	9
Luxembourg	3,533	4,158	+18	11	11	3,533	4,158	+18	11	11
U.A.E.	2,038	2,759	+35	12	12	2,038	2,758	+35	12	12
World Total	117,960	110,030	-1			101,520	100,590	-1		

Development of freight traffic by airlines 2000–2002
(in million RTK)

Airlines	TOTAL WORLD TRAFFIC 2000	2002	02/00%	Ranking 00	02	INTERNATIONAL TRAFFIC 2000	2002	02/00 %	Ranking 00	02
Fedex	10,809	12,992	+20	1	1	4,656	4645	+	6	6
Lufthansa	7,155	7,167	+	2	2	7,036	7,152	+1	1	1
Singapore AL	6,020	6,775	+12	5	3	6,020	6,775	+12	3	2
UPS	6,316	6,602	+4	4	4	2,650	2,659	=	14	13
Korean AL	6,484	6,046	-7	3	5	6,357	5,953	-6	2	3
Air France	4,980	4,862	-2	6	6	4,968	4,855	-2	4	4
Cathay Pacific	4,108	4,764	+16	10	7	4,108	4,764	+16	9	5
China AL	4,139	4,480	+9	9	8	4,133	4,190	+2	8	7
Japan AL	4,607	4,382	-5	7	9	4,323	4,141	-4	7	9
Cargolux	3,523	4,157	-18	14	10	3,523	4,157	+18	12	8
Eva Air	3,558	4,126	+16	13	11	3,558	4,126	+16	11	10
British Airways	4,564	4,124	-10	8	12	4,555	4,116	-10	10	11
KLM	3,964	3,992	+1	11	13	3,964	3,992	+1	10	12
Northwest AL	3,234	2,967	-8	15	14	2,409	2,163	-10	15	17
United AL	3,694	2,790	-24	12	15	2,777	2,156	-22	13	18
Asiana	2,598	2,579	-1	17	16	2,598	2,546	-2	14	14
American AL	2,780	2,577	-8	16	17	2,166	2,011	-7	19	19
Martinair	2,365	2,465	+4	18	18	2,365	2,465	+4	16	15
Nippon AC	2,186	2,202	+1	19	19	2,166	2,202	+1	17	16
Emirates	1,288	1,961	+52	31	20	1,288	1,961	+52	28	20

The regulatory framework
Liberalisation of air transport has been thriving, particularly with regard to traffic rights for cargo flights, which often provide test cases in this field. Nevertheless, the rate of change has been slower than was expected by some liberal forecasters at the beginning of the century. With regard to cargo flights, the situation is as follows:

- East-west-east routes (between Europe, North America and Asia and vice versa) have largely been deregulated;

- North-south routes, with the exception of open skies agreements with the United States, still retain a number of protectionist agreements;

- Cargo flights within the United States, China and Russia remain closed to foreign competition, more out of concern for security and national defence, than for truly commercial reasons.

The international economic environment
During the first quarter of the 21st century, the world economy

has shown an average annual growth rate of around 2.5%. International trade expanded at a visibly faster rate, underpinned by new agreements which were, not without difficulty, reached within the World Trade Organisation, and were promoted by a number of factors.

More than ever, Asia is at the core of world trade, and is the centre of gravity of the airfreight industry. All countries in this continent have made their contribution to this development, but three areas in particular have come to the fore: China, India and central Asia.

China has become "the workshop of the world" in numerous fields. Its domestic air traffic has reached a similar size to that of the United States, which has also expanded. The so-called "China Nebula", an extremely flexible economic and political structure, linking the People's Republic of China, the SARs of Hong Kong and Macao along with Taiwan, has reached the top ranking in the world airfreight industry.

India has succeeded in diversifying its exports, by developing certain leading-edge technologies.

Central Asia, an immense collection of peoples and nations extending from the Caspian Sea to the gates of Xian – the capital of the first emperors of China and the arrival point of the Silk Road – has, thanks to its oil reserves, become a particularly active region, in which American, Russian and Chinese interests are involved in a fierce struggle for supremacy.

Elsewhere, the establishment or the expansion of vast regional economic zones has provided new impetus to commercial trade, which to an increasing degree is operating like domestic traffic. This is the case in the Americas, where North, Central and South America form a large single free-trade area. This is also the case in Europe, which after having integrated the former countries of Eastern Europe over a period of 20 years, has now opened up to Ukraine and Turkey under American pressure.

The competitive world

Competition from other means of transport has increased. Since the year 2000, sea transport has benefited from scale effects and technical progress which has increased its competitiveness:

- The race to produce ever larger ships has continued: the container ships of 6,000 TEU of the mid–1990s were followed by vessels offering 9,000 TEU by 2005, and ships of 12,000 TEU and more now provide the backbone of the world fleet, even if the mammoth 18,000 TEU "Malacca Max" has not yet been built.

- The race for speed has produced "Fast Ships" (Fast Sea Transport Services) which cross the North Atlantic in 3.5 days, following the solution of the problem of marine propulsion. [4]

In Europe, the railways have at last cast off their lethargy. The injection of vast sums of capital to build a cargo rail network, the institution of independent regulatory authorities, and the coexistence of a number of companies competing over the same routes has provided the railways with new vigour, and developed combined transportation. Airfreight zones now possess their own rail connections, and approximately a third of pre- and post-flight shipments is carried by rail. Within Europe, integrators and express specialists are now combining air, rail and road transport.

In spite of a continuous, though irregular, economic growth, the oil prices have only slightly increased in constant currency value, even if temporary "oil crises" have occurred as a consequence of limited international armed conflicts.

Aircraft construction

In a book which appeared in 1995, one could read: "Today, the prospects for new productivity gains in aircraft, resulting in cost reductions, are no longer the same as in the Fifties and Sixties, when the productivity of the aircraft themselves increased by a factor of four every ten years. As a result, the future growth of air traffic will depend much more on the intensity of economic activities and development of world trade than on the technical prowess in aircraft construction." [5] This view has been confirmed, particularly for cargo fleets, which in the majority of cases, still consist of converted passenger aircraft.

The most advanced models of the A300-600F and the B747-400F and ERF still hold a substantial market share. Two aircraft provide the backbone of the world's long-haul network: the Boeing 777 ERF, the cargo version of the passenger machine, and the Airbus A380F with its payload of 150 tonnes, which is well suited to the main routes, and whose awaited economic performances have been confirmed for than 15 years. These two new types of aircraft did not revolutionise the airfreight industry, but allowed it to retain its competitive qualities in comparison with marine transport.

"Outsized shipments" are now being carried mainly by cargo dirigibles, and by heavy helicopters. The road network is suffering less and less from lorry convoys and exceptional loads. These are carried from point to point by helicopters over short distances and by cargo dirigibles for long-haul flights.

A number of projects are in an advanced stage of design: a cargo version of the "Flying Wing" with 250 tonnes payload, and a Civil Unmanned Air Cargo Vehicle. Although the transportation of cargo by means of rockets is still reserved for the construction and re-provisioning of orbital space stations, Fred Smith's successor is following with great interest the studies on hypersonic planes being undertaken by NASA.

The business environment – airlines and freight forwarders

With regard to the airlines, the policy of alliances has been confirmed and expanded. The liberalisation of traffic rights has enabled fleets and cargo programmes to be integrated within the framework of each alliance. Data processing systems have been standardised. Alliances have been expanded to allow the entry of freight forwarders. These are "Open alliances" – their members are linked by reciprocal contracts, but never in the form of exclusive relationships. The authorities in Brussels and the American Department of Justice are keeping a critical eye on the situation.

The close association between airlines and freight forwarders, particularly with respect to data processing within the alliances, has resulted in a blurring of the distinctions between integrators and traditional carriers/freight forwarders, except for true express products. Nevertheless, privileged arrangements have been set up between the integrators and the three major alliances. The latter are beginning to attain new dimensions, due to their inclusion of road, rail and marine transport companies, which enables them to offer to their customers truly world-encompassing transport systems.

With regard to the freight forwarders, the major multinational freight agents have increased their market share, but seem to have reached their limits. In parallel, a large number of specialist freight agents are continuing to prosper.

The products and services offered to customers are the result of joint marketing deliberations between the airlines and the freight agents working together in widened alliances. These elements of cargo traffic have developed according to expectations. A balanced situation seems to have been achieved, resulting from a combination of a long development process and from the maturity of the air transport markets:

The share of "general cargo", or the traditional non-segmented freight sector, has fallen to around 20% and it seems to have stabilised at this level. Added value products (express, time-definite services and special products) therefore represent around 80% of the market:

- Express, in the strict sense of the word, is now the prerogative of the major specialists (the same as in the year 2000) and some postal administrations. With regard to market share, it seems to have reached its peak, partly due to the restriction of night flights. In Europe, the market, which took off again after an explosive expansion in B2C (business-to-consumer) traffic, is essentially in the hands of the German, Dutch and French Post Offices. This situation means that airmail is now considered to be one express service amongst others.

- Time-definite services occupy a range between D+1 and D+4. Consolidation services cover up-market services (TD consolidations) and more economical versions (general cargo consolidations) in areas where fast ships have not put an end to this type of activity.

- Special products, adapted to the physical or commercial peculiarities of an expanding number of goods, give the impression that they still have a certain growth potential compared with other elements of the air transportation market, taking market share from "general cargo" and time-definite services for general merchandise. In many cases, the multiplication of such specific products has led to a personalisation of the supply.

- The civil market charter. The civil charter market for outsize and very heavy cargoes has continued to grow, accelerated by the development of such countries as India, China, and the oil-rich states. Still in the hands of a very few specialists, this market is now operated by heavy helicopters, traditional freighters and lighter than air vehicles.

A more-than three-fold growth in traffic
The traffic on scheduled flights in the year 2025 could reach 450 billion RTK, a more-than three-fold increase on 125 billion in the year 2000. This is equivalent of an annual average growth of about 5.5% over the period of 2000 to 2025. In spite of the dramas and conflicts at the beginning of the 21st century, growth factors have outweighed those influences which were slowing down development.

The braking forces were sufficient to cause a slowdown in growth compared with the last two decades of the 20th century. Among the chief limiting factors were the continuation of regional political and military tensions, the irregular nature of world economic growth, the constraints imposed by the absolute observance of security measures, and the operating limitations of airports (night flights). However, the growth factors, which have been sufficiently strong and numerous to be self-perpetuating, have won the day. Ten major factors played a seminal role:

1. The globalisation of the economy: "The trend towards international commerce is unstoppable." [6]

2. The growing proportion of high added-value, manufactured products in international trade.

3. The relocation of production units – while remaining a source of social upheaval, they represent a physical dislocation between production sites and places of consumption, generating flows of goods.

4. The reduction in product life cycles: "Successful firms will have to be constant innovators, to stay ahead of global imitators, copiers and property rights pirates… Fashion goods and software will move from hot to obsolete in a few months. Delivery time to shelf will separate winners from losers." [7]

5. The international division of labour within the same company. The increasing complexity of products, and the globalisation of production systems led a growing number of companies to spread the various production stages for a single product over separate manufacturing sites, often far removed from one another. The efficiency of this production process, which is very widespread in the electronics industry, depends on the speed, regularity and dependability of the links between the production sites. In these circumstances, airfreight is often an irreplaceable tool.

6. Modern techniques in logistics. The just-in-time, zero stock and tight supply chain techniques, which all aim to shorten the process from order acceptance to delivery to the final consumer, and to eliminate intermediate stocks, require increasingly effective transport systems. The division of the flows of goods into small lots, and the speeding up of decision-making processes, are factors which all favour air transport.

7. The inevitable malfunctions in the increasingly tight logistics chains.

8. The expansion of e-commerce, the development of which depends on the solution of the associated logistics problems.

9. The continuing tendency for air transport prices to fall when expressed in units of constant value.

10. The increasingly energetic and personalised marketing and advertising tactics of the airlines and associated freight forwarders "virtually integrated" within widened alliances, thanks to information technology.

Doubtless, this list is not exhaustive, but these 10 factors represent as many reasons for optimism and confidence in the future of airfreight: "Be not afraid."

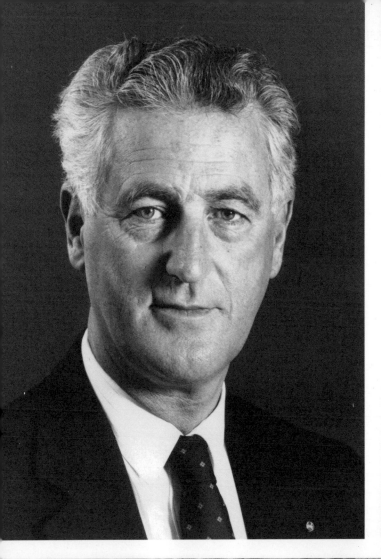

FAR LEFT **J. Martin Schröder founder of Martinair Holland (see page 331).**
Air Cargo News UK

ABOVE LEFT **Sir William Hildred (see pages 173 and 221).** *IATA*

BELOW LEFT **Sir Peter Abeles, TNT Chairman and Ansett joint MD and Sir Raymond Lygo, BAe CEO, signing long-term**

partnership commitment for all BAe146QT aircraft planned for production over the following five years (see page 280).
BAe/Air Cargo News UK

ABOVE **The shape of things to come? Impression of Cargolifter CL-160 semi-rigid cargo airship.** *ABB*

BELOW **An impression of Emirates SkyCargo Airbus A380F.**
Emirates

NOTES TO THE TEXT

PART ONE

CHAPTER 1

1 Charles Hirschauer, "The First Aerial Ascensions from Versailles", 1915 (pp.26-48) and 1918 (pp.57–95).

2 According to Peter Thoene, "La Conquête du Ciel", Paris 1938, pp.67-8

3 Peter Thoene, Op. cit. p.57.

4 Marquis d'Argenson, "Thoughts upon the reform of the State", Paris, P.350.

5 Charles Dollfus, "Les Ballons", Paris 1960, p.7.

6 Rigo de Righi, "Britain's Pioneer Airmails", National Postal Museum London.

7 Throughout the battle of Fleurus, "L'Entreprenant" was in the air all day, and its crew signalled valuable information about the movements of enemy forces to officers on the ground.

8 On this subject, see: Alfred Clément, "Handbuch Der Militär Luftpost", Graz, 1955, pp.5-6; Ernest. M. Cohn, "Postal History Journal", May 1971; E. de Keyser, "Le Vieux Papier", July 1971, No 241, p.282.

9 "Luftpostens Historia I Norden" ("The History of Airmail in Scandinavia"). Örjan Luning, Stockholm, 1978, pp.231-232.

10 Edmund Petit, "L' Atlantique Nord", "Pégase" ("Revu de l' Association des amis du Musée de l'Air" - "Review of the Association of the Friends of the Museum of the Air"), No/53 April 1989 p.14. Edgar Poe, "Tales of the Unexpected", "The balloon hoax" (JMS to find best standard addition & Page nos etc)

11 Charles Dollfus, "Histoire de l'Aéronautique", Paris, 1947, p.87.

12 "Postal History International". Brighton, United Kingdom, Volume XIV, No 1, January 1969 p.37

13 "Icare", No 56 Winter-Spring 1971, pp. 59.

14 "La Cohorte", Quarterly review of the Society for the Mutual aid of members of the Légion d'Honneur, April-May 1995, P.18.

15 Ernst M. Cohn, "Comparison of Belfort & Metz, 1870 balloon mails" Postal History International, September 1976, p.200.

16 The journal "Icare" published three remarkable numbers devoted to the siege of Paris, No 56 Autumn-Spring 1971, No 57 Summer 1976 and No 83 Winter 1977-78. We are very much indebted to these accounts.

17 "Science applied to the art of warfare", compiled by the Réunion des Officiers, Paris 1886, p.355.

18 "Weltpost und Luftschifffahrt" a lecture to the Berlin Scientific Association, Berlin 1874.

19 Charles Dollfus and Henri Bouché, "Histoire de l'aéronautique", Paris, "L'Illustration", 1942, p.152.

20 "Icare", No 135, April 1990, p.73

21 Hans G. Knäusel "LZ1 - Der erste Zeppelin - Geschichte einer Idée: 1874-1908", Bonn, 1985, pp.43 and 58.

22 "Zeppeline und Post", an Exhibition of the Bundes Postmuseum, Frankfurt am Main, 1987, p.15.

23 See Sieger, "Zeppelin Post Katalog", Sieger Verlag-Lorch, Württemberg, pp.10 et seq.

24 "Zeppeline und Post", Op. cit. p.16.

CHAPTER 2

1 Charles H Gibbs-Smith, "Aviation - An Historical Survey", Science Museum, London, 1970 p.8.

2 Revue de L'Aéronautique, 1893.

3 Flight record of the Wright Brothers.

4 Chadeau, "L'industrie aéronautique en France: 1900/1950", Paris 1987, p.39.

5 See article "The first airfreight" by Roger E. Bilstein, Professor of History at Wisconsin State University - "Ohio History", pp. 248-58.

6 Cameron, "The Hungry Tiger", New York, 1964.

7 J. Stroud, "Annals of British Air Transport", London, 1962, p.19

8 See James Mackay, "Air mails - 1870-1970", London, 1971.

9 "Luftfahrt in Berlin Brandenburg", Catalogue of the Historical Exhibition of the ILA '92, Berlin, 1992.

10 "La Poste et l'Aviation", Exhibition catalogue, 17th June-3rd September 1983, Musée de la Poste-Paris, 1983.

11 William M. Leary : "Aerial Pioneers", Smithsonian Institution, Washington 1985, pp.14-16.

12 Carroll V. Glines, "Airmail", Blue Ridge Summit, Pa, 1990, p.36.

13 Regarding the first postal flights in Italy, see: "L'Union Postale", March 1942.

14 James Mackay," Airmails 1870/1970", London 197, pp.68-72.

15 See: Peter Supf, "Das Buch der Deutschen Fluggeschichte", Berlin 1935; Erik Heimann: "Die Flugzeuge der Deutschen Lufthansa", Stuttgart 1980, p.9.

16 "Postal History Journal", New York, Oct.1981, p.32.

17 "Revue des Postes et Télécommunications de France", Paris, 1962, No 4, p.37.

18 Örjan Lüning: "Luftpostens Historia I Norden", Stockholm 1978.

19 Stanley Brodgen, "The History of Australian Aviation", Melbourne 1960, pp. 35-36.

PART TWO

CHAPTER 1

1 Le Corbusier, "Aircraft". The Studio, London, 1935 , p.9.

2 Charles H. Gibbs-Smith, "Aviation - An Historical Survey", Science Museum, London, 1970, pp.178-179.

3 Revue du Secrétariat Général à L'Aviation Civile, No 133/15 Nov.1968, p.100.

4 "Aeroplanes and aero-engines", "Avion", London, 1918

5 Peter Meyer, "Luftschiffe" ("Airships"), 1980, Koblenz/Bonn.

6 Alfred Clement, "Handbuch Der Militär-Luftpost", Graz, 1955.

7 Major General Benjamin D. Foulois, "From the Wright Brothers to the Astronauts", Memoirs, MacGraw Hill, New York, 1968.

CHAPTER 2

1 "L'Aérophile", 1st-15th November 1918.

2 "L'Union Postale", UPU, Berne, March 1942.

3 "Annales des PTT", Paris, 1919, "L'Aviation et La Post", p.216 et seq.

4 "L'Aérophile", 1st-15th June 1918.

5 J. Stroud, "Annals of British and Commonwealth Air Transport - 1919-1960", London, 1962, p.23.

6 "Postal History Society (UK) Bulletin", Jan-Feb 1957, pp.10-11.

PART THREE

CHAPTER 1

1 Mermoz, "Mes vols" ("My flights"), Paris, 1972, p.20.

2 Paul Painlevé, former President of the Council of Ministers, before the "Senatorial Group for Aviation", 11th February 1920.

3 "L'aéronautique", July 1919.

4 "L'Aérophile", 1st-15th November 1922.

5 J. Stroud, "Annals of British and Commonwealth Air Transport, 1919-1960", p.35.

6 "L'Aérophile", 1st-15th July 1920.

7 Or "Lake Constance".

8 Örjan Lüning, Op. cit. p.237.

9 Robert Espérou, "Revue du SGAC", No 133, 1968, p.103 and No141, 1971, pp.184-186.

10 "Il Corriere Philatelico", February 1978.

11 Philip Smith, "Sur les ailes du temps. Air Canada. Les 50 dernières années" ("On the wings of time. Air Canada: the last 50 years"), Montreal 1986, p.17.

12 See: "Postal History Journal". Official organ of the Postal History Society (USA). Vol 15 No 1 January 1971; "Postal Service Today". Republic of China, Nos 286/287 Oct-Nov 1981.

13 Concerning the history of air transport in Japan: Katsu Kohri, Ikuo Komori, "A view of 50 years of Japanese Aviation 1910-1960", Tokyo 1962; Robert Mikesh and Shorzoe Abe, "Japanese Aircraft 1910-1941", London 1990.

14 Unpublished document kindly provided and commented on by the Paris Office of the Asahi Shimbun.

15 Stanley Brogden, "The History of Australian Aviation", Melbourne 1960, p.77.

CHAPTER 2

1 S. Ralph Cohen: "IATA les trente premières années" ("IATA: the first thirty years"), IATA, Montreal, 1949.

2 Ralph Cohen: IATA, p.75.

3 The mechanism of the pool consists of holding in common the revenues taken by several carriers on a specific sector and sharing them according to rules agreed in advance.

4 IATA Bulletin, December 1949, No 10, p.17.

5 Maurice Lemoine, "Traité de Droit Aérien" ("Treatise on Air Law"), Paris, 1947, p.22.

6 Paris Convention Article 15.

7 Eugène Pépin, "Géographie de la circulation aérienne" (Geography of air traffic), Paris, 1956, p.27.

8 "Documents of the Madrid Postal Congress", 1920, Universal Postal Union, Berne, Volume 1, pp.581-582.

9 Stockholm Universal Postal Convention – Article 74 §3. UPU – Documents of the Stockholm Postal Congress. Berne, 1924, p.135 and pp.266-268 – Author's translation.

10 "Annals of the PTT", Paris 1930, p.399.

11 "Documents of the Conference on Aerial Post of The Hague", UPU, Berne.

12 Postal Union – Berne 1938 Speech of the Director-General of the Belgian Post to the Brussels Conference of 1938.

13 Jean-Louis Magdalénat, "Le Fret Aérien – Règlementation Résponsibilités" Airfreight – Règlementation and Responsibilities. Toronto. Paris. p.61. – see also English language edition: "Air Cargo Regulations and Claims", Butterworth's Toronto 1983.

14 J. L. Magdalénat. Op. cit., p.124.

15 Albert Rabut: "La Convention de Varsovie", Paris, 1952, p.23.

CHAPTER 3

1 According to Carl Solberg " Conquest of the Skies. A History of Commercial Aviation in America", Boston-Toronto, 1979, p.17.

2 William M. Leary "Aerial Pioneers – the U.S. Airmail Service – 1918-1927", Washington 1985, p.29.

3 Carrol V. Glines – "Airmail". Blue Ridge Summit Pa, 1990, p.51.

4 First class post consists of sealed letters,

post cards, business papers etc.

5 On this subject: James Woolley, "Airplane Transportation", Hollywood, 1929, p.159.

6 William M. Leary. Op cit. p.127.

7 "Icare", No 154, 1995/3, p.93.

8 Document of the US Postal Service, Washington, Archives of the Air and Space Museum.

9 Lisbeth Freudenthal, "The Airline Business", New York, 1940, tables in appendix.

10 Solberg, Op. cit. p.144.

11 Stanley H. Brewer, "The impact of mail programmes and policies on United States Air Carriers", Seattle/Washington, 1967, p.IV.

12 Archives of the Library of the Musée de la Poste, Paris. Note from the Economic Counsellor to the French Embassy in Washington.

13 American Airlines, Eastern Airlines, Transcontinental and Western Airlines, United Airlines.

14 James Woolley, Op. cit. p.201

CHAPTER 4

1 Raymond Danel, "Les lignes Latécoère", Toulouse, 1986, p.17.

2 Raymond Danelle, Op. cit., p.38.

3 Robert Espérou, Revue du SGAC November 1968, "Le Matériel Volant des Compagnie Aériennes Françaises" (The aircraft of the French airlines), p.97.

4 Marcel Moré, "J'ai vécu l'épopée de l'Aéropostale" ("My first hand experiences of the airmail epic"), Paris, 1970 p.76.

5 Raymond Vanier, "Tout pour la ligne" ("All for the line"), Paris, 1960, p.34.

6 E. Allaz, "La Poste Aérienne" in "Terre et ciel", the personnel magazine of the National Company Air France, June 1947.

7 R. Danel, Op. cit., p.146.

8 Didier Daurat, "Dans le vent des hélices" ("In the draught of the propellers"), Paris, 1956, p.60.

9 Didier Daurat, Op. cit.

10 Antoine de Saint Exupéry, "Terre des hommes", Paris, 1939, p.21.

11 Raymond Vanier, Op. cit., p.33.

12 Air France, "Postal Instruction booklet" of 1st April 1936, p.9. Note the capital letter on the word "Users", a sign of particular consideration towards the customers.

13 "Annals of the PTT", Paris, 1930.

14 Antoine de Saint Exupéry, "Courier Sud" ("Southern Mail"), Paris, 1929.

15 Joachim Wachtel, "Lufthansa. L'Histoire", Cologne, 1975, p.35.

16 Title borrowed from R. Dannel, "L'Aéropostale", p.97.

17 Marcel Moré, Op. cit., pp.150-151.

18 "Deutsche Verkehrszeitung", 28th July 1934.

19 "Lufthansa, l'histoire", Op. cit., pp.48-49.

20 R. Danel, "L'Aéropostale", p.119.

21 R. Vanier, Op. cit. p.167.

22 This was Henri Bouché, Director and Editor in Chief of "L'Aéronautique" and later founder of L'Institut français du Transport Aérien (IFTA) which later became the Institut du Transport Aérien (ITA).

23 Extract of a report of 21 July 1938 by the Inspector General for Aeronautics, Monsieur Hirschauer, "on the situation of the company Air France in 1938". Appendix about the South American service, p.3. Archives Air France, Box HL 383.

24 On this delicate subject see the Hirschauer report of 21st July 1938 already quoted. Appendix concerning the South American service, pp. 20 to 25.

CHAPTER 5

1 Pierre Deffontaines and Louis Charvet, "Géographie des Transports Aériens" ("Geography of Air Transport"), Air France, Paris, 1939, pp.53-54

2 Jean Farrugia and Tommy Gammons, "Carrying British Mail", National Postal Museum London, 1980, p.92.

3 Brig. Gen. F. H. Williamson, "La Grande Bretagne et la poste aérienne" in "l'Union Postale", 1924.

4 John Stroud, Op. cit., p.62.

5 Peter Pigott, Kaï Tak.

6 Regarding the totality of this subject cw Hajening, "Le développement du service postal Aérien aux Indes Néerlandaises" in "L'union postale", Berne, 1932.

7 "Les Ailes", 23 February 1933.

8 Archives of the Postal Museum, Paris.

9 "L'Aviette Postale", 7th November 1930.

10 G. Collot/A.. Cornu, "La Ligne Noguès. Histoire Aérophilatèlique, 1911-1941" ("The Noguès line Aerophilatelic history, 1911-1941"), Paris, 1992.

11 "France Aviation", October 1978, supplement p.4.

12 Robert Espérou, "Le Matériel Volant des Compagnies Aériennes Francaises" ("The aircraft of the French airlines 1919-1939"), "Revue du SGAC", No 134, p.68.

13 Air France archives "Étude de la Ligne Impériale, Marseilles/Saigon/Hanoi", 1/7/1938.

14 "Icare", No 159, 1996/4, p.54.

15 "The Rolls-Royce Magazine", No 62, September 1994.

16 R. Espérou, Articles quoted, Revue du SGAC, No 137, p.103.

17 Ministry of PTT, information bulletin, July-August 1939, "L'Aviation Postale à Madagascar".

18 "L'Aviette Postale", January 1937.

19 Ministry of PTT, quoted article.

20 Letters and postcards.

21 "Highways of the sky - The story of British Airways", British Airways, 1979, p.9.

22 J. Parker Van Zandt, "European Air transport on the eve of war 1939", Norwich University, Northfield, Vermont USA, 1940, p.18.

23 John Stroud, "Annals of British & Commonwealth air transport", London, 1962, p.164.

24 "Freight" is understood in the sense of "traffic".

25 Note from the French Commercial Attaché at The Hague, 22nd May 1937, Archives of the Musée de la Poste, Paris.

CHAPTER 6

1 Lufthansa, "L'histoire" ("The History"), p.4.

2 "L'Union Postale", Berne, 1937, No 7.

3 "Der Nachtluftverkehr" ("Night-time air services"), Berlin, 1936.

4 "Postarchiv", April 1943, Vol 2, pp.116-140.

5 Information Bulletin of the Ministry for PTT, November 1937, "L'aviation postale intérieure".

CHAPTER 7

1 Mackay, Op. cit. p.99.

2 Jean Farrugia and Tony Gammons, "Carrying British Mails", London, National Postal Museum, 1980.

3 "L'Aviette Postale", 15th February 1938.

4 "Icare", No 157, p.13.

5 "Icare", No 157, p.12.

6 J. Stroud, Op. cit., p.408.

7 Philip Smith, Op. cit., p.18.

8 Philip Smith, Op. cit., pp.19-20.

9 "Union postale", Berne, December 1959.

10 "Lufthansa, The History", Op. cit., p.57.

11 "L'Aviette postale", October 1937.

12 "Die Deutsche Post", 25th October 1938.

13 The French protype policy refers to the requirement for tendering manufacturers to build prototypes that often did not lead to series manufacture – and thus many expensive one-off aircraft and few profitable long-running series.

14 "Icare", No 157, p.77.

14 M. Josephson, "Empire of the air", New York, 1944, p.88.

15 FAM9: Foreign Airmail Contract No 9.

16 M. Josephson, Op. cit., p.44.

17 R. E. G. Davies, "Airlines of the United States", p.214.

18 "Icare", No 155, 1995/4, p.104.

CHAPTER 8

1 A company created on 1st January 1923 from the merger of La Compagnie des Messageries Aériennes and La Compagnie des Grands Express Aériens. In particular, it operated the London/Paris route.

2 "L'union postale", Bern, 1929, pp.191-197 and 211-220.

3 Karl Pirath, "Konjunktur und Luftverkehr" ("Economics and air transport"), Berlin, 1935.

4 "Icare", No 103, 1982/4, p.31.

5 Literally: "aircraft-railway".

6 Dr Günter Berendt, "Die Entwicklung der Marktstruktur im Internationalen Luftverkehr" ("The development of the market structure in international air transport"), Berlin, 1961, pp.25 and 53/54.

7 Erich H. Heimann, "Die Flugzeuge der Deutschen Lufthansa", Stuttgart, 1980, pp.122-133.

8 "Icare", No 103, 1982/4, p.77.

9 "Aviation in Canada 1971", Information Canada, Ottawa, 1972.

10 "Forces Aériennes Francaises", Review of the L'Armée de l'Air, No 236, May 1967.

11 "L'Union Postale", Bern, January 1949, p.14.

12 1 ounce = 28.35 grams.

13 Traffic expressed in gross tonnes.

14 J. Parker Van Zandt, "Air Cargo in Latin America", "Air Transportation", January 1943, p.32.

15 Jürgen Ulderup, "Der Stand des Weltluftverkehrs" ("The situation of World Air Transport"), Berlin, 1935, p.59.

16 James Sinclair, "Wings of Gold", Sydney, 1978, p.108.

17 "The World Almanac", The New York World-Telegram, 1941, p.589.

18 Ministry for PTT, "Bulletin d'information", 1932, No 7, p.56.

19 Harry Bruno, "Wings over America", New York, 1942, pp.121-122.

20 House of Representatives, "Hearings before the Committee on the Post Office and Post Roads", 76th Congress, 12th June, 1940, p.7.

21 Stan Cohen: "Flying Boats Work", The story of Reeve Aleutian Airways, Missoula, Montana, 1988, p.11 et seq.

CHAPTER 9

1 Pierre George, "L'URSS" ("The USSR"), Paris, 1947, p.121.

2 Pierre George, Op. cit. p.382.

3 R. E. G. Davies, "Aeroflot, An airline and its aircraft", Rockville, MD, USA, 1992, p.12.

4 Archives of the Musée de la Poste, Paris.

5 Information bulletin of the Ministry for PTT, Paris, 1932, No 5, pp.97-98.

6 Source: Karl Heinz Eyermann, "Die Luftfahrt in der USSR, 1917-1977" ("Air transport in the USSR"), Berlin (East), 1978.

7 XXX, "L'aviation soviétique, Les ailes", 1937. Chapter V.

8 XXX. Op. cit.

9 "L'Odyssée du Tchéliouskine", Compilation. preface by Professor Otto Schmidt, p.13, Paris 1935.

10 The origin of this expression goes back to a journalist on the "Illustration", No 4614, 8th August, 1931.

11 Papanine, "Sur la Banquise en Dérive" ("On the drifting ice flow"), Paris, 1948, p.XIV.

PART FOUR

CHAPTER 1

1 "Bulletin hebdomadaire", No 1035, January 1941.

2 "Il Corriere Filatelico", No 9, Feb 1977.

3 Louis Castex, "Les Compagenies étrangères dans le Réseau Aérien mondial" ("Foreign companies in the world airways network"), 1944.

4 Based on "Postal history journal" (US), Vol. VII, No 2, Dec.1963, pp.3-8.

5 Postal Union, "L'administration des Postes de Grande Bretagne pendant la Guerre", July 1946, pp.170-171.

6 Canada's First Line Paper, Vol. 2, No 7-11/12/1943, quoted in "Philatélie Québec", February 1994.

7 "Archiv für Deutsche Postgeschichte", 1969, Vol.1, p.57.

8 See: "L'union postale", June 1946, pp.126-146. "A postscript to the Postal Historian", Vol III, No 2, May 1953, pp36-46.

9 In order to combine confidentiality with low weight, the Post Office had launched the "sixpenny air letter"on 7th December 1942, to be sent to the BritishForces.

10 "Philatélie Québec", No 162, November 1989.

11 E. C .Baker, "The Airgraph Service" in "A Postscript to...", p.45.

12 "War Department Field Manual", April 1945, "Photomail operations", Washington, Air & Space Museum Archives.

13 See Keith Winston, "V-Mail: Letters of a World War II combat medic", Alconquin Books of Chapel Hill, North Carolina, 1985.

14 "Postarchiv", April 1943, Vol. 2, pp.135-140.

15 "Archiv Für Deutsche Postgeschichte", 1969, Vol. 1, pp.30-55.

CHAPTER 2

1 Charles H. Gibbs-Smith, Op. cit., p.205.

2 Carl. Solberg, "Conquest of the skies", p.251.

3 Rosario Abata, "Aeroplani Caproni", 1910-1983, Trento, 1992, p.93.

4 In 1938, Lufthansa had transported 2 251 tonnes of goods.

5 Generalmajor Fritz Morzik, "German Air Forces Airlift Operations" in "USAF Historical Studies", No 167, New York 1961 and "Die Deutschen Transport Flieger im Zweiten Weltkrieg", Frankfurt-am-Main, 1966.

6 Jean Roeder, "Civil freighters and Military Transports" International symposium on

The future of freight transport aviation, Strasbourg, March 1993, p401.

7 J. Roeder, Op. cit.

8 "Jane's", New York, 1969.

9 Franz Kurowski, "Luftbrücke Stalingrad", Kurt Vohwinckel Verlag, Berg am See, 1983.

10 The West Point Military History Series - "The Second World War, Europe and the Mediterranean", p.131.

11 Ministry of Defence of the USSR, "The Soviet Air Force in World War II", David & Charles, London, 1972, p.142.

12 Ministry of Defence of the USSR, Op. cit., p.143.

13 Ministry of Defence of the USSR, Op. cit. p.236.

14 Fritz Morzick, Op. cit., p.223.

15 Harrison Salisbury, "900 days: The siege of Leningrad", New York, 1985, p.401.

16 The Company Aeroflot was integrated into the Air Force on 25th June 1941.

17 General Karl Drum, "Air power and Russian Partisan warfare", "USAF Historical studies", No 177, March 1962, p.30.

18 Op. cit., p.42.

19 Reginald Cleveland, "Transport at war", New York, 1945, p107/108, p.241.

20 J. Parker Van Zandt, "European Air Transport on the Eve of War", Norwich University, Vermont USA, 1940.

21 Ibid.

22 Charles H. Gibbs-Smith, "Aviation", p.214.

23 ATA: Air Transport Association.

24 Estimate given in N. W. Kendall, "US Overseas Air Cargo Services" - US Department of Commerce, Washington, 1949, p.13.

25 C. Bright, "Historical Dictionary of the US Air Force", p.152.

26 Eiichiro Sekigawa, "Pictorial history of Japanese military aviation", London, 1974. It was unique to Japan that the navy held 70% of the aircraft in use.

27 Anon, "The Japanese air forces in World War II", Arms and Armour Press, London/Melbourne, 1979.

28 R. J. Francillon, "Japanese aircraft in the Pacific War", Putnam, London.

29 Ibid.

30 John Stroud, Op. cit, p.189.

31 Jane's "All the world's aircraft, 1945-1946".

32 "Royal Air Force 1939-1945", Vol. III, p.331.

33 Field Marshal the Viscount Slim, "Defeat in Victory", David McKay Company, New York, 1961, p.455.

34 "Royal Air Force", Op. cit., p.180.

PART FIVE

CHAPTER 1

1 United Nations Charter, (Art. 24).

2 United Nations Charter, (Art. 55).

3 Jacqeline Dutheil de La Rochère, "La politique des États-Unis en matière de l'aviation civile internationale" ("United States policy regarding international civil aviation"), Paris 1971.

4 Idem., p.113.

5 P. P. C. Haanappel, "Pricing and Capacity Determination in International Air Transport", Deventer, The Netherlands, 1978, p. 29.

6 Nawal K. Taneja, "US International Aviation Policy", Lexington/Toronto, 1980.

7 "IATA, Les Trente Premières années" ("IATA, The first thirty years"), Op. cit., p.94.

8 "IATA, Les trente prèmieres années", ("IATA The first thirty years"), Op. cit., p.94.

9 Air France Bulletin de documentation, No 75, p.2.

10 In 1947.

CHAPTER 2

1 TRK: Revenue Tonne Kilometres. The Tonne Kilometre is the unit corresponding to the transportation of one tonne through one kilometre. It combines gross tonnes with kilometres travelled.

2 Excluding the USSR. The USSR did not join the ICAO until 1970.

3 "Esso Air World", Vol. 27, No 3, 1975, pp.58-60.

4 The term "tariff" should be understood in its American sense: it covers both the regulatory arrangements and the conditions of the price tariff.

5 "Here comes American Airlines - Airfreight!", 1944.

6 E. Rath & G. L. Knight, "Air Cargo", New York, 1947, p.40.

7 "Air transportation", No 1, October 1942.

8 Quoted by Frank Cameron, "The Hungry Tiger", New York, 1964, pp.101/102.

9 John F. Foster, Major USAF-retired, "China up and Down", Keen, New Hampshire. Revised 1994, p.39.

10 Frank Cameron, "The Hungry Tiger", New York, 1964.

11 Richard Malkin, "Boxcars in the sky", New York, 1951.

12 "L'aviation marchande", No 24 - Nov/Dec 1949, Paris.

13 Archives of the General Directorate of Civil Aviation, Paris.

14 "Icare", No 115, p.103.

15 Jean Combard, "La SATI" – "Icare", No 117, p.163.

16 Air France, Annual Report 1950, p.18.

17 In the IATA nomenclature, the "European area" includes North Africa.

18 John L. Sutton, "European Commerical Air Cargo", University of Notre Dame, Indiana, Geneva 1949, Chapter VIII.

19 ITA, Study No 269-270, Paris, 1955.

20 "L'Aviation Marchande", No 26, May-June 1949.

21 François Bellec, "Océans des Hommes" ("Oceans of mankind"), Guest, France, 1987, p.167.

22 "IATA Bulletin", January 1948, p.24.

23 "IATA Bulletin", December 1952.

CHAPTER 3

1 Institut Français du Transport Aérien, IFTA, Working note number No 192-193 "Comment developper le transport aérien des merchandises – Le problème de l'avion-cargo." ("How to develop air transport for goods – the problem of the cargo aircraft"), Paris, December 1950.

2 See "Society of Automotive Engineers" – "Cargo aircraft requirements", Kansas City, Dec. 1947.

3 IFTA, "Economie du transport aérien. Le problème du cargo aérien". ("Economics of air transport. The problem of air cargo"), Working note Nos 115-116, Paris, December 1947, pp.33-35.

4 IFTA, Op. cit., p.47.

5 ICAO, "Fret aérien", ("Airfreight"), 1962, p.11.

6 ICAO Circular 97, AT/18, "Fret Aérien, Région Europe – Méditerranée" ("Airfreight, Europe-Mediterranean region"), 1970.

CHAPTER 4

1 Jean Baptiste Duroselle, "Histoire diplomatique de 1919 à nos jours" ("Diplomatic history from 1919 to the present day"), Paris, 1993, p.417.

2 Great Britain Air Ministry, "Berlin Airlift - An account of the British contribution", London, 1949, p.8.

3 GB Air Ministry, Op. cit, p.52.

4 Stanley Brewer, "Military airlift", Seattle, University of Washington, 1967, p.VI.

5 Frost and Sullivan, "The air cargo market", New York, 1972, p. II-129.

6 The CRAF was used for the first time in 1990 during the Gulf War.

7 C. Bright, "Historical dictionary of the US Air Force", New York 1992, pp.156-157.

8 S. Brewer, Op. cit. p.vii.

9 Frost and Sullivan, Op. cit., p.II-131.

10 D. Wragg, "Airlift", Shrewsbury, England, p.70.

11 C. Bright, Op. cit., p.131.

12 Frost and Sullivan, Op. cit., II-144.

13 "Air Transportation", May 1955, p.26.

CHAPTER 5

1 "IATA Bulletin" No 6, January 1948, p.21.

2 "IATA Bulletin" No 19, Mid-year 1954.

3   The French Union, defined in the Constitution of 1946, was the entity consisting of the French Republic, its territories, colonies and protectorates.

4   Edouard Allaz, Course given at the Ecole Supérieure des Transports, 1956, typed copy, p.24.

5   CAB, "Airfreight Forwarding". September 1973, p.50 et seq.

6   "Air Freight Forwarders case", 1948.

7   In American terminology, a "tariff" is a document listing in a very precisely determined form, all the regulatory and tariff conditions of a carrier or a forwarder – considered as an "indirect carrier. These rates cover all rules and rates." Such Rates are documents in the public domain.

8   The AFF only received a 5% commission on international groupage after 1980.

9   At the time, approval was issued office by office. Later it was to be by country.

10 William E. Connor, "An introduction to airline economics", New York, 1972, p.93.

11 Edouard Allaz, Course given at the Ecole Supérieure des Transports, 1956, typed copy, p.24.

CHAPTER 6

1   Sir William Hildred, "IATA Bulletin", December 1956, p.24.

2   Sir William Hildred, "IATA Bulletin", December 1960.

3   ICAO, "Le Fret Aérien" ("Airfreight"), Doc. 8235, Montreal, 1962.

4   See "IATA Bulletin", December 1961, p.101.

5   The London/New York was the standard reference used to determine all the North Atlantic rates and fares.

6   Expression borrowed from R. E. G. Davies in "Airlines of the USA." p.495: "The propellor-turbine interlude".

7   "Interavia", No 8/1950, pp.951-955.

8   We define commonality as follows: "the totality of common features shared by several items of equipment from the point of view of design, manufacture or maintenance". (Translated from "Dictionnaire du transport Aérien", ITA, 1993.)

9   Due to the difficulty of comparing specifications which often vary, we have chosen a B707-320C operated by Air France and a DC-8F-55 operated by Martinair-Holland.

10 See Boeing brochure, "QC - The Double Life Jet", May 1966.

11 "Hommes et Techniques", No 289, November 1968, p.922.

CHAPTER 7

1   "IATA Bulletin" No 16, December 1952, p.6.

2   "Bulletin of Institut du Transport Aérien", 25/01/1960.

3   In tonne kilometres.

4   Gabon was at that time part of French Equatorial Africa (AEF).

5   Letter of Dr Schweitzer, written in Lambarene on 14th November 1953.

6   IFTA (French Institute for Air Transport). Working note 186-187, September 1950. "The adaptation of Air Transport to the needs of Black Africa", p.1.

7   IFTA above-quoted study, p.30.

8   Thóphile Kamoclo, "Réflexions sur certains pays d'Afrique" ("Reflections on certain countries of Africa"), 3rd ITA International Colloquium, ITA, Paris 1968, p.10.

9   Fort Lamy is today known as N'Djamena.

10 ITA, Working Note Nos 341-342, October 1961.

11 Report by Robert J. Garry given before the Institute of Geography of the University of Montreal, 1960. Quoted in Working Note No 341-342 of the Institut du Transport Aérien, Paris, October 1961.

CHAPTER 8

1   ICAO "Etude sur la Poste Aérienne" ("Study on air mail"), 1962, p.12.

2   "IATA Bulletin" No 8, December 1948, p.46.

3   "IATA Bulletin", January 1948, p.37.

4   Edouard Allaz ("La Poste Aérienne" June 1947, in "Terre et Ciel", House magazine for personnel of the Société Nationale Air France.

5   "IATA Bulletin", No 16, December 1952, p.29.

6   "IATA Bulletin", December 1949, p.124.

7   "Union Postale", 1971, p.39.

8   "IATA Bulletin", December 1972, p.31, §95.

9   We should recall that the USSR was not a member.

10 American, Eastern, TWA and United.

11 Stanley Brewer "The impact of mail programs and policies on United States Air Carriers", University of Washington, Seattle, WA, 1967, p.9.

12 "The future of Air Mail Transportation", prepared for the Postmaster General, March 15th 1946, Air & Space Museum archives, Washington.

13 S. Brewer, Op. cit., p.17.

14 Frost and Sullivan, study quoted above, pp.II, 101.

15 René Joder, Dr Gal H. des Postes with Didier Daurat, "Renaissance de la Poste Aérienne" in 1945 in "Icare" No 124, p.15.

16 See G. Beyenburg & H. S. Hilgers, "Les services postaux aériens de nuit en Europe" ("Night airmail systems in Europe"), "Union Postale", 1/1977.

17 Article quoted, "Union Postale", 1/1977, p.13.

18 Article quoted, "Union Postale", 1/1977, p.13.

19 Raymond Vanier, "Tout pour la Ligne" ("All for the Line"), Paris, 1960, p.250.

20 R. Joder, quoted article, "Icare" No 124.

21 "Revue des PPT", No 1, May-June 1946.

22 R. Vanier, Op. cit., p.264

23 R Vanier, Op. cit., p. 295

24 It is interesting to note that these traffic figures are very similar to those of the German postal network, which was operated in a very different manner: 32,500 tonnes in 1970 – 37,200 tonnes in 1975.

PART SIX

CHAPTER 1

1   "Journal pour le Transport International", Basel, 6th April 1979, p.1575.

2   IATA, Annual Report, 26th Annual General Meeting, 1970, pp.84-85.

3   See OECD, Organisation for Economic Cooperation and Development, "La croissance de la production 1960-1980" ("Growth of production 1960-1980"), Paris 1970, p.8.

4   Interview with President Valéry Giscard d'Estaing, "Le Figaro Économique", 16th August 1996.

5   IATA, Annual Report November 1973, p.15.

6   "IATA Bulletin" 22nd November 1976, No 40, p.945.

7   IATA, Annual Report, November 1976, p.11.

8   "Flexibility" refers to the freedom of linking, without intermediate traffic rights, points situated on different routes (eg the right for an American company to operate a cargo service New York/London/Paris/New York by linking London, situated on the route New York/London and Paris, situated on the route New York/Paris). Although this is of limited interest for passenger services, due to increasingly marked aversion to intermediate stopovers, this possibility is highly appreciated by operators of cargo flights. Thus, it allows Air France to operate a service Paris/New York/Chicago/Paris without specific traffic rights on the domestic American section, by linking the terminal points of the route Paris/New York and Paris/Chicago. This kind of circular route allows for the reduction of compensation for possible lack of balance in the traffic in the different directions.

9   Title of an article in "ITA Bulletin", No 24 of 27th June 1977, p.587.

CHAPTER 2

1   "ITA Bulletin", No 29, 26th July 1971, p.701.

2   "Aviation Week & Space Technology", 19th March, 1973, pp61-63.

3   "Nouvelles d'Air France", No 1727, 27.10.1971.

4   "Cargo Plan", 1974.

5   Airbus Brochure, "Airbus A300 Underfloor", p.3.
6   Traffic of the sixth freedom refers to the practice which consists in an airline from country A picking up in country B traffic for country C, and taking it in transit via country A, in the absence of any direct rights under the fifth freedom to carry goods between countries B and C.
7   Fred Smith, "Proceedings", 11th Air Cargo Forum, 1982, p.69.

CHAPTER *3*

1   A. Baltensweiler, President of Swissair, in "ITA Bulletin" No 12, 25th March 1974.
2   IATA, Annual Report September 1972, §59.
3   Jacques Raynaud, "Pétrole et Transport Aérien" ("Oil and Air Transport"), ITA, Etudes et Documents, Vol. 43, p.68.
4   "ITA, Bulletin" No 8, 25 February 1974.
5   "IATA Bulletin", November 1979, p.1.
6   Interview with Joseph Healy, President of Flying Tiger, in the "Journal of Commerce" of 12th December 1981.
7   Fuel has a higher relative weighting in the cost structure for cargo flights than for passenger flights.
8   See "American Airlines Hub Plane Operations", 11th International Air Cargo Forum, 1982.
9   Interview with Peter Bouw – who was then in charge of freight at KLM, and later promoted to President – in "Air Cargo Magazine" in July 1981, p.4. "Combi-Philosophy".
10 Air France, internal document.
11 Airliner Company.
12 See chapter 4, "The express explosion".
13 Dott. A. Trapolino in "XXII International course in Advanced studies on transport Organisation", University of Trieste, September 1981.
14 Aéroport de Paris , Freight Forum 1977, Interview with M. H. Benoit, Managing Director of GEFCO.
15 PAN = Peugeot Automobile Nigeria.
16 Interview with the Managing Director of GEFCO.
17 "Les Echos", 15/09/1979.
18 "Les Échos", 11/06/1981.

CHAPTER *4*

1   "Freight News", 03/12/1984.
2   "Air et Cosmos", 18th January 1986.
3   "Cargo Airlift", July 1972.
4   "Cargo Airlift", September 1973.
5   "History of Plumas, Lassen and Sierra Counties", California, 1882, reprint, Berkley 1974, p. 231 et seq.
6   "Wells Fargo since 1852", San Francisco, 1988, p.11.

7   "Postal History Journal" (USA), official organ of the Postal History Society (USA), Vol.1, No 1, May 1957.
8   See the remarkable article by Levi C. Weir in "100 years of American Commerce: 1795-1895", New York, 1895, Vol.1, p.137/140.
9   Idem, p.139.
10 "Journal pour le transport international", Basel 18/01/1974.
11 Emery annual report, 1974, p.1.
12 Richard Malkin in "Cargo Airlift", April 1973, Vol.63, No 4, Editorial.
13 "Fortune", 10th November, 1997, p.87.
14 Fedex 1997 Annual Report.
15 Jodeau, "Le transport rapide des messageries", ("Rapid package transportation"), Review "Transports", May 1976.
16 POD: Proof of delivery.
17 Emery, Annual Report 1974, p.2.
18 "Business Week", 6th June 1983, p.81.

CHAPTER *5*

1   "Rolls-Royce Magazine", No 57, June 1993, p.8.
2   "Journal pour Le Transport International", Basel, 7/97.
3   "Cargo Logistic Airlift System Study", (Class) Vol.1, p.285, NASA Oct. 1978.
4   AVIAMAG, 970, (15.10.89).
5   IATA, Annual Report, 1970 p. 62.
6   IATA, Annual Report, 1978, p.23.
7   FIATA - Fédération Internationale des Associations de Transitaires et Assimilés (International Federation of Freight Forwarders Associations), whose headquarters is in Zurich.
8   "Journal pour le Transport International", 43/1996, p.4.
9   "Transports Actualités", No 425, 20th March 1992.
10) François Legrez, "La responsabilité du Transporteur Aérien vis-à-vis des usagers" ("The liability of the Air Carrier towards users") in IATA Bulletin No. 26, 1980.
11 Thomas J. Whalen, "The new Warsaw Convention, the Montreal Convention" in "Air and Space Law", Volume XXV, No 1, February 2000.
12 Idem, Thomas J. Whelan.
13 "Aéroports Magazine", No 342, October 2003.
14 "IATA Bulletin", December 1963.

CHAPTER *6*

1   Cargo Automation Research Project, December 1973, Report, Volume I, Executive summary, p. XI.
2   Cargo Automation Research Project, December 1973, Report, Volume 1, p.6-1.
3   EDP: Electronic Data Processing.
4   In this group, a decisive role was played by

Etienne Dreyfous, the delegate of Air France.
5   Journal "Transports", October 1986. Interview with J. C. Berthod, Managing Director of Danzas France.
6   IATA "Air Cargo Automation", p.2.
7   Idem, p.13.
8   International Cargo Forum, Luxembourg 1992. "EDI links between forwarders and airlines" by Peter Kessler, MSAS Cargo International.

CHAPTER *7*

1   Erik Wessberge: "Vers une expérience de déréglementation des transports aériens aux Etats Unis" ("Progress in the experience of deregulating air transport in the United States"), "ITA, Bulletin" No 3, 19th January 1976.
2   ICAO Circular 97, AT/18, 1970, "Fret Aérien, Region Europe – Méditerranée" ("Airfreight, Mediterranean Europe Region"), p.82.
3   "ITA, Bulletin" No 36/1969, p.861.
4   Nawal K. Taneja, "US International Aviation Policy", p.31.
5   "Statement of US International Air cargo policy", Issued by the Department of Transportation, 10th May 1989.
6   "ITA, Magazine" No 44, July/August 1987, p.7.
7   "Air Transport World", 8/97, p.35.
8   "Aviation Week", 15th April, 1998.

CHAPTER *8*

1   The Franco-Soviet Air Agreement of 26th June 1958 had opened the way to the normalisation of aeronautical relations with the Soviet Union.
2   C. B. Y. Panyukon and B. S. Balashov, "Air cargo in the USSR", In: 8th International Forum for Air Cargo, 1975.
3   Quoted article p.54.
4   Michel Mantin, "Fret Aérien et hélicoptères civils et militaires" ("Airfreight and civilian and military helicopters"), International Symposium, Strasbourg, 1993, p.238. (Académie Nationale de l'Air et de l'Espace).
5   John Stroud, "Soviet transport aircraft since 1945", p.168.
6   Extract from brochure "Chartering the An-124-100 Ruslan", Published by Antonov Design Bureau and Air Foyle.

PART SEVEN

CHAPTER *1*

1   "Aviation Week and Space Technology", 16th November, 1988.
2   "The McKinsey Quarterly", 1991, Nos 3 and 4.
3   "Air Transport World", 11/98, p.125.
4   "International Freighting Weekly", 10th

November, 1978, p.10/11.

5 Korean Air cargo schedule/1998.

6 "Cargo Vision", published by KLM Cargo, February 1989, p.22-25.

7 This classification takes up and completes that adopted by the journal "Aviation Week and Space Technology" in its special annual number.

8 "Aviation Week and Space Technology", 16thJune, 1997, p.123.

9 "Journal pour le Transport International", 29-30/2003.

CHAPTER 2

1 ITA, study 64/10F, 1964, "L'emballage des marchandises dans le transport aèrien" ("The packing of goods for air transport"), By R. Maurer, p. 7.

2 SRI - Stanford Research Institute, "How to identify potential uses of airfreight", 1963. SETEC – Société d'Études Techniques et Économiques, "Les avantages de la voie aérienne" (The advantages of air transport), Paris, 1968.

3 "Messager" – Information letter from Air France Cargo, Third Quarter 1997. Interview with the Transport Manager for Rhône-Poulenc Chemicals.

4 Gunnar Fletmo, "Air marketing. Une option nouvelle dans la distribution des produits" ("Air marketing. A new option in product distribution"), SAS, 1974.

5 H. Lewis, J. Culliton and J. Steel, "The Role of Airfreight in Physical Distribution", Harvard University, Boston, 1956.

6 Interview with the Import/Export Director of Parfums Nina Ricci in: "Cargo Frequence", Singapore Airlines, France, January 1998.

7 In "Planet", publication of Lufthansa 2002.

CHAPTER 3

1 Fedex Annual Report 2002, p.11.

2 The familiar nickname given to UPS: "Big" is self-explanatory, and "Brown" because of the livery of its vehicle fleet.

3 Christopher Lovelock, "Services Marketing", Prentice Hall, New Jersey, 2001, p.275.

4 Jagdish N. Sheth and Atul Parvatiyar, "Handbook of Relationship Marketing", Sage Publications Inc, Thousand Oaks, California, 2000, p. 160.

5 Interview with Christopher Foyle, the then President of TIACA, in "Journal pour le transport international", No 35 /1997, p.4/5.

6 See: W. Hubner and P. Sauvé, "Liberalisation Scenarios for International Air Transport", Vol. 35, October 2001, Kluwer Law, The Hague, The Netherlands.

CHAPTER 4

1 This does not mean that there are 4,420 dif-ferent cargo agents, but, since registration is issued country by country, this means that there were 4,420 recent country registrations in 1995.

2 This is the most probable estimate, based on experience, in the absence of any global statistics. Clearly, this refers only to traditional airlines, as integrators work directly with end users, except in a few exceptional cases.

3 IATA text, September 2001.

4 IATA, Annual Report, 1985, p. 28.

5 Danzas, "L'Histoire de Danzas de 1815 à 1919", p. 2.

6 "Mory 1804-1979", pp. 6/10.

7 "Freight News", 27th January 1984.

8 NVOCC: Non-Vessel Operating Common Carrier.

9 H. Grissemann, Director of ASB, stated in 1985 before the Swiss Shippers' Council: "There is no question of an air broker buying aircraft and putting them into service. A forwarder should not play the carrier. Nor should the carrier play the forwarder."

10 Remo Brunschwiller/Danzas/Interview in "International Transport Journal", No 28, 999.

11 Interview with Daniel Delva, Chief Executive of SDV, in "Journal pour le Transport International", No 25, 2001.

12 KLM "Cargo Vision", June 1994, p. 11.

13 Information Letter of Air France Cargo, 2nd Quarter 1997.

14 18th International Air Cargo Forum, Dubai, October 1996.

CHAPTER 5

1 "Union Postale", 1988, pp.126/128.

2 Lufthansa Cargo's "Planet", 2/2002, pp.28/30.

3 "Union Postale", "Un Défi pour les Postes: le Repostage" ("Remail: a challenge to the Post Offices"), 4/1989.

4 "Union Postale", Bern, May 1976.

5 "Union Postale", May 1981, pp. 239/240: "Le Monopole Postal en France" ("The Postal Monopoly in France").

6 "Union Postale", 1986, p.12 F.

7 "Messages PTT", No 354, March 1986. From the Post, that was fighting talk!

8 "Journal pour les Transport International", 51/97.

9 "Union Postale", 1998/3, p.2.

10 "Union Postale", 2002/1, p.5.

11 Headline from the weekly "Transports Actualitiés", No 671, 19th March/1st April 1999.

12 B2B = Business to Business.

13 B2C = Business to Consumer.

14 Now called Astor Air Cargo.

15 "Airline Business", June 2003. p.38, "Fast Forward" by Peter Conway.

16 "Journal pour le Transport International", 5/1993, p.345.

CHAPTER 6

1 "Air Cargo World", April 1996, p.27.

2 Mike Wiebner, "Air Cargo World", April 2003, p.30.

3 "Jane's Airport Review", December 1993, p.23.

4 ACI = Airports Council International.

5 "Air Cargo News", July/August 1994, p.9.

6 KLM Cargo: "Your world-wide partner in animal transportation", 3/96.

7 "ICAO Journal", June 2000.

8 Direction Générale de L'Aviation Civile (France): "Sûreté du Fret Aerien - 4 Règles Simples pour les Enterprises 'customers connus'", Paris, 1997 ("Airfreight Security – 4 Simple Rules for Companies as 'Known Shippers'").

9 "Aviation Week and Technology", March 2000.

10 "Airline Business", September 2001.

CHAPTER 7

1 "Concorde", internal magazine of Air France, 10th June 1997.

2 Expeditors International, Annual Report 1992.

3 Unpublished document: recollections recorded in 1983.

PART EIGHT

1 "ICAO Journal", June 2000, p.9.

2 Lufthansa "Cargo's Planet", 3/2003.

3 "Aviation Week & Space Technology", 10th March, 2003.

4 "Rolls-Royce Magazine", September 2002.

5 Jacques Pavaux, "Le transport Aérien a l'horizon 2020, élément de réflection prospective" ("Air Transport to the year 2020, Prospects and Reflections"), Les Presses de l'Institut du Transport Aérien, ITA, Paris, 1995.

6 Geoff Bridges, "The Global airfreight market – the future" in "International Airport Review", June 2002.

7 Geoff Bridges, Op. cit.

BIBLIOGRAPHY

I ARCHIVES

We were able to consult the archives of the following organisations:

Air France
Air & Space Museum in Washington
General Directorate of Civil Aviation in Paris
Musée de la Poste in Paris
Post Office in London

II – WORKS AND PRINCIPAL ARTICLES

ABATE R., ALEGI G., APOSTOLO G., Aeroplani Caproni, Museo Caproni, Trento, 1992

Académie Nationale de l'Air et de l'Espace (various authors), L'avenir de l'aviation de transport de fret, international Symposium, 1993 Strasbourg, Cépaduès-Editions, Toulouse, 1993.

Air Ministry, Great Britain, Berlin Airlift, an Account of the British Contribution, London, 1949.

AIREVIEW, staff of, "General view of Japanese military aircraft in the Pacific War." Compiled by the staff of Aireview. Kanto-Sha Co. Tokyo, 1st Japanese Edition 1953, 1st English Edition 1956.

ALLAZ, Camille, Air Cargo 2000 les Engeux Actuels du fret aérien, Etudes & Documents Institut du Transport Aérien – ITA – Paris, June 2002.

ALLAZ, Edouard, Transports aériens; tarifs et trafic, Course given at l'École Supérieure des Transports, École Nouvelle d'Organisation Économique et Sociale, Paris, Jan, 1956 (typed copy).

ALLEN, Roy, World Air Cargo Opportunities for European Businesses, Financial Times Management Reports, London, 1995.

ANDERSON, K.J., Outlines and Readings in Air Cargo Transportation, Northwestern University (typed course), 1949

Anonymous, L'aviation soviétique, published in Les Ailes, Paris 1937.

Anonymous, The Japanese Air Forces in World War II, Arms & Armour Press, London/Melbourne 1979.

Anonymous, Wells Fargo since 1852, Wells Fargo & Co, San Francisco, 1988.

ARENS, Geoffrey, Kennedy International, Air Cargo News Inc, New York, 1987.

Marquis d'ARGENSON, René Louis de Voyer, Pensées sur le réformation de l'Ètat, Paris.

Avion, Aircraft and Aero Engines, C. Arthur Pearson Ltd, London, 1918.

BAKER, E.C. "The Airgraph Service, 1941–1945", in A Postscript for Postal Historians, Vol. III, No 2, May 1953.

BARTHÉLÉMY, Raymond, Histoire du Transport Militaire Français Edition France-Empire, Paris – 1981.

BATTELLE Institute Sea and Airfreight – 1980, Frankfurt am Main, 1970.

BAUCHET, Pierre, L'économie du transport international de marchandises, air et mer, Economica, Paris, 1982.

BEITH, R., Scottish Airmail, 1919–1979, published by the author 1981.

BERENDT, Günter, Dr., "Die Entwicklung der Marktstruktur im Internationalen Luftverkehr" in Verkehrswissenschaftliche Forschungen – Band 5, Duncker & Humblot, Berlin, 1961.

BEYENBURG G. & H.J. HILGERS, "Services postaux aériens de nuit en Europe", in Union Postale, Berne, No 8, 1975.

BLISTEIN, Roger E., "Putting aircraft to work, the First Airfreight", in Ohio History, 1980.

BOGGS, WINTHROP S., The Postage Stamps and Postal History of Newfoundland, Quaterman Publication Inc., Lawrence, MA-USA, 1975.

BONAME, Robert, "Contribution des États-Unis aux premières traversées de l'Atlantique Nord", Icare, No 155, 1995. "Air France transatlantique", Icare, Nr157, 1996.

BONOMO, Oscar, L'aviation commerciale, Louis Vivien, Paris, 1926.

BRENSON, Piers, Thomas Cook, Secker & Warburg, London 1991.

BREWER, Stanley & ROSENZWEIG, James, The Domestic Environment of the Air Cargo Industry, University of Washington Seattle, WA, USA, 1967.

BREWER, Stanley H., The Impact of Mail Programs and Policies on United States Air Carriers, Seattle/Washington, 1967.

BREWER, Stanley, Military Airlift, University of Washington, Seattle, WA, USA, 1967.

BREWER, Stanley, S, International Air Cargo Future, Boeing Airplane Cy. Renton, Washington, 1960.

BRIGHT, Charles D., Historical Dictionary of the US Air Forces, edited by Charles D. Bright, Greenwood Press, New York, London, 1992.

BRIMSON, Samuel, Flying the Royal Mail, Dreamweaver books, Sydney, 1984.

BRITISH AIRWAYS, Highways in the air: the story of British Airways, B.A. Public Relations, 1979.

BROGDEN, Stanley, The History of Australian Aviation, Melbourne, 1960.

BROOK, Ernest, "How the Christmas Messengers brought Good Tidings to the Congo", in The Rolls-Royce Magazine, No 62, September 1994.

BROWN, A. Stanley, Customer Relationship Management, John Wiley & Sons Canada Ltd. 2000.

BRUNO, Harry, Wings over America, R.M. McBride, New York, 1942.

BUELL, Thomas and others, Thomas Griess, Series Editor, The Second World War, (The West Point Military History Series), 2 volumes, Avery Publishing Group, Wayne, New Jersey, USA

1984.

CAMBON, Victor, La ligne aérienne France-Afrique-Amérique du Sud, Paris, 1926.

CAMERON, Franck, The Hungry Tigers, McGraw Hill, New York, 1964.

CASTEX, Louis, L'âge de l'air, E. Chiron ed., Paris, 1945.

CASTEX, Louis, Les compagnies étrangères dans le réseau aérien mondial, no publisher, Toulouse, 1944.

de CASTILLON DE SAINT-VICTOR, A., Le transport aérien, de la machine volante au cargo aérien, Dunod, Paris, 1947.

Catalogues:

De l'éole à l'Hermès, cent ans de moteurs dans le ciel, Musée National des Techniques, Paris, 1990.

Il Museo Leonardiano di Vinci, Citta di Vinci 1996.

La poste et l'aviation, Musée de la Poste/Air France, Paris, 1983.

La part du rêve, de la montgolfiére au satellite, Grand Palais, Paris, 1983.

Navigation Maritime, Fluviale, Aérienne. Conservatoire National des Arts et Métiers. Paris 1954.

Zeppeline und Post, Bundespostmuseum, Frankfurt am Main, 1987.

CHADEAU, Emmanuel, L'industrie aéronautique en France, 1900–1950, Fayard, Paris, 1987.

CHIN, Art, Anything, Anytime, Anywhere. The Legacy of the Flying Tiger Line, 1945–1989, Tassels & Wings, Seattle, Washington, 1990.

CHRISTOPHER, Martin, The Strategy of Distribution Management, Gower, Aldershot, England, 1985.

CLARETIE, Jules, Histoire de la Révolution de 1870-1871. Publication de la Librairie Illustrée Paris, 1977.

CLEMENT, Alfred, Handbuch der Militär Luftpost, Graz, 1955.

CLEVELAND, Reginald M., Air Transport at War, New York, 1945.

CLEVELAND, Reginald M., The Coming Air Age, MacGraw Hill, New York, London, 1944.

CLOSTERMANN, Pierre, "Le Grand Cirque", Souvenir d'un pilote de chasse français dans le RAF. Flammarion. Paris, 1948.

COHEN, Ralph, IATA, les trente premières années, IATA ed., Montréal, 1945.

COHN, Ernest M., numerous articles in Postal History Journal and in Postal History International, Brighton, UK.

Collective edition: L'odyssée du Tchéliouskine, Librairie Stock, Paris, 1935.

COLLIER, Richard, Bridge across the Sky, the Berlin blockade and airlift, 1948–1949, MacGraw Hill Book, New York, 1978.

COLLOT, G. et CORNU, A., La ligne Noguès, histoire aérophilatélique, 1911–1941, Ed. Sinais, Paris, 1993.

COLLOT, Gérard et CORNU, Alain, Ligne Mermoz, histoire aérophilatélique, Ed. Bertrand Sinais, Paris, 1990.

COOK, John C., International Air Cargo Strategy, Air Cargo Research Institute, Philadelphia, PA, 1973. Conférence européenne des Ministres des Transports, La télématique dans les transports de marchandises, Paris, 1989.

CUMMING, Michael, The Powerless Ones: Gliding in Peace/War. Frederich Muller Ltd, London, 1966.

DACHARRY, Monique, Géographie du transport aérien, Librairies techniques, Paris, 1981.

DADE, George and STRAND, Frank. Picture history of aviation on Long Island 1908, 1938. Dover Publications, New York, 1985

DANEL, Raymond, I., Les lignes Latécoère, Ed. Privat (Idem I), Toulouse, 1986. II., L'Aéropostale Ed. Privat (Idem I), Toulouse, 1989

DANEL, Raymond, I., Les ligne

DAUGIMONT, A., Aperçu historique de la poste aérien au Congo Belge, no publisher, Bruxelles, 1957.

DAURAT, Didier, Dans le vent des hélices, Editions du Seuil, Paris, 1956.

DAVIES, R.EG, "The History of Air Express in the United States", SAE Technical Papers Series, 12th International Forum for Air Cargo, 1984.

DAVIES, R.EG, Aeroflot: an Airline and its Aircraft, Paladwr Press, Rockville, MD, USA, 1992.

DAVIES, R.EG, Airlines of the United States since 1914, Putnam, London, 1972.

DE CONNINCK, F., European Air Law, Les Presses de L'ITA, Paris, 1992.

De FONVIELLE, W., Histoire de la navigation aérienne, Hachette, Paris, 1910.

DEFFONTAINES, Pierre et CHARVET, Louis, Géographie du transport Aérien published by Air France, Paris, 1939.

DOLLFUS, Charles & BOUCHÉ, Henri, Histoire de l'aéronautique, L'illustration, Paris, 1942.

DOLLFUS, Charles & MAINGENT, Paul, "La merveilleuse historie des 68 ballons du siège de Paris", Icare, No 56, 1971.

DOLLFUS, Charles, Les avions, Delpire, Paris, 1962.

DOLLFUS, Charles, Les ballons, Delpire, Paris, 1960.

DRUM, Karl, General, Airpower and Russian Partisan Warfare, Air University.

DUROSELLE, Jean-Baptiste, Histoire diplomatique de 1919 á nos jours, Dalloz, Paris, 11e édition, 1993.

DUTHEIL de la ROCHÈRE, Jacqueline, La politique des États-Unis en matiére d'aviation civile internationale, Librairie générale de droit et de juris-prudence, Paris, 1971.

ESPÉROU, Robert, "Le matériel volant des compagnies aériennes francaises (1919–1939)", in Revue de Secrétariat Général à l'Aviation Civile, Paris, 1968–1972.

EYERMANN, Karl Heinz, Die Luftfahrt in der USSR, 1917–1977, Transpress Verlag für Verkehrswesen, Berlin, 1977.

FARRAR-HOCKLEY, Student, Ballantine Books, New York, 1973.

FARRUGIA, Jean and GAMMONS, Tony, Carrying British Mails, National Postal Museum, London, 1980.

FAUJAS DE SAINT FOND, "Descriptions des expériences de la machine aérostatique de M.M. de Montgolfier", chez Cuchet, Paris, Tome 1 1783, Tome 2 1784.

FEDERAL EXPRESS CORPORATION. "How time flies – FEDEX delivers the 21st Century". Memphis/TN USA, 1998.

FLEURY, Jean-Gérard, La ligne, Gallimard, Paris, 1939.

FOSTER, John T., China up and down, the 308th Bombardment Group (heavy) of the Flying Tigers, Keene, New Hampshire, USA, 1994.

FOULOIS, Benjamin D., Major General, From the Wright brothers to the Astronauts, Memoirs, McGraw Hill, New York, 1968.

FRANCILLON, R.J., Japanese Aircraft of the Pacific War, Putnam, London.

FREDERICK, John. Commercial Air Cargo Fifth Edition. New York, 1961.

FREUDENTHAL, Elisabeth, "The Aviation Industry", The Vanguard Press, New York, 1940.

FROST & SULLIVAN, The Air Cargo Market, New York, 1972.

GAMMONS, Tony, Halfway Round the World, Exhibition. The

Story of the British Airmail Service, 1919–1934. National Postal Museum, London, 1984.

GEORGE, Pierre, URSS, Haute-Asie, Iran, Presses Universitaires de France, Paris, 1947.

GIBBS-SMITH, Charles, Aviation, an Historical Survey from its Origins to the End of World War II, Science Museum, London, 1970.

GIBBS-SMITH, Charles, The Wright Brothers, The World's First Aircraft Flights.

Sir George Cayley, Her Majesty's Stationery Office, London, 1963–1965

GLINES Carroll V., Airmail, Tab Books, Blue Ridge Summit, PA/USA, 1990.

GORHAM, James E., How to Identify Potential Uses of Airfreight, Stanford, Research Institute, prepared for Emery Airfreight Corporation, South Pasadena, California, USA, 1963

GREEN, William, The War Planes of the 3rd Reich, New York, 1970.

GRUSS, Robert, "Les Flottes de l'Air en 1937". Société d'Editions géographiques, maritimes et coloniales. Paris 1937.

HAANAPPEL P.P.C., Pricing and Capacity Determination in International Air Transport, Kluwer Law Publishers, Deventer/The Netherlands, 1984.

HAJENIUS, W., "Le développement du service postal aérien aux Indes Néerlandaises", in Union Postale, Berne, 1932, p.290 et seq.

"The Riddle of Sweden's Ballbearings". New Background Inc. New York. 1944.

HEIMANN, Erich, Die Flugzeuge der Deutschen Lufthansa, Motorbuch Verlag, Stuttgart, 1980.

HIGHAM, Robin (et al.), Soviet Aviation, 1977.

HILL, D.J., Freight Forwarders, Stevens & Sons, London, 1972.

HIRSCHAUER, Charles, "Les premières ascensions aérostatiques à Versailles", in Revue d'Histoire de Versailles, years 1915 (pp.26 to 48), and 1918 (pp.57 to 95).

HIRSCHAUER, L. and DOLLFUS, C.H., "L'Année Aéronautique". Dunod. Paris 1920–1939.

HOFF, Gerd, Dr., "Entwicklung und Bedeutung des Luftfracht-Verkehrs in der Bundesrepublik Deutschland", in Verkehrswissenschaftliche Forschungen, Band 25, Duncker & Humblot, Berlin, 1972.

HUBNER, Wolfgang and SAUVÉ, Pierre. Liberalization scenarios for international air transport. Vol. 35, No. 5, October 2001, KLUWER LAW INTERNATIONAL, The Hague, The Netherlands.

HUTCHINSON, W.H., History of Plumas, Lassen & Sierra Counties, 1882, Reprint Howell-North Books, Berkeley, California, 1971.

IATA, IATA, les trente premières années, (See Cohen Ralph S).

Il L'aéropostale, Private edition, Toulouse, 1989.

US Air Force, Arno Press, New York, 1962.

INSTITUT FRANÇAIS DU TRANSPORT AÉRIEN, IFTA,
États-Unis, Statistiques du trafic aérien, Working Note, 10 March 1943.

Le transport aérien de marchandises, Working Note, 16 Feb 1944.

À propos du transport aérien de marchandises, Working Note, 15 April 1944.

Le transport spécialisé des marchandises par voie aérienne, Working Note, 25 July 1944.

Le transport des marchandises par la voie des airs aux États-Unis, information note, 20 Feb 1947.

Économie du transport aérien, Working Note, 9 October 1947.

Évolution des courants d'échanges…, Working Note, 24 January 1948.

Caractéristiques d'aménagement et d'exploitation des avions cargo modernes, Working Note no 146-147, December 1948.

Bilan économique du transport aérien de marchandises, Working Note No 157, May 1949.

Avions-cargo à soute détachable ou containers?, Working Note, July 1949.

L'adaptation du transport aérien aux besoins de l'Afrique Noire, Working Note, No 179, No 182/183, No 186/187, 1950.

Le problème de l'avion-cargo, Working Note No 192/193, December 1950.

Les opérations au sol de transport. L'aérogare de marchandises, Working Note, No 228/229, October 1952.

INSTITUT DU TRANSPORT AÉRIEN, ITA
Évolution du transport des marchandises depuis 1939 jusqu'à ce jour, Working Note, No 269/270, March 1955.

Caractéristiques d'aménagement et d'exploitation des avions-cargo modernes, Working Note, No 280/281, November 1955.

Exportations par air des pays européens en 1954: textiles, machines, Working Note, No 273/274.

Le transport aérien, facteur essentiel du prodigieux essor de l'economie canadienne, Working Note, No 341/342, October 1961.

Le rôle du transport aérien dans le développement économique du Sahara, Working Note No 166, March 1962.

Les avions cargo modernes, Working Note, No 345/346, June 1962.

Examen comparatif de quelques prévisions de trafic aérien de marchandises, No 63/5 F. 1963.

La manutention du fret aérien, par René Maurer, No 63/9 F, 1963.

Inventaire des problèmes de manutention et d'emballage intéressant le fret aérien, Par René Maurer, January 1964.

L'avion, maillon d'une chaîne de transport, par René Maurer, No 65/7 F, 1965.

Les prévisions dans le transport aérien: méthodes et résultats, No 66/7 F, 1966.

Le commerce international des fleurs en Europe, No 67/1 F, 1967.

Les droits de trafic devant l'évolution du fret aérien, 1967.

Situation et problèmes du fret aérien, by Jean Mercier, November 1968.

Aspects du fret aérien dans les pays neufs, by Théophile Kamoclo, November 1968.

Containers et palettes dans le transport aérien, by René Maurer, 1970/5 F, 1979.

Le transport aérien face à l'évolution du coût des carburants, 1974/7 F, 1974.

Les transports. clé de développement au Nigéria, by Georges Desmas, 1975/2 F, 1975.

JACKSON, P., BRACKENRIDGE, W., Air Cargo Distribution, Gower Press, London, 1971.

JANE, A. "Pocket Book of Airships". Collier Books, New York,

1977.

JANE'S, Milestones of the Air, MacGraw Hill, New York, 1969.

JANES'S, Jane's 100 Significant Aircraft, MacGraw Hill, New York, 1969.

JELICIE, D. Borislav, The Global Air Cargo Industry, D V B Verkehrsbank, Frankfurt/Main, June 2001.

JOSEPHSON, Matthew, Empire of the Air, Juan Trippe and the Struggle for World Airways, Harcourt, New York, 1944.

KATSU, Kohri, IKUO, Komori, etc., Air View of 50 Years' Japanese Aviation. 1910–1960, Tokyo, 1962.

KENDALL, N.W., US Overseas Air Cargo Services, US Dept of Commerce, Washington, 1949,

KILMARX, Robert, A., A History of Soviet Air Power, London, 1962.

KNAÜSEL, Hans G., LZ1, Der erste Zeppelin, Geschichte einer Idée, Bonn, 1985

KUROWSKI, Franz, Luftbrücke Stalingrad, Kurt Vowinckel-Verlag, Berg-Am-See, 1983.

L'avion, maillon d'une chaîne de transport. Études ITA, 1965. Les unités de chargement, Études ITA, 1976.

La manutention du fret aérien, Études ITA, 1963.

LE CHÂTELIER, Lieutenant-Colonel, Le rôle du transport aérien dans le développement économique du Sahara, École Supérieure des Transports, Paris, 1961.

LE CORBUSIER, Aircraft, The Studio, London, 1935. French edition Adam Biro, Paris, 1987.

LE MOINE, Maurice, Traité de droit aérien, Recueil Sirey, Paris, 1947.

LE MOUËL, Joseph-Jean, "L'Union Postale Universelle et l'Aviation Commerciale", in Bulletin IATA, No 10, Decembre 1949.

LE MOUËL, Joseph-Jean, "La poste aérienne sans surtaxe" in Bulletin d'information du Ministére des PTT, Paris, 1939.

LEARY, Williamm M., Aerial Pioneers, the US Airmail Service, 1918–1927, Smithsonian Institution Press, Washington, DC, 1985.

LEBON, E., "La poste aérienne", in Annales des PTT, year 1928, p.72 et seq.

LEFRANC, Jean-Abel, Les avions, Hachette, Paris, 1922.

LESOUEF, Pierre, La campagne de Birmanie, 1942–1945, Economica, Paris, 1993.

LEWIS, Howard & CULLITON, James, The Role of Airfreight in Physical Distribution, Harvard University, Boston, 1956.

LIDDEL HART, Sir Basil. Histoire de la Seconde Guerre Mondiale. Fayard, Paris. (History of the Second World War. Cassells & Co London 1970).

LOVELOCK, Christopher. "Services Marketing". Prentice Hall, New Jersey, USA. 4th Edition, 2001.

LÜNING, Örjan, Luftpostens Historia I Norden. The History of Airmail in Scandinavia, Sveriges Filatelist Förbund, Stockholm, 1978.

MACKAY, James, Airmails, 1870–1970, London, 1971.

MAGDALÉNAT, Jean-Louis, Air Cargo Regulation and Claims, English Language edition, Butterworths, Toronto, 1983.

MAGDALÉNAT, Jean-Louis, Le fret aérien, réglementation, responsabilité, The Carswell Cy Ltd, Toronto, Éditions A. Pedone, Paris, 1979.

MAINCENT, Paul, "Les ballons de Metz,", in Icare, No 56, 1976.

MAINGUET, F., "La poste aérienne", in Annales des PTT, année 1930, p.393/436, Paris.

MALKIN, Richard, Boxcars in the Sky, New York, 1951.

MASON, Francis K., Lockheed Hercules, Patrick Stephens Ltd, Wellingborough, UK, 1984.

MATHÉ, Hervé et TIXIER, Daniel, La logistique, Presses Universitaires de France, Paris, 1985.

MAURER, René, L'avion-cargo moderne, lecture speech given on 26 January 1957, Edition CGC.

MERMOZ, Jean, Mes vols, Paris, 1937.

MEYER, Peter, Luftschiffe, Wehr & Wissen, Koblenz/Bonn, 1980.

MIKESH, Robert & ABE Shorzoe, Japanese Aircraft, Putnam, London, 1990.

MILLS, Stephen, Alaska Bush Pilots, 1969.

MINISTRY OF DEFENCE OF THE USSR. The Soviet Air Force in World War II. David and Charles. London 1972.

MORÉ, Marcel, J'ai vécu l'épopée de l'Aeropostale, Acropole, Paris, 1980.

MORZIK, Fritz, Die Deutschen Transportflieger im Zweiten Weltkrieg, Bernard und Graefe Verlag für Wehrwesen, Frankfurt am Maim, 1966.

MORZIK, Fritz, Generalmajor, German Air Force Airlift Operations, USAF Historical Studies, Nr 167, Arno Press, New York. International Civil Aviation Oganisation (ICAO), Le fret aérien, Doc 8235, Montréal, 1962. Étude sur la poste aérienne, Doc 8240, Montréal, 1962.

"Etude sur l'Aviation Italienne". Comité français de propagande aéronautique. Paris 1936.

O'CONNOR, William, E., An Introduction to Airline Economics, Praeger Publishers, New York, 1982.

Observatoire Économique et Statistique des Transports, Ministère des Transports (OEST), Les integrators et le fret express en Europe, 1988. Le fret Express au Royaume-Uni, 1988. Acteurs et enjeux du fret express en Europe. 1990. Three studies directed by Patrice Salini.

Office of Technology Assessment (OTA), Congress of the United States, Impact of Advanced Air Transport Technology, The Air Cargo System, Washington D.C., 1982.

Organisation for Economic Co-operation & Development (OECD). La croissance de la production: 1960–1980, Paris, 1970.

PAHL, Walter, Les routes aériennes du globe, translated from German, Payot, Paris, 1937.

PAINET, Jean, "La presse à Paris pendant le Siège", in Icare, No 77, 1976.

PALMER, Adrian, "Principles of services marketing". McGraw Hill, Maidenhead, England. Third Edition 2001.

PANYUKOV, B.Y. & BALASHOV, B/S/, "Air Cargo in the USSR", in 8th International Forum for Air Cargo Proceedings, 1976.

PAPANIN, IVAN, Sur la banquise en dérive, Éditions Albin Michel, Paris 1948.

PAVAUX, Jacques et autres, Le transport aérien a l'horizon 2020, élèments de réflexion prospective, Les Presses de ITA, Paris, 1995.

PÉPIN, Engène, Géographie de la circulation aérienne, Gallimard, Paris, 1956.

PETERSON, C.G., Air Express & Freight, R.E.A. Inc, January 30, 1942.

PETIT, Edmond, Nouvelle histoire mondiale de l'aviation, Hachette Réalitiés, Paris, 1973.

PIGOTT, Peter, Kai Tak. A History of Aviation in Hong Kong, Government Printer, 1990.

PIRATH, Carl, Dr. Ing., Notebooks from Institut für Luftfahrt an der Technischen Hochschule Stuttgart, 1929–1938, Munich-

Berlin.

PLOWMAN, GROSVENOR, E., "Business Logistics", in Air Transportation, February 1969.

POULTON, H.W., New Facts in Papua New Guinea, Air transport, Royal Aeronautical Society, London, 1969.

PUTNAM, "Aéroflot – Soviet Air Transport since 1923". London 1975.

QUENOT, M., "La poste aérienne", "Lecture to Congrès des Transports Aériens", in Bulletin d'Informations du Ministère des PTT, Paris, 1939.

RABUT, Albert, La convention de Varsovie, Librairie Générale de Droit et de Jurisprudence, Paris, 1952.

RATH, E. & KNIGHT, G.L., Air cargo, New York, 1947.

RAYNAUD, Jacques, Pétrole et transport aérien, ITA Études & Documents, Volume 43, Paris, 1996.

RICHARDS, Denis and SAUNDERS Hilary, "Royal Air Force 1939–1945", "Three Volumes officially commissioned as a history of the RAF". London. Her Majesty's Stationery office, 1954.

RIGO de RIGHI, Britain's Pioneer Airmails, National Postal Museum, London.

ROMEYER, Jean, L'aviation civile française, J. de Gigord, Paris, 1936.

ROUSSEL, André, Le rôle économique de l'aviation commerciale, Éditions Domat-Mont-Chrestien, Paris, 1937.

SAINT-EXUPÈRY, Antoine de, Courrier Sud, Gallimard, Paris, 1929. Terre Des Hommes, Gallimard, Paris, 1939.

SALISBURY, Harison E., 900 Days: the Siege of Leningrad, New York, 1985.

SAUTER, Manfred, "Ferdinand von Zeppellin", in Icare, No 135, 1990.

SCHMITT, B. & GERICKE, B., "Die Deutsche Feldpost im Osten und der Luftfeldpostdienst im Zweiten Weltkreig", in Archiv für Deutsche Postgeschichte, Vol 1, Frankfurt, 1969.

SEALY, K. & HERDON, P., Airfreight and Anglo-European Trade, The London School of Economics, 1961.

SEKYGAWA, Eiicniro, "Pictorial History of Japanese Military Aviation". London, 1974.

SERRA, François, L'avion-cargo, Les Éditions Internationales, Paris, 1948.

SHAPIRO, Roy, D. & HESKETT, James, L., Logistics Strategy, West Publishing Cy, Saint Paul/Minnesota, 1985.

SHAW, Stephen, Effective Airfreight Marketing, Pitman Publishing, London, 1993.

SHETH, Jagdish and PARVATIYAR, Atul. "Handbook of Relationship Marketing". Sage Publications Inc. Thousand Oaks, California, USA. 2000

SIMMA, Bruno. "The Charter of the United Nations – a commentary". Edited by Bruno Simms. Oxford University Press, Second Edition, 2002.

SINCLAIR, James, Wings of Gold, Pacific Publications, Sydney, New York, 1978.

SINGER, Kurt, The Riddle of Sweden's Ballbearings, New Background Inc, New York, 1944.

SLETMO, Gunnar K., Air Marketing – Une option nouvelle dans le distribution des produits, SAS, 1974.

SLIM, The Viscount, Defeat into Victory, David McKay Company, New York, 1961.

SMITH, Peter, S., Airfreight, Faber and Faber, London, 1974.

SMITH, Philip, Sur les ailes du temps. Air Canada. Les 50 premières années, Les Éditions de l'Homme, Montréal, 1986.

Société d'Études techniques et Économiques – SETEC, Les advantages de la voie aérienne, Aéroport de Paris, 1968.

SOLBERG, Carl, Conquest of the Skies, A History of Commercial Aviation in America, Little, Brown & Cy, Boston-Toronto, 1979.

STALK, George & HOUT, Thomas, Competing against Time, MacMillan, New York-London, 1990.

STANFORD Research Institute, SRI, How to identify Potential Uses of Airfreight, South Pasadena, California, 1963.

STEPHAN, Heinrich von, Weltpost und Luftschiffahrt, Julius Springer, Berling, 1874.

STROUD, John, Annals of British and Commonwealth Air Transport, 1919–1960, Putman, London, 1962

STROUD, John, Soviet Air Transport Aircraft since 1945, Putman, London, 1968.

SUPF, Peter, Das Buch der Deutschen Fluggeschichte, Berlin, 1935.

SUTTON, John Lawrence, European Commercial Air Cargo, University of Notre Dame, Indiana, Imprimeries Populaires, Genève, 1949.

TANEJA, Nawal K., The US Airfreight Industry, Lexington Books, Lexington/MA-Toronto, 1982.

TANEJA, Nawal K., US International Aviation Policy, Lexington Books, Lexington/MA-Toronto, 1980.

TAPNER, H., Air Cargo, Cassell Company, London, 1967.

THOENE, Peter, La conquête du ciel, Translation from German, Payot, Paris, 1938.

TIACA (The International Air Cargo Association). The Tiaca Manifesto. Paris, 1998.

ULDERUP, Jürgen, Der Stand des Weltluftverkehrs, Berlin, 1935.

VAN ZANDT, J. PARKER, European Air Transport on the Eve of War, 1939, Norwich University, Northfield, Vermont, USA, 1940.

VAN ZANDT, J. Parker, The Geography of World Air Transport, The Brookings Institution, Washington D.C., 1944.

VANIER, Raymond, Tout pour la ligne, Édition France-Empire, Paris, 1960.

VAUX, Jacques de La, Comte, Histoire des montgolfières de 1783 à nos jours, Versailles, 1988.

VEDRINES, Jules. "La vie d'un aviateur". Editions de l'Officine. Paris. 2002.

VER NOY, Stanley. "Airfreight Rates". International Correspondence School, Seranton, Pennsylvania. 1968.

VIÉ-KLAZE, Marie-Paule, Les grands Latécoère sur l'Atlantique, éditions Denoël, Paris, 1981.

VILLIERS, Jacques, Regard sur le transport aérien européen, ITA Études & Documents, volume 34, Paris, 1994.

VOISIN, Gabriel, Mes 10 000 cerfs-volants, La Table Ronde, Paris, 1960.

WACHTEL, Joachim, Lufthansa, l'histoire 1926–1976, éditions DLH-Cologne 1975.

WASSENBERGH, Eric, Principles and Practices in Air Transport Regulation, Les Presses de l'ITA, Paris, 1993.

WEBBER, Michael and RIGBY, David Z, "The Golden Age Illusion". The Guilford Press. New York-London. 1996.

WEIR, Levi C., "The Express"" in One Hundred years of American Commerce, New York, 1885.

WILLERTON, John P. Jr., International Handbook of Transportation Policy, Edited by Tsuneo Ankaha, Greenwood Press, 1990.

WILLIAMSON, Brig. Gen., "La Grande-Bretagne et la poste aéri-

enne", in L'Union Postale, Berne 1924.
WINSTON, Keith, V... – Mail – Letters of a World War II
Combat Medic, Algonquin Books of Chapel Hill, USA, 1985.
WOLKOWITSCH Maurice, Géographie des transports, Armand
Colin, Paris, 1973.
WOOLLEY, James G. & HALL, Earl W., Airplane Transportation,
Hartwell Corp., Hollywood, 1929.
WRAGG, David, Airlift, A History of Military Air Transport, Airlife
Publishing, Shrewsbury, England, 1986.
WYCROFF, D. & MAISTER, D.H., The Domestic Airline Industry,
Lexington Books, Lexington, Massachusetts, Toronto, 1977.
WYKEHAM, Peter, Santos Dumont, Éditions de Trèvise, Paris,
1964.
ZANTKE, Siegfried, ABC des Luftverkehrs, Deutscher Verkehrs-
Verlag, Hamburg, 1985.

III – REVUES AND PERIODICALS

We only mention here the reviews and periodicals most frequently used and consulted, listed by country and in alphabetical order.

• **Belgium**
Lloyd Anversois

• **Canada**
Philatélie Quebec

• **France**
L'Aéronautique
L'Aérophile
Aéroports Magazine
Air Cargo Magazine
Air et Cosmos
L'Antenne (daily)
Aviation Française
Aviation Magazine
L'Aviette Postale
Bulletin d'Information
L'Exportation
France Aviation
Fret Aérien International
Icare
Interavia (review)
Journal de la Marine Marchande
Logistique
Le M.O.C.T.
PTT: Annales des PTT
Revue des PTT
Références
Revue du SGAC, later of DGAC
Transports
Transports Actualités

• **Germany**
Archiv Für Deutsche Postgeschichte
Cargo World Dvz
Deutsche Verkehrszeitung Dvz
Frankfurt Air Cargo Letter

Post Archiv

• **Great Britain**
Airline Business
Air Trade
Financial Times
Flight
Freight Forwarding
Freight News
Postal History International
Postal History Society Bulletin
Rolls-Royce Magazine

• **Hong Kong**
Payload Asia
Shippers Today

• **India**
ACAAI News
Air Cargo News

• **Italy**
Il Corriere Philatelico

• **Japan**
Air & Trade Japan
Airfreighting Guide
Space
World Air Cargo Travel

• **Switzerland**
Journal pour le Transport International

• **United Arab Emirates**
Dubai Cargo Village News

• **United States**
Air Cargo Magazine
Air Cargo News
Air Cargo USA
Air Cargo World
Air Commerce
Air Transport World

Air Transportation
Aviation Week
Cargo Airlift
Journal of Air Law
Journal of Commerce International
Postal History Journal

IV – OTHER

Under this heading we include various documents (annual reports, bulletins, studies, statistics, periodicals etc) published by:

Aircraft manufacturers
Airlines
Airports
Customs authorities
International associations and organisations
Petrol companies
Engine manufacturers
Customs authorities

An attentive reading of the publications of at least four organisations is absolutely necessary for an understanding of the development of post and freight transport: FIATA, IATA, ICAO, UPU (congress papers and monthly publications of L'Union Postale).

In addition, a mine of information and extremely valuable thoughts and remarks can be found in the Proceedings of the International Forum for Air Cargo (later called International Air Cargo Forum) which have been held regularly every two years since 1964, at first under the aegis of the Society of Automotive Engineers of the United States, and today of the International Air Cargo Association.

INDEX